THE GOSPEL
BEHIND THE GOSPELS

SUPPLEMENTS TO
NOVUM TESTAMENTUM

VOLUME LXXV

THE GOSPEL
BEHIND THE GOSPELS

Current Studies on Q

EDITED BY

RONALD A. PIPER

E.J. BRILL
LEIDEN · NEW YORK · KÖLN
1995

The paper in this book meets the guidelines for permanence and durability of the Committee on Production Guidelines for Book Longevity of the Council on Library Resources.

Library of Congress Cataloging-in-Publication Data

The gospel behind the Gospels : current studies on Q / edited by
Ronald A. Piper.
        p. cm. — (Supplements to Novum Testamentum, ISSN 0167-9732 ;
v. 75)
    Includes bibliographical references and indexes.
    ISBN 9004097376
    1. Q hypothesis (Synoptics criticism)   I. Piper, Ronald A.
(Ronald Allen), 1948–   . II. Series.
BS2555.2.G57   1994
226'.066—dc20   94-23349
                                                                    CIP

Die Deutsche Bibliothek - CIP-Einheitsaufnahme

The **gospel behind the gospels** : current studies on Q / ed. by
Ronald A. Piper– Leiden ; New York ; Köln : Brill, 1994
    (Supplements to Novum Testamentum; Vol. 75)
    ISBN 90–04–09737–6
NE: Piper, Ronald A. [Hrsg.]; Novum testamentum / Supplements

ISSN   0167-9732
ISBN   90 04 09737 6

PRINTED IN THE NETHERLANDS

To Faith and Lisette

CONTENTS

PREFACE

The concept for the present volume arose out of the International
Meeting of the Society of Biblical Literature at Vienna in the
summer of 1990, at which a special seminar on Q was arranged to
bring together European and North American scholars. This
planted the seed for a volume which would present an international perspective on the direction of Q studies. I am grateful to
the many eminent scholars who have agreed to contribute to this
effort, many of whom had prepared their essays in late 1991 or
early 1992. I had no idea at that time that within a few months I
would be facing a new administrative position in the University
which would slow progress on this project considerably. My
thanks are due to Hans van der Meij of Brill Publishers, who
inherited the concept of the volume and provided constant
patience and encouragement. In preparing the scripts, I was aided
to a very large extent by Alan McFarlane and Dr Karin Maag,
without whose efforts this volume would still be competing with
day-to-day administrative demands. Finally, I must not fail to
signal my thanks to my family and to my New Testament colleagues in St Andrews for their support in every sense.

Three of the contributions to the current volume have been
translated from German to English. Dieter Lührmann's essay was
translated by my former St Andrews colleague and friend, Robin
McL. Wilson. Paul Hoffmann's essay appeared originally in
German in the *Festschrift* for Frans Neirynck and has been
translated for the present volume by Dr David Orton of Brill.
Luise Schottroff's contribution was originally translated by Dr
Jonathan Reed for the *Occasional Papers* (1991) published by
the Institute for Antiquity and Christianity at Claremont. I am
grateful for permission to reproduce this essay here, particularly
because a version of this paper was originally pressented at the
Vienna conference.

Readers should be aware that throughout the volume contributors have been asked to adopt the convention of the Society of
Biblical Literature's Q Seminar for citing Q texts in the "Q"

format. The Lukan versification is used, preceded by "Q". This notation is used without prejudice regarding either the wording or context of the Q passage. Thus "Q 6:36" refers to the Q-text found at Mt 5:45 // Lk 6:36.

St Mary's College   R. A. Piper
University of St Andrews
St Andrews, Scotland
July 1994

ABBREVIATIONS

The convention for most abbreviations conforms to that given in S. Schwertner (ed.), *Theologische Realenzyklopädie. Abkürzungsverzeichnis* (Berlin / New York: 1976). In addition, the following abbreviations can be found.

BETL	Bibliotheca ephemeridum theologicarum Lovaniensium
ETL	Ephemerides theologicae Lovanienses
GThom	*Gospel of Thomas*
JSNT	*Journal for the Study of the New Testament*
JSOT	*Journal for the Study of the Old Testament*
NovT	*Novum Testamentum*
POxy	*Papyrus Oxyrhynchus*
SBLSP / SBLASP	Society of Biblical Literature Seminar Papers

CHAPTER ONE

IN QUEST OF Q: THE DIRECTION OF Q STUDIES

Ronald A. Piper

As with many areas of scholarly study, the modern investigation of Q has been subject to an uneven history of attention and to the fads and fashions of methodological interests. It is not the purpose of this essay or the present volume to look back over the history of Q studies, even in recent times.[1] The goal is rather to chart from present positions the likely way ahead for scholarly discourse, although necessarily such projections do not emerge from a void. The studies in this volume are also selected to illustrate the breadth of current interests in this field.

It is well documented that Q studies benefited from a surge of interest in the late 1960s and early 1970s. This was largely due to the application of redaction-critical insights to Q and the recognition that Q represented a theologically distinctive entity.[2] Of

---

[1] In 1980, F. Neirynck produced his bibliographical aid entitled "Studies on Q since 1972" in *ETL* 56 (1980) 409-413. In 1982, this was supplemented by a more extensive survey by Neirynck, "Recent Developments in the Study of Q" in *Logia. Les paroles de Jésus – The Sayings of Jesus. Mémorial J. Coppens*, ed. J. Delobel (BETL 59; Leuven: 1982) 29-75. This has been followed by successive contributions of D. Scholer to the SBL Seminar Papers: "Q Bibliography: 1981-1989," *SBLSP* 28 (1989), 23-37; "Q Bibliography Supplement I: 1990," *SBLSP* 29 (1990) 11-13; "Q Bibliography Supplement II: 1991," *SBLSP* 30 (1991) 1-7; "Q Bibliography Supplement III: 1992," *SBLSP* 31 (1992) 1-4; "Q Bibliography Supplement IV: 1993," *SBLSP* 32 (1993) 1-5. Scholer also notes the usefulness of entries under "Q" in T. R. W. Longstaff and P. A. Thomas, *The Synoptic Problem: A Bibliography, 1716-1988* (New Gospel Studies 4; Macon and Leuven: 1988). More recent reviews of Q scholarship include J. M. Robinson, "The Q Trajectory: Between John and Matthew via Jesus" in *The Future of Early Christianity: Essays in Honor of Helmut Koester*, eds. B. A. Pearson *et al.* (Minneapolis: 1991) 173-194; A. D. Jacobson, *The First Gospel. An Introduction to Q* (Sonoma: 1992) 19-60; J. S. Kloppenborg and L. E. Vaage, "Early Christianity, Q and Jesus: The Sayings Gospel and Method in the Study of Christian Origins" in their *Early Christianity, Q and Jesus* (Semeia 55; Atlanta: 1992) 1-13.

[2] A. D. Jacobson (*First Gospel* 33) particularly views this as stemming from the work of H. E. Tödt on the Son of man sayings.

particular significance were studies emanating from the German-speaking world—most notably the monographs of D. Lührmann (1969), P. Hoffmann (1972), S. Schulz (1972), A. Polag (1977)—although dissertations in the States by P. D. Meyer, R. A. Edwards and R. D. Worden also stem from this period. These studies raised the question of the theological characteristics of the Q material, when viewed as a coherent or as a "layered" source, and of course christology became an important focus in the works of Tödt, Schürmann and Polag. In the present volume, D. Lührmann and B. McLean have also suggested that an interest in *Gospel of Thomas* studies at this time, following the Nag Hammadi discoveries, may have been a contributing factor to the parallel interest in Q. This was all the more significant in view of the observations at that time about the *Gattung* of Q in the work of J. M. Robinson and the suggestions of Helmut Koester regarding the relationship of the *Gospel of Thomas* and Q.[3] The 1970s were also marked by the source-critical work of Frans Neirynck, his important studies of the minor agreements of Matthew and Luke against Mark and increasing interest in the relationship between Mark and Q.

A slight sag in the German production of monographs on Q in the late 1970s led to some consolidation at the Louvain Conference on the Sayings of Jesus in 1981. Neirynck's article in this present volume notes that the Logia conference continued to be mainly concerned with the issues of the composition of Q and of the pre-Q collections.

The next major impetus to Q studies came more from the direction of Britain and North America than from Continental Europe. It seems likely that this was due in no small part to the significant revival of discussion in the English-speaking world on the subject of the historical Jesus in the 1980s. The New Quest, deriving from Ernst Käsemann's 1953 lecture, was still heavily indebted to the existential categories of Bultmann. It also seemed still wedded to the consequences of the criterion of dissimilarity, focusing upon the uniqueness of the historical Jesus as seen *over against* Judaism. In the 1980s, however, Jesus studies became

---

[3] J. M. Robinson, "LOGOI SOPHON: On the Gattung of Q" in *Trajectories through Early Christianity*, eds. J. M. Robinson & H. Koester (Philadelphia: 1971) 71-113; H. Koester, "One Jesus and Four Gospels" (pp. 158-204) in the same volume. For a recent evaluation of Koester's contribution, cf. also R. Cameron, "The *Gospel of Thomas* and Christian Origins" in *The Future of Early Christianity: Essays in Honor of Helmut Koester*, eds. B. A. Pearson *et al.* (Minneapolis: 1991) 381-392.

increasingly based on a re-evaluation not only of the nature of Judaism, but also of Jesus as one who sought to renew or reform Judaism *from within*.[4] This was reflected in the titles and sub-titles of several of these works: G. Vermes, *Jesus the Jew* (1973) and *Jesus and the World of Judaism* (1983); J. Riches, *Jesus and the Transformation of Judaism* (1980); E. P. Sanders, *Jesus and Judaism* (1985); G. Theissen, *The Shadow of the Galilean* (1986); and recent books by J. D. Crossan, *The Historical Jesus: The Life of a Mediterranean Jewish Peasant* (1991) and by J. P. Meier, *A Marginal Jew: Rethinking the Historical Jesus* (1991).[5] This increasing willingness, also reflected in several other significant Jesus studies, to write about the historical Jesus has inevitably led to a renewed interest in the earliest sources for Jesus material. So it is perhaps not surprising that the attempt to achieve a critical reconstruction of the text of Q, being undertaken by the International Q Project under the auspices of the Society of Biblical Literature in conjunction with the Institute for Antiquity and Christianity at Claremont, arose in the same era as the (formally distinct) Jesus Seminar which has sought critically to assess the authenticity of the Jesus sayings.

It is likely, though, that other factors too have been at work in the association of Q with the study of Christian origins and the historical Jesus. One such factor was noted in a recent article by J. M. Robinson:[6]

> the early sapiential layer, which may well involve a "paradigm shift" in our understanding of Jesus, is the most important discovery of the current phase of Q research, for which we are primarily indebted to Helmut Koester.

The suggestion of early sapiential, "pre-apocalyptic" material in Q was developed in varying ways in the mid-1980s by D. Zeller,[7]

---

[4] However, the Jewish backgrounds in which Jesus has been located have been exceedingly diverse: cf. J. D. Crossan, *The Historical Jesus. The Life of a Mediterranean Jewish Peasant* (San Francisco: 1991) xxvii-xxviii.

[5] Some figures associated with the New Quest also widened the range of criteria used for reconstructing the historical Jesus, particularly through use of the criterion of independent multiple attestation. This is reflected in J. D. Crossan's work (*The Historical Jesus*), based in part on the Jesus Seminar in the States. He still relies largely, however, on testing sayings material. A more "holistic" approach to developing a historical hypothesis is set forth by E. P. Sanders in his *Jesus and Judaism* (Philadelphia: 1985) 1-58.

[6] "The Q Trajectory" 193-194.

[7] *Die weisheitlichen Mahnsprüche bei den Synoptikern* (FzB 17; Würzburg: 1977)

R. A. Piper[8] and J. S. Kloppenborg.[9] Kloppenborg developed the most comprehensive thesis for Q in this respect, however, arguing for a thoroughgoing stratification of Q in which the earliest formative layer of Q redaction was sapiential rather than "apocalyptic". The growing interest in a sapiential rather than an imminent eschatological proclamation of the kingdom began also to influence recent work on the historical Jesus, with some scholars emphasizing similarities to the message of the Cynics. Q becomes not just a possible early source for such a perspective on Jesus; it is perhaps *the most significant source*. Such views of the nature of the earliest layers of Q have not gone unchallenged, however, as will be discussed further below.

The significance of the investigation of an early sapiential layer of Q can hardly be overestimated for current study in North America. The influence of Kloppenborg's thesis in Europe has been more limited, but European scholars are now beginning to respond to these issues, even if often with caution. The work of Steinhauser, Kloppenborg and Vaage in Toronto, and of Robinson, Mack, and a host of younger scholars from Claremont has led some to identify a "Claremont-Toronto school" of Q studies in North America. Kloppenborg and Robinson have also jointly chaired the International Q Project, which initially emerged in 1983. This project has been a major stimulus to Q research in the North America, although it has had a sprinkling of scholars from other countries associated with it.[10] Recently the participation of a team from Bamberg under Paul Hoffmann[11] has significantly enhanced the international dimension of this effort. Q research inevitably, however, remains broader than is depicted in Claremont-Toronto circles, and it is the intent of the present volume to represent this wider range of Q scholarship rather than any one supposed axis of agreement. It should also become evident that even scholars associated with the so-called Claremont-

---

[8] "Matthew 7,7-11 par. Luke 11,9-13. Evidence of Design and Argument in the Collection of Jesus' Sayings" in *Logia. Les paroles de Jésus – The Sayings of Jesus. Mémorial J. Coppens*, ed. J. Delobel (BETL 59; Leuven: 1982) ; *Wisdom in the Q-tradition. The Aphoristic Teaching of Jesus* (MSSNTS 61; Cambridge: 1989).

[9] Especially his *The Formation of Q. Trajectories in Ancient Wisdom Collections* (Studies in Antiquity & Christianity; Philadelphia: 1987).

[10] Uro, Piper, Hartin, with recent visits by Neirynck, Baarda and Stanton, amongst others.

[11] Also U. Busse.

Toronto school are hardly uniform in their outlook on many of the current debates regarding Q.

The goal of the International Q Project has been to produce a critical reconstruction of the text of Q.[12] There is of course awareness of the dangers of such a project—producing an "agreed" text which masks the evolution of methodology in its production and the inevitable inconsistencies of majority decisions made by a changing board of scholars. Few participants expect the imminent publication of a critical text to resolve all discussion of the wording, sequence and extent of the Q material. Yet the expectation is that a critical text and its database should nevertheless be a valuable resource to the academic community and perhaps to a wider readership, and a substantial revision and updating of the critical text is already being planned to follow its initial production.

The focus in innovative Q research is now being shared between the German-speaking and English-speaking worlds. It is apparent, though, that Q scholarship has tended to have different concerns in its different centres. What is a prominent interest in one region's gospel scholarship may simply not be so pressing a concern elsewhere.

An interesting example is British scholarship. Until recently, at issue has not been the stratification of Q or the precise christology of Q[13] or even the eschatology of Q. The issue has remained the more basic one of whether Q existed at all. Following in the footsteps of the Oxford scholar Austin Farrer, Michael Goulder[14] has continued powerfully to raise the prospect of "dispensing with Q" in favour of a theory which accepts both Markan priority and direct Lukan use of Matthew. Hypothetical sources are unnecessary if redactional efforts, primarily of Luke acting upon Matthew, can be shown to explain what otherwise would be

---

[12] The results of the Project have been regularly reported in *JBL*. See "The International Q Project Work Session 17 November 1989," *JBL* 109 (1990) 499-501; "The International Q Project Work Session 19 November 1990," *JBL* 110 (1991) 494-498; "The International Q Project Work Sessions 12-14 July, 22 November 1991," *JBL* 111 (1992) 500-508; "The International Q Project Work Sessions 31 July-2 August, 20 November 1992," *JBL* 112 (1993) 500-506. Also, cf. J. M. Robinson, "A Critical Text of the Sayings Gospel Q," *Revue d'Histoire et de Philosophie Religieuses* 72 (1992) 15-22.

[13] But cf. G. N. Stanton, "On the Christology of Q" in *Christ and Spirit in the New Testament* (*Festschrift* C. F. D. Moule), eds. B. Lindars & S. S. Smalley (Cam–bridge: 1973) 25-40.

[14] Cf. especially M. D. Goulder, *Luke. A New Paradigm*, 2 vols. (JSNT Supplement Series 20; Sheffield: 1989).

attributed to Q. While his highly economical solution to the synoptic problem has appealed to some British scholars, probably more influential have been his specific attempts to undermine the Q hypothesis by pressing the significance of the minor agreements of Matthew and Luke against Mark in triple tradition passages in order to demonstrate Lukan dependence on Matthew (*contra* Q). The importance of this discussion for the Q hypothesis has also been reflected in the previously-noted monumental work of Frans Neirynck, supporting Q by arguing that the agreements are often due to independent redactional activity by Matthew and Luke.[15] These concerns also gave rise in July 1991 to a symposium on the minor agreements in Göttingen.[16]

At the opposite pole to the economical theory of Michael Goulder, however, is another attack upon the Q-hypothesis which suggests that it is inherently more likely that there were *several* hypothetical lost sources, including different editions of the gospels themselves, with complicated possibilities of copying from one another.[17] In this view, the Gospel of Mark is not always the middle term among the three synoptic gospels. It is argued by E. P. Sanders, for example, that even those who adopt "simple solutions", such as the Two-Source Hypothesis, often have to make exceptions which strictly should lead to more complicated solutions.[18] For some the necessary extra flexibility has been achieved by viewing Q as a floating layer of tradition, rather than as a fixed document. Increasingly, however, those working in Q studies have rejected this understanding of the Q hypothesis. Important among the considerations has been a recognition of a discernible common order to the Q-sayings in Matthew and Luke.[19] This precludes an understanding of the double tradition material as simply having been plucked at random, independently, by Matthew and Luke from a floating body of oral or written traditions. Acceptance of a fixed source then leads to questions

---

[15] *The Minor Agreements of Matthew and Luke against Mark, With a Cumulative List* (BETL 37; Leuven: 1974).

[16] *Die Minor Agreements in den Synoptischen Evangelien* (GTA; Göttingen: forthcoming). Cf. also recently J. Schüling, *Studien zum Verhältnis von Logienquelle und Markusevangelium* (FzB 65; Würzburg: 1991).

[17] Cf. the discussion of M.-E. Boismard and of other "complicated" solutions in E. P. Sanders & M. Davies, *Studying the Synoptic Gospels* (London / Philadelphia: 1989) ch. 6.

[18] *Ibid.* 115.

[19] Cf. V. Taylor, "The Order of Q," *JTS* 4 (1953) 27-31; and "The Original Order of Q" in *New Testament Essays. Studies in Memory of T. W. Manson*, ed. A. J. B. Higgins (Manchester: 1959) 95-118.

regarding compilation, redaction, and social context for the composition and its stages of development.[20]

In Britain these two-pronged, albeit rather different, attacks of Goulder and Sanders have led to some diffidence about Q studies in scholarly circles, although Q research is currently being pursued by Tuckett, Catchpole and Piper. In contrast, the neo-Griesbachian attack in the States seems simply to have led to a polarization of approaches. Adherents of Q in North America have not been diverted into defensive arguments about the Q hypothesis, but have been intent on following up the consequences of the Q hypothesis for the reconstruction of Q, the compositional layers of Q and the accompanying contextual and theological issues. This theological agenda was of course raised earlier in German scholarship, where doubts about the existence of Q have also been relatively rare.

In addition, notice should be taken of the production in recent years of scholarly tools for the study of Q. Q-synopses have been produced according to a variety of styles and principles. Some attempt to give reconstructions of Q, such as A. Polag's *Fragmenta Q* (1979)[21] and W. Schenk's reconstruction in German, *Synopse zur Redenquelle der Evangelien* (1981). Frans Neirynck's *Q-Synopsis. The Double Tradition Passages in Greek* (1988) prints parallel texts, highlighting precise similarities but without a reconstruction. J. S. Kloppenborg's *Q Parallels. Synopsis, Critical Notes & Concordance* (1987) sets out parallel texts in Greek with an accompanying English translation and other parallels. Further portrayal of Q's parallels with the *Gospel of Thomas* are set out in the *Q-Thomas Reader* (1990),[22] although the English translations of Q and Thomas are presented separately, rather than in parallel. Kloppenborg's concordance goes beyond the minimal Q vocabulary (the verbatim Matthew-Luke agreements),[23] but indicates the minimal vocabulary with

---

[20] The reconstruction of the *sequence* of Q is part of the task of the International Q Project. Arland Jacobson, however, notes that this has surprisingly not been a central focus in recent studies of Q. Progress towards this end has been made, however, by his recent book, *The First Gospel*, building upon his very significant dissertation "Wisdom Christology in Q" (Claremont: Ph.D. dissertation, 1978).

[21] With an English translation in I. Havener, *Q. The Sayings of Jesus* (Good News Studies 19; Wilmington: 1986).

[22] Eds. J. S. Kloppenborg, M. W. Meyer, S. J. Patterson, M. G. Steinhauser.

[23] See R. A. Edwards, *A Concordance to Q* (Chico: 1975).

asterisks.[24] The task of critical reconstruction of the text of Q underpins most of Q research and inevitably involves considerable attention to preferences in vocabulary. For this R. Morgenthaler's *Statistische Synopse* (1971) and F. Neirynck and F. Van Segbroeck's *New Testament Vocabulary* (1984) are invaluable. The sheer number of such tools appearing in recent years for the study and reconstruction of Q is itself testimony to the level of activity in the field of Q studies.

*

Essays in the present volume have been selected to reflect these and other strands in Q studies which point the way to future research. The breadth of the studies is itself impressive. Beginning with the basic question of the Q hypothesis itself, and writing in the context of the British debates about the Q hypothesis described above, Christopher Tuckett has presented a renewed defence of the existence of Q in his essay in the present volume. In doing so, he chooses to tackle one of the most critical areas of dispute between adherents of Q and its opponents—the issue of whether Luke used Matthew. Both M. D. Goulder and the adherents of the Griesbach hypothesis appeal to Luke's use of Matthew to explain the double-tradition material without the need for Q. If their explanation for the double-tradition material lacks credibility, as Tuckett argues, then this inevitably bolsters the likelihood of the Q hypothesis at one of its most critical points.[25]

Not unrelated to the question of Luke's knowledge of Matthew is the other vulnerable point of the Q hypothesis, the so-called "minor agreements" of Matthew and Luke against Mark. Their prominence in recent studies has already been noted above. If the minor agreements are explained by extending the range of sayings attributed to Q into triple tradition passages, then they have the potential of seriously enlarging Q. Q thus becomes increasingly gospel-like in form and extent (particularly if it includes material from the passion narrative). One alternative is to posit other common sources for Matthew and Luke, but this raises the

---

[24] Kloppenborg (*Q Parallels* xxi-xxii) also notes other partial or privately-circulated synopses.

[25] Another recent attack on Goulder's position appears in D. Catchpole, *The Quest for Q* (Edinburgh: 1993), chapter 1, in which Catchpole appeals to specific passages in which it is argued that the form of the tradition in Luke is an earlier version than that in Matthew, thus opening up "the space between the theology of Q and the theology of Matthew" (p. 7).

question of the nature of such sources and can lead to theories which seem highly complex and arbitrary. Another alternative is of course to accept Luke's direct use of Matthew, but (as Tuckett argues) this may be implausible on other grounds. A further alternative is argued in the present volume by Frans Neirynck, who carefully considers several examples of such agreements in which independent redactional activity by Matthew and Luke can be used to explain such agreements. The result of such a position is that the minor agreements need not lead to an enlargement of Q or necessitate other more complex solutions.

It is interesting to observe, however, that even among staunch adherents to the Q hypothesis, there has been a tendency to extend the boundaries of Q, as Neirynck notes.[26] Increased study of the theology of Q has sometimes resulted in scholars seeing their findings reflected in other *Sondergut* material or Markan material. The need to maintain some methodological control over such expansions will clearly be a test for future Q studies. The pressures will not only come from those outside the circles of Q scholarship, but from within it.

This is in part because Q is increasingly seen by scholars in the field as a "real" document, not simply a hypothetical construction. It is therefore arguably likely that if Matthew and Luke each independently had a "real" document Q in front of them, then on occasions either Matthew or Luke would choose not to record a saying where the other evangelist did. After all, Matthew and Luke clearly do not agree on reproducing the whole of Mark (on the theory of Markan priority). Thus Q might have included material which to us appears as *Sondergut* material.

The situation is slightly different, however, for the Mark-Q overlaps. The explanation for the overlaps is less clear. Did Mark know and use Q? If so, why did he leave out so much of it? Can one explain these "omissions" in terms of Markan redactional motives? Or, did Mark only know of Q material at secondhand? Were there floating traditions common to Mark and Q or an earlier fixed core tradition?

The willingness to entertain Mark-Q overlaps as indicating Markan dependence upon Q has been more characteristic of some Q scholars than others. David Catchpole's recent analyses of the beginning of Q and the mission charge both allow for Mark's

---

[26] The extent of Q is a major consideration in the construction of the recent Q-synopses. Neirynck has tended to be more restricted in the passages included in his synopsis than either Polag or Kloppenborg: see above.

dependence upon Q,[27] in contrast to C. M. Tuckett,[28] R. Laufen, J. Kloppenborg, M. Sato and R. Uro. These latter scholars tend to be more cautious in describing the extent of the overlaps and take the view that Mark and Q are not *directly* related. The debate has also taken place in Leuven, with Jan Lambrecht arguing against Neirynck in favour of Mark's knowledge of Q in several pericopes. Lambrecht's contribution to the present volume, on the Great Commandment, proposes a relatively-untested example of such a possibility on the basis of minor agreements in Mt 22:34-40 and Lk 10:25-28 against Mk 12:28-34. How far to extend the boundaries beyond "minimal Q" thus continues to be a live issue.

A radical enlargement of the extent of Q might also materially affect estimates of its genre. Traditionally known as the Sayings Source, even this description of Q can mask different assumptions, as the insightful essay in this volume by Dieter Lührmann shows. Lührmann traces the modern discussion back to Schleiermacher's interpretation of Papias' comments about the gospels of Matthew and Mark. J. M. Robinson's designation some thirty years ago of the *Gattung* of Q as λόγοι σοφῶν (rather than *Logia*) was intended to imply not just a collection of sayings, but a *sapiential* collection of Jesus' sayings, on a trajectory extending from Jewish wisdom literature through the *Gospel of Thomas*. The description of the sapiential nature of the *Gattung*, however, has been further modified by J. S. Kloppenborg. Kloppenborg not only expanded the discussion of genre to include consideration of literature outside Jewish and Christian collections, but also suggested a stratification of the material in Q such that some shift of genre has occurred as Q developed from instruction to proto-biography.[29] The identification of the earliest, formative aspect of Q as sapiential and instructional, which then was expanded by chriae and polemical material against Israel, however, has opened up a field of debate both on the front of the stratification of the

---

[27] *The Quest for Q* 63, 152-158. Cf. also W. Schenk with respect to the mission charge in a paper presented to the SNTS Pre-Synoptic Tradition Seminar at Madrid in 1992.

[28] Cf. "Mark and Q" in *The Synoptic Gospels. Source Criticism and the New Literary Criticism*, ed. C. Focant (BETL 110; Louvain: 1993) 149-175. In addition to D. Catchpole and J. Lambrecht, Tuckett cites W. Schenk, W. Schmithals, H. Fleddermann and B. Mack amongst recent scholars arguing for Mark's use of Q.

[29] *Formation*, 1-40, 263-327

material and on the front of whether "formative Q" is best described as sapiential.[30]

Dieter Lührmann had previously attempted to distinguish earlier and later stages of Q in terms of early collections and subsequent redaction.[31] Kloppenborg, however, distinguishes between those blocks of Q material which were permeated with the announcement of coming judgement and attacks on the lack of repentance on the part of "this generation" and other blocks which were sapiential rather than polemical. He argues that the sapiential collections of sayings represent the formative stratum in Q (Q[1]) and the sayings with the theme of judgement represent a later stratum (Q[2]). A third stage followed, marked mainly by the temptation account, and was an example of a historicizing tendency. This stratification theory has been extremely influential in North America and has begun to raise questions about the history of the Q "community" implied in these stages, although the theory of stratification itself is not without challengers.[32] Hoffmann, in his essay in the present volume, finds Kloppenborg's main criterion for the discernment of traditio-historical layers problematic in that it relies on distinctions of *form* and the broad identification of complexes of sayings as being of the "wisdom"-type. Hoffmann appeals instead to literary and

---

[30] The title of the current volume, *The Gospel Behind the Gospels*, may seem to suggest a return to the older views of B. Weiss and B. W. Bacon that Q is of the "gospel" genre. A new defense of the applicability of the term "gospel" is offered, however, by A. D. Jacobson (*The First Gospel*). He states: "The word 'gospel' is used provocatively to suggest that Q by itself represents a view of Jesus, a view which did not necessarily have its principal focus on Jesus' death and resurrection. The use of the word 'gospel' suggests that Q and the canonical gospels are comparable entitities. Simply calling Q a source does not make this point" (pp. 3-4). A detailed argument for the use of the category "Sayings Gospel" has also been recently offered by J. M. Robinson, "The Sayings Gospel Q" in *The Four Gospels 1992. Festschrift Frans Neirynck*, eds. F. Van Segbroeck *et al.* (BETL 100.1; Leuven: 1992) 361-388. Cf. also several recent works by J. S. Kloppenborg, and B. L. Mack in his *The Lost Gospel. The Book of Q and Christian Origins* (Shaftesbury/Rockport/Brisbane: 1993) 1.

[31] *Die Redaktion der Logienquelle* (WMANT 33; Neukirchen: 1969).

[32] Cf. also C. M. Tuckett, "On the Stratification of Q. A Response" in *Early Christianity, Q and Jesus*, eds. J. S. Kloppenborg & L. E. Vaage (Semeia 55; Atlanta: 1992) 213-222; R. A. Horsley, "Logoi Propheton? Reflections on the Genre of Q" in *The Future of Early Christianity: Essays in Honor of Helmut Koester*, eds. B. A. Pearson *et al.* (Minneapolis: 1991) 195-209. Horsley also refers in this essay to his earlier work "Questions about Redactional Strata and the Social Relations Reflected in Q" in *SBLSP (1989)* 186-203, and the response by Kloppenborg in the same volume (204-215).

redaction-critical investigation of units of composition and shows more sympathy with the approach of M. Sato.

The debate over stratification is still continuing, as indicated earlier. In the present volume, Wendy Cotter's essay builds upon, rather than challenges, Kloppenborg's stratification theory and explores the socio-cultural contexts which would apply to the two main strata. This is undoubtedly an important field for future research and involves the application of social-scientific approaches, a developing field of study now being applied to the New Testament world. Cotter's results suggest that while the sapiential stratum of Q reflects a weak sense of group organization and a new value system based in part on a present confidence in God's providence, the later stratum (Q²) shows a stronger group identity in the face of opposition. They continue to enjoy the security of being known as Jews but portray themselves as heirs of the persecuted prophets and patriarchs. This allowed them both to maintain their Jewish identity and to preach their new unconventional wisdom.

Yet the present volume also includes essays which challenge Kloppenborg's thesis. The essay by Migaku Sato is particularly directed this way. Sato's earlier monograph on *Q und Prophetie. Studien zur Gattungs- und Traditionsgeschichte der Quelle Q* (1988) had already argued for a more "prophetic" assessment of the genre of Q, following M. E. Boring, S. Schulz and W. Kelber.[33] D. Catchpole has also recently defended such an assessment, appealing in part to the way in which Q begins with the prophetic figure of John the Baptist, warning that the people of God (and Q) must be prepared for the imminent eschatological crisis, centring on the coming of the Son of man.[34] Sato's case relies on arguing that the allegedly sapiential material often overturns conventional wisdom in a way which is not unlike "prophetic" texts and that the outlook of Q is fundamentally prophetic and eschatological, regardless of the incorporation of sapiential material. This applies to all compositional levels.[35]

---

[33] Cf. also R. Horsley, n. 31 above.

[34] *The Quest for Q* 77-78.

[35] My own work suggests that the early sapiential collections were deliberately non-polemical in tone, because they were attempting to persuade "insiders" to adopt certain attitudes towards sensitive issues such as material and physical welfare and community relationships. Strictly, the *function* of the collections rather than their location in a particular "stratum" accounts for the nature of these clusters, although it must be recognised that a predilection to present material in this way also relies upon a collector or set of "scribes" skilled in such

Recently, C. M. Tuckett has also questioned Koester's concept of a "primitive Wisdom Gospel" based on both Q and the *Gospel of Thomas*.[36]

The debate involves forms, themes and the traditio-historical study of individual units. Regarding leading theological concepts, J. M. Robinson notes in his essay that two of the leading theological categories of Q are often identified as the kingdom of God and the Son of man. Both raise important questions about the nature of Q's eschatology which are relevant also to the discussion of Q's redactional stages. Moreover, Q's treatment of the Son of man is crucial to any discussion of the development of early Christology.

Not surprisingly, various redactional models have been suggested for Q's use of the Son of man category. Paul Hoffmann's contribution to the present volume on the Son of man sayings has these issues firmly in mind. After careful examination of the theories of H. E. Tödt, O. H. Steck, D. Lührmann, A. Jacobson, J. S. Kloppenborg and M. Sato, Hoffmann puts forward the provocative thesis that the Son of man concept gained favour during the period around the Fall of Jerusalem (70 CE) and therefore is likely to represent a very late phase in the redaction of Q. Far from representing an early stage of tradition, this concept owes its incorporation into Q (as in Mark 13) to a late crisis and to the social traumas of the separation of the Q-adherents from the Jewish national community and the rejection of their Palestinian mission to Israel. The concept of the Son of man provides the Q-people with a new universal perspective of their significance; it marks a new beginning as well as a separation. Although Hoffmann shows considerably more sympathy for Sato's

---

techniques. Whether their outlook was unmixed with imminent eschatological concerns when other issues were being considered is more difficult to discern. Note also the recent study by D. Zeller ("Eine weisheitliche Grundschrift in der Logienquelle?" in *The Four Gospels 1992. Festschrift Frans Neirynck*, eds. F. Van Segbroeck *et al.* [BETL 100.1; Leuven: 1992] 389-402), who doubts that the composition of Q as a whole can be regarded as primarily sapiential. On the other hand, in the same volume A. Jacobson challenges those who would argue that an apocalyptic *Naherwartung* dominates the Q material ("Apocalyptic and the Synoptic Sayings Source Q" in *The Four Gospels 1992. Festschrift Frans Neirynck*, eds. F. Van Segbroeck *et al.* [BETL 100.1; Leuven: 1992] 389-402). See also J. M. Robinson's response to Sato in "Die Logienquelle: Weisheit oder Prophetie? Anfragen an Migaku Sato, *Q und Prophetie*," *EvTh* 53 (1993) 367-389.

[36] C. Tuckett, "Q and Thomas: Evidence of a Primitive 'Wisdom Gospel'?" *ETL* 67 (1991) 346-360.

methodology than for Kloppenborg's model of Q strata, he
differs significantly from Sato by locating the Son of Man sayings
at such a late stage.[37]

Distinguishing the earlier from the later stages of Q also has
other major consequences. Not least among these are the consequences for studies of the historical Jesus. The works of J. D.
Crossan[38] and B. L. Mack[39] have firmly raised the issue of
whether the earliest stage of the Jesus tradition, linking closely to
Jesus himself, could be described as reflecting the outlook of a
Jewish Cynic-sage, largely devoid of the millenial or
"apocalyptic"-prophetic perspective attributed to figures like
John the Baptist.[40] Crossan's reconstruction of the historical Jesus
relies heavily on Q and on what he identifies as the earliest stratum
of the *Gospel of Thomas*. For Mack, the focus is more closely on
the earlier, formative stages in Q.

This matter is addressed from different angles by several of the
essays in this volume. Leif Vaage's essay tackles directly the
attack by Christopher Tuckett on the theory of a Cynic Q.[41] Much
of Tuckett's original attack was addressed at the work of F. Gerald
Downing,[42] but not exclusively so, and the discussion has widened
considerably since then. Tuckett questioned both the nature of the
evidence for Cynicism in the first century and the comparison of
Cynicism with Q. Interestingly, Tuckett's case also seems linked to
approval for the prophetic rather than sapiential nature of Q, as
Vaage notes.[43] For his part, Vaage differentiates his own views
from Downing's (and Kloppenborg's[44]) and responds to both

---

[37] In contrast, in a forthcoming review of Colpe's article on the Son of Man,
J. M. Robinson ("The Son of Man in the Saying Gospel Q") argues for a layering
of the Son of man concept in Q such that: "In the older layer the term is infrequent, and refers to Jesus only during his public ministry (Q 6:22; 9:58), but
in the redactional layer it is common, in most cases used in an apocalyptic
sense, so that a directionality in the development is indicated." Cf. also L. E.
Vaage, "The Son of Man Sayings in Q: Stratigraphical Location and Significance" in *Early Christianity, Q and Jesus*, eds. J. S. Kloppenborg & L. E. Vaage
(Semeia 55; Atlanta: 1992) 103-129.

[38] *The Historical Jesus.*

[39] *The Lost Gospel.*

[40] Crossan, *Historical Jesus* 421.

[41] C. M. Tuckett, "A Cynic Q?" *Biblica* 10 (1989) 349-376.

[42] See Downing, *Christ and the Cynics. Jesus and Other Radical Preachers in
First-Century Tradition* (Sheffield: 1988); *idem*, "Quite Like Q. A Genre for 'Q':
The 'Lives' of Cynic Philosophers," *Bib.* 69 [1988] 196-225.

[43] C. M. Tuckett, "A Cynic Q?" 376.

[44] Kloppenborg does not argue that Q itself is Cynic, but he recognizes some
analogies between Q and Cynicism: *Formation*, 324.

spheres of Tuckett's attack. While admitting the late date of many of the texts referring to early Cynics, Vaage argues that the general popularity and the persistance of the movement in the Mediterranean basin make likely the thesis that Cynic ideas were present even in first-century Galilee. With regard to evidence for parallels between Cynic ideas and the sayings in Q, prime attention of course focuses on the mission instructions in Q 10:3-6, 9-11, 16. Other ethical teaching (Q 6:27-35; Q 6:20-21; Q 11:2-4, 14-20; Q 12:22-31; Q 13:18-19, 20-21) and polemics or social critiques (Q 11:39-41, 42, 44, 46, 47-48, 52) are, however, also analyzed in an effort to show that the comparison is sustainable. The similarities, he argues, are not simply incidental. This latter point is likely to be a key feature of further debate. Although similarities can hardly be denied on a superficial level, it is necessary to demonstrate that the underlying perspectives are similar in order to find a truly Cynic Q, much less a Cynic Jesus.

A tentative step in this general direction, however, comes perhaps rather unexpectedly from Risto Uro's study in the present volume on John the Baptist in Q. Because of its prophetic nature, the Baptist material is only rarely considered fertile ground for any Cynic theory, although Ron Cameron has recently presented an argument based on Q 7:18-35.[45] Working on the basis of Kloppenborg's redactional strata, Uro attributes to the second stratum of Q the apocalyptic Baptist sayings in Q 3. Because this corresponds so closely to the redactional strategies of this stratum, it cannot be held that the apocalyptic warnings in Q 3 necessarily reflect the historical John. To do so would involve a complicated theory of an originally apocalyptic John, who then re-emerges in the second stratum of Q after passing through the medium of the sapiential first stratum. Moreover, Uro finds it significant that Q preserves sayings which pit Jesus and John together against common opponents (Q 7:33-34) and notes the lack of hostility even in sayings which subordinate John to Jesus (Q 3:16; 7:28). Taken together, these observations raise for him the possibility not necessarily of a "Cynic" Jesus and John (in partial differentiation from Cameron), but at least a closing of the gap between the historical John and historical Jesus and a questioning of the apocalyptic features of both.

---

[45] Cf. his "'What Have You Come Out To See?' Characterizations of John and Jesus in the Gospels" in his *The Apocryphal Jesus and the Christian Origins* (Semeia 49; Atlanta: 1990) 35-69.

Not all who recognise the sapiential character of Q, or of strata
or clusters within it, necessarily argue for a Cynic model for Q or
Jesus. In this volume, J. M. Robinson puts forward a different
paradigm: "The Jesus of Q as Liberation Theologian".[46] This
stimulating essay takes as its point of departure material such as
Q 11:2-4, 9-13; 12:22-31 and the mission instructions in Q 10.
From these sayings, he argues that the Jesus of Q, although being
neither an ascetic nor a leader with an effective social programme,
did elevate the plight of the masses who were living without the
basic necessities of life to a central point in his theology. The
movement "had its original focus on re-evaluating the status of all
victims of fate, in view of the radical nature of the kingdom of
God." In this sense, the Jesus of Q may be seen as "liberation
theologian". The social implications of this portrait for the
earliest Q community still need to be explored, as well as the
connection between the Jesus of this early stage of tradition and
the historical Jesus.

The connection between the Jesus of Q and the historical Jesus
may indeed be far from simple, despite the relatively early tradition which Q presents. This is clearly depicted in John
Kloppenborg's essay on the parables of Jesus in Q. He argues that
the original dynamic of the parables has been lost because even in
Q the parables have acquired other functions as "proofs" or
"examples" which conform to the compositional strategies of
each stratum of Q. None of the parables in Q function
"parabolically", and only two are explicitly related to the
kingdom. Scribal rhetoric and argument have been at work, in a
way which contrasts strikingly with the *Gospel of Thomas* where
the parables are free-standing and lack such transformation. The
Gospel of Thomas therefore provides better access to the parables
of Jesus. This must be seen as testimony to the strength of the
"scribalizing" of Q.

The relationship of the *Gospel of Thomas* (*GThom*) to Q has of
course been a prominent field of discussion following the discovery of this Coptic text in 1945 and a growing interest in the relationship between the apocryphal and the canonical gospels. The
correspondence between *GThom* and three previously-known
Oxyrhynchus Papyri suggests that *GThom* was widely known in
the early Church, and its genre as a collection of sayings has
provided many scholars with an intriguing parallel to the sup-

---

[46] Robinson describes the Cynic conclusion as "more provocative than convincing" (cf. note 6 of his essay below).

posed genre of Q. Although many *GThom* sayings have no counterparts in the canonical gospels, there are several examples of sayings common to both. Questions initially focused upon whether *GThom* showed direct dependence upon the canonical gospels in these cases. The essay in the present volume by Bradley McLean tabulates the impressive array of scholarly opinion on both sides of this debate and explores more precisely the relationship between *GThom* and Q. If *GThom* is based primarily on oral tradition rather than secondarily upon the synoptic gospels, then it could preserve early testimony to the Jesus sayings tradition, which would place *GThom* on par with Q. Indeed it would support the thesis that *GThom* at times may preserve an earlier form of a given tradition than Q. McLean's essay updates the case for this view. Significantly, he also raises the further issue of how *GThom* may relate to the *various strata* of,Q. In view of Crossan's recent stratification of *GThom* itself,[47] these discussions are increasingly important, but still have some way to go.

Finally, the social organisation of the early Christians who transmitted and were addressed by the traditions in Q has also given rise to considerable interest. Gerd Theissen's model of itinerant prophets as the early transmitters of the Q traditions was based in part on the recognition that the "sayings tradition is characterized by an ethical radicalism that is shown most noticeably in the renunciation of a home, family and possessions."[48] His theory, however, has been either challenged or refined on several fronts. In the essay in this volume by Luise Schottroff, entitled "Itinerant Prophetesses: A Feminist Analysis of the Sayings Source Q," Schottroff re-examines this ethical radicalism from a feminist perspective. She argues that Q depicts Jesus challenging the patriarchal household, despite the generally androcentric perspective of the Q material. This leads her to the inference that *women* prophetesses existed in this community, including some who left the household to become itinerant messengers. This conclusion particularly arises from her analysis of sayings which depict a woman's labour (Q 13:20-21; Q 17:34-35; Q 12:27; Q 17:27; Q 11:11-12) and family conflicts (Q 12:51-53; Q 9:58; Q 17:27).

Scholars such as Kloppenborg and Horsley, however, have begun to question whether even the earliest stages of Q were

---

[47] *Historical Jesus* 427-428.
[48] G. Theissen, *Social Reality and the Early Christians. Theology, Ethics and the World of the New Testament,* trans. M. Kohl (Minneapolis: 1992) 37.

dominated by the concerns of itinerant prophets / prophetesses.
These scholars have, in contrast, insisted that the concerns of Q
were *community*-oriented.[49] Furthermore, Arland Jacobson's essay
in the present volume questions whether the patriarchal household
was rejected because it was "patriarchal". He argues that Q is
simply anti-family, noting that the locus of Jewish religious life
was after all not in the synagogue but primarily in the household.
The household was therefore the battleground for the religious
peculiarities of the Q-people, who in turn formed new family-like
groups. Jacobson notes that although he believes families or
households constitute the most likely social context for the Q
group(s), the study of such families and households has not yet
received the attention it deserves.

The field of Q studies therefore faces an impressive agenda. It
appears to be set not simply for a short-term burst of activity, but
for an investigation of Christian origins, spurred on by renewed
interest not only in these origins but also in the historical Jesus,
which will occupy Q scholarship at least to the end of the present
decade and probably beyond. The present volume is dedicated
both to sketching the parameters of this investigation and to advancing the discussion of "the Gospel behind the Gospels."

---

[49] J. S. Kloppenborg, "Literary Convention, Self-Evidence and the Social
History of the Q People" in *Early Christianity, Q and Jesus*, eds. J. S. Kloppenborg & L. E. Vaage (Semeia 55; Atlanta: 1992) 86-91; R. Horsley, "Q and Jesus:
Assumptions, Approaches, and Analyses" (in the same volume) 197, 205, and
his "Logoi Propheton?" 207-209. Also cf. R. Piper, *Wisdom in the Q Tradition*
70-74, 184-186.

CHAPTER TWO

THE EXISTENCE OF Q

Christopher M. Tuckett

The theory of the existence of a "Q" source is usually regarded as part of the more wide-ranging Two Source theory (2ST) which seeks to account for the agreements between the three synoptic gospels. According to the 2ST, Matthew and Luke are directly dependent on the Gospel of Mark as one of their main sources; the further Matthew-Luke agreements are then explained by common dependence on a lost source, or a lost body of (possibly disparate) source material, usually known as "Q".

The essays in this volume testify to the intense interest today in Q, taking seriously the possibility that Q may have had its own distinctive features and characteristics, and that it may reflect the concerns of a particular group of Christians within primitive Christianity. However, before one considers such possibilities, one should consider the prior question of whether Q ever existed. For if there is one thing about which all are agreed, it is this: *if* Q ever existed, it is now lost and we possess no manuscript copy of it. Further, it appears to have left little or no influence on any extant documents in early Christianity other than the gospels of Matthew and Luke.[1] Is it then justifiable to talk of "Q" as a well-defined

---

[1] Occasionally attempts have been made to try to find evidence of Q (or something closely related to Q) in other texts, e.g. in 1 Corinthians, or in some of the Nag Hammadi texts, notably the Gospel of Thomas. I have examined these claims elsewhere with uniformly negative results: there appears to be no clear evidence for the existence of anything akin to Q lying behind any of these other texts. For 1 Corinthians, see my "1 Corinthians and Q," *JBL* 102 (1983) 607-619; for Thomas, see my "Thomas and the Synoptics," *NovT* 30 (1988) 132-157, and for the other Nag Hammadi texts *Nag Hammadi and the Gospel Tradition* (Edinburgh: 1986). More recently, H. Koester has developed further his views about the possible link between Q and the Gospel of Thomas in his *Ancient Christian Gospels* (London: 1990). I have tried to discuss this in "Q and Thomas: Evidence of a Primitive 'Wisdom Gospel'?" *ETL* 67 (1991) 347-360 The attempt to see evidence of Q in the tradition behind James by P. J. Hartin, *James and the Q Sayings of Jesus* (Sheffield: 1991), suffers somewhat

body of material when the evidence for its existence appears to be so slim?

In general terms one may say initially that the apparent silence elsewhere in the tradition about any evidence of Q is not particularly surprising, and certainly no bar to postulating the existence of a Q source. It is quite clear that our knowledge of primitive Christianity is at best somewhat fragmentary. There are a number of texts whose existence we know of, or can postulate, but which we do not possess. For example, we know of the existence of Jewish Christian gospels such as the Gospel of the Hebrews from citations in the Church fathers, although we have no manuscript copies of these gospels;[2] from Paul's extant letters we can deduce the existence of other letters written by Paul (e.g. to Corinth) which have not been preserved. We know too of areas of primitive Christianity, for example in Egypt or in Rome, that must have developed very quickly but which have left little or no literary deposit. Thus the fact that Q, if it existed, has not left its mark on other preserved elements within primitive Christianity is not necessarily surprising. Such silence may simply indicate the sparse extent of the evidence which has been survived.

Further, we may note that, if Q was used by Matthew and Luke, such use would almost certainly have led to a lessening of concern to preserve Q itself. The situation may not have been dissimilar to that involving Mark and the other two synoptic gospels. If Mark was used by Matthew and Luke, then the very fact of (say) Matthew's existence inevitably led to an eclipse in interest in Mark, since Mark must have appeared to many to be somewhat redundant alongside the fuller Gospel of Matthew.[3] Certainly we know that in the period after the writing of the gospels, Matthew was the most widely used and interest in Mark's Gospel was severely limited.[4] It is easy to conceive of the same happening with Q, if it existed. The appearance of Matthew's and Luke's gospels must inevitably have led to Q's being regarded as somewhat redundant and hence its lack of prominence elsewhere in primitive Christianity is not at all surprising. Nevertheless the nonappearance of Q in any explicit manuscript form has always led

---

by failing to provide clear criteria for identifying what is Q and by being rather optimistic in locating parallels.

[2] See E. Hennecke (ed.), *New Testament Apocrypha: I* (London: 1963) 117-165.

[3] The same is true even if Mark was written after Matthew.

[4] Cf. E. Massaux, *Influence de l'Evangile de saint Matthieu sur la littérature chrétienne avant saint Irénée* (repr. BETL 75; Leuven: 1986).

some to doubt the existence of such a source, and such doubts have continued right up to the present. The question "Did Q exist?" has thus always been a contentious one.

One should however note that the question "Did Q exist?" is not necessarily as straightforward as it appears at first sight, or perhaps better, any alleged straight "yes" or "no" answer to the question might need some further clarification. The theory of the existence of a Q source arose as part of the 2ST to explain the agreements between the texts of Matthew and Luke which were not to be explained by common dependence on Mark. These agreements are often so close, amounting at times to almost verbatim agreement in the Greek texts of the gospels (cf. Q 3:7-9; 11:9f.), that some form of literary relationship seems to be demanded: either one evangelist has used the work of the other directly, or both are dependent on (a) common source(s).

At one level, the Q hypothesis is simply a negative theory, denying the possibility that one evangelist made direct use of the work of the other.[5] However, within such a denial, a variety of positions can be adopted. One could for example argue that Luke and Matthew both had access to a single common source which existed as a self-contained written document. (This is often regarded as "the" Q hypothesis.) Alternatively, whilst still denying any direct use of Matthew by Luke, one could argue that Matthew and Luke depend at various points in the tradition on a variety of different source materials, and the nature and extent of these materials might have been rather varied: some might have formed smaller written collections, some might have constituted isolated traditions preserved orally.[6] On this view, the whole of the so-called Q material may never have been collected into a single document prior to its use by Matthew and Luke and we should perhaps speak of "Q material" rather than "Q" simpliciter. Ad-

---

[5] For various reasons, this is almost always postulated in the form of Luke's dependence on Matthew. Matthean dependence on Luke is hardly ever advocated, though one sometimes wonders why given the tendency of many to believe that Luke's version is very often more original (cf. below). However, Lk 1:1 clearly implies that Luke is aware of the existence of predecessors in writing some account of Jesus' ministry.

[6] Cf. E. E. Ellis, "Gospel Criticism" in *Das Evangelium und die Evangelien*, ed. P. Stuhlmacher (Tübingen: 1983) 27-54, on 37. Cf. too the classic theory of W. Bussmann, *Synoptische Studien* (Halle: 1929), arguing for two quite separate Q sources, one in Greek, one in Aramaic. Similarly, more recently, C. J. A. Hickling, "The Plurality of 'Q'" in *LOGIA. Les Paroles de Jésus—The Sayings of Jesus*, ed. J. Delobel (BETL 59; Leuven: 1982) 425-429.

vocates of such a theory might say "no" to the question "Did Q exist?", meaning by this that they were denying the existence of a single, well-defined (possibly written) "source" or document called Q. But they would not be pleading for any direct dependence of Luke on Matthew. Further, even amongst those who have tended to think in terms of a single well-defined Q, there has been a notable trend in recent years to argue for stages in the development of Q, so that we have Q^1, Q^2, Q^3 etc, and "Q" itself is by no means a static, monolithic entity.[7]

Others again have argued that the "Q" used by Matthew and Luke may have been available to the two evangelists in different forms, a Q^{mt} and a Q^{lk}.[8] Such a theory has an *a priori* plausibility since, if one thinks of Q as a written source, it is hard to conceive of Matthew and Luke having exactly the same copy of Q available to them and hence some degree of variation in the form of Q used by them would be entirely expected. Whether the amount of variation is as great as some have argued is however debatable.

It is also possible to combine some of these theories. For example, the question of whether Luke used Matthew could be answered differently in relation to different parts of the tradition. Thus Luke may have known Matthew's gospel and used it on some occasions; but at other points Luke may have had access to other sources which provided him with his information about the relevant tradition.[9]

There is not enough space in the course of this essay to examine every nuance of every theory that has in some way or other denied the existence of Q as a single source. Thus simply in order to keep the discussion within manageable limits I shall confine attention in what follows to those who have tried to deny the existence

---

[7] See above all J. S. Kloppenborg, *The Formation of Q* (Philadelphia: 1987) and many essays of H. Schürmann, including "Das Zeugnis der Redenquelle für die Basileia-Verkündigung Jesu" in *LOGIA* (note 6 above) 121-200, and "Beobachtungen zum Menschensohn-Titel in der Redequelle" in *Jesus und der Menschensohn* (*Festschrift* for A. Vögtle; Freiburg: 1975) 124-147.

[8] Cf. the survey of F. Neirynck, "Q^{Mt} and Q^{Lk} and the Reconstruction of Q" in *ETL* 66 (1990) 385-390, repr. in *Evangelica II* (BETL 99; Leuven: 1991) 475-480, reviewing especially the work of M. Sato, *Q und Prophetie* (WUNT 2.29; Tübingen: 1988), and D. Kosch, *Die eschatologische Tora des Menschensohnes. Untersuchungen zur Rezeption der Stellung Jesu zur Tora in Q* (Freiburg: 1989).

[9] In recent times the view of R. Morgenthaler, *Statistische Synopse* (Zürich: 1971) esp. 300ff. The view of Farmer and other supporters of the Griesbach Hypothesis often reduces to this: cf. below.

of "Q" by arguing explicitly for Luke's knowledge and direct use of Matthew.

The theory that Luke used Matthew has always had a number of defenders and is still advocated strenuously by some today. Within the history of scholarship, the Q hypothesis arose as part of the 2ST, and hence is frequently coupled with the theory of Markan priority (MP). However, the two theories are not inseparable. Thus some today have retained a belief in MP, but have argued that Luke is directly dependent on Matthew as well as on Mark (see the first diagram below).[10] Other scholars have however questioned MP itself and this in turn has led to a rejection of the Q hypothesis in various ways. Thus for some, Mark is directly dependent on Matthew alone with Luke then dependent on Matthew and Mark (the so-called Augustinian hypothesis: see below).[11] Several recently have argued that Mark's Gospel comes last of the three, dependent on Matthew and Luke and representing a conflation of those two gospels, with Luke directly dependent on Matthew alone (the Griesbach hypothesis [GH]: see below).[12] The "traditional" Q hypothesis is represented by the fourth diagram:

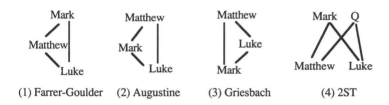

(1) Farrer-Goulder   (2) Augustine   (3) Griesbach   (4) 2ST

---

[10] Cf. A. Farrer, "On Dispensing with Q" in *Studies in the Gospels. Essays in Memory of R. H. Lightfoot*, ed. D. E. Nineham (Oxford: 1967) 55-88; H. B. Green, "The Credibility of Luke's Transformation of Matthew" and "Matthew 12.22-50 and Parallels: An Alternative to Matthean Conflation" in *Synoptic Studies*, ed. C. M. Tuckett (Sheffield: 1984) 131-156, 157-176; and above all the works of M. D. Goulder, especially his "On Putting Q to the Test," *NTS* 24 (1978) 218-234, and *Luke—A New Paradigm* (Sheffield: 1989).

[11] In recent years B. C. Butler, *The Originality of St Matthew* (Cambridge: 1951); J. W. Wenham, *Redating Matthew, Mark & Luke* (London: 1991).

[12] See above all the works of W. R. Farmer, *The Synoptic Problem* (London: 1964) and many other works since; also the relevant essays in D. L. Dungan (ed.), *The Interrelations of the Gospels* (BETL 95; Leuven: 1990). In recent years, advocates of the Griesbach hypothesis have preferred the description "Two-Gospel Hypothesis", though without any change in the hypothesis itself. I have kept the earlier term here.

One must however note that, in relation to the agreements between Matthew and Luke, these all represent rather different solutions. For example, (1) above presumes that Luke used Mark as well as Matthew; hence some of the Matthew-Luke agreements are due to common dependence on Mark. (2) also assumes that Mark is the mediator of some of the material common to Matthew and Luke. On the other hand, (3) presupposes that all the agreements between Matthew and Luke are due to Lukan dependence on Matthew alone since Mark had not yet been written. In (1) and (2) the relationship between Matthew and Luke is rather different from that implied by (3), and explanations of Luke's use of Matthew in non-Markan passages cannot *ipso facto* be regarded as explanations of Luke's use of Matthew in the whole tradition without more ado.

There is clearly not enough space here to discuss all the solutions in detail. In terms of contemporary scholarship, the most influential theories which claim to deny the existence of Q by referring to Luke's direct knowledge of, and use of, Matthew are probably (1) and (3) above: the GH ((3) above) has a small but influential body of support today; and (1) above, accepting MP but denying Q, is argued most strongly by M. D. Goulder. It is on these as the main alternatives to the Q theory that I shall focus attention in the rest of this essay.

*

Before looking at these alternative explanations of the Matthew-Luke agreements themselves, we should perhaps consider the standard arguments used to defend the Q hypothesis and how the evidence to which they refer can be related to these other theories. The arguments are mostly of a negative form, claiming that Luke's use of Matthew seems very improbable. If then one decides that Luke did not know Matthew, the options available within some kind of "Q" theory are not uniform, as we have already seen. However, at this point I shall consider only the problem of whether Luke can plausibly be seen to have known and used Matthew. The main arguments against this view can be considered under four headings.[13]

---

[13] For standard defences of the Q hypothesis, see W. G. Kümmel, *Introduction to the New Testament* (London: 1975) 63ff.; J. A. Fitzmyer, "The Priority of Mark and the 'Q' Source in Luke" in *Jesus and Man's Hope* I (Pittsburgh: 1970) 131-170.

(i) Luke never appears to know any of Matthew's additions to Mark in Markan material. Sometimes, in using Mark, Matthew makes substantial additions to Mark, cf. Mt 12:5-7; 14:28-31; 16:16-19; 27:19, 24.[14] If Luke knew Matthew, why does he never show any knowledge of Matthew's redaction of Mark? It seems easiest to presume that Luke did not know of these Matthean additions to Mark and hence did not know Matthew.

Such an argument clearly presupposes MP and might at first sight appear irrelevant for other hypotheses which deny MP, especially the Augustinian or Griesbach hypotheses.[15] Yet essentially the same problem is still there for both these alternative hypotheses. For the Augustinian hypothesis, the problem is similar though the Matthew-Mark relationship is reversed. The longer Matthean version is now abbreviated by Mark; but why then does Luke consistently ignore the longer Matthean versions? Why too has Mark abbreviated Matthew in the first place?[16] Very similar problems are faced by the GH in these passages, though with different "actors". On the GH, Mark comes third and so is irrelevant to the problem of Luke's use of Matthew, but the problems are fundamentally similar: why does Mark consistently ignore the longer Matthean versions? And why has Luke abbreviated Matthew in the first place? No answer in detail in relation to these passages has (as far as I am aware) been offered by contemporary advocates of the GH. Goulder's answer to the problem is to claim that, when using Mark, Luke generally used that gospel as his main source and did not use Matthew at all in Markan passages. In abstract terms this is quite plausible though, as we shall see, it scarcely explains all the required facts satisfactorily (cf. below).

(ii) After the opening pericopes of the Baptism and the Temptation narratives, none of the non-Markan material which Luke shares with Matthew appears in the same context relative to the non-Markan material in the two gospels. Streeter's (slightly polemical) statement of the facts is often cited in this context:

> If then Luke derived this material from Matthew, he must have gone through both Matthew and Mark so as to discriminate with meticulous precision between Marcan and non-Marcan material; he must then have

---

[14] Further examples in J. A. Fitzmyer, *The Gospel according to Luke I-IX* (New York: 1981) 73f.

[15] Cf. W. R. Farmer, "A Response to Joseph Fitzmyer's Defense of the Two Document Hypothesis" in *New Synoptic Studies*, ed. W. R. Farmer (Macon: 1983) 501-523, on 517f.

[16] The issue is not discussed by Butler or Wenham.

proceeded with the utmost care to tear every little piece of non-Marcan material he desired to use from the context of Mark in which it appeared in Matthew—in spite of the fact that contexts in Matthew are always exceedingly appropriate—in order to re-insert it into a different context of Mark having no special appropriateness. A theory which would make an author capable of such a proceeding would only be tenable if, on other grounds, we had reason to believe he was a crank.[17]

As before the same argument could apply to the Augustinian hypothesis: the problem is to try to explain the Lukan text if Luke had both Matthew and Mark before him, and the precise relationship between Matthew and Mark themselves is immaterial at this point. For the GH the problem is again slightly different, since Mark had not appeared when Luke wrote. Yet that hypothesis must still explain why Luke chose to keep some of Matthew's material in its original context (the material which, for the most part, Mark later decided to include) but to change the order of the rest very considerably.[18] There is also the further problem of explaining why Mark decided to include primarily (but not exclusively) only that material whose *order* Luke kept from Matthew. Goulder himself has attempted to meet Streeter's argument head on and give a very detailed explanation of Luke's ordering of the Matthean material: this will be considered in detail later.

(iii) It is argued that, in the double tradition (i.e. the material common to Matthew and Luke alone), Matthew has no monopoly on the more original form of the tradition. Sometimes Matthew, sometimes Luke, seems to be more original at different points. This, it is said, tells heavily against any theory of direct dependence of Luke on Matthew since in that case we should expect Luke to have the secondary form of the tradition at every point. Examples of Luke's greater originality which are often cited include the Beatitudes (6:20-23), the Lord's Prayer (11:2-4) and the doom oracle (11:49-51).

With this argument the problem is the same for all defenders of Lukan dependence on Matthew. The relative position of Mark is immaterial. However, different scholars have adopted different lines of defence. Some have argued that the case for Lukan originality can at every point be countered: Luke is secondary to Matthew everywhere so that where the two gospels differ, Luke's

---

[17] B. H. Streeter, *The Four Gospels* (London: 1924) 183.
[18] One attempt to explain this is that of B. Orchard, *Matthew, Luke & Mark* (Manchester: 1976); I have tried to respond to Orchard's argument in my *The Revival of the Griesbach Hypothesis* (SNTSMS 44; Cambridge: 1983) 31-40.

version is due to LkR. This might be termed a "hard-line" position and is defended most strongly today by Goulder. Others would adopt a more "soft-line" approach, arguing that, whilst Luke is dependent on Matthew most of the time, there may be occasions where Luke had access to other sources of information which overlapped with Matthew.[19] The last option is of course not far removed from a form of the Q hypothesis (see note 9 above and the discussion below).

(iv) Finally, appeal is made to the presence of doublets in Matthew and Luke. One half of the doublet evidently comes from Mark (assuming MP) and, it is argued, the other can most naturally be explained as stemming from a second common source, i.e. Q. (See for example the versions of the saying about saving / losing one's life in Mt 16:25 / Mk 8:35 / Lk 9:24 and also in Mt 10:39 / Lk 17:33.)

This is perhaps one of the weakest arguments for the existence of a Q source. Certainly the evidence is adequately explained by the Q hypothesis; but the evidence could equally well be explained in other ways. For advocates of Matthean priority, doublets in Matthew could be due to a variety of reasons (e.g., overlapping sources in the pre-Matthean tradition, or Matthew's redactional repetition of material he wished to emphasize). For the Augustinian hypothesis, Mark would then have chosen one half of each doublet and Luke for some reason decided to include a version from Mark and a version from Matthew. (In any case, reasons for Luke's inclusion of a doublet have to be found whether Luke derived the second half of the doublet from Matthew or from Q.) Similarly, on the GH, Luke's doublets simply repeat Matthew's doublets and Mark would then have included only one half of each parallel pair.

These then are some of the main arguments for the existence of Q. As we have seen, they are mostly negative arguments, trying to refute the possibility that Luke knew Matthew. What then are the counter-arguments? As already noted, the most influential theories today which advocate Luke's dependence on Matthew are probably the GH and the Goulder-Farrer theory. I consider therefore each of these in turn.

---

[19] So, for example, Butler, *Originality* 16, 57, 58, 59 etc.; also Farmer, "A Fresh Approach to Q" in *Christianity, Judaism and Other Greco-Roman Cults. Studies for Morton Smith at Sixty. Part One*, ed. J. Neusner (Leiden: 1975) 39-50. Cf. also below.

1. The Griesbach Hypothesis [GH]

Not a great deal of space will be devoted to the GH in this essay. The reasons for this are two-fold. First, the GH has been extensively debated in modern discussions since its contemporary revival in the work of W. R. Farmer and others who have followed him. There is therefore no need to rehearse in detail arguments about the GH which can be found elsewhere.[20] Secondly, it is probably fair to say that the problem of Q and the relationship between Matthew and Luke has not been at the top of the agenda in many modern scholarly discussions of the GH. The hypothesis' most controversial claim concerns the position of Mark in relation to the other gospels. Thus a great deal of attention has been focused on the problem of whether Mark should be regarded as the source of Matthew and Luke, or as a conflation of those two gospels. The precise relationship between Matthew and Luke themselves has not received such detailed examination within discussions of the GH.

This is not surprising, at least at one level. Griesbach himself never really addressed the problem of the relationship between Matthew and Luke in detail. Further, it is logically perfectly possible to maintain a Griesbachian view about Mark and yet claim that Matthew and Luke are not directly dependent on each other. This was the view of De Wette and Bleek in the last century, and is also the view of scholars such as Stoldt and Walker in the current debate.[21] There is thus disagreement even within the ranks of those who might call themselves "Griesbachians" on the question of the precise relationship between Matthew and Luke.

In the most recent discussions of the GH, the Matthew-Luke relationship has still not been very much to the fore. In published discussions in the 1980s from supporters of the GH, most attention has been focused on patristic testimony about the gospels and on the argument from order. Indeed one recent writer called these the "two foundational pillars" on which the hypothesis rests.[22] However, quite irrespective of the question whether these two considerations do give positive support to the GH's claims about

---

[20] See my *Revival* and the relevant essays in Dungan (ed.), *Interrelations* (note 12 above).

[21] H. H. Stoldt, *Geschichte und Kritik der Markushypothese* (Göttingen: 1977); W. O. Walker, "The State of the Synoptic Question," *Perkins Journal* 40 (1987) 14-19.

[22] A. J. McNicol, "The Composition of the Eschatological Discourse" in *Interrelations* (see note 12 above) 157-200, on 200.

Mark,[23] the fact is that neither really says anything about the Matthew-Luke relationship. It is true that some patristic testimony may support the view that the gospels were written in the order Matthew-Luke-Mark; but such witness says nothing about the problem of whether Luke writing after Matthew used Matthew's gospel directly or whether both are dependent on a common source.[24] And the argument from order referred to above, alluding to the absence of Matthew-Luke agreements against Mark in order, relates only to the problem of the relative position of Mark's gospel: it says nothing about the Matthew-Luke relationship.

Nevertheless, for many advocates of the GH, Q is an unnecessary hypothesis and Luke should be seen as directly dependent on Matthew. Arguments adduced by modern Griesbachians against Q very often reduce to a single appeal to "simplicity", and a general mistrust of appealing to hypothetical sources to explain the synoptic data. Farmer made such an argument basic in his 1964 book, inaugurating the modern revival of the GH: he argued there that priority should be given first and foremost to theories which did not suppose the existence of hypothetical sources.[25] And in various other places the same argument has been alluded to and repeated without much change. Thus to take a recent example, A. J. McNicol writes:

> We believe, in balance, that the simplest solution to a literary problem should be preferred unless there is compelling evidence against it. The simpler solution (i.e. *one that does not need to postulate unnecessary hypothetical source[s]*) is to be preferred to a solution which requires such a postulation.[26]

I have argued elsewhere that such a claim is not convincing.[27] Modern Griesbachians have never denied the existence of other traditions, or even "sources", available to all three evangelists. Unless one is prepared to argue that Matthew invented his gospel *de novo*, then Matthew according to the GH must have been heav-

---

[23] See my "Response to the Two Gospel Hypothesis" in *Interrelations* (see note 12 above) 47-62.

[24] The only exception might be Augustine, but that is very late. The earlier witnesses simply state the order without any comment about literary dependence.

[25] Farmer, *Synoptic Problem* 209. For a discussion, and critique, of the importance of this step in Farmer's overall argumentation, see A. D. Jacobson, "The Literary Unity of Q," *JBL* 101 (1982) 365-389, especially 367f.

[26] McNicol, "Eschatological Discourse" 167 (my italics).

[27] See my "Response" 61f.

ily dependent on earlier sources and traditions. The same applies
to Luke in material which is peculiar to his gospel. What is perhaps ironic in the present discussion is that many advocates of the
GH today would adopt precisely this view in relation to several
passages in Luke where Luke runs closely parallel to Matthew.
Such a theory is said to be necessary to account for the fact that
Luke's version sometimes seems to be more primitive than
Matthew's parallel. Thus Farmer has argued that Luke may have
had access to parallel, and more original, traditions in the parables
of the lost sheep and the talents / pounds, as well as for parts of the
eschatological discourse.[28] Similarly the recent detailed discussion
of the eschatological discourse by a team of scholars defending
the GH makes extensive appeal to the existence of such traditions
available to Luke.[29]

The irony of this is that this is effectively some kind of Q theory. It is perhaps not the Q hypothesis that thinks of a single written "document", or "source", called Q. But it is a clear admis-
sion that the parallel versions cannot all be satisfactorily explained
by Luke's direct use of Matthew without recourse to other (lost)
sources or traditions. Further, it is equally ironic that the number
of sources that has to be hypothesized is in danger of growing almost without control. For if one does not wish to argue that all
these parallel traditions available to Luke were united in any kind
of unified Q source prior to Luke, then the number of such
"sources" is greatly increased. To quote my earlier study:

> One could argue that the 2DH [=2ST] is rather 'simpler' in this re-
> spect. If one were to regard the Q material as constituting a unitary
> source in the tradition, then an enormous amount of material in the
> gospels can be ascribed to just two major sources, Mark and Q. By
> appealing to a number of 'earlier traditions' to which Luke had access,
> the 2GH [=GH] potentially multiplies the number of prior sources be-
> hind the gospels to a greater extent than does the 2DH. An appeal to
> 'economy', or 'simplicity', to support the 2GH is thus unpersuasive.
> An appeal to such a criterion would appear to work against, rather than
> for, the hypothesis.[30]

One other point in discussions of Q by Griesbachians should
also be made here. Clearly attempts to isolate a theology, or characteristic features, of Q are worthless for those who do not think
that Q existed. Thus Farmer has claimed that any apparently dis-

---

[28] See note 19 above.
[29] See McNicol, "Eschatological Discourse," e.g. on 161.
[30] Tuckett, "Response" 62.

tinctive features of the Q material arise from the fact that it is Luke who has chosen to include this material in his gospel:

> That 'Q' could have produced an 'intelligible' theology is explained by the fact that Luke selected from Matthew only material that was useful for his Gentile readers.... [Q] is generally free of Jewish *Tendenz* which would be offensive to Gentile readers.... 'Q' is more representative of Luke's version of the Jesus tradition than it is of Jesus himself.[31]

Once again, to repeat what I have written elsewhere:

> All this would be more convincing if recent studies of the theology of Q had produced a theology that was basically Lukan. But this is scarcely the case. Parts of Q show a markedly strong Jewish *Tendenz* particularly in its attitude to the Jewish Law (cf. Mt 5:18 / Lk 16:17; Mt 23:23d / Lk 11:42d). So too the 'Wisdom Christology', often thought to be one of the most distinctive features of the Q material, can hardly be said to be very characteristic of Luke since it does not recur outside the Q passages concerned (Mt 11:19 / Lk 7:35; Mt 23:34 / Lk 11:49).[32]

The fact that the material common to Matthew and Luke turns out to be rather un-Lukan at times (and also perhaps un-Matthean) may be a strong indication against the theory that this material is in Luke because of Luke's redactional decision to select precisely this from Matthew's gospel.

Arguments produced by advocates of the GH against Q are thus unconvincing for many. Even if one wishes to dispute the theory of Q as a unified written "document", the alternative of direct use by Luke of Matthew is not sustained consistently by modern Griesbachians. As often as not, by appealing to independent parallel traditions available to Luke, advocates of the GH are implicitly supporting some kind of Q theory by admitting that the evidence is better explained by a less direct relationship between Matthew and Luke themselves and by common dependence of both gospels on earlier traditions.

2. M. D. Goulder

Whilst most modern Griesbachians have been unwilling to argue that the Matthew-Luke agreements can in their entirety be explained by Luke's borrowing directly from Matthew, precisely

---

[31] Farmer, "The Two Gospel Hypothesis" in *Interrelations* (see note 12 above) 125-156, on 143.
[32] Tuckett, "Response" 59.

this view has been argued in recent years with great clarity and
boldness by Goulder. He has produced probably the most comprehensive series of arguments against the existence of Q
(although, unlike advocates of the GH, Goulder accepts the theory
of MP—hence his arguments only concern those Matthew-Luke
agreements which are not explained by dependence on Mark). He
has published a number of important articles on the subject, and
has recently brought this work to a climax in the publication of a
massive two-volume commentary on Luke (see note 10 above)
seeking to explain the whole of the text of Luke on the basis of
dependence on Mark and Matthew alone. Goulder is by no means
unique in questioning the existence of Q, even from within the
presuppositions of MP (cf. note 10 also). However, his discussion
of the issue is by far the most wide-ranging and comprehensive in
the contemporary debate and I shall therefore restrict my remarks
in this section to the views of Goulder himself. Further, much of
Goulder's work has not yet evoked a detailed response from advocates of other hypotheses.[33] Hence in what follows I shall try to
indicate where Goulder's case is perhaps weak in order to defend
the theory of the existence of Q in some form.

Not every aspect of Goulder's arguments can be considered in
detail here.[34] He starts by arguing that some knowledge of
Matthew by Luke is demanded by the presence of "minor agreements" (MAs) between Matthew and Luke in Markan material
where Q presence is never postulated, e.g. in the passion narrative
(cf. Mk 14:65 and pars.). Clearly the MAs cause some problems
for the theory of MP; yet whether they should be explained by
Lukan knowledge of Matthew is not certain. Further, the MAs
might show at most a subsidiary use of Matthew by Luke in
Markan material; from this one might perhaps deduce a sub-

---

[33] I have tried to respond to some of Goulder's earlier arguments, especially
in relation to some of the minor agreements, in my "On the Relationship between Matthew and Luke," *NTS* 30 (1984) 130-142. Since the writing of this
essay, the work of D. R. Catchpole, *The Quest for Q* (Edinburgh, 1993) has been
published. In chapter 1 of this book, entitled, "Did Q Exist?", Catchpole gives
a detailed critical discussion of many of Goulder's arguments relating to individual passages. This has only become available to me at the proof-reading
stage and hence can only be noted briefly here. It does however represent an
important complement to the argument of this essay.

[34] A full discussion of every point in his two-volume commentary on Luke
would require at least two volumes in return!

sidiary use of Matthew in non-Markan material.[35] But the MAs themselves cannot show, even on Goulder's presuppositions, that Luke used Matthew alone where Mark was not available.

One other preliminary point made by Goulder is about the allegedly "unscientific" argumentation of defenders of the Q hypothesis. He claims that defenders of Q constantly change their theories to meet problems (e.g. the MAs): as a result the theory becomes almost unfalsifiable and hence worthless. By contrast he claims that his own theory is falsifiable: he adopts what might be termed a "hard-line" position, arguing that at *every* point Luke's version is secondary to Matthew. Hence if just one example could be produced where Luke's version is more original than Matthew's, this would be enough to falsify the theory. Goulder thus claims that his own theory is falsifiable, and hence more scientific than those he is opposing. Whether this is in fact the case remains to be seen.

As well as giving a detailed commentary on the whole of the text of Luke, Goulder offers a number of more general arguments by way of criticisms of the Q hypothesis and in favour of his own theories. These may be divided in two major categories: linguistic arguments, and arguments based on the choice and ordering of the material.

(a) Linguistic Arguments

Within this category Goulder's arguments may be sub-divided further into discussions of Matthew and of Luke respectively.

(i) Matthew

Goulder argues forcefully that all linguistic arguments in favour of Q are really fallacious. One such argument he dubs the "Matthean Vocabulary Fallacy". Many, he claims, argue that if there are instances where Matthew and Luke differ and Matthew's version is Matthean, then Luke's version must be more original. In fact, he suggests, Matthew's version turns out to be extraordinarily like Q, and Matthew and Q are almost indistinguishable.[36]

---

[35] See F. Neirynck, "ΤΙΣ ΕΣΤΙΝ Ο ΠΑΙΣΑΣ ΣΕ; Mt 26,68 / Lk 22,64 (diff. Mk 14,65)," *ETL* 63 (1987) 5-47, on 27, repr. in *Evangelica II* (BETL 99; Leuven: 1991) 95-138, on 115.
[36] Goulder, *Luke* 11ff.

With regard to the first point, no defender of the Q hypothesis has (as far as I am aware) argued quite as baldly as Goulder suggests and claimed that simply because Matthew's version is MattR, then *ipso facto* Luke's version is more original. Such an argument might be used by some who are presupposing the Q hypothesis, but also with the proviso that Luke's different version is unlikely to be LkR. However, this will be discussed in more detail when we look at what Goulder calls the "Lucan Priority Fallacy".

Goulder's other point about Matthew deserves more attention. He claims that repeatedly, in terms of language, style and even theology, Q and Matthew are virtually identical.[37] At the level of style and vocabulary, Goulder's argument is repeated with several examples. He refers to many instances where allegedly Q words or phrases turn out upon examination to be highly characteristic of Matthew's terminology. For example, the use of ὀλιγόπιστος in Mt 6:30 / Lk 12:28 is usually taken to be part of Q, assuming some form of Q hypothesis. But the word is distinctively Matthean: it is used by Matthew in 8:26; 16:8; 17:20, all of which are redactional additions to Mark (assuming MP), and in 14:31 which is probably also due to MattR.[38] Thus Matthew's vocabulary and that of Q are indistinguishable. The same applies to the case of the phrase "there will be weeping and gnashing of teeth". It is used once in the allegedly Q tradition (Mt 8:12 / Lk 13:28) and frequently elsewhere in Matthew alone (Mt 13:42; 22:13; 24:51; 25:30). "Thus Q shares Matthew's enthusiasm for the pangs of hell."[39]

The whole argument is however based on a major flaw in logic, part of which Goulder has seen but part of which still remains hidden behind his rhetoric. Practically all the examples Goulder gives concern words or phrases which occur once in alleged Q, but several times in Matthew. Goulder's conclusion is that the *style* and *characteristic* vocabulary of Q are thus indistinguishable from that of Matthew. Now no one would dispute that the features indicated by Goulder are characteristic of Matthew and, to a certain extent, distinctive of Matthew in the synoptic tradition. The question is whether they must be judged necessarily unique to

---

[37] For language and style, see *Luke* 11-15; for theology 52ff.

[38] The argument is conducted within the presuppositions of MP; but even without this assumption, the use of the word 5 times in Matthew (0 in Mark, 1 in Luke) indicates Matthew's distinctiveness here.

[39] *Luke* 12.

Matthew, and also whether a single occurrence of the same phenomenon in alleged Q can be taken as indicative of the *style*, or *Tendenz*, of Q. Goulder is at least alive to the latter problem, though his answer is scarcely convincing. He argues that since there are only *c*. 1800 words common to Matthew and Luke in Q and *c*. 18,000 words in Matthew, one occurrence of (say) ὀλιγό-πιστος in Q as against five in Matthew is about par for the course.[40] This is however special pleading. Whatever the size of Q in relation to Matthew, we cannot deduce from a single occurrence in alleged Q anything about its style or characteristic features. For matters of style, we need recurring features and it is just this which Goulder's examples do not supply *for Q*.

Another more dangerous hidden assumption within Goulder's argumentation is that all the features isolated as characteristic of Matthew can be ascribed to Matthew's own redactional activity: in other words, everything which is characteristic of Matthew has been *created* by Matthew. Such an assumption is of course a dangerous nonsense,[41] and can be seen to be immediately false on a moment's reflection. Matthew does not write out of cultural vacuum, even though his cultural milieu may be different from Mark's or Luke's. Thus Matthew typically refers to the "Kingdom of heaven", rather than the "Kingdom of God". But "Kingdom of heaven" is not a Matthean redactional creation *de novo*—it simply represents a more Jewish terminology which distinguishes Matthew from Mark and Luke but which Matthew shares with many other Jewish contemporaries.

More importantly, it is clear that, on almost any source theory, Matthew collects together teaching material systematically into blocks of thematically related teaching; and he often repeats himself.[42] But is every such doublet then created due entirely, in *both* halves of the doublet, to Matthew's creativity? Goulder himself would agree that this is not the case as Matthew sometimes takes up material from Mark and repeats it.[43] Thus in relation in Mark, Matthew is quite capable of taking up a feature which occurs once

---

[40] *Ibid.* 13.

[41] See M. D. Hooker, "In His Own Image?" in *What About the New Testament?* (*Festschrift* for C. F. Evans), eds. M. D. Hooker & C. J. A. Hickling (London: 1975) 28-44, on 35.

[42] Cf. W. D. Davies & D. C. Allison, *The Gospel according to Saint Matthew* (Edinburgh: 1988) 88-93.

[43] *Luke* 34. Cf. Mt 3:2 + 4:17; 5:32 + 19:9; 10:22 + 24:9; 9:27ff. + 20:39ff.; 9:32ff. + 12:22ff.

in his source and repeating it. The same can equally have happened with the examples from alleged Q cited by Goulder.

Goulder's argument could have been used with different examples to argue for Mark's dependence on Matthew. For example, Matthew is fond of castigating opponents of Jesus as "hypocrites"; yet at one point Mark has Jesus refer to opponents as hypocrites, in parallel with Matthew (Mt 15:7 / Mk 7:6). Matthew's fondness for τότε as a connecting particle is also well known; yet on a few occasions Mark too has τότε in parallel with Matthew (cf. Mt 24:30 / Mk 13:26). These examples are of exactly the same nature as the Q examples adduced by Goulder. Yet they do not necessarily show any dependence of Luke or Mark on Matthew, or any identity between Matthean and Q's / Mark's *style*. They can just as easily be taken as showing Matthew's willingness to take over terminology systematically so that it becomes characteristic and distinctive in its repeated use in his gospel, but not necessarily unique to him.

In fact Goulder himself has argued in precisely this way, replying to Farmer's attempt to prove Mark's dependence on Matthew via exactly the same kind of argumentation. Goulder writes:

> [Farmer's argument] is of the form: If document A (Mark) has favourite expressions not found in document B (Matthew), A is unlikely to be known by B; whereas if B has favourite expressions occurring once in A, it is likely that A has carried them over inadvertently. But this is a fallacy.... Sometimes later B may copy an expression from earlier A inadvertently; and *sometimes a casual expression of earlier A may appeal strongly to B so that he uses it often.*[44]

Goulder then goes on to excuse Farmer by admitting that he made "virtually the same error of method" in a paper to an SNTS seminar in 1981, referring to characteristic Matthean phrases re-occurring in Luke, including the "weeping and gnashing of teeth". "They might just be Q phrases that Matthew liked very much; though there are other reasons in fact for preferring the inadvertence explanation, which I offered." In fact the preface to Goulder's latest book indicates that a 1981 SNTS seminar paper forms the basis of his chapter on Q in his 1989 *Luke* volume. But, as far as I can see, there is no difference in the manner of argumentation from that criticized by Goulder himself in 1984. The argument is still exactly the same, appealing to the Matthean nature of the phrases concerned to argue against Q. No

---

[44] Goulder, "Some Observations on Professor Farmer's 'Certain Results...'" in *Synoptic Studies* (see note 10 above) 99-104, on 100 (my italics).

"other reasons" are offered for these individual cases, even in the later study.

We may conclude that Goulder's reference to the alleged Matthean nature of Q's style is unconvincing. On the 2ST, a consistent picture of Matthew emerges as a writer who is capable of latching on to a word or a phrase in his source material and repeating it frequently. And this happens in the case of both Markan and Q material.

A discussion of Q's theology, and alleged similarity between Q theology and Matthean theology, would probably take us too far afield. As just one possible counter-example, I would refer again to the phenomenon of the so-called "Wisdom Christology" in Q, whereby Jesus appears as the envoy of Wisdom. Matthew regularly "up-grades" the Christology so as to identify Jesus with the figure of Wisdom itself.[45] Hence Q's theology cannot be identified with Matthean theology completely. However, it is also the case that some level of continuity between Q and Matthew is not unexpected on the Q hypothesis.[46] This applies perhaps more at the level of ideas than of style and vocabulary. But the very fact that Matthew used the Q material (if indeed he did) suggests that Matthew must have found it not uncongenial. He may have wished to modify it in places and perhaps did so; but the very fact that he decided to use the material at all indicates a measure of agreement between the ideas of the source and Matthew's own ideas. A measure of agreement between Matthew and Q is thus entirely expected, and Goulder's arguments about the possible overlap between Matthew and Q is thus no bar to the Q hypothesis.

(ii) Luke

A second aspect of Goulder's argument concerns Luke's stylistic features. Goulder criticizes what he calls the "Lucan Priority Fallacy", arguing against claims that Luke's version might at some points be more original than Matthew's.[47] He criticizes excessive use of appeals to isolated *hapax legomena* in Luke's work, referring to the fact that Luke has a very wide vocabulary and is

---

[45] See M. J. Suggs, *Wisdom, Christology and Law in Matthew's Gospel* (Cambridge, Mass.: 1970).

[46] See U. Luz, *Das Evangelium nach Matthäus*, I. *Mt 1-7* (Neukirchen-Vluyn: 1985) 57.

[47] *Luke* 15.

quite capable of rewriting Mark using hapaxes—hence an odd hapax cannot prove anything. Indeed the whole of his massive two-volume work is an attempt to show that Luke's version is at every point LkR when different from Matthew. Goulder also objects to arguments which appeal to the Matthean nature of Matthew's version as showing the pre-Lukan nature of Luke's version. By itself, of course, such a form of argumentation is quite indecisive, but few would in fact argue in this way quite so baldly today. As noted above, attempts to show that Luke's version is pre-Lukan at any one point would always be coupled with arguments seeking to show that Luke's version is in some way uncharacteristic of Luke.

Now such an attempt will inevitably be a delicate operation. Moreover one will never be able to *prove* such a theory one way or the other. It will be a delicate operation because at one level one is trying to show the impossible. Luke can only be said to be "un-Lukan" in a rather unusual sense; for what is "Lukan" is almost by definition what is in Luke. By "un-Lukan" we therefore have to refer to something that is not impossible for Luke to have written, for if it is in Luke's gospel he patently did write it. What we mean is something which is rather unlike what Luke wrote elsewhere and which Luke probably did not invent *de novo*. But this means that we are in the realms of probabilities and not certainties. At most, we can only say that such and such is improbable, unlikely or whatever; we shall never be able to say that such and such is totally impossible. We are not in the realm of mathematics where a result of 0=1 is a total impossibility, nor in the realm of natural sciences where hypotheses can be tested empirically and the untenability of hypotheses established if expected results do not match up to predictions. The same applies to Goulder's theory as well. Thus despite his own claims, his own theory is no more "falsifiable" than alternative hypotheses. Goulder can and does produce arguments to show that Luke's version may be LkR. Others may be rather unconvinced. But one cannot be more than unconvinced! One cannot "prove" that the proposed feature of LkR is not redactional after all and thus "falsify" the theory with mathematical finality.

To take a concrete example, many would argue that at Q 11:49, Luke's version is more original in having the doom oracle spoken by the "Wisdom of God" in the past ("Therefore the Wisdom of God said 'I will send to them...'") by contrast with Matthew's version in which the oracle is spoken by Jesus in the present ("Therefore, behold I am sending to you..."). From the side of the Q hypothesis, Luke's version looks decidedly un-Lukan. Nowhere else in Luke (apart from Lk 7:35 which is also a Q passage, or one borrowed from Matthew) does Wisdom appear as an almost personified being. On the other hand, Matthew's replacement of "Wisdom" with the "I" of Jesus is part of a consistent pattern whereby Matthew's Jesus takes the place of Wisdom in such texts (cf. above). Thus Luke's version seems to represent the more original Q version which Matthew then redacts.

Goulder's reply is to argue that the change can be explained as LkR.[48] Luke has just spoken of OT prophets so he takes the reference to the people sent by Matthew's Jesus (prophets, wise men and scribes) as a reference in part to OT figures. He thus has to change Matthew's "I" (= Jesus) to "God" and in doing so chooses a periphrasis for "God" by writing "the Wisdom of God", prompted perhaps in part by the σοφούς who are sent out by Matthew's Jesus. Now clearly none of this is totally impossible, and if Luke used Matthew he must have made the actual changes involved. At the most a sceptic can say that the proposed reasons seem unconvincing. Why should Luke have interpreted the "prophets" of Mt 23:34 as OT figures? They are (in Matthew) clearly figures sent out by Jesus and Luke certainly knows of Christian prophets (cf. Acts 11:27; 13:1; 21:10). Further, even if Luke did decide to change things here and make God the subject, why did Luke feel obliged to introduce a periphrasis for God, and why this particular periphrasis? Elsewhere Luke has no compunction about talking of God himself sending prophets;[49] and as already noted, this is a highly unusual periphrasis in Luke's writings. Only once elsewhere (in a passage that Q-proponents and Goulder would agree is due to a source in Luke) does Luke refer to the Wisdom of God in personified terms.[50] Thus Goulder's arguments seem weak and uncompelling (to this particular sceptic, at least!)

But the important thing to note here is that that is all we can say. We cannot prove that Luke did not make these changes, perhaps for the reasons Goulder suggests, perhaps for quite different (as yet undiscovered) reasons. In that sense Goulder's theory is not falsifiable. It could have happened that way. Each critic has then

---

[48] *Luke* 523.

[49] For God speaking through, or raising up, prophets: cf. Lk 1:70; Acts 3:13, 21, 22; 7:37.

[50] Cf. above. The other text in Lk 7:35 which is either dependent on Q (according to the 2ST) or on Matthew (according to Goulder).

to make up his / her mind whether things did happen in this way
or whether the cumulative evidence is such that a theory of Lukan
dependence seems less probable than some kind of Q hypothesis.
If Goulder thinks that the only respectable hypotheses are those
which are falsifiable, then his own theory is no more (or less!) respectable than the one he opposes. No theory about the Synoptic
Problem is falsifiable in the strict sense. All are at best the result of
weighing up likelihoods and making more or less coherent
guesses and combinations of hypotheses to try to explain the evidence of the texts themselves. There is not enough space here to
give detailed arguments about other specific texts, but cumulative
arguments similar to those already given have convinced many
that on a significant number of occasions, Luke preserves a more
original form of the tradition than Matthew and hence any theory
of Luke's dependence on Matthew is unconvincing (cf. Lk 6:20-
23; 7:35; 11:2-4; 11:20; 11:30 etc.).

(b) Choice and Order of Material

Goulder's other main line of argumentation concerns the choice
and ordering of material by Luke. A strong part of the argument
for the existence of Q has always been the fact that (a) Luke never
uses any of Matthew's additions to Mark in Markan material, and
(b) Luke never has the Matthean material in the same context
relative to the Markan material (cf. above).

Goulder's answer to (a) is to appeal to a general policy by Luke
of wishing to cut down the length of the preaching discourses in
his sources.[51] This is then the reason for Luke's splitting up the
material in Mk 4, in Matthew's Great Sermon etc. Luke wants
"manageable sections",[52] and long discourses in Matthew and
Mark are "too long and indigestible".[53] Thus Luke "regularly
likes teaching pericopes of about twelve to twenty verses, which he
regards as the amount a congregation (or reader) can assimilate at
one time".[54]

---

[51] Goulder, "The Order of a Crank" in *Synoptic Studies* (see note 11 above)
111-130, on 112; *Luke* 39f.
[52] *Ibid.*
[53] *Luke* 41.
[54] *Luke* 40.

Such a policy may sound reasonable in general terms, but it fails to fit all the facts. Lk 12:22-53 (or even 12:22-59[55]) constitutes a sustained piece of teaching with no real break at all. (Peter's interjection in v. 41 is scarcely enough to stop the flow of thought.) Ch.15 is a long section with admittedly three well-defined parables, but no clear markers between them supplied by Luke. What too of Lk 21 / Mk 13? Here Goulder says that Luke retained Mark's long discourse because it "cannot be broken up".[56] This is however patently false: Mk 13 can be broken up and was broken up—by Matthew (assuming MP): Matthew uses Mk 13:9-13 by itself in Mt 10 (as well as repeating its substance in Mt 24), possibly because Matthew knows that persecution of Christians is not only a preliminary to the End but also a matter of past experience for Matthew's own Christian community. But Luke too knows of Christian persecution (cf. Acts 8:1-3). He could thus have made the same redactional change to Mk 13 as Matthew did. Luke thus did not have to keep Mark's discourse intact here. Indeed on Goulder's theory he does hive off the (substantively related) material in Mt 24-25 which, *ex hypothesi*, he knew and included earlier in his gospel (in Lk 12 and 17).

The argument about the indigestibility of long discourses is thus very fragile. When one compares too the lengths of some of the "pericopes" in Acts (cf. Peter's long Pentecost speech, Stephen's 52-verse oration in Acts 7, the story of Cornelius' conversion in Acts 10), any appeal to the short supply of stamina on the part of Luke's audience / readership becomes even harder to conceive. The appeal to Luke's desire for brevity thus seems unconvincing, The problem therefore remains: why does Luke split up all his material in the way he has?

Goulder's second argument is to appeal to what he sees as Luke's overall policy of using his sources in "blocks". He envisages Luke as using one source at a time,[57] using first Mark, then Matthew, etc. Thus the reason why Luke never includes any Matthean modifications of Mark is simple:

> When he [Luke] is treating Marcan matter he has Mark in front of him, and he has made it his policy not to keep turning up Matthew to see what he had added. So again the problem disappears on examina-

---

[55] The introductory "and he said to the crowds" in v. 54 scarcely stems the flow of the discourse.

[56] *Luke* 39.

[57] "Crank" 113.

tion: Luke does not include the additions because he had decided on a policy which involved letting them go.[58]

However, although this may explain some of the text of Luke, it cannot explain everything: in particular the Mk 13 material again causes problems.[59] Here Matthew has reworked the Markan discourse, expanding it very considerably with other material in Mt 24-25. But now Luke evidently decided not to ignore Matthew's additions to Mark. He must have gone through Matthew very carefully,[60] marking off all those extra bits of Matthew which he would include. Moreover, Luke must then have distributed this material in three quite separate places in his gospel: in chs. 12, 17 and 19. Clearly Luke's "block" policy has been rather different in Mk 13 / Mt 24-25 than elsewhere!

One other feature also casts some doubt on Goulder's overall case. Goulder explains the lack of Matthean additions to Mark as due to Luke's policy of not referring to Matthew to see how Matthew redacted Mark, Yet Goulder elsewhere refers to the MAs as evidence that Luke does know Matthew in Markan passages. But the very nature of the MAs is that they are (individually) very minor. One such agreement referred to by Goulder is in Mk 8:31 pars. where Matthew and Luke agree in using ἀπό instead of ὑπό for Jesus' being rejected "by" the elders etc., and in having no definite article with the "chief priests" and "scribes". Goulder's theory thus implies a situation where Luke resolutely follows Mark in Markan blocks, using one source only (his copy of Matthew being left "on the floor"); so resolutely does Luke follow Mark that any substantial changes which Matthew might have made are studiously ignored by Luke. Yet Luke apparently knows Matthew's Greek text well enough to be influenced to the extent of changing a Markan ὑπό to ἀπό and a Markan "the elders and the chief priests and the scribes" to "the elders and chief priests and scribes". The overall picture does not seem very convincing. The fact that the MAs are so minor makes it hard to believe that Luke has been both influenced positively by Matthew's text in such (substantively) trivial ways, but also totally uninfluenced by any of Matthew's substantive additions to Mark. Undoubtedly the MAs constitute a problem for the 2ST, but precisely their minor nature constitutes a problem for Goulder's theory as well.

---

[58] *Luke* 44.

[59] I owe this point to Professor G. N. Stanton. See his *A Gospel for a New People: Studies in Matthew* (Edinburgh: 1992) 32f.

[60] Goulder actually suggests that Mark used a pen to do so: *Luke* 40.

The rest of Goulder's case depends in part on a detailed argument about Luke's reasons for producing his order of events from Matthew and Mark. Not all of Goulder's case can be discussed in detail here. However, in one recent article, Goulder has attempted to face directly the charge of Streeter (see above) that Luke's ordering of the material, if derived from Mark and Matthew seemed so totally lacking in rhyme or reason that Luke could on this theory only be regarded as a "crank". Goulder boldly sets out to account for the "order of a crank".[61] He claims that Luke first went forwards through the texts of Mark and Matthew, taking some of the material he wanted, and by the end of ch. 13 of his gospel had worked his way through to Mt 25; but then, according to Goulder, Luke realised that there was other material from Matthew which he still wanted to include; he therefore decided to go backwards back through the text of Matthew picking up non-Markan material from Matthew he had missed out up until now, sometimes using it directly, sometimes providing a "substitute" of similar material.[62]

In very general terms such a procedure might seem plausible; however, the theory fails to fit the facts in an uncomfortably large number of cases. Part of Goulder's claim is that Luke's version is as often as not a substitute for Matthew's version: e.g. the worthless salt of Lk 14:35 which is "cast out" is seen as the equivalent of Matthew's appendix to the parable of the Great Supper where the man without the wedding garment is also "cast out" (Mt 22:13). "Not one diamond shall be lost from the Matthean tiara: all must be included."[63] But however delightful the imagery and language, the application is not clear. What is the Matthean tiara? It is scarcely the whole gospel, since some parts of Matthew have no counterpart at all in Luke. For example, the parable of the Labourers in the Vineyard is "left out" by Luke,[64] perhaps because it was redundant after the Two Sons, or perhaps because its theme (Mt 20:16) had already been used in Lk 13:30. Evidently some diamonds from the Matthean tiara are not quite as valuable as others for Luke!

Further, the choice and order which Luke follows is scarcely explained, even on Goulder's theory. For example, the two parables of the tower builder and the king who "sent" an embassy of

---

[61] "Crank" *passim.*
[62] "Crank" 121; also *Luke* 581f.
[63] "Crank" 122; also *Luke* 582.
[64] "Crank" 123.

peace (Lk 14:28-32) are said to be inspired by the parable of the Wicked Husbandmen in Mt 21, these parables being Luke's "substitute" for Matthew's parable.[65] Yet according to Goulder, Luke has resolutely decided to ignore Matthew's use of Markan material and this is a Markan pericope which Luke himself will include later in Lk 20. This section in Luke thus fails to fit Goulder's explanation since (a) it is no substitute but a doublet (Luke does include the Markan parable in his gospel later), and (b) it is material which, on Goulder's own theory, Luke should be ignoring here.

Working backwards, Luke is now said to come across the parable of the Two Sons (Mt 21:28-32) for which Luke provides a substitute in his own "Two Sons" parable in Lk 15:11ff.[66] But before that Luke must have skipped back three whole chapters in Matthew to rescue the small parable of the Lost Sheep from Mt 18. This is quite a jump, including leap-frogging over material which (according to Goulder) Luke will include later anyway (at least via substitution: Mt 18:23-35 cf. Lk 16:1-13). Thus again the theory scarcely explains the actual Lukan order.

There is a similar failure for the theory to explain the facts later. According to Goulder, Lk 16:1-13 is inspired by Mt 18:23-35; but then instead of following Matthew backwards through his scroll, Luke now moves forwards—this time into Mt 19 where his attention is allegedly caught by v. 24, the saying about it being easier for a camel to go through the eye of a needle than for a "rich man" to enter the Kingdom. This is supposedly the inspiration for the story of the rich man and Lazarus in Lk 16:19ff. and the discussion about the Law.[67] Again this seems both difficult to envisage in itself and also contradictory of Luke's alleged general policy. Luke is meant to be working backwards, not forwards, through Matthew, and also ignoring Matthew's treatment of Markan material. Yet Goulder's theory suggests that Luke's eye was caught by a saying 24 verses ahead of the point in Matthew he has reached (and 24 verses is not just one line!); and in any case this is all Markan material in Matthew which Luke is supposedly ignoring!

These are some of the problems that seem to beset Goulder's theory. His discussion of Luke's order still provides no very convincing explanation for why Luke should have selected and di-

---

[65] "Crank" 122f.
[66] "Crank" 123.
[67] "Crank" 124f.

vided up the material in Matthew in the way he must have done if he knew it in its Matthean form and order. When one couples this with Luke's very conservative treatment of the order of Mark, the problem becomes even more acute. Why should Luke have had so much respect for the order of Mark, scarcely changing it at all, and yet change the order of Matthew at almost every point? Streeter's comment that such a procedure seems like that of a "crank", although expressed somewhat polemically, still has force. Not even Goulder's defence of the "order of a crank" seems sufficient to meet the problem.

Goulder's theory thus seems to many untenable. Further, the problems encountered by Goulder in seeking to explain the Matthew-Luke agreements whilst still assuming MP are very similar to those faced by the Augustinian hypothesis. For both theories, problems arise in trying to explain Luke's text as the result of Luke's redaction of Matthew and Mark together. Thus many of the objections mentioned above in relation to Goulder could apply, with only slight modification of the argument, to the Augustinian hypothesis.

*

In this essay I have tried to discuss the major theories currently proposed which claim that the agreements between Matthew and Luke are to be explained by Luke's direct knowledge and use of Matthew. For those who regard these theories as unsatisfactory, the alternative is to accept some sort of Q theory: the agreements between Matthew and Luke in the material which they have in common and which they have not derived from Mark is to be explained by their common dependence on prior source material.

Whether this "source material" ever existed in a unified form prior to its inclusion by Matthew and Luke is perhaps a further question, as I tried to show earlier. It is certainly possible to deny the existence of Q at one level by refusing to accept that the material common to Matthew and Luke ever existed independently in a fixed (written?) form. In this case "Q" would be rather more a mass of amorphous unrelated material than a single "source", or even "document". However, it may be that this issue could be decided in relation to the possible order and the nature of the Q material.

Several scholars have attempted to defend the view that Q was a unified source by seeking to show that the Q material exhibits a clear order. The lack of agreement in the order of this material in the gospels of Matthew and Luke was a key point in Streeter's argument against any theory of direct dependence between the two gospels, as we have seen. However, in two important articles, Vincent Taylor has argued that, provided one takes note of Matthew's redactional policy, a clear ordering of the Q material may be discernible.[68] Matthew has a clear policy of collecting related teaching material into his great discourses (e.g. in Mt 5-7, 10, 13, 18, 24-25). Taylor then showed that, if one compares the order of Q material in Luke with that in each Matthean discourse in turn, there is a remarkable correlation in the order. This suggests that the Q material may have existed in a fixed order: Luke then (in line with his general redactional procedure of preserving the order of his sources, cf. his treatment of Mark) kept the Q order mostly intact; Matthew (in line with his general redactional procedure) changed the order at times to bring substantively related material together in his teaching discourses. This would then suggest that the Q material existed in a fixed order and hence may have constituted a unified source.

Taylor's arguments are not fool-proof, and not all the evidence quite fits the facts.[69] Nevertheless, many have accepted the general conclusions suggested by Taylor's work in seeing (at least the bulk of) the Q material as forming a unified and ordered whole at some stage in the development of the tradition, with Luke preserving the order of Q more faithfully than Matthew.

The same conclusion about the unity of the Q material may also follow from attempts to determine a "theology" or Q, or to see Q as reflecting the beliefs and practice of a specific group of Christians in the early church. At first sight, such attempts would appear to be heavily dependent on arguments for the existence of Q. One cannot find a "theology of Q", or locate a "Q community", if "Q" did not exist. However, it may be that attempts to isolate a distinctive Q theology can provide, in a back-handed way, further support for the theory of the existence of Q as a unified source. If it can be shown that the Q material exhibits a distinctive theological profile, then this in turn may show that this material did exist in a unified form at some stage of the developing tradition. There is clearly not enough space here to

---

[68] V. Taylor, "The Order of Q," *JTS* 4 (1953) 27-31; and "The Original Order of Q" in *New Testament Essays. Studies in Memory of T. W. Manson*, ed. A. J. B. Higgins (Manchester: 1959) 95-118.

[69] See Kloppenborg, *Formation* 68f.

write a "theology of Q" to justify this. But one example to illustrate the point may be appropriate here. I refer once again to the so-called "Wisdom Christology" of the Q material, where Jesus is presented as one of the prophets sent by Wisdom, all of whom suffer violence and rejection. I have already tried to show that this Christological schema is neither Matthean nor Lukan (cf. above). And the combination of motifs (the rejected prophets, and rejected Wisdom) is also not evidenced outside these Q texts as far as I am aware.[70] The schema thus seems to be a distinctive feature of the Q tradition in the gospels. As such it may then reflect the beliefs of a specific group of Christians within early Christianity. Others too have sought to identify other features of Q and to build up a Q theology. The measure of distinctiveness will of course vary from case to case; and, as noted earlier, it is inherently likely that there will be a high degree of continuity between the theology of Q and that of both Matthew and Luke. Still many are convinced that such a theological profile in relation to the Q material can be built up. And in turn, if successful, this can be used to argue more strongly for the existence of Q as a unified source.

It may of course be that, even if "Q" was more than an amorphous mass of unrelated traditions, "Q" was not a static entity. Indeed the trend in recent Q studies has been to postulate (at times quite complex) developments in the growth of Q. Nevertheless such theories would still assume that it is indeed sensible to talk of Q as a unified source in some sense. It is precisely this belief in the existence of a Q source, coupled with a realisation that we can no longer think in the static terms that has characterized New Testament studies in the past, that has led to the quickening of interest in Q as an entity worthy of study in its own right and as possible evidence of a distinctive stream, or "trajectory", within early Christianity. That interest is reflected in the rest of the essays in this volume.

---

[70] See my *Revival* 164f.; S.Schulz, *Q. Die Spruchquelle der Evangelisten* (Zürich: 1971) 340.

CHAPTER THREE

THE MINOR AGREEMENTS AND Q

Frans Neirynck

"Although there is some hesitation about one or another isolated saying, a rather general tendency can be observed to include only passages attested by both Matthew and Luke and to include all of them. The possibility that a *Sondergut* passage may stem from Q is not denied but it is seen as too uncertain to be reckoned with."[1] This was, it seems to me, a fair description of the situation in the study of Q in 1981. Contributors to the Louvain Colloquium of that year were mainly interested in the composition of Q and pre-Q collections, i.e., the "formation" of Q rather than the expansion of its extent with Sondergut passages. In the past ten years, however, there seems to be a shift of scholarly interest. It is noticeable that J. S. Kloppenborg explicitly included Lk 9:61-62 and 12:13-14, 16b-21 in his list of Q pericopae.[2] In his edition of *Q Parallels* (1988) he distinguishes between the generally accepted extent of Q and "probable" and "possible" extent of Q printed in parentheses and in square brackets. His first category (Q origin likely) comprises the following pericopae: Mt 5:41; 7:2a; 10:23; 11:23b-24; Lk 6:24-26; 6:34-35b; 6:37c-38b; 7:3-5; 7:20; 9:61-62; 11:21-22; 11:27-28; 11:36; 12:13-14, 16-21; 12:49; 13:25; 15:8-10; 17:28-29. For all passages from Luke (and Mt 10:23) Kloppenborg can refer to suggestions made by H. Schürmann (1968, 1969), and although he opposes his own "limited selection" to Schürmann's "substantial expansion of

---

[1] F. Neirynck, "Recent Developments in the Study of Q" in *Logia. Les paroles de Jésus - The Sayings of Jesus*, ed. J. Delobel (BETL 49; Leuven: 1982) 29-75, especially 35-41: "The Reconstruction of Q" (37); = *Evangelica II* (BETL 99; 1991) 409-455 (417).
[2] *The Formation of Q. Trajectories in Ancient Wisdom Collections* (Philadelphia: 1987) 92 note 5.

the extent of Q",[3] one can speak of a return to a more positive attitude toward Sondergut candidates for membership in Q. A more reserved position is shown in my *Q-Synopsis*,[4] where Mt 10:23; 11:23b-24; Lk 11:27-28; 11:36; 12:13-14, 16-21; 15:8-10 are not retained in the text, and small print (uncertain Q text) is used for all other passages, with the exception of Lk 13:25 / Mt 25:11. M. Sato (1984, 1988),[5] followed by D. Kosch (1989),[6] has opted for a middle position ascribing Lk 6:24-26; 6:37c-38b; 7:3-6a; 9:61-62; 11:36; 12:16-21; 17:28-29 not to the common source Q but to the Lukan recension of it. Other Sondergut pericopae, printed in square brackets in *Q Parallels* (Q origin unlikely), are also assigned to Q^{Lk} by Sato: Lk 3:10-14; 7:29-30; 10:18-20; 11:5-8; 12:35-38.[7] All these passages appear in Schürmann's list of Q pericopae, and for some of them the ascription to Q has received new support in recent special studies. D. R. Catchpole's essay on Lk 11:5-8[8] and R. A. Piper's investigation of Lk 16:9-12(13)[9] are among the most notable examples.

The expansion of Q is not limited to Sondergut material with verbal reminiscences in Matthew or Luke and structural similarities in the double tradition. The phenomenon of the minor agreements in triple-tradition passages is also cited as evidence for Q. This argument takes an extreme form in E. Hirsch's suggestion[10] that the Q source contained a passion narrative, on the basis

---

[3] *Q Parallels. Synopsis, Critical Notes & Concordance* (Sonoma, CA: 1988) xxiv (the name of Schürmann is missing in the list of authors, see xxvii). Cf. "A Synopsis of Q" *ETL* 64 (1988) 441-449 (= *Evangelica II* 465-473).

[4] *Q-Synopsis. The Double-Tradition Passages in Greek* (SNTA, 13; Leuven: 1988).

[5] *Q und Prophetie. Studien zur Gattungs- und Traditionsgeschichte der Quelle Q* (WUNT 2/29; Tübingen: 1988; [Diss. Bern, 1984]).

[6] *Die eschatologische Tora des Menschensohnes. Untersuchungen zur Rezeption der Stellung Jesu zur Tora in Q* (NTOA 12; Göttingen: 1989; [Diss. Freiburg, 1988]). See also his "Rekonstruktion und Interpretation. Eine methodenkritische Hinführung mit einem Exkurs zur Q-Vorlage des Lk," *FZPT* 36 (1989) 409-425.

[7] For more detailed information, cf. "Q^{Mt} and Q^{Lk} and the Reconstruction of Q," *ETL* 66 (1990) 385-390 (= *Evangelica II* 475-480).

[8] "Q and 'The Friend at Midnight' (Luke xi.5-8/9)," *JTS* 34 (1983) 407-424. But see: C. M. Tuckett, "Q, Prayer, and the Kingdom," *JTS* 40 (1989) 367-376; and "A Rejoinder" by Catchpole 377-388.

[9] *Wisdom in the Q-tradition. The Aphoristic Teaching of Jesus* (MSSNTS 61; Cambridge: 1988) 86-99: "Lk 16:9-13".

[10] *Frühgeschichte des Evangeliums*, vol. I (Tübingen: 1941) 243-246. Cf. Kloppenborg, *Formation* 86.

of *Kleinübereinstimmungen* in Mt 26:50 / Lk 22:48; Mt 26:64 / Lk 22:69; Mt 26:68 / Lk 22:64; Mt 26:75 / Lk 22:62; Mt 28:19 / Lk 24:47.[11] G. Schneider wrote a reply to Hirsch in his dissertation on Lk 22:54-71,[12] but he himself, impressed by the Mt-Lk agreements against Mk 11:27-33, hesitantly raised the question: "Vielleicht ergibt sich daraus, dass die Redenquelle (Q) doch eine P[assionsgeschichte] erhalten hat und somit eine Evv-Schrift gewesen ist."[13] The evaluation of the minor agreements, first in Lk 9[14] and then in general, has led E. E. Ellis to another radical conclusion: "When these agreements are given their full weight, Q could well be understood as a (derivative of a) primitive Gospel or Gospels postulated by earlier criticism on which all three Synoptics are in one way or another dependent."[15] The great B. Weiss cast a long shadow upon 20th-century Gospel studies. His *ältere Quelle* (Q)[16] provides indeed an easy explanation of the Matthew / Luke agreements. It includes sayings material *and* narratives and is used by Matthew and Luke in combination with Mark. I cite three examples:[17]

---

[11] For description of the agreements, cf. F. Neirynck, *The Minor Agreements of Matthew and Luke against Mark, with a Cumulative List* (BETL 37; Leuven: 1974) 175, 178, 179, 182, 195; *The Minor Agreements in a Horizontal-line Synopsis* (SNTA 15; Leuven: 1991).

[12] *Verleugnung, Verspottung und Verhör Jesu nach Lukas 22,54-71* (StANT 22; München: 1969) 47-60 (on Mt-Lk agreements).

[13] *Ibid.* 117 (cf. 56: Lk 22:68a). For a critique, cf. *ETL* 58 (1972) 570-573, 572; D. R. Catchpole, *The Trial of Jesus* (SPB 22; Leiden: 1971) 276-278.

[14] E. E. Ellis, "The Composition of Lk 9 and the Sources of Christology" in *Current Issues in Biblical and Patristic Interpretation. Festschrift M. C. Tenney*, ed. G. F. Hawthorne (Grand Rapids, MI: 1975) 121-127; F.T. in J. Dupont (ed.), *Jésus aux origines de la christologie* (BETL 40; Leuven: 1975; ²1989) 193-200, especially 196-197.

[15] "Gospels Criticism. A Perspective on the State of the Art" in *Das Evangelium und die Evangelien*, ed. P. Stuhlmacher (WUNT 28; Tübingen: 1984) 27-54, especially 38 (E.T.: *The Gospel and the Gospels* [Grand Rapids, MI: 1991] 26-52, especially 36).

[16] "Note on the Siglum Q" in *Evangelica II* 474: on the use of "Q" (with reference to B. Weiss) in E. Simons, *Hat der dritte Evangelist den kanonischen Matthäus benutzt?* (Bonn: 1880(!)).

[17] *Die Evangelien des Markus und Lukas* (KEK 1/2; Göttingen: ⁹1901) 422, 431 note 1, 600. In each of these three instances B. Weiss's position is at least indirectly alluded to in J. A. Fitzmyer's commentary on Luke (1981, 1985): 763: "not impossible, but can scarcely be proved" (cf. 766); 806 ("a shorter 'Q' form... So B. Weiss"); 1278 ("but such a position counters the basic understanding of 'Q'"). For more complete references to Weiss's Q hypothesis in Markan sections with "Lk-Mt contacts", see B. S. Easton, *The Gospel accord-*

Lk 9:10-17 Wie in der Einleitung V. 11, so sind die Reminiscenzen an die vielfach noch bei Mt erhaltene kürzere Erzählungsform (Q) in V. 13. 14. 17 unleugbar.

Lk 9:37-43 ...er kannte noch eine kürzere Erzählungsform dieser Geschichte, die sich im Wesentlichen noch bei Mt 17,14ff. erhalten hat.... Diese Form wird dann aus Q stammen.

Lk 20:9-19 ...es fehlt nicht an Anzeichen, wonach ihm dies Gleichnis noch in einer älteren Gestalt vorlag, und da eine solche auch noch bei Mt durchblickt, so wird dieselbe in Q gestanden haben.

The first example is M.-É. Boismard's test case, and the Synoptic solution he proposes is that of B. Weiss (Proto-Matthew).[18] For H. Hübner, too, the minor agreements against Mk 2:23-28 can be explained by acceptance of a shorter form of this story (without v. 27) in the second source Q.[19]

The minor agreements also have their bearing on the Q hypothesis in a quite different direction. A. Fuchs and his school[20] emphasize the unitary character of the minor agreements and their relatedness to the text of Mark: they are secondary to Mark and explainable by Matthew's and Luke's common dependence on a hypothetical Deutero-Markan redaction. In a first stage of this theory, dependence on *Deuteromarkus* was suggested for the location of Q material that is found in the same Markan context in Matthew and Luke. In a second stage, the double-tradition pericopae overlapping with Mk 1:7-8 (the preaching of John the Baptist); 1:12-13 (the temptations of Jesus); 3:22-26 (the Beelze-

---

ing to St. Luke (Edinburgh: 1926). Q influence is assumed by Easton in Lk 9:10-17 (137); 5:17-26 (67); and, with less probability, 5:12-16 (64).

[18] "The Two-Source Theory at an Impasse," *NTS* 26 (1979-80) 1-17. For a response, cf. *Evangelica II* 75-94 and 29-34.

[19] *Das Gesetz in der synoptischen Tradition* (Witten: 1973; Göttingen: ²1986) 117-119. For a response, cf. my "Jesus and the Sabbath" (1975) 270 note 157 (= *Evangelica* 1982, 680): "a typically B. Weiss solution"; J. Kiilunen, *Die Vollmacht im Widerstreit* (AASF 40; Helsinki: 1985) 199-203; H. Sariola, *Markus und das Gesetz* (AASF 56; Helsinki: 1990) 84-86.

[20] See especially A. Fuchs, *Die Entwicklung der Beelzebulkontroverse bei den Synoptikern* (SNTU B/5; Linz: 1980) and numerous contributions in *SNTU*, from 3 (1978) to 16 (1991); F. Kogler, *Das Doppelgleichnis vom Senfkorn und vom Sauerteig in seiner traditionsgeschichtlichen Entwicklung* (FzB 59; Würzburg: 1988). Cf. T. A. Friedrichsen, "The Matthew-Luke Agreements against Mark. A Survey of Recent Studies: 1974-1989" in *L'Évangile de Luc—The Gospel of Luke*, ed. F. Neirynck (BETL 32; Leuven: 1989) 335-392, especially 360-365.

bul controversy); 4:30-32 (the mustard seed parable) are subtracted from Q, and a strict definition of the second Synoptic source is urged by Fuchs: "*Rede*quelle" or "*Logien*schrift" without narrative elements.[21]

In a more drastic way the minor agreements are used as an argument against the very existence of Q by M. D. Goulder: "The issue...is central because if Luke knew Matthew, we should have lost the main reason for believing in the existence of Q"; and: "if there were one significant and clear MA in the Passion story, then we should know that Luke was following Matthew; and Q, and with it the whole structure, would be undermined."[22] In answer to this "putting Q to the test", one can observe that "If [*dato non concesso*] Lukan knowledge of Matthew would be the conclusion to be drawn for the minor agreements, then Luke would have used Mark notwithstanding his knowledge of Matthew, and the inference could only be that elsewhere, where Luke is using another source, a similar subsidiary influence of Matthaean reminiscences can be expected."[23]

As indicated above, the point of departure of this paper is the list of double-tradition pericopae commonly accepted as the contents of Q. Without espousing B. Weiss's position, a more modest expansion of Q on the basis of the minor agreements is suggested anew in some recent studies.[24] Possible candidates for inclusion

---

[21] Fuchs, *Entwicklung* 199; *SNTU* 5 (1980) 142; 9 (1984) 144. Kogler seems to propose further limitations to the Q source (*Doppelgleichnis* 219: "nicht...ohne Einschränkungen").

[22] *Luke. A New Paradigm* (JSNT SS 20; Sheffield: 1989) 6; see also 47-50 ("The Arguments against Q: 2. The Minor Agreements"). On Mt 26:68 / Lk 22:64 (6-7), see my response in *Evangelica II* 27-28 (and 95-138); on Lk 9:22, Goulder's example of "the accumulation of uncharacteristic Lucan changes" (48-50), see *Evangelica II* 43-48.

[23] *Evangelica II* 144 (= "The Study of Q" 34).

[24] For Sato (see note 5 above), Lk 3:2-4; 10:25-28 are possibly Q texts; 6:20a: uncertain; 3:21-22: probably (25: "nicht völlig sicher, aber wahrscheinlich"). The mention of "sonstige 'minor agreements' zwischen Matthäus und Lukas" (diss. 23: "höchst unwahrscheinlich") is deleted in the published text (21). Kosch (see note 6 above) ascribes to Q: Lk 3:2-4; 3:21-22 (217: probably); 6:12a ("vielleicht"), 17a, 20a (229: ὄχλος and μαθηταί: "vermutlich"); not 6:13-16 (226); 12,1b (83, cf. 79); but not 10:25-28 (93: "kaum nachweisbar"). Lk 3:3-4; 3:21-22a(!); 6:12-16 (and 8:9-10: cf. Pesch-Kratz) are mentioned by J. Schüling, *Studien zum Verhältnis von Logienquelle und Markusevangelium* (Diss.; Giessen: 1987) 59 (57-59 and 203-206 are not reprinted in the published text: FzB 65; Würzburg 1991).

Compare A. Polag's reconstruction of Q: [3:2b-4]; [3:21-22]; 6:12a, 17a, 20a; [17:2]; 17:31 (*Evangelica II* 417-419; = "The Study of Q" 37-39). None of

will be examined one by one, in the reversed order: first individual sayings in Luke's central section with a distant parallel in Mark,[25] and then sayings material in the Markan order prior to the Sermon Q 6:20-49.[26]

The basic assumption of Markan priority will be my guiding methodology in this paper: in triple-tradition passages where Matthew's and Luke's independent redactions provide a satisfactory explanation of their agreements against Mark there is no need to suggest the existence of a second non-Markan source (Q).

I. Mark, not Q, in Luke's Central Section

1. Luke 17:31 (Mk 13:15-16 / Mt 24:17-18)[27]

The text of Lk 17:31 is printed in A. Polag's reconstruction of Q, with two omissions (καὶ τὰ σκεύη αὐτοῦ ἐν τῇ οἰκίᾳ and ὁμοίως, both peculiar to Lk) and one conjecture (τὰ ἐν τῇ οἰκίᾳ):[28]

---

these passages, except 6:20a, is included in my *Q-Synopsis*. Cf. Kloppenborg's "Critical Notes" in *Q Parallels* 6 (3:2-4), 16 (3:21-22), 22 (6:12a, 17a, 20a), 118 (12:1), 182 (17:2), 194 (17:31). His *Q Thomas Reader* (Sonoma, CA: 1990) includes <6:20a>, 17:2 (cf. *Q Parallels*) and also <Q 3:3> (incorrectly cited as 3:2).

[25] On the argument of "der markusferne Kontext," cf. *Evangelica II* 427-432 (= "The Study of Q" 47-52). The placement in Luke's central section by itself is not a valid reason for ascription to a non-Markan source, L or Q.

[26] The overlapping of Q and Mark (Mk 1:7-8; 1:12-13; 3:22-26; 4:30-32) is a related problem but neither these "major" agreements nor the influence of the Q-doublet on Lk 8:16,17; 9:1-5; 20:46 (par. Mk) are directly considered here. See now the contributions on Mk 3:22-26 and 4:30-32 in *The Four Gospels 1992. Festschrift F. Neirynck* (BETL 100; Leuven: 1992) 587-619: M. E. Boring, "The Synoptic Problem, 'Minor' Agreements and the Beelzebub Pericope" (587-619); T. A. Friedrichsen, "'Minor' and 'Major' Matthew-Luke Agreements against Mk 4:30-32" (649-676). On Mk 1:7-8, see C. M. Tuckett, "Mark and Q" in *The Synoptic Gospels*, ed. C. Focant (BETL 110; Leuven: 1993) 149-175, especially 168-172: "Mk 1:7-8 / Q 3:16".

[27] On Lk 21:21bc, Luke's substitute for Mk 13:15-16, cf. my "The Eschatological Discourse" in *The Interrelations of the Gospels*, ed. D. L. Dungan (BETL 95; Leuven: 1990) 108-124, especially 116. On the hypothesis of a special source in Lk 21, see the critical remarks by J. Verheyden, "The Source(s) of Luke 21" in *Luc-Luke* (note 20 above) 491-516, especially 510.

[28] *Fragmenta Q* 78-79.

ἐν ἐκείνῃ τῇ ἡμέρᾳ
ὃς ἔσται ἐπὶ τοῦ δώματος [ ]
  μὴ καταβάτω ἆραι (τὰ ἐν τῇ οἰκίᾳ)
καὶ ὁ ἐν ἀγρῷ [ ]
  μὴ ἐπιστρεψάτω εἰς τὰ ὀπίσω.

Matthew's and Luke's common use of a plural object of ἆραι (Mt 24:17 τὰ ἐκ τῆς οἰκίας αὐτοῦ and Lk 17:31 αὐτά resuming τὰ σκεύη αὐτοῦ ἐν τῇ οἰκίᾳ, against Mk 13:15τι ἐκ τῆς οἰκίας αὐτοῦ) and their common omission of μηδὲ εἰσελθάτω (after μὴ καταβάτω in Mk) are noted by J. Lambrecht as traces of the Q saying which he supposes to be the source of Mk 13:15-16.[29] I. H. Marshall mentions a third agreement: the preposition ἐν (diff. Mk 13:16 εἰς).[30] Contrary to Polag, he holds that Luke's phrase καὶ τὰ σκεύη αὐτοῦ ἐν τῇ οἰκίᾳ and αὐτά belong to the Q saying.[31] R. H. Gundry (1982) too draws attention to the omission of "neither let him enter" and to the use of the plural τά "It looks as though Matthew has conflated the two forms of the saying."[32]

For J. A. Fitzmyer, Lk 17:31 is not a parallel to Mk 13:15-16 ("the wording is quite different") and 17:28-31 "should be regarded as a unit, probably derived from L."[33] Such a solution, however, seems to neglect the double-tradition parallel Mt 24:39b /Lk 17:30. With regard to Lk 17:31, even Marshall could not deny that "the language, it is true, is close to that of Mk."[34] The main differences are in the first part. The beginning is distinctively Lukan, in contrast to καὶ ὁ in the second clause (= Mk/Mt).

---

[29] "Die Logia-Quellen von Markus 13," *Biblica* 47 (1966) 321-360, 342; *Die Redaktion der Markus-Apokalypse* (Analecta Biblica 28; Rome: 1967) 157-159, especially 157: the Mt/Lk agreements "machen es zugleich unwahrscheinlich, dass Lk 17,31 in Abhängigkeit von Mk 13 redigiert wurde" (incorrectly rendered by J. Zmijewski, *Die Eschatologiereden* [see note 40 below] 474 note 43).

[30] *Luke* 665: "the correction may be coincidental or due to non-Marcan tradition." Cf. D. Wenham, *The Rediscovery of Jesus' Eschatological Discourse* (Gospel Perspectives 4; Sheffield: 1984) 189-192: the three agreements point to "the existence of a pre-synoptic form of the tradition", but ἐν for εἰς "could be coincidental" (190).

[31] *Ibid.* See also J. Jeremias, *Die Sprache des Lukasevangeliums* (Göttingen: 1980) 269: the anacolouthon is pre-Lukan.

[32] *Matthew* 483. The omission of δέ and the use of ἐν (for εἰς) are not treated as agreements with Lk. For a full description of the minor agreements, cf. my *The Minor Agreements* § 84. Mk 13:15 δέ (om. N): TR T h S V B [N²⁶] Greeven.

[33] *Luke* 1165.

[34] *Luke* 665.

Lk 17:31 is placed by Luke in a Q context,[35] and the wording of the saying may have been influenced by this context:

30 κατὰ τὰ αὐτὰ (Mt οὕτως) ἔσται ᾗ ἡμέρᾳ...
31 ἐν ἐκείνῃ τῇ ἡμέρᾳ ὃς ἔσται...
34 ταύτῃ τῇ νυκτὶ ἔσονται δύο...35 ἔσονται δύο...

"On that day" refers back to the day when the Son of Man is revealed. In v. 31 Luke speaks of people outside the house, on the roof or in the field, and in vv. 34-35 he speaks of people inside the house, in bed or at the mill. Luke cannot be blamed for writing the relative ὃς ἔσται...καὶ τὰ σκεύη αὐτοῦ ἐν τῇ οἰκίᾳ (= οὗ τὰ σκεύη...).[36] This introduction of the man on the roof "and his goods in the house" was suggested to Luke by Mk's μηδὲ εἰσελθάτω and τι ἐκ τῆς οἰκίας αὐτοῦ,[37] which he can simply replace by a resumptive αὐτά. The addition of ὁμοίως and the change of εἰς to ἐν in the second clause[38] are clearly due to Lukan redaction. A more important modification is the omission of ἆραι τὸ ἱμάτιον αὐτοῦ at the end and v. 32, "Remember Lot's wife", directly connected with μὴ ἐπιστρεψάτω εἰς τὰ ὀπίσω.

A quite different, typically Matthean care for parallel structure is at the origin of the minor changes in Mt 24:17-18:

ὁ ἐπὶ τοῦ δώματος μὴ καταβάτω[39] [ ]   ἆραι τὰ ἐκ τῆς οἰκίας αὐτοῦ

καὶ ὁ ἐν τῷ ἀγρῷ   μὴ ἐπιστρεψάτω [ ] ὀπίσω ἆραι τὸ ἱμάτιον αὐτοῦ.

The agreements with Lk 17:31 are coincidental resemblances in two independent redactions of Mk 13:15-16 and "do not justify positing a Q Vorlage."[40]

---

[35] Lk 17:30, 34-35; 32 is redactional and 33 stems from Q=Mt 10:39, or Mk 8:35 (cf. "The Study of Q" 49-50 = Evangelica II 429-430).

[36] For examples of this usage, cf. Kühner-Gerth, Grammatik, II. 432-433.

[37] By treating καὶ τὰ σκεύη αὐτοῦ ἐν τῇ οἰκίᾳ as "clearly a Lucan addition" Kloppenborg seems to neglect this connection (Formation 159). Is it not rearrangement rather than addition? In good Lukan style the prohibition is preceded by an appropriate "setting".

[38] The anarthrous ἐν ἀγρῷ (12:28; 15:25) may be formula-like but is it therefore pre-Lukan? Ctr. Jeremias, Sprache 269; cf. 218.

[39] Greeven: καταβαινέτω (TR S). In Mk 13:15 Greeven reads εἰς τὴν οἰκίαν: TR S V; τι ἆραι (word order): H S V M N (both diff. Mt/Lk).

[40] Kloppenborg, Formation 157 note 247. See also A. Ennulat, Die 'Minor Agreements' (Diss.; Bern: 1989) 302-303. On Lk 17:31-33, cf. J. Zmijewski, Die Eschatologiereden des Lukas-Evangeliums (BBB 40; Bonn: 1972) 465-489 (478: "Die Anhaltspunkte für Q [in Lk 17:31] sind...keineswegs überzeugend").

2. Luke 17:2 (Mk 9:42 / Mt 18:6)

The saying on scandals is printed in Polag's reconstruction in square brackets: *vermutlich* in Q. The saying is given in the order of Luke, preceded by Q 17:1b, and the reconstruction is based on the text of Luke, with two exceptions: μύλος ὀνικός (Lk λίθος μυλικός) and ἕνα τῶν μικρῶν τούτων (Lk 2-4,1), both from Mt=Mk.[41]

ἀνάγκη ἐλθεῖν τὰ σκάνδαλα,
πλὴν οὐαὶ τῷ ἀνθρώπῳ δι' οὗ τὸ σκάνδαλον ἔρχεται.
[λυσιτελεῖ αὐτῷ,
εἰ μύλος ὀνικὸς περίκειται περὶ τὸν τράχηλον αὐτοῦ
καὶ ἔρριπται εἰς τὴν θάλασσαν,
ἢ ἵνα σκανδαλίσῃ ἕνα τῶν μικρῶν τούτων.]

In a short study on Lk 17:2 J. Schlosser has defended the Q origin of the saying (*"wahrscheinlicher...als oft angenommen"*, "nicht sicher").[42] He notes that there is at least one minor agreement against Mark: "Mt and Lk...(haben) nach 'es ist besser' je einen ἵνα-Satz als Subjekt."[43] To Schlosser's list of defenders of Q 17:2 (up to 1981) we can now add Fitzmyer, Kloppenborg, Davies and Allison.[44]

My position is correctly described in Kloppenborg's critical note: "Luke 17:1-2 is a combination of Q (17:1) and Mark 9:42 (17:2)."[45] Schlosser refers to a comment I wrote in 1966, from which I quote here a few sentences:[46]

It is hardly strange that Matthew [18:6, 7] brought together sayings about scandal from Mk and Q.... Lk 17:2 shows no specific similarity with Mt 18:6 and negative agreements against Mk (καλόν ἐστιν, βέβληται) only confirm that Mk 9:42 has been handled in two different

---

[41] *Fragmenta Q* 74-75. Like most authors, I accept the Q origin of Q 17:1b. On M. Sato's reserve concerning the scattered sayings between Lk 14:26 and 17:6 (and D. Kosch's reply: sequence Q 17:1, 3-4, 6; but see *Tora* 147: "unsicher"), cf. *Evangelica II* 476, 478. W. Schenk's reconstruction of Q 17:1b (*Synopse*, 1981) is identical with Polag's. J. Schlosser (cf. below note 42) deletes τὸ σκάνδαλον (77: "plumbe Wiederholung", MtR).

[42] "Lk 17,2 und die Logienquelle," *SNTU* 8 (1983) 70-78, especially 78.

[43] *Ibid.* 73-74, in reply to R. Laufen's statement: "Übereinstimmungen zwischen Matthäus und Lukas gibt es nicht" (87). This MA is not included in my list, *The Minor Agreements*.

[44] Fitzmyer, *Luke* 1137; Kloppenborg, *Q Parallels* 182; W. D. Davies and D. C. Allison, *Matthew* II (1991) 761. Cf. Schlosser's list: 74 note 21.

[45] Cf. *Evangelica II* 432 ("The Study of Q" 52).

[46] "The Tradition of the Sayings of Jesus: Mark 9,33-50," *Concilium* (1966): cf. *Evangelica* (BETL 60; 1982) 811-820, 817.

ways.... For the connection of Mk 9:42 with 17:1b(Q) Luke may have been inspired by the word about the traitor in Mk 14:21. The scheme is identical: it is necessary (as is written)—woe to him who—it would be better for him...

Mt 18:6 is closely parallel to Mk 9:42, and all changes can be redactional: δέ (for καί), συμφέρει (καλόν ἐστιν...μᾶλλον), ἵνα (εἰ), κρεμασθῇ (περίκειται), καταποντισθῇ ἐν τῷ πελάγει + gen. (βέβληται εἰς + acc.). Quite understandably, none of them is retained in Polag's reconstruction of Q. Polag takes the three verbs from Lk 17:2. He is followed by Schlosser, but with hesitancy: λυσιτελεῖ (for καλόν ἐστιν) could be "ein von Lk ausgesuchtes, gut griechisches Wort"; περίκειται is borrowed from Mk (Schlosser conjectures the verb περιτίθημι in Q, cf. 1 Clem 46:8); ἔρριπται (for βέβληται) is "gut lukanisch" (Lk 4:35, diff. Mk; Acts 22:23; 27:19, 29).[47] On the other hand, Schlosser differs from Polag regarding λίθος μυλικός and the postposition of ἕνα (Lk=Q, against Mt=Mk). The first case is irrelevant for us (though Lukan correction of μύλος ὀνικός is likely). He argues more specifically about εἷς + partitive genitive: there are only two other occurrences of the postposition in the Synoptics, Lk 15:4 and 16:17, which are "allgemein anerkannte Q-Texte".[48] But the text of Lk 17:2 is not wholly certain: ἕνα τ. μ. τ. (TR) is read by Kilpatrick and Greeven,[49] and in the two other instances the word order in Q is scarcely "allgemein anerkannt".[50]

There is one more divergence from Polag in Schlosser's reconstruction of Q, λυσιτελεῖ...ἵνα[!]... ἢ ἵνα (cf. Mt συμφέρει...ἵνα): in place of the first ἵνα Lk wrote εἰ under the influence of Mk's καλόν ἐστιν...εἰ.[51] The force of this minor agreement is weakened in two ways. First, the redactional use of συμφέρει + ἵνα (Mt) for καλόν ἐστιν is well attested in Mt 5:29, 30 (doublet of 18:8, 9, par. Mk 9:43, 45, 47). Second, the direct parallel is Lk 17:2a (λυσιτελεῖ αὐτῷ cf. Mk) and not the second

---

[47] "Lk 17,2" 77-78, cf. 71, 72.

[48] Ibid. 75.

[49] See also Davies and Allison, II. 761. Schlosser refers to Aland's Konkordanz without noticing the lacuna at Lk 17:2 (no mention of TR).

[50] Q 16:17 μία κεραία...ἀπὸ τοῦ νόμου (= Mt): Polag, cf. Harnack, Schmid. Q 15:4 stresses the contrast: ἑκατὸν πρόβατα, ἐξ αὐτῶν ἕν (diff. Mt), τὰ ἐνενήκοντα ἐννέα (cf. v. 7).

[51] "Lk 17,2" 77.

clause ἢ ἵνα in v. 2b. Schlosser adduces several considerations against the dependence of Lk 17:2b on Mk 9:42a.[52]

(1) The *Tobspruch* in Lk 17:2 is more original than the broken form in Mk/Mt. But the "full form" of καλόν ἐστιν with ἤ and a second clause in the immediate context (Mk 9:43, 45, 47) may have influenced Luke's reworking of Mk 9:42.

(2) The absence of a comparative before ἤ is unusual in Lk. But this is apparently not the case with λυσιτελεῖ in a comparative sense.[53]

(3) The normal construction is λυσιτελεῖ with infinitive, and not with εἰ. But the direct parallel (and source) is καλόν ἐστιν + εἰ in Mk.[54]

(4) The unclassical use of ἵνα in a non-purpose sense (in Q 4:3; 6:31; 7:6) is not favoured by Luke: he shows "eine deutliche Zurückhaltung" (with reference to Jeremias).[55] But Jeremias cites Lk 9:45 as an example of redactional use; Lk 8:32 (diff. Mk 5:12) can be added, and other occurrences in the Sondergut may be redactional as well (7:36; 16:27; 21:36).[56]

(5) The main reason is "das Fehlen des Partizips πιστευόν-των".[57] But this is really a strange argument in Schlosser's theory. If omission by Luke is "durchaus unwahrscheinlich", is it then thinkable that the same Luke who depends on Mk 9:42b in 17:2a (εἰ...περίκειται for ἵνα + conj. in Q) would be unaware of this parallel in Mk 9:42a when he copies his Q source in v. 2b? The debate on the identity of "the little ones" is not closed.[58]

---

[52] *Ibid.* (1): 75; (2), (3): 71; (4): 75; (5): 73-74.—Schlosser also rejects the (less probable) explanation of Lk 17:2b ἢ ἵνα... (= Mk 9:42a) as added to Q (v. 2a) by Luke. Cf. H. Fleddermann in *CBQ* 43 (1981) 68; Davies and Allison, II. 761: "from Q or Mark?"

[53] Cf. Tobias 3:6 BA λυσιτελεῖ μοι ἀποθανεῖν ἢ ζῆν. Andocides, *Or.* 1.125: τεθνάσαι νομίσασα λυσιτελεῖν ἢ ζῆν.

[54] On the *"magna vis"* in this use of εἰ + indicative, see M. Zerwick, *Graecitas Biblica* § 311. Cf. BDR § 372.3.

[55] *Die Sprache* 58. The figure of the omissions in Lk, diff. Mk ("Von den 22 Belegen...behielt er nur 8 bei und beseitigte er 14") needs correction. Seven instances have a parallel in Lk: Mk 5:18, 23, 43; 8:30; 15:21 (infinitive); 6:8; 15:11 (*oratio recta*), but in the seven other instances either the ἵνα clause or the verb + ἵνα or both are lacking in Lk (Mk 6:12; 9:9, 30; 11:28; 12:15; 14:35, 49).

[56] Cf. P. Lampe, art. ἵνα, *EWNT* II. 460-466: "Die lk *Red.* zeigt 4 unklass. Beispiele: 7,36; 8,32; 17,2; 9,45" (463).

[57] Schlosser (72 note 12) prefers the shorter reading against N[26] [εἰς ἐμέ], par. Mt.

[58] Cf. D. P. Moessner, *Lord of the Banquet* (Minneapolis: 1989) 201-202.

3. Luke 12:1b (Mk 8:15 / Mt 16:6)

"There is one slight agreement with Mt. 16:6 diff. Mk., which supports the hypothesis that it is derived from Q and not from Mk." (Marshall).[59] The saying in Lk 12:1b is now assigned to Q in some recent commentaries on Matthew, though with less emphasis on the minor agreement: "the use of προσέχετε...need not point to a common source."[60] The location of Mt 16:6 is strictly parallel to Mk 8:15 and the change to "Pharisees *and Sadducees*" is characteristically Matthean. For Mk's ὁρᾶτε, βλέπετε ἀπό Matthew writes first ὁρᾶτε καὶ προσέχετε ἀπό (16:6) and then repeats the saying in v. 11 with προσέχετε (without ὁρᾶτε) and again in his own comment, v. 12 (εἶπεν) προσέχειν. He uses προσέχετε ἀπό in 7:15; 10:17 (diff. Mk 13:9 βλέπετε...) and προσέχετε μή in 6:1.

For Fitzmyer Lk 12:1b is more likely derived from Q and not from Mk, "since only five words are common to Mark and Luke".[61] But in this short saying the five words ἀπὸ τῆς ζύμης τῶν Φαρισαίων are rather a high percentage of common words. In 12:1 Luke writes προσέχετε ἑαυτοῖς ἀπό for Mk's double imperative ὁρᾶτε, βλέπετε ἀπό, and again in 20:46 προσέχετε ἀπό for βλέπετε ἀπό: "He substitutes a characteristic verb *prosechein* for the Marcan *blepein*" (Fitzmyer, at 20:46).[62] Προσέχετε ἑαυτοῖς is Lukan usage: Lk 17:3; 21:34; Acts 5:35; 20:28.

The relation of Lk 12:1b to the preceding Q section (11:39-52) is cited as a second argument for its ascription to Q: Matthew's designation of the Pharisees as "hypocrites" (in the Woes, Mt 23, diff. Lk) is supposed to be a reminiscence of ὑπόκρισις in the Q

---

[59] *Luke* 510 (cf. 511, with reference to Schürmann). The saying is classified with the uncertain texts in Polag's *Fragmenta Q* 86. Cf. *Der Umfang der Logienquelle* (Diss.; Trier: 1966) 57, 124a: probably from Q (*Sondervers*, without parallel in Mt; note 271: "Das προσέχετε in Mt 16,6 genügt nicht").

[60] Davies and Allison, *Matthew* II (1991) 589. See also Gnilka, *Matthäusevangelium* II (1988) 43 ("Ein Einfluß des Q-Logions auf Mt ist nicht feststellbar"). Cf. W. Wiefel, *Lukas* (1988) 232 ("aus Q", but no comparison with Mt).

[61] *Luke* 953. "The saying is often ascribed to Q" (*ibid.*, with reference to Marshall and Schneider); contrast Kloppenborg, *Q Parallels* 118: "Not in Q: Most authors." But see above, note 60.

[62] *Luke* 1316. It is less evident that the verb in Lk 20:46 "may have been drawn from Luke's source in 12:1" (Marshall 749). Nor can the use of βλέπετε μή in Lk 21:8 (par. Mk 13:5) offer evidence for a non-Markan source in Lk 12:1 and 20:46 (ctr. D.M. Sweetland in *Biblica* 65 [1984] 65 note 22).

saying.[63] Such a position is not irreversible,[64] but if the clause ἥτις ἐστὶν ὑπόκρισις is a Lukan insertion,[65] it can suffice to refer to 11:39-44 (Q) and the criticism in v. 44 that "the Pharisees conceal their true nature".[66] Luke's understanding of their ὑπόκρισις (Mk 12:15) is made clear in Lk 20:20, ὑποκρινομένους ἑαυτοὺς δικαίους εἶναι. "Ein in Lk 12:1 erhaltenes Q-Logion gibt es nicht."[67]

The use of Mk 8:15 in Lk 12:1b is not unique. Compare Luke's framing of the Q sections in Lk 11:16, 29 (cf. Mk 8:11); Lk 11:37-38 (cf. Mk 7:1, 5); Lk 12:1 (cf. Mk 8:14-15): all from the great omission and all referring to the Pharisees.[68]

4. Luke 10:25-28 (Mk 12:28-34 / Mt 22:34-40)

The Great Commandment was not included in my 1981 survey of current reconstructions of Q,[69] and ten years later there is not much change in this situation.[70] The combination of Mk and Q in Mt 22:34-40 and Lk 10:25-28 is of course a possible solution for their well-known minor agreements against Mk.[71] Defenders of

---

[63] Marshall, *Luke* 512 (cf. Schürmann).

[64] U. Wilckens (*TWNT* 8 566 note 45): ὑπόκρισις in Lk 12:1 LkR derived from "hypocrites" in Q (cf. Mt 23). Compare E. Simons (see note 16 above) 72-73: Luke's dependence on Mt 23.

[65] "Perhaps" the more likely alternative for Davies and Allison (see note 60 above).

[66] Marshall's comment (*Luke* 499). Cf. Fitzmyer, *Luke* 954 ("their dissemblance in conduct"): "This explains why Jesus could call some Pharisees 'unmarked graves' (11:44)."

[67] U. Luz, *Matthäus* II (1990) 466 note 4. Cf. B. Weiss, *Lukas* (⁹1901) 484.

[68] Cf. D. Zeller, in *Logia* (see note 1 above) 398. On Lk 11:37-39a (LkR), cf. Kosch, *Tora* 63-73. Less convincingly, Kosch proposes a pre-Lukan transition in 12:1a (83: ἤρξατο λέγειν τοῖς μαθηταῖς αὐτοῦ).

[69] Cf. "The Study of Q" 36-37, 53 (= *Evangelica II* 416-417, 433): P. Hoffmann, R. Laufen, D. Lührmann, R. Morgenthaler, A. Polag, W. Schenk, W. Schmithals, P. Vassiliadis.

[70] "In der Mehrzahl der modernen Q-Arbeiten (wird) mit einer Q-Parallele nicht gerechnet" (Kiilunen [see note 74 below] 17 note 5, and a similar observation by Ennulat [see note 73 below] 269, both in 1989). Cf. Kloppenborg, *Formation* (1987); *Q Parallels* (1988); Neirynck, *Q-Synopsis* (1988). The possibility of a Q version is mentioned by D. Zeller (1984, 70) and by M. Sato: "möglich, aber unsicher" (22) and finally not taken into consideration because of uncertain location in Q (39).

[71] Cf. *The Minor Agreements* § 77.

this solution now recognize that it is not wholly satisfactory,[72] and other scholars prefer for instance the suggestion of a Deutero-Markan recension.[73] But do we really need a source-critical solution other than the priority of Mark? Is the true alternative to Mk+Q not Matthew's and Luke's independent redaction of Mk 12:28-34?[74]

I will concentrate here on Lk 10:25-28 because, as so often with the minor agreements, the problems are mainly on the side of Luke.[75] Mk 12:28-34 is omitted by Luke but the remains of the episode are still there: Lk 20:39 ἀποκριθέντες δέ τινες τῶν γραμματέων (cf. v. 28 εἰς τῶν γραμματέων) εἶπαν· διδάσκαλε, καλῶς εἶπας (cf. v. 32a). 40 οὐκέτι γὰρ... (v. 34b καὶ οὐδεὶς οὐκέτι...). We cannot simply say that Mk 12:32-34 is "a later addition to Mark's text" and that this "appendix" is missing in Luke.[76] Lk 20:39-40 at least shows some traces of it. Moreover, it is not completely absent in Lk 10:25-28. The structure of Lk 10:25-28 is more complex than the question-and-answer in Mt 22:34-36, 37-40, par. Mk 12:28, 29-31:

---

[72] K. Kertelge, *Das Doppelgebot der Liebe im Markusevangelium* in *À cause de l'Évangile. Festschrift J. Dupont* (Lectio Divina 123; Paris: 1985) 303-322, especially 307-312: "Trotz der bestehenden Schwierigkeiten.... Mit den immer noch offenen Teilfragen..." (309). Cf. Marshall, *Luke* 441: "although Matthew might then have shown more influence from it [Q]"; Sato 39: "Falls [Lk 10:25-28] wirklich zu Q gehörte, wäre ihre Stellung dort ganz unklar" (see also Ennulat 271). Defenders of the Q version are listed, e.g., by Kertelge (310 note 17), Kiilunen (17 note 5), Ennulat (269 note 2), Friedrichsen (in *Luc-Luke* [see note 20 above] 389).

[73] A. Ennulat, *Die 'Minor Agreements'* (Diss.; Bern: 1989) 269-278 (brief discussion of all agreements against Mark 12:28-34). See also D. Kosch, *Tora* 94 note 142.

[74] See esp. J. Kiilunen, *Das Doppelgebot der Liebe in synoptischer Sicht* (AASF B.250; Helsinki: 1989) *passim* (with references to J.-G. Mudiso Mbâ Mundla [1984], J. Gnilka [1988], W. Weiss [1989], *et al.*); review in *ETL* 67 (1991) 432-433.

[75] "There is not the least difficulty in expounding Mt. 22.34-40 as a redaction of Mark" (M. D. Goulder, *Luke* 486, with reference to Gundry's commentary). This is apparently also the opinion of Fitzmyer who ascribes the Lukan form of the story to 'L' (*Luke* 877). For both Goulder and Gundry (*Matthew*, 1982) the agreements in Luke can be ascribed to Matthean influence. See now also R. H. Gundry, "Matthean Foreign Bodies in Agreements of Luke with Matthew against Mark: Evidence that Luke Used Matthew" in *The Four Gospels 1992* (see note 26 above) 1468-1495, especially 1480-1482.

[76] H. Koester, *Ancient Christian Gospels* (Minneapolis: 1990) 277; 343 note 3.

question	Lk 10:25	Mk 12:28	scribe (question)
counter-question	26	29-31	Jesus (answer)
answer	27	32-33	scribe
reply	28	34	Jesus

In contrast to the answer given by Jesus in Mk 12:29-31 (par. Mt), the answer is spoken by the scribe/lawyer himself in Mk 12:32-33 and Lk 10:27 and he receives approval by Jesus: he saw that he answered wisely, νουνεχῶς ἀπεκρίθη (Mk 12:34a), ὀρθῶς ἀπεκρίθης (Lk 10:28). The distinction between the first and second commandment—πρώτη ἐστίν and δευτέρα αὕτη (Mk 12:29, 31, cf. Mt)—is lacking in Lk 10:27 (ἀγαπήσεις...καὶ...), and this formulation is closer to that of Mk 12:32-33 (τὸ ἀγαπᾶν...καὶ τὸ ἀγαπᾶν..., in contrast with "sacrifices").

The three main positive agreements are found at the beginning: νομικός, ἐκπειράζων, διδάσκαλε (Lk 10:25).[77] Νομικός is a customary Lukan term,[78] and the opening phrase is undeniably Lukan style: καὶ ἰδοὺ νομικός τις ἀνέστη (for καὶ προσελθὼν εἷς τῶν γραμματέων in Mk 12:28a). The lawyer's question is taken from Mk 10:17, par. Lk 18:18: λέγων· διδάσκαλε (om. ἀγαθέ), τί ποιήσας ζωὴν αἰώνιον κληρονομήσω;[79] the agreement with Mt 22:36 can be no reason for excising διδάσκαλε from this parallel.[80] Ἐκπειράζων (Mt πειράζων) is a more significant agreement: by this addition the school debate turned into a controversy dialogue (Bultmann). In Gundry's opinion, Luke lacks Matthew's reasons for making this change: "Hence, influence from Matthew

---

[77] Mt 22:35: ...[νομικὸς] πειράζων αὐτόν· 36 διδάσκαλε, "eine dreifache Übereinstimmung...derart massiv" (Ennulat 273, 275).

[78] Cf. "Luke 14:1-6. Lukan Composition and Q Saying" in *Der Treue Gottes trauen. Beiträge zum Werk des Lukas. Festschrift G. Schneider*, eds. C. Bussmann and W. Radl (Freiburg: 1991) 243-263, especially 249-251 (=*Evangelica II* 190-193). Schürmann's retraction (*ibid.* note 51) is more explicit in *SNTU* 11 (1986) 59 note 77. On the other hand, "Luke's predilection for νομικός" is now discarded by Gundry (1992). However, his word statistics (1480 note 27) need correction by distinguishing between plural and singular in Luke's use of γραμματεύς (cf. *Evangelica II* 191).

[79] Ctr. Marshall (*Luke* 442) who suggests influence of the pre-Lukan source (10:25 Q) upon 18:18!

[80] Moreover, διδάσκαλε, lacking in the scribe's question in Mk 12:28, appears in his comment in v. 32a (cf. Lk 20:39). Occurrences of διδάσκαλε in Lk (besides 10:25): 9:38; 18:18; 20:21, 28, 39; 21:7 (cf. Mk 13:1): all par. Mk; 3:12; 7:40; 11:45(!); 12:13; 19:39. In Lk 11:45 (redactional transition) there is a new intervention of τις τῶν νομικῶν, again with διδάσκαλε.

seems likely."⁸¹ But is ἐκπειράζων (for ἐπηρώτησεν in Mk)
really a "foreign body" in Luke? Lk 10:25-28 should be read in
connection with the "example" in 10:29-37.⁸² The introduction
of the lawyer's new question in v. 29, ὁ δὲ θέλων δικαιῶσαι
ἑαυτόν (cf. 16:15; 18:9, 14), seems to confirm the hostile intent of
the "testing" question in v. 25. Jesus replies with a counter-
question in v. 26, as he did in Mk 10:3 (cf. v. 2 πειράζοντες
αὐτόν) and Mk 12:15 (τί με πειράζετε).⁸³

Lk 10:26 contains a fourth⁸⁴ minor agreement: ἐν τῷ νόμῳ, in a
slightly different context in Mt 22:36, the lawyer's question:
μεγάλη ἐν τῷ νόμῳ (diff. Mk: πρώτη πάντων). Jesus' counter-
question is formulated as a double question: ἐν τῷ νόμῳ τί γέγραπται; πῶς ἀναγινώσκεις;⁸⁵ The motif of this reply can be
compared with Mk 10:17 followed by τὰς ἐντολὰς οἶδας in v. 19
(Lk 18:18, 20).⁸⁶ For ἐν τῷ νόμῳ + γέγραπται, cf. Lk 2:23 καθὼς
γέγραπται ἐν νόμῳ κυρίου and 24:44 πάντα τὰ γεγραμμένα ἐν
νόμῳ Μωϋσέως...,. Other minor agreements in Lk 10:25-28 are
'minor' (Ennulat's "neutrale Grauzone") and less decisive in a
debate on Q.⁸⁷

---

⁸¹ *Matthew* 448. See now also his "Matthean Foreign Bodies" (see note 75
above) 1481. Here, too, no consideration is given to the context in Luke, including 10:29-37.

⁸² The (Lukan) framing of the parable repeats the same structure (question—
counter-question—answer—final reply): 10:29, (30-)36, 37a, 37b. On the
priest and the levite (*Kultpersonen*) in the parable (10:31-32) and a possible
link with Mk 12:33b, cf. Kiilunen, *Doppelgebot* 76-77; see also M.-É. Boismard, *Synopse II* 350.

⁸³ Cf. Lk 20:20 ὑποκρινομένους ἑαυτοὺς δικαίους εἶναι. See also πειράζοντες in Mk 8:11 and Lk 11:16. The use of the compound verb in Lk 10:25
does not necessarily imply the motif of "testing the Lord" (Dt 6:16 in Q 4:12).

⁸⁴ In Ennulat's classification this is the last of the minor agreements of category I (highest probability for Dmk). He also mentions the omission of
Mk 12:29b (Shema') as category II (276). Cf. Fitzmyer, *Luke* 877-878: "The
use of 'lawyer' instead of 'one of the Scribes' and the omission of the first part
of the Shema' (Deut 6:4; cf. Mark 12:29b) could easily be explained by Luke's
redactional concern for the predominantly Gentile audience for whom he was
writing."

⁸⁵ Luke retained a few of Mk's double questions: Lk 4:34; 5:21; 5:22-23;
13:18 (single question in Q?); 20:2; 21:7, and wrote a double question in 7:31
(single question in Q?) and 13:15-16. Cf. *Evangelica II* 432 (and 495 note 4).
See now also T. A. Friedrichsen's study of the double question in Lk 13:18
(see note 26 above), 662-675.

⁸⁶ Kiilunen 59.

⁸⁷ See Kiilunen's study. Cf. K. Salo, *Luke's Treatment of the Law* (AASF 57;
Helsinki: 1991) 104-111: "In my previous work I favoured the theory of the Q-

II. The Beginning of Q

There is a broad consensus about the beginning of Q, at least in its final form,[88] with Jesus' inaugural sermon preceded by John's preaching and the temptations of Jesus. In each of the three sections, however, the existence of a prepositive unit has been suggested, and the argument of the minor agreements against Mark has been advanced in each case:

[3:2b-4]   3:7-9,16-17

[3:21-22]   4:1-13

[6:12a,17a,20a]   6:20b-49

Regarding "The Setting of the Sermon in Q", I can refer to a recent critical note: "All we can possibly retain...is the assumption that the Q introduction had the disciples as the audience of the Sermon."[89]

5. Luke 3:21-22 (Mk 1:9-11; Mt 3:13-17)

Mt 3:16 ἠνεῴχθησαν οἱ οὐρανοί: "That Luke has ἀνεῳχθῆναι τὸν οὐρανόν can scarcely be taken as the firm sign of a common source"; ἐπ᾽ αὐτόν: "The coincidental use by both Matthew and Luke of ἐπί is probably just that, coincidental: both have independently corrected Mark" (Davies and Allison). But their first

---

source being behind this pericope, but after being introduced to Kiilunen's work I had to change my mind" (107 note 18).

[88] In Kloppenborg's analysis, 3:7-9, 16-17 (Q^2); 4:1-13 (Q^3); 6:20-49 (Q^1). Cf. J. M. Robinson, in *Q Thomas Reader* (see note 24 above) viii: "The opening line in the original form of Q was probably the first beatitude, which initiates Jesus' inaugural sermon in Q". On the temptations as an integral part of Q, see C. M. Tuckett, "The Temptation Narrative in Q" in *The Four Gospels 1992* (see note 26 above) 479-507.

[89] Cf. my "Matthew 4:23–5:2 and the Matthean Composition of 4:23–11:1" in *The Interrelations* (see note 27 above) 23-46, especially 36-38 (38), with reference to R. A. Guelich (1982); T. L. Donaldson (1985); K. Syreeni (1987). On Matthean redaction in Mt 4:23–5:2, see *ibid.* 26-36; on Lukan redaction in Lk 6:12-19, see *Evangelica* (1982) 761-764 (= *ETL* 49 [1973] 808-811). See now also Kosch, *Tora* 223-226, on Lk 6:13-16. The correspondence between Lk 6:20a and Mt 5:1-2, μαθητ(αἱ)...αὐτοῦ...λέγ(ειν) is noted by Sato (24), Kosch (229), *et al.* (cf. *Q-Synopsis*). For Kosch, the mention of the mountain is "gut denkbar" (228; 229: "vielleicht"); but both Lk 6:12 and Mt 5:1 depend on Mk 3:13. "Aufgrund von Mt 4,25...ist zu vermuten, dass in Q von ὄχλος (πολύς) die Rede war" (229); but Mt 4:25 is "gut mt" and Lk 6:17 ὄχλος πολὺς μαθητῶν αὐτοῦ "LkRed" (*ibid.*)!

sentence receives a continuation: "Nevertheless, because Q contained an account of the Baptist preaching shortly followed by a temptation narrative which presupposes Jesus' divine sonship, it is likely that...there was a notice of the baptism."[90] The real argument is clearly not that of the agreements against Mark but the fact that the temptations in Q presuppose the Son of God title (Mk 1:11 parr.)[91] One can reply, with Kloppenborg, that this title "does not require an explanatory narrative any more than does the title 'Son of Man,' which is by far the more common title for Q."[92] C. M. Tuckett has proposed a more pertinent suggestion: the Greek in Q 4:3, 9 lacks an article with υἱός and, within the context of Q, εἰ υἱὸς εἶ τοῦ θεοῦ can possibly be interpreted in a non-Christological way.[93] The connection with πνεῦμα (Mk 1:10 parr.)[94] is a much weaker argument. The Mt/Lk agreement in the narrative introductions, Mt 4:1 (ἀνήχθη εἰς τὴν ἔρημον ὑπὸ τοῦ πνεύματος) and Lk 4:1 (ἤγετο ἐν πνεύματι ἐν τῇ ἐρήμῳ), can be the result of independent redaction (cf. Mk 1:12 τὸ πνεῦμα αὐτὸν ἐκβάλλει εἰς τὴν ἔρημον)[95] and is too easily accepted in reconstructions of Q.[96] Together with Jesus' "fasting" and hunger the location in the wilderness can be an appropriate setting for the first temptation in Q, but the link with the account of Jesus' baptism and the motif that "he was led by the Spirit" may derive from Mk 1:12.[97]

A full description of the Mt/Lk agreements against Mk 1:9-11 includes besides the verb ἀνοίγω (for σχίζω) and the preposition ἐπί (for εἰς), already mentioned, the participial construction

[90] *Matthew* I. 329, 334.

[91] See, e.g., Luz, *Matthäus* I. 160; Sato, *Q und Prophetie* 25: "Hier wird über die vorher proklamierte Gottessohnschaft neu reflektiert."

[92] *Formation* 85. Cf. A. Vögtle, "Herkunft und ursprünglicher Sinn der Taufperikope Mk 1,9-11" (1972) in Id., *Offenbarungsgeschichte und Wirkungsgeschichte* (Freiburg: 1985) 70-108, especially 72-75: "Zur Erklärung der Anknüpfung des Versuchers an den Gottessohntitel verbleiben auch andere Möglichkeiten" (74, with reference to P. Hoffmann, 1969).

[93] "The Temptation Narrative in Q" (see note 88 above) 495-496 (cf. 483, 492).

[94] Luz, *Matthäus* I. 151 note 2. Cf. Sato, *Q und Prophetie* 25 ("nicht völlig sicher").

[95] Cf. *Evangelica II* 321-322: post-Markan redaction (not Deutero-Markan, ctr. A. Fuchs, *SNTU* 9 [1984] 101-106).

[96] Cf. Schulz, Polag, *et al.* Cf. Schenk (1981), but see now *Die Sprache des Matthäus* (1987): εἰς, ἔρημος, πνεῦμα = Mk (229, 248, 413); ὑπό "dupl. von V. 1b (= Mk)" (450); ἀνάγω derived from QLk 4:5 (12: "permutiert").

[97] Cf. Vögtle, "*Herkunft*" 74: "innerhalb der Q-Versuchungsperikope (wird) nicht auf den Geistbesitz Jesu abgehoben."

βαπτισθείς / βαπτισθέντος (for ἐβαπτίσθη), τοῦ θεοῦ / τὸ ἅγιον (added to τὸ πνεῦμα), and an agreement in word order (against ὡς περιστερὰν καταβαῖνον).[98] There is no need to repeat here the demonstration that these agreements are easily explained as redactional changes of Mark.[99]

6. Luke 3:2b-4 (Mk 1:2-6 / Mt 3:1-6)

The problem of the minor agreements already arises in the very first Synoptic pericope. The presence of Q material overlapping with Mk 1:2-6 has been suggested because of (a) the omission of the quotation from Mal 3:1; (b) the inverted order, the introduction of John before the quotation; (c) the verbal agreement between Mt 3:5 and Lk 3:3, πᾶσα ἡ περίχωρος τοῦ ᾿Ιορδάνου / (εἰς) πᾶσαν τὴν περίχωρον τοῦ ᾿Ιορδάνου.[100] It is less difficult to accept that "both Matthew and Luke realized independently that the quotation of the OT as given in Mark was not adequately covered by the introductory formula."[101] By placing the presence of John before the quotation, Matthew adopts the scheme of his fulfilment quotations; Luke rearranges the order in view of his extended quotation of Isaiah at the conclusion of the section.[102] The striking verbal similarity in the third agreement is more fascinating, or at least, as recently shown by Kloppenborg, it can give rise to fascinating theory.[103]

Kloppenborg's essay is written in response to a reconstruction of "The Beginning of Q" by H. Fleddermann: Q 3:7b-9, 16b-17,

---

[98] Cf. *The Minor Agreements* § 3. On ᾿Ιησοῦς / ᾿Ιησοῦ, cf. Easton, *Luke* (see note 17 above) 43.

[99] Kloppenborg, *Formation* 85 note 157; Fitzmyer, *Luke* 480 (ἀνοίγω). Cf. M. Devisch (see note 104 below) (1975) 444-451 (in response to Schürmann and Polag).

[100] Sato, *Q und Prophetie* 21. Cf. Luz, *Matthäus* I. 143 note 1 (Mt 3:5 / Lk 3:3): "Ob das Jesajazitat aus Q stammt, muss offenbleiben."

[101] Fitzmyer, *Luke* 461. "Of course, the later use of this quotation in 11:10 and Luke's agreement with Matthew in the present omission and later use (Luke 7:27) suggest that these evangelists are following a source different from Mark (see also vv 7-10)" (R. H. Gundry, *Matthew* 44). On the overlap Mk 1:2b and Q 7:27, cf C. M. Tuckett, "Mark and Q" (see note 26 above): Q 7:27 is not redactional in Q and provides no evidence for concluding that Mark was dependent on Q (in reply to D. R. Catchpole; cf. note 121 below).

[102] On Mt 1:2-6 and par., cf. *ETL* 44 (1968) 141-153; = *Jean et les Synoptiques* (BETL 49; Leuven: 1979) 299-311, especially 306-309.

[103] J. S. Kloppenborg, "City and Wasteland: Narrative World and the Beginning of the Sayings Gospel (Q)," *Semeia* 52 (1991) 145-160.

with a short phrase εἶπεν Ἰωάννης to introduce these sayings of John:[104]

> Fleddermann is undoubtedly correct in concluding that "Pharisees and Sadducees" is Matthean and that ὄχλοι ("crowds") is Lukan, and that Luke's wording of 3:7a has been influenced by Mark 1:5. Nevertheless, John's question "Who warned you to flee?" presupposes precisely what Luke 3:7a envisages: a group of persons coming out to John (cf. Q 7:24). Moreover, John's own clarification of the nature of his baptism in contradistinction to that of the Coming One is intelligible if the audience has come either to participate in or perhaps simply to be spectators at John's baptism.[105]

Kloppenborg's personal suggestion concerns more specifically the presence of the phrase πᾶσα ἡ περίχωρος τοῦ Ἰορδάνου in this introduction:

> ...the opening lines of the Sayings Gospel framed John's speech as an address to persons...seeking out John *in the circuit of the Jordan*....The phrase itself is firmly anchored in the Lot narrative.... Q 3:(3a), 7-9 raises the specter of Sodom's destruction and seals off the most convenient avenue of escape, offering moral reform as the only route.[106]

The acceptance of πᾶσα ἡ περίχωρος τοῦ Ἰορδάνου in the Introduction of Q is a new step in Kloppenborg's Q studies.[107] His basic observation is that "the technical term for the southern Jordan basin" is used "quite awkwardly" by both Matthew and Luke. Is it then no longer "unwise to include it in Q"?[108]

In Mt 3:5 it is part of a threefold subject in parallel to Mk 1:5,

---

[104] H. Fleddermann, "The Beginning of Q," *SBLSP (1985)* 153-159. Fleddermann relies on the work of a student of mine: "Michel Devisch has shown that the linguistic evidence does not support a Q text behind Luke 3:3-6... I will follow Devisch's reconstruction of Q 3:7-9" (153). Cf. M. Devisch, *De geschiedenis van de Quelle-hypothese* (Diss.; Leuven: 1975) 402-421 (Lk 3:3-6), 491-509 (Lk 3:7a), 509-515 (Lk 3:7b-9). For Fleddermann's reconstruction of Q 3:16b-17, cf. "John and the Coming One (Matt 3:11-12 // Lk 3:16-17)," *SBLSP (1984)* 377-384.

[105] "City and Wasteland" 149.

[106] *Ibid.* 151 (italics mine).

[107] Conjectural reconstruction in *Q Thomas Reader* (1990) 35: <John came into *all the region about the Jordan...*>.

[108] *Q Parallels* 6; on Q 3:2-4: "The agreements of Matthew and Luke against Mark are slight and can be explained without recourse to a Q *Vorlage*." Cf. *Formation* 74.

(a) Ἱεροσόλυμα   (b) καὶ οἱ Ἱεροσολυμῖται πάντες

(b) καὶ πᾶσα ἡ Ἰουδαία   (a) πᾶσα ἡ Ἰουδαία

(c) καὶ πᾶσα ἡ περίχωρος τ. Ἰ.   χώρα

The phrase looks like a duplication of Mk's Ἰουδαία χώρα, used by metonymy for the inhabitants who went out to John.[109] The term περίχωρος occurs once in Mk, εἰς ὅλην τὴν περίχωρον τῆς Γαλιλαίας (1:28), with a secondary parallel in Mt 4:24, εἰς ὅλην τὴν Συρίαν, i.e., the region around Galilee.[110] There is one other occurrence in Mt: οἱ ἄνδρες τοῦ τόπου ἐκείνου ἀπέστειλαν εἰς ὅλην τὴν περίχωρον ἐκείνην, i.e., the surrounding region (14:35, diff. Mk 6:55 περιέδραμον ὅλην τὴν χώραν ἐκείνην).[111] Is it so awkward that in 3:5, "Then went out to him (Jerusalem and all Judaea), and were baptized in the Jordan", Matthew added "and all the region about the Jordan"?[112] "His intent is probably to anticipate the description of the locales from which Jesus' followers come in Matt 4:25."[113]
Kloppenborg correctly indicates how Luke "distinguishes between the ἔρημος where John's call occurs and the circuit of the Jordan where he preaches","suggesting that John is an itinerant in the 'region of the Jordan', a notion which is otherwise unattested, but which parallels the itinerancy of Jesus which Luke elsewhere stresses."[114] It is less clear for me how then he can conjecture that Lk 3:3a καὶ ἦλθεν εἰς πᾶσαν τὴν περίχωρον τοῦ Ἰορδάνου derives from Q. The phrase itself may be known to Luke

---

[109] On Jerusalem, for Jerusalemites, cf. Mt 2:3 (and 21:10).

[110] On περίχωρος in Mt 3:5, "suggested perhaps by Mark 1:28", cf. Gundry, *Matthew* 45; in Mt 14:35, "eine nicht gebrauchte Wendung aus Mk 1:28", cf. Luz, *Matthäus* II. 413.

[111] There is a notable difference in Mt: the people of that place "sent" to all the region around and (from there) they come to Jesus (*stabilitas loci* in contrast to Jesus' itinerancy in Mk).

[112] Cf. Schenk, *Die Sprache* (see note 96 above), art. Ἰορδάνης: "3,6 (= Mk)...und von daher 3,5 (+Mk) dupliziert zum 'Umkreis des Ἰ.'" (85). There is no need to conclude with G. Theissen that "sich der Täufer nicht direkt am Jordan befinden (kann)"; cf. *Lokalkolorit und Zeitgeschichte in den Evangelien* (NTOA 8; Göttingen: 1989) 41-42 (= *The Gospels in Context* [Edinburgh: 1992] 40). See above note 111.

[113] "City and Wasteland" 150. Cf. my "Matthew 4:23–5:2" (see note 89 above) 32-33: Mt 4:25, cf. Mk 3:8: Judaea/Jerusalem (inverted in Mt) and πέραν τ. Ἰ.

[114] "City and Wasteland" 150, with references to Lk. Contrast F. Bovon, *Lukas* 170: "das Bild eines Wanderpredigers (aus Q; vgl. Mt 3,1)" (*sic*).

from the LXX (Gen 13:10, 11 πᾶσα ἡ περίχωρος τοῦ Ἰορδάνου; 19:17 πᾶσα ἡ περίχωρος). It is less evident, however, that it directly alludes to the story of Lot.[115] R. C. Tannehill's reserve with respect to Q applies to its use by Luke as well:[116]

> Although Kloppenborg's description of city and wasteland in Q may be valid, his interpretation of the beginning of Q depends on his assertion that it reflects the Lot and Sodom story in Gen 19. I doubt that there is sufficient evidence to support this connection.... But is this phrase sufficiently distinctive to remind one of the Lot story? "The region of the Jordan" also occurs in 2 Ch 4:17 in a context that has nothing to do with Lot, and περίχωρος is frequently followed by the name of a geographical area or of the people occupying that area in the LXX and NT.[117]

Kloppenborg can cite a further allusion to the story of Sodom in Q 10:12, which provides a conclusion to 10:2-11 and a transition to 10:13-15, the woes against the Galilean towns.[118] Q 10:13-15 also shows how sayings without framing introduction are included in Q and such an introduction is secondarily added in Mt 11:20. The motifs of 10:13-15, reproach of impenitence and announcement of judgment, are those of the preaching of John in the first Q segment, Q 3:7-9, 16-17. Here the reconstruction of the Q introduction is mere conjecture. One can guess that the name of the speaker was indicated: John said (or used to say). It appears in the saying that the addressees are children of Abraham and that he baptizes (them) with water. In the light of Mk 1:5 both Matthew and Luke can project this data into a narrative introduction of their own. Their agreement in Lk 3:7a and Mt 3:7a is only partial: "crowds" or "Pharisees and Sadducees," coming "to be baptized by him" or "to the baptism" (for critical observation), and "it may be that neither Matthew nor

[115] Ctr. F. Bovon, *Lukas* 170 ("Denkt Lukas an Lot und Abraham...?"); 365-366 (Lk 7:17). Bovon's interpretation of τῆς περιχώρου τῶν Γερασηνῶν in Lk 8:37 is quite correct: "die Gegend der Gergesener selbst; περι- weist auf die Umgebung hin, nicht auf Nachbargegenden" (438); cf. 8, 26 τὴν χώραν τῶν Γερασηνῶν. Compare (par. Mk 1:28 πανταχοῦ εἰς ὅλην τὴν περίχωρον τῆς Γαλιλαίας) Lk 4:37 εἰς πάντα τόπον τῆς περιχώρου (cf. v. 31 τῆς Γαλιλαίας); 4:14b καθ᾽ ὅλης τῆς περιχώρου (14a Galilee); 7:17 (ἐν ὅλη τῇ Ἰουδαίᾳ περὶ αὐτοῦ καὶ πάση τῇ περιχώρῳ: synonymous?); Acts 14:6.
[116] "Beginning to Study 'How Gospels Begin'," *Semeia* 52 (1991) 185-192, especially 190.
[117] His references are: Dt 3:4, 13, 14; 34:3; 1 Chr 5:16; 2 Chr 16:4; 2 Esdras 13:9, 12, 14, 16, 17, 18; Mk 1:28; Lk 8:37.
[118] "City and Wasteland" 151. Cf. *Formation* 146, 243.

Luke has the Q introduction."[119] In this case I prefer to follow the old B. Weiss: "Es muss in ihr [Q] noch jede Angabe darüber gefehlt haben, an wen die Rede gerichtet war."[120]

Conclusion

Since the completion of this paper (December 1991) the problem of the beginning of Q has received extensive treatment in two essays published in *NTS* 1992 by D. R. Catchpole and J. Lambrecht.[121] Both propose, on the basis of the Mt / Lk minor agreements against Mk 1:2-6, the reconstruction of a Q text preceding the introduction of John's preaching (Q 3:7a). For Catchpole[122] πᾶσα ἡ περίχωρος τοῦ Ἰορδάνου appears in an awkward combination in Mt 3:5 and "there must be a preference for the Lucan setting of the phrase": [Ἰωάννης ὁ βαπτίζων] ἦλθεν εἰς πᾶσαν τὴν περίχωρον τοῦ Ἰορδάνου κηρύσσων βάπτισμα μετανοίας εἰς ἄφεσιν ἁμαρτιῶν (= Lk 3:3), καθὼς γέγραπται ἐν τῷ Ἡσαΐᾳ τῷ προφήτῃ· φωνὴ...αὐτοῦ (= Mk 1:2a, 3). The possibility of Lukan editorial intervention in Lk 3:2 *and* 3a is not even taken into consideration. On the other hand, the Matthean version in Mt 3:5 is declared to be an awkward combination without making any effort at understanding this "combination" in its relation to Mk 1:5. If the awkwardness is seen in the use of the verb ἐξεπορεύετο (= Mk),[123] is it then less awkward that Luke replaces ἐρχομένοις (Catchpole's reconstruction of Q 3:7a) by Mark's ἐκπορευομένοις, said of "the crowds" without the

---

[119] Davies and Allison, *Matthew* I. 303 note 36. Cf. J. Ernst, *Johannes der Täufer* (BZNW 53; Berlin and New York: 1989) (41-)42: "Der ursprüngliche Wortlaut wird sich kaum noch rekonstruieren lassen."

[120] *Markus und Lukas* (see note 17 above) (⁹1901) 324; cf. ⁶1878: 316.

[121] D. R. Catchpole, "The Beginning of Q: A Proposal," *NTS* 38 (1992) 205-221; J. Lambrecht, "John the Baptist and Jesus in Mark 1.1-15: Markan Redaction of Q," *NTS* 38 (1992) 357-384.

[122] See especially 217-218. It is quite correct that Matthew and Luke agree in introducing John before the quotation (218), but it is rather amazing that obvious redactional explanations are not even mentioned. The form of the quotation "which makes ἐν τῇ ἐρήμῳ define the location of the herald and not that of the way of the Lord" (*ibid.*) is not an agreement against Mark.

[123] "It hardly makes sense to say that the surrounding area of Jordan went *out* to the Jordan" (217). But Matthew reads: ἐξεπορεύετο πρὸς αὐτόν (to him, and not: to the Jordan). And is it not a dubious criterion that awkwardness indicates secondary redaction and smoothness is the property of original tradition (cf. 214)?

connotation of Mark's Judaea and Jerusalem? Lambrecht's reconstruction is slightly different:[124]

John came in the wilderness
preaching a baptism of repentance
as it is written...
All the region about the Jordan went out to him,
and they were baptized by him in the river Jordan.

By retaining the coming of John ἐν τῇ ἐρήμῳ and, after the quotation, a parallel to Mk 1:5 (the Matthean setting of the phrase "all the region about the Jordan"), the hypothetical Q text is made more similar to Mark, and Mark's redaction of Q more easily arguable. But the existence of minor agreements is the starting point of this reconstruction. Matthean and Lukan redaction can explain each of them taken separately, but: "Will such an explanation do for the four taken together? Hardly."[125] Without real discussion of these explanations, the argument is once more the (high) number of minor agreements. I may repeat my comment: "In fact, it is hardly conceivable that the total number of *explained* agreements could become *unexplainable*."[126]

Q 3:2-4; 3:21-22; (6:12-16); 10:25-28; 12:1b; 17:2; 17:31 are proposed in some recent studies as candidates for inclusion in the double-tradition source Q. In none of them, however, the Matthew-Luke agreements against Mark seem to provide conclusive evidence.[127]

---

[124] See especially 363-364. That both continue John's coming immediately with John's preaching (363) is hardly an argument against Mark.

[125] *Ibid.* 363. On one of the "four" agreements, cf. note 124 above. Lambrecht presents his own approach as "careful guessing" (364). Compare also his enumeration of the five agreements against Mk 1:9-11: without analysis of the individual instances, or confrontation with the pertinent studies, the minor agreements are supposed to be "highly unlikely...fortuitous coincidence" (367).

[126] Cf. *Evangelica II* 40.

[127] Additional note on Lk 10:25-28: see now my "Luke 10:25-28: A Foreign Body in Luke?" in *Crossing the Boundaries. Essays in Biblical Interpretation in Honour of M. D. Goulder* (Leiden: 1994) 149-165 (cf. note 75 above). See also H. Schürmann's retraction in *Das Lukasevangelium* II/1 (Freiburg: 1994) 138-139; cf. my review in *ETL* 70 (1994), especially 172.

CHAPTER FOUR

THE GREAT COMMANDMENT PERICOPE AND Q

Jan Lambrecht, S.J.

A number of minor agreements are present in Mt 22:34-40 and Lk 10:25-28. This might suggest the existence of a Q-variant of the Markan great commandment pericope. Yet nothing of such a possibility is mentioned in the more recent Q synopses of, e.g., A. Polag, J.S. Kloppenborg and F. Neirynck.[1] Is this possibility or hypothesis not worth considering? We think it is, for several reasons. If the existence of a Q pericope becomes probable, not only can more insight be reached regarding Luke's redaction within 10:25-28 and that of Matthew in 22:34-40, but the question must also be asked whether or not Mark himself has known that Q text:[2] in view of a (hypothetical) dependence on Q, does his redaction of 12:28-34 perhaps become more comprehensible?

---

[1] A. Polag, *Fragmenta Q. Textheft zur Logienquelle* (Neukirchen-Vluyn: 1979); J. S. Kloppenborg, *Q Parallels: Synopsis, Critical Notes and Concordance* (Sonoma: 1988); F. Neirynck, *Q-Synopsis. The Double Tradition Passages in Greek* (Leuven, 1988). See also, however, G. Sellin, "Lukas als Gleichniserzähler: Die Erzählung vom barmherzigen Samariter (Lk 10:25-37)," *ZNW* 65 (1974) 166-189; 66 (1975) 19-60, especially 20-23; R. H. Fuller, "Das Doppelgebot der Liebe. Ein Testfall für die Echtheitskriterien der Worte Jesu" in *Jesus Christus in Historie und Theologie. Festschrift H. Conzelmann*, ed. G. Strecker (Tübingen, 1975) 317-329; R. Pesch, *Das Markusevangelium. II* (HThK; Freiburg-Basel-Wien: 1977) 244-248.

[2] Cf. D. Lührmann, *Das Markusevangelium* (HNT; Tübingen: 1987) 205: "Könnte man daraus [= aus den Übereinstimmungen] schliessen, dass Mt und Lk an dieser Stelle nicht nur den Mk-Text, sondern ausserdem eine parallele Überlieferung (vielleicht Q) zur Verfügung hatten, wäre gesichert, dass Mk die Szene als ganze im wesentlichen vorgelegen hat." I have tried to demonstrate Mark's knowledge and use of Q in several pericopes. See "Die Logia-Quellen von Markus 13," *Bib* 47 (1966) 321-360; *Die Redaktion der Markus-Apokalypse. Literarische Analyse und Strukturuntersuchung* (AnBib 28; Rome: 1967); *Marcus interpretator. Stijl en boodschap in Mc. 3:20-4, 34* (Brugge: 1969); "Redaction and Theology in Mk. IV" in *L'Evangile selon Marc. Tradition et rédaction*, ed. Maurits Sabbe (BETL 34: Leuven: 1974, 1988) 269-308; "Jesus and the Law: An Investigation of Mk 7:1-23," *ETL* 53 (1977) 24-82, reprinted in *Jésus aux origines de la christologie*, ed. Jacques Dupont (BETL 40; Leuven, 1989) 358-415

It would seem that in this investigation three steps have to be taken. First, it is necessary to have a clear view of Luke's editorial activity in 10:25-28. Then, the minor agreements between Mt 22:34-40 and Lk 10:25-28 should be brought together and carefully analyzed. If this analysis leads us to the postulate of a Q text and, therefore, to its reconstruction, then, in a last section, the possibility of Mark's knowledge of this Q passage and his use of it in 12:28-34 must be examined.

Lukan Redaction in 10:25-28

In Lk 10:25-37 there are two sections of dialogue (vv. 25-29 and 36-37) separated by a monologue, i.e., the parable about the good Samaritan spoken by Jesus (vv. 30-35).[3]

Lukan Creative Activity

We focus here mainly on verses 28-29. "*Do* this, and you will *live*" in v. 28 constitutes an eye-catching inclusion with v. 25: "what shall I *do* to inherit eternal *life*?"[4] The verb "to do" (ποιέω), moreover, is employed twice in the final verse 37: "the one who *did* mercy" and "go and *do* likewise". Such a frequency is most probably the result of Luke's editorial activity.[5]

V. 29 also appears very Lukan. First of all, there is the striking fact that the idea of the lawyer's "desiring to justify himself" occurs in the gospels only here and in another Lukan text, 16:15, where it is said that the Pharisees justify themselves before others. What is decisive, however, in leading us to view this transitional v.

---

and 428-429; "Q-Influence on Mark 8,34-9,1" in *Logia. Les paroles de Jésus – The Sayings of Jesus*, ed. Joël Delobel (BETL 59; Leuven: 1982) 277-303; "John the Baptist and Jesus in Mark 1.1-15: Markan Redaction of Q?" *NTS* 37 (1992) 357-384.

[3] In what follows in "Lukan Redaction in 10:25-28" and in the first paragraph of "Minor Agreements and Q", I have utilized my *Once More Astonished: The Parables of Jesus* (New York: 1981, ²1983) 57-68.

[4] Cf., e.g., J. Kiilunen, *Das Doppelgebot der Liebe in synoptischer Sicht. Ein redaktionskritischer Versuch über Mk 12:28-34 und die Parallelen* (Annales Academiae Scientiarum Fennicae, B/250; Helsinki: 1989) 68: "Die Inklusion ist vollkommen."

[5] According to M.D. Goulder, *Luke: A New Paradigm* (JSNT Supplement Series 20; Sheffield: 1989) 485, Luke "reformulates the man's question..., replacing the Jewish-theoretical interest with a Lucan, practical one." Cf. also, e.g., Kiilunen, *op. cit.* 57-58.

29 as a purely Lukan creation is the question which it contains: "And who is my neighbor?" This question stands in a certain tension with that of v. 36: "Which of these three became neighbor to the man ...?" Verse 29 is evidently formulated by the same redactor who had just previously written at the end of v. 27, "(Love) your neighbor as yourself", and who, with this commandment in mind, reads the parable about the good Samaritan and wishes to use it as a commentary on that commandment, its clarification. Luke makes the lawyer ask: Who, concretely, is my neighbor? The expected answer is: the wounded traveller. But later, at the end (v. 36), comes the other question, Jesus' question: Which of these three—priest, Levite or Samaritan—became a neighbor? The answer now is: the good Samaritan.

What can be concluded from these remarks? Since verses 28 and 29 appear to be highly redactional transitions from dialogue to parable, since verse 28 constitutes a redactional inclusion with v. 25 and the editorial verse 29 stands in a certain tension with v. 36, and since v. 30 contains the phrase "a certain man" with which many other originally independent parables in Luke begin, it seems best to ascribe the connection between dialogue and parable to Luke himself. The evangelist realized that he could explain and illustrate the commandment of love of neighbor by means of the parable about the good Samaritan. As he wrote, however, he may not have noticed that his parable commentary actually explains only the second commandment and not the first concerning the love of God.

Luke's Dependence on Lk 18:18-20 (= Mk 10:17-19)

It would seem that Luke's use of "to do" and "life" is not purely redactional. In v. 25 he writes, διδάσκαλε, τί ποιήσας ζωὴν αἰώνιον κληρονομήσω;[6] The formulation of this question is verbally almost the same as that of Lk 18:18 in the pericope of the rich man: "(Good) Teacher, what shall I do to inherit eternal life?" (cf. Mk 10:17).[7] In Lk 10:26 Jesus answers: "What is written in the

---

[6] Cf. T. Schramm, *Der Markus-Stoff bei Lukas. Eine literarkritische und redaktionsgeschichtliche Untersuchung* (MSSNTS 14; Cambridge: 1971) 48: "Gut lukanisch wird die theologische-spekulative Frage durch eine solche nach dem praktischen Tun ersetzt". Schramm admits fur Luke "eine Nicht-Mk-Traditionsvariante" (p. 49).

[7] The texts of the questions in Lk 10:25 and 18:18 are strictly identical except for the qualification ἀγαθέ in 18:18 which is absent in 10:25. In Mk 10:17

law?[8] How do you read?[9]" In the pericope about the rich man
Jesus says: "you know the commandments" (Lk 18:20 =
Mk 10:19) and cites the law (Ex 20:13-16 and 12 = Deut 5:17-20
and 16). Twice, thus, in Lk 10 and 18, we have also a reference to
scripture.

One can hardly avoid the impression that in his editing of 10:25-
28 Luke was influenced by the beginning of the pericope of the
rich man[10] which he presents in 18:18-30.

Luke's Use of Mk 12:28-34

"The crucial problem in the [= Luke's] narrative is its relationship to Mk 12:28-34".[11] There are a great many differences
between Lk 10:25-28 and Mk 12:28-34. For a moment, however,
we should focus our attention on Luke's dependence on Mark
since Luke "enthält Elemente aus Mk 12,28ff. und zwar aus
höchstwahrscheinlich *redaktionellen* Wendungen".[12] In regard to
Lk 10:25-28 (and 20:39-40) five items must be mentioned.

(a) It cannot but strike the reader that, between Lk 20:39 and 40
(or 40 and 41), the Markan pericope of the great commandment is
missing. The most probable explanation of this fact is that Luke
wants to avoid a repetition here.[13] He must have realized that

---

"to do" is the main verb: διδάσκαλε ἀγαθέ, τί ποιήσω ἵνα ζωὴν αἰώνιον
κληρονομήσω;

[8] νόμος is absent in Mark's gospel. For the connection of "what is written"
and "law" in Luke, see 2:23 (cf. 2:24: κατὰ τὸ εἰρημένον ἐν νόμῳ κυρίου) and
24:44.

[9] For ἀναγινώσκω see Lk 4:16 and 6:3. In Acts Luke employs the verb quite
frequently: 8:28, 30 and 32 (Isaiah the prophet); 13:27 (the prophets); 15:21
(Moses); 15:31 (a letter from the Jerusalem authorities); 23:34 (a letter of the
tribune). The question πῶς ἀναγινώσκεις is probably Lukan. Otherwise I. H.
Marshall, *The Gospel of Luke* (New Intern. Greek Test. Comm.; Exeter: 1978)
441.

[10] There can scarcely be any doubt that the question which Luke takes over
from Mk 10:17, is more original in the pericope about the rich man (18,18)
than in Lk 10:25.

[11] Marshall, *op. cit.* 440. Cf. Fuller, *art. cit.* 318; and Sellin, *art. cit.* 20:
Lk 10:25-28 "stellt in seinem Verhältnis zu Mk 12:18-34 / Mt 22:34-40 immer noch ein literarkritisches Rätsel dar."

[12] Sellin, *art. cit.* 20.

[13] Although the so-called consistent avoidance of "doublets"
(*Dublettenvermeidung*) by Luke must not be accepted without qualification, it
provides, we think, an adequate reason for the absence of the great commandment pericope in chapter 20. Cf., e.g., J. A. Fitzmyer, *The Gospel According to
Luke (X-XXIV)* (AncB; Garden City, NY: 1985) 877.

10:25-28 is very much the same as that Markan pericope.[14] Therefore he omits it in chapter 20.

(b) Lk 20:40 concludes the Sadducees' question concerning the resurrection: οὐκέτι γὰρ ἐτόλμων ἐπερωτᾶν αὐτὸν οὐδέν. The fact that one does not easily see how the motivation (γάρ) properly functions may point to a somewhat clumsy Lukan editing; two verses are linked which originally do not belong together.[15] It would seem that Luke has taken this verse from Mark's conclusion of the great commandment passage, 12:34c: καὶ οὐδεὶς οὐκέτι ἐτόλμα αὐτὸν ἐπερωτῆσαι. It should be noted that already in 20:39 Luke is influenced by Mark's pericope of the great commandment. Compare not only v. 39b with Mk 12:32b but also τινὲς τῶν γραμματέων in v. 39 with εἷς τῶν γραμματέων in Mk 12:28 and καλῶς in both these verses.[16]

(c) In Lk 10:27, it is the lawyer who answers and quotes the double commandment of love of God and neighbor; in Mk 12:29-31, it is Jesus who does so. In Mark, the two commandments are neatly separated into the first (see πρώτη in Mk 12:28 and 29; vv. 29-30 cite Deut 6:4-5, love of God) and the second (see δευτέρα in Mk 12:31; here Lev 19:18 is quoted, love of neighbor). These two facts—that in Luke's text the two Old Testament quotations are fused into a single sentence and that it is the lawyer and not Jesus who makes the daring equation of the two commandments—strongly suggest that the Lukan text is less original than its Markan parallel.[17] It is not impossible that in "fusing" the two quotations Luke was influenced by Mk 12:33 since in this Markan verse the scribe combines Jesus' twofold answer: it becomes one long sentence.[18] Two small agreements may point to a Lukan

---

[14] Cf. Marshall, *op. cit.* 440: "...it is incontestable that Luke knew Mark's form of the story and regarded his own as an equivalent to it."

[15] Cf. Kiilunen, *op. cit.* 29-32. One more detail strikes the reader, at least at first sight: "In dem V. 40 fällt...das Adverb οὐκέτι auf. Dass die Schriftgelehrten keinen Mut zu weiteren Fragen hätten, ist befremdlich, denn nicht sie, sondern die Sadduzäer haben im vorangehenden Abschnitt 20:27-38 Jesus befragt" (p. 30).

[16] Cf. *ibid.* 31-32: "Beide Verse stammen aus dem sonst ausgelassenen Mk 12:28-34, während die Konjunktion γάρ—in schwerfälliger Weise—versucht, das ausgelassene Textstück zu überbrücken."

[17] Cf. Sellin, *art. cit.* 22-23: "die ursprünglich pointierte Verbindung von Dtn 6:5 und Lev 19:18 wird schon als überliefert und bekannt vorausgesetzt" (p. 22). Goulder, *op. cit.* 485, notes: "this reversal of the position, with Jesus asking the question and the scribe answering, enables Luke to let down the guillotine ['You have answered right', 10:28] as at 7.42ff." (see also p. 490).

[18] Cf. Fuller, *art. cit.* 319.

dependence on Mk 12:29. The prepositional phrase of the first faculty in Lk 10:27 has ἐξ (the others have ἐν) and Luke possesses the same four faculties (not three as in the Septuagint), be it in an order different from that in Mark.

(d) Jesus' reaction in Lk 10:28b, "You have answered right" is reminiscent of Mk 12:34a, "And when Jesus saw that he answered wisely". Luke must have been influenced by this Markan statement. Further, in Lk 10:28, as in Mk 12:34, "Jesus behält das letzte Wort".[19]

(e) The idea of illustrating the quotation in Lk 10:27—above all Lev 19:18: "and your neighbor as yourself"—by the parable about the good Samaritan perhaps came to Luke's mind from reading Mk 12:33b: "And 'to love one's neighbor as oneself',— this is much more important than all whole burnt offerings and sacrifices".[20]

We may conclude this analysis as follows: Lk 10:25-28 has most probably not been written without the influence of Mk 12:28-34, a pericope which Luke omits in his parallel chapter 20.[21] In using the Markan text Luke betrays himself as redactionally secondary.

Minor Agreements and Q

It is clear that the evangelist Luke has not mechanically or blindly reproduced the traditions which he received. In respect to this peri-cope, he was perhaps more active as a redactor than might be ap-parent after a first reading. It would, however, be wrong to con-clude from the literary data just mentioned that Luke merely transposed and rewrote Mk 12:28-34[22] with a view to using it in his

---

[19] Sellin, *art. cit.* 21. Cf. K. Kertelge, "Das Doppelgebot der Liebe im Mark-usevangelium" in *A Cause de l'Evangile. Festschrift J. Dupont* (LeDiv 123; Paris: 1985) 304-322, especially 306. See also Goulder, *op. cit.* 487: "ὀρθῶς ἀπεκρίθης echoes Mk 12:34 νουνεχῶς ἀπεκρίθη".

[20] Cf. Fuller, *art. cit.* 319.

[21] C. Burchard, "Das doppelte Liebesgebot in der frühen christlichen Über-lieferung" in *Der Ruf Jesu und die Antwort der Gemeinde. Festschrift J. Jeremias*, ed. E. Lohse (Göttingen: 1970) 42-43, is (too) minimalist: "Abgesehen von Lk 20:39f. scheint die Markusfassung im dritten Evangelium keine oder nur geringe Spuren hinterlassen zu haben."

[22] Cf., e.g., G. Schneider, *Das Evangelium nach Lukas. Kapitel 1-10* (Ökum. Taschenb.-Komm. N.T.; Gütersloh and Würzburg: 1984) 247: "Für die Annahme, dass Lukas in den VV 25-28 Mk 12:28-34 und keine Sondervorlage benutzt hat..., gibt es wohl die besten Argumente." J. Gnilka, *Das Matthäusevangelium. II* (HThK; Freiburg-Basel-Wien: 1988) 257, writes about Mt 22:34-40: "Die tra-ditionskritische Analyse bereitet besondere Schwierigkeiten". He refers to

gospel as an introduction to the parable about the good Samaritan. A comparison with Mt 22:34-40 seems to indicate that Luke had access to a second source which was more or less similar to the version known to him from Mark's gospel. The reason for postulating this second source is that Matthew and Luke exhibit a number of quite remarkable agreements in this passage against the Markan parallel text which can, it would seem, only be explained in terms of a second common source.

Agreements

The points on which Matthew and Luke agree with one another and at the same time differ from Mark are the following:[23]

(1) Unlike Mk 12:29, their quotation of the first commandment does not begin with "Hear, O Israel: the Lord our God, the Lord is one".

(2) Both Matthew and Luke offer a much shorter version. They have no parallel to Mk 12:32-33. This means that they do not offer a monotheistic comment (cf. Mk 12:32: "there is no other than he") nor a critique on sacrifices (cf. Mk 12:33: "much more than all whole burnt offerings and sacrifices").

(3) Jesus is initially addressed as διδάσκαλε ("teacher"), a title not found at the beginning of the Markan pericope (12:28) but only subsequently in 12:32.

(4) The question in Mt 22:35 and Lk 10:25 is asked by a νομικός ("lawyer"),[24] whereas in Mk 12:28 it is posed by εἷς τῶν γραμματέων ("one of the scribes").

"Gemeinsamkeiten des Mt mit dem Lk Text" and mentions that "vielfach die Auffassung vertreten (wird), dass neben der Mk-Vorlage noch eine zweite Vorlage der Perikope existiert habe, von der Mt und Lk zusätzlich abhängig seien." Yet he states: "Hier soll die Auffassung von der zweiten Vorlage nich übernommen werden." —As is well known, Goulder, *op. cit.* 484-487, believes that Luke is dependent on (both Mark and) Matthew.

[23] For a similar list see Burchard, *art. cit.* 41 n. 4; Fuller, *art. cit.* 318; Pesch, *op. cit.* 244-245; Kertelge, *art. cit.* 308; Kiilunen, *op. cit.* 18-19. We should not forget the old, but not dated, discussion in J. Schmid, *Matthäus und Lukas* (BSt[F] 23,2-4; Freiburg [Breisgau]: 1930) 142-147. After mentioning most of the "minor" agreements, he writes: "Eine solche Häufung von an sich geringfügigen Übereinstimmungen ist jedenfalls beachtenswert" (p. 145).

[24] "Die Ursprünglichkeit des Terminus" in Mt 22:35 "kann textkritisch nicht restlos gesichert werden" (Kiilunen, *op. cit.* 37 n. 9). Cf. B. M. Metzger, *A Textual Commentary on the Greek New Testament* (London-New York: 1975) 59. In Mt 22:35 family 1 and "widely scattered versional and patristic witnesses" omit the term νομικός. Since, in addition, "Matthew nowhere else uses the word" the

(5) By his question the lawyer intends to put Jesus to the test (see Mt 22:35: πειράζων and Lk 10:25: ἐκπειράζων), while Mark's scribe questions Jesus "seeing that he answered them (= the Sadducees) well" (12:28c; cf. Lk 10:28b). The scribe in Mark appears to be well-disposed toward Jesus.

(6) Both Matthew and Luke have the expression ἐν τῷ νόμῳ, be it in a different context. Compare Mt 22:36, "Teacher, which is the great commandment 'in the law'?" with Lk 10:26, "(Jesus) said to him, What is written 'in the law'?"[25] The expression ἐν τῷ νόμῳ is not present in Mark.

(7) In the enumeration of Mt 22:37 and Lk 10:27, both evangelists use the preposition ἐν, while Mark in 12:30, as well as in 33, always writes ἐξ.[26]

(8) Both Matthew and Luke end the series of human faculties on διανοία ("mind"). Mark has ἰσχύς ("strength") as the fourth and last term.

Committee is of the opinion that "it is not unlikely, therefore, that copyists have introduced the word here from the parallel passage in Lk 10.25." Yet there "seems to be an overwhelming preponderance of evidence supporting the word", so that "the Committee was reluctant to omit the word altogether, preferring to enclose it within square brackets." Gnilka, *op. cit.* 258, clearly underestimates the testimony for the presence of νομικός: "trotz relativ guter Bezeugung". R. H Gundry, *Matthew: A Commentary on His Literary and Theological Art* (Grand Rapids: 1982) 448, more correctly speaks of "the relative weakness of the support for omission". W. Schenk, *Die Sprache des Matthäus. Die Text-Konstituenten in ihren makro- und mikrostrukturellen Relationen* (Göttingen: 1987) 65, mentions possible Q-influence. See now the lengthy discussion of νομικός in Matthew and Luke in F. Neirynck, "Luke 14:1-6. Lukan Composition and Q Saying" in *Evangelica II* (BETL 99) 183-204, especially 190-193: νομικός does not belong to the Q vocabulary; all occurrences in Luke are Lukan; in Mt 22:35 the term is either not authentic or due to Matthean editing. Once more, a minor agreement is explained away.

According to Burchard, *art. cit.* 43 n. 14, νομικός is "bei Matthäus...wohl Adjektiv". It is better taken as a noun in the so-called attributive position (Schenk: "eine nachgestellte Apposition"): "one of them, a lawyer".

[25] Cf. Burchard, *art. cit.* 60: "Matthäus hat schon in die Frage des Schriftgelehrten V. 36 ἐν τῷ νόμῳ eingefügt, möglicherweise nach der auch bei Lukas vorliegenden Überlieferung."

[26] Actually, Luke follows Mark in beginning with ἐξ, but immediately after the first faculty, probably under Q influence, switches to ἐν. N[26] and the Synopsis of Huck-Greeven accept in Lk 10:27 four nouns, of which the first is introduced by ἐξ, the other three by ἐν. There are, however, minor variants regarding the nouns, their number (three or four) and their prepositions. Cf. Kiilunen, *op. cit.* 43-45 and 64-67; K.J. Thomas, "Liturgical Citations in the Synoptics," *NTS* 22 (1975-76) 205-214, especially 205-206 and 209-215.

(9) Matthew and Luke agree in that they have, respectively in
22:37a and 10:26a, ὁ δέ (without "Jesus"), a verb of saying and
the indication of the addressee: compare ὁ δὲ ἔφη αὐτῷ (Matthew)
with ὁ δὲ εἶπεν πρὸς αὐτόν (Luke). In Mk 12:29a we read:
ἀπεκρίθη ὁ ᾽Ιησοῦς. This last agreement, thus, is threefold.
(10) Both Matthew and Luke have Jesus' answer in direct speech
without a ὅτι which we find in Mk 12:29a.[27]

A Second Version

The number of agreements in these four verses of Luke is very
impressive indeed. Of course, some of them are very minor (e.g., 6,
7, 8, 9, 10) and, without a common second version, could have
been the result of mutually independent but identical or similar
rewriting of the Markan text. Further, if there were only two or
three items, one would be justified in reckoning with accidental
correspondence. For the isolated agreement, a possibility of independent redaction on Mark can almost always be brought forward,
however stretched and strained the reasoning sometimes appears.
The number of the agreements is, however, too high and several
of them (e.g., 1, 2, 4, 5) are really too striking to be explained by
mere coincidence. It is not very likely that Matthew and Luke
would have, independently of a second source, made all these similar editorial changes to the common Markan text. For these sometimes verbatim agreements they most probably are indebted to a
competing version from Q. One should concede, however, that, to a
certain extent, the judgment in such matters remains the result of a
personal evaluation and prudential assessment. Moreover, the existing texts scarcely allow a rigorous proof.
Quite recently, J. Kiilunen analyzed in great detail all agreements
of the great commandment pericope. He is convinced that the way
in which Matthew and Luke, each according to his own style and
concerns, rewrote the Markan text adequately explains their
versions: "als selbständige Redaktionarbeit des Matthäus und
Lukas an der Mk-Vorlage erklärbar";[28] no second source-text is

---

[27] In Mk 12:29 it could also be direct speech, but with ὅτι this remains uncertain.
[28] Kiilunen (full reference in note 4), quotation on p. 19. Cf. P.J. Farla, *Jesus' oordeel over Israël. Een form- en redaktionsgeschichtliche analyse van Mc
10:46-12:40* (Kampen: 1980) 240-271, especially 241-254; J.-G. Mudiso Mbâ
Mundla, *Jesus und die Führer Israels. Studien zu den sog. Jerusalemer Streitge-
sprächen* (NTA NF, 17; Münster: 1984) 110-233, especially 110-119: "Es dürfte

needed. Yet it must be repeated: even though each of these agreements, taken separately, could be regarded as independent
Matthean and Lukan redactions of the Markan text alone, this type
of solution hardly works for all of them taken together. Could two
independent redactors agree so often? This is hardly believable. It
would seem that here coincidence no longer is acceptable.

There must have been, therefore, in addition to the Markan great
commandment pericope, another text telling a similar story. Both
Matthew and Luke must have known this second version which
most probably belongs to Q. Each in his own way realized that
both accounts dealt with the same incident and, therefore, both
evangelists narrated it only once in their respective gospels. In their
redactions, however, they clearly drew upon both sources, Mark
and Q.[29]

---

also klar geworden sein, dass es sich unter literarkritischen, kompositorischen
und redaktionskritischen Gesichtspunkten plausibel machen lässt, dass Lk und
Mt über keine andere Vorlage als Mk verfügen" (p. 119); F. Neirynck, "Paul and
the Sayings of Jesus" in *L'apôtre Paul. Personnalité, style et conception du min-
istère*, ed. A. Vanhoye (BETL 73; Leuven: 1986) 265-321, reprinted in
Neirynck, *Evangelica II* (BETL 99) 504 n. 150: the author agrees with those
"who explain the version of Mt 22:34-40 and Lk 10:25-28 as relying on the
sole basis of Mark"; Gnilka, *op. cit.* 257-258.

The fact that elsewhere in his gospel Mark has utilized Q heightens the probability of his knowledge of the pericope about the great commandment in Q as
well. In my article "John the Baptist" (see note 2) I mentioned, moreover, the
corroborating or confirmative factor that in Mt 3-4 = Lk 3-4 numerous minor
agreements are present in *a cluster* of pericopes.

[29] We may quote Kertelge, *art. cit.* 310: "Die Übereinstimmungen zwischen
Matthäus und Lukas gegen Markus sind nicht ohne weiteres durch voneinander
unabhängige Redaktionen der beiden Evangelisten zu erklären." After having
considered all data, F. W. Beare, *The Earliest Records of Jesus* (Oxford: 1962)
158-159, concludes: "This would indicate that the Lucan version comes from
'Q'...; and that Matthew has conflated Mark with the 'Q' story." Cf. K. Berger,
*Die Gesetzesauslegung Jesu. Ihr historischer Hintergrund im Judentum und im Al-
ten Testament. I: Markus und Parallelen* (WMANT 40; Neukirchen-Vluyn: 1972)
56-208 (without mentioning Q: "eine fur Mt und Lk gemeinsame Tradition", p.
203).

See also G. Bornkamm, "Das Doppelgebot der Liebe" in *Neutestamentliche
Studien für Rudolf Bultmann*, ed. W. Eltester (BZNW 21; Berlin: [2]1957) 85-93;
also in Bornkamm, *Geschichte und Glaube. I* (BEvTh 48) 37-45: Matthew and
Luke each had before him "eine eigene Variante unseres Mk-Textes" (p. 44);
Schramm, *op. cit.* 47: "Die Unterschiede zu Mk 12:28-34 sind evident und am
besten erklärt, wenn man Lk aus einer Mk-fremden Tradition schöpfen lässt...";
Fitzmyer, *op. cit.* 877-878, who admits another version but ascribes it to "L"
(Luke's special material); Marshall, *op. cit.* 444.

R. Bultmann, *Die Geschichte der synoptischen Tradition* (Göttingen: 1970)
22, postulates a second version for, it would seem, a less appropriate reason:

Reconstruction

The Markan and Q versions almost certainly narrate the same incident.[30] Which of the two is older and, perhaps, more original?
Within the most obvious working hypothesis we postulate that it is
Q.[31] Moreover, as a second hypothesis in this paper, we presume
that Mark has known Q, and that he thus may have used and
rewritten the Q-text about the great commandment and integrated
it into his gospel. In order to investigate Mark's editing we must,
therefore, first try to reconstruct the Q version of this pericope.

Within the reconstructed text of Q the common elements of
Matthew and Luke should certainly find a place. Since the two
evangelists, however, did their own rewriting, it is possible that
some features of Q have been preserved only in Mark.

a) Basic Structure

The original structure is decidedly that of Matthew / Luke (without
Mk 12:32-34): the inimical question addressed to Jesus by a
lawyer and the double answer given by Jesus who connects "love
of God" with "love of neighbor".[32] This is the backbone of the
fairly simple pericope.

"Möglicherweise ist diese Kombination (10:25-28 and the good Samaritan)
schon vor Lk vollzogen gewesen; denn die Formulierung der Frage und die
Gegenfrage (Lk 10:25f.) scheinen zu zeigen, dass hier eine andere Fassung des
Textes benutzt ist als die Mk Redaktion."

[30] Cf., however, the cautious opinion of Fitzmyer, *op. cit.* 876-879:
"Whether the Marcan and Lucan forms of the story go back to the same incident
in the ministry of Jesus is hard to say" (p. 876). Yet "it is more likely that the
different forms...emerged in the post-Easter transmission..." (p. 878). Marshall,
op. cit. 441-442, with reference to T. W. Manson, M.-J. Lagrange and J.
Jeremias, seems to opt for different incidents: "There is nothing surprising in
the question being asked on more than one occasion, since it was a rabbinic
theme" (p. 442).

[31] Otherwise, V. Taylor, *The Gospel According to St. Mark* (London: 1952)
484 (with reference to Bultmann and M. Albertz).

[32] Lührmann, *op. cit.* 206, notes: "Da eine solche Verbindung...nur in der
sich im griechischen Horizont definierenden jüdischen Überlieferung
nachzuweisen ist, geht die Szene nicht auf die historische Situation Jesu zurück"
(cf. also p. 207). See in the same sense, e.g., Burchard, *art. cit.* 51-62; Sellin,
art. cit. 21. Otherwise, however, Fuller, *art. cit.* 329; Pesch, *op. cit.* 246:
"Gegen die Herkunft dieser Beantwortung einer prüfenden Frage einer Schriftgelehrten von Jesus selbst lassen sich keine durchschlagenden Bedenken mehr
erheben."

Luke has rewritten the text in view of the parable about the good Samaritan. As long as the pericope of the great commandment stood alone, it was, logically speaking, Jesus himself who in his answer must have made this connection between the two commandments and thus created a challenging new way of behavior. Luke's attention was, however, so exclusively focused on what he wanted to illustrate by the parable about the good Samaritan that, in his introductory presentation, he did not hesitate to place the connection on the lips of the lawyer. Jesus' reaction to the lawyer's question now is: "What is written in the law? How do you read?" The lawyer answers and quotes, within the same long sentence, both commandments; he only once uses the verb ἀγαπήσεις: "You shall love the Lord your God with all your heart, and with all your soul, and with all your strength, and with all your mind; *and* your neighbor as yourself".

b) Vocabulary

The reconstruction of words, phrases and whole sentences cannot be completely effected because of the mixed state of the existing texts. We must proceed cautiously and indicate what of the evangelists is either present or absent in the Q pericope. We do not intend to engage in a word-by-word reconstruction of the entire hypothetical Q-text.[33]

Q 10:25a: It must be assumed as good as certain that the introductory clause contained the noun νομικός (most probably without τις[34]) and the participle (ἐκ)πειράζων[35]. Much uncertainty remains concerning the expression καὶ ἰδού at the beginning[36]

---

[33] See for a reconstruction of the text in Greek, Fuller, *art. cit.* 322; and in German, Pesch, *op. cit.* 245-246. Cf. the discussion of these reconstructions in Kiilunen, *op. cit.* 81-84.

As is often done nowadays in this study the Lukan versification is used for designating the Q text.

[34] For its Lukan character, cf., e.g., Sellin, *art. cit.* 21-22 and n. 110: "einem Substantiv nachgestelltes τις: Nie in Mt, 1mal in Mk, 29mal in Lk, 39mal in Act". Fuller, *art. cit.* 321, and Pesch, *op. cit.* 445, are of the opinion that the Semitism εἰς ἐκ (Mt 22:35) belongs to Q; but see also Kiilunen, *op. cit.* 36-37.

[35] We may prefer here the simplex since Luke likes to use compound verbs. However, Q employs both πειράζω (Mt 4:11 = Lk 4:2; Mt 16:1 = Lk 11:16) and ἐκπειράζω (Mt 4:7 = Lk 4:12). The compound is also present in Deut 6:16.

[36] We have the Septuagintism καὶ ἰδού certainly twice in Q (Mt 12:41 = Lk 11:32 and Mt 12:42 = Lk 11:31) and ἰδού occurs seven times in Q

and in regard to the main verb.[37] It is quite possible that the name Jesus was mentioned in this introduction.

Q 10:25b: This clause is a question in direct speech. Its first word is the vocative διδάσκαλε. Then, for what follows, we must perhaps turn to Matthew: "Which commandment is great [= the greatest] in the law?".[38] Instead of ποία, the interrogative pronoun τίς may be preferable for Q. Most probably the expression ἐν τῷ νόμῳ was part of the same question.[39]

Q 10:26a: The clause which introduced Jesus as speaker contained ὁ δέ, a verb of saying and the indication of the lawyer by means of (presumably the dative of) αὐτός.[40]

(Lk 10:26b-27a must, of course, be omitted.)

Q 10:27bc: This long clause, the citation of Deut 6:5, comes immediately after Q 10:26a. The question "Which commandment...?" is followed by the answer which cites the commandment. The repeated preposition within the Old Testament quotation is in the Septuagint ἐν plus dative. In Q, as in Mt 22:37, most probably three nouns (heart, soul, mind) were present.[41] We may

---

(Mt 10:16 = Lk 10:3; Mt 11:8 = Lk 7:25; Mt 11:10 = Lk 7:27 [Mal 3:1]; Mt 10:19 = Lk 7:34; Mt 23:38 = Lk 13:35; Mt 24:26 = Lk 17:23 [twice]). According to Sellin, *art. cit.* 21, the phrase here is decidedly Lukan. He may be right. See also Goulder, *op. cit.* 486; Kiilunen, *op. cit.* 54-55; Fuller, *art. cit.* 320 (with reference to Schramm, *op. cit.* 91-92): "eine lukanische Einführung..., nach dem Stil seines Sondergutes gefasst".

[37] It may have been a simple verb of coming or approaching or, perhaps, as in Lk 10:25 ἀνίστημι (cf. for Q: Mt 12:41 = Lk 11:32). For Fuller, *art. cit.* 320, this last verb is pleonastic and Lukan redaction. Moreover, Fuller (320-321) and Pesch, *op. cit.* 245, reconstruct the "Semitic" sequence: verb-subject.

[38] Cf. Pesch, *op. cit.* 245, who, again, points to Semitisms: "Verwendung des Positivs statt des Superlativs" and "Fehlen der Kopula"; see also Fuller, *art. cit.* 321. Otherwise Kiilunen, *op. cit.* 40-42, who in a not too convincing reasoning defends the meaning "great". The use of μείζων by Mark in 12:31 seems to indicate that he, too, read μεγάλη in his source.

[39] However, Matthew's interest in the law within this pericope is most evident from 22:40, and Luke read "You know the commandments" in 18:20 almost immediately after 18:18, the very verse he used in 10:25. Cf., e.g., Goulder, *op. cit.* 486; Gnilka, *op. cit.* 258: "die Wendung ἐν τῷ νόμῳ... hat jeweils einen anderen Bezug und ist beiden Evangelisten auch sonst vertraut". On the other hand, redactional tendencies do not exclude (supplementary) Q influence. Moreover, it is possible that Matthew retained νομικός (a *hapax legomenon* in his gospel) precisely because of the presence of ἐν τῷ νομῳ in Q 10:25b.

[40] As is well known, Luke often uses πρός plus accusative after a verb of saying for the addressee(s). Cf., e.g., Goulder, *op. cit.* 487; Kiilunen, *op. cit.* 58; Sellin, *art. cit.* 22 n. 122: "εἶπεν πρός ist Lukanismus (Lk: etwa 75mal; Mk: 6mal; Mt: nur 3, 15)."

[41] Cf. Pesch, *op. cit.* 245.

accept that in Q καὶ ἐν ὅλῃ διανοίᾳ concluded the enumeration.[42] Pesch thinks that the first question was followed by "This (is) the great [= greatest] commandment" (v. 27c).[43]

Q 10:27de: Was the second part of Jesus' answer separated from the first by an introductory formula as we find it in Mt 22:39: "and a second [is] like it" (v. 27d)?[44] This is not impossible. Then, in v. 27e, the quotation of Lev 19:18 follows. In Q, as in both Mt 22:39 and Mk 12:31, the verb ἀγαπήσεις is repeated.

Q 10:27f: It would seem that Jesus' answer also contained a concluding statement similar to the one present in Mk 12:31c: "There is no other commandment greater than these".

Was this the end of the pericope, as Matthew suggests? We cannot be completely certain, although the continuations of Mk 12:32 and Lk 10:28 each introduce a secondary addition.

All in all, not too much guesswork is necessary. In Q 10:25a we hear about a (certain) lawyer who came to Jesus to test him; in v. 25b he asks his question probably as follows: "Which commandment is the greatest in the law?" Jesus is introduced as replying in v. 26a; the first part of the answer follows in v. 27b, the second part in 27e. The Greek Q text of v. 27b and v. 27e can to a great extent be recovered. If the clauses of v. 27c, d and f are present in Q—which is somewhat doubtful—their vocabulary remains

---

[42] We may refer to the extensive discussion in Berger, *op. cit.* 177-183 and also draw the following synopsis:

LXX Dt 5:5	Mk 12:30	Mk 12:33	Mt 22:37	Lk 10:27
καρδία	καρδία	καρδία	καρδία	καρδία
ψυχή	ψυχή	ψυχή	ψυχή	ψυχή
	διάνοια			ἰσχύς
δύναμις	ἰσχύς	ἰσχύς	διάνοια	διάνοια

A variant of the first noun in the LXX is διάνοια.
Cf. Lührmann, *op. cit.* 206: "Drücken die drei urpsrünglichen Substantiva [= die drei anthropologischen Grundbegriffe] die Totalität der Gottesbeziehung aus, so tritt im griechischen Sprachbereich der Verstand hinzu, diese Totalität zu wahren"; Pesch, *op. cit.* 240, comments: "Vermutlich sind in der viergliedrigen Formel die beiden ersten Glieder (Herz-Seele) als Benennung der ganzen, ganzheitlichen personalen Existenz und die beiden letzten Glieder (Denken-Kraft) als zur Hervorhebung der all-umfassenden Kräfte einander zuzuordnen." See, however, also, e.g., E.P. Gould, *The Gospel According to St. Mark* (ICC; Edinburgh: 1907) 232: "There is no attempt at classification, or exactness of statement, but simply to express in a strong way the whole being."

[43] Cf. Pesch, *op. cit.* 245 n. 26. Again Semitisms: no "Kopula"; "great" in the sense of "greatest".

[44] So Pesch, *op. cit.* 245 n. 26. The adjective ὅμοιος, although (together with its cognates) very much favored by Matthew, is also present in Q (cf. Mt 11:16 = Lk 7:32; Mt 13:31 = Lk 13:18; and Mt 13:33 = Lk 13:21).

uncertain. This applies to v. 25b to a lesser extent as far as the vocabulary is concerned. We may summarize our findings in the following tentative text (the square brackets indicate our hesitation):

Q 10:25a	A lawyer stood up to put Jesus to the test,
b	"Teacher, [which commandment is the greatest in the law?]"
26a	He said to him,
27b	"You shall love the Lord your God with all your heart, and with all your soul, and with all your mind.
c	[This is the greatest commandment.]
d	[And a second is like it,]
e	You shall love your neighbor as yourself.
f	[There is no other commandment greater than these]".

Place in the Q Document

To determine the original place of this passage in Q is quite a difficult, if not an impossible, task. Matthew is of no help here since he follows the Markan disposition. Insofar as Mark is using Q elsewhere, he does not seem to respect its order to any great degree. In Luke the great commandment pericope follows the section on "Discipleship and Mission" (Q 9:57-10:24)[45] and could be the concluding pericope of this section, or the pericope might belong to the cluster "Controversies with this Generation" (Q 11:14-52 and 13:34-35). The pericope of Q 10:25-28 stands in fairly close proximity to it, and within this section, in Q 11:46 and 52, Luke uses the noun νομικός.

To be sure, Lukan disposition is always a valuable argument in the matter of Q's order.[46] To a lesser extent, the controversial character of our pericope could also be helpful in determining its position in Q. The reappearance of νομικός, however, is hardly an indication of order. Moreover, we must not forget that the pericope

---

[45] For the titles and the extension of this "cluster" and the following, see Kloppenborg, *op. cit.* xxxi-xxxii.

[46] Cf., e.g., V. Taylor, "The Order of Q," *JTS* (1953) 27-31; and "The Original Order of Q" in *New Testament Essays: Studies in Memory of T.W. Manson*, ed. A. J. B. Higgins (Manchester: 1959) 246-269. Both studies are reprinted in Taylor, *New Testament Essays* (London: 1970) 90-94 and 95-118.

is employed by Luke in function of the parable. Such a secondary adaption may have caused a transposition.

In regard to the precise position of the great commandment pericope in Q, it would perhaps be better simply to confess our ignorance because of lack of clear data. A similar ignorance is to be admitted regarding the stage of Q into which the pericope was integrated.[47]

Markan Redaction of Q

Is there any ground for positing another text than the reconstructed Q version as the immediate source of Mark?[48] The main reasons which are brought forward to postulate a pre-Markan text different from Q are the following.[49]

(1) There is a certain tension between v. 34c and what precedes. "Dass niemand mehr Jesus eine Frage zu stellen wagt, bezieht sich nur einschlussweise auf diese Gesprächsszene, sachlich gesehen aber eher auf die vorhergehenden Konflikte...".[50]

(2) That Jesus and the scribe agree is unlike the picture of the scribes which Mark presents elsewhere in his gospel.

(3) The criticism contained in the preference of love of neighbour to sacrifices is better understandable in a Jewish-Christian than in a (Markan) Gentile-Christian setting.

But do these reasons really force us to admit a pre-Markan text which could then be seen as an intermediate stage between Q and Mark?

If one accepts (as a working hypothesis) Mark's knowledge of this Q pericope, then his editorial activity, it would seem, becomes more evident and understandable. To be sure, Mark quite heavily rewrote and expanded the pericope of the great commandment.[51]

---

[47] For the stages in Q, see, e.g., my remarks in "Q-Influence" (see note 2 above) 298-304. Does a consideration such as that of Lührmann (see note 32 above), if correct, not plead for a rather late stage?

[48] Burchard's position (*art. cit.* 43) is diametrically opposed to our hypothesis. The "zweite Fassung [= Q] mag Matthäus oder Lukas oder beiden vorgelegen haben.... Wie dem auch sei, die Fassung hat jedenfalls mit Markus literarisch nichts zu tun, auch nicht über eine gemeinsame Vorlage, sondern fusst auf einer mündlichen Einzelüberlieferung"; Mk 12:28-34 has "keine literarische Vorgeschichte".

[49] Cf. Kertelge, *art. cit.* 311-124.

[50] Kertelge, *art. cit.* 306.

[51] Cf. Lührmann, *op. cit.* 205: "Der markinische Anteil ist...höher zu veranschlagen, als das üblicherweise geschieht." As can be expected, Pesch, *op. cit.*

He made it the last of the three questions (12:13-17; 12:18-27 and 12:28-32) addressed by non-disciples to Jesus in the temple complex after he told the parable about the vineyard (12:1-12).⁵² "Ein Gesetzesapophthegma aus Q...wird von Mk erweitert in eine Art Lehrgespräch".⁵³ We may go into greater detail.⁵⁴

Markan Rewriting

Mk 12:28: The first clause is a thorough rewriting of Q 10:25a. Mark does not employ νομικός. The genitive construction with γραμματεύς, "one of the scribes", can be compared with 2:6 and 7:1 ("some of the scribes").⁵⁵ According to Mark's narrative, the scribes have been present since 11:27. The construction of 12:28a: καὶ προσελθὼν εἷς τῶν γραμματέων...ἐπηρώτησεν αὐτόν, is very similar to that of 10:2a: καὶ προσελθόντες Φαρισαῖοι ἐπηρωτῶν αὐτόν. This is all the more striking because in 10:2 Mark has πειράζοντες, the negative participle which, in 12:28, is omitted by him from Q. He wants to depict the scribe as a sincere person. At the end of the pericope the Markan Jesus will even praise him (see 12:34). This is at first sight strange enough since in Mark's gospel the scribes are consistently Jesus' opponents: "Nicht die Pharisäer,

---

236, sees Mark's editing as mimimal: "Der Konservative Redaktor Markus greift in die Überlieferung selbst nicht ein."

⁵² According to Pesch, *op. cit.* 236, the connection with 12:18-27 is "vormarkinisch".

⁵³ Sellin, *art. cit.* 21. Cf. Kertelge, *art. cit.* 307: "Der Schriftgelehrte wird zum gelehrigen Schüler des Meisters Jesus." Burchard, *art. cit.* 49-50, pleads for the opposite evolution: from "Schulgespräch" to "Streitgespräch", i.e., from "apologetisch-missionarische Theorie" to "christliche Paränese". Cf. also Fuller, *art. cit.* 323 (with reference to Bultmann): "Nach den Erkenntnissen der Formgeschichte ist das Streitgespräch gegenüber dem Schulgespräch sekundär." M. Kinghardt, *Gesetz und Volk Gottes. Das lukanische Verständnis des Gesetzes nach Herkunft, Funktion und seinem Ort in der Geschichte des Urchristentums* (WUNT II/32; Tübingen: 1988) 137-139, does not accept the hostile character of the verb here: "Trotz das (ἐκ)πειράζων der Mt-Lk Fassung ist nicht ersichtlich, dass es sich dabei um ein Streitgespräch gehandelt hat" (p. 137). This is hardly correct.

⁵⁴ See, e.g., Kertelge, *art. cit.* 314-321.

⁵⁵ Within Mark's gospel the scribes are very prominent and active. Twice it is stated that some of them come down from Jerusalem to Galilee (see 3:22 and 7:1). In 3:22 Mark, too, most probably inserted "scribes" into a Q-pericope (cf. Lk 11:14: οἱ ὄχλοι; 11:15: τινὲς δὲ ἐξ αὐτῶν). See Lührmann, *art. cit.* especially 243, and also *op. cit.* 51: "Von allen jüdischen Gruppierungen eigneten sich die Schriftgelehrten am meisten als Identifikationsfiguren für aktuelle Auseinandersetzungen mit den Juden." Cf. Pesch, *op. cit.* 243.

sondern die Schriftgelehrten sind...die Hauptgegner Jesu bei Mk
und—so möchte ich folgern—die aktuellen Gegner der Gemeinde
des Mk von jüdischer Seite".[56]

There can hardly be any doubt that v. 28bc has been added by
Mark. The two clauses refer to the preceding pericope, the controversy of Jesus and the Sadducees about the resurrection: "having
heard them disputing and knowing that he answered well". The
scribe apparently admires Jesus. His question, in its essence taken
over from Q, could no longer be brought forward in order to test
or entrap Jesus. Not in an adversary sense, but being well-inten-
tioned, he asks: "Which commandment is the first of all?" Since
the scribe uses διδάσκαλε in v. 32, nothing can be deduced from
its omission in v. 28. Mark writes "first" instead of "great" (=
greatest), probably influenced by "second" in Q 10:27d (at least,
if this term was present in Q, cf. Mt 22:39); he "numbers" the
commandments, more than his source. Mark, who in his gospel
does not use νόμος, replaces "in the law" by "of all
(commandments)".[57] The adverb καλῶς is most probably Markan
(see 7:6, 9, 37 and 12:32). It is well known that ἐπερωτάω is a fa-
vorite verb of Mark.[58] "Die einleitende Fragepartikel ποία ersetzt
ein τίς, hebt zugleich aber auch auf die *Qualität* des 'ersten
Gebotes' ab".[59]

Mk 12:29: Jesus is introduced explicitly as "answering". Mark
adds ὅτι πρώτη ἐστιν which corresponds to his question of v. 28.
The double use of "first" betrays a "Systematisierung im
markinischen Text, wo die Gebote als erstes und zweites eingeführt
werden".[60] The origin of the addition of v. 29b, "Hear, O Israel:
the Lord our God, the Lord is one" is disputed. It was not present
in the Q pericope. It does not seem impossible that Mark himself
inserted the "Hear, O Israel", perhaps under some Jewish-Hel-

---

[56] Lührmann, *art. cit.* 183. Cf. Id., *op. cit.* 51: "Dass mit einem einzelnen
Schriftgelehrten Jesus gegenseitige Übereinstimmung erzielen kann..., was nie
von den Pharisäern gesagt wird, zeigt, wie nahe sich ein solches von den
Schriftgelehrten vertretenes Diaspora-Judentum und das Christentum der Leser
des Mk standen." See also the same author in the preceding note.

[57] πάντων may be feminine (cf. ἐντολή). The numeral πᾶς is becoming inde-
clinable; cf. M. Zerwick, *Biblical Greek* (Rome: 1963) number 12.

[58] ἐπερωτάω is used 25 times in Mk, 8 times in Mt and 17 times in Lk. We
cannot accept Fuller's reconstruction of "die früheste erreichbare Form" (= older
than Q): καὶ ἐπηρώτησεν αὐτὸν εἷς ἐκ τῶν γραμματέων (*art. cit.* 322-324),
which retains both ἐπερωτάω and γραμματεύς.

[59] Kertelge, *art. cit.* 315.

[60] Pesch, *op. cit* 238 and 245 n. 26 (but on the pre-Markan level).

lenistic influence in his community.[61] Monotheism is thus stressed. We will see how, in v. 32, Mark comments on that sentence.

12:30: Mark alters the first citation through the minor shift from ἐν back to the Septuagintal ἐκ[62] and through the replacement of δύναμις by (διάνοια and) ἰσχύς.[63]

12:31: If v. 27d ("and a second [is] like it") was present in Q 10, Mark retains δευτέρα, adds the announcing demonstrative αὕτη, but omits ὁμοία αὐτῇ. As the introductory clause now stands, it could suggest a rather subordinating nuance: Love of neighbor is only the second commandment. This, however, is hardly Mark's idea. The second quotation (Q 10:27e = Lev 19:18) is taken over and, probably, also "there is no other commandment greater than these" (Q 10:27f).

12:32-33: Verses 32-34 constitute a most impressive Markan expansion of Q. A first remark should focus on the function of the repetition of the O.T. quotations in vv. 32-33. Since the figure of the scribe in Mark remains thoroughly positive throughout the pericope, this repetition is needed from a narrative point of view. By his reaction the scribe must, as it were, manifest his agreement with Jesus, so that he can be praised by Jesus in v. 34.

In vv. 32-33 we must appreciate "the evident enthusiasm with which the Scribe received the statement of Jesus, and his ability to enter into the spirit of it so as to develop it in his own way".[64] The Markan scribe "wiederholt zustimmend und weiterführend Jesu Antwort"[65] and thus provides a double comment. The first ex-

---

[61] Cf. Fuller, *art. cit.* 323: "offentsichlich für heidnische Leser hinzugefügt" (by Mark?). According to Pesch, *op. cit.* 239, the clause is inserted before Mark. J. Gnilka, *Das Evangelium nach Markus. II* (Zürich and Neukirchen-Vluyn: 1979) 165, writes: "Wenn Markus...mit der Zitierung von Dtn 6:4 auf die Einzigkeit Gottes abhebt, wird erneut der hellenistische Grund erkennbar." Bornkamm, *art. cit.* 39-40, assumes the presence of 12:29b in the Jewish-Palestinian pre-Markan pericope but states that its sense must have been changed in a Jewish-Hellenistic milieu.

[62] Dt 6:5 (LXX): καὶ ἀγαπήσεις κύριον τὸν θεόν σου ἐξ ὅλης τῆς καρδίας σου καὶ ἐξ ὅλης τῆς ψυχῆς σου καὶ ἐξ ὅλης τῆς δυνάμεως σου.

[63] Cf. Gnilka, *Markus* 165: "...zwei aus dem rationalen bzw. psychologischen Bereich stammende Begriffe". For Gnilka διάνοια is "die Verstandeskraft". "ἰσχύς wurde zu einem psychologischen Term, der die Gesamtkraft der Seele bezeichnet." See also note 42 above.

[64] Gould, *op. cit.* 234.

[65] Lührmann, *op. cit.* 205.

plains the "Hear, O Israel..."; the second deals with the two commandments.[66]

For the editorial καλῶς, see v. 28. As already mentioned above, the vocative διδάσκαλε is transferred from Q 10:25b. For the expression ἐπ' ἀληθείας (and διδάσκαλε), see 12:14 which is also of interest as to its content: "...you truly (ἐπ' ἀληθείας) teach the way of God...". Is this not what takes place in 12:28-31 as well?

Within the resumption in v. 32, neither the first two words ("Hear, O Israel") nor "God" and "Lord" are repeated. The end of v. 32 ("and there is no other but he") quotes Deut 4:35 and explains how we have to understand the term εἷς in vv. 29 and 32: "one", in the sense of "unique, no other foreign gods"[67].

In v. 33 σύνεσις seems to replace διάνοια Only three faculties remain; the second (ψυχή) of v. 30 is omitted.[68] Mark twice "substantivizes" the verb "you shall love": τὸ ἀγαπᾶν. Although both τὸ ἀγαπᾶν-clauses function in this long sentence as the grammatical subject, the predicate ("is much more than all whole burnt offerings and sacrifices") apparently refers more particularly to the second clause. We must understand: love of neighbor is better than all sacrifices; love of neighbor is by far the best proof of true love of God.[69] K. Kertelge comments: "Die 'Ethisierung' des Gottesdienstes und damit verbunden die Entwertung des Opferkultes entspricht einer gesetzeskritischen Tendenz, die Markus auch an anderen Stellen seines Evangeliums erkennen lässt".[70]

12:34: Notwithstanding the fact that the adverb νουνεχῶς is a *hapax legomenon*, the construction of v. 34a is almost certainly Markan. We may compare ἰδὼν [...] ὅτι νουνεχῶς ἀπεκρίθη with what we have in v. 28: ἰδὼν ὅτι καλῶς ἀπεκρίθη.[71] Not only among Hellenistic Jewish Christians but also in a Gentile Christian

---

[66] Cf. Bornkamm, *art. cit.* 38-39: "Man wird an der Formulierung V 32f. beachten müssen, dass sie Jesu Wort in zwei Sätze zerlegt, und zwar nicht, wie man erwarten sollte, den beiden Geboten...entsprechend...."

[67] In the Old Testament different senses of εἷς have been proposed, e.g., besides that which is present in Mk, another sense of "one, unique", namely against the many Yạwheh cult places and / or traditions.

[68] σύνεσις, perhaps, replaces both ψυχή and διάνοια. According to Gnilka, *Markus* 166, the new term again emphasizes "das Verstandesmässige".

[69] Cf. in the O.T. 1 Kings 15:22 and Hos 6:6.

[70] Kertelge, *art. cit.* 520. He refers to Mk 2:18-22; 2:23-28; 3:1-6; 7:1-23; 11:15-19; 14:58.

[71] A variant reading in v. 28 has εἰδώς. Cf. Lührmann, *op. cit.* 206: "Die Bezeugung...ist etwa gleichwertig; das textkritisch unumstrittene ἰδών in 34 könnte zu einer Änderung von ursprünglichem εἰδώς geführt haben."

setting is this criticism possible. Mark himself could have composed it. Together with the verb ἐπερωτάω (in both vv. 28 and 34)
the clause forms an artful inclusion of the whole pericope.

This pericope is the only place in Mark's gospel where the evangelist presents a scribe in a positive way. However, for Jesus' ap-
preciative statement ("you are not far[72] from the kingdom of
God"), we may refer to 15:43 where Joseph of Arimathea is called
εὐσχήμων βουλευτής and qualified as follows: "he was himself
looking for the kingdom of God". This last verse, moreover, has,
like 12:34, the verb τολμάω. For Mark the "kingdom of God" is
the central theme of Jesus' proclamation (cf. Mk 1:14-15). The
expression is here used ecclesiastically rather than eschatologi-
cally.[73] Does the litotes "not far from" (= within reach) imply that
the scribe refuses to accept this proclamation?[74] Hardly. Further,
because this sympathetic scribe is an exception in Mark, we should
not conclude too easily that for this presentation Mark depends on
a non-Q tradition.[75]

"And after that no one dared to ask him any question" (v. 34c)
is the conclusion not only of this pericope but of the three controversies together (12:13-34ab) and even of the whole section 11:27-
12:34ab. One must therefore not exaggerate the so-called tension
between the pericope proper and v. 34c. The clause marks a pause
in the narrative.

Markan Context and Content

Through comparing Mk 12:28-34 with its probable source,
Q 10:25-28, we are able, it would seem, to reach a better insight
into Mark's thorough rewriting and editing. First of all, the evangelist integrated the Q text into his gospel. He provided it with a
particular controversy-context. The pericope became the third and
final discussion while Jesus, during the last days of his public life,
was walking in the temple. After Jesus had spoken the parable
about the workers in the vineyard, some Pharisees and Herodians

---

[72] The adverb μακράν is a *hapax legomenon* in the N.T. For Markan preference for μακρόθεν, cf. 5:6; 8:3; 11:13; 14:54; 15:40; see also the neutral plural
μακρά in 12:40.
[73] Cf. Pesch, *op. cit.* 244.
[74] Cf. Lührmann, *art. cit.* 184, and *op. cit.* 207: "Trotz aller Nähe bleibt also
ein unüberbrüchbarer Gegensatz". Contrast Kertelge, *art. cit.* 320: "Dieses Wort
schränkt die Anerkennung Jesu für den Schriftgelehrten nicht ein, sondern setzt
sie voraus."
[75] So Taylor, *op. cit.* 485.

were sent to entrap Jesus by means of the question about paying
taxes to Caesar (12:13-17). Then, some Sadducees came to him
with their question about rising from death (12:18-27). Finally,
one of the scribes approaches Jesus and asks the question about the
greatest commandment. At the close of this third discussion nobody dares to ask Jesus any more questions.[76]

What must strike everyone who knows the Q pericope, as well as
everyone who takes into account its present Markan context of
controversy, is the presentation of the scribe as a sincere and re-
ceptive person. As already mentioned above, in the Markan gospel
itself such a scribe is an exception (but see "the respected member
of the council" in 15:43). The scribe comes to Jesus because he is
convinced that Jesus has given the Sadducees a good answer. Otherwise than in Q, he asks his question out of a sincere disposition.
By expressing his assent ("you are right, Teacher", 12:32) and by
resuming Jesus' answer the scribe proves that he is in accordance
with what Jesus proposes. Jesus notices that the reaction of the
scribe is wise and does not hesitate to say: "You are not far from
the kingdom of God" (12:34b). That is to say: not far from what
Jesus himself preaches in his gospel. "Dass der 'Schriftgelehrte'
im zweiten Teil in die Nähe der Gottesherrschaft gerückt wird, ver-
rät eine werbende Absicht missionarischer Bemühung im jüdisch-
hellenistischen Milieu".[77]

By inserting "Hear, O Israel: The Lord our God, the Lord is
one" at the beginning of the first quotation (that from Deuteron-
omy), Mark stresses the uniqueness of God. The scribe reacts to Jesus: you are right in saying that there is only one God, that there is
no other god but he (cf. 12:32). Apparently, monotheism matters
to Mark.

Mark has added, in v. 29, "the first is". It remains somewhat uncertain whether, in v. 31, he underlined the numbering by "the
second is this". Probably a clause such as "there is no other
commandment greater than these" was already present in Q. In
Mark, as in Q, the two commandments are joined together. However, one could argue: the second is but the second. Does this involve a subordinating nuance which differs from the coordinating
one in Mt 22:39 and, possibly, in Q: δευτέρα δὲ ὁμοία αὐτῇ?[78]

---

[76] Cf. Kertelge, *art. cit.* 305-306.

[77] Pesch, *op. cit.* 248.

[78] See Gundry, *op. cit.* 449: In Matthew "'second' refers...to order in quotation, not to order of importance." According to Matthew the second commandment is equal to the first in importance. The same applies to Q. However, Burchard, *art. cit.* 61, presents an interesting comment on Mt 22:39a: "Das bedeutet

Most probably not since, in the scribe's comment of v. 33, Mark emphasizes the importance of the second command, love of neighbor.[79] By themselves, sacrifices should manifest the respectful, submissive and loving attitude towards God. The scribe, however, rightly concludes from Jesus' words that "to love one's neighbor as oneself" is a true manifestation of love of God, much more and much better "than all whole burnt offerings and sacrifices".

Conclusions

Three important conclusions can be drawn from this investigation.

a) It appears impossible to explain adequately Lk 10:25-28 and Mt 22:34-40 without the postulate of a second source, a text which is different from Mk 12:28-34, the first source of Matthew and Luke. The second text can be reconstructed in its outline and even, to a great extent, with its vocabulary. There is no reason why this text should not be called a Q passage. Its place in the Q document, however, is difficult to determine. As to its content, the main point of the Q pericope is Jesus' joining of love of God with love of neighbor. Notwithstanding the brevity of the passage, Jesus' answer is a radical and truly revolutionary statement. We must also note the negative, "testing" intention of the lawyer who asks the question.

b) The two texts, Q 10:25-28 and Mk 12:28-34, apparently deal with the same incident. Ultimately they must go back to one and the same narrative. But, as far as Mark is concerned, must we look for a narrative different from that of Q? Other Markan texts strongly suggest that Mark knew sections of Q. The analysis of Mark's version of the great commandment leads to the conclusion that there is no need for supposing another text as source for Mark than the Q passage itself. Mark has most probably known and used this Q pericope as well.

---

mehr, als dass beide Gebote gleichgeordnet werden. Es ist Gleichordnung trotz Differenz. Obwohl das Gebot der Liebe zu Gott das grösste und erste ist, und nur eins kann das sein, ist das Gebot der Liebe zum Nächsten ihm gleich."

[79] For Mark, cf. Gnilka, *Markus* 165: "Zwar ist dieses [= the second commandment] bei Markus dem ersten nicht gleichgestaltet wie bei Mt 22:39..., aber das nebeneinander beider bereitet die Gleichwertung vor"; Pesch, *op. cit.* 238-239 (however, on the pre-Markan level).

c) Once again, by detecting how Mark radically edited Q, while incorporating sections of it into his gospel, we have encountered the evangelist whom we may still call *Marcus interpretator*, to be sure, not so much as Peter's translator or interpreter, but more as the explaining and actualizing *interpretator* of older traditions, Q included.

CHAPTER FIVE

Q: SAYINGS OF JESUS OR LOGIA?

Dieter Lührmann

After my book on the redaction of the Logia source in 1969, I did not write anything further about Q until 1989.[1] There are only a few reviews, for naturally I followed the further discussion with interest. There are also occasional remarks on Q in other connections; but there has been no continuous work of my own in this field. Here I present only a few observations from the area of my present interests, the gospels which were classed as apocryphal and the history of exegesis since the period of the Enlightenment. I hope that they may contribute something to Q research, even if in a limited field.

The starting point is a few sentences in an article "Logion" which I had to write for an English-language dictionary.[2] I have always used the designation "Logienquelle" (logia source), without reflecting on the history which lies behind this apparently harmless concept. Only now has it become clear what this description means, and with this the following essay is concerned.

I consider the assumption that Matthew and Luke used a second source in addition to Mark to be assured, despite all criticism. Neither the priority of Matthew nor proto-Luke hypotheses can resolve the Synoptic Problem to any comparable extent. The two-document hypothesis has thus become independent of the circumstances in the history of theology out of which it arose. I think, however, that it is worthwhile to recall these circumstances.

The thesis of this study is that at the beginning of Q-research there was a misunderstanding, namely Schleiermacher's interpretation of Papias' comments on the gospels of Matthew and Mark. The two-document hypothesis was developed in the 19th

---

[1] This present essay has been translated into English by R. McL. Wilson. *Die Redaktion der Logienquelle* (WMANT 33; Neukirchen: 1969); "The Gospel of Mark and the Sayings Collection Q," *JBL* 108 (1989) 51-71.

[2] Art. "Logion" in *A Dictionary of Biblical Interpretation*, ed. R. J. Coggins and J. L. Houlden (London and Philadelphia: 1990) 406f.

century in part independently of this, and in part appealing to it. At the end of the 19th century it became separated from this interpretation, but to some extent was now substantiated by new discoveries of apocryphal gospels.

In the 20th century the two-document hypothesis was taken up under new circumstances and with the raising of new exegetical questions. However, the question of the significance of the Jesus tradition for theology still remained, and this question has been handled in very controversial fashion. One aspect of this development can be displayed in the varying interpretation of the Greek word λόγιον, which at the beginning was a given factor through the text of Papias. I think that some very fundamental exegetical questions lie concealed in the semantic problems.

1. The Two-Document Hypothesis and Papias

At the beginning of the 19th century the Synoptic Problem represented one of the fundamental questions, at least in German Protestant theology. Historical criticism since the period of the Enlightenment made it necessary, and then the debate with David Friedrich Strauss made it positively essential, to attain to statements about Jesus which were historically verifiable. The solution was provided by the two sources for the historical Jesus, from which such a reliable portrait could be obtained: the Gospel of Mark and the second source which could be reconstructed from Matthew and Luke. It was outlined for the first time by Christian Hermann Weisse in 1838[3] and comprehensively presented by Heinrich Julius Holtzmann in 1863.[4]

Friedrich Schleiermacher's 1832 treatise *Über die Zeugnisse des Papias von unseren beiden ersten Evangelien*[5] was an important step along this road. It finds an echo right through the entire 19th century, for from it comes the justification for the existence of a pre-Synoptic collection of sayings of Jesus and the description of this collection, typical for the German tradition, as "Logienquelle". In English this would have to be reproduced as "Logia source", but this designation was evidently hardly ever used.

---

[3] *Die evangelische Geschichte kritisch und philosophisch bearbeitet*, 2 vol. (Leipzig: 1838).
[4] *Die synoptischen Evangelien* (Leipzig: 1863).
[5] *Sämmtliche Werke*, erste Abteilung, zweiter Band (Berlin: 1836) 361-392.

Schleiermacher examined the well-known statements about Matthew and Mark[6] in Eusebius (*HE* III 39.5 f), with the conclusion that Papias here did not mean either the Gospel of Mark or that of Matthew in the form known to us. The comment on Matthew was rather to be understood to mean that in the Gospel named after Matthew a collection of utterances of Jesus had been used, and to this collection he traced back in essentials the great discourses of Jesus in that Gospel. Schleiermacher's interpretation of Papias' comment on Mark is less interesting for our theme. Here he sees behind the text known to us a collection of speeches and acts of Jesus which goes back to the sermons of Peter.

This is recognisably not yet the two-document hypothesis. Yet there are insights to be found here which have come to fruition in form criticism: the existence of collections of the Jesus tradition and its kerygmatic character. In the era of source criticism only a part of this was at first taken up, namely the theory of a source containing utterances of Jesus behind the Gospel of Matthew. The advance consisted in the expansion of this into a solution of the Synoptic Problem. Schleiermacher was not able to take up a stance on this point; he died in 1834.

His interpretation of the Papias text is the basis for a quarter of the two-document hypothesis. It is of no significance for the priority of Mark; but for the second source it postulates, at least for Matthew, the existence of a collection of sayings of Jesus, and this thesis was then extended to include Luke. Thus the modern two-document hypothesis appeared to have a foundation in early church tradition, and indeed as early as the 2nd century. The assumption of the priority of Matthew in Johann Jakob Griesbach and the Tübingen school appealed to Augustine. The two-document hypothesis on the other hand now seemed to answer the claims of historical criticism, and also of the patristic tradition. Over against the challenge which D. F. Strauss presented for Protestant theology, this was a two-fold safeguard: the two-document hypothesis was modern, and at the same time it was rooted in the tradition of the early Church.

In the theological turbulence of that time, the comprehensive presentation of the two-document hypothesis by H. J. Holtzmann signified a further step beyond Weisse and Schleiermacher. In explicit debate with D. F. Strauss, Holtzmann sketched a foundation for the Christian faith which was guaranteed by a source A ("Urmarcus") and a second source which he designates

---

[6] Cf. below in part 5.

by the Greek letter Λ, an abbreviation for λόγια corresponding to Schleiermacher's interpretation of the Papias fragments. Since then "Logienquelle" has become the most usual designation in German research.

In the further course of the 19th century Schleiermacher was perhaps no longer so highly esteemed as a theologian, but rather as a philologist; he had translated the whole of Plato into German. His interpretation of the Papias fragments however met with opposition from the side of philology. Here we need mention only the contesting of his rendering of λόγια as "Aussprüche" (utterances). Early critics already referred to the fact that λόγια in Greek means '"divine utterances, oracles", not simply "utterances" of any kind, sayings. The quest for the historical Jesus in the 19th century was however in search of sayings of the human being Jesus, not oracles of divine origin!

Schleiermacher by no means ignored his lexicons. He was perfectly aware that λόγια generally, where it occurs, means "divine utterances, oracles", and so also in the Septuagint and the New Testament. He ruled this meaning out for Papias, however, for the latter could only mean utterances of *Jesus*, and these were no oracles.[7] Holtzmann took up this argument and repeated it against Schleiermacher's critics. Since in the time of Papias there was still no canon of the New Testament, only the words or sayings of Jesus could be meant by λόγια here: for Holtzmann, Papias thus provides the proof for the existence of λόγια; indeed according to Holtzmann the apostle Matthew may have perfectly well have been the author of this collection of Logia Jesu.[8]

Despite their distance from the pure source-criticism of their teachers, the representatives of the History-of-Religion school held fast to the two-document hypothesis. With detective accuracy the Belgian Frans Neirynck has shown that one of them, Johannes Weiss, in 1890 made use for the first time of the siglum Q for the second source, now so familiar to us.[9] Since Weiss took over from Holtzmann the siglum A as a designation for "Urmarcus", the introduction of Q betokens a conscious substitution for Λ. Q as an abbreviation of the German word Q(uelle) ("source") is admittedly a little enigmatic, since it is not immediately clear

---

[7] 366f.
[8] 251.
[9] "The Symbol of Q (= Quelle)," *EThL* 54 (1978) 119-125; "Once More: The Symbol Q," *EThL* 55 (1979) 382f.; "Note on the Siglum Q" in *Evangelica* II, *EThL* 99 (1991) 474.

which source is meant, whereas Λ precisely describes the Logia mentioned by Papias. The siglum Q can therefore only be employed in contexts in which it clearly describes the (second) *synoptic* source.

The reason for the replacement of Λ by Q is rightly seen by later authors to lie in the fact that "Q" is a more neutral designation than "Λ", for now the theory of a second source common to Matthew and Luke was no longer linked with the Papias fragment. Thereby the two-document hypothesis did indeed lose its alleged foundation in early church tradition; but it could no longer be criticised on the basis of other interpretations of the Papias text, or by reference to the semantics of the Greek word. The modern solution of the Synoptic Problem thus freed itself from the early church tradition. On the other hand it should not be forgotten that for Albert Schweitzer the two-document hypothesis belongs among the major errors in the quest for the historical Jesus. He adhered to the priority of Matthew, and developed his picture of the apocalyptic Jesus from the Gospel of Matthew.

In the German-speaking area the designations "Logienquelle", "Spruchquelle", "Spruchsammlung" are orientated largely to the origins in Schleiermacher, Weisse and Holtzmann. On the other hand the terms "Redenquelle", "Redensammlung", which are also used, emphasise that Q consists not only of individual sayings of Jesus, but that larger compositions can be identified. English-speaking scholars took over the siglum Q, but in part detached it from its German origin, in that Q was seen as the next letter after P (=Peter, the 'Urmarcus' A of Holtzmann). The fundamental studies on the Synoptic Problem have taken up the German terminology, but have also rendered "Quelle" by "document" and not only by "source". But today—so far as I can see—"the Sayings Collection (Q)" is in English the most usual description of this second source common to Matthew and Luke.

Nobody today argues for the existence of Q on the basis of the Papias quotation in Eusebius. For all who follow the two-document hypothesis, it results from the analysis of the Synoptic Gospels. But even those who appeal to Augustine in favour of the priority of Matthew cannot simply cite his authority, but must also justify it by an analysis of the Synoptic Gospels. Nevertheless it remains as a legacy of the history of the Synoptic Problem that a particular interpretation of the "Logia of Matthew" mentioned by Papias as Q in the sense of the two-document hypothesis be-

longs to the beginnings of the two-document hypothesis. This interpretation is still influential in the terminology
("Logienquelle"), but also describes a problem of substance, as
will be shown in the following sections.

2. Logia and Sayings of Jesus

So far we have followed the history of Q down to about 1900.
The first new discoveries of non-canonical Jesus tradition,
including the *Oxyrhynchus Papyri* 1, 654 and 655, also fall in this
period about the turn of the century. It is no accident that among
their first interpreters were the same scholars who at the time were
also concerned with Q. These papyri were described from the
beginning as the *Oxyrhynchus Logia*.[10] This has no basis in the
text of the fragments, but is evidently an echo of the Papias text
and accordingly of the description of the source common to
Matthew and Luke as λόγια. By about 1900 Papias could no
longer prove its existence. All the more did these newly
discovered papyri appear better suited to the purpose. They were
dated to the beginning of the 3rd century and showed that in
early Christianity there had been collections of sayings of Jesus.
Admittedly they were for the most part non-canonical, but the
traditional canon was also in the meantime subject to historical
criticism.

The term *logia* occurs again not only in relation to these new
discoveries, but also in the new exegetical investigations of form
criticism. Rudolf Bultmann describes the "Logia (Jesus as the
Teacher of Wisdom)" as a sub-division of the "Dominical Sayings".[11] As Wisdom sayings they are distinct from prophetic,
apocalyptic and other sayings. In Bultmann, Martin Dibelius and
others there is however a more general usage, in which "Logion"
is employed as more or less synonymous with "Spruch"
("saying") or "Ausspruch" ("utterance"); the semantic
problem of translating the Greek word λόγιον is thus no longer
seen.[12]

---

[10] B. P. Grenfell and A. S. Hunt, *Logia Iesou. Sayings of Our Lord* (London:
1897).

[11] *The History of the Synoptic Tradition* (Oxford: 1968) 69-108.

[12] 'logion n. (pl. logia) a saying attributed to Christ, especially one not
recorded in the canonical Gospels (Gk. = oracle f. *logos* word)': *the Concise Oxford Dictionary of Current English* (1991) 698.

Since the first reference to the Coptic *Gospel of Thomas*, discovered after the Second World War, people have spoken as a matter of course of its *logia*, and in editions of the text the division into 114 such *logia* has become usual, in contrast to most other texts from Nag Hammadi, which are cited according to codex, page and line. In the case of the *Gospel of Thomas* it soon became clear that it has parallels in the *Oxyrhynchus Papyri* 1, 654 and 655, already mentioned; it is this that explains the taking over of the term *Logia*, and not the Coptic text itself.

Although the siglum Λ had been prudently replaced by Q at the end of the 19th century, the term *Logia* thus survived in New Testament research. It occurs on the one hand in the terminology of form criticism. On the other hand it helped to characterise the Coptic *Gospel of Thomas* and its Greek parallels. Not only does the German term "Logienquelle" continue to be used, but *"Logia"* was also the title of the collective volume on Q published by Joel Delobel in 1982 with the subtitles "Les paroles de Jesus" and "The sayings of Jesus". In the modern Greek phrase πηγὴ τῶν λογίων, λόγιον has also returned to the original language–the Greek alphabet does not know the letter Q!

In Q the sayings of Jesus are never described as λόγια. At the end of the programmatic speech Q 6:20b-49 this is summarised as Jesus' λόγοι (Lk 6:47/Mt 7:24, repeated once again in Mt 7:26 diff. Lk 6:49), and Q 7:7 directly following reflects the authoritative character of the Word of Jesus. In these passages the Greek word λόγος is rightly translated as "word"; likewise in many other passages where λόγος occurs in the New Testament a translation by "word", "saying", "sermon" etc. is appropriate. In the light of our starting-point in Papias it should be emphasised that Matthew too in his gospel describes the speeches of Jesus as λόγοι (7:28; 19:1; 26:1), but himself never employs λόγια. Papias' comment is therefore not to be explained from Matthew's usage.

In the Coptic *Gospel of Thomas* neither λόγιον nor λόγος appears as a Greek loan-word. Where a Greek substratum has survived, only λόγος occurs. Above all, what in the *subscriptio* of the Coptic text runs as εὐαγγέλιον κατὰ Θωμᾶν is characterised at the beginning of *POxy* 654 as οἱ λόγοι [ἀπόκρυφοι οὓς ἐλά]λησεν Ἰη(σοῦ)ς ὁ ζῶν, "the secret sayings which the living Jesus spoke" (line 1f.).[13] This is taken up in lines 3-5:

---

[13] H. W. Attridge, "Appendix: The Greek Fragments" in *Nag Hammadi Codex Ii, 2-7*, ed. B. Layton (NHS 20; Leiden: 1989) 95-128.

[ὅστις ἂν τὴν ἑρμηνεί]αν τῶν λόγων τούτ[ων εὑρίσκῃ θανάτου] οὐ μὴ γεύσηται

In the *Gospel of Thomas*, and in the Greek behind it, the reference is thus to sayings of Jesus, to λόγοι, not to λόγια. James M. Robinson in an influential article in 1964 pointed to this difference, and therefore assigned Q to a *Gattung* of λόγοι σοφῶν instead of characterising it as *Logia*.[14] For this he referred not least to the Papias text, and emphasised the distinction between λόγος and λόγιον, in order to throw into relief the independent *Gattung* of the λόγοι. It may be questionable whether one can actually speak of a *Gattung*. Robinson himself has in the interval modified this in favour of John S. Kloppenborg's definition of Q.[15] What is important is the abundance of the material which Robinson brought together, and just as important is the question of the relation of such a *Gattung* of λόγοι to the *Logia*.

3. The Shift from Logia to Sayings

We have seen how in the history of research λόγιον has become a merely technical term, used as synonymous with "saying". In the literature in German the term "Logienquelle" has long since meant not the Matthean *Logia* of Papias but Q, the common source of Matthew and Luke, which in contrast to Mark's Gospel contains above all sayings or discourses of Jesus.

The siglum Q as such contains no information of its own. The Greek letter Λ first employed clearly pointed to the Greek word λόγια and accordingly to Papias' Matthean *Logia*. The letter Q is indeed used in German maps to mark the source (=spring) of a river, but otherwise is not a current abbreviation. Phonetically Q sounds like "Kuh" (=cow), and thus affords occasion for all kinds of witticism, as "queue" probably also does in English. To speak in German of the "Logienquelle Q" or in English of the "Synoptic Sayings Source Q" points more precisely to what the siglum Q by itself cannot designate.

The history of research shows that the solution of the Synoptic Problem with the aid of the two-document hypothesis was inspired by the Papias text. Its interpretation by Schleiermacher paved the

---

[14] "LOGOI SOPHON: On the Gattung of Q" in *Trajectories through Early Christianity* (Philadelphia: 1987) 71-113.
[15] Cf. Robinson's "Foreword" to J. S. Kloppenborg, *The Formation of Q* (StAC, Philadelphia: 1987) xi-xiv.

way for a new complex theory. In this, two apparently contradictory models come together. On the one hand there had been a
search since the period of the Enlightenment for the lost *one*
Gospel behind those which became canonical–to some extent Q
corresponded to this. On the other hand the relation of the
canonical Gospels to one another was thought of in terms of the
use of one or more by others–this was the dependence of Matthew
and Luke upon Mark.

The two-document hypothesis thus combined elements of these
two models with one another. Surprisingly, however, Mark
became the oldest gospel, and no longer Matthew. No less
surprisingly John became the latest gospel; throughout church
history it had borne the burden of proof for the traditional
Christology. We should not forget that it had been above all the
interpretation of the Gospel of John by D. F. Strauss which had
led to the strictly historically based two-document hypothesis.
Now there were two sources or documents, Mark and Q, from
which the historical Jesus could be known, over against Matthew
and John, which traditionally had had the function of showing
who Jesus was.

Schleiermacher's interpretation of the Papias text had inspired
this development. At the end of the 19th century it was however
possible to renounce the dubious Papias text, and write Q instead
of Λ. The *Oxyrhynchus Logia* appeared to provide a very much
more modern proof for the possibility of a sayings source. In
form criticism, in the strict German sense, *Logia* = wisdom sayings
of Jesus signified little over against the kerygma as the all-
controlling basis of Christianity. In place of the *two* sources Mark
and Q there appeared a single source, the kerygma.

Logia and also Q had accordingly become terms which had
purely technical value: Matthew parallel to Luke minus Mark = Q.
James M. Robinson however called to mind the difference between λόγοι and λόγια, but with it at the same time some fundamental problems not only in gospel research but in theology as a
whole. It is certainly no accident that the revival of Q research in
the 60s shows a connection with the new quest for the historical
Jesus.

My own work on Q began more than 25 years ago, without my
being conscious of such connections. I used the term
'Logienquelle', without knowing whence it really came and what
it implied. The whole history of research is very meagerly presented in my book, and Papias evidently not once mentioned. The
actual situation at the time was more important. On the one side

Hans-Theo Wrege claimed to have proved that there never was
any Q.[16] On the other side William R. Farmer's battle against the
two-document hypothesis began at that time.[17] As it has proved,
there was a future for Q, but at the end of the 60s that future
could have appeared altogether more gloomy for anyone who was
seeking a place in the academic world with a work on Q.

The abundance of works on Q since then does not indeed prove
the existence of the sayings source, but rather that the theory
which lies at the base of its affirmation is plausible. My reflections
in this essay do not call Q into question. They may however perhaps contribute something to the history of the Jesus tradition in
the *second* century, when the λόγοι became λόγια. From this
there may possibly emerge perspectives both for the history of
synoptic research and also for problems of contemporary
research into Q.

4. When the Sayings of Jesus Became Logia

We return therefore to our starting point, the Papias fragment in
Eusebius. Little is known about the person of Papias. Not even the
dates of his life are reliably handed on, but he must have written
in the first half of the second century, probably as early as about
110.[18] It is the more regrettable that his work is preserved only in
fragments: Λογίων κυριακῶν ἐξήγησις in five books (λόγοι or
βίβλια). This title is mentioned in Eusebius, but appears also in
other witnesses, in Latin in Jerome: *explanatio sermonum Domini*,
while Rufinus translates *verborum dominicorum explanatio*. This
corresponds to ἐξήγησις τῶν κυριακῶν λόγων in a fragment of
Apollinaris of Laodicea culled from the catenae; *verba* is the
Latin translation of λόγοι, *sermones* of λόγια.

It is to be noted that the several columns of Papias' work could
be called λόγοι or βίβλια, while at the same time the title is
quoted with the key-word λόγιον. There is therefore in the
tradition clearly a distinction between the two words λόγος and
λόγιον. This holds in particular for the passages in which sayings
of Jesus or the apostles are called λόγος or λόγοι. The distinction

---

[16] *Die Überlieferungsgeschichte der Bergpredigt* (WUNT 9; Tübingen: 1968).

[17] *The Synoptic Problem* (New York and London: 1964). I had read this book
as early as 1965 or 1966, when Bill Farmer visited Heidelberg.

[18] Cf. Ulrich H. J. Körtner, *Papias von Hierapolis* (FRLANT 133; Göttingen: 1983), including a new edition of the fragments.

in the use of λόγια and λόγοι and other terms is to be noted especially in the longer fragment in Eusebius.

For the Greek word λόγιον, Liddell and Scott's *Greek-English Lexicon* (1056a) gives first of all: "oracle, esp. one preserved from antiquity,...more freq. in pl., oracles,...distd. fr. χρησμοί, Th, 2:8". From this it distinguishes: "2. τὰ λόγια κυρίου the *sayings* of the Lord. LXX Ps. 11 (12).6, cf. Act.Ap. 7:38, Ep.Rom. 3:2, 1 Ep.Pet. 4:11." Liddell and Scott thus assume that in the Greek of the Bible there was a meaning of λόγιον/λόγια ("sayings") which is different from that elsewhere in Greek ("oracles"). Yet the usual meaning of λόγιον is adequate both for the Old Testament references in the Septuagint and also for those in the New Testament. In every case the λόγια could be understood as "oracles, esp. one(s) preserved from antiquity".

This holds good for the Septuagint and for other Jewish literature in Greek. It also holds for the few New Testament references. In Acts 7:38, Rom 3:2 and Heb 5:12 λόγια (in the plural!) are "oracles" preserved from the antiquity of Israel. In the remarkable use in 1 Pet 4:11, εἴ τις λαλεῖ, ὡς λόγια θεοῦ, what is required in the speaker is evidently the same quality possessed by God's own speech, namely to be as reliable as λόγια.

New Testament scholars are probably irritated by the catch-word "oracle", especially in the German tradition, which is pledged to a theology of the *Word*. But in other respects also oracles today scarcely rank any longer as reliable. Yet we should note the aspect "preserved from antiquity". We should also call to mind the fact that in the New Testament sayings of Jesus are never described as λόγια, and that even in the second century it is still λόγος not λόγιον, that is dominant when sayings of Jesus are quoted.

G. W. H. Lampe in his *Patristic Greek Lexicon* (805b-806a) also prefers a special significance "sayings of Christ" for the Christian occurrences. He gives first of all, as a translation for λόγιον, "utterance, saying", and notes under 3. "esp. of oracular or inspired utterances: a. pagan...,b. of utterances of OT prophets, prophecies." Under 3b. he mentions Papias' comment on Matthew, "if λ. here denotes OT prophetic proof-texts; to be included under d. infra, if λ. here denotes sayings of Christ", and the title of Papias' work, "where λ. may similarly denote either *prophecies* relating to the Lord or *sayings* of the Lord". Under 3c. he notes: "plur. of OT scriptures in gen.", under 3d. "sayings of the Lord", for which he adduces Polycarp, *Phil* 7.1 in addition to Papias.

Like Liddell and Scott, Lampe also thus assumes a special Christian significance "sayings (of the Lord)" for λόγια.[19] The logic behind this is presumably the same as we found in Schleiermacher and Holtzmann: in the 2nd century there was still no New Testament canon; hence sayings of *Jesus*, with which we are here concerned, could not be understood as λόγια in the proper sense ("preserved from antiquity"!). In the interval however it has become beyond dispute that in the 2nd century the canon of the New Testament was still in its beginnings, even the canon of the (four) Gospels. No defence against a misunderstanding is therefore any longer necessary, but it is possible to ask why we should find in Papias and other authors of the second century a tendency to describe sayings of Jesus as λόγια, not merely as λόγοι, and thus to understand these sayings of Jesus as inspired divine utterances from the past.

If we accept the definition of the Greek word λόγιον as "divine utterance, especially one preserved from antiquity, more frequently in the plural", then it gives good sense in regard to the Papias fragments. For κυριακὰ λόγια (plural!) are then sayings of the Lord gaining the quality of divine utterances ("oracles") from the past. Papias knew the gospels of Matthew and Mark, both of which he examined with an eye to such λόγια. In both he found deficiencies, which he sought to remove with his work Λογίων κυριακῶν ἐξήγησις. But in that Papias understood the sayings of Jesus as λόγια in the strict sense, he gave a new significance to *them*, not to the Greek word λόγιον. He thus stands at the beginning of a development which can be traced in the 2nd century.

Before we turn briefly to this further development, a possible objection to my view of the Papias text must be cleared away. Papias' interest, it might be said, lies in the *oral* tradition. This is naturally correct, for that is why Papias whenever he could endeavoured to learn what had been handed down through the presbyters from the first generation of the apostles. In this connection however the key-word λόγια, with the use of which I am concerned, never occurs, but instead a whole series of familiar terms for the transmission of tradition. It is Papias' own aim in the first place to create from such tradition a λογίων κυριακῶν ἐξήγησις.

Apart from this title of his work, the word λόγιον occurs *only* in the comments on Matthew and Mark. Evidently he saw in these two gospels, as *written* compilations of the Jesus tradition, the first efforts on the way in which he himself wished to carry to comple-

---

[19] Cf. also G. Kittel, *ThWNT* IV 140-145.

tion with his work. The deficiencies which he censured can thus be defined more exactly. Mark did indeed note down the sermons of Peter, but not in the requisite τάξις. The reason for this was his source: Peter had not orientated his teachings (διδασκαλίαι) towards a σύνταξις of the Lord's λόγια. Matthew on the other hand had brought the λόγια together in the Hebrew tongue, but there were in Papias' opinion varying ἑρμηνεῖαι.

Papias wished to remove the shortcomings of the two *written* presentations of the Jesus tradition, and to this end he attempted to obtain as much as possible of the *oral* tradition. The reason for this view was however that he regarded such Jesus tradition as *Logia*, and accordingly gave to it a new quality. In the interpretation of the Papias text we therefore have to distinguish between the semantic problem of the meaning of the Greek word λόγιον, or in the plural λόγια, and the relation of oral and written material in the Jesus tradition. The two problems lie on different levels and should not be confused with one another.[20]

A use of λόγια comparable to that of Papias occurs only rarely in the 2nd century. These few passages are all the more striking. Polycarp, *(2) Phil* 7:1, has already appeared in our summary of Lampe's exposition. Otherwise probably only Justin, *Dial.* 18.1, calls for mention. In both authors it is to be observed that in other passages they presuppose normative written versions of the Jesus tradition. It is only with Irenaeus that we find throughout the combination τὰ λόγια τοῦ κυρίου, or in Latin *Domini sermones*, as a description of Jesus tradition.[21]

This is on the one hand not surprising, for Irenaeus knew Papias' work and we owe to him one of the few fragments that have survived. On the other hand it is surprising that Irenaeus still employs the category of the λόγια/*sermones* alongside the four Gospels. It had been the tendency in the 2nd century to single out as normative a particular version of the Jesus tradition, be it Papias' work, or Marcion's expurgated Gospel of Luke, Gospel harmonies as in Justin, Tatian and others, or finally local peculiarities in the preference for individual Gospels. Over against this Irenaeus declared *four* Gospels (and Acts) to be normative. In this he had long-standing success, for in the West at least it was scarcely ever debated in the further discussion on the canon; the only

---

[20] Unlike Körtner, whose "Doktorvater" I was, I would not explain Papias' work on the basis of his comment on Mark, and hence understand the Logia as what Jesus said and did.

[21] Cf. *Haer.* IV praef. 1; 41.4.

questions were the compass of the Apostolicon and the validity of the Apocalypse.

In Irenaeus the λόγια τοῦ κυρίου remained normative beside the four Gospels.[22] The Latin translation *Domini sermones* indicates a certain shifting of the term. Irenaeus with the whole of the 2nd century understood the Gospels as witnesses to the preaching of the apostles. The λόγια τοῦ κυρίου or *Domini sermones* were contained *in* them, and not to be sought outside of them. But the retention of this category made it possible for church fathers to adduce also sayings of Jesus which did not correspond with those versions of the text of the four Gospels which ranked as canonical.

The problem of the canon was thus brought to a solution, so far as the Gospels were concerned, in Irenaeus. Nevertheless the λόγια τοῦ κυρίου continued to survive as an independent category alongside them. This meant acceptance of Papias' attempt to understand the Jesus tradition as divine utterances preserved from the past, if not from antiquity. However, this was done no longer in a new work alongside the Gospels but within the canon of the four Gospels.

A second aspect is the bringing together of λόγια and ἑρμηνεία(ι). It appears in Papias from the point of view of the translation and interpretation of the λόγια. Mark worked as translator (ἑρμηνευτής) of the teachings of Peter, in which the λόγια were contained.[23] Matthew's compilation of the λόγια in the Hebrew tongue met with various translations or interpretations (ἑρμηνεῖαι). What Papias wanted to present was an ἐξήγησις of the λόγια. Both ἑρμηνεῖαι and ἐξήγησις could however also be understood as communication from the divine sphere in human language. In the New Testament writings there is the problem of the ἑρμηνεῖαι of glossolalia, but also the statement in John 1:18 about the imparting of revelation through the Son (ἐξηγήσατο). In the case of both words linguistic investigations lead into the world of poesy, of divination, and also that of oracles.[24]

Less attention has so far been paid to a type of early Christian literature which in such fashion combines sayings of Jesus with ἑρμηνεῖαι. The discovery of a papyrus from the fourth (?) cen-

---

[22] Cf. Hans von Campenhausen, *The Formation of the Christian Bible*, (Philadelphia: 1972).

[23] Cf. alongside this the tradition about a certain Glaucias as Peter's interpreter: Clem. Alex., *Strom.* VII 106.4.

[24] On this (very briefly) J. Behm, *ThWNT* II 659-662 and 910.

tury, included in New Testament manuscript lists as 𝔓⁸⁰, has however shown that it is not simply a late phenomenon to conceive of
sayings of Jesus as oracles or fortune telling. Rather does such a
use reach back to a relatively early period.[25]

Here it is a question chiefly if not exclusively of texts from the
Gospel of John. In each case a quotation from a discourse of
Jesus is set at the beginning, and then after the stereotyped
catchword ἑρμηνεία there follows a short interpretation. For this
there was evidently a well-defined repertoire, which could however
be applied at will to different texts. For our purpose such a brief
reference is sufficient. It shows a use of sayings of Jesus in which
they were provided with ἑρμηνεῖαι, and the sayings of Jesus were
understood as oracles. That they ranked as divine utterances preserved from antiquity may surprise us; but this is the claim with
which the sayings of Jesus are quoted.

The interpretation of the Papias fragment in Eusebius is in the
first place a philological problem. Usually it is resolved by inserting "sayings of Jesus" for κυριακὰ λόγια, "translation" and
"translator" for ἑρμηνεία and ἑρμηνευτής, and "explanation"
or "interpretation" for ἐξήγησις. In view of the concentration of
words which as logion, hermeneutics and exegesis have entered
not only into technical language, it is not surprising that the treatments of the text often become mirrors for their authors' conceptions of the tasks of New Testament scholarship.

The solution here proposed is not in any way intended to define
afresh what should be done in New Testament scholarship. But it
gives the Papias text–in my opinion–a good sense in the context
of the 2nd century. Papias was the first to understand the sayings
of Jesus as oracles preserved from antiquity, but down to his own
time found only poor or even false translations and/or interpretations of such oracles, and wished himself to supply the interpretation which with oracles is always necessary. He knew the gospels
of Mark and Matthew, but for various reasons considered them
unsatisfactory. He wanted to set his own work in their place. He
offered a new collection of his own of the Λόγια, which was
founded on the written versions and also upon oral tradition.

---

[25] Cf. Bruce M. Metzger, "Greek Manuscripts of John's Gospel with
'hermeneiai'" in *Text and Testimony* (*Festschrift* A. F. J. Klijn), ed. T. Baarda *et
al.* (Kampen: 1988) 162-169; Kurt Treu, "*P.Berol.* 21315: Bibelorakel mit
griechischer und koptischer Hermeneia" *Archiv für Papyrusforschung* 37 (1991)
55-60, who admittedly would date 𝔓⁸⁰ very much later.

Papias did not succeed with his venture. The 2nd century produced a large number of other attempts to preserve binding versions of the Jesus tradition. For the West at any rate they end with
Irenaeus' solution of a canon of the four Gospels. Combined with
the speeches of Acts they ranked as documents of the teaching of
the apostles. But in them were contained also τὰ λόγια τοῦ
κυρίου/*Domini sermones*, although this now meant something
other than what Papias aimed at in his work.

Papias found a late echo in Jerome. He probably did not know
Papias' work at first hand but had read the quotations in Irenaeus
and Eusebius and took from them the information about a
"Hebrew Gospel of Matthew", and even asserted that he had himself translated it.[26] This contributed materially to the confusion
which reigns in research into the so-called "Jewish Christian"
gospels. But as mediator of the Greek tradition to the Latin-
speaking area he kept alive the memory of gospels of this kind
outside the canon.

From Schleiermacher to Walter Bauer the Gospel of the
Hebrews, or the other traditions associated with this title, played a
major role. Schleiermacher saw the λόγια of Matthew, of which
Papias speaks, as the common basis for the Jewish-Christian
gospels, including the only one that became canonical, that of
Matthew. For Bauer, the Gospel of the Hebrews and that of the
Egyptians formed the two sources for the early period of Christianity in Egypt; he assigned the *Oxyrhynchus Logia* to the Gospel
of the Hebrews.[27]

5. Papias, The Oxyrhynchus Logia and the Gospel of Thomas

The canon of the four Gospels ensured an uninterrupted transmission of their versions of the text, whereas otherwise early Jesus
traditions are preserved only in fragments. We do not have complete texts of the Gospels which became canonical before the
great codices of the 4th and 5th centuries. Older manuscripts than
these have only become known in the last 100 years, among them
𝔓45 (3rd century) with text from the four canonical Gospels and
Acts. This papyrus is at the same time the only manuscript of the
Gospel of Mark before the 4th century. Without their

[26] Commentary on Mt 12:13.
[27] *Rechtgläubigkeit und Ketzerei im ältesten Christentum* (Tübingen: 1934)
55f. ([ET: *Orthodoxy and Heresy in Earliest Christianity* (Philadelphia: 1971)
50ff.])

canonisation we should possess, for Mark and the other Gospels which rank as canonical, only fragments from a period from which we now have more and more discoveries of apocryphal gospels. The fixation of the canon of the four Gospels and Acts in Irenaeus is evidently also the presupposition for the extensively preserved papyrus codex $\mathfrak{P}^{45}$.[28]

At first only papyrus was available as writing material, not yet parchment. The special climatic conditions of Egypt made it possible for papyrus to be preserved there over centuries. Our knowledge of the early tradition of the gospels therefore rests almost exclusively upon their reception in Egypt. Here the Gospel of John enjoyed a clear pre-eminence, with Matthew following at some distance.

It is to these special conditions in Egypt that we also owe our knowledge of the *Gospel of Thomas*. It was only through the discovery of this gospel in a codex from Nag Hammadi that it became possible to determine that the three manuscripts of the *Oxyrhynchus Logia* belong together. And it is only the Coptic text which enables us to assign sayings of Jesus in the church fathers to this gospel. For the *Gospel of Thomas* we thus possess a complete text in Coptic, in a single manuscript dating from about 400, three fragmentary Greek manuscripts from the 3rd century for a fifth or less of the total text, and a few quotations in early fathers. Who would venture to reconstruct one of the Gospels which became canonical on such a basis? But again, who would, for example, without knowledge of the Gospel of Mark, interpret $\mathfrak{P}^{88}$ (4th century) as a fragment of an independent work, and not merely as a variant to Matthew or Luke?

That there is no "Papyrus Q" cannot therefore be any argument against the assumption that Matthew and Luke independently of each one another used such a sayings collection in addition to Mark. The circumstances of the transmission of the Jesus tradition are so haphazard that Q would have had to be known in Egypt for us to possess a fragment of it. Even for the Gospel of Mark, as was said above, there is only a single manuscript, and that derives from circles which already accepted the canon of Irenaeus.

Q is a product of modern gospel research. This has taken its origin from three models one after another: Papias, the *Oxyrhynchus Logia* and the *Gospel of Thomas*. At the beginning

---

[28] A papyrus discovery shows that Irenaeus was already known in Egypt at an early date.

stood Schleiermacher's misunderstanding of the Papias fragment. In what was for his time a modern fashion he interpreted it in the sense of what could pass as the task of gospel research: older sources had to be sought behind the extant gospels; it was a question of translation (ἑρμηνεία) and interpretation (ἐξήγησις).[29] But above all sayings of Jesus were understood no longer as divine utterances, oracles, especially ones preserved from antiquity, but as "words of the Lord".

Schleiermacher's interpretation of the Papias text helped Holtzmann, against Strauss, to find in Q the sayings of the *historical* Jesus. Strauss had founded his picture of Christianity upon the Gospel of John. Against this Holtzmann set up Mark and Q as the two sources which in his opinion were alone historically reliable. Yet the Gospel of John is the best attested of all the Gospels in the early period!

The discovery of the *Oxyrhynchus Logia* again helped to cut the two-document hypothesis free from the dubious interpretation of the Papias fragments. Now it seemed to be possible, in a fashion modern for this period, to give Q a foundation from archaeological evidence. Hence one could dispense with the siglum Λ and set the apparently more neutral siglum Q in its place. The sayings of Jesus in *POxy* 1, 654 and 655 did not however match the portrait which the History-of-Religion school had drawn of the historical Jesus as an apocalyptist. In Bultmann's *History of the Synoptic Tradition* they therefore remain *wisdom* sayings, and as such were not typical for Jesus.[30]

There were various reasons for the new beginning of Q research in the 60s. One of them was that the two-document hypothesis became acceptable for Catholic exegesis, which opened the way for a concern with Q in the proper sense.[31] Another was the New Quest for the historical Jesus. But with this new interest in Q the new texts from Nag Hammadi were also connected, and especially the *Gospel of Thomas*, which became accessible in full in 1956 or 1959, and through it again *POxy* 1, 654 and 655, for which

---

[29] Schleiermacher here expressed his sympathy for Papias over against the negative judgements handed down from the early Church.

[30] Cf. the remarks of James M. Robinson, "The Q Trajectory: Between John and Matthew via Jesus" in *The Future of Early Christianity (Festschrift* Helmut Koester), ed. B. A. Pearson (Minneapolis: 1991) 173-194.

[31] Cf. however Josef Schmid, *Matthäus und Lukas: Eine Untersuchung des Verhältnisses ihrer Evangelien* (BibS[F] 23/2-4; Freiburg: 1930), who worked on Q without mentioning Q.

Joseph A. Fitzmyer and Otfried Hofius put forward reconstructions in 1959 and 1960.[32]

There appears to be a widespread consensus that Q is stamped
by the motif of opposition to "this generation", but with it also
the motif of final judgement. Here the apocalyptic interpretation
of the History-of-Religion school lives on. The question is however in debate as to whether there were older versions of Q which
did not yet interpret the preaching of Jesus apocalyptically, in this
comparable to the *Gospel of Thomas* or older strata contained in
it.

This question may here be left aside. In the *Gospel of Thomas* a
redactional framework can be recognised in its prologue (Logion
1). What is requisite is a ἑρμηνεία of the λόγοι ἀπόκρυφοι which
Jesus spoke (ἐλάλησεν).[33] The introduction of the individual
sayings then follows with λέγει in the present tense. The Greek
text of *POxy* 654 however shows that this prologue does not present the first of the logia, but sets at the head of all the logia what
Thomas said: "Whoever finds the interpretation of these sayings
will not experience death."

Here the sayings of Jesus are understood not yet as λόγια but
λόγοι of the living Jesus. With the passing of time, however, the
question must have become the more urgent: in what manner Jesus could be the living one. Mark already, then Matthew and
Luke, John, Papias, Tatian and many others right down to
Irenaeus attempted to establish in a specific textual version what
Jesus had said in the past, and this *Gospel of Thomas* also does.
But over and above that there was always the question of the
ἑρμηνεία, of how one should deal with the texts of the Jesus
tradition.

For the understanding of Q, Q 10:16 in the more original Lukan
version is important: "Whoever hears you hears me, and whoever
rejects you rejects me; and whoever rejects me rejects him who has
sent me." Here the sayings of Jesus are not "oracles preserved
from antiquity". They also do not need any ἑρμηνεία, translation
or interpretation. The living Jesus is present in those whom he has
sent out. Although Q was a text in written form, that which Jesus

---

[32] J. A. Fitzmyer, "The Oxyrhynchus Logoi of Jesus and the Coptic Gospel
according to Thomas," *ThSt* 20 (1959) 505-560, revised version in Id., *Essays
on the Semitic Background of the New Testament* (London: 1971) 355-433; O.
Hofius, "Das koptische Thomasevangelium und die Oxyrhynchus-Papyri Nr. 1,
654 und 655," *EvTh* 20 (1960) 21-42, 182-192.
[33] Cited above in note 13.

says is yet what they say whom he has sent. Their words are divine utterances, but as the words of contemporary prophets.

The *Gospel of Thomas* on the other hand demands a ἑρμηνεία of the sayings of Jesus in the present. Here there is a reflection of the problem of the distance between the time of the living Jesus and the present time, and this problem appears not only in the *Gospel of Thomas* but in all strata of the Jesus tradition. Papias first of all and then, in a manner influential for the future, Irenaeus declare the sayings of Jesus to be λόγια, and I need not repeat the semantic definition of λόγια yet again.

In 1988 we might have celebrated "150 years of Q", but who wanted to celebrate when it was only 150 years old and not 1950 *ab Q condita*? Q, the "Logienquelle", the Synoptic Sayings Source or Gospel–there are many names. Q was invented under circumstances that can be identified historically. Since then the two-document hypothesis belongs to the common heritage of various traditions of New Testament exegesis. Even today it is in rivalry with other solutions of the synoptic problem. But it has never been a problem of hypotheses or theories only; it is a question of the ἑρμηνεία of the sayings of Jesus decades and centuries later. What we call Q has had its consequences right through church history, even if as tradition taken into the Gospel of Matthew. The same holds for the Gospel of Mark. Only for a relatively short period, by comparison with the centuries of church history, has there been an influence from Q and Mark themselves on theology.

The Gospel of John however has been the most important throughout church history. Here the christological questions found their answers, or did not. The modern christological question on the other hand appears to be founded upon a historical Jesus won from Mark and Q. The sayings of Jesus are scrutinised for their authenticity, and do not in any way rank as *Logia* in the strict sense. But it would be too little to understand ἑρμηνεία and ἐξήγησις merely in a philological sense as translation or historical interpretation, if the tasks of New Testament exegesis are to be mirrored in the Papias fragment.

CHAPTER SIX

PRESTIGE, PROTECTION AND PROMISE: A PROPOSAL FOR THE APOLOGETICS OF Q^2

Wendy Cotter, C.S.J.

The discussion of Q's stratigraphy naturally leads to a probing of the possible social contexts which would explain the orientation of the material. Although scholarly consensus is not unanimous, there is a general and growing support for the position of John Kloppenborg that of the two major strata of Q, the Wisdom speeches belong to an earlier stage of the document (Q^1) while the Judgement material demonstrates the controlling influence indicative of a later development in Q's composition (Q^2).[1] The shift in the character and scope of Q^2 has been attributed to an apologetic in the face of a failed Jewish mission. The proposal is well supported by the deuteronomistic pattern evinced in the argumentation and the prophetic rebukes.[2] At the same time these elements are part of what appears to be a broader and more public engagement of the world in general.

This paper will first discuss Q^1 and Q^2 with attention to three prominent areas of difference: a. Religious Identification; b. Cultural Script; c. Incentives and Rewards. The shift that is ob-

---

[1] For Q^1, we refer to six sets: (a) Q 6:20b-23b, 27-35, 36-45, 46-49; (b) 9:57-62; 10:2-11, 16; (c) 11:2-4, 9-13; (d) 12:2-7, 11-12; (e) 12:22b-31, 33-34; (f) 13:24; 14:26-27; 17:33; 14:34-35; perhaps 15:4-7, (8-10?); 16:13; 17:1-2, 3b-4, 5-6. For Q^2 we refer to five blocks of sayings: (a) Q 3:7-9, 16-17; (b) 7:1-10, 18-28, 31-35; 16:16; (c) 11:14-26; (27-28?), 29-32, 33-36, 39b-42b, 43-44, 46-52; (d) 12:39-40, 42-46, 49, 51-59; (e) 17:23-24, 26-30, 34-35; 19:12-27; 22:28-30. To this collection also we assign nine interpolations into the material of Q^1: (a) 6:23c; (b) 10:12; (c) 10:13-15; (d) 12:8-9; (e) 12:10; (f) 13:25-27; (g) 13:28-30; (h) 13:34-35; (i) 14:16-24. [Q^3 is assigned: (a) 4:1-13; (b) 11:42c; (c) 16:17.] Cf. John S. Kloppenborg, an unpublished paper, "Redactional Strata and Social History in the Sayings Gospel," n. 1.

[2] John S. Kloppenborg, *The Formation of Q* (Philadelphia: 1987) 167; Ivan Havener, *Q: The Sayings of Jesus* (Wilmington: 1987) 100-101; Burton L. Mack, *A Myth of Innocence* (Philadelphia: 1988) 85-86.

served in Q² will then be discussed in relation to the culture of the Greco-Roman world.

1. Q¹

Q¹ and Religious Identity

In examining Q¹ for the religious tradition in evidence one might suggest a search for the identity of the presumed Deity, the obligations concommitant with the participation in the movement, and any mention of heroes which signal a particular religious tradition.

The God of Q¹ is referred to as "the Most High" (6:35), and as "Father" (6:36; 11:2, 13; 12:30).[3] Both epithets find a place in the general religious climate of the Greco-Roman world. Ὑψίστος is a frequent appellation for the central divine force such as Zeus[4] and ὁ πατήρ is applied to both the god of the Stoic Epicurus[5] and of the Jewish prophet Malachi (2:10).

The obligations imposed by the Deity include a trustful surrender to this great kindly Providence (Q 12:4-7, 11-12, 22-30, 33-34), an imitation of God's magnanimity in all dealings with others (Q 6:27-28, 30-36), the preaching of the nearness of the God's "reign" or "kingdom" and the healing of the sick (Q 9:59-62; 10:2-9).

Only one person is mentioned by name in Q¹ and this is the Jewish king Solomon (Q 12:27). In order to understand the reference in the saying, the listener should know that Solomon is an example of the epitome of worldly magnificence. No other knowledge of him is required. Since this hero is Jewish, one wonders if there might be other signals on the material to indicate that either the composer or the presumed reader share that particular religious tradition. There is no mention of Law, or of the prophets. There is no reference to Scripture. Q 12:30 refers to the

---

[3] Even should Q 10:21 be accepted as Q¹ material the title, "Lord of heaven and earth" cannot be appropriated as an indication of the God of the Jews.

[4] A. D. Nock, "The Gild of Zeus Hypsistos," *Essays on Religion in the Ancient World* (2 vols; Oxford: 1972) 1.414-443. Cf. G. H. R. Horsley, *New Documents Illustrating Early Christianity* I (North Ryde, NSW: 1981) 25-28; Franz Cumont, *Oriental Religions in Roman Paganism* (New York: 1956) 62-63.

[5] Epictetus, "That God is the Father of Humankind," *The Discourses of Epictetus* (2 vols; London: 1956) 1.1.3.

world by "the nations" and this does suggest that the audience is presumed to be Jewish.

The major religious theme which seems to dominate the community's strivings is the nearness of the "kingdom of God" (6:20; 9:60, 62; 10:9, 11; 11:2; 12:31; 13:20). Yet this expression does not occur in the canonical Hebrew scriptures. Futhermore, attempts to trace it to apocalyptic influence have met with difficulty. Burton Mack's recent research causes him to conclude, "The combination of ideas that early followers of Jesus invested in the term kingdom of God does not appear anywhere in the canonical or apocalyptic literature."[6] However it does occur in three works of the Greco-Roman world, two of them from Jewish sources (Wisdom of Solomon 10:10; and Philo's *De specialibus legibus* 4) and the other a document from the second century (*Sentences of Sextus* 311).[7]

Q¹ and Cultural Script[8]

The injunctions of Q plainly propose a perception and a behavior which run counter to the Mediterranean culture of first century. In Lucian's dialogue *Nigrinus* the new convert to philosophy recalls the "blessings" which he once sought to obtain, "wealth and reputation, dominion and honour, yes and purple and gold."[9]

Within that honour / shame society[10] the dynamics of the institutions follow rules which guarantee public esteem or public disgrace. As Nigrinus' disciple tells us, "It is not so much being rich that they like as being congratulated on it."[11] In this system one's honour is open to constant challenge. In the case of equals, one of two responses is required to maintain one's public esteem. Either the challenge is disdainfully rejected, or it is accepted in a pugilis-

---

[6] Cf. Mack, *A Myth of Innocence* 70, and for a review of the scholarly argumentation, n. 13.

[7] *Ibid.*, 73 n. 16.

[8] Bruce Malina, *Christian Origins and Cultural Anthropology* (Atlanta: 1986) 11. Sheldon R. Isenberg and Dennis E. Owen, "Bodies, Natural and Contrived: The Work of Mary Douglas," *Religious Studies Review* 3.1 (1977) 5-8.

[9] Lucian, *Nigrinus* 4.

[10] Malina, *The New Testament World* (Atlanta: 1981) 25-50, especially 30-33.

[11] Lucian, *Nigrinus* 23.

tic spirit, with retaliation blow for blow. A silent acceptance of the challenge incurs loss of one's honour.[12]

Nigrinus distanced his disciples from their society's value system by presenting them with the alternate example of Athens, a city where "Philosophy and Poverty have ever been their foster-brothers".[13] The ostentatious behavior of wealthy and pretentious visitors is curbed by the citizens' audible asides to each other about their amusing appearance and behavior. In this way, the strength of this society's "group" causes the visitors to modify their behavior and at least consider the values of Athens' society ("grid").[14]

Q's similar dissatisfaction with the society's superficial preoccupations of wealth, ambition and ultimately their honour before others closely resembles that of the philosophers. In particular the almost parallel counsels to Q's "missionaries" and those of the Cynics have drawn considerations of possible influence.[15]

The wisdom speeches of Q^1 engage the chief value of Greco-Roman society: one's honour before others. In Q 6:20-23 persons who are understood to be disgraced by their state, i.e. the poor, the hungry, the sorrowful, the objects of hatred and agression, are assured that their honour is secure for it is God who esteems and loves them. The kingdom is theirs (Q 6:20-23). Likewise, those who are victims of what would be considered dishonouring events, i.e. the blow of an enemy, the robbery of one's clothing, are encouraged to behave as though they were not being shamed. Therefore there is no pugilistic retaliation. But there is no passive submission either. The disciple is counselled to respond

---

[12] Malina, *The New Testament World* 32.
[13] Lucian, *Nigrinus* 13.
[14] Malina, *Christian Origins* 13-27.
[15] Carl Schneider, *Geistesgeschichte des antiken Christentums* (2 vols; München: 1954) 1.35; W. L. Knox, *Sources of the Synoptic Gospels* (Cambridge: 1957) 48, who also recognizes Stoic elements in the "kingdom" theme; *idem, Some Hellenistic Elements in Primitive Christianity* (London: 1944) 30; Howard C. Kee, *Community of the New Age* (Philadelphia: 1977) 104 and also Stoicism; Paul Hoffmann, *Studien zur Theologie der Logienquelle* (Münster: 1972) 318 and similarities with other philosophers / ascetics: Pythagoras and Bannus; Martin Hengel, *The Charismatic Leader and His Followers* (New York: 1981) 28, who amazingly, after his strenuous, convincing study of similarities between the philosophical materials and Q, dismisses the possibility of influence and returns to a scenario of Jewish, eschatological prophets: 88; Gerd Theissen, "Wanderradikalismus," *ZThK* 70 (1973) 256; Mack, *A Myth of Innocence* 68-69; and see also the discussion of the Cynics in John Kloppenborg's *Formation of Q* 306-325.

actively and positively with understanding and kindness, offering the other cheek, offering an even more important piece of attire. The paradigm for this behavior is God, who is kind to the "ungrateful and selfish" (Q 6:27-35). To adopt this perspective and behavior is to have a reward in heaven and to become a child of God. According to this wisdom teaching, since one's honour is secure in God, one cannot be robbed of it by another. And each person is free to manifest God's own kindness to even the most hostile.

Once liberated from the binding institutions which barter on one's honour, one is no longer involved in the various sorts of indebtedness. Not surprisingly, the "kingdom of God" sayings engage the freedom of this new reality. Thus, as we have seen, the poor who are the shamed publicly are blessed and the kingdom is theirs. They are to be freed from the controls of a system that forces them into situations of "debts" to secure some scraps of honour.

In the second mention of the kingdom (Q 9:60) the would-be follower expresses a conventionally pious desire to stay to bury his parents and is told, "Leave the dead to bury their own dead; but as for you, go and proclaim the kingdom of God." The disciple is asked to be free of the bonds of society's expectations regarding filial duties. Likewise in Q 9:62 the disciple's return to say goodbye to parents makes one unworthy of the call. They are still bound to the respectability code of the society.

Q 10:9 and Q 10:11 address the imperative of preaching the nearness of the kingdom and healing while living with the people of the town. The work of healing the sick seems to actively express the message of the preaching. We can only surmise that the nature of the message is positive and promises wholeness.

The possibility of a town's rejection elicits advice on how to properly respond. Without retaliation or scornful verbal abuse, and without simply slipping away, the disciples go into the streets for a pronouncement. That saying formally severs the disciples from the town. They take nothing with them, not even the dirt from its streets. But they remind the town of the fact that they have left something for which the town is responsible, and that is the preaching of the nearness of the kingdom. In this scenario the disciples do not behave as though they had lost face. Furthermore, Q 10:16 reminds the disciples that they are the representatives of God. Since no one can dishonour God, the rejection of the disciples rebounds back upon the town.

Finally in Q 13:18-19, and Q 13:20-21, the kingdom of God is compared to a mustard seed and leaven. Both are images that express the idea of rapid growth from something small, yet interestingly, these plants are often mentioned in a negative context. For example, Pliny the Elder observes,

> ...mustard, which with its pungent taste and fiery effect is extremely beneficial for health. It grows entirely wild, though it is improved by being transplanted: but on the other hand when it has once been sown it is scarcely possible to get the place free of it, as the seed when it falls germinates at once.[16]

As for leaven, it is mentioned in the Hebrew scriptures as a forbidden substance in the bread of the Passover (Ex 12:15-20; 13:3-7; 34:18). In the New Testament, with the exception of these two sayings from Q, the context is also pejorative: (a) the leaven of the Pharisees (Mt 16:5-12 / Mk 8:14-21 / Lk 12:1) which Matthew interprets as their arrogance; (b) Paul's exhortation to cast out the old leaven (1 Cor 5:6) with reference to sexual impurity infecting the community; and (c) his observation to the Galatians (5:9) that "a little leaven leavens the whole lump" referring to the false doctrine that is spreading through his communities.

Therefore, although both mustard and leaven are excellent images for a type of natural agent demonstrating amazing growth, both are somewhat too powerful, a little too much beyond human control. And here one wonders if there is not a wry humour at work in their choice as images of the kingdom's strong and counter-cultural effects.

The call of the disciple to leave the superficial values of society, to actively adopt a new perception of honour-designation and to live in such a way as to replace the stifling institutions which foster those values with a new relating signifies a community of low-grid. At the same time, although the disciples are living a life contrary to the expectation of the majority, they do not seem to manifest much interior organization as a group. There are counsels concerning their living within the towns they serve but no guidelines for roles within the community itself. And we do not sense any group pressure on an individual to conform to this new perception. Each person is to make his or her own responsible decision. For this reason, the Q[1] material suggests a community tend-

---

[16] Pliny the Elder, *Natural History* 19.170.

ing towards "weak group". This combination of "weak group / low grid" produces its own type of community:

> Weak group / low grid social formations might best be imagined as groupings of individuals each of whom feels that he or she stands alone even in the presence of other individuals. The main criterion for meaningful living in this quadrant is contentment, a contentment deriving from opposition to the social thrust of the quadrant from which the individual derives.[17]

Within this grouping there is no conflict between the society and the individuals. The belief is one of effervescent enthusiasm that the positive power of love and kindness can change the world. Concommitant with this perspective of the innate goodness in the world there is also a sense that prayer is simple, warm and direct. In this quadrant the important element is the wonderful freedom of the spirit so that although one's own body may need attention, one can also undergo great renunciation with no alarm (Q 12:4-7).[18]

The orientation of the "weak group / low grid" community coheres well with the positive spirit in the wisdom speeches of Q^1. There are no reproaches or demands for repentance from sin. The hostile acts of opponents are not to be understood as damaging to honour. The proponents are to receive understanding and kindness. The community has its own fresh prayer in which it addresses God as "Father". Everyone is urged to trustful reliance on the Providence of God both in the body's necessities and in times of persecution. The disciples are willing to renounce the comforts of a stable home life to take on the life of the emissary of the Kingdom.[19]

Q^1: Incentives and Rewards

The specific mention of a reward occurs in only three of the ninety-five sayings attributed to Q^1. Those who have endured hatred on account of the Son of man will rejoice because their reward is great in heaven (Q 6:23). Similarly those who treat the hostile with kindness will have their reward in heaven and be children of God (Q 6:35). Finally, those who have sold all to give to the poor will have treasure in heaven that will never fail. But

---

[17] Malina, *Christian Origins* 58.
[18] *Ibid.* 13-27, especially 14.
[19] Havener, *Q: The Sayings of Jesus* 165.

what does μισθός actually mean? And in what way will one experience the treasure in heaven? With no images or further teachings we can only surmise that the subject of these rewards was not an issue of particular importance. The subject which does seem to occupy the community is the kingdom and the way in which disciples may faithfully spread the news of its nearness. It must be that the incentives and rewards of the community are found there, in the actual participation in the kingdom's coming. The news of the kingdom bestows a new dignity on the ordinary populace, assures God's watchful providence over their life, calls for a life of love that makes the disciple a child of God. We can only surmise that it was chiefly the quality of their present, their participation in the nearing kingdom which gave the community of Q^1 their sustenance and their joy.

Conclusion

The sayings of Q^1 do not clearly identify one particular religious tradition. The center of the religious striving is located in the bright and reassuring teaching that God's kingdom is near. With respect to cultural script the community of Q^1 demonstrates the characteristics of a "weak group / low grid". The values of the society and the institutions that support them are supplanted. A new value system featuring honour and love takes its place. On the issue of institutions to foster this system, Q^1 is not strong. Neither is the sense of group organization. Nevertheless the spirit is confident relying on God's providence. The incentives and rewards for the members are located in the present for the most part. Membership as a disciple brings its own sense of honour and worthiness and assures them of God's special considerations and even a hope for a heavenly reward.

2. Q^2

Q^2 and Religious Identity

The God of Q^2 is defined as the God of the Jews, not by the addition of new epithets but by the associations of the material with the Hebrew scriptures and heroes.

The scriptures are quoted twice by Jesus, once to verify his identity as the Coming One (Q 7:22; cf. Is 61:1-2; 42:6b-7; 35:5-6a; 29:18, 19) and again to authenticate John as the Precursor

(Q 7:27; cf. Ex 23:20 / Mal 3:1). Q 11:49 also makes an appeal to "the Wisdom of God" (although the text-if the allusion is not to Wisdom herself-is not found in either the MT or LXX): "I will send them prophets and apostles, some of whom they will kill and persecute." Scriptural allusions may be present in Q 10:15 (cf. Is 14:13a, 15), 12:52-53 (cf. Micah 7:6), 13:35 (cf. Jer 22:5; Ps 117:26 [LXX]), and 13:27 (cf. Ps 6:9a).[20]

The direct mention of the Law occurs in Q 16:16 and Q 16:17 and the abuses of its observance are the criticisms brought against the Jewish leaders (Q 11:39b, 41, 42, 46). The only groups identified are the Jewish societies of the Pharisees and Scribes (Q 11: 39b-42; 46-52).

In particular, the heroes who set precedent in Q² all belong to Jewish tradition: Abraham (Q 3:8; 13:28), Isaac, Jacob (Q 13:28), Jonah (Q 11:30, 32), the Queen of the South (Q 11:31); Solomon (Q 11:31), Abel (Q 11:51), Zechariah (Q 11:51), Noah (Q 13:26-27), Isaac (Q 13:28), Jacob (Q 13:28), and Lot (Q 17:28). Unlike the reference to Solomon in Q¹ (Q 12:27), the reader would be expected to know something of the sagas connected with all of these figures in order to understand the import of the sayings. In other words the community adopts the figures of the Jewish tradition to communicate the significance of their own identity.

The theme which dominates the material of Q² is one of coming judgement. Unlike the "reign of God" material of Q¹, this call to repent before the judgement of God finds ample parallels in the Jewish scriptures. What O, H. Steck has demonstrated as the Deuteronomistic motif[21] provides the pattern for Q²'s posture toward Israel: the people sin; they are sent a prophet who warns them of punishment; they will not repent and so they face the coming wrath of God.[22]

Against this Jewish background the Q community clearly identifies itself with the role of the Jewish prophets (Q 6:23c; 11:47-51; 13:28-29, 34; 22:28-30.)

---

[20] O. H. Steck, *Israel und das gewaltsame Geschick der Propheten.* (WMANT 23; Neukirchen-Vluyn: Neukirchener Verlag, 1967).

[21] The theme of repentance as necessary to receive the kingdom is not found in Q¹ with the exception of Q 17:3-4 and even here Luke's μετανοία does not find concurrence in Matthew's ἀκούω. Furthermore the context of this saying deals with the forgiveness of a repentant brother or sister, not a primary prerequisite for entering the kingdom.

[22] Malina, *The New Testament World* 41.

Q^2 and Cultural Script

Q^2 shares the "low grid" of Q^1. But the manner in which Q^2 makes its protest is quite distinct . The community finds its identity in the ancient role of Israel's persecuted prophets (Q 6:23c; 11:47-51; 13:28-29, 34; 22:28-30).

Once this role is adopted any rejection or resistance to the community is given an honourable significance. And the material of the Q^2 stratum indicates that the honour of the community is an issue of importance, as it is not for Q^1. We notice that Q^2 adopts one or other of the two methods to save face. The criticism of their heroes John and Jesus receive either a scornful dismissal (Q 7:31-35) or tough retaliatory condemnation (Q 11:39-42; 13:34-35). Similarly the rejection of the Pharisees and the Scribes are countered by the prophetic woes against them (Q 11:39b-44, 46-48, 49-52).

Even the speeches of Q^1 which call the disciple to relinquish the quest for public honour in order to rely on Providence are shifted to serve Q^2's perspective. In Q 6:20b-49 the poor, hungry and hated are said to be blessed but the reason changes. Q 6:23c connects the suffering with the lives of the prophets. Because this speech is placed after the dark threats of John against the smug (Q 3:7-9, 16-17), Q 6:23 carries the threat of punishment against all who have caused suffering to the members of the community.

Similarly, in the case of the rejected missionaries (Q 10:2-16), the injunctions that teach non-retaliation (Q 10:10-11) are changed. The saying of Q 10:13-14 dramatically condemns the towns in a fiery backlash of prophetic judgement.

It is clear that the representatives of religious presumption in Q^2 are the unrepentant Jews. And as we have seen, Q^2 denounces their hypocrisy. At the same time, Q^2 uses this prophetic strength to affirm the Gentiles. In fact all examples of sincere conversion in Q^2 are Gentiles: the centurion whose faith surpasses anything Jesus has ever seen in Israel (Q 7:1-10); the Ninevites who respond to Jonah's preaching (Q 11:30, 32); and the Queen of the South who journeys "from the ends of the earth" to receive Solomon's wisdom (Q 11:31). These converted Gentiles will rise to judge "this generation" for their hard-heartedness because "something greater" than either Jonah or Solomon is here. And in Q 12:8-9 and Q 22:28-30 it is clear that the community of Q^2 is open to Gentile membership.

By means of the prophetic identification then, the community has an honourable explanation for any Jewish opposition against their movement, and a ready argument for their openness to Gentile membership. In this way, the community can continue to claim for itself the public esteem connected with an ancient religion, while opposing the conventions that it sees as a hypocritical collusion with society.

These observations indicate that Q² is "low grid" as is Q¹. But the character of its social formation seems quite distinct. There is a stronger sense of community pressure in Q 12:39-46 and Q 19:12-27. The teaching on family divisions in Q 12:52-53 take on a different character than in Q 9:59-62. In the Q¹ sayings it is the social system's expectations which are challenged. But in Q 12:49-53 the examples suggest that the disciple is still at home or nearby, and the saying justifies the rifts that occur right within the larger family complex. Furthermore, this circumstance is given a holy authority in that Jesus claims that this situation fits precisely into his expectations and deliberate plans. The Jesus who brings fire to the earth echoes the promise of John (3:16-17). Another sign of community formation occurs in Q 12:57-59 where it appears that members of the community are being brought to court. Unlike the Q¹ counsel of Q 12:11-12 where the disciple waits for the Spirit to direct his or her defense, this saying urges the disciple to quickly settle matters beforehand. Now, the reason given is that it will be less expensive to do so. And this is hardly a consideration in Q¹. The prosaic character of this advice suggests a settled community with practical problems.

These sayings indicate a community which demonstrates an inclination to "strong group". The "strong group / low grid" communities are described by Malina as a network of interrelated sets of circles:

> Each circle represents a group related in multiple fashion to other groups while vying with still other groups in the attempt to acquire what the society considers significant and to maintain those acquisitions in spite of porous boundaries...The problem is how to maintain what one inherits, has ascribed to him or her or acquires. Life is a constant challenge and hassle. Thus strong group / low grid perceives all human beings as divided into insiders and outsiders.[23]

Q² demonstrates that it regards the community's honour and credibility as significant values to be defended and hopefully maintained. The good reputation of its heroes matters and the esteem of its members in the midst of external and internal conflicts

---

[23] Suetonius, *Divus Augustus* 93.

is a vital concern. All of these problems are addressed, and favourably so, by the identification with the ancient and recognized religion of the Jews, and then by appropriating the particular traditions and sagas of the prophets. In this way the Q^2 community is almost *expected* to be marginal. And therefore it can both contest its society and still win an honourable place for its membership as it does so.

Q^2 and Rewards

In Q^1 we saw that only three of the sayings mentioned rewards for membership and they were rather vague. In Q^2 there are four sayings and they display more definition. Two of these are indirect, appearing in statements of coming judgement against unrepentant Jews. Q 3:17 promises that "he will gather his wheat into the granary, but the chaff he will burn with unquenchable fire." Believers can expect to be among those saved from destruction. Q 13:28 warns the presumptuous Jews that the Judgement will hold ignominy and suffering for them as they see Abraham, Isaac and Jacob and all the prophets enter with the faithful Gentiles while they are refused entrance. And Q 13:29 promises that everyone—the patriarchs, prophets and those who are faithful— will banquet together in the kingdom. The other two sayings are directed to community members. Q 12:9 is an ultimatum that warns the members against any denial of the Son of Man "before people". Their choice to confess the Son of man or not will merit the same behaviour of the Son of man before the angels of God. In this saying a type of city is presupposed where the angels function as the rulers who authorize the credentials of incoming officials. The Son of man will be there to speak on behalf of all those faithful to his reputation on earth. The fourth saying closes the document promising that those who have been with the Son of man will become the magistrates pronouncing judgement on the twelve tribes of Israel.

The first observation to be made is that the subject of eternal reward is much more of an issue here than in the Q^1 stratum. Second, the time for the reward seems to be located only in the forthcoming future. Third, the reward comes to the faithful via a frightening visitation of the "Coming One" who will destroy the unrepentant with fire. Punishments are nowhere mentioned in Q^1. Fourth, the kingdom concept adopts the conventions of a city with its administrators, prominent figures, and magistrates. All of the positions and the activities are ones that connote great honour, mutual respect and the luxury of plenty. That is, the main feature of the kingdom is the security and prestige that it awards to all of its members. Fifth, the privilege of membership makes one a prophet and a fitting child of Abraham. Thus the promises to Abraham belong to all. Sixth, universality marks the membership of the kingdom. There is no exclusivity on the basis of either Jewish birth or observance of laws. The Law is recognized (Q 16:17) but Q² does explain how it is observed. Seventh, these rewards can be assured by means of any appeal to the saving God of the scriptures.

Conclusion

The religious identity claimed by Q² is clearly Jewish. Within that ancient tradition the community finds coherence with the prophetic tradition and its call to repentance and preparation for the coming Judgement. Although the community chastises the representatives of Jewish "respectability", the Pharisees and the Scribes, Q² shows that it searches for a respectability of its own in the face of humiliation and challenges. And although Q² will castigate "this generation" for its false wisdom and its obstinacy the community longs to be found wise and worthy by those who would listen and repent. Q² demonstrates the characteristics of the "strong group / weak grid" community that strives to protect its borders and maintain whatever gains it has made. There is the impression that there is not much in the present which acts like an incentive or a reward for the members, except their honour to be in continuity with the great prophets of Israel and the promise of their honour and happiness when they feast with the patriarchs and prophets in the kingdom.

3. The Apologetics of Q²

It is the forensic character of Q² which has suggested a defence for the community in the face of a failed Jewish mission. And this may well be the case. Yet it is the extent of the changes which suggests a much broader circumstance and purpose.

The Q² community appropriates to itself the promises of the Hebrew Scriptures as its right. According to this community the inheritors of the promise are God's prophets and holy ones. Being a "Jew" is not a factor in whether one may join the patriarchs and prophets in the kingdom, as Q^2 harshly warns.

As we have seen, the concept of "kingdom" occurring in Q^1 finds no parallel in the Hebrew Scriptures. The community responsible for Q^2 has defined the kingdom as a social entity and embedded it within the prophetic tradition of the Jews, and then has announced themselves as the true and only authentic heirs. The key factor for the community is repentance from sin, faithful vigilance and a confession of Jesus "before people". The works of righteousness and not the state of being Jewish take precedence.

By their identification with and indeed appropriation of Jewish religious tradition, Q^2 can claim public advantages which Q^1 neither possesses nor desires to possess.

Prestige

The first and most striking gain is the prestige of antiquity. At a time when the world was engulfed in new and exotic cults the religions that could boast ancient roots had a surer hope of survival. Suetonius gives us an example in the administration of Augustus who "showed great respect towards all ancient and long-established foreign rites, but despised the rest."[24] According to Dio Cassius, Maecenas had advised Augustus to obstruct the authorization of these foreign cults because:

> such persons by bringing in new divinities in place of the old, persuade many to adopt foreign practices, from which spring up conspiracies, factions and cabals, which are far from profitable to a monarchy.

The *unknown* cult was the suspect one. Tacitus offers an aristocratic view of a recent cult in his description of the Roman Christians who were persecuted by Nero in 64 CE.

> Nero fabricated scapegoats—and punished with every refinement the notoriously depraved Christians (as they were popularly called). Their originator, Christ, had been executed in Tiberius' reign by the governor of Judaea, Pontius Pilate. But in spite of this temporary setback the deadly superstition had broken out afresh, not only in Judaea (where the mischief had started) but even in Rome. All degraded and shameful practices collect and flourish in the capital.[25]

---

[24] Dio Cassius, 52. 36.
[25] Tacitus, *The Annals* 15.42.

But in speaking of the Jews, even though Tacitus despises their customs, he recognizes their tradition as a *religio* not a *superstitio*. In the *Histories* for example he presents a selection of etiological surmisings by Gentiles about the Jewish year of Jubilee:

> In the course of time the seductions of idleness made them devote every seventh year to indolence as well. Others say that this is a mark of respect to Saturn, either because they owe the basic principles of their religion (*seu principia religionis*) to the Idaei, who, we are told, were expelled in the company of Saturn and became founders of the Jewish race, or because, among the seven stars that rule humankind, the one that describes the highest orbit and exerts the greatest influence is Saturn. A further argument is that most of the heavenly bodies complete their path and revolutions in multiples of seven. *Whatever their origin, these observances are sanctioned by their antiquity.*[26]

Tacitus' opinion is that the Jews are simply lazy. But he presents three opinions from less hostile sources which plainly situate Jewish Sabbath observance within the general religious sensitivities of respectable religions: the custom which honours divine founders; the philosophical reverence for the hierarchy of the heavenly bodies; and the religious observance which honours the cosmic harmony. Then finally he admits that the custom continues due to its great age.

But Jewish men of letters were also keenly conscious of the importance of their religion's antiquity in securing tolerance among their conquerors.[27]

The Romans themselves had sought the prestige of antiquity for their people and claimed descent from Aeneas, a son of Venus and the veteran of the Trojan wars who was to be the ancestor of Romulus.[28] The concept of Aeneas as an instrument of Destiny was to fire the imagination of Augustus and his ambition as well. The prophecies that claimed Rome's instrumentality in bringing civilization to the world became the patterns to which the conquerors adhered religiously: "Fortune had already engaged as it were, to grant the Roman rule over the east."[29] These prophecies

---

[26] Tacitus, *The Histories* 5.4-5. Italics are my own.

[27] We consider here Demetrius, Artapanus, Pseudo-Eupolemus, Eupolemus, Pseudo-Hecateus, Philo, Theodotus, and Josephus. Also cf. John J. Collins, *Between Athens and Jerusalem* (New York: 1983) especially 25-59; George W. E. Nickelsburg, *Jewish Literature Between the Bible and the Mishnah* (Philadelphia: 1981) 161-193.

[28] Virgil, *Aeneid* 3; Livy 1.1-2,6.

[29] Livy 26.37,5.

appeared to be appropriate and expected since it was clear that Destiny had favoured the Romans from their inception with Aeneas.[30] What is important here is that the aspect of antiquity was so valued by the Romans that they were to create and sustain this historical link between their own people and the Greeks.

When Augustus revived the old shrines and temples within Rome[31] he made two statements that were guaranteed to win him the acclaim of the people. First he gave a respect to old Roman religion which was reserved for some of the more prestigious religions of the East. Second, in doing so he assigned public honour to Roman identity.

The cultural values and perspectives which are disposed to recognize the credibility of religions and institutions depending on their rootedness in antiquity seems fully engaged in the Q^2 stratum. The clear, constant and various references to Jewish sagas, Jewish patriarchs and prophets as well as the appeal to Jewish scriptures for verifications plainly demonstrate that the community has consciously identified itself with an ancient recognized religion in a most deliberate and indeed necessary manner. The issues which are raised and especially addressed in Q^2 point to problems of: (a) the credibility of the wisdom / prophet Jesus to the community members (Q 7:22; 12:8-9; 22:28-30); (b) the honour of Jesus in the face of the opponents' denunciations of his holiness (Q 7:33; 11:14-26); (c) criticisms by members of Jewish religious groups, including Pharisees and Scribes (?) (Q 11:39b-44, 46-48, 49-52); and other unrepentant children of Abraham (Q 3:7-9, 16-17; 10:12-15; 13:25-27, 28-29, 34-35); (d) a critical and recalcitrant public "this generation", (Q 7:31-34; 11:29-32) and the troubles of a community in danger of buckling under pressure (Q 11:49; 12:8-9; 12:52-53, 57-59).

Interestingly, Q^1 gives no evidence of these problems, with the exception of its expectation that members will be brought before local authorities (Q 12:11-12). But even here the message is one of calm hope in the providence of God. There is no appeal to the prophet archetype of the Jewish scriptures. In fact, as we have seen, Q^1 does not identify itself with one particular religious tradition. It is only in Q^2 where the deliberate identification of the community with Israel's tradition becomes not only prominent but indeed takes control of the document.

---

[30] Moses Hadas, *Hellenistic Culture* (New York: 1959) 253-257.
[31] Suetonius, *Divus Augustus* 31.

The various problems of which the Q² community gives evidence require a strong argument to ratify the authenticity of the community and its heroes. By directly invoking its continuity with Jewish religious tradition the community prevents itself from being classified with the outrageous new cults springing up in the East and it gains prestige through their identification with a religion publicly known and recognized within the Greco-Roman world.

Protection

From Cicero we learn that even in spite of the ban on ordinary *collegia* in Rome the Jews were permitted their community meetings both in Rome and the provinces as well.[32] Jewish synagogue communities were distinct from other voluntary organizations[33] in that (a) their decisions affected all facets of their social life within the larger polis; (b) membership came automatically to any Jew from the moment of birth whereas in other *collegia* one had to present oneself and volunteer; (c) there was a strong exclusivity of worship in this religious society to a degree not found in other religious communities; (d) since they could have only one temple, and it was in Jerusalem, Jews required a place to meet and pray on their Sabaath. In these ways Jewish communities presented a special case for Roman laws.[34]

Caesar's recognition of the Jewish religion set an important precedent within the law. Just as his interdict against newly-formed *collegia* went beyond Rome to include the Provinces,[35] so

---

[32] Cicero, *Pro Flaccus* 66.

[33] Of course, all *collegia* were "religious" ("à l'époque lointaine dont nous parlons, une corporation sans culte ne se conçoit pas"; cf. J. P. Waltzing, *Etude historique sur les corporations professionelles* (4 vols; Louvain: 1895-1900) I:75.

[34] Cf. E. Mary Smallwood, *The Jews Under Roman Rule* (Leiden: 1976) 133-134.

[35] Caesar took measures against the guilds of riff-raff which his one-time colleague Claudius had initiated, abolishing them all. Only the most ancient were permitted to continue. The precise wording of the *Lex Julia* is no longer extant; we must rely on historians and inscriptions for the evidence of its actual content and its application. Consider, e.g.,the titulus of the *Collegii Symphoniacorum* from 1st century BCE: Dis Manibus. Collegio symphoniacorum qui sacris publiscus praestu sunt, quibus senatus c[oire] c[onuocari] c[ogi] permisit e lege Julia ex auctoritate Aug[usti] ludorum causa. *Fontes Iuris Romani Antejustiniani*, ed. S. Riccobono, J. Baviera, C. Ferrini, J. Furlani, V. Arangio-Ruiz (3 vols; Florence: 1941) III, 111; cf. also Suetonius, *Divus Julius* 42.3: Francesco

too his recognition of the Jewish community meant that their
rights were ensured right across the empire.

Josephus records a letter from Caesar to the people of Parium in
which the rights of the Jews are particularized: to observe "their
national customs and sacred rites...to collect contributions of
money...to hold common meals."[36] Furthermore, Caesar was to
declare his own special esteem for their tradition:

> Similarly do I forbid other religious societies but permit these people
> alone to assemble and feast in accordance with their native customs
> and ordinances. And if you have made any statutes against our friends
> and allies, you will do well to revoke them because of their worthy
> deeds on our behalf and their good will towards us.[37]

Caesar's largesse to Jews in Rome and throughout the empire
came not so much from his love of their ancient roots but his
inimitable political acumen. This was a broad reward for Antipater
who had assisted him in his war against Alexander. Caesar had a
good relationship with Hyrcanus II and the Jews of Palestine were
favourably disposed towards him. Caesar knew that his public and
generous political gestures to the Jews would cast him in the role
of their benefactor and retain their loyalty to him in the eventual-
ity of another war.

But Caesar's approval of the Jews was to influence their history
from that time onward. The Roman reverence for Caesar's laws
secured them as a type of solid precedent. This served to bring a
measure of protection to them during the stormier days of the
Imperial period. No matter how grudgingly, the state was to
recognize the Jewish tradition as a permissable religion in the
Empire. And even when their assemblies might be disallowed for
a time, their other religious customs were permitted to be
continued.

With regard to these rights it is interesting to note that the
administration of Gaius "Caligula" (37-41 CE) was a time when
the usual controls on clubs and guilds were relaxed. When
Claudius took office in 41 CE he began restorations of order at
every administrative level within the Empire. Dio Cassius tells us
that "he disbanded the clubs that had been reintroduced by

M. de Robertis, *Storia delle Corporationi e del Regime Associativo nel Mondo
Romano* (2 vols; Bari: 1934) I:195ff. For a swift survey of approaches to *collegia* throughout the Imperial period, cf. de Robertis *Corporationi* I:244-245, and
his *Il Diritto associativo Romano* (Bari: 1938) 216-217.

[36] Josephus, *Ant.* 14.8.
[37] *Ibid.*

Gaius. As for the Jews he was afraid of their numbers in Rome. He forbade them to meet but permitted them to observe their other religious customs."[38]

Then Suetonius tells us that Claudius expelled the Jews from Rome because they "caused continual disturbances at the instigation of Chrestus".[39] The aggression of Claudius must have sent a warning alarm to all Jews throughout the Empire. With the new scrutiny of this administration a guild's survival lay in its coherence with a religion already recognized by the state.

At the same time, we do not have clear evidence of how Claudius' policies in Rome actually affected the provinces. We have no proof for example that tighter restrictions were applied to religious groups. But it seems reasonable to accept that in Claudius' reaction to the disastrous neglect and abuse of Caligula's reign, his concern for stability would reach farther than the gates of Rome.

Given the likelihood of Q²'s composition during Claudius' reign or perhaps Nero's, we can only observe that its claim to be in direct continuity with the patriarchs and prophets, its reliance on Jewish sagas and its use of Jewish scripture would have been a prudent decision. This is not to imply that the community represented by Q¹ did not consider itself Jewish, but only to note that there is no seeming effort to make that identity clear. Whereas in the case of Q², it is immediately apparent from the first prophetic denunciation of John as he castigates the presumptuous children of Abraham.

Promise

This aspect of Q² engages the community's interpretation of the significance of the present, of the expectations that would explain and control the communities' life and work.

In the comparison of the material concerning reward in Q¹ and Q² we have already noted that whereas the earlier stratum of sayings shows little interest in time beyond the present, Q² demonstrates a more deliberate attempt to define the imminent future. Q¹ seems to find the reward for membership right here, while Q² conveys the idea that the present is largely painful for the community. Coordinate with these layers is the context of

---

[38] Dio, *Dio's Roman History* 60.6.6.
[39] Suetonius, *Divus Claudius* 25.

kingdom perceptions. It could be held easily that Q^1 interprets the nearness of the kingdom as the breaking in of a new order. It is not clear in any case what the "reign" or "kingdom" precisely signifies. So, it might mean a reality already in motion, or one that is just on the threshold. Either way the prospect seems to be a joyful one. The healing of the sick seems a powerful clue to interpret the wholeness that God's "reign" brings.

In the stratum of Q^2 sayings, the kingdom concept has been perceived as a type of city, with magistrate angels before whom the faithful will be affirmed by "the Son of man". These followers will seat themselves on the judgement thrones to judge the twelve tribes of Israel. Everyone in the kingdom, the great patriarchs and prophets of Israel and all those who have suffered together with the Son of man, share the heavenly banquet.

It is clear that the community has situated "the kingdom" outside the immediate present, and situated it in the proximate future.

Bruce Malina's article, "Christ and Time: Swiss or Mediterranean", observes that the hierarchical importance of "past, present and future" for the peasant of Greco-Roman antiquity was first the present, then the past and only after that, the future.[40] In the context of his investigations the shift which seems to occur in the kingdom concept of Q^1 and Q^2 is from a present reality which is also forthcoming to one which lies in the imminent future. That shift would seem to require a new or more defined perception of the significance of the immediate present. Where alternatives are proposed Malina observes:

> traditional present-oriented people make their choices in terms of present utility only. An inferior product available now is better than a superior product in the future since the future is generally discounted.[41]

If the kingdom or reign of Q^1 was in fact an expectation of a changing new order, it did not happen. What we can see in the Q^2 material is the type of kingdom which does not grow from a seed, or spread through what is already here. It presupposes the breaking in of a new reality which signifies the final destruction of the earth (Q 3:7-9, 16-17) and the moment of judgement.[42] The

---

[40] Bruce Malina, "Christ and Time: Swiss or Mediterranean," *CBQ* 51 (1989) 1-30, especially 5-9.

[41] *Ibid.* 29.

[42] John Kloppenborg demonstates that while Q^2 exhibits many of the elements found in apocalyptic literature, it is distinct from the genre by its lack of true dualism with regard to nature, an absence of anomie, and a relatively posi-

nature of this kingdom is a type of replacement for the city-society already known within the Greco-Roman society: the Son of man testifying to the chief administrators (the angels) on behalf of the faithful; the magistrates (the true disciples who have suffered with the Son of man) conducting judgement against the evil doers (the smug children of Abraham and the hard-hearted people of "this generation"); and the celebratory banquet where all are welcome. Outside the gates, the rejected Jews gnash their teeth. The "kingdom" has taken on a the clear concept of a rival superior city.

This concept of the coming kingdom would seem credible to the kingdom because it would explain why the expectations of a new order growing from within the present society was disappointed. Further it provides a point of hope under the present situation of confrontation. It is the chief threat and incentive to wavering believers (Q 12:8-9, 39-40, 42-46; 22:28-30); and the chief threat to critics of the community (Q 3:7-9, 16-17; 10:13-15; 11:29-32, 39b-44, 46-52; 13:25-27, 28-29, 34-35).

But since this kingdom is not part of the "experienced world" but in the realm of the "possible", it requires a strong testimony to its credibility. Without that, the community can neither hope to retain a troubled membership or to retain an honourable defense against its detractors.

In the gospels the credibility factor rests on Jesus Christ and the Easter event. In Q^2 the Son of man will acknowledge the faithful before the angels, and those who belong to him will sit as judges upon the thrones. But the credibility the promised kingdom does not rest with the Son of man. Its chief credibility is found in the proclaimed pattern which places the community in continuity with Israel's great persecuted prophets. That is, Q^2 assures its promise of the future to a present-oriented people by anchoring it in the ancient promises of Israel's past.

Conclusion

In these three ways the Q^2 stratum took on a credibility within the Greco-Roman world. First, it had a religious tradition with which to identify in a public way. Second, by this association this community was far safer in those times than would have been the case

---

tive perspective of cosmic order. God is still present in the creation. "Symbolic Eschatology and the Apocalypticism of Q," *HThR* 80 (1987) 1-20.

otherwise. Third, the deliberate and expressed engagement of the ancient patriarchs and in particular Abraham gave a holy security to the promises they claimed as their own. We may have the creative product of a failed mission to the Jews. We suggest we have a masterpiece of effective apologetic which allows the community a traditional Jewish identity and at the same time the freedom to preach its wisdom in its own unconventional way.

CHAPTER SEVEN

WISDOM STATEMENTS IN THE SPHERE OF PROPHECY

Migaku Sato

1. In recent years one of the important controversies concerning
Q has been whether the source is in its essence prophetic or sapiential. Elsewhere I have argued for the former cause.[1] In the last
few years, however, several important studies have appeared
which try to define the nature of Q as sapiential.[2] This motivates a
more detailed examination of the issue.

In discussing "wisdom" in Q, we basically have to distinguish
three levels of the problem: (1) whether the *genre* of Q as a literary product (*macro-genre*) can be defined as sapiential; (2) how
the sapiential speech genres (*micro-genres*) or wisdom sayings—
"statements" and (imperatival) "admonitions" being two main
categories—in the source are to be interpreted in relation to its
clearly prophetic speech genres; (3) whether one can speak about

---

[1] The tendency to look at Q as a sapiential writing virtually originated with
J. M. Robinson, "LOGOI SOPHON. Zur Gattung der Spruchquelle Q" in *Zeit und
Geschichte* (*Festschrift* R. Bultmann), ed. E. Dinkler (Tübingen: 1964) 77-96;
further elaborated in his "LOGOI SOPHON: On the Gattung of Q" in *Trajectories
through Early Christianity*, J. M. Robinson / H. Koester (Philadelphia: 1971)
71-113; cf. also H. Koester in the same volume, 114-157, and in *HThR* 73
(1980) 105-130. Those who see Q from a prophetic point of view are: S.
Schulz, *Q. Die Spruchquelle der Evangelisten* (Zürich: 1972); M. E. Boring,
Sayings of the Risen Jesus. Christian Prophecy in the Synoptic Tradition
(MSSNTS 46; Cambridge / New York: 1982) especially 137ff., and *idem, The
Continuing Voice of Jesus. Christian Prophecy and the Gospel Tradition*
(Louisville: 1991) especially 191ff.; W. H. Kelber, *The Oral and the Written
Gospel. The Hermeneutics of Speaking and Writing in the Synoptic Tradition,
Mark, Paul, and Q* (Philadelphia: 1983) especially 199ff.; M. Sato, *Q und
Prophetie. Studien zur Gattungs- und Traditionsgeschichte der Quelle Q* (WUNT
II/29; Tübingen: 1988).

[2] J. S. Kloppenborg, *The Formation of Q. Trajectories in Ancient Wisdom
Collections* (Studies in Antiquity and Christianity; Philadelphia: 1987); R. A.
Piper, *Wisdom in the Q Tradition. The Aphoristic Teaching of Jesus* (MSSNTS
61; Cambridge / New York: 1989); H. von Lips, *Weisheitliche Traditionen im
Neuen Testament* (WMANT 64; Neukirchen-Vluyn: 1990) especially 193ff.,
267ff., to mention the most noted studies.

"wisdom christology" in Q, particularly in view of those sayings which reflect "speculative wisdom" concerning the personified "Sophia" (Q 7:35; 11:49-51; 13:34-35; etc.).

Regarding the first problem, it has been my contention that Q as a whole is far more similar to an Old Testament prophetic book than to a sapiential sayings collection.

> One of the most extensive researches done recently on Q, as well as on the *macro-genre* of Q, is undoubtedly the work by J. S. Kloppenborg.[3] He claims that the "formative stratum", composed of six units of wisdom sayings functioning as instruction, was then redactionally expanded with polemical materials against "this generation" as well as with five blocks of apocalyptic and prophetic words, formulated mostly as "chriae". The last step, the addition of the temptation story (4:1-13), suggests a development into "proto-biography". This trajectory is a natural development within the framework of the "wisdom collection".[4]

> I am not quite convinced by this clear-cut layer analysis, which seems to follow a rather schematic conception. It is possible to find sayings of prophetic nature already in the "formative stratum": e.g. Q 6:20b-21, 22-23b. Kloppenborg himself comments on these sayings: "The beatitudes are 'anti-beatitudes': they stand in contrast to the views of the conventional wisdom...in Q the criticism of wealth is based not on philosophical reflection but upon an apprehension that the imminent kingdom will bring about a radical transformation of human life."[5] This is, however, precisely what "prophecy" is expected to be. One wonders, on the other hand, if the blocks of the "chriae collections" really constitute a single redactional layer: how is it possible to line up such salvation-prophetic words as Q 7:22 or Q 10:23-24 on the same level as the darkest doom sayings of Q 11:49-51; 13:34-35? The category "chriae", defined as "short, pithy sayings which are given a brief introduction or setting",[6] is to my mind too formal and abstract to convey anything about the content of these sayings. In fact, many of the Old Testament prophetic books which are often provided with some kind of introductory remarks could also be classified as "chriae collections". How meaningful, then, is "chriae collection" as the name of a *genre*?

---

[3] *Formation.*

[4] *Formation* especially 166, 238, 242, 317-328. F. G. Downing ("Quite Like Q. A Genre for 'Q': The 'Lives' of Cynic Philosophers," *Bib.* 69 [1988] 196-225) develops J. S. Kloppenborg's position further to the extent that Q is, in his opinion, a kind of Cynic *vita*. To this, cf. the extensive criticism by C. M. Tuckett, "A Cynic Q?" *Bib.* 70 (1989) 349-376.

[5] *Formation* 188-189.

[6] *Formation* 168.

The third of the issues listed above—regarding a "wisdom christology" in Q—was briefly addressed in my previous book.[7] To elaborate further on this matter is the subject for a future study. As for second issue, one half of that problem was dealt with rather extensively in the same book. It was argued that the sapiential *admonitions* in Q are more or less overshadowed by prophetic dynamism so that they do not constitute an alternative to the prophetic understanding of the nature of the source.[8] In the present article, therefore, I will concentrate on the other half of this issue, which was not so fully discussed in my book: the significance of the *wisdom statements* in Q in their relationship to prophecy.

2. But what is prophecy? Traditional prophecy in Israel has, in my opinion, four fundamental constituents.[9]

(1) Prophecy takes place through *inspirational possession* by a deity.

(2) Prophecy has actual *addressees*, usually a collective body of people (example par excellence: the entire people of Israel) in a critical situation, to whom it speaks usually in oral speech.

(3) Prophecy manifests an *eschatological* time-perception that something decisive for the fate of the addressees is soon coming or has already begun.[10]

(4) Prophecy consciously relates itself to the established *prophetic tradition* by employing typical speech genres, motives, etc.

As for wisdom sayings, it is clear that they basically do not attest to any "inspirational possession", since they are based upon experiential evidence. On the other hand, we know that Old Testament prophets often took up apparently wisdom-type speech

---

[7] M. Sato, *Q* 160-161: there is hardly a "wisdom christology" in Q in the sense that Jesus is identified with the personified Sophia; the understanding that Jesus is an envoy of the heavenly Sophia (Q 7:35; 11:49a) derives from a redactor in Q who tried to style the Q-Source like an Old Testament prophetic book.

[8] M. Sato, *Q* 202-226: on "Mahnwort".

[9] For the following description, cf. M. Sato, *Q* 96-107.

[10] I understand the word "eschatology" in a wider sense than usual; apocalyptic end-expectation is merely *one*—though noteworthy—form of "eschatology". Unapocalyptic, inner-historical expectations among the Old Testament prophets are also called "eschatological" as long as they await or witness something decisively new for the destiny of the people.

genres and employed them in their public preaching.[11] The wisdom materials are integrated into their eschatological time-conception and are given the same or similar functions as the typically prophetic speech genres: e.g. in an "announcement of doom" (*Unheilsankündigung*), as Is 18:5:

> For before the harvest, when the blossom is over and the flower becomes a ripening grape, he will cut off the shoots with pruning hooks, and the spreading branches he will hew away

or in an "announcement of salvation" (*Heilsankündigung*),[12] as Is 55:10-11:

> For as the rain and the snow come down from heaven, and do not return there until they have watered the earth, making it bring forth and sprout, giving seed to the sower and bread to the eater, so shall my word be that goes out from my mouth; it shall not return to me empty

or in an "invective" (*Scheltwort*),[13] as Jer 13:23:

> Can Ethiopians change their skin or leopards their spots? Then also you can do good who are accustomed to do evil

or in a "prophetic admonition" (*prophetisches Mahnwort*),[14] as Jer 4:3:

> Break up your fallow ground, and do not sow among thorns.

This procedure, namely to *propheticize* non-prophetic genres of speech, is in itself a characteristic of prophetic-inspiratory dynamism.

---

[11] In general, cf. J. Lindblom, "Wisdom in the OT Prophets" in *Wisdom in Israel and in the Ancient Near East* (VT.S 3; Leiden: 1955) 192-204; W. McKane, *Prophets and Wise Men* (SBT 44; London: 1966) 65-130; D. Hill, *New Testament Prophecy* (London: 1979) 20-21. Specifically for Amos, cf. H. W. Wolff, *Amos' geistige Heimat* (WMANT 18; Neukirchen-Vluyn: 1964); J. L. Crenshaw, "The Influence of the Wise upon Amos. The 'Doxologies of Amos' and Job 5:9-16; 9:5-10," *ZAW* 79 (1967) 42-52; for Isaiah, cf. J. Fichtner, "Jesaja unter den Weisen" (1949) in ders., *Gottes Weisheit. Gesammelte Studien zum Alten Testament* (AzTh II/3; Stuttgart: 1965) 18-26; J. W. Whedbee, *Isaiah and Wisdom* (New York / Nashville: 1971); etc.

[12] An "announcement" is a short saying announcing an impending or already inaugurated eschatological reality. This is the most important speech genre for the prophets. It is divided into two kinds according to the character of the eschatological: "announcement of doom" or "announcement of salvation". For these and the following prophetic speech genres, cf. M. Sato, *Q* 125ff.

[13] A saying which accuses the addressees of committing a fault.

[14] An imperative sentence accompanied by reason. The "reason" is usually formed with an eschatological reference.

The procedure in the present article will be as follows. Methodologically presupposing that Q witnesses a prophetic movement,[15] I shall first consider whether and / or how the respective wisdom statements in Q reflect a prophetic-eschatological time-understanding (i.e. the third constituent of prophecy) and are similar to the functions of typically prophetic speech genres. Then the non-eschatological statements in Q will be discussed in view of their possible relation to prophecy.[16]

3. Recently H. von Lips published an extensive work on the wisdom traditions in the Old Testament, early Judaism, and (most intensively) the New Testament. There he organizes the wisdom statements (Aussageformen)—along with wisdom admonitions— in Q into the following groups,[17] which I would like to present, in a slightly modified form, as the basis for our analysis:

a. sentences (Sentenzen)

Q 3:9; 6:39; 6:40; 6:43-44; 6:45; 9:58; 10:7b; 11:10; 11:11-12; 11:17; 11:23; 11:33; 11:34-35; 12:2; 12:34; Q[?] 14:34-35; 16:13; Q[?] 17:1; Q[?] 17:33; 17:37b; Q[?] 19:21b; Q[?] 19:26.[18]

b. comparisons (Vergleiche)

Q 7:8; 10:3; 11:13; 12:6-7; 12:24, 27-28; 12:39-40; 13:34; Q[?] 17:6; 17:24.[19]

---

[15] H. von Lips (Traditionen 226) seems to be against such a procedure. But otherwise one would simply end up confirming that there are two streams in Q, prophecy and wisdom, without gaining any deeper insight into their interrelation.

[16] Due to lack of space, I shall not deal with the *history* of the wisdom statements in Q.

[17] H. von Lips, Traditionen 204-214.

[18] The sign Q[?] means that I have certain doubts whether these sayings belong to Q at all, although von Lips (and also many others) ascribes them to Q. See M. Sato, Q 17ff. Von Lips names further Lk 13:30; 14:11; 14:34-35; 22:26 par. But these statements hardly constitute Q-sayings, cf. M. Sato, Q 20-23. Lk 11:42c par, which von Lips considers also to be a sapiential saying, has scarcely anything to do with wisdom. These passages are, therefore, not considered in the following discussion. Lk 9:62 is a Q-Luke saying, that is, a saying which probably did not belong to the orignal version of Q, but was later added to the Lukan version of Q (cf. M. Sato, Q 47ff.; for Q-Luke and Q-Matthew, cf. D. Kosch, *Die eschatologische Tora des Menschensohnes. Untersuchungen zur Rezeption der Stellung Jesu zur Tora in Q* [NTOA 12; Göttingen / Fribourg: 1989] 28ff.). Therefore, it is omitted in the following discussion.

[19] Lk 12:(54-55,) 56 par and 14:5 par are hardly Q-materials (Lk 12:54-56=QLk?), contra H. von Lips, Traditionen 207-208. Von Lips (ibid. 208) lists

c. parables (*Gleichnisse*)

Q 6:47-49; 7:31-32; 11:21-22[20]; 12:42-46; 13:18-19; 13:20-21; 13:(25,) 26-27; Q[?] 14:16-24; Q[?] 15:4-7; Q[?] 19:12-27.

d. metaphoric speech (*bildliche Redeweise*)

Q 3:17; 6:41-42; 10:2a; 13:24[21].

Total number: 45 (36 + 9 cases with Q[?])

3.1. Let us first consider those wisdom statements which are employed to imply a future-eschatological time conception.[22] I shall begin by making an inventory of the relevant passages while paying attention to the following questions: (1) what prophetic speech genres can *functionally* be compared with the respective wisdom statements found in their immediate context in Q; and (2) who are supposed to be the *primary addressees* of the respective statements.

Q 3:9("Even now the axe is laid to the root of the trees; every tree therefore that does not bear good fruit is cut down and thrown into the fire."[23]) Part of the Baptist's strong warning to "bear a good fruit"

---

as "Anhang" what he names "geschichtliche Vergleiche" (Q 10:13-15; 11:30; 11:31-32; 17:26-30; 17:32 [Lk 17:32 is a redaction by Luke]). However, these sayings are not considered in the following because, as von Lips himself acknowledges (*ibid.*), they are "nur bedingt als weisheitliche zu bezeichnen...(hier) liegt eher ein prophetisch-eschatologisches Schema vor."

[20] Lk 11:21-22 may represent a Q-parable. Cf. the argument and authors cited in J. S. Kloppenborg, *Q Parallels: Synopsis, Critical Notes & Concordance* (Sonoma, Ca.: 1987) 92.

[21] Von Lips also lists here Lk 11:35-36 par, but v. 35 is to be considered with 11:34; v. 36 is probably a Q-Luke verse.

[22] Also C. E. Carlston ("Wisdom and Eschatology in Q," in *Logia. Les Paroles de Jésus – The Sayings of Jesus*, ed. J. Delobel [BETL 59; Leuven: 1982] 114-115) divides the Q-wisdom sayings into "texts illustrating the presence of the eschatological" and those "illustrating the futurity" of the eschatological. However, he classifies and appraises the texts differently—hence the significance of our own attempt. For the eschatological time-perception in Q in general, cf. D. Zeller, "Der Zusammenhang der Eschatologie in der Logienquelle" in *Gegenwart und kommendes Reich (Festschrift* A. Vögtle), eds. P. Fiedler / D. Zeller (Stuttgart: 1975) 67-77; K. Woschitz, "Reflexionen zum Zeitverständnis in der Spruchquelle 'Q'," *ZKTh* 97 (1975) 72-79.

[23] Regarding the reconstruction of the text, cf. S. Schulz, *Q*, A. Polag, *Fragmenta Q. Textheft zur Logienquelle* (Neukirchener-Vluyn: 1979); W. Schenk, *Synopse zur Redenquelle der Evangelien* (Düsseldorf: 1981); J. S. Kloppenborg *et al.*, *Q-Thomas Reader* (Sonoma, Ca.: 1990); J. M. Robinson, "The International Q Project. Work Session 17 November 1989," *JBL* 109 (1990) 500-501.

against the near ["even now"] Judgment. *Function*: admonition; *addressees*: people of Israel.

Q 3:17("His winnowing fork is in his hand, and he will clear his threshing floor and gather his wheat into the granary, but the chaff he will burn with unquenchable fire.") "Gathering his wheat into the granary" is in itself an announcement of salvation; on the other hand, "the chaff he will burn..." is an announcement of doom. The saying is thus structurally a warning, demanding a right decision. However, if we see the primary emphasis in the latter part of the statement, the image of severe doom becomes primary. *Function*: admonition / announcement of doom; *addressees*: people of Israel.

Q 6:47-49("Everyone who hears my words and practices then will be like a man who built his house upon the rock. [And the rain fell,] and the torrents came [and the winds blew and beat] upon that house, and it did not fall, for it had been founded on the rock. And everyone who hears my words and does not practice them will be like the man who built his house upon the sand. [And the rain fell,] and the torrents came [and the wind blew and beat] against that house, and it fell; and [its fall was] great.") This promise and / or warning concludes the inaugural sermon Q 6:20-49. In its parabolic language—"rainstorm"—the pericope seems to anticipate an imminent catastrophe; the images of "rain", "torrents", "wind", "fall of a house", etc. manifest an affinity to the language used in the prophetic books of the Old Testament.[24] More exactly the statement shows the same stance as the "conditioned announcement of doom" of the Old Testament prophets: "if..., then... (salvation); if not..., then...(doom)."[25] *Function:* admonition; *addressees*: disciples.[26]

Q 7:31-32 ("To what shall I compare this generation, and what are they like? It is like children seated in the agora and addressing their playmates, 'We piped to you, and you did not dance; we sang a dirge, and you did not mourn.'") The parable is used prophetically to accuse "this generation", i.e. contemporary Israelites understood as the last generation before the End. *Function:* invective; *addressees*: people of Israel.

The English translation is chiefly based upon the translation of the gospel / Q texts by J. S. Kloppenborg, *Q Parallels*.

[24] U. Luz, *Das Evangelium nach Matthäus*, I: *Mt 1-7* (EKK I/1; Zürich / Neukirchen-Vluyn: 1985) 414 with n. 13.

[25] M. Sato, *Q* 121.

[26] By "disciples" I mean in this article not only the so-called "wandering missionaries" who must have constituted the main body of the prophetic Q-movement, but also the "resident believers" in local communities. For the structure of the Q-circle with these two "poles", cf. M. Sato, *Q* 379ff.

Q 12:39-40("But know this, that if the houseowner had known in what part of the night the thief was coming, he would not have let his house be dug into. You also must be ready; for the Son of man is coming at an hour you do not expect." Q 12:39 is a parable which shows how unexpectedly the doomsday comes. It is then compared to the coming of the Son of man in v. 40. *Function*: admonition; *addressees*: disciples.

Q 13:25, 26-27("...'Lord, [open for us....We ate and drank with you and you taught in our street.'] And I will [declare to them], 'I never kn[ew] you; depart from me, you [who act against the law].'") This depicts how the addressees will ruthlessly be cast out at the End in spite of their earlier acquaintance with Jesus. *Function*: announcement of doom; *addressees*: people of Israel.

Q 13:34 ("O Jerusalem, Jerusalem, you kill the prophets and stone those who are sent to you! How often would I have gathered your children together as a hen gathers her own brood under her wings, and you refused!") The comparison strengthens the accusation against the entire poeple of Israel. This verse is part of Q 13:33-34, a typical "pronouncement of doom" (*Unheilswort*).[27] *Function*: invective; *addressees*: people of Israel.

Q 17:24 ("As the lightning comes from the east and flashes to the west, so will the Son of man be in his day.") The saying about the sudden advent of the heavenly Son of man is employed to explain why people should not run after false messiahs on the earth. *Function*: ambiguous (anouncement of doom / salvation); *addressees*: people of Israel / disciples.

Q 17:37b("Wherever the corpse is, there the eagles will be gathered.") Employed to visualize the inevitable coming of "the day of the Son of man". *Function*: announcement of doom; *addressees*: people of Israel.

Q[?] 17:1("It is necessary that scandals come, but woe to him by whom they come!") V. 1a expects the coming of "scandals", which could derive from an everyday sapiential experience that difficulties in life are inevitable. Here it might be understood as the inescapable distress before the eschaton. The "woe" warns the addressees not to be a carrier of the "scandals". *Function*: admonition; *addressees*: disciples(?).

Q[?] 17:33("Whoever finds his life will lose it, and he who loses his life will find it.") A parenesis to put one's own life at stake--possibly

---

[27] A combination of "invective" or "cause (of doom)" and "announcement of doom"; cf. M. Sato, *Q* 146ff.

against the approaching End. *Function*: admonition; *addressees*: disciples(?).

Of the 11 examples listed above, 6 cases are employed in quite a prophetic way (Q 3:9; 3:17; 7:31-32; 13:(25,) 26-27; 13:34; 17:37b). With their strong end-expectation they function like prophetic speech with its "announcement of doom", "invective", or "admonition", and they envisage the entire people of Israel as their primary addressees. Two of these derive from John the Baptist (Q 3:9; 3:17).

Three of the remaining cases can also be related to prophetic speech. One case (Q 6:47-49) is virtually a "conditioned announcement of salvation / doom", and two cases (Q 12:39; 17:24) are employed to strongly admonish the addressees against the unexpectedly assailing eschaton—although the addressees may be restricted to the inner-circle of believers.

If the remaining two cases (Q[?] 17:1; Q[?] 17:33) are Q-sayings, Q[?] 17:1 might also approach prophetic dynamism, but the lack of detailed information regarding its context forbids us further speculation. It is also unclear if Q[?] 17:33 reveals something prophetic, for, even if the aphorism is a Q-saying, its original context cannot be fully ascertained.

3.2. What about those wisdom statements which are employed under the present-eschatological time perception? By "present eschatology" I mean that form of intensified eschatology according to which the eschaton is already considered to be dawning in the present time. As is generally acknowledged, this type of eschatology exists alongside the futurist eschatology in Q— most probably as the legacy of Jesus. Here is an inventory of relevant passages:

> Q 10:2a("The harvest is large, but the workers are few.") The harvest is "bereits gewachsen"; (die) "Erntearbeit ist Arbeit, die vorliegt, die nicht gesucht werden muß; eine Arbeit, die zu Ende geführt werden muß."[28] *Function*: unspecified; *addressees*: disciples.

> Q 11:21-22("[When a strong man, fully armed, guards his own court-yard, his goods are safe; but when one stronger than he overpowers him and conquers him, he takes away his armor in which he trusted, and divides his spoil].") The context implies that the "strong one" is the devil, the "stronger one" Jesus; that the victory of Jesus has al-

---

[28] H. -J. Venetz, "Bittet den Herrn der Ernte. Überlegungen zu Lk 10,2 / Mt 9,37," *Diakonia* 11 (1980) 154.

ready become reality can also be inferred from the preceding verse
Q 11:20. *Function*: announcement of salvation; *addressees*: people
of Israel / disciples.

Q 11:23("Whoever is not with me is against me, and whoever does
not gather with me scatters.") "Whoever does not gather with me" implies that there is already something to be gathered at present: the
"harvest". One can either work for it or oppose it; it is *"neutrality
that the saying categorically denies"*.[29] *Function*: admonition;
addressees: disciples.

Q 11:33 ("They do not light a lamp and put it under a grain basket,
but on a lampstand, and it gives light to all in the house.") "The
light" is possibly a metaphor for Jesus' or the Q-circle's offer of the
ultimate salvation (cf. Q 11:31-32); it has now become visible and
should not be hidden from people's eyes. But the position of this verse
in Q is enigmatic and its meaning is not quite certain. *Function*: ad-
monition(?); *addressees*: disciples(?) / people in Israel(?).

Q 12:2 ("Nothing is covered that will not be revealed, or hidden that
will be known.") The eschatological transformation, which has already
been inaugurated but still remains "covered" and "hidden" will soon
manifest itself. *Function*: announcement of salvation; *addressees*:
disciples (especially wandering missionaries, cf. v. 3).

Q 12:42-46 ("Who then is the faithful and wise servant, whom his
master has put in charge of his household, to give them their meals on
time? Happy is that servant whom his master when he comes will find
so doing. Amen, I tell you, he will put him in charge of all his possessions.") The master's putting the servant in charge of his own
household, leaving, and then returning presuppose a special time-span
preceding the eschaton. *Function*: admonition; *addressees*: disciples
(especially the leaders of resident communities).

Q 13:18-19 ("What is the reign of God like? And to what shall I
compare it? It is like a grain of mustard seed which a man took and
put into his garden; and it grew and became a tree, and the birds of the
sky made nests in its branches.")

Q 13:20-21 ("To what shall I compare the reign of God? It is like
leaven which a woman took and hid in three measures of flour, till it
leavened the whole mass.") These parables presume a special interim
time: the mustard seed has (already) been sown, and it will soon grow
enormous; the leaven has (already) been put into the flour, and it will
soon leaven the whole flour. The positive images with which these

---

[29] J. D. Crossan, *In Fragments. The Aphorisms of Jesus* (San Francisco:
1983) 50 (italics by Crossan).

parables come to an end hint that the time thus initiated has a quality of salvation. *Function*: announcement of salvation; *addressees*: people of Israel / disciples.

Q[?] 14:16-24 (The parable of the great supper: on the whole, the Lukan version is older.) The declaration that the great supper (Lk) / the wedding (Mt) is now "ready" must indicate that the eschatological time has already begun. *Function*: announcement of doom (if the Lukan version is original); *addressees*: people in Israel.

Q[?] 14:34-35 ("Salt [is good;] but if salt becomes insipid, with what could it be salted? [It is fit neither for the soil nor for the dunghill; they throw it] away.") The "salt" may be something similar to the "light" in Q 11:33. *Function*: admonition; *addressees*: disciples.

Q[?] 15:4-7 ("Which of you, having a hundred sheep, if he has lost one of them, does not leave the ninety-nine in the wilderness, and go after the one which is lost? And when he has found it, I tell you, he rejoices over it more than over the ninety-nine.") The joy of re-finding the lost one is not something expected in the future, but a reality already palpable at present. *Function*: announcement of salvation; *addressees*: people in Israel.

Q[?] 19:12-27 (The parable of the talents / minas: the original version can hardly be reconstructed.) A similar time-conception as in Q 12:42-46. See the following case. *Function*: admonition; *addressees*: disciples.

Q[?] 19:26 ("To everyone who has will be given more; but from the one who has not, even what he has will be taken away.") Employed to show that the disciples must make the best of their eschatological "money", which is entrusted to them in the interim time, until the day of the last Reckoning. *Function*: admonition / warning; *addressees*: disciples.

The above survey shows that 5 (4 + 1Q[?]) cases of 13 (8 + 5Q[?]) can functionally be paralleled with an "announcement of salvation" (Q 12:2; 11:21-22; 13:18-19; 13:20-21 + Q[?] 15:4-7). They draw the attention of the whole people of Israel to the new world that has now begun to take shape. On the other hand, Q[?] 14:16-24—if it is a Q-parable at all—would function as an "announcement of doom" to the people of Israel for rejecting the invitation to the already manifest salvation. These cases are, therefore, functionally quite close to prophetic speech.

   Five (2 + 3Q[?]) cases address the disciples in an admonitory or warning tone in view of the now inaugurated eschaton (Q 11:23;

12:42-46 + Q[?] 14:34-35; 19:26; 19:12-27). Here the prophetic dynamism is confined to the dimension of a single circle, but in so far as the Q-circle envisages the whole of Israel as a missionary group, the prophetic thrust is still tangible.

One case, Q 10:2a, addresses the disciples in a tense atmosphere of commencing eschaton; yet its function is not comparable to any prophetic speech model. As for Q 11:33, no concrete meaning can be inferred, although it probably breathes a present-eschatological air.

Thus far (in Sections 3.1 and 3.2), out of 24 (17 + 7Q[?]) cases which are clearly permeated with an eschatological ambiance, 12 (10 + 2Q[?]) cases have been shown to serve a highly prophetic function, while 8 (5 +3Q[?]) of the remaining cases serve the same function to a lesser extent. This suggests that the wisdom statements in the source are, to say the least, no obstacle to its having an essentially prophetic orientation.

3.3. However, before we can draw that conclusion, we must examine the *uneschatological* wisdom statements, which are not scarce in Q. And with this group of sayings we come into the most problematic area. How could the seemingly non-eschatological wisdom statements in Q co-exist with the clearly eschatological sayings without interfering with the source's prophetic nature?

3.3.1. First we focus upon several cases which, despite the lack of any eschatological connotation, can possibly be integrated into a present-eschatological time-perception.

Q 11:10 ("For everyone who asks receives; and everyone who seeks finds; and for everyone who knocks, it is opened") The tone is scarcely eschatological; what is striking, however, is the strong exaggeration ("Everyone [πᾶς] who..."), which is hardly sanctioned by our experience. However, this "optimism" is quite *compatible* with the present-eschatological message of Q. What underlies its optimistic stance may well be the time-understanding that God's eschatological salvation has already begun—therefore the absolute confidence in God's loving response *hic et nunc*.

Q 11:11-12 ("Who among you, if his son asks him for bread, will give him a stone? Or if he asks for a fish, will give him a snake?") "Who among you...?" calls for experiential verification. This verse is an introduction to the following comparison.

Q 11:13 ("If you then, being wicked, know how to give good gifts to your children, how much more will the heavenly Father give good things to those who ask him?") The examples in Q 11:11f. serve as material for the logic *a minori ad majus*, an argument which supports God's positive desire for our salvation. Characteristic in this saying is also the unshakable trust that "God gives good things" to his followers. The argument reminds us of, e.g., Is 49:15:

> Can a woman forget her nursing child, or show no compassion for the child of her womb? Even these may forget, yet I will not forget you.

When we remember that Deutero-Isaiah is the most notable Old Testament prophet who announces the already initiated salvation-eschatology (cf. Is 43:18-19), this parallel is all the more interesting. In both cases the divine will for salvation latent in his original Creation is decisively intensified and made manifest by the new actions of salvation which have now begun.

Q 12:6-7 ("Are not five sparrows sold for two assaria? And not one of them will fall to the ground without your Father. But even the hairs of your head are all numbered. Fear not, therefore; you are worth more than many sparrows.") V. 7a is probably an insertion into the original admonition composing vv. 4-7[30]; it is employed so as to stress God's perfect providence. V. 6 focuses on God's complete protection even for the most insignificant beings. Here God's original will for the well-being of all creation is not only presupposed but proclaimed with utmost clarity. This intensification of the original will of God to save his creatures is perfectly *congenial*, to say the least, with the eschatological con-

---

[30] R. A. Piper (*Wisdom* 52-55) sees in this composition (and further in the larger context Q 12:2-9) what he believes to be the common "structure" or "pattern" of the other five sayings-groups (Q 11:9-13; 12:22-31; 6:37-42; 6:43-45): (a) a general opening saying, (b) an initial supporting argument, (c) a further supporting argument, often in a rhetorical question, and (d) a final application which provides the key to the entire composition (cf. also *ibid* . 35-36, 61-65). He considers this pattern to be "a design and argument unique in the synoptic tradition", or as a proof for "an unique 'compositional activity'" in Q (*ibid.* 64). Yet he himself acknowledges that the same pattern exists also in Prov 6:25-9; Sir 13:15-20. Something similar can also be found among the Old Testament prophets, e.g. Am 6:11-12; Jer 6:13-15 (= 8:10b-12); 13:20-24. On the whole, what Piper has convincingly disclosed is a certain "tendency to work from very general principles to more specific application by carefully graduated steps" (*ibid.* 37). Is this not a general rhetorical pattern more or less common elsewhere?

sciousness of the inaugurated salvation. The whole stance is even further intensified by the "anthropocentric" argument of *a minori ad majus.*

Q 12:24, 27-28 ("Look at the ravens: they neither sow nor reap nor gather into granaries, and yet God feeds them. Are you not worth more than the birds? Who of you by being anxious can add one cubit to his span of life?...Consider the lilies of the field, how they grow; they neither toil nor spin; but I tell you, even Solomon in all his glory was not arrayed like one of these. But if God so clothes the grass of the field, which is growing today and tomorrow is thrown into the oven, will he not much more clothe you, O weak in faith?") These famous verses are part of the larger composition Q 12:22-31, in which v. 31 witnesses a clearly eschatological background ("reign of God"). Some commentators think, however, that v. 31 was added later to the original unit which is not at all eschatological in nature.[31] Let us for a moment suppose that this is correct and narrow our focus to 12:24, 27-28. Here, too, the extremely optimistic view concerning God's care for his creatures captures our attention. Although nature is fundamentally ambivalent with its goodness as well as its mercilessness, no negative aspects concerning nature are elaborated in these verses. Instead, even the ostensibly catastrophic aspect of "being thrown into the oven" is depicted as a demonstration of perfect protection by God. And we see again that this *selectiveness* of viewpoints[32] can go hand in hand with a present-eschatological time perception. We would, therefore, go one step further and conclude that it is awareness of the newly inaugurated salvation-eschatological era which motivates and supports this selectiveness. In fact, such statements as Q 12:24, 26-27 would have been virtually impossible if Jesus' eschatology had been a purely futuric one. It is the present-eschatological time-perception, characteristic of salvation-prophecy both for Jesus and the Q-circle, that takes up, reinforces and amplifies the manifestation of God's

---

[31] E.g., H. von Lips, *Traditionen* 225, writes: "Man darf sie nicht vor schnell dem eschatologischen Aspekt unterordnen, so wenn man Lk 12,22ff ganz von 12,31 her liest" (criticism against my view).

[32] For the "selective" use of aphoristic materials in Q, cf. R. A. Piper, *Wisdom* 180-181. Also noteworthy is his argument from the reverse side: "It is true...that the 'certainty' of this (sc. "Jesus' proclamation of God's eschatological rule") may be reinforced by reference to God's creative activity" (*ibid.* 268 n. 135).

will for the welfare of creatures, which is innate in the creation and has found traditional expressions in wisdom literature.[33]

Here opens up a possibility of convergence between the prophetic stance and the wisdom stance. Certain sapiential observations on the creation can be utilized by prophecy to visualize the eschatological salvation already in process.[34] This means that the above-mentioned wisdom statements which are employed in a seemingly uneschatological way could well be utilized within the scope of prophetic eschatology in Q. In other words, they can be *indirectly propheticized*. And that is exactly what happened to Q 12:24, 27f. within the framework of Q 12:22-31 (with v. 31).

This leads to another consequence: although Q doubtlessly awaits a future collapse of the universe (Q 3:7-9, 17; 12:39; 17:24, 26-27, 30, 34-37; etc.), this does not mean a *total* rupture with what has already been going on in this world under divine power.[35] The existing world will soon perish, but something will continue to abide in spite of the discontinuity. It is, more precisely, continuity *through* discontinuity. What continues to exist is, first of all, God's sovereign rule and his will for salvation, which has remained basically unaltered since the Creation; it has only been decisively intensified and activated since the new era began.[36] Its sign in Q is its visible victory over the anti-godly

---

[33] Cf. L. Goppelt, *Theologie* 125: "Von dieser eschatologischen Offenbar–ung Gottes aus zurückblickend weist Jesus die Zeichen der Leben erhaltenden Güte des Schöpfers in einer vom Bösen und vom Übel gezeichneten Welt auf.... Wie Israel einst vom Bundesgott her das Bekenntnis zu Gott dem Schöpfer fand, so läßt Jesus im Licht der hereinbrechenden Gottesherrschaft die Spuren der Güte des Schöpfers in dieser Welt aufleuchten." More generally, cf. W. Grundmann in *Die Kirche des Anfangs* (*Festschrift* H. Schürmann), eds. R. Schnackenburg / J. Ernst / J. Wanke (Leipzig: 1978) 175-199, with the title (which is his *These* it-self) "Weisheit im Horizont des Reiches Gottes".

[34] For these examples, Deutero-Isaiah is an outstanding "storehouse" among the Old Testament prophets: see Is 44:1-5; 43:1-3a; 45:15; 46:3-4; 49:15; 54:10; 55:10-11.

[35] Cf. H. von Lips, *Traditionen* 252; R. A. Piper (*Wisdom* 155) also argues for the aspect of "continuity". Von Lips (*ibid.* 247-248) makes an important observation concerning the wisdom materials in the synoptic gospels: "...daß Beispiele aus der Natur in Analogie verwendet werden, Beispiele aus dem mens-chlichen Leben dagegen teils in Analogie, aber mehrfach in Kontrast zur alltäglichen Erfahrung" (cf. further *ibid.* 235-240).

[36] That God stays "with" the faithful and stands by them is a well-known theme attested both in sapiential writings (e.g. Ps 37:24-28; 73:23; 139) and in prophetic books (e.g. Is 7:14; Ez 39:27-29; Hos 3:1-5; Mi 2:13; Zech 8:23). Cf. also apocalyptic works (e.g. 1 En 39:7-8; 45:6; 62:14; 71:16; Rev 21:3). That God's sovereign rule stretches from the creation

powers (cf. Q 11:20) who will be completely eliminated when the
definitive end breaks in. Secondly, the creatures' faithful obedience to God will also abide in the next world throughout the
last catastrophe, just like the "the ark of Noah" which was intact
even amid the deluge which destroyed the rest of the creation
(Q 17:27), or—more figuratively speaking—like that pitiable
"sparrow" which fell to the ground but was "with" God
(Q 12:6), that is, in God's perfect protection. In fact, without the
conviction of this continuity, no exhortations to stay faithful
despite the present hardship (e.g. Q 6:22-23; 12:8-9) would have
any meaning at all.[37]

3.3.2. There still remain 16 (14 + 2Q[?]) uneschatological wisdom statements which cannot be classified into any of the above
groups. However, it is interesting to note that—except for 3 (2 +
1Q[?]) cases[38]—all of these statements concern the theme of
"disciple ethics".

> *Q 6:39* ("Can a blind man lead a blind man? Will they not both fall
> into a pit?") If the present location of this verse in Luke is its original
> context, it seems to criticize the disciples' "blindness" or warn them
> against it (possibly in their mission to convert the "blind" Israelites).

> *Q 6:40* ("A disciple is not above the teacher. [It is enough for the dis-
> ciple to] be like his teacher.") Both the Lukan and Matthean locations
> relate the saying to discipleship, although the concrete meaning of the
> Lukan sequence, if original, is not quite clear.

> *Q 6:41-42* ("Why do you see the speck that is in your brother's eye,
> but do not notice the beam that is in your own eye? Or how can you
> say to your brother, 'Let me remove the speck from your eye,' when
> behold there is the beam in your own eye? Hypocrite, first remove the
> beam from your own eye, and then you will see clearly to remove the
> speck from your brother's eye.") A saying requiring the disciples to
> examine their own faults and to endeavor to eliminate them before crit-

---

through the present time to the eschaton is presupposed even in the apocalyptic
literature with its abrupt coming of the eschaton, e.g. Dan 2:20-23; 3:33;
4:31-32; 6:27-28; 1 En 93:1-10. Cf. C. E. Carlston (*Logia* 116, 118) who
sees in the "the divine will" the unchangeable element before and after the eschaton; similarly A. P. Winton, *The Proverbs of Jesus. Issues of History and
Rhetoric* (JSNT Supplement Series 35; Sheffield: 1990) 162-163.

[37] Also the apocalyptic writings with their strong end-expectation could
emerge only with this conviction; in 1 En 93:1-10 (the "Ten-Week Apocalypse") the "righteousness" abides throughout the whole of history, even beyond the eschaton.

[38] Cf. note 45 below.

icizing others. The intention is to maintain harmony among "brothers".

Q 6:43-44 ("No good tree bears bad fruit, nor again does a bad tree bear good fruit; for by its fruit the tree is known. Are grapes gathered from thorns, or figs from thistles?")

Q 6:45 ("The good man out of the good treasure produces good things, and the evil man out of his evil treasure produces bad things; for from what overflows the heart the mouth speaks.") Admonitions toward the disciples to do good deeds, especially to use right speech (v. 45b).

Q 9:58 ("Foxes have holes, and birds of the sky have nests; but the Son of man has nowhere to lay his head.") This experiential truth (v. 58a) is utilized to form a sentence urging a missionary candidate to abandon home and family.

Q 10:3 ("Behold, I am sending you out as lambs among wolves.") The implication is "that the messengers will experience rejection and even persecution."[39] Precisely because of that, the saying calls implicitly for determination and mindfulness.

Q 10:7b ("The worker deserves his wages.") A proverb used to establish the right of itinerant missionaries to free accomodation and / or to solicit resident believers to welcome and accommodate the missionaries.

Q 11:34-35 ("The eye is the lamp of the body. When your eye is generous, your whole body is [/ will be] full of light; but when your eye is evil, your whole body is [/ will be] full of darkness. If then the light in you is darkness, how great is the darkness!") This saying presumably "encourage(s) self-examination and commitment among those who have received light."[40]

Q 12:34 ("Where your treasure is, there will your heart be also.") This statement is used to conclude the previous admonition Q 12:33: the disciples should "lay up treasures in heaven" with all sincerity.

Q 13:24 ("Enter through the narrow gate; for the gate is wide that leads to destruction, and those who enter through it are many. But how narrow is the gate that leads to life, and those who find it are few.") The way how this saying is employed is not very clear, but it seems

---

[39] A. D. Jacobson, "The Literary Unity of Q. Lc 10,2-16 and Parallels as a Test Case" in *Logia. Les Paroles de Jésus – The Sayings of Jesus*, ed. J. Delobel (BETL 59; Leuven: 1982) 422.

[40] R. A. Piper, *Wisdom* 130.

to be "a summons to discipleship"[41] despite the severe conditions expected for disciples.

Q 16:13 ("No one can serve two masters; for either he will hate the one and love the other, or he will be loyal to one and despise the other. You cannot serve God and mammon.") The original location of this verse in Q is uncertain,[42] but its meaning is clear enough: it is necessary to despise money in order to serve God.

Q[?] 17:6 ("If you have the faith as a grain of mustard seed, you could say to this sycamine tree, 'Be uprooted, and be planted in the sea,' and it would obey you.") A solicitation for faith as pre-condition for a great and difficult task (if this is a Q-verse, the task could be the mission in Israel).

Of these 13 (12 + 1Q[?]) statements, 4 depict the *difficulty of discipleship*, while encouraging the disciples, either explicitly or implicitly, to persevere with their present load (Q 9:58; 10:3; 13:24; possibly also 16:13). Q 9:58; 10:3 are specifically related to the itinerant messengers who are on the mission to convert the Israelites before the eschaton. Another 7 cases express an *exhortation to self-criticism* (Q 6:39; 6:40; 6:41-42; 6:43-44; 6:45; 11:34; 12:34). Five of these 7 belong to Q 6:37-49, that is, to the latter part of the so-called "programmatic speech" (Q 6:20-49); perhaps this fact reveals the intention of this special sayings collection in its present form. At any rate, the main concern of these special sayings is to maintain the integrity of the group as committed disciples of Jesus. They know themselves to be a specially qualified prophetic-eschatological group (cf. Q 6:23), sent to convert the whole of Israel before the eschaton. Since they have already decided to accept the message of Jesus / Q, it is not always necessary to keep announcing the eschatological reality to these "insiders".[43] The problem is rather how to free themselves from various temptations and difficulties assailing them from outside as well as from inside.[44] Any lack of integrity within the circle could damage the entire mission. Sapiential statements encouraging them to sincere self-criticism are, therefore, quite

---

[41] J. S. Kloppenborg, *Formation* 235.

[42] Cf. M. Sato, *Q* 24.

[43] Cf. D. Zeller, *Die weisheitlichen Mahnsprüche bei den Synoptikern* (FzB 17; Würzburg: 1977) 172 about "wisdom admonitions".

[44] In this connection we can again refer to the wisdom statements with eschatological-admonitory application, which were dealt with earlier (Q 6:47-49; 11:23; 12:39-40; 12:42-46; etc.).

meaningful as a way to keep them aware of their own weaknesses. Therefore, these statements, even if they show no explicit echatological connotations, can rightly co-exist with the prophetic sayings in Q.[45]

4. *Conclusion.* Of 45 (36 + 9Q[?]) wisdom statements in Q, 24 (17 + 7Q[?]) statements are employed to manifest either the future-eschatological coming of the eschaton or the present-eschatological commencement of the new age; more than four-fifths of these examples witness to a more-or-less prophetic application, i.e. they are *propheticized.* Another 5 wisdom statements, which are not particularly eschatological in their wording, are so constructed that they are highly compatible with the notion that the new era of salvation has already begun. They are presumably sustained by and formed with this time-understanding in the background. In this sense, they are born and move within the sphere of prophecy. The other group of wisdom statements without any direct eschatological connotation, 13 (12 +1Q[?]) in number, concerns the ethics for disciples as an eschatological group; more than half of them invite hearers / readers to self-examine whether or not they are worthy followers of Jesus with his eschatological message.

Therefore, we may conclude that the existence of numerous sapiential statements in Q—together with sapiential admonitions—does not contradict the fundamental character of Q as a prophetically-oriented book, but rather can even support it. That the source contains a number of wisdom sayings—more than any of the Old Testament prophets—derives from the fact that Jesus was *also* skilled in wisdom teaching and employed many wisdom sayings as an auxiliary to his prophetic-eschatological proclamation. And this influenced the general outlook of the source itself.

If we were to presuppose, on the other hand, that Q is basically sapiential, it would become extremely difficult to explain why and how such a strong prophetic vein could come into the source,

---

[45] Three statements remain yet undiscussed: Q 7:8 ("I myself am a man under authority, with soldiers under me; and I say to one, 'Go,' and he goes, and to another, 'Come,' and he comes, and to my slave, 'Do this,' and he does it"); Q 11:17 ("Every kingdom divided against itself is laid waste; and a household divided against itself will not survive"); [Q?]19:21b (["You reap where you did not sow, and gathered where you did not scatter"]). These have, however, little to do either with eschatology or with disciple ethics. These three sayings are used in dialogues to demonstrate metaphorically the speaker's point—which is a common way sapiential materials are utilized in all types of literature.

unless we resorted, for example, to overvaluing the early-Judaic
tendency toward a "mixture of traditions" between wisdom and
prophecy,[46] or to treating the prophetic elements as a kind of
Fremdkörper.

---

[46] This viewpoint is in itself valuable (cf. M. Hengel, "Jesus als messiani-
scher Lehrer der Weisheit und die Anfänge der Christologie" in *Sagesse et Religion* [Colloque de Strasbourg, Octobre 1976; Paris: 1979] especially 180; H.
von Lips, *Traditionen* 188), but it should not be pushed too far. For even in a
"mixture of traditions" between prophecy and wisdom we can ask which element
is primary: e.g., the fact that Sirach imitates prophetic speech in a few places
does not make this wisdom teacher a true prophet.

CHAPTER EIGHT

THE REDACTION OF Q AND THE SON OF MAN: A PRELIMINARY SKETCH

Paul Hoffmann

Many points of detail would of course need to be addressed for a conclusive judgment to be possible concerning the literary genesis of the sayings source Q and its position in the history of early Christianity. If these were put aside, current discussion could be focussed on three main problem areas.[1] These concern the genre of Q—"wisdom collection" (so also J. M. Robinson, and most recently J. S. Kloppenborg), or "prophetic book" (M. Sato)—secondly its redactional history and finally—somewhat by the way—the old question of the relationship between Mark and Q.[2] My present occupation with redactional history is at the same time an attempt to repair a deficit in my Habilitationsschrift, *Studien zur Theologie der Logienquelle*.[3] In my view, the redaction-critical problems are very closely connected with a matter that is not only of central importance for Q, but also for the history of early Christian christology as a whole: the question of the Son of Man (SM).[4] This connection is not a new one for redaction-critical discussion, since no construction can avoid settling the matter of the tradition-historical position of the SM sayings in Q. It seems to me, however, that by linking these two questions in a more focused way—taking account of progress that has been made in the SM

---

[1] This essay has been translated into English by David E. Orton and corresponds to my contribution to the Neirynck *Festschrift*. On the genesis of Q and its position in early Christianity, see also the overview of F. Neirynck, "Recent Developments in the Study of Q" in *Logia*, ed/ J. Delobel (Leuven: 1982) 29-75.

[2] On this see recently J. Schüling, *Studien zum Verhältnis von Logienquelle und Markusevangelium* (Würzburg: 1991).

[3] Presented to the Faculty of Catholic Theology of the University of Münster: 1968 (published Münster: 1972, 3rd edn: 1982).

[4] On this see my essay "Jesus versus Menschensohn, Matthäus 10,32f und die synoptische Menschensohnüberlieferung" in *Salz der Erde—Licht der Welt. Exegetische Studien zum Matthäusevangelium. Festschrift für A. Vögtle*, eds. L. Oberlinner & P. Fiedler (Stuttgart: 1991) 165-202, in which in various respects I correct my earlier position on this question.

discussion—progress will also be possible in our appreciation of the nature and tradition-historical classification of the redaction of Q (QR). For this purpose I have elected to proceed via a review of the history of scholarship, but restricting myself—for reasons of space for one thing—to what I consider to be the essential stops en route, marked out by the work of H. E. Tödt, O. H. Steck, D. Lührmann, A. D. Jacobson and M. Sato, with sideways glances at studies that are less illuminating for my question. In this manner not only may the premises which motivated discussion to date be clarified, but also those premises which established the discussion; and perhaps the latter may be overcome.

1. The Basis of Recent Discussion

The most incisive and significant contribution to the study of the sayings source, and also the foundation and impetus for recent discussion, is the exegetical dissertation of the Heidelberg ethicist Heinz Eduard Tödt, entitled *Der Menschensohn in der synoptischen Überlieferung*.[5] Whereas earlier research (P. Wernle, A. von Harnack) initially found Q to be a catechetical collection of sayings and then, under the influence of J. Wellhausen and form criticism, saw it as a less significant complement to the (passion) kerygma as represented by Paul—in their view the real centre of the early Christian proclamation (R. Bultmann, M. Dibelius, etc.)—Tödt showed that the tradition of the Jesus sayings in Q presupposes an independent "kerygmatic programme".[6]

---

[5] The dissertation was presented to the Faculty of Protestant Theology of the University of Heidelberg in 1956 with the title, "Hoheits- und Niedrigkeitsvorstellungen in den synoptischen Menschensohnsprüchen"; it was published in 1959.

[6] Tödt's teacher, G. Bornkamm, also emphasizes the distinctive "theological conception" of Q in his article "Evangelien" in *RGG* II (3rd edn: 1958) col. 759. Tödt's perspective has clear points of contact with R. Bultmann's characterization of the early Palestinian proclamation of the message of Jesus, which the latter, however—unlike Tödt—sees as still adherent to Judaism and qualitatively distinct from the Pauline kerygma (*Theologie des Neuen Testaments* [2nd ed; Tübingen 1954] 34, 37).

Already T. W. Manson (*The Sayings of Jesus* [London: 1937]) assessed Q as an independent early Christian strand of tradition at the centre of which stands Jesus as the teacher, and showed the eschatological character of Q in its concern with the idea of judgment, which determines the beginning and the end of the collection (p. 16), but at the same time saw Q as of less importance than the passion kerygma (p. 9).

After the emerging redaction-critical research (as opposed to form criticism) had taught scholars to appreciate that the evangelists were not just collectors and tradents but also authors and theologians, they also began to ask more directly about the specific intentions of the redaction of Q as distinct from the body of tradition summarized in Q, and about the *Sitz im Leben* of the collection.

Even though Tödt does not explicitly make the question of the redaction his topic, in distinguishing the authentic sayings of the coming SM from the later, post-Easter sayings about the earthly SM, preserved especially in Q, his investigation aims to assess the christological conception of Q as opposed to the historical Jesus and integrate it into the content of what the sayings source as a whole has to say. Tödt thus certainly enquires into the specific level of theological knowledge and the interests which guided the bearers of the tradition. He does this, admittedly, without distinguishing individual stages in the history of the traditions. Since Q primarily preserves those materials which go back to Jesus' own announcement of the coming SM,[7] Q can also be seen as a prominent witness for that "second independent source for christology" (p. 215, cf. 245), independent of the passion kerygma, which is recognizable precisely *in the development of the Son of Man sayings*. What Tödt has particularly in mind at this point is the movement from the originally soteriological relation between Jesus and SM, as can be perceived in Q 12:8f., to the christological identification of the SM with Jesus in the understanding of the earliest community, which is the condition for the development of the sayings concerning the earthly work of the SM (cf., e.g., p. 210). The catalyst for this is the Easter experience. In the resurrection of Jesus, God confirmed the *exousia* of Jesus, which had been placed in question by the crucifixion, but also the community which in his *exousia* he had given to the disciples.

> It is understandable, then, if the early church again takes up and spreads the proclamation of the one whom God has confirmed, at the same time including in this proclamation the proclaimer himself, who effectively

---

Evidently independently of Tödt, W. D. Davies has disputed the paraenetic character of Q and drawn out the christologically oriented idea of judgment as the primary theme of this collection of Jesus' ethical teaching: "Q sets forth the crisis constituted in the coming of Jesus, and it is as a part of this crisis that it understands the ethical teaching of Jesus: it is itself an expression of this crisis" (*The Setting of the Sermon on the Mount* [Cambridge: 1964] 385).

[7] "Careful criticism" leads him to view as authentic: Lk 11:30; 12:8f. par.; Mt 24:27, 37, 39, 44 par.; Lk 17:30 (cf. p. 206).

brought about the kingdom in his announcement of it. The promise
that the coming Son of Man would acknowledge those who confessed
him remained in force. But if Jesus himself, as the resurrected one, had
turned his community again to the disciples, how then could the re-
newer of the community in the kingdom of God, that is, the Son of
Man, be any other than Jesus? *(p. 230)*

The death and resurrection of Jesus do not form the content of
the message of Jesus, but they do form the basis for the re-procla-
mation of the message, initiated at Easter (p. 228). The passion
kerygma, on the other hand, can only become the centre of the
content of the proclamation at the point where "the soteriological
significance of the death (of Jesus) is acknowledged and unfolded.
But this is precisely what does not happen in Q" (p. 229). With
Bultmann, Tödt takes the sayings of the earthly work of the SM as
a whole as constructions of the early church (pp. 105ff., especially
116). Unlike Bultmann, however, he understands them not as a
relatively late hellenistic product which owes its existence to the
misunderstanding of the original SM in the sense of "person" or
"I" in the translation of the term from Aramaic into Greek.
Rather, he tries to ground its origin from the early Palestinian
community precisely by making plausible "an illuminating
tradition-historical and material cooperation of both groups"
(p. 105f.).

> At the place where Jesus' claim stands in the sayings concerning the
> coming Son of Man, the term Son of Man is brought into play in the
> sayings concerning his present work. It means nothing other than Jesus
> himself in his sovereign activity, i.e. it replaces *Jesus'* "I", but at the
> same time gives him the expression of a special sovereignty....*(p. 108)*

When Tödt repeatedly emphasizes that here "the term Son of
man does not call down on Jesus the sovereignty of the transcendent Son of Man" (p. 108, cf. 116), he is obviously concerned to
counter the objection that such a sovereignty could not be trans-
ferable to the earthly Jesus, since in the traditional conception, the
SM is subject to "no earthly restriction". However, at the same
time he tries to avoid the consequence of this, that the title is due to
a misunderstanding or has been reduced to a mere self-designation, or means the SM who exists in concealment.[8]

Tödt's interpretation seems, however, to correspond more to the
redaction of the gospels, in which the title cannot be reduced to a

---

[8] Cf. pp. 208f. as well as 116 and 248 in debate with Bultmann, *Theologie*
30f. (on which see also Tödt 15).

simple self-designation either. He is correct to emphasize that Q is concerned to draw out the specific *exousia* of Jesus. The strict separation of the *exousia* of the earthly from the coming SM is not, however, able to explain sufficiently well the ambiguous use of the title. Though the sovereignty of the transcendent SM is not brought down on Jesus by this title, nonetheless with the title Jesus' historical *exousia* is placed in the perspective of the authority of the transcendent SM. The apocalyptic cipher qualifies Jesus as the decisive eschatological authority.[9] In Jesus' original claim the hearer encounters the claim of God's coming representative. The function of the transfer consists precisely in claiming for the earthly Jesus and his message the authority of the coming one. If we take the identity of both not in a static way but dynamically— the historical Jesus *is* already what he *will be* as the coming (again) one—the agreement in content in the use of the title can be preserved without the problems arising of which Tödt was afraid.[10]

In his analysis of the sayings material, Tödt then draws attention to a second aspect that is decisive for subsequent research: "It is the contrast to the *people* or this *generation*" which determines the SM sayings (p. 115, cf. also 206f.). In the

> parousia sayings the contrast was not between the transcendent Son of Man and *people*, but between Jesus and them. In the sayings concerning his earthly work, the *Son of Man* is drawn into this opposition and steps into the position in which in the Parousia sayings Jesus stood with his claim to authority. *(p. 115)*

Here, too, Tödt observes a correspondence to the rest of the Q material: "The same opposition which dominates the Son of Man sayings also runs through the Sayings Source" (*ibid.*). For this Tödt cites Q 6:22; Mt 11:16f.; Lk 11:29f., 31f.; 12:8f. and also the wisdom saying "Lk 11:50f." (strangely, however, not Q 13:34f.), in which the community detected "surely the charge" against that generation that "kills Jesus and thereby shows that it is guilty of the continued murder of the prophets..." (p. 242). Here he is referring to a context of motifs whose relevance for Q, however, would not become fully recognized until O. H. Steck's *Das gewaltsame Geschick der Propheten* became influential.

---

[9] Cf. Tödt's apt comment on Q 17:24: "The transcendent eminence of the Son of Man thus acquires such strong validity that God's prerogatives are transferred to the figure of the one who brings everything to consummation" (p. 48).

[10] On this compare my critique of Tödt: *Studien* 143-147.

Tödt's impressive overall picture of the development of early christology proceeds from the premise that the bulk of the sayings of the coming SM go back to Jesus himself. This dictates that he also brings the expectation of the return of Jesus, which was prompted by the Easter experience, into direct association with the formation of the SM christology—with the result that for him "Son of Man christology and the Sayings source...belong together both in terms of content and in terms of tradition history" (p. 245), the Q tradition appears to have been linked with the SM christology right *from the beginning*, and the continued proclamation of Jesus' message and thus the collection of the sayings of Jesus have their origin here. Accordingly, Tödt understands those sayings in which—without any direct reference to the SM—the eschatological significance of Jesus is the subject in correspondence with the development of the SM christology.[11] In light of this the saying of the confessor in Lk 12:8f. (with SM) gains a fundamental significance for the explanation of the genesis of post-Easter SM christology. The soteriological relation between Jesus and the SM, which Jesus himself proclaimed, was to be reinterpreted after Easter by the early church as a christological relation (by identifying the two).

The problems that arise from this are already evident in the fact that Tödt—correctly—always speaks of the SM as the eschatological guarantor of those that are his. But this formulation obscures the religio-historical problems thrown up by this. The SM is not understood elsewhere as guarantor, just as he cannot in general be counted as the "judge" (if we disregard for a moment *1 Enoch* and later Christian reception). This difficulty points to a problem that requires another explanation than that offered by Tödt. He correctly observes that the SM—especially if we also include the sayings of the earthly SM—forms a kind of leading idea of the collection of dominical sayings preserved in Q and that the mention of these sayings in the framework of the composition as a whole is evidently executed in a carefully planned way (cf. pp. 246-248). If, however, one does not share Tödt's premise of the authenticity of the sayings of the coming SM, the early start for the SM christology loses its strict necessity. The possibility cannot be immediately excluded that the reception of the SM idea and its careful outworking did not occur until a later stage in the Q tradi-

---

[11] Cf. especially 231-242: "The bonding of the disciples to Jesus; the understanding of the future promises and the earthly authority of Jesus according to the Q materials that results from that bond".

tion. The urgent question is then how the SM christology relates to QR. To answer this question it is necessary to seek a more nuanced model for the development of early christology. Subsequent research has made a start in this direction.

Before we pursue this question further, however, brief reference at least should be made to another seminal work that has become essential for the understanding of the redactional profile of QR. The work in question is O. H. Steck's dissertation, *Israel und das gewaltsame Geschick der Propheten* (Heidelberg, 1965; published Neukirchen, 1967). According to Steck, Q's notion of the sending of the prophets and the violent rejection of their preaching of repentance by stiff-necked Israel, the consequence of which will be judgment, constitutes a firm topos of the deuteronomistic tradition (the oldest form of which is found in Neh 9:26). As the history of the reception of this topos in early Judaism demonstrates, it clearly determined Jewish thought in many variant forms well into the post-New Testament period. Two strands of it can be discerned in its Christian reception: one in hellenistic Jewish Christianity, in which it is seen in reference to the killing of Jesus (Mk 12:1b-9; 1 Thess 2:15f.; Acts 7:52), and one in Palestinian Jewish Christianity, in which the notion "is held up polemically against the scribes but is also drawn upon for understanding the fate of its rejected preachers and probably also the killing of Jesus" (p. 289). The main prooftexts for this are found in the sayings source and in the Gospel of Matthew. Both of these attest the present significance which evidently was attached to the concept for the self-understanding of the (Israel-) preachers working in their areas of tradition.[12]

It is in line with the framework of ideas of the deuteronomistic depiction of history when great emphasis is given in Q "to repentance and obedience towards the will of God in view of the imminent turn of the ages". According to this there arises "a division of the people in the present which is understood as the last time; some go to their imminent salvation...,the others are subjected to definitive rejection" (p. 286). The interest that motivates Q is the "quickening of Israel". The Jewish Christian preachers understand their task and their fate as "corresponding to that of 'the prophets'..." (p. 287).

Against this background Steck determines the *Sitz im Leben* of Q as a "logia-collection for the instruction of these Israel-preach-

---

[12] In this context special reference should also be made to Käsemann's studies on early Christian prophecy, to which Steck also refers.

ers..., from which they could extract their message to Israel, words
to their supporters and words for themselves, but also words of woe
and judgement to the stiff-necked" (p. 288). The relationship to
the deuteronomistic tradition is not unbroken: "The confession of
allegiance to *Jesus* as the SM who has worked on earth and will
come, expressly or implicitly determines the whole of what Q has
to say" (*sic*).[13] "The content of their proclamation (is) above all
the message of Jesus himself." For their work for Israel they understand themselves to have been "sent not by God or by Wisdom,
but by Jesus" (cf. Q 10). They experience their "fate of rejection" for his sake (cf. Q 6:22), and in his work, but "no longer
directly in 'the prophets'", have they "the example for their
task" (p. 288).

The special connection of the message of the prophets with the
(pre-existent) divine Wisdom in Lk 11:49f., which has there assumed the place of God both as the one who sends the prophets
and also as the "proclaimer of judgment", can in his view be understood from the connection between the wisdom tradition and
the deuteronomistic prophetic tradition which is already evident in
the hasidic movement (pp. 224-226). Steck views Lk 11:49f. as
traditional material taken over from Q (p. 223), which first receives
its Christian accent "in the authoritative word of Jesus" (v. 51b),
so "that it is this *present* generation that falls guilty of the blood of
the prophets" (p. 283). In Lk 6:22f. the prophets' saying is
connected "with the traditional notion of the suffering of the just"
(p. 283) and with the concept of the SM. Steck also sees the
invective of Lk 13:34 as a place of Jewish tradition (pp. 227f.), the
original subject of which is personified Wisdom. He assigns v. 35
also to this subject and finds here an expression of the threat that
Wisdom will withdraw from Israel and return only with the SM on
the occasion of the judgment (pp. 236f.). The saying derives from
the situation of the Jewish War (pp. 237-239) and regards the
impending destruction of Jerusalem as an expression of the
judgment that will not even be reviewed at the final assize.

This is not the place for a detailed critique of these ideas, which
would have to deal in particular with the reconstructions of the Q
text as well as the Jewish origins of Q 13:34f.[14] The circles in
which the deuteronomistic view of history was maintained also
need no separate discussion, since there is at least a consensus as
regards the notion that this view of history was largely determina-

[13] P. 288, with reference to Tödt 245ff. in note 7.
[14] On this, cf. *Studien* 158-190, and further below (p. 191).

tive for Jewish thought in early Christian times.[15] There is, however, a problem in Steck's wholesale interpretation of Q from the perspective of the deuteronomistic prophets saying. His identification of the *Sitz im Leben* of Q can therefore at best apply to individual traditions in Q, but not for QR, as D. Lührmann would object.

2. *First Attempts at a Redaction History*

In his Habilitationsschrift, *Die Redaktion der Logienquelle*,[16] Dieter Lührmann was the first of recent scholars (if we may for a moment disregard the investigations of A. Polag and H. Schürmann, as well as that of S. Schulz[17]) to deal programmatically with the redaction

---

[15] See e.g. the critique of M. Sato, *Q und die Prophetie* (Tübingen: 1988) 343f. Mention at least should be made of the dissertation of J. A. Williams, Jr, *A Conceptual History of Deuteronomism in the Old Testament, Judaism, and the New Testament* (Southern Baptist Theological Seminary: 1976), the essential parts of which were written without knowledge of Steck's work. It is not a fruitful study as regards the question of QR. On Q 11:47-51 and 13:34f., see 289-297. Williams' desire to trace these traditions back to the circles of Stephen and Philip (290), like the traditions in Acts 3 and 7 and 1 Thess 2:15f., is scarcely convincing.

[16] Accepted by the Faculty of Theology in Heidelberg in 1968 and published in 1969.

[17] In the context of this study I would rather not deal in more detail with the authors named above, since this would unnecessarily extend the scope without materially advancing the discussion. I shall therefore restrict myself to a few basic observations. In the framework of his studies on the Gospel of Luke H. Schürmann has repeatedly expressed his views on the sayings source since the beginning of the 1950s. Of particular interest as regards the present matter is his essay, "Beobachtungen zum Menschensohn-Titel in der Rede(n)quelle" in *Jesus und der Menschensohn* (*Festschrift* for A. Vögtle), eds. R. Pesch and R. Schnackenburg (Freiburg: 1975) 124-147 (= *idem*, *Gottes Reich—Jesu Geschick* [Freiburg: 1983] 153-182). In his view, the SM concept is attributable neither to the oldest discernible level of tradition of the dominical sayings nor to the final redaction of Q. Rather, it constitutes the "property of the early transmission of, or commentary on, the logia" (175, cf. 172), and was therefore not "the basic and fundamental christology of the final redaction" (179f.) either. This understanding, except as regards some individual interpretations, seems doubtful to me; his application of his ideal model of a four-stage sequence of *composition forms* in the genesis of the logia source (individual saying + additional sayings; series of proverbs; discourse composition; concluding redactional compilation of the discourse compositions into the sayings source) for his assessment is too directly *tradition-historical*, and he underestimates the overlapping function of the SM sayings in the compositions (cf. 174f.). Schürmann himself has again nuanced this model in his essay, "Das Zeugnis der Redenquelle für die Basileia-Verkündigung Jesu" in *Logia*, ed. J. Delobel (Leuven: 1982) 121-194 (=

of Q. For this he builds on Bultmann's distinction between "collection" and "redaction". Collection means "the placing together" according to particular principles, which, it is true, can become "redaction", or conscious "emphases and elaborations". In his opinion, the "principles of the collection" shown by Bultmann make possible "a distinction between a tradition that follows them and a redaction that consciously interprets". His first concern, then, is the question "whether within the material Q wishes to include an intention can be discerned, according to which the tradition collected here was put together" (p. 19). Here Lührmann transfers the redaction-critical way of viewing the evangelists onto the "larger collections" in the tradition that was "taken over" by them (p. 16). He further asks, critically, whether Bultmann's "concept of an organic process of the transmission of Q from the Palestinian community into the hellenistic community" (a concept developed "clearly under the influence of Wellhausen") could not be replaced by the more probable hypothesis "that at some stage various traditions were put together into the logia source, so that a single redaction of Q could be demonstrated" (p. 16). The form-critical approach opens a window on the "history of the tradition" underlying Q, more

---

Geschick 65-152), and (if somewhat inadequately) outlined its problems (cf. *ibid.* 74-79, especially 78f.).

In his doctoral dissertation, *Christologie der Logienquelle* (Trier: 1969, published in a revised form in Neukirchen in 1977), A. Polag took further the findings of his licenciate thesis, "Der Umfang der Logienquelle" (Trier: 1966), as regards the redaction-critical questions, and made them the basis for his presentation of the christology of Q. His distinctive description of a main collection, which presupposed smaller, earlier groups of sayings and was subjected to minor elaborations from a late and especially christologically-oriented "late redaction", is not sufficiently well demonstrated by an analysis of the compositions. Particularly problematic, however, is his assumption that the SM designation in the sayings that belong to the early layer—even when they speak of the future SM—refer to the speaker himself in a "qualified, indefinite manner of speaking" (*Christologie* 111-115) and was not taken as a title until the time of the translation into Greek in the late redaction (cf. 132f.). On this, see my treatment of Polag in *Studien* 92-98.

Finally, when S. Schulz (*Q. Die Spruchquelle der Evangelisten* [Zürich: 1972], e.g. 382) ascribes the coming SM sayings to the oldest Palestinian layer, but the earthly SM sayings only to the later hellenistic / Jewish-Christian Q communities of Syria, the distinction is not reinforced by a literary and redaction-critical analysis of the individual Q compositions and of the source as a whole. The omission of such analyses in general makes his whole scheme problematic. I have dealt with his theses—though on the basis of my earlier overall view of Q—in detail in a review (*BZ* 19 [1975] 104-115).

precisely on "the history of particular pieces of tradition brought together in Q" (p. 101). The distinction between "collection" and "redaction" can here also "reveal a form-history..., insofar as in the course of the compilation of originally isolated individual instances of the various forms, new forms, frameworks or mega-forms come into being, in the case of Q mostly the form of the extended apophthegm" (p. 101).

As far as method is concerned, there is a choice of three ways of looking at the redaction. Lührmann correctly demands, first, that one start with those

> larger passages...which are found in the same order in Luke and Matthew and can thus be deduced to have already been placed together in Q. When the form-critical investigation shows that we are dealing with several units which were originally transmitted in isolation, the question arises whether there is any evident intention behind the compilation of these units. All results only have any validity if they can be shown to appear not only in one place, but be typical of Q at several places. *(p. 20)*

Secondly, a comparison with the parallels in the Markan tradition can "demonstrate tendencies within the Q-tradition" (*ibid.*). Lührmann prefers—like classical literary criticism—not to take the double tradition as indicating the literary dependency of the different sources, but to see "tradition-historical connections in it". "Sources" are "not static entities with no history which were formulated once and for all in a particular way, but discernible intermediate and final stages in a history of transmission, which leads from Jesus himself, via the early Palestinian and Hellenistic church to a provisional fixing in Mark and Q and its further elaboration in Luke and Matthew" (p. 21).

Thirdly, the "community constructions" in Q make it possible to draw conclusions concerning QR. However, since it is not clear "from which stage of the transmission" they derive, they can only be turned to account "insofar as they clearly go back to the redactor himself or to the most recent layer before the redactors, from which the redaction might derive" (p. 22).

In his work Lührmann restricts himself to "making a provisional test of the possibility of the question cited with some relatively straightforward examples" (p. 22). He proceeds from a careful selection of units of tradition, which he summarizes thematically under the three rubrics, "Jesus and 'This Generation'" (pp. 24-48), "The Community" (pp. 49-68) and "Eschatology" (pp. 69-83). In his concluding chapter, "Q in the History of Early

Christianity", he evaluates the individual results for the tracing of the redactional profile of Q and its position in the history of early Christian theology.

Proceeding from Q 7:34f.; 11:30; 11:49f., 51 + 13:34f., which he ascribed to QR as an addition or a creation, he designated the "contrast between Jesus and this generation" and the related "proclamation of judgment against Israel" as the main concern of the redaction (p. 84). An examination of the sections Q 12:2-7 + 8f. (+ R); 6:22f.; 10:2(R) + 3-11 + 12(R) + 13-15 + 21f. (concerning the disciples) shows clearly that the disciples enter into this contrast—"extended to *all* who refuse to hear the proclamation of the disciples" (pp. 84, 64)—which is legitimated by the revelation given to them by the Son. Here QR assumes that Gentiles belong to the community, for which Lührmann finds evidence in Q 7:1-10 (pp. 57f.). Analysis of the eschatological passages that conclude Q—Q 17:24, 26-30, 34f., 37; 19:12-27 (and possibly Q 22:30) again confirms the dominance of the threat of judgment in the whole of the collection. Q 12:39f., 42-46 and Q 19:12-27 show that the "admonition of watchfulness" in the context of Q "must be understood against the background of the delay of the parousia" (p. 75).

As the analysis shows, if QR is drawing on collections of sayings that are already in existence and is deliberately forming these according to theological features, this indicates "that Q already stands at the (provisional) end of a lengthy process of transmission and that, accordingly, the material taken up in Q is not homogeneous" (p. 84; cf. 20f., 16). Since Q 10:21f. derives from the hellenistic community (p. 85; cf. 64-68, 99f.) and some sayings reflect the delay of the parousia, while others give reason to assume that Gentiles belong to the community (cf. pp. 86-88), QR is to be situated "in the hellenistic community of the 50s or 60s.... A likely setting would be the Syrian area (without being more precise)—in which Matthew is also probably to be situated" (p. 88).

Associated with this tradition-historical placement are two problem areas that are central for forming a theological profile of QR. The "proclamation of judgment against this generation" makes the "contrast between Jesus and the community on the one hand, and Israel on the other, a definitive one; only judgment remains for Israel" (p. 93). Steck's view, therefore, that "the leading concern in Q, also, is the 'revival of Israel'", Lührmann can see as true only of "the original sense" of "the passages that arose in the context of the dispute between the early Christian mission and

Israel", i.e. as true only of the tradition, but not of QR.[18] This important distinction does indeed merit consideration, along with the observation that the proclamation of judgment is valid "no longer for Israel alone" but has been "extended" (p. 96 with reference to 64) and thus has a universal horizon, as is clear precisely from the SM sayings in Q 17.[19]

His assessment of the christology of Q also has to do with these emphases. Like Tödt, he stresses that the passion kerygma is not significant for Q but that, on the other hand, despite its omission Q certainly does have a christological orientation. Accordingly, he seeks to give precision to Tödt's thesis that "Q's leading christological motive" is to be seen "in the further proclamation of the message of Jesus" concerning the nearness of the kingdom (p. 96).

> Through the strong predominance of the announcement of judgment—so significant precisely for the Q redaction—this proclamation is taken up in the apocalyptic expectation of judgment. Even if this expectation of judgment goes back to Jesus himself, in Q it is at least emphasized one-sidedly and has become the decisive factor in the redaction's interpretation of Jesus' proclamation of the kingdom. *(p. 94)*

One might, then, speak of a "reapocalypticization of the proclamation of Jesus in Q.[20] For christology...this means that the continuity between Jesus and the community is to be found in eschatology, not in the kerygma. It is not Jesus who is proclaimed, rather the content of the proclamation is the coming judgment, in which Jesus, as the SM, will save his church" (p. 96).[21] The titles SM and Kyrios,[22] which occur in Q—quite apart from the Son-title—confirm "how determinative eschatology is for Q" (p. 97).

---

[18] Accordingly, for him it is also questionable "whether Q is so exclusively coloured by the deuteronomistic view of history as Steck thinks" (p. 88).

[19] But what, then, of Q 22:30 / Mt 19:28?

[20] How this can be reconciled with the delay of the parousia which he discerns, Lührmann correctly sees as a problem, though his statement that this shows the delay of the parousia was "not the only concern of the redaction of Q" (p. 94) is hardly satisfactory.

[21] When Lührmann (96 n. 5) reduces the continuity between Jesus and Q to the "taking up of the proclamation of judgment", he overlooks the fact that QR also accepts other traditions and is concerned to qualify the proclamation of judgment precisely in its eschatological sense. On this, compare the view of Davies (see note 6 above).

[22] "The latter—with the exception of Lk 7:6 / Mt 8:8—designates the eschatological judge" (p. 97).

Although Lührmann views the message of QR in this way, he rejects any contemporary relevance for the SM title for QR. This obviously has tradition-historical presuppositions. The identification of the coming SM with Jesus, along with Tödt and the majority of scholars he assumes, belongs "already to the tradition before Q". It "evidently goes back to the Palestinian church". To this extent it cannot be maintained with the exclusiveness that Tödt implies that SM christology and Q belong so closely together. This association is true only for the tradition, while for QR "the sayings of the Son of Man coming for judgment"...are—only(!)—"a means of carrying through its motive of the proclamation of judgment, but only one, which stands next to such a saying as Lk 11:49-51 which reflects completely different tradition-historical conditions, and serves the same purpose" (pp. 85f.).

The question in which stage of the tradition Jesus came to be identified with the SM should for the moment be left open. Here Lührmann shows himself to be rather uncritically indebted to Tödt's view. It is surely right that the SM christology cannot be maintained to be exclusively the province of Q, as Tödt claims, and that in Q christology becomes a topic only indirectly. But can the observation that QR ascribes a fundamental role to the proclamation of judgment be reconciled with the notion that for the redactor, who gives this proclamation of judgment central place, there was no significance to the agent of the eschatological event, who is mentioned by name in the proclamation? Precisely because its agent is for QR (also) identical with Jesus, his message is relevant for QR as well, the proclamation of judgment is put on his lips, and justification in the judgment is made dependent on the response to this message.

The contradictions in the argument are evident in the details. In his analysis, Lührmann designates Q 7:31-35 as a redactional addition (31), through which the whole unit Q 7:18-35 receives the "new direction...towards the contrast with this generation" (p. 30), which is subsequently shown to be typical of QR. On the other hand, with his argument on p. 83 that the sayings which identify Jesus with the SM (e.g. Q 7:34 or 9:58) belong to the tradition before Q and are not attributable to QR, Lührmann denies any significance of this identification for QR. But then why does the already traditional motif of "contrast" have significance for QR, while the SM-designation that is so closely associated with it and with the proclamation of judgment does not? The SM saying Q 11:30 Lührmann in fact classes as one of the few compositions of the redaction (pp. 40-42, 99). But as the comparison with the "person of Jonah" shows, the saying refers equally to the "person" of the SM who is identical with Jesus, who becomes the sign of judgment for this generation. When Lührmann cites Q 11:49-51 in order to show that QR can articulate the proclamation of judgment even without any reference to the SM christology, he ignores the fact that, for example in the related passage Q 13:34f., the proclamation of judgment is also christologized.[23] Finally, the statement in Q 7:34f., connected tradition-historically with the wisdom / prophetic tradition, in which John and the SM are understood as messengers of Wisdom, confirms this christological interest of QR.[24]

The question of the relationship of the SM designation of Jesus to QR thus becomes the decisive problem. In these logia, which are characterized by "late-Jewish wisdom", Lührmann correctly sees the "latest and therefore, temporally if not tradition-historically speaking the nearest layer of the tradition to the redaction of Q" (p. 98). But the same is true of the judgment motif. "It is beyond dispute that this tradition found essential motifs, such as the proclamation of judgment in particular, in the existing tradition; but the uniformity with which this motif is treated in several studies indicates that the redaction uses it consciously in the shaping of the material" (p. 101).

3. The Wisdom-Deuteronomistic Redaction in Q

Arland Dean Jacobson further develops the ideas of Steck and Lührmann in his dissertation, "Wisdom Christology in Q" (Claremont, 1978), which was inspired by J. M. Robinson, and his 1982 essay, "The Literary Unity of Q".[25] I shall deal first with the dissertation.

It is clear to him, precisely from the characteristically wisdom-type sections—as distinct, for example, from the "primitive structure" of the Gospel of Thomas—that Q constitutes a "coherent document" (p. 6). At the same time, however, it is clear to him "that Q underwent development beyond the stage of a mere ran-

---

[23] Lührmann himself would even like to assume that the two sayings were originally linked and attached to the discourse to the Pharisees, though even he brings out the christologization in the case of Q 13:35.

[24] Lührmann (97 n. 6) assigns this passage expressly to "late Jewish wisdom".

[25] *JBL* 101 (1982) 365-389.

dom collection of unrelated sayings" (p. 5). Access to the theological tendencies of the compilers is gained "through analysis of the structure of the document and the interior dynamics of its parts" (p. 8). With N. Perrin he distinguishes "composition criticism" from "redaction criticism" in the narrower sense.[26] The former is concerned with "the sequence of the material and the thematic relationship of the various pericopes".[27] In scope he limits the investigation to Q 3:1–11:52, since in these compositions—unlike the materials that follow in Q 12:2ff.—the Q-akolouthia is recognizable with some certainty. He distinguishes three "sections": Q 3:7–7:35; 9:57–10:16 and 11:14-52, which owe their present form and order to a uniform redaction. Since the most intensive reworking of the traditional material is evident here, he designates this layer as the "composition stage of Q".[28] From this stage he wishes to separate two later re-workings: an "intermediate redactional stage" which he assigns to Q 3:16c;[29] 7:18-23 (indicated as final redaction on pp. 94 and 222); 7:28 and 10:21f. (belonging rather to the final redaction according to pp. 144 and 221). Finally he sees this redaction at work only in the first section in the context of the Baptist. To the "final redaction", which interests him in the concluding summary only,[30] he ascribes Q 4:1-12; 10:21f., and in close association with this 11:2-4, 9-13 (pp. 156, 221) and cautiously also 12:2-10; 12:22ff. (p. 222); 17:5f., 18-23 (p. 221). He wants to see this layer of reception as determined by a "highly enthusiastic form of Christianity" and in dispute with it (pp. 221f.; cf. also 232). Here he suspects also connections with Paul and the Gospel of John (pp. 219f.): "We can see how at its last stage Q seemed to have been steered into a more orthodox course, preparing for its demise as an independent document" (p. 222).

---

[26] P. 8, with n. 20 and n. 19 (with further bibliographical references).

[27] Pp. 8f., with the three steps: Reconstruction of the Sequence of Q; Analysis of the Reconstructed Q Material; Determining the Stages in the Composition of Q. The detailed literary-critical questions, however, as well as the reconstruction of the Q text, are all dealt with together, with reference back to earlier discussion.

[28] In the interests of simplicity I abbreviate this stage of redaction with my siglum QR, although, as will become apparent, to this stage I also assign in large part the later stages of redaction distinguished by Jacobson.

[29] Cf. 33-35, 73f., 94: by means of the insertion, the baptism of fire by Yahweh is associated with Jesus' baptism of the spirit; on this see also my own analysis, *Studien* 15-33.

[30] Pp. 215-224, cf. 231ff.: "A Later Redaction of Q", with brief reference to the intermediate redaction on p. 231.

As regards the question of QR and the SM one needs to refer to his analysis of the first stage of redaction. The wisdom-influenced sayings Q 7:31-35; 10:21f.; 11:29-32, 49-51; 13:34f. are characteristic of this stage. At the same time they are—with the exception of 10:21f.— also influenced by the deuteronomistic view of history, in particular by the prophetic utterance and the proclamation of judgment against this generation. For the first section he indicates this in his analysis of Q 7:31-35, which in his view were connected to the Baptist sayings Q 7:24-27 by means of Mt 11:12f. (here Jacobson prefers the Matthean order over Lk 16:16):

> The views it expresses coincide with those found elsewhere in the compositional stage of the first section of Q: John and Jesus are placed on the same level, both are rejected and there is polemic against "this generation". But this pericope goes beyond the previous material in showing how John and Jesus are related—namely as messengers of Wisdom. This pericope thus provides the theological basis for the composition of the whole first section of Q. The "children" of Wisdom are those who, in contrast to "this generation", respond to the call to repentance issued by John and Jesus, and who thus "justify" Wisdom because they acquiesce in Wisdom's judgment on this generation, uttered by her messengers, John and Jesus. Thus, the Wisdom pericope in Lk 7:31-35 par is not a foreign intrusion into the surrounding Q material; rather, it brings to clearer expression the tendencies at work in the composition of Q. *(pp. 96f.)*

By the insertion of Q 6:39, 42 (perhaps also 43-45) into a collection of wisdom admonitions which was originally addressed to the disciples, the compositional unit Q 6:20-49 is given a polemical (anti-Pharisaic) tone directed against the religious leaders (pp. 95f., 227; cf. also 65f.). The insertion of the pericope concerning the pagan centurion, Q 7:1-10 corresponds with this note of polemic towards Israel (p. 96). The addition of Lk 6:23c introduces the prophetic aspect into the last beatitude (pp. 53-55). Finally, the addition of 3:8b, which questions the guarantee of Israel's salvation, in the Baptist's sermon indicates the same redaction (p. 31f.).

In the analysis of the second section, Q 9:56–10:16, Jacobson does not distinguish so clearly between tradition and redaction. Evidently he finds the specific redactional tendencies particularly discernable in the saying of 9:58, which is to be attributed to the myth of the rejection of Wisdom (pp. 131-133), and in the words of judgment in 10:13-15. Here there is no question of a "real mission", as in the traditional material that has been reworked by the redaction, but rather of an "errand of judgement", an errand which serves only to announce judgment against Israel (p. 145; cf. also 134f.).

In the third section, Q 11:14-20, 23, 29-32, 24-26 (27-)28, 33-36, 46, 42, 39-41, 47-48, 49-51 (cf. p. 193 on this sequence), 11:47f., 49-51 is correctly evaluated as the main redactional statement. Jacobson also finds redactional tones in the sayings in Q 11:19f., with its threat of judgment (p. 164; cf. 193), which in this respect correspond to the sayings inserted by the redaction in Q 11:31f. Jacobson would like to relate the sign of the SM in Q 11:30 in a non-apocalyptic way to the preaching of Jesus in analogy with that of Jonah and see it as a pre-redactional elaboration, which QR has then placed with the sayings in 11:31f. (pp. 168f.). With their polemic against this generation they also betray how close they are to the deuteronomistic tradition (p. 171). By then leaving the saying concerning the unclean spirit at the end of the unit of tradition, with Matthew, and understanding it, like the latter, as a woe against this generation, he again makes out the polemic "against this generation" to be the redactional intention.[31]

In the woe against Jerusalem in Q 13:34f., which Jacobson prefers not to link with 11:49-51, even if its original position in Q (after Q 12:2ff.) can no longer be discerned, the deuteronomistically flavoured critique of Israel is expressed in its sharpest form (cf. pp. 210-14, here 211).[32]

Jacobson is no doubt successful in demonstrating the significance of the wisdom-deuteronomistic elements for the first comprehensive redaction of the Q material. When it comes to the details, he too is left with questions which must be addressed before we discuss his second contribution.

His assumption of a second or third layer of redactional interference seems particularly problematic to me. I would question the

---

[31] When in this section too Jacobson relates the polemic to "Jewish leaders" (thus 193), his view is justified only by the woes in 11:37ff. There are no grounds for it in the text itself. But it can be seen precisely in 11:37ff. too that QR generalizes the concrete accusation into "this generation" (Lk 11:51!). Is Jacobson's judgment influenced by the analysis of Lk 6:20ff., where he supports the orientation against the "leaders of Israel" only upon the saying Q 6:39, which is extremely dubious in its position (cf. pp. 65f.)? Do the observations above not rather lead to the conclusion that QR extends a polemic which in the tradition before him is against the Pharisees and Scribes into a polemic against all Israel, which is identified with "this generation"?

[32] To this extent this woe deserves, in my view, special attention as far as the historical classification of QR is concerned.

redactional character of Lk 3:8b as well as the ascription of
Lk 3:16c; 7:18-23; 7:28 to a later layer of tradition "which served
the purpose of driving a wedge between John and Jesus by
assigning John to the old aeon. One could sense here the emergence of a high Christology" (p. 231). In contrast with this, he
reclaims for the first redaction a certain equal ranking of John and
Jesus as messengers of Wisdom. Can this distinction really be
maintained? Here we are back again with my primary question
concerning the relationship between QR and the SM tradition.
Jacobson has consistently to play down the significance of the
characterization of Jesus as SM, by ascribing it to the pre-redactional tradition, as in Q 6:22f. and 11:30 (here with a rather unconvincing literary-historical manoeuvre), or on the other hand by
emptying the title of its content.[33] Has he achieved this convincingly?

In Q 11:30 he reduces the reference to the SM, in its content, to
the statement "that Jesus or his preaching is what is compared to
Jonah..." (p. 168). It speaks against this that in 11:30 the demand
for signs in v. 29 is moved into the perspective of judgment by
the—in his view redactional—juxtaposition of 11:31f. The sign of
Jonah thereby receives a clear reference to the future—precisely
for QR as well. For even without this context v. 30 moves attention
from the present situation of the demand for signs (v. 29) to a future event (ἔσται).

The SM title is not assured in Q 6:23. If, however, "SM" did
stand here, though—as Jacobson together with Perrin correctly
points out against Tödt—the title cannot be reduced to the earthly
exousia. Still, his open definition, "not...simply as a reference to
the apocalyptic figure of judgement" (p. 54 note 103), is not
satisfactory either. For precisely this distinctive break with
apocalyptic usage and its combination with the notion of the suffering righteous man demand an explanation, and this is scarcely
provided by means of an interpretation that devoids the content of
significance.

Jacobson has no explanation at all for the use of SM in Lk 9:58
(cf. pp. 131f.), although he emphatically points out that the saying
should be seen "as essentially a statement about Jesus" and thus
possesses christological relevance and represents "a kind of
frontispiece to the second section of Q" (p. 132). He correctly
sees, too, that Q 10:21f. was added—in his view at a later stage of
redaction, however—in order "to reinterpret the preceding ma-

---

[33] On this cf. "Unity" (see note 25 above) 388f.

terial" (p. 143). But then can the statement of Q 9:58 really be reduced to the motif of the rejection of Jesus and his designation as SM be simply passed over?

Decisive for our question, finally, is the redactional conclusion to the first section in Q 7:31-35, to which Jacobson too attaches central importance for QR. He correctly states that the primary contrast is not between John and Jesus but between "this generation" and these two messengers of Wisdom. He correctly observes, also, that Jesus' statement is given greater weight, on the one hand by its length, and on the other by the SM-designation: "the designation 'Son of Man' might indicate Jesus' superior status" (p. 87). With M. Black, he considers it conceivable, too, "that originally 'Son of Man' was simply an elliptical way of saying 'I'" (p. 88, with note 187). But since "here" too it is "clear" for Q 'that 'Son of Man' does not designate the apocalyptic end-time judge" (p. 88), he concludes:

> Therefore, the meaning of "Son of Man" will have to be determined from its present context. In that case, either the earlier apocalyptic use of the designation had already been worn down through familiarity into little more than a name (analogous to Jesus Christ), or the Q tradition did not understand "Son of Man" exclusively in the sense of an apocalyptic end-time judge. I consider the latter to be more probable. (*ibid.*)

One may acknowledge that the distinctive unevenness in the use of the title has been adequately observed. But what does it mean to suggest that SM here is not used exclusively in the sense of the apocalyptic end-time judge? And above all, why does QR then use, or take over, the designation here and in other passages that are significant for the redaction? How can it be reconciled with this interpretation that in Q 12:40 and Q 17 QR takes over apocalyptic SM-sayings? Q 13:35 shows that for QR too Jesus assumes a unique position in the events of the end-time which can certainly be related to the traditional content of the SM title. Could QR not yet have known this in 7:34? The more likely assumption, then, is that according to QR Jesus here not only shares with John the fate of the rejected messenger of Wisdom but also—unlike John—is to be named as the decisive authority in the end-time event.

Already in the material that Jacobson ascribes to QR, therefore, the concern is not only with the equal juxtaposition of John and Jesus, but also with the special eschatological position of Jesus, as the use of the SM designation shows. This is unaffected by QR's still valid insight that John marks the turn of the ages and that with him the time of the *Basileia* has begun, as Jacobson correctly brings out in his interpretation of Mt 11:12f. (p. 81). If this is accepted as the genuine view of QR, the next question is whether there is indeed such a serious difference between Q 7:18-23, 28; 3:16c and QR that those sayings have to be ascribed to a later stage in the development of christology, in which the desire was to emphasize the fundamental difference between John and Jesus and even exclude John from the *Basileia* (p. 95). The latter, in my view, cannot be concluded from Q 7:28 either, to the extent that the saying wants to draw out the overwhelming significance of Jesus in the eschaton *at the same time* as acknowledging the present significance of John.[34] This is also true then for 7:18-23 and 3:16c.[35] These so-called later additions have certainly become part of the ambivalent presentation of Jesus in QR. So I see no reason not to ascribe these passages to QR. As a result, the problem of the combination of quotations in 7:27 is more open to a solution. For the recourse to Isa 40:3, which Jacobson ascribes to Q in Q 3:4, does not alter the fact that the relationship between John and Jesus as coming SM is a theme in the context of QR at this point (cf. pp. 77f.). John's "more than a prophet" is expounded with reference to the coming SM through his function as predecessor / precursor. This is confirmed by the overall construction of Q. The position of the Baptist pericope with the message of the coming judgment and the proclamation of the future Baptizer in fire expresses this relationship *before* the preaching of Jesus, if we assume that for QR the expectation of the end-time coming of Jesus, as inherited from the oldest interpretation of Jesus, was taken for granted and that the overall composition reached its conclusion in Q 17. Q 11:29-32 and 13:34f. individually confirm that QR associates the notion of Israel's rejection of the prophets with the notion of the decisive eschatological agent of divine action (my wording is deliberately broad) in the figure of Jesus. Independently of the question in what stage of the tradition the SM concept was received by Q, we have to assume that the ambivalence observed in the relationship between John and Jesus must have determined the post-Easter tradition right from the beginning, even if

---

[34] See my interpretation of this in *Studien* 219-224.

[35] Incidentally, it is instructive that the supposed difference from others as well is brought into the argument and—reversing the tradition-historical relationships—the emphasis on the difference is ascribed to an earlier stage in the dispute with the Baptist's disciples and the equality of status between the two is ascribed to a later stage. It is true of both models of interpretation that they play down the value of the SM title in 7:34. In my view this is methodologically unjustified.

it was articulated in different ways. It is rooted in the Jesus story itself, to the extent that the former disciple of John and later
Basileia-messenger, Jesus, was after his violent death expected by
the disciples as the coming Kyrios.

Against this background, the logion 10:21f. too—even if its religio-historical background and its interpretation continue to be
disputed in the details—does not represent something totally new,
as Jacobson, Lührmann and others assume when they assign the
saying to the latest stage of tradition or see it as a hellenistic
construction. In my view the first saying—perhaps transmitted independently—could certainly be situated in the life of Jesus.[36] The
theme of opposition between those in Israel who are counted as
"wise", from whom the mystery of God is hidden, and those
"little ones" (νήπιοι) to whom it has been revealed in accordance
with God's will, only reflects the opposition between those who reject Jesus' message and those who accept it, by attributing it theologically to the will of God. In this respect it can certainly be reconciled with QR's statement in Q 7:34f. The second saying, which
can scarcely have been originally transmitted in isolation, can be
understood as an interpretation of the first statement as long as the
identity of Jesus with the coming representative of God's
sovereignty is presupposed. It is certainly plausible that in the light
of this previous indication the former messenger of Wisdom
should become the one who himself reveals to the elect the divine
secret of his end-time eminence. If one can ascribe such a statement to—I freely admit—a relatively later stage of reflection, then
such an explanation would certainly be consonant with that line of
interpretation of QR which acknowledged (with qualifications) eschatological eminence for the former messenger of Wisdom. From
a religio-historical point of view it is not unusual for wisdom and
apocalyptic motifs to be linked together here in such a particular
manner, as is shown for example by the Similitudes of *1 Enoch*.
Against a one-sidedly wisdom interpretation of the Father–Son
metaphor it should be borne in mind that precisely the early evidence for the "Son-Christology" is found in markedly eschatological contexts (cf. Mk 13:32 or 1 Cor 15:28). Whatever
redaction-critical decision one makes, it is not justifiable to play off
the wisdom references against an apocalyptic background, especially as such a connection is evident also in the use of the SM title
in wisdom-deuteronomistic statements.

---

[36] On this cf. *Studien* 109-118 and 118-142.

An explanation is, however, needed for the question why that wisdom-deuteronomistic layer of redaction brings precisely the SM designation into its text at passages which are clearly relevant for the redaction, even when it is "only" a matter of the reception of the available tradition. Jacobson's unconcerned interpretation is not convincing, especially since christological tendencies of the redaction can be discerned outside those passages shaped by the SM christology, as Q 13:35 documents. The findings require an explanation, even if it is right that these "christological tendencies" are not articulated in explicit, christological confessional statements but rather become operative indirectly in the formulations. Christological reflection does not directly become a topic— or hardly so—but still remains latently operative. It determines the deeper dimension of the statements rather than their outward dimension.

In his first investigation Jacobson restricted himself to the first, in his structure more easily reconstructable, part of the sayings source, and apart from some rather hypothetical remarks he did not take account of the Q material following in Lk 12–17. As far as the understanding of QR is concerned, but in particular also as far as the significance of the SM for QR is concerned, the effect of this is rather negative. For in Q 12:40 and 17:23-37 (perhaps also in Q 12:8f.) we encounter precisely the statements that refer unambiguously to the coming SM. Besides these, however, there are further statements which, without designating Jesus as SM, deal with his end-time function (cf. Q 13:25-27, 28f. or the parables Q 12:42-46 and 19:11-27). In this part of Q too there appear statements that are determined by the deuteronomistic view of history. Jacobson himself mentions Q 13:34f; 14:16-24. Even if the reconstruction of the Q akolouthia is still disputed because of the strong redactional intervention by Luke, these traditions must be brought into the investigation if we are to make progress on the questions that are raised. Jacobson himself dealt with these problems in his 1982 article, "The Literary Unity of Q", and attempted to integrate them into the view of QR he reached in his dissertation. To begin with, on the basis of a comparison of the strands of tradition represented by Mark and Q, he regards his thesis as confirmed that "the organizing principle which gives literary unity to Q and provides coherence to its various characteristics" is given in the tradition affected by wisdom-deuteronomistic influences. He sees the first half of Q in particular as predominantly characterized by this tradition, but here he does make a qualification:

It is not being claimed that in identifying the source of literary unity of
Q we have explicated the theology of Q. Put otherwise, the
deuteronomistic and Wisdom perspective is not the content of the Q
proclamation but simply the vehicle for its expression. The
deuteronomistic tradition seems to have provided a framework within
which to reflect theologically upon the disappointments of the Jesus
movement among their fellow Jews. The integration of the figure of
Wisdom into the deuteronomistic sketch of history served to draw John
and Jesus into Israel's *Heilsgeschichte* as the last in a series of Wisdom's envoys. *(p. 388)*

This finding changes, however, with the sections from Q 12:2
onwards:

Beginning at Luke 12:2 par, one comes upon a section of Q in which
apocalyptic paraenesis dominates and where traces of the
deuteronomistic-Wisdom perspective are infrequent.... All of the apocalyptic Son of Man sayings occur in this latter portion of Q
(Luke 12:8, 10 par; 12:40 par; 17:23-24 par; 17:26-27, 30 par). In
contrast to most of the material in the first part of Q, the material in
the latter part is usually addressed to the community itself. It deals with
typical apocalyptic concerns: exhortations to remain faithful during persecution (Luke 12:2-9 par), the promise of God's care (Luke 12:11-12
par; 12:22-31 par), calls to be watchful (Luke 12:35-45 par), exhortations concerning radical discipleship and faithfulness (Luke 12:49-53
par; 14:26-27 par; 17:5-6 par), calls to righteousness in view of the
coming judgement (Luke 12:57-59 par; 13:23-24, 25-29 par; 16:16-18
par) and warnings about the end-time to come (17:23-37 par). Such
apocalyptic paraenesis is by no means alien to the deuteronomistic tradition. Nevertheless, the material in this second portion of Q (the material interspersed from Luke 12:2 par to Luke 22:30 par) must be regarded as representing an older block of material (with exceptions such
as Luke 13:34-35 par). *(p. 388)*

Jacobson justifies this with the thesis of his dissertation, that in the
first part of Q the apocalyptic SM christology is not characteristic
of QR but is older than QR. From this he concludes, finally, "that
the whole block of apocalyptic paraenesis, buttressed as it is by
imminent expectation of the Son of Man, must underlie a later
layer of deuteronomistic-Wisdom material" (p. 389). In this over-
laying of material, he believes, evidence surfaces of "the beginning of a tradition history of Q". The deuteronomistic redaction
presents "a shift away from the earlier view focused on the imminent expectation of the Son of Man". This change, he claims, also
indicates a change in the self-understanding of the group in its relationship to Israel:

In the block of apocalyptic paraenesis, the community sees itself as the righteous minority, the community of the elect within Israel who must remain faithful and watchful during difficult times, while the majority are portrayed as heedless of the gravity of the hour. But in the material subjected to redaction from the deuteronomistic-Wisdom perspective, we find an intensification of polemic. "This generation' is not only heedless, it shows its solidarity with past impenitent generations by violently opposing the prophets. Indeed, Israel is being redefined and those who now call themselves Israel will be replaced by others. (p. 389)

The emphasis upon judgement is now so strong that it is no longer clear whether there is any hope of Israel's awakening.[37]

He sees this change as on the one hand conditioned by the persecutions of the church, on the other by the successes in the Gentile mission. Both experiences are mirrored in the texts that are affected by the deuteronomistic redaction.

This interesting continuation and elaboration of the dissertation also raises some questions. Clarification is necessary for the presupposition that, from a literary-critical and tradition-historical point of view, in Q 12–17 we are dealing with a unified block of tradition which was marked by apocalyptic paraenesis, in particular by the SM expectation, and which QR took over together *en bloc*. A more exact analysis would have to test whether—as in the case of Q 3–11—groups of sayings of various origins were placed together secondarily, and who is responsible for this compilation. Perhaps QR again, or a pre-QR redaction, whose specific profile however would then have to be verified on the basis of these texts? Or are we dealing here with smaller, isolated series of sayings which should rather be ascribed to the oral stage of tradition?[38] Is

---

[37] *Ibid.* 389 n. 109 with Lührmann, against Steck.

[38] For example, in the course of my own investigation of the sayings concerning worries in Q 12:22-31 I have gained the impression that an older Jesus tradition which was directed to people living at subsistence level in general was at first related to travelling missionaries who were to do without all life security for the sake of the *Basileia*; their reference was not to the coming SM until a last stage because of the sayings in 12:39ff. which follow. For an analysis of the compositional units see my essays: "Die Sprüche vom Sorgen" in *Artikulation der Wirklichkeit (Festschrift* Siegfried Oppolzer), eds. H. Hierdeis and H. S. Rosenbusch (Frankfurt/M: 1988) 73-94 (89), and "Jesu 'Verbot des Sorgens' und seine Nachgeschichte in der synoptischen Überlieferung" in *Jesu Rede von Gott und ihre Nachgeschichte im frühen Christentum (Festschrift* Willi Marxsen), eds. D.-A. Koch *et al.* (Gütersloh: 1989) 116-141 (124-127); see also C.-P. März,

it really only in this part that the church is the direct addressee? Do we not find in the first part of Q also sections which refer to the church (such as Q 6:20ff. or Q 10:2ff.)? Does the use of the SM designation in the sayings sections from Q 12:2ff. onwards—if we set aside the frequency in Q 17—differ from that in Q 3–11 to such an extent that there is justification for a constitutive distinction from Q 3–11? It is in any case striking that here too one can speak of Jesus' eschatological function without the SM title. In Q 12:8, for example, if Mt 10:32f. is original with its I-form, Jesus appears as the end-time guarantor of his own.[39] In Q 13:25-27 Jesus is addressed as the Kyrios who makes the decisions regarding admittance into the eschatological community of salvation. Nor do the parables Q 12:42-46 and Q 19:11-27 give any indication of an original relation to the SM concept. If the decisive active agent in each of them is the householder, in material terms the figure corresponds rather with the Kyrios expectation of the early church. The apocalyptic SM title only occurs in Q 12:40 (then in 12:42-46, qualifying) and Q 17 and perhaps Mt 19:28 (diff. Lk 22:28-30). The aspect of the end-time *judge* is not so clearly brought out as is often assumed. Rather, the function of the SM remains in the air. The decisive thing is only that his coming implies the definitive in-breaking of the eschaton, signifying salvation for some, perdition for others. This SM slips into the role of judge only in the secondary connection with the servant parables, in which in the person of the unexpectedly returning householder he decides matters of payment and punishment. It is right that through the powerful final vision in Q 17, Q as a whole in its redactional final form is oriented towards the imminent arrival of the SM—in correspondence with John's announcement of the coming baptizer in fire at the beginning.[40] So there is no decision as yet concerning the age of the individual traditions and their relationship to one another.

Anyone who can no longer accept Tödt's thesis, that the sayings concerning the coming SM go back to Jesus himself and that following the Easter experience the earliest Palestinian church arrived at an identification of Jesus with this SM, as a necessary prerequisite for the reconstruction of the early development of chris-

---

"'...laßt euere Lampen brennen!'" in *Studien zur Q-Vorlage von Lk 12,35–14,24* (Leipzig: 1991).

[39] But even if the SM is original in the "confessor" saying, his particular function as guarantor rather than judge should be noted.

[40] As T. W. Manson already pointed out (see note 6 above).

tology,[41] to such a person the assumption that the SM concept was received only at a later stage cannot be excluded *a priori* as a possibility. Are there grounds for justifying this assumption? Should its absence from the Antiochene—Pauline sphere of tradition be attributable only to the fact that the title was suppressed out of consideration for the need to be understood by the hellenists being addressed?[42] Remarkably enough, the evangelists writing later, in their reception and elaboration of the SM christology—Matthew even with an intensified apocalypticization—do not recognize this problem when they even construct SM sayings themselves.

Jacobson also assumes that QR is responsible for the connection between Q 3–11 and Q 12–17. But then the conclusion must be that QR too was interested in the prospect of the coming SM (who was identical with Jesus). When on the one hand in Q 12–17 the SM statements are added secondarily to other units,[43] but on the other hand the SM designation crops up already in Q 3–11 in passages that are relevant to QR (Q 6:22; 7:34; 9:58; 11:30), the possibility cannot be excluded that behind this too there is a redactional intention. What right do we have to take the motif of contrast with this generation and the threat of judgment as typical of QR and not do the same in respect of the SM sayings that are connected with it? In view of his overall redaction-critical view, this question should be addressed even more pointedly to Jacobson than to Lührmann.

The suspicion expressed is further reinforced when we observe other instances of redactional intervention in the text which betray the fact that QR has a christological interest.[44] A reason to ascribe these passages to a later redaction is only present on the condition that QR is not allowed to have had a christological interest. If we take seriously the arrangement in the macro-text, there is no avoiding the impression that QR (also!) is concerned with the inte-

---

[41] On this cf. my essay, "Jesus versus Menschensohn" (195f. see note 4 above). Like Vögtle, I see the oldest stage of the process of christologization as indeed discernible in the Maranatha cry, which should not be interpreted too hastily as a SM address.

[42] That 1 Thess 1:9f. or 4:13-17 presuppose a SM christology is pure speculation. In the latter passage it seems, as is clear from the use of the coined phrase "Parousia of the Kyrios", that the Kyrios title was determinative, which again alludes to the ancient Maranatha cry.

[43] Cf. 12:39f. following 12:22-31 or Q 17 as the conclusion to the whole collection.

[44] Q 3:16; 7:18-23; 7:27, 28b; 13:(34), 35, possibly also 10:(21), 22 or 6:46 (-49), if these sayings belong, together with Lk 6:20-23, to the redactional framework.

gration of various (or rather unspecific) christological statements in the tradition under the leading idea of the coming SM. It is precisely this that explains the brokenness (correctly observed by Jacobson) in the application of the SM designation in reference to the earthly Jesus. These SM passages are evidently given a double function. In the units of composition and between them they specify "Christologoumena" given in the context with reference to the SM expectation, as in the case of Q 6:22f. in correspondence to 6:46 and to the announcement of the judge by fire in Q 3:16;[45] Q 7:34 in correspondence with 7:19 and 3:16, Q 9:58 in correspondence with 10:22. There is a sequence within the overall concept of the units (of Q 3–17) in which the SM statements trace a line from the "enigmatic" use of the title in the sayings concerning the earthly SM, through statements that are unambiguous and relate to his eschatological function (Q 11:30; 12:40), to the concluding prospect of the "Day of the Son of Man" in Q 17. Before I go into this question any further, an appreciation should be given of two recent models.

4. Two Recent Alternative Models

John S. Kloppenborg (*The Formation of Q. Trajectories in Ancient Wisdom Collections* [Philadelphia: 1987]) follows Lührmann's and Jacobson's approach in his redactional analysis, though he modifies it significantly in line with the assumption, which he derives from J. M. Robinson, that the genesis of Q should, in form-critical terms, be understood against the background of the development of wisdom-saying collections. But this involves the differences in form—in Q mainly wisdom instructions and earlier groups of prophetic-apocalyptic sayings—becoming the decisive criterion for the discernment of tradition-historical layers, which is extremely problematic as far as method is concerned. Accordingly he divides the Q material up in the two main sections of his investigation: "The Announcement of Judgement in Q" (Q 3:7–9:16f.; 7:1-10, 18-35; 11:14-26, 29-33, 39-52; 12:39-59; 17:23-35 [pp. 102-170]) and "Sapiential Speeches in Q" (Q 6:20b-49; 9:57-62 + 10:2-16, 21-24; 11:2-4, 9-13; 12:2-12; 12:22b-31, 33f.; 13:24–14:34 [pp. 171-245]), and a section on its own, Q 4:1-13 (pp. 246-262). Drawing a comparison with ancient sayings collections he then distinguishes three stages in the process of the

---

[45] Note the general redactional correspondence of Q 6:43-45 to Q 3:7-9 in the fruit-bearing motif, to which Jacobson also draws attention.

formation of Q. At the beginning are collections of wisdom sayings with a Jewish character; at the second stage—analogously to Greek chreia-collections—these are then overlaid with those sayings units that are marked by a judgment motif (do these really go together?); finally, at the third stage they are given a bio-graphically-oriented introduction in the temptation story (cf. pp. 317-327). The second stage broadly corresponds to Jacobson's wisdom-deuteronomistic redaction. Kloppenborg, however, supplements this by material from the "apocalyptic block" (Q 12–17), which is thus—correctly in my view—no longer seen as a pre-existing unit. Kloppenborg does not continue to argue like Jacobson on the basis of precise references in content; the criterion of the "judgment motif" is conceived in such general terms for ordering the sayings that it is insufficient for an exact redaction-critical classification. A further question would be whether such a "prophetic-apocalyptic" re-working of the original wisdom collection assumed by Kloppenborg does not destroy the category "collection of wisdom sayings". In principle one may be able to agree with Kloppenborg that pre-existing complexes of logia were re-worked by QR.[46] But they can scarcely be lumped together as Kloppenborg does in his twofold division. The determination of their extent in detail, but also of their context, presupposes the literary-critical investigation of the units of composition discernible in the Q text as we have it. It is only on the basis of a "relative chronology" arrived at in this way that the further questions concerning redaction-critical contexts can then be asked. The decision cannot be made in the framework of form criticism. The main problem in method lies in the giving of priority to form criticism over literary and composition criticism, which effectively determines Kloppenborg's assessment.

It cannot be ruled out that the very same author has linked mate-rial of different types together because he found them already in such variety in the Jesus tradition and because they were useful for his own concerns. The notion that there was a closed collection of exclusively wisdom-type admonitions in the first stage remains pure hypothesis until proved by literary and redaction criticism. Kloppenborg's rather formal observations are of no help here. The classification together of the groups of so-called wisdom say-ings is not convincing, either. Why is the judgment motif, or the call to repentance, omitted in Q 10:2-16 (cf. p. 101)? Are these

---

[46] On this, cf. D. Zeller, *Die weisheitlichen Mahnsprüche bei den Synop-tikern* (Würzburg: 1974) 191.

mission instructions really a "wisdom discourse" at all? Q 6:20-
46 too contains a reference to the judgment in its concluding
parable and beatitudes with an originally eschatological orientation. Kloppenborg himself concedes the possibility of
"interpolations made from another perspective" (*ibid.*) and
judges the Q complex in Q 13:24–14:35 to be "mixed speech",
but he still consigns it to the category of "wisdom discourses".
Does he not here betray the fact that his whole conception cannot
be maintained? Though his model may work impressively at first
sight, it seems to me that, despite many noteworthy individual observations as far as the question of QR is concerned, it leads into a
cul-de-sac.

Migaku Sato's Berne dissertation, *Q und die Prophetie. Studien
zur Gattungs- und Traditionsgeschichte der Quelle Q* (1984/5;
published Tübingen, 1988), unlike those studies so far mentioned
which are inclined to assign Q to the wisdom tradition, classifies it
in the category of "prophetic book". By so doing, he does rather
more justice, historically speaking, to the genesis of Q in the
framework of the early Christian missionary movement in the area
of Syria-Palestine. Presupposing H. Schürmann's four-stage development model (p. 33), he first aims to distinguish two larger
redactional blocks. In the context of a broad redactional process,
these blocks summarize already extant collections of sayings,
which themselves grew out of groups of sayings, and to that extent
form "consciously composed literary units" (p. 35). He distinguishes Redaction A for the "John complex, Lk 3:2–7:35"
(pp. 33-37) and Redaction B for the "mission complex Lk 9:57–
10:24" (pp. 37f.), which possibly derive from the same redaction
too (p. 44). The isolated groups of sayings which follow these
blocks of material were then put into order by a Redaction C and
combined with blocks A and B. Since, however, he assumes a
"continued, successive reshaping" of the Q collection, he thinks
we have here, as already in the first two blocks, "various,
unsystematic insertions and additions from a later—or previous?—
time" (pp. 43, 45). More recent additions to blocks A and B—
after or perhaps even before Redaction C—might be seen in
Q 6:43-45 or 6:39, 40, certainly in Q 7:27 as well as Q 10:22 and
4:1-11. Underlying the latter two is "the earlier embedded account
of the baptism of Jesus" (p. 38). The woes of Q 10:(12), 13-15,
however, he ascribes to Redaction C. In Q 14:16–17:6 in particular
he is not keen to presuppose a "continuous" redaction, since no
"clear thought process" can be discerned here (p. 43).

"Characteristic of Redaction C are the polemical accusation or the proclamation of judgment against the whole people of Israel and the accentuation of the motif of divine wisdom" (p. 45). So this Redaction C corresponds to the redactional layer of a wisdom-deuteronomistic character expounded by Lührmann and Jacobson. This redaction formed Q 7:31-34, 35 as a bridge to the disciples complex (p. 45, cf. 34). Q 11:14-32, 39-52 in particular, probably QLk 13:23-35 and possibly 12:2-34 should also be ascribed to it. Similarly, the position of the "fixed collection of sayings, Lk 17:23-37" may derive from it. Even though the motifs characteristic of Redaction C are missing here, "the perspective of universal judgment" fits "not badly" with its main concerns (pp. 42, 45). In the later addition of further material, too, their final position was retained because their "concluding character" also continued to be acknowledged. "The picture of the coming of the Son of Man" could to this extent have continued to work as a "principle of composition" (p. 44). The present position of Lk 17 at the end of the whole collection may therefore show "how central for the whole source was the expectation of the Son of Man Jesus coming for judgment" (p. 44).

This "christological interest" recognizable in the SM sayings is, in his opinion, of central significance for the whole composition of the collection. It not only marks Redaction A, which expressly makes "the position of Jesus in relation to the Baptist" a theme in its composition (p. 35), but also the "other redactions and re-workings", as the leading position of the SM sayings (or of other christological statements) in the compositions reveals. In this connection Sato refers to Q 3:16 (for Redaction A), 6:22 (at the beginning of the programmatic discourse composition), 7:34 (Redaction C), 9:57 (Redaction B), 13:35 (presumably Redaction C), and 17:24, 26, 30 (as the introduction to the concluding collection of sayings). On the basis of this division he concludes there was "a relatively firm continuity" among the tradents of Q (*ibid.*). The "present form" of Q he wishes to situate before 70 CE, "since there is no clear reflection of the destruction of Jerusalem, and the temple and the temple system are presupposed (Lk 4:9 par.; 11:42 par.)". Q 13:34f. offers "no indication", moreover, for "the sayings having necessarily arisen *ex eventu*" (p. 47), even though in his detailed analysis he understands the saying as a "farewell saying": "The city and the people are irrevocably marked for destruction" (p. 160).

Sato's study cannot be assessed in full detail in this context. For the purposes of our discussion it is instructive that his redaction-critical model is the first to grasp, with good grounds, the significance of the SM christology even for the final redactional phase. Unlike my own proposal, he does, it is true, presuppose this interest for the previous redactional stages as well, and even for the historical Jesus, who in his view saw himself in a "personal"—albeit "paradoxical"—"continuity with the coming world judge" (p. 174 with reference to Q 12:8f.). This is a perspective which I cannot share, in view of my assessment of the SM problem. As a consequence of his approach, however, it is understandable that tradition-historically he is able to situate the concept in all stages of the development. But does this do justice to the findings regarding the tradition, which alongside the SM statements also reveals other, more open, christological tendencies which seem to be overlaid by the SM concept? Finally, there is also the redaction-critical question whether the correctly observed christological character of the A block of redaction can be ascribed to an independent earlier tradition or—especially if Q 7:31-35 derives from Redaction C—should not also be seen as the work of Redaction C. The consequence of this for the redactional history of Q would be that in the pre-C Redaction phase we can reckon only with larger or smaller groups of sayings (similar to those which Sato posits for the concluding part). These groups of sayings would have been structured to a greater or lesser degree—in some individual cases perhaps composed in writing—but would have been on the whole more a component of the oral tradition which was transmitted by the Jewish Christian missionaries behind the Q tradition. The committing of this material to writing would then have been the consequence of an experience that was evidently decisive for the Palestinian Jesus movement, an experience which—as the judgment sayings against Israel show—meant the end of its mission to Israel.[47]

5. The Son of Man and the Fall of Jerusalem

Is QR responsible for the reception of the SM concept, or at least for its literary-theological integration, in the rest of the Q material? Can the process perhaps also be clarified through the historical situation that may be supposed for QR?

---

[47] On this cf. also the observations of D. Zeller, "Redaktionsprozesse und wechselnder 'Sitz im Leben' beim Q-Material" in *Logia*, ed. J. Delobel (Leuven: 1982) 395-409.

Steck, and also Jacobson, are right to see Q 13:34f. as the clearest and the most massive threat of judgment against Israel among the deuteronomistically-coloured statements of QR. It is striking that here Jerusalem is at the centre of the accusation. The announcement in v. 35a that God will abandon the city means "that the destruction of the city could be understood traditionally as judgment upon it".[48] On the basis of the closeness of the proclamation to Josephus' reports regarding various portents for the disaster threatening Jerusalem, Steck has dated the saying concerning Jerusalem to the time of the Jewish-Roman War.[49] Though I consider improbable his assumption that Q 13:34, 35a was already connected with v. 35b originally, and derives from Jewish circles which belonged to the "peace party" and saw the resistance movement as the reason for the divine judgment threatened in the saying, the historical context of the saying has evidently been appropriately determined. Precisely in comparison with the Sophia saying Q 11:49f., the saying shows a distinctive concentration on the speaker's (in the Q context this is Jesus himself) specific experiences with Jerusalem, while the allusions to the general prophetic statement—already clear from the grammatical structure—form only the background of the statement. This seems rather to argue in favour of seeing this as a Christian adaptation of the general prophetic announcement to the envoy of Wisdom, Jesus, whose experiences with Jerusalem and "its children"—including the experiences of the disciples' mission—are the *final* concern, as is clear from the use of the aorist. The reference to the speaker who is "coming (again)" for the ruin of the Jerusalemites addressed, can also be derived more easily from the Christian expectation of a return.[50] The proclamation of judgment is then to be

---

[48] Steck, *Geschick* 228f.

[49] *Geschick* 237f. Here he refers to the nocturnal auditions of the priests in the temple: "when...the priests came into the inner court of the temple by night...they would have heard, as they say, first a movement and a disturbance, but then a repeated cry: 'Let us go away from here' (*Bellum* 6.299)". He refers also to the appearance of Jesus b. Ananias with his proclamation of destruction for Jerusalem "four years before the war": "A voice of rising, a voice of falling, a voice from the four winds, a voice concerning Jerusalem and the temple, a voice concerning bridegroom and bride, a voice concerning the whole people" (*Bellum* 6.301). Cf. also the voice from the inner part of the temple mentioned in *SyrApocBar* 8.1f.: "Penetrate here, you enemies, and come here, you haters, for he who watches the house is departed."

[50] For critical discussion of Steck, cf. *Studien* 171-180. Underlying the unusual motif of stoning there is possibly recourse to Christian experience (Stephen?). I would, however, depart from my discussion in the *Studien* in seeing

understood with Lührmann and Jacobson, against Steck, as a
definitive one. The saying looks back to the vain efforts on Israel's
behalf and reflects the imminently expected, or perhaps already
completed(?),[51] destruction of Jerusalem in the framework of the
deuteronomistic view of history as the consequence of the rejection
of the envoys. At the same time in v. 35b, however, the traditional
deuteronomistic framework is blown apart under the influence of
the expectation of the return of Jesus, and expanded
christologically. The proclamation of the imminent judgment concerning this generation (cf. Q 11:49-51 with the redactional
emphasis in v. 51) turns into the proclamation of the eschatological "executor of judgment" Jesus, who for QR is the decisive representative of God's end-time action.[52]

If we assume this to be QR's situation, various characteristics of
QR find a plausible explanation. I would mention first of all the
intensification of imminent expectation as expressed in the acceptance of the Baptist's sermon as the opening for the whole collection, but also, for example, in the concluding parable of Jesus' first
discourse in Q 6:47-49. Also, the experience of the delay of the
Parousia, as Lührmann claims, is reflected in Q 12:39-46 and
19:11-27, which appears to be in tension with the imminent expectation. These statements—precisely because of their evident polar-
ity—can scarcely be understood as in line with Luke's adaptation
of the early Christian imminent expectation under the influence of
the delay of the Parousia. It seems more plausible to relate them to
the final phase of the Jewish-Roman war. In the situation of political crisis in Jewish, especially Zealot circles,[53] but also in the Christian groups, as the re-worked Palestinian piece of tradition in
Mk 13 shows,[54] that phase brought about the expectation of the
imminent in-breaking of the end times. The emphasis on the un-

---

as correct the reference to the situation in the Jewish-Roman war, which Steck
expounds.

[51] Steck's rejection of a *vaticinium ex eventu* (238f.) is not compelling.
Which "public, historical evidence" is opposed to such an assumption? Steck
disagrees here with H. Braun, *ThR* 28 (1962) 146 (=*Qumran und das Neue Testament* [Tübingen: 1966], vol. I.50).

[52] On this, cf. my own thoughts, inspired above all by E. Brandenburger in
"Jesus versus Menschensohn" 196 with notes 74, 75 (see note 4 above).

[53] On this, cf. M. Hengel, *Die Zeloten. Untersuchungen zur jüdischen Frei-
heitsbewegung in der Zeit von Herodes I. bis 70 n. Chr.* (Leiden / Köln: 1961)
316.

[54] Cf. especially E. Brandenburger, *Markus 13 und die Apokalyptik*
(Göttingen: 1984).

expected coming of the Kyrios, or the SM, and the admonition to watchfulness is then—against the background of the heightened expectation and motivated by it—to be seen as the attempt to overcome the indifference of those addressed by pointing out their critical situation. The reception of the partly traditional statements in Q that are characterized by the imminent expectation is then less the legacy of an eschatological fervour that has been going on for decades, but rather an indication of a renaissance of the early Christian imminent expectation in response to the challenge of the general socio-political situation of crisis in the late 60s.[55] This would also correspond better with the general sociology-of-religions insight that apocalyptic expectations generally appear in waves and are reactions to concrete crisis situations.

The Palestinian tradition from the time of the Jewish-Roman war, preserved in Mk 13, which—apart from Q—represents the earliest evidence of the Christian reception of the SM expectation of Dan 7 (though already transformed in its own way), now also sheds light on the appearance of the SM sayings in Q. I quite appreciate that the relationship between the two traditions requires an investigation of its own, and that we cannot make hasty tradition-historical or even literary connections between them at this point. Nonetheless, the parallel appearance of this expectation in Mk 13 and in QR could indicate that the SM concept gained special significance for Christian circles during this late phase in the transmission of Q, i.e. in the period around 70 CE, and that it was then that its reception and theological integration into the traditional Q material that was not previously characterized by it came about.[56] This does not settle the question of when the Christian reception of the SM concept occurred. QR takes up this idea because it clearly had a special contemporary significance.

If the thesis of some scholars is correct, that the Similitudes were not composed until the first century[57] or that at least "in Jewish

---

[55] The temptation story of Q 4, too, the interpretation of which is of course much debated, could find its place in this situation, as dealing with various contemporary messianic concepts. On this cf. my essay, "Die Versuchungsgeschichte in der Logienquelle," *BZ* 13 (1969) 207-23.

[56] The question of the age and origins of the genuine SM sayings, as assembled especially in Q 17, is in need of further investigation in this context. In doing so, we should take final leave from the often too "self-evident" assumption that in the SM sayings we are dealing with the oldest Christian or even dominical tradition. In this respect I wish expressly to correct my own position.

[57] Cf. the overview of the discussion in S. Uhlig, *Das Äthiopische Henochbuch* (JSHRZ V.6; Gütersloh: 1984) 573-575.

circles"(!) "the definitive redaction...was undertaken in the first century CE, at which time LXXf was also added on to the corpus",[58] the SM reception in Christian circles would gain a contemporary Jewish context. Particularly interesting, in this case, would be Steck's claim that the circle responsible for the transmission of the tradition collected in *Ethiopic Enoch*, as is evident in the Apocalypse of Weeks and the Animal Apocalypse, was influenced "by the conceptual legacy of the deuteronomistic view of history" and that here too the "Similitudes—with their Son of Man concept—, though admittedly they were composed later, were integrated into the Enoch circle's conceptual legacy of the deuteronomistic view of history".[59] *1 Enoch* would therefore offer correspondence to the secondary connection between deuteronomistically influenced traditions and the SM concept. The elevation and identification of Enoch with the transcendent SM reported in the latest part of the collection, chs. 70f., as C. Colpe already emphasized, represented the nearest analogy to the Christian identification between Jesus and the SM.[60] So long as the date of the Similitudes remains open, the evidence elucidates only the currency of the concept in the milieu of Palestinian Jewish Christianity.

Should M. Hengel be correct in his assumption that the Zealot expectation of God's intervention at the moment of the sacking of the temple (cf. Mk 13:14, 26) was determined by Dan 9:27 and Dan 7, then there would even be evidence for the contemporary significance of the SM expectation for the time of the Jewish war.[61] Finally, we also find a similar process of the combination of deuteronomistic tradition with a messianic tradition characterized by the SM concept in the thirteenth chapter of *4 Ezra*, the author of which is trying to work through the catastrophe of the year 70 theologically.

---

[58] So, Uhlig himself (*ibid.* 575); more precisely "in the first decades after the turn of the era" (494). Some do, however, maintain a later time of composition: the end of the first / beginning of the second century or even the third (cf. Uhlig, *ibid.* 574). J. Theisohn (*Der auserwählte Richter* [Göttingen: 1975]), who places the Similitudes too vaguely between Daniel and Matthew, will at least be correct in his determination of the *terminus ad quem*, since MtR shows points of contact with the Similitudes.

[59] *Geschick* 154-157, especially 155 n. 1.

[60] *TWNT* 8 428f.

[61] According to *4 Ezra* 13:35 too, the place of the revelation of the SM-Messiah is Zion; according to *SyrApocBar* 40:1f. the last enemy ruler is killed on Mount Zion. Cf. M. Hengel, *Zeloten* 248f. (see note 53 above), with reference to Josephus, *Bellum* 6.285f.

The "late dating" of QR proposed here would, finally, provide an explanation for the currency of the SM concept in Christian circles in the second half of the first century. It would then explain plausibly how it was that the SM concept could still have current significance for the Apocalypse of John's Jewish-Christian communities in Asia Minor around the turn of the century—especially if the assumption is correct that these prophetically organized communities recruited from Jewish Christians who emigrated from Palestine to Asia Minor in the wake of the Jewish-Roman war.[62] The intensive re-working and elaboration of the SM tradition in the Gospel of Matthew, which incidentally clearly displays influence from the Similitudes, also suggests we can take it that in the Syrian area in which the Gospel was composed in the second half of the century there was broad acceptance of this concept. The proximity to QR is evident at the same time in the broad reception and contemporization of the deuteronomistic traditions which MtR re-works in the framework of his massive critique of Israel and the theological justification for the replacement of Israel as the chosen people by the church's community of disciples from all nations.[63] If Steck's view is correct that "unlike Luke...for Matthew the deuteronomistic prophetic proclamation in its traditional connection with the element of judgment...is not an association of ideas that was transmitted only literarily, but one which was current and familiar",[64] then the evidence would lead us to conclude that Matthew and his community stood not only in historical proximity to those circles that were responsible for QR, but were clearly linked with them in a lively continuity. The redactional reshaping of the wisdom saying in Mt 23:34: "Behold I send you prophets and wise men and scribes" (cf. also 10:17ff.) may be read as the shorthand version of the history of the Palestinian Jewish-Christian prophetic movement and of its development into the Matthean community with its scribes (cf. 13:52; 23:8-11). Matthew however permits us to recognize the conflicts of these early preachers (the tradents of Q?) with their Jewish compatriots. The (later) interpretation of Jesus by MtR as the non-violent Messiah of peace, whose rejection led the Jewish people into the catastrophe of the Jewish-Roman war, can be understood as the christological transformation of the further proclamation, focused on the com-

---

[62] Cf. A. Satake, *Die Gemeindeordnung in der Johannesapokalypse* (Neu-kirchen: 1966) 192f.
[63] On this, cf. especially Steck 289-316.
[64] *Geschick* 304.

mand to love one's enemies (cf. Q 6:20ff.), the message of Jesus in the Q tradition.[65]

Do these observations provide a basis for a closer identification of the historical setting of QR—at least as a hypothesis? In his editing of the Jesus tradition QR stands equally at the beginning of that ecclesial-historical and theological development which was in the last decades of the first century to lead finally, in the Syrian area, to the Gospel of Matthew. MtR was to take up these traditions and combine them with the extra-Palestinian traditions represented by the Gospel of Mark into the "Gospel of the *Basileia*", whose binding nature for disciples of all nations is declared by the risen one, elevated to the SM, before the disciples on the mountain in Galilee. At the same time, however, QR signifies the end-point of the early Palestinian Jewish-Christian missionary movement. Its traditions are indeed received by the redaction and regarded as the only decisive norm in the coming judgment of the SM Jesus. However, this occurs against the background of the experience of a sorrowful history of permanent rejection which clearly forced the tradents to the insight that the early Christian Jesus movement had failed in its attempt to move the whole of Israel to repentance. In their opinion, all that remained for Israel was catastrophe, both in history and in the Eschaton.

In the history of Palestinian Jewish Christianity, then, QR marks the decisive turning point in the separation of those Jewish-Christian groups of followers of Jesus out of the hitherto clearly evident national-religious association with the Jewish national community, and it marks the constitution of a separate religious grouping which was conscious of its own identity in its belonging, as the "children of wisdom" and as "chosen recipients of the revelation of the Son", to Jesus, the SM. They thus stand in contrast to their former compatriots and fellow believers, who for them are now identified as "this (wicked) generation" and burdened with the stigma of eschatological losers. The deuteronomistic prophetic idea, which quite probably gave the lead to the preachers of Israel in their proclamation, now serves the redaction no longer for the contemporary dispute with Israel, but for the stabilization of the newly-won group identity in conscious contrast with Israel. At the same time, however, the redaction is concerned to maintain the

---

[65] On this, cf. my essay, "Tradition und Situation. Zur 'Verbindlichkeit' des Gebots der Feindesliebe in der synoptischen Überlieferung und in der gegenwärtigen Friedensdiskussion" in *Ethik im Neuen Testament*, ed. K. Kertelge (QD 102; Freiburg: 1984) 50-118, especially 82-93.

continuity with the Jesus tradition transmitted to it through those erstwhile preachers of Israel. The reception of the SM concept makes it possible for the redaction unambiguously to secure their *universal* significance in the horizon of the contemporary, eschatological expectation and thus to keep confronting its own adherents with the claim of the former prophet Jesus who will come again as SM. The fact that the explicit phrase "upon this generation" is absent from Q 17 could be the consequence of this newly gained perspective.

The question whether the followers of Jesus who present themselves in QR are still to be situated in the Palestinian area or have possibly left Palestine as a consequence of the armed conflicts and have moved to the Syrian area, as Steck posits,[66] is to be given the latter answer. It supports this too that, for instance in Q 7:1-10, QR displays a positive attitude to the Gentiles and, by drawing attention to the "converted" Gentiles of the Old Testament and pagan cities in central passages, plays them off against Israel which has closed itself to the message of Jesus.[67] This is no justification, however, for assuming that QR was already associated with an active Gentile mission or even a mixed Gentile / Jewish-Christian community. The conscious step in this direction, in my view, follows only later, and in this area of tradition first becomes expressly programmatic in Matthew. Here too, then, QR evidently stands at the beginning of a new way.

The above considerations presuppose a fair proximity, in both space and time, to the Gospel of Matthew. If we suppose the period around 70 for QR and the 80s for MtR, we are dealing with a span of ten or at most twenty years. It thus becomes clear again, that QR indeed represents only an "intermediate stage" in the process of early Christian tradition from the Jesus of history through to the Gospel of Matthew. Perhaps this is also one of the reasons why Q has not survived as an independent document but only in its reception by the great evangelists.

These thoughts, which may seem to some perhaps to be rather too speculative, constitute a working hypothesis. They aim to stimulate further discussion concerning QR, not to decide it already. I realize that this hypothesis needs to be maintained in

---

[66] *Geschick* 310, with reference to Hengel's assumption (*Zeloten* 231) that the Palestinian Jewish-Christians did not participate in the Zealot rebellion. I have sought to give further grounds for this view in "Studien zur Theologie".

[67] Cf. Q 10:12, 13f. or 11:31f.

many individual analyses. These can only be carried out in the context of a commentary on Q.

CHAPTER NINE

Q AND CYNICISM:
ON COMPARISON AND SOCIAL IDENTITY

Leif E. Vaage

The present article is, in large measure, a response to Christopher Tuckett's recent inquiry, "A Cynic Q?"[1] Tuckett's negative reply is answered here with a reciprocal: Yes. At the same time, the present article seeks to clarify the conditions under which such a comparison between Q and Cynicism alone has validity. In fact, at issue is finally less the particular question of Q and Cynicism and more the general enterprise of comparison itself, specifically with regard to the determination of social identity. Given that virtually everything (a) can be compared with anything else (b) provided it is clear in which respect (c) the comparison is made, the only criticism which conceivably might hold against current conjunctions of Q and Cynicism is how the similarities and differences between them have been drawn; not, however, whether this comparison should be made in the first place.

The preceding remarks reflect the results of Jonathan Z. Smith's recent book, *Drudgery Divine: On the Comparison of Early Christianities and the Religions of Late Antiquity*, a devastating critique of the naive and disingenuous manner in which many modern New Testament scholars have set about the task of understanding the place of their texts and the social movements they embodied in antiquity.[2] Of relevance here is especially Smith's second chapter on comparison itself. Smith's principal conclusion quite simply stands on end the widespread habit among New Testament scholars of equating the attribution of parallel materials with a statement about origins or genealogical derivation. Smith contends that the purpose of comparison is not to determine something's primordial character, but a means—perhaps, the only means—whereby, on the

---

[1] See Christopher M. Tuckett, "A Cynic Q?," *Bib.* 10 (1989) 349-376.
[2] See Jonathan Z. Smith, *Drudgery Divine: On the Comparison of Early Christianities and the Religions of Late Antiquity* (Chicago: 1990).

basis of our own theoretical and practical interests, we may achieve a new appreciation—Smith's term is "disciplined exaggeration"—of a given document or group of persons. It is only the abiding conceptual confusion of comparison with genealogy, I suggest, that still impedes recognition of the strong degree of similarity that exists between Q and the Cynics.

1. A Cynic Q?

Tuckett's article, "A Cynic Q?" is to be welcomed for its explicit discussion and recognition thereby of this line of inquiry as both possible and worthy of debate. A number of Tuckett's critical observations regarding the nature of the evidence for Cynicism are, moreover, germane and helpful. At the same time, however, Tuckett's main argument against the comparison of Q and Cynicism is, it seems to me, fundamentally flawed. Without rehearsing every detail, but honouring the specificity of Tuckett's assessment, I wish to respond first to each of his main objections to "a Cynic Q", leading in this fashion in the second part of the article to a short synthetic description of Q's formative stratum as a Cynic document.[3]

Tuckett begins his article by reviewing quickly a number of recent publications that consider some of the possible relations between early Christianities and Cynicism. Implied appears to be that the comparison of Q and the Cynics belongs to a current "fad" of scholarship—a pursuit, in Tuckett's opinion, best abandoned as soon as possible. Tuckett's own proposal, however, that we return to the great tradition of prophecy as the more appropriate analogue to Q is simply a reassertion of the previous prevailing paradigm.[4]

---

[3] Unless otherwise indicated, I presuppose the literary stratigraphy for Q established by John S. Kloppenborg in *The Formation of Q: Trajectories in Ancient Wisdom Collections* (Studies in Antiquity and Christianity; Philadelphia: 1987). It is Q's formative stratum, essentially as Kloppenborg describes it, that best compares with Cynicism. Kloppenborg himself (*Formation of Q* 324-325) only considers the correlation between them with regard to certain features—the chreia—of Q's secondary redaction.

[4] See Tuckett, "A Cynic Q?" 376. Reference is approvingly made by Tuckett to Migaku Sato's 1984 dissertation, now published as *Q und Prophetie: Studien zur Gattungs- und Traditionsgeschichte der Quelle Q* (Tübingen: 1988); cf. the critical reviews of this book by Kloppenborg in *JBL* 109 (1990) 137-139; *idem, CBQ* 52 (1990) 362-364. Beyond myself, Kloppenborg, and Downing, Tuckett also refers to the work of Abraham J. Malherbe on Paul, certain asides by Paul

Tuckett's conflation throughout his article of the comparative work of John S. Kloppenborg, F. Gerald Downing, and myself is misleading.[5] To be sure, a certain sympathy exists between these various labours. But they are finally rather different from one another. As Tuckett himself recognizes, "Kloppenborg explicitly denies" that Q itself is Cynic.[6] Kloppenborg's treatment of the analogy between Q and Cynicism—specifically regarding the literary form of the chreia in the document's secondary stratum—is 225 sake of contrast than similitude; though, in fact, it is only a sense of the similarity between them that eventually permits the identification of difference.

Downing's comparative programme is both more ambitious and less tightly focused than my own. In many ways, it seems that Tuckett's displeasure at a Cynic Q has principally to do with Downing's work. I will not attempt here to defend what Downing himself can clarify and correct. At the same time, it is important to recognize that *prima facie*, at least in *Christ and the Cynics*, Downing has done nothing methodologically different from what Strack-Billerbeck, for example, provide with their Rabbinic parallels to the New Testament; or Herbert Braun, to name but one scholar, for the writings from Qumran; or Jacob Wettstein, with Greco-Roman materials in general.[7] It is, again, only the confusion, as Smith portrays it, of comparison with genealogy that has made

---

Hoffmann and Gerd Theissen in their writings on Q, and Burton L. Mack's suggestive remarks about Jesus in *A Myth of Innocence* (Philadelphia: 1988) 67-69.

[5] Bibliographically, Downing is clearly the main target: see Tuckett, "A Cynic Q?" 350 notes 6, 7. Regarding Kloppenborg and myself, only Kloppenborg's *Formation of Q* and my dissertation, "Q: The Ethos and Ethics of an Itinerant Intelligence" (The Claremont Graduate School, 1987) are cited. See also my "The Woes in Q (and Matthew and Luke): Deciphering the Rhetoric of Criticism" in *SBLSP* 27 (1988) 582-607; *idem*, "Q(1) and the Historical Jesus: Some Peculiar Sayings," *Forum* 5/2 (1989) 159-176; *idem*, "'Amen a sus enemigos' y otras estrategias de resistencia," *Revista de interpretación bíblica latinoamericana* 9 (1991) 81-96; *idem*, "Monarchy, Community, Anarchy: The Kingdom of God in Paul and Q" in *Scriptures and Cultural Conversations: Essays for Heinz Guenther at 65*, eds. Kloppenborg and Vaage (= *Toronto Journal of Theology* 8/1 [1992] 48-65).

[6] See Tuckett, "A Cynic Q?" 350; Kloppenborg, *Formation of Q* 324; cf. Vaage, "Q: Ethos and Ethics" 51-54.

[7] See Downing, *Christ and the Cynics: Jesus and Other Radical Preachers in First-Century Tradition* (Sheffield: 1988); Herman L. Strack and Paul Billerbeck, *Kommentar zum Neuen Testament aus Talmud und Midrasch* (6 vols.; München: 1961-63); Herbert Braun, *Qumran und das Neue Testament* (Tübingen: 1966); Jacob Wettstein, *Novum Testamentun Graecum* (2 vols.; Graz: 1962 = repr. of 1752 ed.).

the creation of one set of parallels seem more likely or less problematical than another.

Regarding Cynicism itself, Tuckett is correct in his depiction of it as an understudied, still somewhat loosely constituted field of investigation. Actually, Tuckett suggests that the disparate quality of the evidence produced "especially in the work of Downing and Vaage" is due not to the nature of ancient Cynicism, but rather results from a less than exact citation of diverse materials as Cynic.[8] This problem, however, is itself part of a debate, in many ways yet to be had, about the proper sources for the study of Cynicism, not to mention the pertinent categories of interpretation.

The relationship between Stoicism and Cynicism is simply one facet of this complex issue. Indeed, it may be the least of our worries. It is now generally recognized—far more so than Tuckett's tentative note to this effect would suggest—that the traditional habit among New Testament scholars of referring to "Cynic-Stoic" materials is clearly a misnomer lumping together through the facile convenience of a hyphen two quite distinct moral-philosophical styles.[9] Already in antiquity, Seneca had depicted well, albeit with evident bias, the pertinent differences between them:

> Inwardly [as Stoics], we ought to be different in all respects, but our exterior should conform to society [unlike the Cynics]....it is quite contrary to nature [*pace* the Cynics from a Stoic point of view] to torture the body, to hate unlaboured elegance, to be dirty on purpose, to eat food that is not only plain, but disgusting and forbidding.... [Stoic] Philosophy calls for plain living, but not for [Cynic] penance; and we may perfectly well be plain and neat at the same time. This is the mean of which I approve; our [Stoic] life should observe a happy medium between the ways of the sage and the ways of the world at large; all persons should admire it, but they should understand it also [unlike the Cynic way of life].[10]

Another index of the same contrast between the Cynics and the Stoics would be their mutual invocation of "nature" to defend and explain otherwise distinct social styles as being both "in accordance with nature". Of the two, only the Stoics had a body of

---

[8] See Tuckett, "A Cynic Q?" 351.

[9] See Tuckett, "A Cynic Q?" 352 note 13. For a succinct description of the differences between "Stoic and Cynic theology", see Malherbe, "Pseudo Heraclitus, Epistle 4: The Divinization of the Wise Man," *JAC* 21 (1978) 45-51; also *idem,* "In Season and Out of Season: 2 Timothy 4:2" in *Paul and the Popular Philosophers* (Minneapolis: 1989) 141.

[10] See Seneca, *ep. mor.* 5.2, 4f.

"theory" to back up the cultural criticism centred in this term.[11] The Cynics, by contrast, if required to clarify what they meant by such language, could only tell another story, usually about Diogenes, of unconventional behaviour.[12] Yet the fact that both Cynic and Stoic shared the same broad nomenclature is not thereby rendered irrelevant. For when, from a Stoic point of view, the "excesses" of Cynicism, as above with Seneca, were not in view, much of what a Cynic said (less likely, did) would also have been useful to a Stoic. While we must "beware of equating Cynicism and Stoicism," we cannot therefore conclude that having labelled a particular person or piece of writing "Stoic" thereby disqualifies him, her, or it from ever supplying "Cynic" data.[13]

The difficulty of using certain "Stoic" writers for a description of Cynicism belongs, in fact, to a much larger problem, which is the highly biased character of virtually all our ancient sources regarding these persons. By highly biased, I do not mean merely the partiality of perspective or a specific ideological tendency. By highly biased, I mean the polarized tendency when discussing the Cynics either to idealize or to villify, mockingly to disparage or impossibly to praise them. We simply have no "indisputably" Cynic sources, insofar as everything said in any text about them, both ancient and modern, must inevitably be subject to a thoroughgoing debate regarding its historical veracity.

For example, the pseudonymous Cynic epistles, or book six of Diogenes Laertius' *Lives, Teachings, and Sayings of Famous Philosophers*, or the "wandering" orations of Dio Chrysostom, all are suspect for their general celebration of what was likely a more motley and scurrilous set of performances in reality. On the other hand, the scrupulous self-serving distinctions of Cicero and Seneca, the lampooning portraits of the Cynics painted looking down his nose by Lucian of Samosata, and the earnest defense of "true" Cynicism by Epictetus and Julian versus its all too real present-day representatives, equally fail to allay doubt regarding their reliability, given the obvious desire in this case either to debunk or to dis-

---

[11] See, e.g., Diogenes Laertius 7.148f.

[12] See, e.g., ps-Diogenes, *ep.* 16, 42.

[13] For the warning against "equating Cynicism and Stoicism", see Tuckett, "A Cynic Q?" 352. At the opposite end of the spectrum stands the problem of "genuine" Cynic sources that contain "properly" Stoic material: see, e.g., Marie-Odile Goulet-Cazé, "Un syllogisme stoïcien sur la loi dans la doxographie de Diogène le Cynique. A propos de Diogène Laërce VI 72," *Reinisches Museum* 125 (1982) 214-240; *idem, L'ascèse cynique: un commentaire de Diogène Laërce VI 70-71* (Paris: 1986).

cern a hidden truth beyond the "dog's breakfast" before them. Every witness to ancient Cynicism is thus essentially untrustworthy, and our only source of information about it.

Of equal, if not greater import for the definition of Cynicism—and, in some respects, the flip-side of the preceding problem of strongly divergent testimony regarding it—is the question of the "very wide variety of thought [and action] permitted" among the Cynics.[14] Tuckett is quite mistaken in asserting that I question "whether there is really as great a variety within genuine Cynicism as Malherbe claims."[15] Even a superficial reading of Diogenes Laertius or the Cynic epistles makes clear that all Cynics were not cut from the same cloth. It is rather the meaning of this diversity that must be established and where, incidentally, I differ from Malherbe.

It is precisely the division by Malherbe and others of "genuine" Cynic difference into two "pure" breeds: rigorous / ascetic and milder / hedonistic, that I question.[16] Not that I assume that the al-

---

[14] See Tuckett, "A Cynic Q?" 352.

[15] See Tuckett, "A Cynic Q?" 353 note 18.

[16] Malherbe refers especially to G. A. Gerhard (*Phoinix von Kolophon* [Leipzig / Berlin: 1909] 64-72, 165-168; *idem,* "Zur Legende vom Kyniker Diogenes," *ARW* 15 [1912] 388-408) in support of his distinction between "two types of Cynicism: an austere, rigorous one, and a milder, so-called hedonistic strain" ("Self-Definition among the Cynics" in *Paul and the Popular Philosophers* 14). Elsewhere, however, Malherbe recognizes that the same distinction—leaving aside the question of its validity *per se*—does not account for the full variety of flesh-and-blood Cynics in antiquity. For example, when discussing "the Cynic background to 1 Thessalonians 2", Malherbe (*Paul and the Popular Philosophers* 38-47) reviews the *five* types of mainly "Cynic" philosophers, plus an ideal sixth type, mentioned in Dio Chrysostom, *or.* 32.

Regarding the distinction itself between two kinds of Cynicism, it is not clear that Gerhard's characterization of Cynic divergence in these terms was in fact intended or is able to constitute a proper typology instead of being merely an *ad hoc* effort to articulate the fact of "difference" within the various traditions about Diogenes and his followers. Note, moreover, that the original debate concerning "hedonistic" versus "rigorous" or ascetic Cynicism had as its centre of gravity a strangely familiar quest for the historical Diogenes. Beyond Gerhard, see, e.g., Kurt von Fritz, *Quellenuntersuchungen zu Leben und Philosophie des Diogenes von Sinope* (*Philologus,* Supplementband 18.2; Leipzig: 1926); Ragnar Höistad, *Cynic Hero and Cynic King: Studies in the Cynic Conception of Man* (Uppsala: 1948) 132-135; *idem,* "Cynicism" in *Dictionary of the History of Ideas* (1968) 1.631-632; Jan Fredrik Kindstrand, *Bion of Borysthenes: A Collection of the Fragments with Introduction and Commentary* (Uppsala: 1976) 64-67. For Gerhard and von Fritz, the terms "hedonistic" and "rigorous" finally function as the tradition-historical key to sorting out the seemingly confused and contradictory anecdotes associated with the dog-philosopher from Sinope. The

ternative is simply to imagine as constitutive of Cynicism a mo-
mentary mongrel mating of whatever seemed good wherever. But
too quickly to collapse the wide range of apropos pronouncement
and public performance equally labelled "Cynic" throughout
Greco-Roman antiquity into separate "schools" is to ignore the
problem how it is that all practitioners of this variable "dog's life"
were nonetheless still generally identifiable as "Cynic."

The issue of the date of the Cynic evidence becomes irrelevant,
once the enterprise of comparison is understood not to be about
producing "background" material for the sake of determining
genealogy, developmental "influence", or erstwhile
"dependency". Furthermore, the late date of certain texts regarding the—early—Cynics does not erase the fact that Cynicism as a
social phenomenon and living moral philosophical tradition per-
dured throughout the Mediterranean basin for roughly a thousand
years: from the founder figures, Antistheses and Diogenes, in the
5/4th century BCE to Sallustius in the 5/6th century CE, with inevitable, if unpredictable, peaks and valleys in the general popularity of the movement and its notable embodiments. In terms of
Cynicism, Q—not to mention Jesus and the rest of early Christianity—emerges at the mid-point of this millenial trajectory. It hardly
seems out of line, comparative methodology aside, to inquire how
the document and its tradents might be related to what both preceded and followed their own brief existence.

The question of provenance is like the issue of date: it matters
only if we understand a statement of origin to be at stake in the
comparative enterprise. Even so, Tuckett at this point betrays certain erroneous habits of thought, to wit, an implied opposition between "Judaism" and the wider Hellenistic world. Only in this
fashion can one avoid finding a non-sequitur in the reasoning of
his paragraph that begins with "the question of whether Cynicism
permeated the society from which Q emanated", placed by most

---

significance of Cynic "diversity" was thus reduced to a question of confessional
perspective (e.g., misanthropical *versus* philanthropical).

Hoïstad's characterization of the Cynics as followers of Socrates'
"eudaemonistic asceticism" is more promising, insofar as it allows for an understanding of these persons as sharing a common goal—and, therefore, all being
properly called "Cynic"—at the same time that behaviour and pronouncement
might vary in accordance with immediate circumstances. Hoïstad, however, does
not extend this vision of Cynicism beyond Alexander the Great, believing that
later Cynic "extremists" were influenced by the contact with "oriental" asceticism and its practice of abnegation for abnegation's sake. Dramatic demonstration of self-control became in this way a virtue without concern for attaining
contentment. This is much less certain.

scholars "somewhere in Galilee or the environs", and proceeds
with the observation that "most would agree that the Christian
group which preserved Q was in some kind of relationship
(however hostile) with Judaism", to end with the question: "Is it
then reasonable to think of Cynic preachers, and Cynic ideas, as
present in such a situation?"[17]

Why would a relationship of Q with one or more examples of
early Judaisms diminish in any way the likelihood of Q being
Cynic? The implied unbridgeable gap between "Judaism" and
"Cynicism" is meaningful—though unverifiable—only when key
terms such as "Judaism" function, as they have in the history of
New Testament scholarship, according to Smith, as a kind of covert
theological code for an exclusive—Protestant—imagination of
Christian origins.[18] In fact, as is now increasingly clear, early
"Judaisms" in their multiple forms belonged as much to the Hel-
lenistic world as did "Cynicism" in its various guises.

Equally in error is the assumption that Cynicism was somehow
restricted in the extent of its cultural manifestations to only a few
regions of the ancient Mediterranean world. Even a superficial review of Cynic geography establishes the range of these homeless
hounds as roughly coterminous with the contours of Greco-Roman
civilization in general (the exceptions being, perhaps, northern
Africa—excluding Egypt—and the western provinces of Spain and
northern Gaul). It is important that our schematic "disciplinary"
maps of antiquity not be confused with its mingled cultural state.

2. A Cynic Q!

The contrasting styles of Rudolf Bultmann and Martin Dibelius in
the initial stages of the development of form criticism reflect two
competing prejudices regarding how best to describe the link between a literature—both the process of its production and its subsequent use—and contextual social reality—its *Sitz im Leben*. One
approach (Dibelius) begins with the concrete historical situation of
a given social group insofar as this can be reconstructed and then
attempts to locate within the same context the variety of extant texts
ascribed to it, characterizing these writings in accordance with their

---

[17] See Tuckett, "A Cynic Q?" 356.
[18] See Smith, *Drudgery Divine* 79-83, esp. p. 83. Regarding "Judaism" and
"Cynicism", cf. H. A. Fischel, "Studies in Cynicism and the Ancient Near East:
The Transformation of a Chreia" in *Religions in Antiquity: Essays in Memory of
Erwin Ramsdell Goodenough* (SHR 14; Leiden: 1968) 372-411.

imagined situation in life. The other approach (Bultmann) begins with the extant texts, characterizing them in terms of their literary genre or linguistic type and then, assuming a certain correspondence between discursive form and social function, posits the cultural setting in which such speech was originally at home. Why the latter approach (Bultmann) won out over the former (Dibelius) among New Testament scholars of this century must be the subject of a separate essay.

The comparison of Q and Cynicism by Downing (and Kloppenborg) proceeds in accordance with the form-critical style of Bultmann. It is first via consideration of literary genre and then regarding discursive content that similarities and differences are noted and the possibility of a certain correspondence between Q and the Cynics is posited (or denied). My own approach, on the other hand, is more like Dibelius', insofar as it was first the question of the "community" of Q—the specific character of the persons whom the document may be said to represent—that made the analogy of Q and Cynicism not only possible, but compelling. For this reason, I begin discussion of "a Cynic Q" with the so-called "mission" instructions in 10:2-16, a set of sayings which, in the history of Q research, have been repeatedly the crucial text for all determinations of the document's underlying social group formation.[19]

Note that Tuckett, once past his initial questions about Cynicism, reads all work comparing Q and the Cynics by beginning with the document's literary genre and proceeds from there to discuss certain of its contents. Again, the quarrel is primarily with Downing (and Kloppenborg). The same line of attack, however, inclines Tuckett to focus on broad issues of excessive generality and / or insufficient necessity in the comparisons that have been made. What Tuckett does not perceive in approaching the discussion in this way—or which considerations of space and the inevitable "blind spot" of any methodological orientation did not allow him explicitly to engage—is the inability of previous interpreters to account convincingly for the different signs in Q of a peculiar social style on the part of its original tradents. It is, however, precisely the striking and uncommon similarity in this regard between Q and the Cynics that finally grants every other possible, if less peculiar comparison between them whatever cogency it may possess.

---

[19] See Vaage, "Q: Ethos and Ethics" 1-71.

(a) Q 10:2-16

Tuckett essentially side-steps the "mission" instructions in his assessment of "a Cynic Q", although he recognizes that "One of the most striking apparent agreements between Q and Cynicism concerns the Q mission charge."[20] Tuckett's critique does not exceed the long scholarly tradition of quibbling about the fact that in 10:4, unlike the usual garb of many Cynics, the persons whom Q represents are told not to take with them either a *pēra* or a staff.[21] Otherwise, the "number of substantive parallels between Cynic traditions and the Q mission discourse in Q 10,3-12", *viz.*, 10:3-6, 9-11, 16, whose display Tuckett attributes to my dissertation, are simply passed over in silence.[22]

Let me respond first to the difference that Tuckett with other scholars underscores between the get-up laid down for the Q people in 10:4 and the stereotypical outfit of a Cynic, i.e., the negative significance assigned to Q's supposedly un-Cynic-like prohibition of a *pēra* and a staff. The contrast as such does not need to be debated. But the assumptions do, both that the Cynics *qua* Cynic always dressed the same and that Q's augmented severity in this regard self-evidently means a self-conscious self-differentiation of the persons whom Q represents from the Cynics versus, e.g., intramural competition between them or the internal up-grading of the same dress code. If, moreover, prohibition of the staff and *pēra* diverges from the usual Cynic pattern, the other recommendations in the same verse (10:4) of a penniless and shoeless existence as well as frontal disregard for the customary habits of greeting and social intercourse fall squarely in line with "normal" Cynic practice.

Not all Cynics dressed alike, however. Beyond the fact that stereotypes are just that—a generalized image, not a hard and fast rule—we know of Cynics, whose Cynicism is usually not disputed, whose clothing, though outrageous, was not the standard uniform. Take Menedemus, for example:

---

[20] See Tuckett, "A Cynic Q?" 367.

[21] See, e.g., Martin Hengel, *Nachfolge und Charisma* (Berlin: 1968) 31-37, especially 36; Heinz Schürmann, *Das Lukasevangelium* I (Freiburg: 1969) 502; Paul Hoffmann, *Studien zur Theologie der Logienquelle* (Münster: 1972) 240-242; Iris Bosold, *Pazifismus und prophetische Provokation* (Stuttgart: 1978) 71; Wolfgang Schenk, *Synopse zur Redenquelle der Evangelien* (Dusseldorf: 1981) 52; Richard A. Horsley, *Jesus and the Spiral of Violence* (San Francisco: 1987) 230f.; *idem, Sociology and the Jesus Movement* (New York: 1989) 47, 117.

[22] See Tuckett, "A Cynic Q?" 349.

Menedemus was a pupil of Colotes of Lampsacus.... This was his attire: a grey tunic reaching to the feet, about it a crimson girdle; an Arcadian hat on his head with the twelve signs of the zodiac inwrought in it; buskins of tragedy; and he wore a very long beard and carried an ashen staff in his hand.[23]

Even the reports concerning Diogenes' dress, progenitor of the traditional Cynic outfit, do not suggest that, in his case, the staff was indispensable:

He was the first, some say, to fold his cloak because he was obliged to sleep in it as well, and he carried a wallet to hold his food, and he used any place for any purpose, for breakfasting, sleeping, or conversing.... He did not lean upon a staff until he grew infirm; but afterwards he would carry it everywhere, not indeed in the city, but when walking along the road with it and with his wallet; so say Olympiodorus, once a magistrate at Athens, Polyeuctus the orator, and Lysanias the son of Aeschrio.[24]

As already noted, Tuckett repeats the stock observation of many commentators, not incorrect as far as it goes, that "the *distinguishing marks* of the Cynic were the πήρα, the staff and cloak. However, for the Q missionaries, *no* πήρα and *no* staff are allowed." Tuckett immediately concludes: "Thus even at the level of visible outward appearance to others, the Q missionaries must have looked rather *un*-like Cynic preachers."[25] Much less so, however, than Menedemus! And rather like Diogenes as a young man and later on in his life as well around the city (except for the *pēra*). Moreover, how different would a "stripped-down" Cynic as described in Q 10:4 have looked vis-a-vis the "fully equipped" model seen elsewhere? The lack of a *pēra* and staff would hardly have caused any onlooker suddenly to mistake the Q people for, say, a displaced temple priest or travelling Essene (who, after all, also took a staff as a weapon) or hustling scribe or even sorry peasant. The abnegation of the *pēra* and staff in Q 10:4, if not typical or widely attested, is certainly in line with the ascetic logic of the Cynics, and therefore hardly contradicts or annuls at this point the comparison between Q and Cynicism, certainly not in the facile way that Tuckett and the scholars whom he cites superficially suggest.

---

[23] See Diogenes Laertius 6.102.
[24] See Diogenes Laertius 6.22-23.
[25] See Tuckett, "A Cynic Q?" 367.

A detailed comparison of Cynic-traditions and the instructions in Q 10:3-6, 9-11, 16 depends upon two further considerations for the theoretical relationship between them to become compelling. One derives from the history of Q research, namely, the inability of any other set of comparisons to account concretely for the specific character of the sayings that we find here in the document. The prophetic analogue to which Tuckett approvingly points at the end of his article is case in point. The Cynics present themselves not simply as the best, but on more than one occasion as the only instance of a similar style of behaviour and reasoning in antiquity. It is not enough, therefore, to disagree with broad descriptive categories or abstract theological reasoning, when the text at hand so plainly deals with utterly mundane issues: how to un/dress oneself, address others, manage rebuff and further risks resulting from the same instructions.

The second consideration is the cumulative strength of the comparison between Q 10:3-6, 9-11, 16 and the Cynics. The conclusion that the persons described by these sayings (10:3-6, 9-11, 16) were like the Cynics is based not upon a few scattered associations here and there, but the fact that every one of these sayings can be shown to share certain fundamental features with not a few such utterances in Cynic literature. No single element is primordial; nothing, the cornerstone, lynch pin, or Achilles' heel of the present convergence. It will not suffice, therefore, in order to dismantle the proposed correlation merely to dispute an aspect or two of it. Not just the strength of the individual parts, but their general cohesion in a coordinated whole must be disassembled, if the suggestion of a Cynic Q is to be convincingly rejected.

(i) Q 10:3

The formative stratum of Q's "mission" instructions began with the observation: "Look, I send you out as sheep in the midst of wolves."[26] Likewise, Crates used to say that "those found among flatterers are defenseless [erēmous] like calves [mosxous] found in the midst of wolves."[27] I assume that the variation in the specific animal (sheep / calves) used in the two sayings to symbolize the same position of proneness, susceptibility, and / or exposure to

---

[26] For 10:2, 7b, 12, 13-15 as the work of Q's redaction, see, now, Vaage, *Galilean Upstarts: Jesus' First Followers According to Q* (Valley Forge, PA.: 1994) 107, 111-114..

[27] See Diogenes Laertius 6.92.

threat will not impede perception of their structural similarity to one another. It is clear, furthermore, from the Cynic text—and this is the point of the comparison—that the language of "sheep in the midst of wolves" need not suggest a more "serious" conflict than "moral" danger.

The Q people are depicted in 10:3 as dispersed and aware that the persons among whom they will find their way are likely ill-disposed to support and may even be hostile to the project they embody. But neither physical "persecution" nor fierce "vituperative" polemic over group rights to the sacred title of being the "true Israel" must be understood as implied by the use of such an expression; unless, like Tuckett, in the name of "the Jewish background" one feels compelled for other reasons to assume that a harsher struggle is *de rigueur* in the imagination of Christian origins.[28]

The sense in 10:3 of being "sent" is equally shared with Cynicism, if not exclusively. A favourite trope of Epictetus was precisely this one. Zeus, says the teacher from Nicopolis, has sent the Cynic into the world, whom the Cynic now serves. The Cynic should know that he is both a messenger sent by God and his scout, as Diogenes put it. Indeed, in Epictetus' judgement, the Cynic deemed worthy of God's sceptre and diadem can say: "Behold, God has sent me to you as an example, that you may see yourselves, O humans, that you are looking for happiness and serenity, not where it is, but where it is not."[29] Likewise, the persons whom Q represents appear to have conceived of their indigent state not as mere vagrancy but, rather, as a movement of mendicant heralds, announcing a surer route to felicity.

(ii) Q 10:4

New Testament scholars have been singularly unsuccessful at finding anything with which to compare the instructions in 10:4. The usual comment remarks how "unparalleled" or "impossible" the saying is. But, as already noted, at least three of the items prohibited in 10:4 were likewise typically foresworn by the Cynics.

---

[28] See Tuckett, "A Cynic Q?" 370-371.

[29] See Epictetus 1.24.6; 3.22.23-24, 38, 56, 59, 69, 97. For the quotation, see Epictetus 4.8.30-31; further, 2.16.47; 3.22.26, 23.34; also Margarethe Billerbeck, *Epiktet: Vom Kynismus* (Leiden: 1978) 78. Billerbeck notes that the term, *martys,* is also relevant here. See, e.g., Epictetus, 1.29.46-47; 3.24.112-113.

These are: "Take no money...no sandals...[and] greet no one."
Thus, for example, we read:

> Diocles relates how Diogenes persuaded Crates to give up his property
> to sheep-pasture, and throw into the sea any money he had.[30]

> Therefore, my appearance [as a Cynic] is, as you see, to be dirty and
> unkempt with a worn cloak, long hair, and bare feet.[31]

> Seek out the most crowded places, [says the Cynic,] and in those very
> places try to be solitary and antisocial, greeting neither friend nor
> stranger; for to do so is to lose hegemony.[32]

(iii) Q 10:5-6

Interpretation of 10:5-6, which give instruction regarding the
proper procedure for approaching and entering an unknown resi-
dence, depends heavily upon whatever we decide, at the level of our
"preunderstanding" of the text, is going on here. Some scholars
have paid special attention to the fact that a *house* is mentioned.
Others find the language of *peace* most noteworthy. Still others
worry about what it means for this peace to be able to move about
and *return*. And some have wanted more than anything else to
identify the *son of peace*.

Few, however, have asked why anyone—especially if Q were to
recall popular "peasant" communities or certain lower-level
scribes—in mid-first century CE Galilee would routinely have tried
to establish amicable, but fleeting relations with an open-ended series of previously unknown and soon forgotten households.[33]
Anachronistic notions of door-to-door evangelism and intensive
neighbourhood marketing are clearly out of the question. If, however, we may imagine the persons whom Q represents suddenly
appearing without warning on the threshold of a villager's home in
the vicinity of ancient Capernaum, un/dressed and ill/equipped as

---

[30] See Diogenes Laertius 6.87.
[31] See Pseudo-Lucian, *cyn.* 17.
[32] See Lucian, *vit. anc.* 10.
[33] For Q (and Mark) as originally recalling popular "peasant" communities,
see Horsley, *Sociology*. For members of the lower levels of the administrative
and scribal classes as the persons initially responsible for the production of Q,
see Kloppenborg, "Literary Convention, Self-Evidence and the Social History of
the Q People," *Semeia* 55 (1992) 77-102.

10:4 describes them, it hardly seems unreasonable to assume with the inhabitants of the house, if only as a first impression, that beggars had arrived: the "dogs" at the door were seeking a hand-out.

It is well-known that the Cynics begged. Lucian has them "going from house to house" for this very reason.[34] Though not always welcomed with open arms, their epiphany on the porch was neither inevitably rebuffed. Demonax is a case in point:

> Toward the end, when he was very old, he used to eat and sleep uninvited in any house which he chanced to be passing, and those who lived there thought that it was almost a divine visitation, and that good fortune had entered their house.[35]

At the same time, like the Q people, the Cynics knew that the best thing to do with a hostile reception was often simply to take it and leave. Thus, Diogenes "once begged alms of a statue, and when asked why he did so, replied, 'To get practice in being refused.'"[36]

(iv) Q 10:9

Like 10:5-6, interpretation of the present saying depends heavily upon our preunderstanding—or misunderstanding—of the significance of its language. The overwhelming tendency has been for scholars simply to assume that miracles and an eschatological message are meant when reference is made here to "treating the weak", *viz.*, healing the sick and that "the kingdom of God has arrived." This, despite the fact that reference to miracles is otherwise virtually absent from Q, and the "kingdom of God" sayings in the document must first be read in relation to one another.

Tuckett contends on the basis of the prevailing prejudice that here (10:9) "alleged parallels between Q and Cynic texts should probably be rejected completely."[37] Cynic efforts to achieve moral health and physical contentment through the ascetic practice they called a "shortcut" to felicity have, says Tuckett, "really nothing in common with Jesus as a miracle-worker, giving health miraculously to someone else and doing so by his powerful, authoritative word."[38] Tuckett rejects an understanding of the in-

---

[34] See Lucian, *fug.* 14.
[35] See Lucian, *Dem.* 63.
[36] See Diogenes Laertius 6.49.
[37] See Tuckett, "A Cynic Q?" 375.
[38] *Ibid.*

junction to treat the weak "in metaphorical terms", claiming that it "seems very forced" and that "such an outlook does not really fit the healing stories which actually occur in Q."[39]

Both key terms, *therapeuein* and *asthenēs/eō,* in 10:9a are found only here in Q. Their precise meaning, therefore, especially regarding the formative stratum of the document, can hardly be considered self-evident, not to mention the fact that both terms in antiquity were otherwise subject to a variety of—metaphorical(!)—usages. Malherbe, for example, has recently described the way in which reference to the "weak" formed part of the general vocabulary of ancient moral psychagogy:

> the weak are those who have difficulty in living up to the demands of the virtuous or philosophic life. Their condition is frequently likened to a physical disease or disposition. This condition Cicero and Diogenes Laertius describe as weakness (*imbecillitas,* ἀσθένεια) a condition that accompanies moral illness, exemplified, for example, by 'a fond imagining of something that seems desirable', such as fame, love of pleasure, and the like. Chrysippus, already, had held that by way of analogy souls could be spoken of as being weak or strong, diseased or healthy, just as bodies are, and the notion of weakness found a place in the Stoic theory of cognition: it is because of our weakness (ἀσθένεια), they said, that we assent to false mental images. Erroneous behaviour, then, is due to the slackness (ἀτονία) and weakness (ἀσθένεια) of the soul. Weakness is a vice, and every transgression issues from weakness *(imbecillitas)* and instability.[40]

The Q people are told in 10:9a to treat the plight of persons such as these.

Beyond the question how properly to translate 10:9a, Tuckett's contention that "the [other] healing stories which actually occur in Q" establish "Jesus as a miracle-worker" lacks evidence.[41] There are only two such "healing stories" in Q (7:1-10; 11:14-20). Both have been assigned by Kloppenborg to the document's secondary redaction.[42] Both, moreover, in the end are not especially interested in the miraculous as such, if "miraculous" is the only way in which we can refer to what for us—and only for us—would be unconventional medical activity in antiquity. If Jesus is depicted in

---

[39] See Tuckett, "A Cynic Q?" 375 note 85.

[40] See Malherbe, "'Pastoral Care' in the Thessalonian Church," *NTS* 36 (1990) 379-380.

[41] See Tuckett, "A Cynic Q?" 375.

[42] See Kloppenborg, *Formation of Q, passim.* I myself would place 11:14-20 along with most of the rest of Q 11 in the document's formative stratum, excluding 11:29-32, 49-51.

these sayings (7:1-10; 11:14-20) as able to handle disease and the debilities identified with demon-doing, it is only for the sake of the moral lesson to be learned from the exchange that follows in each case. In neither instance in Q is the recovery of the enfeebled patient more than the occasion for displaying once again, in the finest Cynic fashion, Jesus' triumphant powers of reasoning and rebuke.

(v) Q 10:10-11

I know of no parallels to the gesture depicted in this saying: "going out of that city [which rejects you], remove the dust from your feet", except for its repetition in later Christian literature. One of the problems faced by interpreters has been the ludicrous figure actually cut, if one were physically to do what is here prescribed. Perhaps, however, a certain element of the ridiculous was not unintended. The Cynics likewise, on occasion, courted ridicule through strange symbolic gestures, making blatant in this fashion the wrong they felt that they had suffered. Thus, for example, "having exasperated the musician Nicodromus, [Crates] was struck by him on the face. So [Crates] stuck a plaster on his forehead with these words on it: 'Nicodromus' handiwork'."[43] Far from constituting eschatological judgement, the "sign" performed by the persons whom Q represents in 10:10-11 was rather more a comic retort, like the Minnesotan Norwegian bachelor farmer's "tehellwidem".

(vi) Q 10:16

Face to face since 10:3 with the threat of "wolves" and other mean-minded men and women, looking to be taken in by any peaceable soul (10:5-6) but knowing complete rejection as well (10:10-11), just why the vagrant (10:4) therapists embodying God's reign (10:9) whom Q represents ought to have been accorded better treatment seems a reasonable question. 10:16 provides a rationale for their (irregular) reception, at the same time that we hereby return to the beginning of the "mission" instructions in 10:3 with the affirmation that the Q people, despite appearances, are finally divine messengers whose hospitable acceptance is equivalent to being visited by God himself. Similarly, the part-time Cynic, Dio Chrysostom, could identify himself as "a man

---

[43] See Diogenes Laertius 6.89.

who has come...having no connection with you from any point of view...by divine guidance to address and counsel you."[44] O r likewise in one of the Cynic epistles: "For I am called heaven's dog, not earth's, since I liken myself to it, living as I do, not in conformity with popular opinion but according to nature, free under Zeus, and crediting the good to him and not to my neighbour."[45]

Described in the different "mission" instructions of Q's formative stratum (10:3-6, 9-11, 16) is thus a particular ethos. This "way of life" constitutes the concrete context in which the various other sayings from the same literary layer of the document should be read, if we are not to assume a sort of social "schizophrenia" or deep divorce between the "practical" measures outlined above and the ethical, ideological, and critical pronouncements now to be discussed.[46]

(b) Q 6:27-35

We begin with the ethics of Q as exemplified by the well-known admonition to "love your enemies" (6:27-35) at the heart of the formative stratum's inaugural discourse.[47]

Gerd Theissen asks the appropriate question regarding this famous "hard" saying of Jesus: What is the concrete *Sitz im Leben* that we must imagine for the ethics enjoined here, if taken at face value, not to register in practice merely an open invitation to repeated abuse by others and ultimately self-destruction?[48] I assume that moral maxims like those brought together in Q 6:27-35 were not initially proposed and repeated simply to make life miserable for their adherents but, instead, to help them out by suggesting a better way of dealing with the different difficulties and displeasures

---

[44] See Dio Chrysostom, *or*. 34.4.

[45] See ps-Diogenes, *ep*. 7.

[46] Horsley (*Sociology* 116-119) is plainly perturbed by the term "way of life" or "life-style", perceiving in such speech an anachronistic category reflective not of ancient (traditional) agrarian social reality, but of modern "individualism" and, it seems, contemporary "yuppie" sensibilities. I mean with the term what Diogenes Laertius (6.104) referred to regarding the Cynics as *enstasis biou*.

[47] For further discussion, see my "'Amen a sus enemigos' y otras estrategias de resistencia" (see note 5 above).

[48] See Theissen, "Gewaltverzicht und Feindesliebe (Mt 5,38-48 Lk 6,27-36) und deren sozialgeschichtlicher Hintergrund" in *Studien zur Soziologie des Urchristentums* (Tübingen: 1979) 160-197, especially 191.

of (their) immediate human existence. In this regard, the language of the text has meaning only if and when it works in practice.

To state Theissen's question another way: What makes of "love your enemies" and the related recommendations in Q 6:27-35 more than merely "lousy" advice? It is this necessary inquiry that both permits and insists that similar statements by the Cynics be seen as parallel to what we find here in Q. With such speech, the Cynics sought to outline a strategy for handling the same sort of social conflict apparent in Q, which the Cynics too provoked and suffered; unlike certain theological disembodied interpretations of 6:27-35 that imagine, in the name of Christian faith or eschatology or a "radical reversal" of usual social experience, an otherwise impossible code of behaviour whereby "love", regard for others, and / or mercy would somehow be free of all self-interest, self-centredness, self-regard, and / or concern for self-preservation.[49] By contrast, the Cynic parallels to "love your enemies" make plain both that and the conditions under which the repertoire of responses in 6:27-35 served in practice to convert situations of adversity into moments of successful "self-rewarding" management and triumph.

Tuckett admits that "Epictetus' description in III. xxiii. 53f. about the duties of a Cynic to love those who are beating him may provide a genuine parallel to the gospel tradition." The separate fact, however, that "Diogenes is often portrayed as very far from exhibiting such a generous attitude to his 'enemies'" is immediately taken to imply that, therefore, "Epictetus' description is no more than an ideal which he (as a Stoic) would wish to see in Cynics. Many other Cynics were considerably less loving."[50] That the Cynics were not doctrinaire pacifists or early advocates of complete non-violence goes without saying, much as animals that "play dead" to protect themselves on one occasion will devour their own prey on another. Strategies are, by definition, not universal programmes, principles or postulates, but contextually determined (limited) probings of particular possibilities.

At the same time, Tuckett's rejection of the possibly "genuine parallel" in Epictetus to "love your enemies" in Q on the basis of Cynic inconsistency, if understatement is here not equivalent to error, would apply equally well to Q itself, or to Jesus as portrayed in

---

[49] See, e.g., John Piper, *Love Your Enemies: Jesus' Love Command in the Synoptic Gospels and in the Early Christian Paraenesis: A History of the Tradition and Interpretation of Its Uses* (New York: 1979).
[50] See Tuckett, "A Cynic Q?" 366.

the synoptic tradition. For both Q and Jesus, like the Cynics, alternately advocate forbearance and acquiesence under siege together with outbursts of polemical rage and promises of retribution.

(i) Q 6:27-28

Compare the opening imperatives in 6:27-28, "Love your enemies; pray for those who revile you", with the statement by Diogenes: "When asked how to repulse an enemy, he replied, 'You be kind and good to him.'"[51] Or the perspective of Bion of Borysthenes:

> [who] said to his intimate friends that they might well think that they were making progress when they could listen to their revilers as though they were saying: "Friend, since you have not the look of one who is base and unthinking, health and great joy be yours, and God grant that you may ever prosper."[52]

(ii) Q 6:29

Regarding the difficult advice in 6:29, "If anyone strikes you on the cheek, offer them the other one as well; and let the person who takes your cloak, also have your tunic", the words of admiration for Antisthenes expressed by the orthodox church father, Gregory Nazianzus, are instructive:

> How great a man was Antisthenes! When struck publicly by a certain daring and impudent person, he simply wrote on his forehead the name of the one who struck him, just as one writes the name of the artist on a statue—to accuse him more caustically in this way.[53]

(iii) Q 6:30

Consider the proposal in 6:30, "Give to the one who begs from you, and do not refuse the one who wants to borrow from you", in

---

[51] See *Gnomologium Vaticanum* 187, ed. L. Sternbach (Berlin: 1963) 76; further, Plutarch, *Moralia* 21F, 88B.

[52] See Plutarch, *Moralia* 82E; Léonce Paquet, *Les cyniques grecs: fragments et témoignages* (Ottawa: 1975) 131. The opposite is described by Teles (56H) in *Teles [The Cynic Teacher]*, ed. and trans. Edward N. O'Neill (Missoula, MT: 1977) 65.

[53] See Gregory Nazianzus, "Oratio IV. Contra Julianum I" in *PG* 35.596B.

the light of Crates' answer to the person who asked him why he should become a philosopher:

> Crates said: "You will be able to open your purse easily and to give away freely what you draw out with your hand: not as you do now, calculating, hesitant, trembling, as those with shaky hands. But you will regard a purse which is full as full and after you see that it is emptied, you will not complain."[54]

(iv) Q 6:31, 32-33

The "golden rule" in 6:31 and the subsequent rhetorical questions in 6:32-33 seem at first glance to be less distinctive in their moral outlook than the preceding sayings (6:27-30). Indeed, the "golden rule" expresses common wisdom in the ancient world.[55] At the same time, however, a certain mockery is made here of the general convention in antiquity of reciprocity among peers.[56] If "those who collect taxes for Rome" and other "outsiders"—both groups being stereotypical "bad guys"—are known to treat one another with respect and care, doing likewise can hardly exemplify the highest virtue. Thus, far from recommending such behaviour, the sayings in 6:31, 32-33 serve to establish a moral bottom-line, whose worth is immediately relativized by the surrounding pronouncements.

(v) Q 6:35

Behaving as proposed especially in 6:27-30, Q concludes in 6:35 by assuring its unsettled readership that those who practice such responses to ill-will and aggression will soon be "sons of God, because he makes his sun shine on the wicked" and the like. How exactly to interpret this last statement is less than clear, for it seems to suggest that divinity is defined precisely by ignoring all "normal" codes for assessing personal character in antiquity and acting in a manner "beyond good and evil". On the other hand, it may be that the general superiority implied by the term "God" is evinced precisely through the same ability to ignore mean-spirit-

---

[54] See Stobaeus 4.33.31 in Paquet, *Les cyniques grecs* 113 (see note 52 above).

[55] See Albrecht Dihle, *Die Goldene Regel* (Göttingen: 1962).

[56] Cf. Paul Ricoeur, "The Golden Rule: Exegetical and Theological Perplexities," *NTS* 36 (1990) 392-397.

edness and basic badness for the sake of achieving well-being in another form.

The preceding interpretation of 6:27-35 is just one example of the correlation able to be drawn between Q's "Cynic" ethos and its recorded ethics. Ethical discourse is in its own right a second-order reflection on the embodied understanding of existence realized in the social practice of a group. Ethical discourse tries to clarify this understanding either by resolving problems—such as the menace of inimical opposition—related to the group's on-going ability to re/produce itself or by refining through detailed specification various aspects of its current social style. Similarly, it attempts to systematize the different positions assumed by a particular socio-political persuasion by giving them a certain organizational "stamp". In the case of Q, we are speaking about the various "kingdom of God" sayings found in the document's formative stratum (6:20b; 10:9b; 11:2, 20; 12:31; 13:18-19, 20-21). Here, too, the analogy between Q and Cynicism sustains itself.[57]

(c) Q 6:20b-21

The first "kingdom of God" saying in Q is the well-known beatitude which declares that the "poor" are happy, because theirs is the kingdom of God. Note that the saying is not itself about the kingdom of God but, rather, about the poor, just as the subsequent two sayings in 6:21ab address those who are hungry and weep. Reference to the kingdom of God in 6:20b is simply one way of explaining how it is that the poor, a word traditionally associated with sorrow and hardship, could be thought of as content. At issue is what poverty means.

The theme of poverty is widespread in the moral literature of antiquity. Everyone knew that being poor makes life more difficult. Most, therefore, considered it an evil. Not everyone, however, held this point of view. Thus, we read in one of the Cynic epistles: "Practice needing little, for this is nearest to God, while the opposite is farthest away."[58] Elsewhere, the same perspective is spelled out in greater detail, arguing that a position of dominance can be

---

[57] For further discussion, see my "Monarchy, Community, Anarchy: The Kingdom of God in Paul and Q" (see note 5 above).

[58] See ps-Crates, *ep.* 11 in *Ascetic Behaviour in Greco-Roman Antiquity: A Sourcebook*, ed. Vincent L. Wimbush (Studies in Antiquity and Christianity; Minneapolis: 1990) 119.

achieved over life's misfortunes and vicissitudes precisely by assuming the predictable and proverbial trials of an impoverished life.[59] It is clear that in 6:20b, a share in God's kingdom means not going along with the customary understanding of misery and bliss, if only because one is convinced that present tears and hunger will soon give way to laughter and satisfaction (6:21ab), just as Diogenes used to say regarding hunger that it was the best way to give food its fullest flavour.[60]

The kingdom of God in 6:20b is this ability—call it wisdom, if you will—to incorporate adversity into the experience of contentment. The dramatic "reversal" of the usual order of things often seen here by New Testament scholars is simply this: in Nietzsche's terms, an *Umwertung der Werte*; in Diogenes', a "defacing the currency" of ancient beliefs about what made for the good life.

(d) Q 10:9

Despite everything made of the statement in 10:9b that "the kingdom of God has arrived", it is not at all a widespread formulation in early Christian literature. Indeed, at least in the New Testament, it borders on being a rare expression. Except for Mk 1:14—the source of much speculation about the historical Jesus and Christian origins by New Testament scholars, although the phrase is never again repeated in the rest of Mark—the same statement that "the kingdom of God has arrived" occurs only here in Q (10:9b), excluding all texts otherwise dependent literarily on either Mark or Q. If such speech in Mark is demonstrably at the service of an apocalyptic imagination, the same conclusion can hardly be assumed for Q.

The context of 10:9 itself suggests that, in Q, the reference to God's kingdom arriving formed part of a general "therapeutic" practice by the saying's tradents. When the persons whom Q represents treated the weak, they were to tell them that the kingdom of God had arrived. Just as in 6:20b the life of poverty was made a means of participating in divine aseity through association with the kingdom of God, so here the same expression "kingdom of God"

[59] See, e.g., ps-Crates, *ep.* 18 (see note 58 above)
[60] See Teles 7H (see note 52 above).

serves to identify the experience of—renewed / moral / physical
—health obtained at the hands of the Q people.[61]

(e) Q 11:2-4

It is not uncommon for the first lines of the "Lord's prayer" to be
read by scholars as somehow related to the Jewish "Kaddish"
prayer, which begins similarly. But the comparison, in my opinion,
cannot be sustained beyond a certain superficial correspondence.[62]
In terms of Q itself, there are good reasons for understanding what
is meant by "your kingdom come" in 11:2 together with the petition in 11:3 for daily bread. The kingdom of God is here a matter
of bodily sustenance, just as in 6:20b having a share in God's
kingdom meant being happy, and in 10:9b the experience of
complete well-being. For the persons whom Q represents, without a
beggar's bag or any other visible means of support (10:4), depending on the hospitality of strangers (10:5-6), hoping that the
good fortune of the ravens and the lilies would be theirs as well
(12:22-31), regular nutrition could reasonably be called a kingdom come.

(f) Q 11:14-20

The claim in 11:20b that "the kingdom of God has appeared to
you" opposes the reference made in 11:18b to "his kingdom",
namely, Satan's. One might think that here, at least, the "kingdom
of God" is understood apocalyptically as the new aeon about to
replace the old and evil one. But the reference to "his kingdom"
in 11:18b merely repeats in terms of the initial accusatory figure of
Beelzebul = Satan (11:15) the logical problem posed by 11:17:
"every kingdom divided against itself is laid waste." 11:18b is part
of a rhetorical elaboration that recalls in the midst of refuting it the
defamatory language of the opening charge in 11:15: "he casts
out demons by Beelzebul, the prince of demons."

The fact observed in 11:19a that the "sons" of the accusers do
the same as the accused makes it clear that the debate is finally not
about two opposing realms of being, but the exercise of a certain
power and competing claims to legitimacy. Technically, the state-

---

[61] For similarities in Cynicism, see Diogenes Laertius 6.102 (Menedemus);
Lucian, *Peregr.* 28, 41; J. Bernays, *Lucian und die Kyniker* (Berlin: 1879) 10;
Malherbe, *Paul and the Popular Philosophers* 128-135.

[62] See Vaage, "Q: Ethos and Ethics" 462-464.

ment in 11:20b that "the kingdom of God has appeared to you" is an illative conversion, marking the logical inversion of the initial accusation (11:15) and thereby constituting its ultimate disproof. As "the negation of the negation", the saying represents a piece of discursive legerdemain worthy of Diogenes at his best, not to mention Socrates, Kierkegaard, and Hegel.

(g) Q 12:22-31

The basic problem addressed in 12:22-31 is worry about what to eat and wear. The text's extended reasoning elaborates the somewhat cryptic equation made in 6:20b between poverty and happiness, just as 11:14-20 defends at length the terse identification in 10:9 of health and the kingdom of God. The poor are those who suffer most the insecurities mentioned in 12:22 regarding food and clothing. The saying as a whole argues for the possibility of a full and ultimately satisfying life at the edge of subsistence.

Unlike 11:14-20, two distinct "zones" of existence with their respective rules and rulers are juxtaposed in 12:22-31. On the one hand, there is the animal kingdom, the realm of nature, the rule of God; on the other hand, the orders of human civilization, exemplified by Solomon in all his glory. The cultural enterprise as such is hereby called into question. Instead of struggling to get more of what human society offers as food and clothing, 12:31 urges: "Seek [God's] kingdom, and all these things will be yours as well." To seek "his" kingdom means to seek the father who, in 12:30b, knows what you need, as demonstrated in the sufficient nurture of the ravens (12:24) and the lilies (12:27). If not exactly an argument to follow nature, it is nonetheless "nature" that provides the best analogy for how God's kingdom works.

At this point, we are extremely close to what the Cynics meant when they proposed as a shortcut to felicity the mode of life which they deemed to be most "in accordance with nature". Consider in this regard the following section from Dio Chrysostom's tenth oration, "On Servants":

> Are you not going to try to secure first that which will enable you to profit from everything and to order all your affairs well, but in preference to wisdom are you going to seek money or land or slaves or teams of horses or ships or houses?... Do you not see the beasts there and the birds, how much freer from sorrow they live than human beings, and how much more happily also, how much healthier and stronger they are, how each of them lives the longest life possible, although they have neither hands nor human intelligence. But to counterbalance these

and other limitations, they have one very great blessing—they own no property.[63]

(h) Q 13:18-19, 20-21

The final two kingdom of God sayings in Q's formative stratum attempt to explain to what exactly the term itself, "kingdom of God", refers. The expression, "kingdom of God", used elsewhere in the document to shape perception, here becomes itself the object of reflection. As with all dictionary definitions, additional language is used to explicate the meaning of a given word. Thus, the "kingdom of God" is compared in 13:18-19, 20-21 to a mustard seed and leaven. No new "parabolic" reality is revealed.

It is the happiness of the poor (6:20b), the treatment that the weak receive from the tradents of Q (10:9; 11:20), the fulfilled desire for daily bread (11:2), the lack of worry about what to eat or wear and "all these things" (12:31) that are said in 13:18-19, 20-21 to be "like a mustard seed" and "like leaven". In both instances, it is the disproportion between immediate appearance and projected reality, start and finish, origin and destiny that is at stake.

At the time of planting (for whatever purpose), no seed is what it proves to be; especially, perhaps, the mustard seed. The person who takes the seed and sows it in the ground confides not in the evidence of his or her senses—the mustard seed's resemblance to a worthless speck—but in a knowledge of potentialities: the possible benefits (or disturbances) residing at the centre of ostensible insignificance. What is now for all intents and purposes socially invisible, like leaven "hidden" in a lump, is nonetheless capable of generating great change: the whole lump will soon "all" be leavened. The "kingdom of God" is thus depicted as a permeating power at work within a cultivated mass: a particular social posture whose source of strength, once tapped, is hard to isolate, but whose practical truth, at least from Q's point of view, would soon be evident.

Beyond ethos, ethics and ideology, there is finally the discursive practice of polemic and social critique. The "woes" in Q's formative stratum (11:39-48, 52) assess the life and work of the Pharisees: their piety and public morality, in ways akin to the Cynics' repeated tweaking of their culture's ordained religiosity and os-

---

[63] See Dio Chrysostom, *or.* 10.15-16.

tensible uprightness.[64] As with much social criticism, the woes' "attack" often tells us more about the speaker than they do about the intended "target".[65]

(j) Q 11:39-41

The first woe plays explicitly with the quotidian dichotomy between the inside and the outside (of a cup), distinguishing between the dictates of a system of purity and the actual attainment of moral virtue. The point appears to be that however complete one's treatment may be of "externals", without a corresponding internal reality the former is void of value: "the outside of the cup...you clean..., but inside...full of rapacity." Similarly: "Seeing someone perform an act of religious purification, [Diogenes] said, 'O unhappy one, don't you know that you can no more get rid of errors of conduct by sprinkling than you can mistakes of grammar.'"[66]

(k) Q 11:42

The second woe says essentially the same thing as the first; but instead of using the pursuit of purity as its foil, it employs the im/perfection of accomplished righteousness as the case in point. The Pharisees' attempt to elaborate the truth of their tradition to the utmost degree by dwelling on the smallest of daily details is declared long on effort, but short on principle: "you tithe mint...and neglect...justice." Likewise, Diogenes "was moved to anger that persons should sacrifice to the gods to ensure health, and in the midst of the sacrifice feast to the detriment of health."[67] Similarly: "Once he saw the officials of a temple leading someone

---

[64] For further discussion, see my "The Woes in Q (and Matthew and Luke)" (see note 5 above).

[65] About the Pharisees before 70 CE, we know very little. For the historian of Pharisaism, the synoptic gospel traditions are among the earliest evidence. See Mack, *A Myth of Innocence* 41-44; further, Morton Smith, "Palestinian Judaism in the First Century" in *Israel: Its Role in Civilization*, ed. Moshe Davis (New York: 1956) 67-81; *idem, Palestinian Parties and Politics that Shaped the Old Testament* (New York: 1971); Jacob Neusner, *From Politics to Piety: The Emergence of Pharisaic Judaism* (Englewood Cliffs, NJ: 1973); Anthony J. Saldarini, *Pharisees, Scribes and Sadducees in Palestinian Society: A Sociological Approach* (Wilmington, DE: 1988), especially ch. 12.

[66] See Diogenes Laertius 6.42.

[67] See Diogenes Laertius 6.28.

away who had stolen a bowl belonging to the treasurers, and said, 'The great thieves are leading the little one away.'"[68]

(l) Q 11:44

The invective of the third woe, which compares the object of its outrage to the graveyard, "because you are like unseen tombs...", recalls the equally direct and abrasive rudeness *(parresia)* of the Cynics. Beyond this, however, because of the fragmentary quality of the text, it is difficult to know exactly what the original point of the comparison was.

(m) Q 11:46

The fourth woe sketches once again the contrast between the official posture of the Pharisees as legislators and their human, all too human inability or unwillingness to make possible—less onerous— the fulfillment of their norms and regulations: they "load people with burdens hard to bear, and...do not move...own finger." Just so, Diogenes would wonder, among other things, "that the orators should make a fuss about justice in their speeches, but never practice it; or that the avaricious should cry out against money, while inordinately fond of it."[69]

(n) Q 11:47-48

In the fifth woe, a fundamental contradiction is decried at the heart of the customary reverence of former "national" figures—the prophets—by the descendants of those who earlier opposed them: "you build the tombs of the prophets...your fathers killed them." Contemporary esteem masks a history of rejection. The golden praise of present-day memorials is founded on the slippery clay of yesterday's disdain and hostility. Current civic pride makes heroes out of ancient enemies, but not to set the record straight: "you are witnesses...and consent to the deeds of your fathers." Thus, too, Diogenes "the dog", disparaged while still living, in keeping with his former way of life and understanding of it, "left instructions that [his disciples] should throw him out unburied" or the like when he died. But, instead, there "arose a quarrel among his dis-

---

[68] See Diogenes Laertius 6.45.
[69] See Diogenes Laertius 6.27-28.

ciples as to who should bury him; indeed, they even came to blows; but when their fathers and men of influence arrived, under their direction he was buried beside the gate leading to the Isthmus", the gravesite being further honoured with "a pillar and a dog in Parian marble" and other "bronze statues" with laudatory inscriptions.[70] He who while living had respected nothing that was "upstanding" in his social world, challenging the legitimacy of all "men of influence" and their normative codes, could finally be domesticated in death: "stood up" and fixed as the fathers directed in the guise of a noble hero.

(o) Q 11:52

The final woe of Q's formative stratum puts in question the pretense of privileged (religious) knowledge and power: "Woe to you...because you lock up...you do not go in and those going in, you prevent." Human folly is once more in view, though not without a certain edge to it. Diogenes lampooned the same aspiration to exclusiveness:

> when the Athenians urged him to become initiated, and told him that in Hades those who have been initiated obtain first place. "It would be ludicrous," he said, "if Agesilaus and Epaminondas are to dwell in the mire, while certain folk of no account will live in the Isles of the Blessed because they have been initiated."[71]

Likewise, if what the subjects of Q's final woe have "locked up" truly mattered, they would finally not be able to deny anyone truly worthy of it access to it. On the other hand, if they were to succeed in keeping people away, then the experience is hardly worth the effort in the first place.

In one way or another, all of the preceding woes turn about the axis of appearance versus reality. Appearance is typically synonymous with pretense; reality is always less exalted. As said, the constant tweaking of this contrast also characterized the Cynics, who never ceased to bring their rhetorical inventiveness and sardonic sense of humour to bear upon the gap.

---

[70] See Diogenes Laertius 6.78-79.
[71] See Diogenes Laertius 6.39.

3. Conclusion

In this article, I have sought to respond to Christopher Tuckett's recent inquiry, "A Cynic Q?", first by clarifying a number of issues related to comparison and the study of Cynicism as such, and then by comparing selected sayings of Q's formative stratum and the Cynics in terms of social ethos, ethics, ideology, and critique. The comparison between Q and Cynicism can be sustained in all four instances, which together constitute fundamental features of any group's existence, and suggests therefore that the extensive similarity between Q and the Cynics should not be perceived as either simply the result of tendentious attribution or merely a curiosity. Rather, summarizing briefly, the formative stratum of Q was for all intents and purposes a "Cynic" document.

In the introduction, I defended the legitimacy of comparing Q and Cynicism by referring to Jonathan Z. Smith's recent book, *Drudgery Divine*, and its evaluation of the habits of comparison evident in modern New Testament scholarship and other histories of early Christian religion. Most of Tuckett's concerns and arguments against a "Cynic" Q derive from the generalized confusion described by Smith of comparison with genealogy, understood as a statement about origins.

Limitations of space have not permitted me to discuss in detail every juxtaposition of Q and Cynic materials, nor even to review the whole of Q. But enough has hopefully been said to indicate in which regard(s) a high degree of homogeneity may be posited between the persons whom Q represents and the Cynics. Indeed, the extent of similarity is such that the issue of their social identity must be raised. How significant is it—or should it be—for the historian's effort to locate the Q people on a socio-political "map" of the ancient Mediterranean world that the persons whom Q represents can be shown to have practiced a way of life and style of cultural criticism, not to mention ethical reflection and ideological discourse, quite like those of Cynicism?

Recognizing that the specific diction of Q cannot simply be equated with the speech of other Cynic documents, Q nonetheless shares with Cynicism the same basic socio-rhetorical strategy. Both the formative stratum of Q and the Cynics pursued in word and deed a posture of committed marginality, programmatically suspicious of local society's promises to provide through conformity to its norms and codes a measure of happiness. Both the persons whom Q represents and the Cynics opted instead for a different way, some of whose more notable peculiarities have been reviewed in the preceding pages. If the first followers of Jesus in Galilee were not "just" Cynics, they were at least very much like them.

CHAPTER TEN

JOHN THE BAPTIST AND THE JESUS MOVEMENT: WHAT DOES Q TELL US?

Risto Uro

One of the most significant results of the renewed interest in the Sayings Gospel Q during the last 30 years has been a change in the view of Q from a vague and hypothetical collection of Jesus' sayings to a more precise description of a writing in its own right. This change is signalled in the tendency to use the designation "gospel" instead of "source", shifting the emphasis from the perspective of the canonical gospels to the lost gospel known to us through Matthew and Luke. Intensive analyses of the Q material have been able to reveal a coherent writing with distinctive textual and symbolic worlds.[1] All this has an indisputable pertinence to our understanding of the earliest Christian movements and Christian origins.

The train of the New Testament scholarship moves slowly, however, and it may be that we have not yet fully realized the significance of this newly discovered gospel we are reconstructing. A balanced view of Christian origins which takes into account the results achieved in Q research does not emerge in one or two decades. We are in the process of constructing a new picture piece by piece, reviewing old views in the light of the information gained by the textual analyses of the Q material. This paper will focus on

---

[1] The underlying theoretical framework and terminology of this paper are indebted to the Three World Model developed by K. Syreeni (for a convenient description, see K. Syreeni & M. Myllykoski, "Text, Ideology, and Concrete Reality in the Gospels: A Three World Model for Hermeneutical Exegesis" forthcoming in *ANRW* II.26,4). Syreeni's model provides a heuristic tool for exegetical analysis by making a distinction between the "text-world", "symbolic world" and "concrete world" of the gospels (or any other text under hermeneutic scrutiny). The influence of the model on the present paper can be seen in the attempt to make distinctions between the literary phenomena (e.g., the function of John in the "narrative" of Q), the symbolic world (the symbolizing and mythmaking process attached to John and Jesus in the text), and the concrete social and historical situations (the movements around John and Jesus).

one such piece of construction, John the Baptist, and particularly his preaching as reported in Q 3. The Baptist undoubtedly is a figure of importance both in Q and in the history of the earliest Christianity. Therefore any progress achieved in understanding the message and function of John the Baptist in Q will inevitably have its effects on the reconstruction of the nascent movements around John and Jesus, and ultimately on the history of these figures themselves. The purpose of this paper is to demonstrate the importance of the Q research to such crucial issues by making John's preaching the focal point. As I hope to able to demonstrate, in spite of the vast number of treatises on the Baptist, this particular question has not been duly raised in research.

1. The Consensus

The great majority of scholars take it for granted that the sayings preserved at the beginning of Q (3:7-9, 16-17) are essentially of Baptist provenance, although a slight Christian modification of John's preaching of the Coming One is usually suggested. The characterization by C. H. H. Scobie still represents a consensus among scholars:

> There can be little doubt that the keynote of John's teaching and preaching was the proclamation of the imminent approach of the end of days and of the judgement. This is evident from John's sayings preserved in Q, with their vivid pictures of the vipers fleeing the wrath to come, the tree about to be cut down, and the separating of the wheat from the chaff.[2]

Q's description of John as a fiery preacher of the apocalyptic judgment and as a prophetic figure in his own right (cf. Q 7:30-35) seems indeed more primitive and original than the portrayal of Mark, who presents the Baptist as the less independent forerunner

---

[2] C. H. H. Scobie, *John the Baptist.* (London: 1964) 60. R. Bultmann (*The History of the Synoptic Tradition.* [Oxford / New York / Evanston: Blackwell Harper, 1968] 117 and 247) regards the Baptist preaching in Q 3: 7-9 as a Christian formulation, but even he thinks that the kernel of Q 3:16-17 goes back to the proclamation of the historical John. A recent massive study on John the Baptist by J. Ernst (*Johannes der Täufer. Interpretation - Geschichte - Wirkungsgeschichte* [Berlin / New York: 1989]) simply concludes that "die Logienquelle hat die ursprüngliche Täuferpredigt ohne wesentliche Änderungen tradiert..." (p. 55). Similar optimism pervades another recent book on John, R. L. Webb, *John the Baptizer and the Prophet. A Socio-historical Study* (JSNT Supplement Series 62; Sheffield: 1990).

Elijah (Mk 1:2-3; 9:9-13). The imminent expectation of the end by John also seems to provide a conceivable basis for the further development of the movement: for Jesus' proclamation of the approaching Kingdom and for the apocalyptic fervour among the early Christian congregations (e.g., those of Paul). It is also customary to suggest a shift or break between the gloomy message of John and the more merciful ministry of Jesus, which would correspond to the difference between the more ascetic John and Jesus as "a friend of tax collectors and sinners" (Q 7:34).

Yet there are factors which should make us cautious in assessing the "authenticity" of John's proclamation in Q. The contrast between Jesus and John in Q 7:33-34 has not to do with the preaching of these two prophets, but rather with their *lifestyle* (similarly Mk 2:18-19). There is no need to doubt that John was more hostile to forms of urban civilization than was Jesus (cf. Mk 1:4-6; Q 7:24-25). But this does not say anything specifically about the content of their preaching. Mark's more "advanced" treatment of the Baptist material is also somewhat relative, since in Q too the Baptist's role is clearly subordinate to that of Jesus (Q 7:28). More importantly, we should not forget that the common view of John's message is essentially based on Q. Except for the shorter parallels in Mk 1:7-8 and Jn 1:26-27, 33-34, we have only the so-called *Standespredigt* in Lk 3:10-14 and the Christological statements by the Baptist in the Fourth Gospel, which are usually deemed to add nothing to our knowledge of the message of the historical John. The acceptance of the historical accuracy of the few sayings in Q among scholars is surprisingly confident, at least if one thinks of the usual critical attitude toward the bulk of *Jesus'* sayings.

It is of course possible that Q truthfully preserves the message of John, but before historical evaluations we should undertake the normal procedure of analyzing the sayings as part of the textual entity in which they have been preserved for us. As already noted, recent studies have made it clear that Q has its own symbolic world; it reflects a mythmaking process of its specific social situation. A reference to Q as an old "non-kerygmatic" block of information compared to more "kerygmatic" Mark is simply no longer possible. Any historical conclusion about the Baptist has to be preceded by careful literary analyses of the Q text. There is no short cut from text to social world.

2. The Text of Q 3

The comparison of Matthew and Luke makes it obvious that Q opened with a collection of John's sayings. The first of these sayings, John's preaching of repentance (Q 3:7-9), has been preserved by the evangelists in forms that are very close to each other. The oracle itself can be reconstructed without any great difficulties, but the original text of the introduction (3:7a) is less certain. It is common to think that Matthew introduced "Pharisees and Sadducees" as the addressees of John's preaching, since the first evangelist alone presents these two groups together as opponents (cf. Mt 16:1-12). On the other hand, there is evidence that the plural "crowds", to whom the saying is addressed in Luke, is a Lukan favourite expression.[3] Considering the negative tone of the saying, one may argue that Matthew is closer to the original in that the speech is directed to the *opponents*, although the peculiar union of Pharisees and Sadducees derives from him. Moreover, it is possible that the addressees in the Q introduction were characterized as those who were coming for baptism,[4] because both Matthew and Luke report this and the threat against those fleeing "from the wrath to come" in the saying (3:7b) would make sense in such a context.[5]

The second saying, John's announcement of the Coming One (Q 3:16-17), has a close parallel in Mark (1:7-8), in which there is a similar saying of John on two baptisms. However, agreements in structure and content in Matthew and Luke against Mark are significant enough to show that the saying was also in Q. In spite of the Mark / Q overlap, the passage can be reconstructed with relative certainty. For our purposes, the following points are of importance:

Matthew's characterization that John's water baptism was "for repentance" (εἰς μετάνοιαν) is likely to be the evangelist's addition (cf. the omission of "repentance" at Mk 1:4).[6] It is, furthermore, likely that Matthew's description of the one who is to

---

[3] For the linguistic data, see J. Jeremias, *Die Sprache des Lukasevangeliums: Redaktion und Tradition im Nicht-Markusstoff des dritten Evangeliums* (Göttingen: 1980) 14.

[4] *Contra* H. Fleddermann, "The Beginning of Q," *SBLSP* 24 (1985) 154-155.

[5] S. Björndahl, "Database for Q 3:7-9" in The Archives of the International Q Project. The Institute for Antiquity and Christianity, Claremont, CA (1988) 14.

[6] Matthew (3:1) omits Mark's "preaching a baptism of repentance for the forgiveness of sins" transposing "the forgiveness of sins" to the word over the cup at the Last Supper (26:28) and making John's proclamation (3:20) an exact copy of Jesus' initial proclamation in 4:17. See J. P. Meier, "John the Baptist in Matthew's Gospel," *JBL* 99 (1980) 388.

come, ὁ δὲ ὀπίσω μου ἐρχόμενος, preserves the original Q reading. Luke seems to follow Mark (ἔρχεται δὲ ὁ ἰσχυρότερός μου) at this point except that he omits the phrase ὀπίσω μου, probably wanting to avoid a sense of inferiority (cf. 9:23; 14:27; cf. also the use of μετά in Acts 13:25 and 19:4). The choice of the Markan phrase emphasizing the superiority of the Coming One rather than the coming itself is understandable in the light of Luke's redactional introduction 3:15, 16a, in which people were wondering whether John might be the Christ.[7] Moreover, the use of the participial form of ἔρχομαι with the definite article in Acts 19:4 reveals that Luke knew the Matthean form (cf. also the appearances of the phrase in Jn 1:15, 27). The arguments for the view that Q was more like Mark and that Matthew changed it to ὁ δὲ ὀπίσω μου ἐρχόμενος to make a sharper distinction between John and the coming Messiah are less convincing.[8]

It is more difficult to assess whether Q also stated that the Coming One is *stronger* than John (ἰσχυρότερός μού ἐστιν),[9] or whether this feature derives from Mark, with Matthew's diction combining Q and Mark. Kloppenborg has argued for the latter alternative by referring to Jn 1:27 (ὁ ὀπίσω μου ἐρχόμενος, οὗ οὐκ εἰμὶ ἐγὼ ἄξιος...) and suggests a similar construction for Q.[10] But one can object to his suggestion by noting that the characterization of the one who is to come as stronger is not necessary in the Johannine context, which emphasizes the unrecognized coming of Jesus. Furthermore, the formulation in Jn 1:15 (ὁ ὀπίσω μου ἐρχόμενος ἔμπροσθέν μου γέγονεν; cf. Jn 1:30) may be seen as a Johannine interpretation of the synoptic phrase "stronger".[11] If so, John provides no evidence for a tradition which lacked a reference to the stronger one. We should also note that another saying in Q shows similar language (Q 7:28b: ὁ δὲ μικρότερος ἐν τῇ βασιλείᾳ τοῦ θεοῦ μείζων αὐτοῦ ἐστιν). Since this saying is about John the

---

[7] H. Fleddermann, "John and the Coming One. Matt 3:11-12 // Luke 3:16-17," *SBLSP* 23 (1984) 378.

[8] For such an argument, see V. Trilling, "Die Taufertradition bei Matthäus," *BZ* 3 (1959) 286, and Ernst (note 2 above) 50.

[9] The phrase is included by R. Laufen, *Die Doppelüberlieferungen der Logienquelle und des Markusevangeliums* (BBB 54; Bonn: 1980) 96 and Fleddermann (see above note 7) 378.

[10] J. S. Kloppenborg, "City and Wasteland: Narrative World and the Beginning of the Sayings Gospel (Q)," *Semeia* 52 (1990) 149.

[11] For this suggestion, see W. D. Davies and D. C. Allison, *The Gospel According to Saint Matthew* I: *Introduction and Commentary on Matthew I-VII* (ICC; Edinburgh: 1988) 314.

Baptist, the formulation may well be a reminiscence of John's preaching.[12]

Fleddermann[13] has argued that Matthew simplified the image of unworthiness in Mt 3:11c by changing Mark's and Q's λῦσαι τὸν ἱμάντα τῶν ὑποδημάτων αὐτοῦ to τὰ ὑποδήματα βαστάσαι. However, it is not impossible to interpret the expressions as two different images, that of untying the master's shoes (Mk and Lk) and that of carrying them (cf. the RSV translation of Mt).[14] Since "carrying sandals" possibly occurs in Q 10:4: μὴ [[βαστάζετ]]ε ... ὑποδήματα,[15] I give slight preference to the Matthean diction, although much uncertainty is involved in the decision.

In spite of the fact that Matthew and Luke agree in having ἐν πνεύματι ἁγίῳ καὶ πυρί in connection with the coming baptism, a few scholars[16] regard "the Holy Spirit" as an insertion from Mark. Such arguments, however, usually rely on speculations about the original message of John the Baptist, which, as we shall see, may be questioned and in any case are not decisive for the reconstruction of the Q text. It is safe, therefore, to conclude that Q had both "fire" and "spirit", and the latter was not coincidentally added by Matthew and Luke. Neither have we sufficient reason to exclude the epithet "holy" before the "spirit". "Holy Spirit" occurs in Q 12:10 (see also 12:12) and is thus not foreign to Q. Moreover, we should not read too much Christian Pentecostal theology into the phrase, since it appears elsewhere in early Judaism (see 1QS 3:7-9; 1QH 16:1-2; note also 7:6; 17:26).[17]

What else did Q 3 contain in addition to the two oracles of John in Q 3:7-9; 16-17? Most of the other materials on John the Baptist in Mt 3 and Lk 3 closely parallel Mk 1:1-11 and may therefore be understood as deriving from Mark. Yet at times scholars have argued that there were more overlapping Baptist materials in Mark

---

[12] Fleddermann (see above note 7) 378.

[13] *Ibid.* 379.

[14] See Davies & Allison (note 11 above) 315. It is true, βαστάζειν can also mean "remove". Yet in most cases the connotation of "carry" is present in the use of the verb.

[15] I follow here the sigla and the reconstruction of the International Q Project (SBL and the Institute for Antiquity and Christianity, Claremont, CA). For Q 10:4, see J. M. Robinson, "The International Q Project Work Session November 1990," *JBL* 110 (1991) 494-498.

[16] E.g., B. S. Easton, *The Gospel According to St Luke. A Critical and Exegetical Commentary* (New York: 1926) 41; T. W. Manson, *The Sayings of Jesus* (Grand Rapids: 1957) 40-41; S. Schulz, *Q: Spruchquelle der Evangelisten* (Zürich: 1972) 368.

[17] J. D. G. Dunn, *Baptism in the Holy Spirit* (SBT 15; London: 1970) 9.

and Q than just the saying on two baptisms (Q 3:16 / Mk 1:7, 8). Several have paid attention to the agreement in the words πᾶσα ἡ περίχωρος τοῦ Ἰορδάνου in Mt 3:5 and Lk 3:3, which although used differently by Matthew and Luke are not simply explained as deriving from the Markan geographical description (Mk 1:5). Kloppenborg[18] has recently added strength to the argument by suggesting that "all the region about the Jordan", which seems to allude to the biblical story of Lot and Sodom (see LXX Gen 13:10-11; 19:17, 25, 28-29), would make sense in Q in the light of other references to the Lot-Sodom story (Q 12:10; 17:28-30; cf. also the expressions of "fleeing" and "we have Abraham for a father" in 3:7-9). If this reasoning is sound, we have textual evidence that the first saying of John was preceded by a geographical note of the locale of his activity, although the reconstruction inevitably remains fragmentary.

Further evidence of overlapping materials comes from the fact that both in Mark and Q the appearance of the Baptist was followed by the Temptation of Jesus (Q 4:1-13; Mk 1:12-13). In Mark, the Temptation was closely linked with the Baptism of Jesus (1:9-11), in which the Spirit descends upon Jesus (Mk 1:10) and then drives him into the wilderness to be tempted by Satan (1:12; note the absolute τὸ πνεῦμα in both stories). One has often noticed that in Q too the Temptation seems to assume a preceding account about Jesus' authority, especially the Devil's words "if you are the Son of God" (Q 4:3), which would be much more understandable were they preceded by the designation of Jesus in the baptismal scene ("Thou art my beloved Son": Mk 1:11). Furthermore, a few minor agreements of Mt 3:16-17 / Lk 3:21-22 could give some support to the claim that the baptism of Jesus was in Q.[19] Recently, J.M. Robinson[20] has elaborated the argument by adding several points to the discussion. From his analysis, the following arguments emerge to support the inclusion:

> (1) the minor agreements (the participial form of βαπτίζω; the use of ἀνοίγω in place of σχίζω; ἐπ᾽ αὐτόν; the placement of καταβαίνω);

---

[18] Kloppenborg (see above note 10) 145-160.
[19] A list of scholars who include the Baptism in Q is conveniently found in J. S. Kloppenborg, *Q Parallels: Synopsis, Critical Notes and Concordance* (Sonoma: 1988) 16.
[20] J. M. Robinson, "The Sayings Gospel Q," in *The Four Gospels. Festschrift Frans Neirynck*, eds. F. Von Segbroeck, C. M. Tuckett, G. van Belle and J. Verheyden (BETL 100, Vol. 1; Leuven, 1992) 361-388.

(2) the Son of God Christology presupposed by the temptations demands the existence of a baptismal account containing this motif;

(3) the reference to the Spirit in Q 4:1 would be awkward without any preparation in the preceding material;

(4) if Q began with a collection of John's sayings, the "narrative logic" would demand a recognition of Jesus' authoritative status before the Inaugural Sermon;

(5) the agreement ἐπ' αὐτόν reflects passages from Isaiah (42:1; 61:1-2) and this would be in accord with the central role Isa 61:1-2 plays as a biblical prooftext in Q (7:22; cf also 6:20).

Robinson's arguments can, however, be weakened by several objections: with respect to (3) above, Q does have a reference to the Spirit in the Baptist's preaching on the Coming One (Q 3:16), which contrasts John's water baptism with the baptism of the Coming One "with the Holy Spirit and fire". After such a promise of a more powerful, spirit-filled baptism, the description of Jesus led up by the Spirit into the wilderness to prepare his ministration would not be too awkward. Moreover, it is not perfectly clear whether the absolutely used τὸ πνεῦμα derives from Q. As noted, Q has "the Holy spirit" elsewhere (3:16; 12:10; 12:12?). In Matthew, τὸ πνεῦμα for God's Spirit appears only in these two Markan contexts (the Baptism and the Temptation) and Luke's ἐν τῷ πνεύματι seems to be Lukan (cf. Lk 2:27; 4:14; Acts 19:21; 20:22 and Acts 16:18; 19:1). Therefore, one has to consider the possibility that Matthew follows Mark in using the absolute "Spirit" in Mt 4:1 and Luke modifies Mark with his own favourite expression. Regarding (4), as I shall later argue, the John / Jesus relationship in the "narrative world" of Q can also be construed otherwise than by suggesting the Baptism to be a transitional link between John's and Jesus' teaching. As for argument (5), both Matthew and Luke elaborate the Isaianic texts independently (Mt 5:3-4; Lk 4:18-19), and hence the presumed reference of ἐπ' αὐτόν (Mt 3:16 / Lk 3:22) to Isa 61:1a (or 42:1) may be coincidental. Regarding (1), since the other agreements in Mt 3:16-17 and Lk 3:21-22 are, as Robinson admits, "notoriously inconclusive", we are driven back to the principal argument (2).

Partly, at least, the argument based on the Son of God Christology depends on how much narrative logic we demand from Q. Kloppenborg has argued that we should not expect too much narrative development from Q in such matters and he may well be correct.[21] On the other hand, there *is* considerable coherence between John's preaching on the Coming One and other Q materials (see later), and the Son of God Christology in the Temptation (or in the Baptism *and* Temptation) is in any analysis somewhat anomalous in Q. Perhaps the suggestion that the Baptism was in Q makes this anomaly somewhat easier than it would be otherwise, but it will be there in any case.

All this is perhaps not enough to invalidate completely the arguments for the inclusion of the Baptism story. But it adds so much uncertainty about such a decision that I do not think it wise to include the Baptism in the reconstruction of Q 3 (see Appendix).

3. The Function of John's Preaching in Q

Why was a collection of *Jesus'* sayings introduced by a collection of John's sayings? This question leads us to consider the function of Q 3 in the literary plan of Q and its relation to the rest of the document.

The preaching of the Baptist contains several thematic and other links with important sections in Q. As already noted, one such link between the beginning and the rest of Q is the allusion to the Lot / Sodom story of Gen 18-19, which is echoed in Q 10:12 and 17:28-30. Related to this may be the positive role that "wilderness"—in the sense of uninhabited place—has as a location of John's appearance (7:24; "all region of Jordan" in Q 3:3).[22] According to Kloppenborg, this motif reveals Q's prophetic criticism of the hierocracy in Jerusalem (Q 13:34f.) and a typical peasant stance against cities as places of unbelief and immoral life. The positive symbolic value of "wilderness" is, however, somewhat relativized at the end of Q. The so-called Q-apocalypse (Q 17:23ff.) warns *not* to go out (Mt: μὴ ἐξέλθητε Lk: ἀπέλθητε) after those who say "here" or "there", which recalls the language in the saying on

---

[21] J. S. Kloppenborg, *The Formation of Q: Trajectories in Ancient Wisdom Collections* (Studies in Antiquity and Christianity; Philadelphia: 1987) 84-85. See also A. Vögtle, "Die sogenannte Taufperikope Mk 1,9-11. Zur Problematik der Herkunft und des ursprünglichen Sinns" in *EKK Vorarbeiten 4* (Neukirchen / Zürich / Einsiedeln / Köln: 1972) 109.

[22] The "wilderness" as a scene of John's activity does not seem to refer to a desert, deprived of water, where one would hardly expect to find "a reed shaken by the wind" (Q 7:24). See C. C. McCown, "The Scene of John's Ministry and Its Relation to the Purpose and Outcome of His Mission," *JBL* 59 (1940) 113-131.

the Baptist in Q 7:24-26 (τί ἐξέλθητε εἰς τὴν ἔρημον θεάσασθαι). Especially if Matthew's more concrete words "in the wilderness" and "in the inner rooms" represent Q, as is often argued, we have at the end of Q one more reference to the "wilderness".[23] This means that at the beginning we have John as a true prophet of the "wilderness" preaching the Coming One—i.e., Jesus—who is not in the wilderness (except for the period of preparation), and therefore any exhortation to "go out" after other prophets or apocalyptic signs is by definition false.

The most obvious catchword link with other Q sections is the expression "coming one" (ὁ ἐρχόμενος), which characterizes the Q form of the saying on two baptisms (cf. the "mightier one" in Mark). The title appears three times in Q, at the beginning (3:16), in the middle (7:19) and near the end (13:35), and seems to be an important organizing factor in the overall plan of the document.

There has been plenty of discussion whether the "coming one" was a current messianic title in early Judaism. The evidence for such a fixed use of the absolute participle in Messianic contexts is vague, however, and the whole question would hardly have arisen without the appearances in the synoptic gospels.[24] One suspects that the Coming One as a title belongs to the textual world of Q, rather than to the traditional language of Q's environment. This suspicion is confirmed by further considerations. The question of John's disciples in Q 7:19 (σὺ εἶ ὁ ἐρχόμενος ἤ ἕτερον [Lk: ἄλλον] προσδοκῶμεν;) clearly invokes the Baptist's preaching in 3:16 (ὁ δὲ ὀπίσω μου ἐρχόμενος ἰσχυρότερος μού ἐστιν). Since the Coming One in Q 7:19 makes a reference to John's preaching, it is not so much an independent messianic title as a literary device pointing to the beginning of the document. One could therefore appropriately translate it: "Are you the coming one John predicted or shall we look for another?" Apparently, the compiler of the document wanted to create a clearly visible bridge between Q 3:16 and 7:19. The latter not only refers to the former, but the construction also organizes the material under the major theme presented at the beginning.

It is important to notice how the "narrative" logic goes in this first major section of Q. After John's preaching on the Coming

---

[23] For Q 17:23-24, see R. Uro, "Neither Here Nor There: Lk 17:20-21 and Related Sayings in Thomas, Mark, and Q," *Occasional Papers* 20 (Institute for Antiquity and Christianity at Claremont, CA: 1990) 20-26.

[24] R. Laufen (see above note 9) 407-409, for example, in his survey of the discussion can only refer to Hab 2:3 / Heb 10:37 outside the Q passages and Mk 11:10 par.

One, the temptation of Jesus (Q 4:1-13) presents a transitional scene moving the focus from John to Jesus, from the wilderness to inhabited areas (cf. [Ναζαρά] in Q 4:16).[25] Jesus' authoritative teaching in the Inaugural Sermon (Q 6:20-49) and his powerful word in the Healing of the Centurion's Boy (Q 7:1-10) then inevitably create the question articulated by the disciples of John. In this reconstruction, the Baptism of Jesus is not necessary for the development from John to Jesus (see above), since the question posed to the reader is not whether Jesus is the Son of God, but whether he is the "one coming after me" predicted by John. In other words, what is at stake is not Jesus' status as the Son of God, but his role as one who comes after John and is more powerful than John. The answer to this can only be given properly after Jesus' teaching and healing in the materials between Q 3:16 and 7:19.

Jesus' answer to John's disciples in Q 7:22-23 makes an appeal both to his healing activity and proclamation to the poor (πτωκοὶ εὐαγγαλίζονται) and refers back to the Centurion's Boy and to the beginning of the Sermon (6:20 μακάριοι οἱ πτωχοί).[26] The whole section on John and Jesus in Q 7:18-35 is a collection of miscellaneous sayings of different origins. It culminates in a parable and its explanation (Q 7:31-35) in which the ascetic John and less abstaining Son of man—who, however, has nowhere to lay his head (Q 9:58)—are aligned against "this generation", which rejects both. In spite of the negative opinion of this generation in 7:33 (δαιμόνιον ἔχει), one gets the impression that John's authority as a true prophet is largely accepted among the readers and it has been used to support the authority of Jesus as an even more powerful figure.[27]

---

[25] See note 15 above.

[26] For the "poor" as a self-designation of the Q community, see J. M. Robinson (see above note 20).

[27] Cf. the estimation by E. P. Sanders and M. Davies that "from the evidence available, it appears that John attracted more attention than did Jesus" (E. P. Sanders and M. Davies, *Studying the Synoptic Gospels* [London: 1989] 312-313). They give the following reasons for this suggestion (352 note 8): "(1) Josephus wrote that John attracted 'multitudes' and that a subsequent defeat of Antipas' army was commonly believed to be a punishment for the execution of John (*Antiq.* 18.116-119).... (2) John created enough disruption to be executed by Antipas, while Jesus did not. (3) Jesus' question, 'Was the baptism of John from heaven or from men?' (Mk 11.30) which was posed to justify his own authority, implies that John the Baptist was widely regarded as a prophet, as the continuation of the passage makes clear, while Jesus' status was doubted." For a

The same argument dominates in later sections of Q. The authority of Jesus as a figure of word and deed continues in the Mission, where Jesus delivers his power to teach and heal to his messengers (Q 10:9). Those sent by Jesus are expected to meet resistance and hostility (10:3, 10-12), and this negative prospect is confirmed by the saying against Galilean cities (10:13-15), the tenor of which comes very close to John's preaching against those who say "We have Abraham as our father" (3:7-9). Jesus' status as a powerful figure comes up explicitly in the Beelzebul Controversy, in which Jesus is accused of using demonic forces and the accusation is annulled by the claim that the exorcisms show Jesus' victory over the power of the Devil (Q 11:14-23; cf. the Temptation). The Sign of Jonah (11:29-32), which probably followed the dispute about Jesus' exorcist powers, presents people as asking Jesus to give them a sign. Jesus' answer takes the form of a correlative which parallels Jonah, a preacher of penitence like John, with the Son of man. Similar language of being "greater" or "something more" (πλεῖον) characterizes this pericope (cf. ἰσχυρότερος μου in 3:16). Moreover, "this generation" is condemned here as in 10:13-15 and the "sons of Abraham" in 3:7-9. Jesus preaches the same message of judgment and repentance as Jonah and John did, but at same time his ministry is greater than Jonah's and mightier than John's.

The sign of Jonah already plays with the ambiguity that the Son of man in Q is both present (7:34; 9:58) and futuric (12:40; 17:24, 26-30). This has resulted in difficulties for scholars in deciding whether the correlative refers to the eschatological coming of the Son of man (note the parallelism between 11:30 and 17:24) or to his present activity. Whereas in Q 7 the Coming One is clearly Jesus the healer and preacher, whose success proves his authority (7:35), the final appearance of the phrase ὁ ἐρχόμενος (Q 13:35) unambiguously refers to Jesus as an eschatological figure. The phrase appears in the quotation of Ps 117:26a LXX, which Mark and John have in the context of the Triumphal Entry (Mk 11:9 pars.; Jn 12:13) but in Q follows the Lament over Jerusalem and its final comment: "I tell you, you will not see me until the time comes when you say, 'Blessed is he who comes in the name of the Lord'" (13:35). The oracle charges Jerusalem with killing the prophets and messengers sent to it and pronounces that her "house" will be abandoned. The speaker, in Q no doubt Jesus,

---

generally convincing picture of John as a leader of a popular movement, see R. Webb (see above note 2) 349-378.

uses language and imagery derived from Wisdom speculation and in effect takes the role of divine Wisdom.[28]

Unfortunately we have problems in the precise location of the Lament, since both Matthew and Luke seem to have been responsible for its present positions in their gospels. But it is obvious from the sequence of the Q material in the gospels that the oracle was located near the end of the document. If the Lukan Q material in Lk 13:18-21, 24-30; 13:34-35 14:16-24 reproduce the essence of a section which preceded the eschatological discourse Q 17:23-37, we have a unit in which the basic motifs of John's preaching reach their final culmination.[29] The Coming One predicted by John is now speaking through the mouth of a divine figure who has sent messengers and prophets (cf. Q 10:3; 11:49) to Israel and will come back to judge "this generation". All this will happen as in the days of Noah and Lot, when catastrophes came upon unprepared and impenitent people (17:26-30). Appeal to Abraham as father will be of no help. As John anticipated, redefinition of God's people is already underway: "God is able from these stones to raise up children to Abraham". "People will come from east and west to sit at the table with Abraham, Isaac and Jacob", but the original sons will be thrown out (13:28-30).

The above survey leads us to conclude that the preaching of John is an integral part of the text-world and the symbolic world of Q. The opening section of the Sayings Gospel not only presents the major theological motifs of the document but it also functions as an important organizing factor around which the "narrative" development of Q is constructed. John's preaching on the Coming One is the main thread in Q, running from Q 3 via Q 7 to the final eschatological discourse in Q 17.

4. The Collection of Q 3: Prehistory and Relation to Mark

The collection in Q 3 gathers originally separate traditions and sayings under the figure of the Baptist. An important connective element is the imagery of "fire" which recurs three times (3:9, 3:16 and 3:17) and makes the apocalyptic judgment the major theme in the whole section: every bad tree bearing no fruit and chaff separated from the wheat will be thrown into the fire. How-

---

[28] For the Wisdom language in Q 13:34-35, see R. Uro, *Sheep Among the Wolves: A Study on the Mission Instructions of Q* (Annales Academie Scientarum Fennicae. Dissertationes Humanarum Litterarum 47; Helsinki: 1987) 236-237.

[29] For this section in Q, see *ibid.* 217-220.

ever, the imageries and sayings used are heterogeneous enough to reveal that the section is not an original unity.

It is widely recognized that the two sayings, Q 3:7-9 and 3:16-17, did not originally belong together. Although the announcement of the imminent judgment occurs in both sayings, the first is simply a threat of judgment and a call to repentance, while the latter focuses on a figure who will bring a more powerful baptism and fiery judgment.[30] But even the sayings themselves seem to be composite. Schürmann[31] observed that in 3:7-9 two different criticisms of false confidences are juxtaposed: the confidence that baptism by itself will save ("who warned you to flee from the wrath to come") and that national privilege will save from judgement ("...do not begin to say to yourselves, 'We have Abraham as our father'"). One can argue that these accusations have different groups or situations in view, since the appeal to Abraham as father appears to indicate a rejection of baptism altogether. Schürmann thought that the latter is more original, reflecting the use of the saying in early mission among Jews, whereas the first applies John's preaching to early Christian prebaptismal catechesis. However, the reversed order in tradition history is more probable. Q 3:8bc interrupts the flow of thought from 8a ("Bear fruit that befits repentance...") to verse 9 ("Even now the ax is laid to the root of the trees")[32] and is therefore likely to be a later addition. Moreover, the criticism against those who appeal to Abraham as father in 8:bc is in accord with the redactional layer of Q which is dominated by the "deuteronomistic" criticism[33] and by the conviction that Israel has lost her prerogative as covenant people (cf. above and Q 13:28-30; 14:16-24).

In this reconstruction, the hypothetical early form of Q 3:7-9 was a *chria* with a short mention of people coming to baptism (7a) and with a response by John warning of false confidence and calling to true repentance (7b, 8a, 9). It was later expanded by the insertion of 3:8bc, which makes the saying a more general criticism of the impenitent Israel.[34]

---

[30] See, e.g., H. Schürmann, *Das Lukasevangelium. Erster Teil: Kommentar zu Kap. 1,1–9,50* (HThK 3; Freiburg / Basel / Wien: 1969) 183.

[31] *Ibid.* 182.

[32] Davies and Allison (see above note 11) 317.

[33] This has been emphasized by A. D. Jacobson, *The First Gospel. An Introduction to Q* (Sonoma, 1992) 31-32.

[34] For a different reconstruction of the composition of Q 3:7-9, see Kloppenborg (note 21 above) 105. He thinks that the introduction 3:7a is secondary, attached to join the two Baptist oracles (Q 3:7b,8a,9 + 8bc and 3:16a,c, 17).

The tradition history of Q 3:16-17 is closely related to the question of the relationship between the Markan and Q forms (Mk 1:7-8) of the saying. The vast majority of the scholars argue that Q has preserved the more original form and Mark has changed the apocalyptic tenor of the saying to a contrast between John's water baptism and the later Christian baptism bestowing the Holy Spirit.[35] This common solution, however, uncritically presupposes that an apocalyptic baptism with "wind and fire" was the focus of John's preaching and hence Q represents more faithfully the historical proclamation of the Baptist. I do not think we should start with such a presumption; instead, we should employ methods similar to those used in analyzing the Jesus traditions.

Two points are of pertinence here. Firstly, since Lührmann[36] Q research has largely accepted the judgment of the impenitent Israel as representing a significant and clearly recognizable redactional motif in the composition of the document. Secondly, many of those who have worked with the Mark / Q problem think that the best hypothesis for the relationship of these two gospels is a "common tradition" model, a hypothesis that Mark / Q overlaps are due to common traditions or sources used by the authors.[37] This model has recently fallen into disfavour among a few scholars,[38] but what is not always noticed is that in many sections of Q these two results fall together in an inseparable way. One of the clearest examples is the Mission Discourse.[39]

> Several analyses confirm that behind the Markan and Q Mission Charges one can recognize a common pattern consisting of instructions for the equipment, "houses", and "towns" or "places" (Mk 6:8-11 / Q 10:4-11).[40] Such a structure, which in both gospels has been framed

---

[35] In contrast with the mainline interpretation, E. E. Ellis (*The Gospel of Luke* [NCB; London: 1974] 90) regards the Markan form as original and "fire" as a Christian *pesher*-ing to the Pentecostal fulfillment.

[36] D. Lührmann, *Die Redaktion der Logienquelle* (WMANT 33; Neukirchen-Vluyn: 1969).

[37] M. Devisch, "La relation entre l'évangile de Marc et le document Q" in: *L'evangile selon Marc. Tradition et rédaction*, ed. M. Sabbe (BETL 34; Leuven: 1974) 59-91; Laufen (see note 9 above).

[38] See, e.g., H. Fleddermann, "The Mustard Seed and the Leaven in Q, the Synoptics, and Thomas," *SBLSP* 28 (1989) 216-236; B. Mack, "Q and the Gospel of Mark: Revising Christian Origins," *Semeia* 55 (1991) 15-39; D. Catchpole, "The Mission Charge in Q," *Semeia* 55 (1991) 147-174.

[39] Compare also Mk 8:11-12 and Q 11:29-32 (The Sign of Jonah); Mk 13:21-23 and Q 17:23 (Neither Here Nor There). See Uro (note 23 above).

[40] Laufen (note 9 above) 206-301; Kloppenborg (note 21) 190-203; Uro (note 28).

by further narrative (Mk 6:7, 12-13, 30) or sayings material (Q 10:2, 3, 12, 13-15, 16), points to a common antecedent used independently by Q and Mark rather than to a *direct* literary dependence. Lührmann's[41] path-breaking observations also support this hypothesis: Q 10:12 is best explained as a redactional bridge linking the secondary woes on the Galilean towns (10:13-15) with the instructions about towns (10:8-11) and utilizing the language of the woes. The tone of these "frame sayings" (10:3; 12, 13-15) is conspicuously negative and reflects a stage of redaction in which Israel's unbelief and the Gentiles' positive response are prominent themes. On the other hand, the Markan narrative framework also reveals signs of redaction and can largely be understood as a creative fiction by the evangelist.[42] So we have a common kernel of mission instructions with an astonishingly similar pattern, on the one hand, and different redactional frameworks of Mark and Q, on the other. To suggest that Mark is literally dependent on Q is to suggest that the evangelist succeeded in striking out all redactional elements from the Q instructions and substituting his own redaction for them.

Now, accepting this "common tradition" hypothesis in the case of the Mission we can recognize the same model at work in Q 3 (see Appendix). From this perspective, the kernel of the tradition is a saying on two baptisms appearing both in Mark (1:7-8) and Q (3:16). As in the Mission Charge, the common tradition in Q 3 was framed by sayings which focus on Israel's recalcitrance and the coming judgment (3:7-9 and 3:17). If the mention about God being able to raise children from stones (3:8bc) is a secondary intrusion, as I argued, John's saying on repentance has been moulded into Q's general pattern either before or simultaneously with the attachment to 3:16-17. In the redaction of the section, the words "and fire" in 3:16 were formed as an editorial bridge (cf. 10:12), which made it possible to use the saying on two baptisms as part of the "fire" scheme and to add further imagery of fiery judgment committed by the coming powerful figure (3:17).[43] The entire speech thus created was also preceded by a short narrative description of John's appearance (3:3), although most of it has been covered under the later redactions by Matthew and Luke.

Mark used the Two Baptisms as part of the prologue of his gospel (Mk 1:1-15). In contrast to Q, he does not make the saying

[41] Lührmann (note 36 above) 62-63.

[42] Uro (note 28 above) 26-39.

[43] For a similar observation, see W. Cotter, "Yes, I Tell You, and More Than a Prophet. The Function of John in Q," a paper presented at the SBL Annual Meeting in Kansas City, November 23-26 (1991).

a preaching of judgment but uses it to serve his forerunner Elijah concept already evoked in the composite quotation of 1:2-3 (cf. Mal 3:1; Exod 23:20 and Isa 40:3).[44] The citation from Mal 3:1 (cf. also Exod 23:20) also occurs in Q 7:27, which indicates that the forerunner idea was not a Markan invention, although he developed it consistently (cf. Mk 9:11-13). The saying on Two Baptisms is adapted to the narrative context with the use of aorist (ἐβάπτισα) referring to the earlier mention of John's baptismal activity (1:4-5) and relegating it to the past period in the salvation history.[45] The emphasis of the Markan prologue is undoubtedly on the baptism of Jesus, which provides a model for Christian baptism and in which the crucial Christological secret of Jesus' divine sonship is first revealed in the narrative (cf. Mk 9:7; 15:39). In Q, at least if the baptism of Jesus is not included, the point is not the baptismal activity of John but his preaching repentance and judgment, which makes him a precursor and a colleague of Jesus at the same.

It is difficult to decide whether the chiastic form of the saying in Q or the Markan construction is more original. The Johannine version (1:26-27) would perhaps provide evidence for the Q form,[46] but firm decisions on such "performancial variants" is neither necessary nor possible.[47] The same is probably true of the difference between the participial construction of Q (ὁ δὲ ὀπίσω μου ἐρχόμενος) and Mark's finite form (ἔρχεται). As we have seen, there is no reason to read an established messianic ideology into the phrase used in Q.

5. The Saying on Two Baptisms: The Sitz in the Jesus Movement

If the above sketch of the tradition and composition history is on the right track, the compiler of the collection in Q 3 had two basic traditions available: the *chria* on John's preaching of repentance

---

[44] See W. Wink, *John the Baptist in the Gospel Tradition* (Cambridge: 1968) 1-8; R. Pesch, "Anfang des Evangeliums Jesu Christi. Eine Studie zum Prolog des Markusevangeliums (Mk 1,1-15)" in *Die Zeit Jesu (Festschrift H. Schlier)*, eds. G. Bornkamm and K. Rahner (Freiburg / Basel / Wien: 1970) 108-144; Vögtle (see above note 21) 105-137.

[45] Pesch (see note 44) 121; J. Gnilka, *Das Evangelium nach Markus (Mk 1-8,26)* (EKK II /1; Zürich / Neukirchen-Vluyn: 1978) 48; P. Hoffmann, *Studien zur Theologie der Logienquelle* (NTA 8; Münster: 1972) 20.

[46] For such an argument, see Laufen (note 9 above) 98.

[47] J. D. Crossan, *In Fragments. The Aphorisms of Jesus.* (San Francisco: 1983) 41.

(3:7, 8a, 9) and the saying on Two Baptisms (3:16; the extension of 3:17 was hardly an originally independent saying). Since the latter circulated widely in early Christianity (Mark, Q, John),[48] it is reasonable to examine it more carefully and to raise the question of the provenance and the *Sitz* of the saying.

Although one has often seen a Christian influence in the saying, especially in its Markan version, most scholars confidently assume that it in some form goes back to the historical John. At times, though, the saying has been divided into two parts, one about the coming of the mightier one and one about the baptism. Bultmann thought it possible that the first is a Christian addition reflecting the rivalry between the Christians and the disciples of John,[49] while the saying on the baptism with fire would represent the earliest phase in the tradition. The problem of such attempts, however, is the vague form of the hypothetical original saying: "I baptize you with water, but he will baptize you with fire". To be able to treat such a statement as an independent saying, one has to put "the Coming One" in the place of "he",[50] which makes sense only if one presumes a titular use for the phrase. To avoid such arbitrary presumptions, it is best to assume that the contrast between the water baptism of John and the baptism of a more powerful figure is original.

The most crucial problem in the interpretation of the saying, however, is that the baptism with "fire" has almost universally been accepted as part of the original saying. If the "spirit" has been included, too, then the epithet "holy" has often been dropped and the word read in the sense of "wind", functioning together with "fire" as imageries of the divine judgment. The apocalyptic interpretation of the saying therefore rests upon the word "fire", which according to the above analysis is a redactional addition in Q. If we leave the word out, it is not clear that the contrast between baptisms with water and spirit should be understood in an apocalyptical sense. Neither is it necessary to speak

---

[48] The use of the Johannine versions as witnesses of the circulation of the saying depends on the traditional view of John's independence from the synoptics (for a challenge of this view and the recent discussion, see F. Neirynck "John and the Synoptics 1975-1990" in *John and the Synoptics*, ed. A. Denaux [BETL 101; Leuven, 1992] 3-62). This part of the argument fails, if John has known and used the synoptic gospels, but there would still remain the appearances in Mark and Q.

[49] Bultmann (note 2 above) 246-247; see also Hoffmann (note 45 above) 25.

[50] So does Hoffmann (see note 45 above) 25.

of the "wind" instead of the "Holy Spirit", which is attested both by Mark and Q.

However, let us for a moment accept the standard view that fire metaphor was present in the earliest tradition. How then, would the coming more powerful baptism be understood in the context of the historical John? The usual explanations are that John meant the baptism with fire (or wind and fire) to refer to the coming judgment accomplished either by God himself or some future messianic figure (e.g., the "Son of man").[51] Clearly, the first alternative is not a very happy one. The basic problem was already stated by Schlatter: "Who can speak of the thongs of God's sandals!"[52] The anthropomorphic language of the saying strongly indicates that the contrast is between John and a more powerful human figure. Otherwise the comparison would not be reasonable.[53]

But even assuming that John's preaching was about a coming messianic figure we are involved in difficulties. The crucial question is: are we able to reconstruct a conceivable picture of how John understood his own baptism to be inferior to the baptism of someone more powerful than he? Without entering into a detailed discussion about the background and the function of John's baptism, one can safely argue that for him it was not only an act anticipating the future judgment but a rite having a positive meaning: initiation into salvation or the like. Mark reports that John came "preaching a baptism of repentance for the forgiveness of sins" (Mk 1:4). That John's baptism was for the remission of sins is unlikely to be a later Christian invention.[54] It is worth noting that

---

[51] For the latter alternative, see J. Becker (*Johannes der Täufer und Jesus von Nazareth* [BSt 63; Neukirchen-Vluyn: 1972] 34-37) who thinks it possible that the "Coming One" in John's preaching refers to the Danielic "Son of man" figure.

[52] A. Schlatter, *Johannes der Täufer*, ed. D. Wilhelm Michaelis (Basel: 1956) 103.

[53] J. H. Hughes, "John the Baptist: the Forerunner of God Himself," *NovT* 14 (1972) 191-218, argues that the coming figure preached by John is Yahweh himself. Hughes refers to Ps 60:8 and 108:9 ("Moab is my washbasin; upon Edom I cast my shoe") and to the fact that in the Old Testament and apocalyptic literature God is often described as "mighty". These objections do not, however, remove the difficulty of the direct comparison between John and the coming figure in the saying. For a convincing criticism of Hughes' argument, see R. L. Webb (see note 2 above) 284-286.

[54] See H. Thyen, *"BAPTISMA METANOIAS EIS APHESIN HAMARTION"* in *Zeit und Geschichte (Festschrift R. Bultmann)*, ed. E. Dinkler (Tübingen: 1964) 97-125; *Idem, Studien zur Sündenvergebung im Neuen Testament und seinen alttestamentlichen und jüdischen Voraussetzungen* (Göttingen: 1970) 131-145.

Matthew omitted Mark's εἰς ἄφεσιν ἁμαρτιῶν and transposed it to
the word over the cup at the Last Supper (26:28), thus revealing
that he felt it inappropriate to speak of the remission of sins within
the context of John's baptism. Moreover, Josephus' report (*Ant.*
XVII.5.2) also indirectly witnesses to there being some associative
connection between John's baptism and forgiveness of sins,[55] although Josephus' own interpretation was that the baptism must *not*
be employed "to gain pardon for whatever sins" (μὴ ἐπί τινων
ἁμαρτάδων παραιτήσει χρωμένων) and was rather for "a
consecration of the body" (ἐφ᾽ ἁγνείᾳ τοῦ σώματος; cf. the description of the washing practiced by Bannus in *Vita* 11).

If, then, "forgiveness of sins" was attached to the baptismal rite
either by John or his immediate followers, the problem inevitably
arises of why this salvific rite was contrasted with another
"baptism" used metaphorically for God's fiery or stormy judgment. Many scholars[56] believe that the imagery of a fiery stream in
Dan 7:10 (4 Ezra 13:10) is what connects the two baptisms in the
saying. But they are at pains to explain that this "river of fire" is
meant to be a purification for those who have been baptized by
John and perdition for others. Sato,[57] for example, takes the saying
as a threat: if you don't let me baptize you, you will find
yourselves in the fiery stream! But if John's intention was to say
that his baptism *saves* people from the coming judgment, the
contrast in the saying totally distorts the idea.

However, the possibility remains that John spoke of *two* baptisms,
one with Holy Spirit and one with fire. In this reading, John's water
baptism is contrasted with two different kind of activities, one
towards those who will be destroyed and one towards those who
will be saved.[58] But even this interpretation is burdened with
difficulties. The reading presupposes either that those addressed in
the first part of the saying are not the same group addressed in the
latter half, in spite of the close connection drawn between the two
statements ("I baptize *you*....but he will baptize *you*..."), or that
the first "you" includes also half-hearted or renegade followers
among those baptized by John. The latter would emphasize the

---

[55] H. Lichtenberger, "Täufergemeinden und frühchristliche Täuferpolemik im
letzten Drittel des 1. Jahrhunderts," *ZThK* 84 (1987) 44-45; Webb (see note 2
above) 190.

[56] E.g., C. H. Kraeling, *John the Baptist* (New York: 1951) 116; Scobie
(note 2 above) 68.

[57] M. Sato, *Q und Prophetie* (WUNT 2/29; Tübingen: 1988) 127.

[58] J. D. G. Dunn, "Spirit-and-Fire Baptism," *NovT* 14 (1972) 81-92; Ernst
(note 2 above) 305-308; Webb (note 2 above) 289-295.

ineffectiveness of John's baptism in a way that is historically hardly credible. Moreover, even if we accept the view that John preached of two baptisms, the emphasis of the Q saying (3:16-17), on which this reading is based, is in any case on the destructive side of the coming baptism. The problem, therefore, is essentially the same as in the interpretation which assumes only one baptism of judgment.

These kinds of difficulties in the interpretation have led me to reject the standard reading of the saying. In view of what has been said above, the simplest explanation is that Mark's contrast between baptisms with water and (Holy) Spirit represents the original idea of the saying. This is in accord with the composition history reconstructed above. If this conclusion is sound, the common assumption of the Baptist origin of the saying is also on shaky ground. In fact, it becomes quite possible to imagine that the saying on two baptisms came into existence among the Jesus movement to reflect the relationship between John and Jesus. It is a widely accepted view that the Jesus movement emerged as a branch of the Baptist movement. It is therefore natural to suggest that at an early stage there arose a need among the Jesus people to explain their relation to the mother movement. The charismatic phenomena among the movements around Jesus may have given a justification for the claim that according to John's own witness that after him (ὀπίσω μου—whether it implies a master / student relationship or not)[59] there comes a more powerful figure baptizing with Spirit. The baptism with Spirit could thus reflect the fact that Jesus was not a baptizer but a charismatic healer and / or the later conviction that the Christian baptism bestows Spirit. One should also notice that several traditions use "strong man" or "stronger one" language (Mk 3:27; Q 11:21-22; *GThom* 35) and propagate Jesus to be stronger than Satan (Mk 3:22-26; Q 11:14-20). Jesus' being a "stronger one" is therefore a deeply rooted notion in the sayings tradition.

However we interpret the original *Sitz* of the saying, the retrospective perspective and the improbability that the historical John would have spoken of his baptism *only* as a water rite points to a provenance among the Jesus people rather than in John's own movement. A further proof for this suggestion comes from the fact that several other sayings appear to repeat this same model, in

---

[59] For a recent treatment of the issue with a negative conclusion, see J. Ernst, "War Jesus ein Schüler Johannes des Täufers?" in *Vom Urchristentum zu Jesus*, eds. H. Frankemölle & K. Kertelge (Freiburg / Basel / Wien 1989) 13-33.

which Jesus and John (or their representatives) are in some way
contrasted. For example:

> John baptizes with water / Jesus baptizes with the Holy Spirit (and fire)
> (Mk 1:7-8; Q 3:16)

> John's disciples fast / Jesus' followers do not (Mk 2:18-19)

> John is greatest among those born of women / yet he who is least in
> the kingdom is greater than he (Q 7:28)

> John is ascetic / Jesus is a glutton and a drunkard (Q 7:33-34)

> Jesus must increase / and John must decrease (Jn 3:30)[60]

The frequency of such "contrast sayings" demonstrates that the
comparison between Jesus and John is a common theme in the
tradition. It appears that the saying on two baptisms belongs to this
same apologetic tradition which either tends to juxtapose John and
Jesus in favour of the latter or aligns both against some third front
(cf. Q 7:33-34). In sum, what we have in these traditions is not the
historical John but John as seen and as used by the Jesus
movement.

6. John the Baptist and the Q People

How should one evaluate the "frame materials" in Q 3 added in a
secondary redaction? As argued above, Q 3:7-9 may go back to an
earlier *chria* which presented John's warning against those who
falsely put their confidence in baptism and were unwilling to
repent. There is no reason to doubt the general view that John was
a preacher of repentance and demanded a conversion from sins
(cf. also Mk 1:4). In terms of modern sociology, one could indeed
call John's movement a "conversionist sect".[61] This, however, is
not to accept all of Q 3:7-9 and 3:17 as an authentic report of what
John proclaimed on the banks of the Jordan.

---

[60] For an analysis of the traditions behind Jn 3:25–4:3, see E. Linnemann,
"Jesus und der Täufer" in *Festschrift für Ernst Fuchs*, eds. G. Ebeling & E. Jüngel
& G. Schunack (Tübingen: 1973) 219-236.

[61] For such a characterization of the Baptist movement, see D. E. Aune,
Prophecy in Early Christianity and the Ancient Mediterranean World (Grand
Rapids, Mich.: 1983) 127.

Sometimes the incorporation of the Baptist material into Q has been explained by the suggestion that at some stage the Q people came into contact with Baptist circles,[62] who delivered sayings of their own leader to followers of Jesus. On a more ideological level, one has attempted to trace an apocalyptic trajectory which would go from John the Baptist to the later layer of Q (and further to Matthew) and from which the pre-apocalyptic layer of Q and the historical Jesus to some degree diverge.[63] This would provide one possible scenario, but several factors have led me to question it and to consider alternative explanations. These factors are comprised of tentative questions rather than final results of the analysis:

1) On a sociological level, such explanations presuppose the existence of independent Baptist circles by the time editions of the Q document came into being. A common assumption is that after John was put to death his disciples continued his work and gradually formed a rival movement parallel with Christian groups in Palestine and elsewhere. One can refer to Luke's stories about Apollos and a dozen other "disciples" in Ephesus, who knew only John's baptism (Acts 18:24-28; 19:1-5), or to the Lukan infancy narrative (Lk 1), where John appears to have ranked much higher than just as a forerunner of Jesus (especially in the *Benedictus*). In the Pseudo-Clementine *Recognitions* (1.60), one reads a fictive post-resurrection disputation between the apostles and John's disciples, who assert that "John was the Christ".[64]

It is beyond the possible scope of the present paper to discuss whether John's later followers formed a messianic movement or not. The only critical point I want to make is to ask whether the

---

[62] E.g., J. S. Kloppenborg, "Redactional Strata and Social History in the Sayings Gospel Q," a paper presented at the SBL Annual Meeting in Chicago, (19-22 November 1988) 23. Note also my earlier comment in Uro (see above note 28) 132-133.

[63] J. M. Robinson, "The Q Trajectory: Between John and Matthew via Jesus" in *The Future of Early Christianity: Essays in Honor of Helmut Koester*, ed. B. A. Pearson (Minneapolis: 1991) 173-194.

[64] See also *Recognitions* 1.52. The disputation in 1.60 is as follows:

"And, behold, one of the disciples of John asserted that John was the Christ, and not Jesus, inasmuch as Jesus Himself declared that John was greater than all men and all prophets. 'If then,' said he, 'he be greater than all, he must be held to be greater than Moses, and than Jesus himself. But if he be the greatest of all, then must he be the Christ.' To this Simon the Canaanite, answering, asserted that John was indeed greater than all the prophets, and all who born of women, yet that he is not greater than the Son of man. Accordingly Jesus is also the Christ, whereas John is only a prophet..." (*Ante-Nicene Fathers* VIII, eds. A. Roberts and J. Donaldson [Grand Rapids, Michigan: 1951]).

apocalyptic material in Q 3 can easily be imagined to derive from such a Baptist sect. Since the role of John in Q is not that of a rival prophet, one has usually assumed a period of fraternity between John's disciples and Jesus' followers, later giving way to one of intense rivalry.[65] That would parallel a development from the sayings placing John and Jesus on the same level to those with a clear subordination of John (e.g., Q 7:28b). But how credible is such a scenario sociologically and historically? The Jesus people, a messianic movement in the process, came into contact with the John people, in which a similar mythmaking process was underway. The former would have used the latter's traditions, indeed moulded several Jesus traditions into the form of John's apocalyptic preaching. Yet by the time of the final Q, these people exalted Jesus to the position of a divine figure and at the same time preserved their high respect for the founder figure of the rival movement. Would one not expect to recognize much stronger hostility in the traditions about John than there now exists?

2) The second critical point emerges from the present analysis of John's preaching. It has become obvious that the apocalyptic sayings in Q 3 have very much in common with the materials usually assigned to the secondary redaction of Q. Since Vielhauer's seminal article,[66] there has been a growing skepticism about the historicity of the Son of man sayings of *Jesus*. If this trend is correct, one has to at least raise the question of whether it is reasonable to hold to the apocalyptic sayings of *John*, since similar arguments can be raised against them, as can be done against the secondary apocalyptic layer in Q. This is a relevant issue because the usual hypothesis presupposes a relatively complicated development from John's fiery apocalypticism to the alleged revival of John's preaching in Q^2 via the non-apocalyptic serenity of Jesus' ministry and the earlier layers of Q.

3) Finally, if many of the sayings on John in the gospels reflect an apologetically oriented picture of John, how can we be sure that the sayings attributed to him are somehow free from the Christian imagination? It is, of course, not impossible that Q 3 provides a direct channel to the historical John in contrast to other traditions, but such a deep-freezing theory stretches the credulity.

Let me express myself explicitly: I am not claiming that the historical John did not preach anything about God's judgment or

---

[65] E.g., Kraeling (note 56 above) 175.

[66] P. Vielhauer, "Gottesreich und Menschensohn in der Verkündigung Jesu" in *Festschrift für G. Dehn*, ed. W. Schneemelcher (Neukirchen: 1957) 51-79.

lacked all apocalyptic imageries whatsoever. Neither am I willing to go as far as those who want to replace the apocalyptic paradigm with pictures of John and Jesus as Cynic preachers.[67] With regard to John at least, the baptismal rite—the indisputable characteristic of the historical John—and perhaps also the notion of the "remission of sins" hold John apart from the Cynic model, although he surely shares some common features with the popular philosophers. However, I think that the above analysis has provided abundant evidence that we should be cautious when we make assessments about the preaching of the historical John. We probably know much less than we tend to believe. Clearly, such assertions that John was "the gloomiest preacher of repentance within Judaism"[68] should be re-evaluated. Moreover, the common comparisons between the dark apocalyptic message of John and the more merciful proclamation of Jesus are not as firmly grounded as has been thought.

---

[67] R. Cameron, "'What Have You Come Out To See?' Characterizations of John and Jesus in the Gospels," *Semeia* 49 (1990) 35-69. For the Cynic hypothesis, see also L. Vaage's article in this volume.

[68] Becker (see note 51 above) 25: "...freilich dominiert die Gerichtsbotschaft derart umfassend, dass Johannes nicht zu einer ausmalenden Darstellung eines Heils kommt. Die Radikalität des Zorns hat diese Möglichkeit verdrängt, so dass Johannes wohl in der Tat der dunkelste Bussprediger des Judentums gewesen ist, den die Überlieferung kennt."

Appendix: The Preaching of the John the Baptist[69]

Q 3:2-3, 7-9, 16-17

3² ...'Ιωάννη ...
³ [[...πᾶσα.. ἡ.. περίχωρο... τοῦ 'Ιορδάνου...]]

⁷ε[[ἶπ]]εν τοῖς ἐ[[ρχ]]ομένο<ι>ς... [[ἐπὶ τὸ]] βάπτισ[[μα αὐτοῦ]]·
γεννήματα ἐχιδνῶν.
τίς ὑπέδειξεν ὑμῖν φυγεῖν ἀπὸ τῆς μελλούσης ὀργῆς;
⁸ ποιήσατε οὖν καρπὸν ἄξιον τῆς μετανοίας,
καὶ μὴ δόξητε λέγειν ἐν ἑαυτοῖς· πατέρα ἔχομεν τὸν
'Αβραάμ.
λέγω γὰρ ὑμῖν ὅτι δύναται ὁ θεὸς ἐκ τῶν λίθων τούτων
ἐγεῖραι τέκνα τῷ 'Αβραάμ.
⁹ ἤδη δὲ ἡ ἀξίνη πρὸς τὴν ῥίζαν τῶν δένδρων κεῖται·
πᾶν οὖν δένδρον μὴ ποιοῦν καρπὸν καλὸν ἐκκόπτεται καὶ
εἰς **πῦρ** βάλλεται.

¹⁶ ἐγὼ μὲν ὑμᾶς βαπτίζω [[ἐν]] ὕδατι
ὁ δὲ ὀπίσω μου ἐρχόμενος ἰσχυρότερος μού ἐστιν
οὗ οὐκ εἰμὶ ἱκανος τ[[ὰ]] ὑποδήματα [[βαστά]]σαι·
αὐτὸς ὑμᾶς βαπτίζει ἐν πνεύματι ἁγίῳ
καὶ πυρί

¹⁷ οὗ τὸ πτύον ἐν τῇ χειρὶ αὐτοῦ
καὶ διακαθαριεῖ τὴν ἅλωνα αὐτοῦ,
καὶ συνάξει τὸν σῖτον εἰς τὴν ἀποθήκην αὐτοῦ,
τὸ δὲ ἄχυρον κατακαύσει **πυρὶ** ἀσβέστῳ.

Mark 1:7-8

⁷ ἔρχεται ὁ ἰσχυρότερός μου ὀπίσω μου,
οὗ οὐκ εἰμὶ ἱκανὸς κύψας λῦσαι τὸν ἱμάντα τῶν
ὑποδημάτων αὐτοῦ.
⁸ ἐγὼ ἐβάπτισα ὑμᾶς ὕδατι,
αὐτὸς δὲ βαπτίσει ὑμᾶς ἐν πνεύματι ἁγίῳ.

---

[69] Sigla as used by the International Q Project. The reconstruction of Q 3:2-17 is very close to that of the IQP, but includes some slight deviations. Cf J. M. Robinson & M. C. Moreland "The International Q Project Work Sessions 31 July—2 August, 20 November," *JBL* 112 (1993) 501-502.

John 1:26-27

²⁶ ἐγὼ βαπτίζω ἐν ὕδατι
μέσος ὑμῶν ἔστηκεν ὃν ὑμεῖς οὐκ οἴδατε,
²⁷ ὁ ὀπίσω μου ἐρχόμενος,
οὗ οὐκ εἰμι ⟦ἐγὼ⟧ ἄξιος ἵνα λύσω αὐτοῦ τὸν ἱμάντα τοῦ
ὑποδήματος.

CHAPTER ELEVEN

THE JESUS OF Q AS LIBERATION THEOLOGIAN

James M. Robinson

I

The two-fold problematic of the title "The Jesus of Q as Liberation Theologian"[1] should be obvious to us all.

First, there is the problem of speaking of Jesus, when all we have is a secondary text. The very process of discussing what may and may not be ascribed to Jesus, and the divergence of opinions among respected colleagues, serves to keep us painfully aware of the problematic of this whole undertaking.

But there is an alternative to this never ending and ultimately rather frustrating process of trying to recover genuine mosaic stones and then to fit them into the same coherent picture from which they originally came. For there is an overriding directionality to the earliest stages of the tradition, which shows the flow, the *Tendenz* of the transmitting process, the main direction in which revisionism was moving. Thus, when analysed in reversed chronological sequence, the trajectory points toward the originative point, the approximate position where Jesus would have to be located. To this extent one can at least mock up a silhouette of the historical Jesus—the black box gains contours and directionality.

This does not in concrete factual biographical terms bring Jesus out of obscurity, but does point to his relative position: He was more *this* than the ensuing tradition; he was less *that* than, for example, the canonical Gospels. Thus the way he cuts, as a role model, as an authority, as a precedent, a pointer, may be clearer than are the actual biographical facts. Back to Jesus, *ad fontes*, means going *this* way, not *that* way. Hence his relevance for us may not ultimately be dissolved by the obscurity in which his biography lies. Indeed the direction he points may be ascertained with sufficient clarity to be uncomfortable.

---

[1] This paper was presented at the Jesus seminar of the Westar Institute in Edmonton, Canada at its semi-annual meeting of 25-27 October 1991.

Second, there is the problem of the often latent apologetic inherent in the association of Jesus, as an authority figure of the past,
with a movement one seeks to support in the present, such as the
dominant theological movement that the third world has contributed to ecumenical discussion, liberation theology.

Of course, Jesus cannot be simply identified with any modern
alternative. But since all Christian theologies claim him as their
own, it is relevant to pose the question of the relative legitimacy of
such claims.

It is more customary to adjust Jesus to one's theology rather than
to adjust one's theology to Jesus. Hence it may be of some
relevance toward transcending such drastic relativity to detect the
main direction the interpretation was taking in the middle third of
the first century, as one moved away from Jesus and toward the
canonical gospels.

The redaction criticism of Matthew and Luke, based upon their
editing of Mark, may have disappointingly few implications concerning Jesus. For Mark had already superimposed on the traditions about Jesus the overlay of the Messianic Secret, which
Matthew and Luke in turn water down. Thus they are often moving
more directly away from Mark than from Jesus.[2] But, on the other
hand, their editing of Q, once the reconstruction of a critical text of
Q makes this kind of redaction criticism possible,[3] has to do
directly with some very old Jesus traditions, affecting the
transmission of what Jesus had to say, in spite of there also being
later traditions in Q, which do not necessarily conform to the layering of Q,[4] although by and large this would seem to be the situation.[5]

---

[2] William Wrede, *Das Messiasgeheimnis in den Evangelien* (Göttingen:
1901); ET *The Messianic Secret* (Cambridge: 1971). An analogous modern
analysis of Mark is Burton L. Mack, *A Myth of Innocence* (Philadelphia: 1988).

[3] "The International Q Project Work Session 17 November 1989," *JBL* 109
(1990) 499-501. "The International Q Project Work Session 19 November
1990," *JBL* 110 (1991) 494-498. "The International Q Project Work Sessions
12-14 July, 22 November 1991," *JBL* 111 (1992) 500-508. "A Critical Text of
the Sayings Gospel Q," *Revue d'Histoire et de Philosophie Religieuses* 72
(1992) 15-22. "The International Q Project Work Sessions 31 July-2 August, 20
November 1992," *JBL* 112 (1993) 500-506.

[4] The current status of the discussion of the layering of Q has its centre in
John S. Kloppenborg, *The Formation of Q* (Studies in Antiquity and Christian-
ity; Philadelphia: 1987): The formative layer (Q^1) contains six discourses, (1)
Q 6:20b-23b, 27-49; (2) Q 9:57-62; 10:2-11, 16; (3) Q 11:2-4, 9-13; (4)
Q 12:2-7, 11-12; (5) Q 12:22b-31, 33-34; (6) Q 13:24; 14:26-27, 34-35;
17:33 and perhaps Q 15:4-7, (8-10); 16:13; 17:1-2, 3b-6. This listing is very

To anticipate the outcome of such an investigation directed backward toward Jesus, which the discussion that follows is intended to begin.[6] In terms of modern theological alternatives, Jesus was more nearly a liberation theologian, if one may refer to such an untrained leader as a theologian at all, than a Prefect of the Congregation for the Doctrine of the Faith (Magisterium), not to speak of Protestant theologians of various kinds. Thus a redaction-critical investigation of the move from Jesus via Q to the canon provides a much-needed canonical precedent for the church's efforts to play down and control liberation theology, as well as pointing up liberation theology's relatively higher claim to the historical Jesus.

---

similar to and no doubt suggested by that in Dieter Zeller, *Die weisheitlichen Mahnsprüche bei den Synoptikern* (FzB 47; Würzburg: 1977) 191. A redactional layer (Q²) interpolated five blocks of material, (1) Q 3:7-9, 16-17; (2) Q 7:1-10, 18-28, 31-35; 16:16; (3) Q 11:14-26 (27-28?), 29-36, 39b-44, 46-52; (4) Q 12:39-40, 42-46, 49, 51-59; (5) Q 17:23-24, 26-30, 34-35; 19:12-27; 22:28-30. The redaction of Q² also involved interpolations into Q¹ (which is an argument for the sequence of the layers): Q 6:23d, 10:12-15; 12:8-10; 13:25-27; 19:18-20; 13:34-35; 14:16-24. This second layer corresponds to Dieter Lührmann, *Die Redaktion der Logienquelle* (WMANT 33; Neukirchen-Vluyn: 1969), and the most significant interpolation reflects Odil Hannes Steck, *Israel und das gewaltsame Geschick der Propheten: Untersuchungen zur Überlieferung des deuteronomistischen Geschichtsbildes im Alten Testament, Spätjudentum und Urchristentum* (WMANT 23; Neukirchen-Vluyn: 1967). Of course this analysis may not ultimately be definitive, and has indeed undergone minor revision of the extent of Q by the International Q Project, as well as fluctuations in detail as to what belongs in which layer by supporters of the basic approach; but it does, in addition to its own cogently argued presentation, tend to represent a convergence of quite different kinds of analysis leading to much the same structuring of priority to the sapiential strand. See my essay "The Q Trajectory: Between John and Matthew via Jesus" in *The Future of Early Christianity: Essays in Honor of Helmut Koester*, ed. Birger A. Pearson (Minneapolis: 1991) 173-194.

[5] It is remarkable how much congruence there is between the layering of older and younger traditions in Siegfried Schulz, *Q. Die Spruchquelle der Evangelisten* (Zürich: 1972), and the two main literary layers that Kloppenborg has disengaged. It would of course weaken considerably Kloppenborg's position if what he identified as the younger literary layer contained primarily traditions older than the older literary layer. Conversely the congruence with the analysis of layers of tradition by Schulz is one reason that Kloppenborg's analysis has much to commend it.

[6] The discussion of Q and the historical Jesus in general dependence on this layering has hardly begun. Leif E. Vaage, "Q¹ and the Historical Jesus: Some Peculiar Sayings (7:33-34; 9:57-58, 59-60; 14:26-27)," *Forum* 5.2 (1989) 159-176, reaches a Cynic conclusion more provocative than convincing; see note 61 below.

The two-fold problematic of, on the one hand, discussing the Jesus of Q and, on the other, discussing him as liberation theologian, should stay in our awareness throughout the discussion, even if not repeatedly mentioned.

II

When thinking of Q's leading theological categories, one normally focusses upon the kingdom of God and the Son of man. But, for Q, important though usually overlooked theological categories are also such mundane matters as bread and rock.

To catch sight of these metaphors, one should visualise a small loaf of bread, or roll (since bread came not in slices but in loaves), and a fist-size stone, the Palestinian dimension with which we are familiar from David-and-Goliath to the Intifada.

The Jesus of Q thought of loaves roughly resembling stones,[7] much as a fish resembles a snake.[8] His trust in God was to the effect that God, like a human father, would not replace the daily loaf for which one prayed with an inedible stone. In the next layer of Q (Q[2]), traditions associated with John saw such common field stones as God's universal source of children of Abraham.[9] But in a still further stage of the Q trajectory (Q[3]), Jesus, as exclusive son of God, becomes the role model for those who do not force God's hand in expecting stones to become loaves from God, but let stones stay stones. By now asking for bread from stones amounts to an inappropriate temptation.[10] The painful human awareness that one

---

[7] Q 11:12 / Mt 7:9. Texts in Q are cited by their Lucan chapter and verse numerations (to which is added the Matthean reference when the Q wording in question happens not to be in the Lucan verse, as here). I first defined this practical procedure, now widely accepted, in "The Sermon on the Mount / Plain: Work Sheets for the Reconstruction of Q," *SBLSP* (1983) 451-452:

> We might adopt the policy of citing Q as follows: Q 6:20 (rather than Lk 6:20 par., or Luke 6:20 //, or Mt 5:3 // Lk 6:20). This practice would mean that one regards something in Luke 6:20 as coming from Q (though not necessarily implying that Luke, rather than Matthew or some wording or sequence diverging in pattern from both, preserves the wording or sequence of Q). This would be a crisp way of referring to Q as an entity in its own right, without the problem of numbering the Q sayings in a different numbering system from that of Luke (e.g., like the numeration of the 114 sayings of the *Gospel of Thomas*). Thus we could refer to a specific verse without prematurely settling upon a numeration system that would soon become antiquated, or without the problem of constantly renumbering (both of which problems have emerged in the case of the *Gospel of Thomas*).

[8] Q 11:11.
[9] Q 3:8.
[10] Q 4:3-4.

needs to be able to count on bread, not stone, from God, is overridden by the religious concern not to permit such trust, when it falters, to test God by asking for bread from stones. The issue is no longer food, but faith.

To return to the painful human point of departure: The Q Prayer has at its centre a loaf of bread: "Give us for today a day's ration of bread."[11] One may recognize the petition "thy will be done"[12] as a secondary Matthean interpretation of "thy kingdom come", comparable to other Matthean moralizing additions such as seeking the kingdom of God *and his righteousness*,[13] hungering *and thirsting after righteousness*.[14] Conversely one may suspect that in Q it was the loaf of bread[15] that was intended to give the interpretative clarity to the immediately preceding petition for the kingdom to come,[16] by making the kingdom as specific as a day's ration.

The petition for bread is meant literally. For in Q's commentary on the prayer, which stands in sharp contrast to the Matthean religious interpretation oriented to forgiveness by humans and hence by God,[17] one finds the reassurance that if one asks, seeks, knocks, one will be provided, as with bread and fish by humans, with good things by God.[18] Luke also first interprets the petition for bread literally, in that he interpolates between the prayer and its Q interpretation an illustration of a person who asks for three loaves for a late-arriving guest and finally gets what he needs.[19]

Yet the Q interpretation does have a dimension *a minore ad majorem* in that God's giving moves beyond the specifics, to good things more broadly.[20] And yet to persons who do not have to worry about where their next meal is coming from (for example, non-liberation theologians), this may still seem to be something of a let-down. For it could suggest a crass materialism to the Q folk: a real feast. So Luke appends a corrective spiritualizing reformulation of the Q interpretation:[21] To those who ask, God will give the

---

[11] Q 11:3.
[12] Mt 6:10 at Q 11:2.
[13] Mt 6:33 at Q 12:31.
[14] Mt 5:6 at Q 6:21. See also Mt 6:33 at Q 12:31.
[15] Q 11:3.
[16] Q 11:2.
[17] Mt 6:14-15 at Q 11:4 // Mt 6:12.
[18] Q 11:9-13.
[19] Lk 11:5-8.
[20] Q 11:13.
[21] Lk 11:13 at Q 11:13.

Holy Spirit—with which however the prayer itself was not at all concerned.[22] But one need only recall Paul's spiritualizing exegesis:[23] "The kingdom of God is not food and drink but righteousness and peace and joy in the Holy Spirit." Paul thus stopped the "rice Christians" of his day—the Q people—in their tracks. The Q people had been led to expect that trust in the coming of the kingdom would involve daily bread, a hope which was ultimately reduced to the eschatology of the Messianic banquet.[24]

It is as if Christian charitable organizations should in our world air-lift in to the Kurdish refugees on the Turkish border or to the famine areas of Somalia or besieged cities of Yugoslavia not bread and blankets so much as—a stack of Bibles.

To be sure, the triple formulation: ask, seek, knock,[25] can not only be interpreted as rough synonyms all exhorting to prayer, but also as distinct metaphors pointing to distinct facets of the Q stance.

One not only "asks" for the kingdom and bread in the Prayer;[26] one "seeks" the kingdom, rather than scrounging food and

---

[22] This came to expression in a spiritualizing corruption of the Lucan text as early as Marcion. See B. H. Streeter, *The Four Gospels: A Study of Origins* (New York: 1925) 277, who advocated this reading as the Lucan text of the prayer itself, which led to the conclusion that the Prayer was not in Q:

> Here we find that **B**, as usual, has been less affected by assimilation than most other MSS.; but here also there is evidence that **B** has not entirely escaped. For **700, 162,** instead of "Thy kingdom come," read "thy holy spirit come upon us and cleanse us" (ἐλθέτω τὸ πνεῦμα...ἐφ' ἡμᾶς) And **D** has ἐλθέτω ἡ βασιλεία ἐφ' ἡμᾶς, where Rendel Harris pointed out, ἐφ' ἡμᾶς is only explicable as a remainder of the other reading which a corrector of **D** omitted to strike out, and this reading was in the text of Luke used by Gregory of Nyssa in Cappadocia in 395; he says so plainly twice, and moreover gives no hint that he had even heard of any other reading. It is also quoted by Maximus of Turin, *c.* 450. So the reading was current both in the East and in the West to quite a late period. But it also stood in the text of Marcion (AD 140), and from Tertullian's comment on this it is not at all clear that his own text was in this respect different from Marcion's. Now in view of the immense pressure of the tendency to assimilate the two versions of this specifically familiar prayer, and of the improbability that various orthodox Fathers should have adopted (without knowing it) the text of Marcion, the probability is high that the reading of **700, 162,** which makes the Gospels differ most, is what Luke wrote. Matthew's version is here the more original.
>
> Now, even if we accept the reading of **B**, the difference between the two versions of the Lord's Prayer, Lk. xi.1-4 and Mt. vi.9-13, is so great as to put a considerable strain on the theory that they were both derived from the same written source. But, if we accept the reading of **700** and its supporters, that theory becomes quite impossible.

[23] Rom 14:17. cf. also Jas 1:5: "But if someone among you lacks wisdom, let him ask from God—who gives to all without hesitation and without grumbling—and it will be given to him."

[24] Q 13:29.

[25] Q 11:9.

[26] Q 11:2-4.

clothing by human means.[27] For the Father, who knows our needs,[28] will just as surely provide for us without our lifting our hands as he does for birds and wild flowers.[29] This way the food and clothing will be ours as well.[30] Thus there is no contradiction between asking God for bread and not seeking from human resources food and clothing, even though God answers through human action.

One also "knocks", of course on a door, which in Q is thought of as having food and lodging on the other side.[31] If one's greeting of Shalom is reciprocated, and one is admitted, then the host is by definition a "son of peace".[32] This was not originally meant as the selection of an already-identified "safe-house", an incipient house church,[33] but rather involved knocking at an unknown address, where God, not a sympathizer, is counted on for food and lodging. Nor does one drop in on relatives or friends for a break from the rigors of the mission.[34] There were no "rest and recreation" centers free of the call of duty.

---

[27] Q 12:31.
[28] Q 12:30.
[29] Q 12:22-31.
[30] Q 12:31.
[31] Q 13:25-29.
[32] Q 10:6.
[33] This may be the meaning in Mt 10:11, reflecting the situation a generation later when circuits of "safe houses" were being developed, such as the Essenes used. This may explain Matthew's rearranging of the order of his Mission Instruction so as to list first not a house but a city or village, where there is a choice of houses. One searches out someone who is worthy, by which Matthew means someone who is a disciple, Mt 10:37-38. This practice is documented in Acts 21:7. Perhaps Q 13:26 has its place in this development.
[34] This may be the meaning of the very obscure injunction, Q 10:4, "Salute no one on the road" (RSV). Bernhard Lang, "Grussverbot oder Besuchsverbot? Eine sozialgeschichtliche Deutung von Lukas 10,4b," *BZ* n.F. 26 (1982) 75-79, ascribes the statement to Q (p. 78). He develops a suggestion made in the Lukan commentary of G. L. Hahn in 1894, to the effect that one should translate "Visit no one during the trip". For ἀσπάζεσθαι can mean not just to greet, but also to visit someone for a period of time (Acts 18:22; 21:7; 25:13). It was the normal custom in that society that one could drop in unannounced at friends or relatives, and count on food and lodging (Lk 11:6). Risto Uro, *Sheep among the Wolves: A Study on the Mission Instructions of Q* (AASF. Dissertationes Humanarum Litterarum 47; Helsinki: 1987) 136 n. 80, rejects this interpretation, since he understands by "son of peace", in analogy to "sons of light", as "one who has a share in the new faith or at least sympathizes with it", "a sectarian designation" (140-141). But this is not attested anywhere as a Christian self-designation. Uro seems to put more theological meaning than is intended in the common, everyday exchange of greetings: "The 'peace' probably had a specifically

Thus the injunction to ask, seek, knock was not a program such as a Protestant work ethic, Ghandian cottage industries, agricultural missions, or the Peace Corps, and to this extent not as developed in practical terms as is modern liberation theology. The emphasis is on sustenance as a gift of God, even if in practice this meant being dependent on a son of peace providing room and board.

Yet the loaves are not spiritualized away in Johannine style, as manna from heaven that points christologically toward the Son whom the Father sent from heaven, or sacramentally as the tidbits that only whet one's appetite for the word of God. Rather they are a square meal, a real loaf of bread. The Johannine Jesus "tempted" Philip[35] with the idea of buying loaves to feed the hungry.[36] Once they are miraculously fed, they recognize Jesus as the Prophet, the Coming One,[37] and are ready to make him King,[38] much as in Q John's disciples are referred to Jesus's healings and his evangelizing the poor to prove he is the Coming One.[39]

The Q people are hence characterized not fully inappropriately by the Johannine Jesus:[40] "You seek me not because you saw signs, but because you ate of the loaves and were filled." Of course there was for the Q people no such dichotomy—the very experience of being filled was a reality of the kingdom, not an overlooking of the kingdom, and hence indeed a sign of the

---

Christian connotation and in the mouth of a wandering charismatic functioned as an effective blessing providing magical protection to the household" (141). Mt 10:12 interprets "Peace" as just a normal greeting: "As you enter a house, salute it." The statement that the peace would rest upon the son of peace or return to the speaker if no such welcoming host opens the door does in fact suggest a potential meaning in the common greeting, which would be unpacked, if one were admitted, in terms of the kingdom of God (Q 10:9), or, as Lk 10:11 interprets wiping the dust of one's feet off on leaving an unreceptive town, "nevertheless know this, that the kingdom of God has come near." But it could hardly function as a "password" (141 n. 100), since it was the standard greeting with no more distinctive connotation than our well-worn greetings of today. Its use may have been mentioned to clarify just how indeterminate the reception was, i.e. whether one would be heard only in a superficial "secular" way or whether one would be received as a bearer of the kingdom. The householder who responds positively to such an opening greeting by replying Shalom and opening the door is all that needs to be ascribed to the designation "son of peace".

[35] Jn 6:6.
[36] Jn 6:5.
[37] Jn 6:14.
[38] Jn 6:15.
[39] Q 7:22.
[40] Jn 6:26.

kingdom, though not just a sign. But in John, one should rather seek the nourishment that lasts to eternal life,[41] not even manna from heaven,[42] but Jesus the true bread from heaven,[43] whose believers will metaphorically never hunger and thirst,[44] for he is the bread of life.[45]

Of course the disciples found this word to be difficult,[46] and a schism resulted:[47] "After this many of his disciples drew back and no longer circulated with him." Yet the twelve (including Judas son of Simon Iscariot[48]) stuck by him, led by Simon Peter, all of whom are missing in Q. The twelve apostles thereupon moved with Jesus not only toward Jerusalem and away from Galilee,[49] but also moved toward the canon—and away from the oldest layer of Q. Those that "no longer circulated with him" are those "that did not believe",[50] that is to say, those who would have enthroned him on the grounds of the unspiritualized loaves,[51] with which the oldest layer of Q was in fact concerned.

To be sure, this Johannine text is a spiritualizing not of Q, but of the Signs Source, specifically its Feeding of the Five Thousand.[52] But these two most firmly established pre-canonical sources, though quite different, in that one is a collection of sayings (Q), the other of miracle stories (the Signs Source), do have much in common, perhaps due to the early period in which they share, that is to say, their relative proximity to Jesus. Indeed the one miracle story of Q is shared with the Signs Source, the Capharnaum Healing of the Centurion's Boy.[53]

The Capharnaum connection goes even further. For they share the questionability of Capharnaum. Just as John locates the schism over heavenly bread at Capharnaum,[54] just so Q pronounces con-

---

[41] Jn 6:27.
[42] Jn 6:31.
[43] Jn 6:32-35a.
[44] Jn 6:35b.
[45] Jn 6:48-58.
[46] Jn 6:60.
[47] Jn 6:66.
[48] Jn 6:67-71.
[49] Jn 5:1, if John 6 originally followed John 4, or Jn 7:10b, after shaking off his brothers (Jn 7:1-10a), if one prefers the present canonical order.
[50] Jn 6:64.
[51] Jn 6:15.
[52] Jn 6:1-13.
[53] Q 7:1-10; Jn 4:46b-54.
[54] Jn 6:24.

demnation on Capharnaum for exalting itself to heaven.[55] If there actually was a schism among Jesus' followers at Capharnaum, it may well be that the Signs Source and Q would have been on the same side, in that both focussed on the down-to-earth dimension of what Jesus had to offer. The role of the Fourth Gospel as spiritualizing the Signs Source may provide a model for understanding the relation of Matthew and Luke to Q.

The Q people were thus originally somewhat reminiscent of a grazing-and-gathering (but not storing) prehistoric ecological system still witnessed to, as God's way, by the flourishing birds and flowers. For the outcome of not seeking food and clothing, but instead God's kingdom, is that these things, the necessities of life,[56] are supplied to them. Q does not really favor privation, any more than the really poor appreciate the romance of poverty. Liberation theology recognizes such romantic illusion as just a ploy of the suppressors. The Q people just have a different, God-given route to a square meal: Get through the door! Knock![57] Don't knock it down, but with a smile on your face, say Shalom![58] Eat anything they will give you![59] Don't demand it be Kosher. Or: Don't be uptight about killing vegetables by plucking them to make food, as reflected in the debates between Mani and the Jewish Christian Elkesaites among whom Mani grew up. Or: Don't insist that it be locusts and wild honey.[60] Or: Don't be abstemious in what one eats and drinks, as befits an ascetic. In one way or the other, eat whatever God provides.

The Q movement then was not ascetic, in the sense of physical privation being an end or goal in itself. Dig in! Eat what is set before you! Be like Jesus, eating and drinking, or, in caricature, a glutton and drunkard, carousing with tax collectors and sinners,[61]

---

[55] Q 10:15.

[56] Q 12:31.

[57] Q 11:9-10.

[58] Q 10:5.

[59] Q 10:7-8.

[60] John's menu according to Mk 1:6.

[61] Q 7:34. Leif A. Vaage, "Q[1] and the Historical Jesus," does not distinguish between what is presented as descriptive (ἦλθεν) and what is presented as hostile caricature (λέγετε). This facilitates his characterization of Jesus as "a bit of a hellion and wanderer on the wild (or, at least, illicit) side of things" (166), "an imp, in Socrates' terms a social gad-fly, an irritant on the skin of conventional mores and values, a marginal figure in the provincial context of Galilee and Judea" (175). However the use of the caricature as objective description would, in the adjoining and structurally parallel case of John (Q 7:33), make of him a demoniac, which is hardly true of the historical John. The point of the text is to

but quite unlike John, the ascetic who neither ate bread nor drank wine, or in caricature, was demon-possessed.[62] John's diet was apparently what he was able to scrounge from nature,[63] and he may have made a virtue of fasting,[64] as did Jesus' disciples at a later time.[65] But in the case of Jesus' disciples this is set over against an earlier time when they did not fast.[66] The practice reflected in the Mission Instructions would tend to indicate that when a host provided a banquet, there was no reason not to accept it. If what could be offered was much more modest, one would accept that too. To judge by the success Jesus may well have had (in contrast to the probable failure of the ongoing Mission of his disciples), he might well have ended up looking like Buddha, had he not headed for Jerusalem, but rather stayed in the Galilee that heard (and fed) him gladly.[67] There is no justification in the Jesus of Q for asceticism in its own right, or for poverty as an ideal to be imposed (by the well-to-do) on the poor.

If Shalom works, one exchanges gifts of healings and food, under the auspices of the kingdom of God.[68] This content of the Mission is presented by Mark in narrative form,[69] when Jesus goes home with Peter to heal his sick mother-in-law and eat the food she serves. He may well not have gone from house to house, but stayed there and made it his headquarters, which the Franciscan brothers who now own and have excavated "Peter's House" in Capharnaum will be glad to show you. In fact when Jesus was invited by a centurion to another Capharnaum home for a healing, he declined the implicit offer of hospitality, while providing from a distance the healing.[70]

If the Q folk were not ascetics in a doctrinaire sense, they were of course also not merely *bon vivants*. The usual understanding of the policy not to go from house to house, but to stay where one was

---

indicate that Jesus coming eating and drinking is distorted by hostile caricature, just as John coming not eating bread and drinking wine is distorted by hostile caricature. The caricatures, to the extent they go beyond the descriptions, are historical evidence only to there having been efforts at hostile caricatures of the diverging lifestyles.

[62] Q 7:33.
[63] Mk 1:6.
[64] Mk 2:18.
[65] Mk 2:20; Mt 6:16-18.
[66] Mk 2:18.
[67] Mk 12:37 uses this familiar phrase of the Jerusalem crowd.
[68] Q 10:6-9.
[69] Mk 1:29-31.
[70] Q 7:1-10.

first received,[71] is that one stays even after the fatted calf there has
been consumed. Nor does one from the pantry stash away supplies
in one's backpack for the next day's road, much less for a rainy
day, for again and again one sets out in the morning empty-
handed.[72]

Why the deprivation, if not derived from ascetic ideology? Perhaps as a show, to attract attention, a visual advertisement for the
illiterate masses, like the chimney-sweep's blackened face, top hat
and ladder, or other *sigla* or sounds of Medieval trades people
hawking their wares on the streets, or like the contemporary Cynics,
whose disdain for respectable society's values was visible in their
distinct primitive garb as far as the eye could see. Though this may
not be the point of the injunction not to greet anyone on the
road,[73] since this may indeed refer more nearly to an injunction
against dropping in on friends for rest and recreation, other traits
which seem to us to have served no earthly good other than to
dramatize their message, such as barefootedness, may have to be
thus explained, at least until we have a better explanation—a sign
of penance?[74]

---

[71] Q 10:7.

[72] Q 10:4. The policy of not accepting provisions for the continuation of the
trip seems to have been violated by the Maltese, who provided Paul with
provisions for the journey in return for his healings (Acts 28:10), consistent
with the Lucan revocation of carrying purse and bag (Q 10:4) as the passion narrative begins (Lk 22:35-38).

[73] I. Bosold, *Pazifismus und prophetische Provokation. Das Grussverbot
Lk 10,4b und sein historischer Kontext* (SBS 90; Stuttgart: 1978), interpreted
this statement as intentionally provocative, to draw attention and thus to serve
as propaganda. It would seem counter-productive to seek to attract attention, in
order to provide an opportunity for the message, by means of refusing a greeting
that usually opens a conversation. Lang's argument (see note 34) is presented as
a corrective of that view. Bosold, 43-51, ascribes the statement to Q. "The
International Q Project: Work Session 16 November 1990," *JBL* 110 (1991)
496, followed Bosold's interpretation, but expressed considerable doubt about
the reading in Q, omitting completely κατὰ τὴν ὁδόν. Lang's interpretation
might make the ascription of the saying to Q more certain.

[74] Norbert Krieger, "Barfuss Busse Tun," *NT* 1 (1956) 227-228, especially
227:

Busse aber wurde und wird unter Juden seit jeher ohne Schuhe begangen.

2 Sam xv 30; Ez xxiv 17, 23; Mi i 8...

Bedeutung des Wegnehmens wie Jo xii 6; xx 13-15.

Doch geht es Mt iii 11, meiner Meinung nach, nicht um ein Abnehmen zu gelegent-
licher Bequemlichkeit; es ging dort vielmehr um ein Wegnehmen zu ständiger Unbe-
quemlichkeit, so dass ein Barfüsserorden der Johannesjünger denkbar wäre.

The Love-Your-Enemies composition at the heart of the Sermon[75] would seem to provide a more specific explanation for the weird life-style. For one is not merely to love an occasional enemy, but even to act lovingly toward the pervasive sponger. Give the shirt off one's back! Even give away one's money! Lending to those who can never repay can only for politeness' sake be called lending—it's a bald hand out! The traveller's usual equipment of purse and pack is rejected in the Mission Instructions, no doubt

---

Krieger is followed by Walter Bauer, *A Greek-English Lexicon of the New Testament and Other Early Christian Literature*, ET by William F. Arndt and F. Wilbur Gingrich, 2nd edition revised and augmented by F. Wilbur Gingrich and Frederick W. Danker from Walter Bauer's 5th edition, 1958 (Chicago / London: 1979), s.v. βαστάζω, 3.a, "remove", citing also *PGM* 4,1058: βαστάξας τὸ στεφάνιον ἀπὸ τῆς κεφαλῆς.

[75] Walter Bauer, "Das Gebot der Feindesliebe und die alten Christen," *ZThK* 24 (1913) 37-54 (Wilhelm Herrmann *Festschrift*), wrote the history of the injunction to love one's enemy in the early church, to the effect that, though the apologists often refer to the Christian practice of loving one's enemy for its apologetic value, this ideal was not nearly so well implemented as this boastful claim might suggest. Matthew (pp. 39-40) has removed it from the central role it had in the Q sermon just after the Beatitudes, and states it only once (Mt 5:44), rather than twice (Lk 6:27, 35). The way in which the tax collectors and Gentiles, types of those to whose conduct one does not want to condescend (Q 6:33-34 / Mt 5:46-47), "who represent the crowd of the unbaptised, are pushed to one side with indifferent coolness," as the model for the way in which an excommunicated person is treated (Mt 18:17), or "the satisfaction with which Matthew reports how the king avenged the death of his emissaries on the unwilling invitees" (Mt 22:6-7) "do not particularly lead one to expect that he would have been inclined to react to expressions of animosity from non-Christians with expressions of love." Luke (p. 40) seems more sympathetic with the love of enemies, in refraining from destroying the Samaritan village (Lk 9:51-56) and in presenting Jesus (Lk 23:34) and, in imitation, Stephen (Acts 7:60), as dying with a prayer for their tormentors. But the widow's plea for justice (Lk 18:6-8) is already reminiscent of the hateful demand for justice of Rev 6:9-11. Mark (p. 48) is completely silent about love to enemies; nor does John, who has a very different view, call for a love of enemies (p. 48). Paul, the only contemporary of the Q Sermon, seems more influenced by the original view (p. 39):

> He did not at all only praise love in general in lofty tones. He called for love to one's fellow human, and in fact not only to such as belonged to the same community of faith, even though he often called for brotherly love, but rather to people in general (Rom 13:8-10; 1 Thess 3:12; Gal 6:10). The opponents and oppressors of the Christian he does not want to consider excluded. Rather he calls for the attitude of love toward them in a way that almost permits the conjecture not only that the spirit of his Lord has touched him, but that his requirements echo in his ear (Rom 12:14-21; 1 Thess 5:15; cf. 1 Cor 4:12).

Occasional sharp words (1 Thess 2:14-16) are compared to Q 11:49-50; 13:34-35, precisely the two Q passages that were later (from O. H. Steck on) recognized as most distinctive of the Deuteronomistic redaction of Q.

272 J. M. ROBINSON

since they can be there only for one reason—to hold on for oneself to what the beggar on the street calls out for, an appeal which,
if always acceded to, would soon leave one empty-handed, oneself
in the same fix as the beggar. This, rather than baptism, may have
been the *rite de passage* into the Q movement. Barnabas may illustrate the way a sympathizer's sale of property for charitable
purposes leads to itinerancy.[76]

This correlation between the composition Love-Your-Enemies
and the Mission Instructions would also suggest that turning the
other cheek[77] may have meant in practice not carrying a weapon.[78]
A graduate student from Kenya first made me aware that it was of
course obvious that the "staff" one was not to take was thought of
as a weapon, a "club". I then recalled that, the first time I had an
interview with the *fellah* who discovered the Nag Hammadi codices
in Upper Egypt, he carried a thick, solid, heavy, polished, two-
meter-long staff which I hardly noticed at the time. I did not see it
again until, a couple of years later, I had a first interview with his
brother. In retrospect, wised up by the student from nearby Kenya,
I realise that these interviews apparently had been entered into with
apprehension, but had a disarming effect. The *Los Angeles Times*
of 17 December 1992, reporting on the new sense of security
provided by the arrival of U.S. military forces in the famine-ridden
town of Baidoa in Somalia, provides the anecdote:

> Wednesday, the feeding centre was filled with optimism and a new sense
> of security; commodities as rare as grain in this parched land. 'Where's
> your gun?' Rice teased Abduhakim, 19, one of the centre's security
> guards. Only a day before, he had been carrying an automatic weapon.
> Wednesday, he was carrying a walking stick.

The stick was obviously not due to a sudden lameness, but rather
was a weapon permissible in the presence of U.S. forces in a way
that a gun would not be. On 14 March 1993 another *Los Angeles
Times* article included a photograph bearing the caption

> Two Somali men walk through the ruins of what was once the Hotel
> Aruba in the capital, Mogadishu. They carry sticks for protection.

---

[76] Acts 4:32-37; 11:22.
[77] Q 6:29.
[78] Q 10:4 / Mt 10:10. Since the staff is in Lk 9:3, but not in Lk 10:4, it is
not a certain reading, but has been graded C by the International Q Project; see
"The International Q Project Work Session 16 November 1990," *JBL* (1991)
496.

Luke may also have understood the staff as a weapon. For when he undoes the Mission Instructions to introduce the Church Militant, he points out that swords have now become part of the approved equipment.[79] A sword is a middle-class equivalent to a poor person's club, just as in the Holy Land today an automatic rifle is a prosperous equivalent to throwing stones. The Q movement was originally defenceless. It had no alternative to loving one's enemy.[80] One may recall the injunction to make peace with one's accuser on the way to court, where one was sure to lose, i.e. was guilty of unpaid debts.[81] The system kept the poor guilty—as liberation theologians know all too well.

The spiritualizing trajectory of the Q movement that we have already observed is also quite apparent in the Beatitudes. Apparently there was an initial triad of blessing the poor, hungry, mourning,[82] perhaps brought together on the basis of a random practice of blessing any and every victim of fate that one came across. The triad became a representative cluster standing for all such victims, with the *primus inter pares* awarded to what may have become a self-designation of the Q movement, the Poor, the Proto-Ebionites.[83] Thus this triad may already by implication have shifted the blessing away from any-and-every victim of fate to Jesus' disciples, thus marking a decisive if only gradually perceptible social formation. This becomes explicit with the secondary appending of a fourth Beatitude, where it is not a matter of victims of fate in general, but rather people of Q who are victimized because of their identification with Jesus.[84] Q later adds blessings explicitly on those who take no offence in him,[85] but behold what he does,[86] that is to say, on the Q people themselves.

This Christianizing trend is then expanded in the Matthean community by adding Beatitudes created to designate the virtues of the Q / Matthean folk: the meek, the merciful, the pure in heart, the

---

[79] Lk 22:36, 38.

[80] Q 6:27, 35.

[81] Q 12:58-59.

[82] Q 6:20-21.

[83] Cf. my essay, "The Sayings Gospel Q," in *The Four Gospels 1992: Festschrift F. Neirynck*, ed. F. Van Segbroeck *et al.* (BETL 100; Leuven: 1992) I.361-388.

[84] Q 6:22-23.

[85] Q 7:23.

[86] Q 10:23. The Beatitude on those who keep God's word in Lk 11:28 may also be in Q.

peacemakers.[87] And the Beatitudes that had originally been
formulated prior to or apart from this social formation are recast or
updated to reflect this trend, as poor *in spirit*,[88] hungering *and
thirsting after righteousness*.[89] The Matthean, or pre-Matthean
emphasis on righteousness may explain an additional beatitude for
those persecuted for righteousness sake.[90]

Thus a movement that had its original focus on re-evaluating the
status of all victims of fate, in view of the radical nature of the
kingdom of God, came to identify itself as the *beati possidentes*.
The Church had become aware of itself as the distinct people of
God. An original liberation theology was transmuted into the social
concerns of the Church.

To be sure, in quite obvious senses Jesus was not a modern liberation theologian. He was not guilty of covertly presupposing
Karl Marx's system; it is more nearly the reverse. Nor did Jesus
engender an effective program to counter the abysmal plight of the
masses. His movement died out in Galilee with hardly a trace.[91]
One hopes for a better outcome in the case of liberation theology.
But Jesus did recognize the plight of the masses living without the
bare necessities of life as systemic—that in any case is inherent in
his otherwise obscure talk of the kingdom of God. Jesus elevated
that plight to the central theme of theology, as has been
rediscovered by the liberation theologians of today. And, like
them, he went about doing something about it. His implementation
was not successful, and in any case is not suited to meet our needs.
But that we should implement his message is itself central to that
message, as liberation theologians have put at the center of their
message.

---

[87] Mt 5:5, 7-9.
[88] Mt 5:3 at Q 6:20.
[89] Mt 5:6 at Q 6:21.
[90] Mt 5:10. The usual assumption that this is Matthean redaction is challenged by Helmut Koester, *Ancient Christian Gospels: Their History and Development* (London and Philadelphia: 1990) 65, who on the basis of 1 Pet 3:14
postulates "a Jewish-Christian document that Matthew used in chapters 5-7".
[91] Acts 9:31.

CHAPTER TWELVE

JESUS AND THE PARABLES OF JESUS IN Q

John S. Kloppenborg

Contemporary scholarship has discovered in the parables of Jesus paradigms of brilliance and wit, exemplifying Jesus' verbal acumen, his narrative skill, and his incisive commentary on the human situation before God. The parables are commonly regarded as a distinctive, if not the most distinctive, feature of the speech of the historical Jesus,[1] and, hence, the most promising avenue of historical Jesus research. At the same time, the fate of the parables in Christian tradition illustrates what has been imagined as a more general shift from the message of the Kingdom in its original freshness to its domestication in the language of the Church, from proclamation to dogma, from metaphorical language to theology. Books on the parables regularly cite the elaborate allegorical exegesis of the Good Samaritan by Origen or Augustine to illustrate how far from the "original" sense patristic writers strayed. But one does not have to look as far as the third or fourth centuries to detect such deviations. It is clear from the editing of the parables by the synoptic evangelists themselves that they did not treat the parables as fresh and lively narratives, combining the everydayness of Palestinian village society with playful inversions and resonant metaphors; instead, the parables offered mere surfaces upon which to inscribe instructions on salvation history, christology, ecclesiology and morals.

The subject of this essay is not the parables at the level of oral performance by Jesus, but their literary appearance—perhaps the

---

[1] For explicit statements to this effect, see Adolf Jülicher, *Die Gleichnisreden Jesu*, 2. Aufl. (Tübingen: 1910; repr. Darmstadt: 1976) 1.149; C. H. Dodd, *The Parables of the Kingdom*, rev. ed. (London: 1961) 1; Joachim Jeremias, *The Parables of Jesus*, rev. ed. (New York: 1972) 12; Norman Perrin, *Jesus and the Language of the Kingdom: Symbol and Metaphor in New Testament Interpretation* (Philadelphia: 1976) 199; Robert H. Stein, *The Method and Message of Jesus' Teachings* (Philadelphia: 1978) 34; John R. Donahue, *The Gospel in Parable: Metaphor, Narrative, and Theology in the Synoptic Gospels* (Philadelphia: 1988) 2.

earliest literary appearance—in the Sayings Gospel Q and the way in which the "Jesus of the parables" becomes the "Jesus of Q".

From Parable to Didactic Narrative and Back

Even before the attention of scholarship turned to the poetic character of the parables, they were regarded simultaneously as key to the understanding of the kingdom proclaimed by Jesus and as showcase examples in the history of exegesis. In a devastating *tour de force* Jülicher had shown how from Clement of Rome to his own day parables had been treated as allegories, and how allegorical exegesis had resulted in a plethora of interpretations, none of them particularly convincing.[2] "Simplex sigillum veri" was the alternative and for Jülicher this meant that parables ought to be interpreted in a way that acknowledged that they were framed in simple, vivid and everyday language.[3] From the imagery (*das Bild*) of the parable the *tertium comparationis* had to be determined and applied to the real matter (*die Sache*) under discussion, the kingdom.[4] Jülicher discovered in the parables a kingdom of God characterized by "a fellowship in God..., a fellowship of brothers and sisters under the protection of their father...", a kingdom "in which spiritual effort and endeavour is demanded of all its members, not one in which preference is given to high birth or standing or intellectual capacity, but to reconciliation, humility, love, trust, patience, vigilance, prudence, self-denial, faithfulness...".[5] The parables illustrated these virtues, and, hence, for Jülicher the parables functioned in an essentially didactic manner. His view of Jesus as a teacher of humane morals, indeed, as the "apostle of progress"[6], epitomized the German liberal view later articulated in Harnack's *Das Wesen des Christentums*.[7]

---

[2] See Jülicher, *Gleichnisreden Jesu*, especially 1.202-322: "Geschichte der Auslegung der Gleichnisreden Jesu."

[3] Jülicher, *Gleichnisreden Jesu* 1.322.

[4] Jülicher, *Gleichnisreden Jesu* 1.149: "Sie [die Gleichnisse] beschäftigen sich zum grossen Teil mit dem Himmelreiche, diesem Grund- und Hauptbegriffe in Jesu Gedankenwelt, der neuerdings denn auch allgemein in die Mitte des 'Lehrsystems' Jesu gerückt wird; wie Christus das Reich Gottes sich gedacht hat, würden wir aus einer andern Quelle, wenn die Parablen uns fehlen, nur schlecht ersehen."

[5] Jülicher, *Gleichnisreden Jesu* 1.149.

[6] *Ibid.* 2.483.

[7] ET: Adolf von Harnack, *What is Christianity?* (London: 1901).

Even though Jülicher's liberal Protestant view of the kingdom of God as the product of spirit-guided human efforts was soon supplanted by the apocalyptic kingdom of Johannes Weiss and Albert Schweitzer—a kingdom not made with hands[8]—Jülicher's rejection of allegory continued to serve as a benchmark of parables research. So too did the view he popularized concerning the use of parables by early Christians: later usage departed from the freshness and vigour of Jesus' vision of the kingdom and overlayed it with dogmatic concerns. To put it somewhat differently, the parables, properly explained, put the interpreter in contact with the pre- and nondogmatic Jesus. In this sense Jülicher and those who followed him imagined the task at hand to be one of removing the later editorial and dogmatic accretions in order to arrive at an undogmatic Jesus—a quest as old as Reimarus and Schleiermacher.

Jeremias' epoch-making *Parables of Jesus*, though it disagreed with Jülicher's view of the kingdom and with Schweitzer's notion of *konzequent Eschatologie*, concurred with their general approach in two crucial respects. First, parables remained didactic and illustrative in function. The Prodigal Son, the Lost Sheep, the Lost Drachma, and the Vineyard Workers, for example, defended Jesus' proclamation to sinners;[9] the Mustard, the Leaven, the Sowers and the Seed Growing Secretly provided assurance and consolation;[10] while the Treasure, the Pearl, and the Good Samaritan illustrated self-sacrifice and the "law of love".[11]

---

[8] For Weiss and Schweitzer, the parables of the Mustard and the Leaven, for example, were not about "the certainty that with the kingdom of heaven the period of perfection would follow the period of incompleteness", as Jülicher (*Gleichnisreden Jesu* 2.581) held, but instead dramatized the apocalyptic character of the kingdom by contrasting the inconspicuousness of the cause with the overpowering result. See Johannes Weiss, *Die Predigt Jesu vom Reiche Gottes*, 3. Aufl. (Göttingen: 1964) 82-83; Albert Schweitzer, *The Quest of the Historical Jesus* (New York: 1968) 356: "In these parables it is not the idea of development, but of the apparent absence of causation which occupies the foremost place. The description aims at suggesting the question, how, and by what power, incomparably great and glorious results can be infallibly produced by an insignificant fact without human aid.... What the parables emphasize is, therefore,...the in itself negative, inadequate, character of the initial fact, upon which, as by a miracle, there follows in the appointed time, through the power of God, some great thing. They lay stress not upon the natural, but upon the miraculous character of such occurrences."

[9] Jeremias, *Parables of Jesus* 131, 136, 139.

[10] *Ibid.* 149, 151, 153.

[11] *Ibid.* 200-201, 205-206. Perrin (*Jesus and the Language of the Kingdom* 105-106) observes that despite Jeremias' rejection of Jülicher's moralizing in-

Second, Jeremias accepted the view that this message was gradually obscured and overlaid. More than those before him, Jeremias saw that this process had already begun with the editing of the synoptic gospels. Alterations were not restricted to minor changes resulting from the translation of the parables into Greek; they included more substantial alterations occasioned by changes in the audience, changing ecclesial situations (e.g., the delay of the Parousia) and the introduction of allegory.[12] Jeremias, nevertheless, was quite sanguine that the "return to Jesus from the Primitive Church"—the title of his second chapter—could be accomplished once the "laws of transformation" were understood. For this reason, he remained persuaded that the parables afforded an unsurpassed route to the message of the historical Jesus.[13]

Although the notion of allegorical and dogmatic "overlays" and "accretions" has endured, the view of Jülicher and Jeremias that the parables are essentially didactic in function has not. The major reevaluation occurred when Amos Wilder in the United States and in Germany, Ernst Fuchs and his two students, Eta Linnemann and Eberhard Jüngel, challenged the prevailing view of the function of the parable. The parables were not didactic, illustrative of Jesus' message; they were revelatory and verbalized Jesus' own vision of the kingdom.

While C. H. Dodd, like his contemporaries, treated the parables as didactic stories, commending, defending and illustrating Jesus' gospel, Dodd's famous definition of the parable already provides the antecedants for Wilder's and Fuchs' view. For Dodd the parable was

> a metaphor or simile drawn from nature or common life, *arresting the hearer by its vividness or strangeness*, and leaving the mind in sufficient doubt as to its precise application *to tease it into active thought*.[14]

The parables combine realism with surprise and thereby confront the hearer with a new vision and therefore, a choice. Wilder stressed both the realism of the language of the parables and their "focus and depth". He distinguished between parables which illustrate particular points—example stories such as the Good

---

terpretation of the parables, he continued to relate the parables to the "message of Jesus" and thus reduced them to illustrations of that message rather than treating them as texts in themselves, with their own integrity and power to "give rise to thought" (Dodd's phrase).

[12] Jeremias, *Parables of Jesus* 23-114.
[13] Jeremias, *Parables of Jesus* 11.
[14] Dodd, *Parables of the Kingdom* 5 (emphasis added).

Samaritan and the Rich Farmer—and symbolic narratives like the Lost Sheep. The latter, far from enjoining a particular course of action, provides "an extended image—the shepherd's retrieval of the lost sheep and his joy—a narrative image which reveals rather than exemplifies".[15] In parables such as the Lost Sheep, the Sower, the Mustard Seed, the Leaven, the Pearl and the Treasure what is revealed is Jesus' own vision. "For us, too, to find the meaning of the parable we must identify ourselves with that inner secret of Jesus' faith and faithfulness."[16] They do not merely illustrate, but rather present a challenge and a personal appeal. One might add that although the editorial "tags" such as "Listen" and εἴ τις ἔχει ὦτα ἀκούειν ἀκουέτω are doubtless later additions, these features recognize and underscore this dimension of challenge and appeal.

For Fuchs and Linnemann the parable is a "language event". It does not merely provoke thought; it mediates Jesus' understanding of existence and creates the possibility for the hearer to share that understanding.[17] In the case of the parable of the mustard seed, for example,

> the parable indicates that God in his coming accommodates himself to our circumstances, so that we are the seed from which the Kingdom will miraculously spring up, and spring up it will....But the parable is no longer a pious discourse, nor even a toying with irony; instead, it acts like a lightning flash, illuminating the night. The parable is now irresistible and self-sufficient. It is now a text, a preaching-text. It provides people with a context for which they could *not* hope and with which they could *not* reckon. This is what is miraculous: what no one sees, he already hears: his *call* by God.[18]

Jüngel invested parables with similar significance. The parables are not *about* the kingdom and hence the search for a *tertium comparationis* is doomed from the outset. Rather, "the Kingdom

---

[15] Amos Niven Wilder, *The Language of the Gospel: Early Christian Rhetoric* (New York: 1964) 80. There are some precedents to this view: e.g., Günther Bornkamm, *Jesus of Nazareth* (New York: Harper & Row: 1960) 69: "The parables are the preaching itself and are not merely serving the purpose of a lesson which is quite independent of them."

[16] Wilder, *Language of the Gospel* 93.

[17] Ernst Fuchs, *Studies of the Historical Jesus* (SBT 1/42; Naperville and London: 1964) 220-221; Eta Linnemann, *Parables of Jesus: Introduction and Exposition* (London: 1975) 30-33.

[18] Ernst Fuchs, "Was wird in der Exegese des Neuen Testaments interpretiert?" in *Zur Frage nach dem historischen Jesus*, Gesammelte Aufsätze. 2 (Tübingen: 1960) 290-291 (emphasis original).

comes to speech *in* the parable *as* a parable."[19] Viewed from the
vantage of the beginning, a mustard seed is nothing. But when
seen from the vantage of the result, the power of the result is seen
to be at work in the beginning. Analogously,

> the power of the coming Kingdom of God already defines the present.
> The parable in which the present is expressed is related to the unseen
> beginnings of Kingdom. But the power of the coming Kingdom of God
> is there in the parable....Confident in the power of the Kingdom that is
> already at work in the unseen beginning, Jesus can venture to gather
> people with the parable of the mustard, to call them for the Kingdom,
> with the result that those who have been called themselves belong to
> the beginning of that miraculous end.[20]

While the New Hermeneutic advocated by Fuchs and his students
did not find a permanent footing, the view that the parables
function as autonomous preaching or revelatory texts became part
of the *sensus communis*. Robert W. Funk crystallized this
consensus when he described the parables as *metaphors*. Jülicher
was right to reject allegorical interpretation, and Dodd and
Jeremias were correct in resisting the reduction of the parables to a
single moralizing point and in asserting the provocative and argumentative character of parables. But for Jülicher, Dodd and
Jeremias, the parables nonetheless were thought to yield *ideas*.
This search for the *tertium comparationis* of the parable presupposes a logic of predication, not the logic of metaphor.
"Metaphor", writes Funk, "raises the potential for new meaning.
Metaphor redirects attention, not to this or that attribute but, by
means of imaginative shock, to a circumspective whole that presents itself as focalized in this or that thing or event."[21] Since
Funk's initial discussion, scholarship has identified the several
ways in which Jesus' parables depart from conventional patterns
of plot[22] or use imagery in unusual ways.[23] It is precisely these

---

[19] Eberhard Jüngel, *Paulus und Jesus: Eine Untersuchung zur Präzisierung der
Frage nach dem Ursprung der Christologie*, 5. Aufl. (HUTh 2; Tübingen: 1979)
135: "Die Basileia kommet *im* Gleichnis *als* Gleichnis zur Sprache" (emphasis
original). For this reason, Jüngel refuses to distinguish between the imagery
(*Bildhälfte*) and the subject (*Sachhälfte*).

[20] *Ibid.* 153-154.

[21] Robert W. Funk, *Language, Hermeneutic, and Word of God* (New York:
1966) 138.

[22] For example, John Dominic Crossan (*Finding is the First Act: Trove
Folktales and Jesus' Treasure Parable* [Semeia Supplements 9; Philadelphia:
1979] 89) notes that the parable of the Treasure departs from plot conventions of
other trove stories by locating the treasure on someone else's land. See also
Robert W. Funk, "Participant and Plot in the Narrative Parables of Jesus" in

unusual features that resist any ideational reduction and which constitute the "parabolic" dimension of parables. Funk concludes:

> the parables as pieces of everydayness have an unexpected "turn" in them which looks through the commonplace to a new view of reality. This "turn" may be overt in the form of a surprising development in the narrative, an extravagant exaggeration, a paradox; or it may lurk below the surface in the so-called transference of judgment for which the parable calls. In either case the listener is led through the parable into a strange world where everything is familiar yet radically different.[24]

Between Jesus and the Parables in Q: Three Puzzles

1. If one accepts the current assessment of the nature and function of Jesus' parables, a number of puzzles present themselves when we turn to the gospels and Q. First, the "parabolic" character of the parables of Jesus was lost, overlooked and overlaid with other meanings almost immediately. It did not take several generations for these lively and subversive stories to be allegorized or converted into example stories; this happened in the synoptic gospels themselves. This means, of course, that in order to use the parables to reconstruct the "original" message of Jesus one must

---

Parables and Presence: Forms of the New Testament Tradition (Philadelphia: 1982) 35-54; *idem*, "Parable, Paradox, and Power: The Prodigal Samaritan" in *ibid*. 55-65.

[23] See, e.g., Bernard Brandon Scott, *Hear Then the Parable: A Commentary on the Parables of Jesus* [Minneapolis: 1989] 379-387) who argues that the Mustard Seed associates the kingdom of God with something small, insignificant and unclean. In regard to the same parable, Douglas E. Oakman (*Jesus and the Economic Questions of His Day* [Studies in the Bible and Early Christianity 8; Lewiston, NY: 1986] 127-128) notes that the mustard seed was a weed and hence the parable creates the spectre of a threat to the current order of production. See also Robert W. Funk, "Beyond Criticism in Quest of Literacy: The Parable of the Leaven," *Interp*. 25 (1971) 149-170.

[24] Funk, *Language* 161. The recent literature recognizing the metaphoric character of parables is vast. See, e.g., John Dominic Crossan, *In Parables: The Challenge of the Historical Jesus* (New York: 1973); *idem, The Dark Interval: Towards a Theology of Story* (Niles, IL: 1975); Dan Otto Via, *The Parables: Their Literary and Existential Dimension* (Philadelphia: 1967); Sallie McFague, *Speaking in Parables: A Study in Metaphor and Theology* (Philadelphia: 1975); Madeleine Boucher, *The Mysterious Parable: A Literary Study* (CBQ.S 6; Washington: 1977); Amos Niven Wilder, *Jesus' Parables and the War of Myths: Essays on Imagination in the Scripture*, ed. James Breech (Philadelphia: 1982); James Breech, *The Silence of Jesus: The Authentic Voice of the Historical Man* (Philadelphia: 1983); Scott, *Hear Then the Parable*.

be prepared to posit a kind of resilience and resistance on the part of the parables which allowed them to be put to other uses without their original nature being thereby irretrievably lost.

It is not much of an exaggeration to say that *none* of the parables in the Synoptics or—as will be seen below—in the Sayings Gospel Q is presented *as* a parable, i.e., "parabolically". Thus while Mark reports the tradition that "Jesus spoke in parables" (4:2, 11, 33-34), he construes the parables as riddles, in need of decoding. Burton Mack comments:

> The odd thing about the collection of parables in Mark 4 is that, with the exception of the explanation that the parables refer to the kingdom of God, Jesus' teaching according to Mark consisted only of parables. This indicates more than astute observation on Mark's part. He was not taking up the parables because he was impressed with the effective function of parabolic discourse as modern parable theory purports. He was not suggesting that Jesus' parables inaugurated the kingdom. The parables were about the kingdom, but they did not function "parabolically". Their "secret" was known only to those already on the "inside" of the kingdom by means of explanation. For those outside, the meaning of the parables remained a mystery.[25]

For the Sayings Gospel comprehension of the parables does not serve as a test to divide insiders from outsiders, although Q also bases a distinction between insiders ("the simple") and outsiders ("the sages") on the communication of secret revelation (Q 10:21-22). But like Mark, the Sayings Gospel apparently remembers that Jesus was (among other things) a parabler and seeks to incorporate parables into its discourses. Q does not elevate discourse in parables to the programmatic level of Mk 4:11, 33-34. And while two pairs of parables are found in Q (13:18-19, 20-21; 15:4-7, 8-10), they are not grouped into a parabolic discourse paralleling Mark 4 or Matthew 13. In fact, Q does not single out "parables" or any other genre of sayings as characteristic of Jesus' discourse. Nevertheless, while Q treats parables somewhat differently than Mark, it is also true that just as in Mark, Q's parables do not maintain their putative original "parabolic" function. Instead, they function for the most part as demonstrative "proofs" and ornaments with both exemplary and allegorical features.

2. This is not the only curiosity concerning the parables in Q. A second notable fact concerns the term παραβολή itself. This is

[25] Burton L. Mack, *A Myth of Innocence: Mark and Christian Origins* (Philadelphia: 1988) 156-157.

nowhere securely attested in Q. Although the term occurs in Q contexts, it is redactional in most. Matthew's introduction of the Mustard and the Leaven with the formula ἄλλην παραβολὴν παρέθηκεν ἐλάλησεν αὐτοῖς (λέγων) (13:31, 33) is probably due to Matthew rather than to Q.[26] This formula is the same as that used to introduce the preceding Parable of the Weeds in 13:24 and is perhaps partially influenced by Mark's πῶς ὁμοιώσωμεν τὴν βασιλείαν τοῦ θεοῦ ἢ ἐν τίνι αὐτὴν παραβολῇ θῶμεν; (4:30). While Luke takes over Mark's use of παραβολή in Lk 8:4, 9, 10, 11 (Mk 4:2, 10, 11, 13), he does not use the term when introducing the parables of the Mustard and the Leaven in chap. 13—in a Q context. The only other Q parable introduced by Matthew as a παραβολή is the Great Supper (22:1-10 [11-14]) where, again, the Lukan parable lacks the term.[27] Matthew's placement of the parable directly after the parables of the Two Sons (21:28-32) and the Tenants (21:33-45) suggests that his introductory formula, ὁ Ἰησοῦς πάλιν εἶπεν ἐν παραβολαῖς αὐτοῖς λέγων, is a redactional connection.[28]

Luke also uses the term παραβολή in connection with Q materials, but as with Matthew, the use of the term is suspect. Q scholarship is nearly unanimous that Lk 6:39a (εἶπεν δὲ καὶ παραβολὴν αὐτοῖς), found in the middle of a sequence in Q's opening speech, is due to Lukan redaction.[29] Similarly, the same is

---

[26] Cf. Mt 21:33, where Matthew has transformed Mark's καὶ ἤρξατο αὐτοῖς ἐν παραβολαῖς λαλεῖν (12:1) into ἄλλην παραβολὴν ἀκούσατε. See the convincing analysis by Jack D. Kingsbury, *The Parables of Jesus in Matthew 13: A Study in Redaction-Criticism* (London: 1969) 12-13; also Rudolf Laufen, *Die Doppelüberlieferungen der Logienquelle und des Markusevangeliums* (BBB 54; Konigstein: 1980) 174; Robert H. Gundry, *Matthew: A Commentary on his Literary and Theological Art* (Grand Rapids: 1982) 263, 265, 268; William D. Davies and Dale C. Allison, *A Critical and Exegetical Commentary on Matthew VIII-XVIII* (ICC; Edinburgh: 1991) 411, 417, 422.

[27] Lk 14:7, however, introduces the hortatory material preceding the parable of the Great Supper with the formula, Ἔλεγεν δὲ πρὸς τοὺς κεκλημένους παραβολήν, ἐπέχων πῶς τὰς πρωτοκλισίας ἐξελέγοντο, λέγων πρὸς αὐτούς.

[28] Siegfried Schulz, *Q: Die Spruchquelle der Evangelisten* (Zürich: 1972) 392. Gundry (*Matthew* 432) notes that "in parables" is a stereotyped Matthaean formula but suggests that the terms might "have been suggested by the omitted material leading up to the parable (see Lk 14:7)".

[29] See Shawn Carruth's database on Q 6:39 and the responses by Rees Conrad Douglas and James M. Robinson, prepared for the International Q Project ("The International Q Project Work Sessions 12-14 July, 22 November 1991," *JBL* 111 [1992] 500-508). Among the most important arguments is the fact that the phrase also occurs redactionally at Lk 5:36; 20:9, 19; 21:29 and in non-Markan contexts at 4:23; 12:6, 41; 13:6; 14:7; 15:3; 18:1, 9; 19:11. δὲ καὶ is also

true of the question interjected by Peter in Lk 12:41: εἶπεν δὲ ὁ Πέτρος, Κύριε, πρὸς ἡμᾶς τὴν παραβολὴν ταύτην λέγεις ἢ καὶ πρὸς πάντας; Since this question does not appear in the parallel Matthaean passage (Mt 24:45-51) and because it betrays various Lukanisms, it too is normally treated as editorial.[30] Luke introduces the parable of the Lost Sheep with the formula εἶπεν δὲ πρὸς αὐτοὺς τὴν παραβολὴν ταύτην λέγων (15:3) where the Matthaean parallel employs a completely different introduction (18:12: τί ὑμῖν δοκεῖ;). A similar introduction is found in Lk 12:16 (εἶπεν δὲ παραβολὴν πρὸς αὐτοὺς λέγων), introducing the story of the Rich Farmer, which some ascribe to Q.[31] But the presence of clearly Lukan features, such as the use of a verb of speaking followed by πρός[32] and εἶπεν δέ,[33] makes it extremely precarious to ascribe either introduction to Q.[34] Finally, the word "parable" appears in the introduction to the Parable of the Entrusted Money (Lk 19:11). But as was the case with the other Lukan Q parables, the Matthaean parallel lacks a corresponding introduction that mentions parables.[35] It is obvious that this verse is replete with Lukanisms, including the use of the genitive abso-

---

Lukan: see Henry J. Cadbury, *The Style and Literary Method of Luke* (HThS 6; Cambridge: 1920) 146.

[30] For a tabulation of arguments, see Philip Sellew, "Reconstruction of Q 12:33-59," *SBLASP* 26 (1987) 636; John S. Kloppenborg, *Q Parallels: Synopsis, Critical Notes, & Concordance* (Foundations & Facets. New Testament; Sonoma, CA: 1988) 140.

[31] See below, n. 84 and Kloppenborg, *Q Parallels* 128 for a tabulation of opinion.

[32] See Cadbury, *Style and Literary Method* 202-203; Joachim Jeremias, *Die Sprache des Lukasevangeliums: Redaktion und Tradition im Nicht-Markusstoff des dritten Evangeliums* (Göttingen: 1980) 33.

[33] εἶπεν δὲ αὐτῷ/οῖς / πρὸς αὐτόν is redactional at Lk 6:9, 39; 8:25; 9:9, 14, 20, 50; 11:2, 39; 18:19; 20:41; 22:67 and is found in unparalleled material at 1:13, 34; 4:26; 7:48, 50; 9:61, 62; 10:18, 28; 12:15, 16, 20; 13:7; 16:31; 17:1, 22; 19:9; 22:36; 24:17, 44. It appears in Q contexts at 4:3 (Mt 4:3: καὶ προσελθὼν ὁ πειράζων εἶπεν αὐτῷ); 12:22 (diff Mt); and 15:3. See also Jeremias, *Sprache* 33.

[34] Thus, with regard to Lk 15:3: Schulz, *Spruchquelle* 387. On both formulations, see Joseph A. Fitzmyer, *The Gospel According to Luke* (AB 28-28A; Garden City, N.Y.: 1981-85) 599, 973, 1076; I. Howard Marshall, *The Gospel of Luke: A Commentary on the Greek Text* (Exeter: 1978) 523, 600; Jeremias, *Sprache* 215, 245.

[35] Matthew has Ὥσπερ γὰρ ἄνθρωπος (25:14).

lute,[36] an articular infinitive as object of a preposition,[37] and the journey motif. Thus Lk 19:11 cannot be ascribed to Q.[38]

We conclude, therefore, that the term "parable" was probably not used by the Sayings Gospel to designate any of its sayings. Even though Q represents Jesus as speaking in parables, it does not call attention to them as "parables" (or anything else for that matter). In the Synoptic tradition—which has forty-eight of the fifty occurrences of παραβολή in the New Testament—the strongest influence was Mark. Matthew's usage was influenced by Mark's, and even though Luke displays greater scope in his use of the term, there is no evidence that this was due to the Sayings Gospel; his usage too derives ultimately from Mark. It could be noted additionally that our other principal source of parables, the *Gospel of Thomas*, lacks the term entirely.

This raises a methodological point. What materials should be treated as "parables" in Q? Only those stories that modern parables research has identified as parables? In Q this would mean the Wise and Faithful Servant, the Mustard, the Leaven, the Feast, the Lost Sheep, the Entrusted Money, and possibly the Rich Farmer and the Lost Drachma.[39] Or should we include other materials as well? Modern definitions of parables are usually much more restrictive than ancient usage. In fact "parable" is not a discrete genre at all. If one views the Sayings Gospel through the lens of ancient literary and rhetorical theory, it clearly contains more than just eight "parables" even if it refrains from the use of any technical designations.

---

[36] Cadbury, *Style and Literary Method* 133-134.

[37] This is a favourite Lukan construction, appearing at 1:8, 21; 2:4, 6, 21, 27, 43; 3:21; 4:10; 5:1, 12, 17; 6:48; 8:5 [=Mk], 6 [=Mk], 40, 42; 9:7, 18, 29, 33, 34, 36, 51; 10:35, 38; 11:1, 8, 27, 37; 12:5, 15; 14:1; 17:11, 14; 18:1, 5, 35; 19:11, 15; 22:15, 20; 23:8; 24:4, 15, 30, 51; Acts 1:3; 2:1; 3:19, 26; 4:2, 5; 7:4, 19; 10:41; 11:15; 12:20; 15:13; 18:2, 3, 28; 19:1, 21; 20:1; 23:15; 27:4. Only twice is it taken from Mark.

[38] Thus Schulz, *Spruchquelle* 288; Marshall, *Luke* 703 (who regards εἶπεν παραβολήν as Lukan but thinks that other portions of v. 11 may be pre-Lukan); Fitzmyer, *Luke* 1231. Jeremias (*Sprache* 277-278) notes that ἀκούω in the absolute genitive is only attested in the Lukan corpus; προστίθημι is a favourite Lukan word; εἶπεν παραβολήν is Lukan, as are the articular infinitive, the form Ἰερουσαλήμ, and παραχρῆμα.

[39] Bernard Brandon Scott's definition of a parable as "a *mashal* that employs a short narrative fiction to reference a transcendent symbol" ("Essaying the Rock: The Authenticity of the Jesus Parable Tradition," *Forum* 2/1 [1986] 3; similarly, *Hear Then the Parable* 34) excludes not only the Tower Builder (Lk 14:30) and the King Going to War (Lk 14:31-32) but apparently also the Builders (Q 6:47-49) and the Children in the Agora (Q 7:31-32).

Marsh McCall observes that for Aristotle "the identifying features of the παραβολή do not...seem to include a particular genre. This is indicated both by the careless phrasing of the illustration of παραβολή [in *Rhet.* 2.20.1393b4-8] and by the similar form given to the surrounding illustrations of historical examples and fables (λόγοι)."[40] "Comparisons" (or "parables") belong to the larger class of παραδείγματα (examples), subdivided into παραδείγματα (historical anecdotes)[41] and manufactured examples, the latter group being further divided into "comparisons" (παραβολαί) and fables (λόγοι).[42] Quintilian's discussion of *similitudo*, the usual Latin translation for παραβολή, makes it clear that these need not entail full narratives and may be nonmetaphorical in character.[43] While the contemporary definition of parable, which excludes nonnarrative comparisons, may be appropriate to a discussion of the parables of Jesus in so far as they were orally performed and had to be capable of oral transmission, when it comes to documents like Q (or the synoptic gospels), we enter the realm of literary composition where no such restrictions apply. It is Aristotle's or Quintilian's broader literary and rhetorical definition that should be employed.

Strictly speaking, this broader definition would qualify the comparison of the Q "workers" with sheep going among wolves (Q 10:3) as a "parable."[44] Nevertheless, there is some warrant for distinguishing between brief similes and longer, more nearly narrative, comparisons,[45] the latter more closely approximating

---

[40] Marsh H. McCall, *Ancient Rhetorical Theories of Simile and Comparison* (Loeb Classical Monographs; Cambridge, MA: 1969) 27.

[41] Both Aristotle and Quintilian use the terms παραδείγματα or *exempla* both in the broad sense of examples and in the narrower sense of historical anecdotes.

[42] Aristotle, *Rhet.* 2.20.1393a28-29. Similarly, Quintilian 5.11.1: Tertium genus ex iis, quae extrinsecus adducuntur in causam, Graeci vocant παράδειγμα, quo nomine et generaliter usi sunt in omni similium adpositone et specialiter in iis, quae rerum gestarum auctoritate nituntur.

[43] Quintilian (5.11.22-24) restricts *similitudo* to a nonmetaphorical analogy where the subject matter closely approximates the subject of the proof and prefers this to the most common usage of the term, which allows for more disparate comparisons, sometimes metaphorical in character. On this, see McCall, *Ancient Rhetorical Theories* 197-199.

[44] Quintilian (8.3.74-75) classifies brief similes as the comparisons (*similitudines*) usable in ornamentation: "as the soil is improved and rendered more fertile by culture, so is the mind by education" and "as physicians amputate mortified limbs, so must we also lop away foul and dangerous criminals, even though they be bound to us by ties of blood."

[45] Demetrius (*On Style* 89) distinguishes between παραβολή and the briefer εἰκασία, advising that the former is poetic and should be used in prose only with

historical anecdotes and thus having greater force as proofs. In Q, in addition to the eight fully narrative parables listed above, at least the Builders (6:47-49) and the Children in the Agora (7:31-32) would also seem to belong.

The consequences of this expansion of the list of parables of Jesus should not be underestimated. Not only are authentic parables of Jesus presented in a way that does nothing to underscore their revelatory (Wilder) or kerygmatic (Bornkamm, Fuchs) or extravagant (Funk) character; they are also placed alongside other "parables"—the Builders and the Children in the Agora or the simile of sheep among wolves—which are anything but extravagant or shocking. A new discursive context has been achieved in Q.

3. The third puzzle has to do with the connection of Q's parables with the kingdom of God. Since Jülicher it has been taken as virtually self-evident that parables were about the kingdom. Yet the kingdom is mentioned in only two Q parables, the Mustard (13:18-19) and the Leaven (13:20-21); it is missing in the other eight.[46] There is little doubt that Jesus' activity had in some way to do with the kingdom of God. Yet it is remarkable how few of the parables—not only in Q but parables in general—directly invoke the kingdom.

The association of the kingdom with parables, like the use of the term "parable" itself, is due in part to the construction of Mark 4. The entire discourse of Mark 4, which contains three of Mark's six parables, is controlled by the statement ὑμῖν τὸ μυστήριον δέδοται τῆς βασιλείας τοῦ θεοῦ ἐκείνοις δὲ τοῖς ἔξω ἐν παραβολαῖς τὰ πάντα γίνεται (4:11). With this Mark problematizes parabolic discourse as he problematizes Christology and the reception of the kingdom. Parables become riddles, just as the kingdom and the identity of Jesus become mysteries for insiders alone to grasp. Even though the parable of the Sower (4:3-9) lacks an introductory formula like Mk 4:26 and 4:30 which associates the parable with the kingdom, the framing of chap. 4 nevertheless makes the association patent.

---

care. Quintilian may reflect the same distinction when he refers to brief similes (sunt et illae breves) that can be used in ornamentation (8.3.81). See McCall, *Ancient Rhetorical Theories* 148, 227.

[46] I.e., the Builders (6:47-49); the Children in the Agora (7:31-32); the Rich Farmer (12:16-20); the Stewards (12:42b-46); the Feast (14:16-24); the Lost Sheep (15:4-7); the Lost Drachma (15:8-10); and the Entrusted Money (19:12-26).

Matthew, in particular, reinforces Mark's connection between parables and the kingdom. He takes over and enhances the terminology of Mark 4.[47] When he introduces parables elsewhere in the gospel, it is with the "kingdom formula" (18:23; 20:1; 22:2; 25:1). Or, he inserts parables into contexts where the Kingdom is discussed.[48] In fact, so strong is Matthew's association of parables with the Kingdom that all of the "M" parables—i.e., those for which he does not depend upon written sources (the Planted Weeds, the Treasure, the Pearl, the Fishnet, the Vineyard Workers, the Unmerciful Servant and the Ten Maidens)—are introduced with some variation of the formula ὡμοιώθη ἡ βασιλεία τῶν οὐρανῶν ἀνθρώπῳ. Only the parable of the Children in the Agora (11:16-17) is not directly linked with the kingdom, although in this case too, the kingdom is mentioned in the immediately preceding verses (Mt 11:12-13).

Luke, by contrast, suffers under no compulsion to associate parables with the Kingdom. He takes over Mk 4:11 (Lk 8:10) and Q's introductions in Lk 13:18-19 and 13:20-21. Elsewhere, however, he is content to introduce the parables with a range of formulae, none of them mentioning the kingdom. If there is an association of the parable with the kingdom at all, it is by way of contrast. The parable of the Rich Farmer (12:16-21), for example, epitomizes conduct which is just the opposite of "seeking the kingdom" (Lk 12:31); the parable of the Great Supper is told in response to—and as a warning about—the enthusiasm implicit in Lk 14:15; and the parable of the Entrusted Money functions to correct the *Naherwartung* implied in Lk 19:11.

---

[47] Matthew takes over the βασιλεία vocabulary from his sources at 13:11 (Mk 4:11); 13:31 (Mk 4:30; Q 13:18); 13:33 (Q 13:20), but adds it at 13:19, 38, 41, 43, 52, introducing parables with the formula ὡμοιώθη ἡ βασιλεία τῶν οὐρανῶν (13:24) or ὁμοία ἐστὶν ἡ βασιλεία τῶν οὐρανῶν (13:44, 45, 47).

[48] The parable of the Builders (7:27-29) is interpreted by Matthew as an illustration of who will "enter" the kingdom (Mt 7:21). The parable of the Lost Sheep (Mt 18:10, 12-14) is directly related by Matthew to the ecclesiological discussion of greatness in the kingdom (18:1, 3, 4, 23); the application parable of the Two Sons (21:28-32) mentions entry into the kingdom (21:31) and immediately precedes the parable of the Tenants, to which Matthew has added a statement about the kingdom (21:43); and the parable of the Ten Maidens (25:1-13) is placed immediately after the parable of the Faithful and Unfaithful Servants (24:45-51) and immediately prior to the parable of the Talents (25:14-30). The latter begins with a formula that links it with 25:1-13 (ὥσπερ γὰρ ἄνθρωπος) and concludes with the motif of exclusion into outer darkness (25:30), a phrase used earlier with respect to exclusion from the kingdom (8:11-12). It is followed by the story of the last judgment, which refers to inheriting the kingdom (25:34).

Were it not for the *Gospel of Thomas* (hereafter, *GThom*), one might suspect that the connection of parables with the kingdom was based on an extrapolation from the occurrence of the kingdom formula in two Q parables, the Mustard and the Leaven, the first of which Mark used. The *GThom*, however, introduces eight of its fourteen parables with the kingdom formula: the Mustard Seed (20); the Planted Weeds (57); the Pearl (76); the Leaven (96); the Empty Jar (97); the Assassin (98); the Lost Sheep (107) and the Treasure (109). The appearance of the formula in Thomas' version of the Planted Weeds, the Pearl and the Treasure suggests that the formula may not be entirely the work of Matthew in Matthew 13.[49] While the *GThom* agrees with the Sayings Gospel in interpreting the Leaven as a kingdom parable, and with Q and Mark with respect to the Mustard Seed, it is also worthwhile noting that Q and the *GThom* concur in not using the Kingdom formula for the Rich Farmer (Q 12:16-20; *GThom* 63) and the Feast (Q 14:16-24; *GThom* 64) on the one hand, and that Q lacks the kingdom formula used in *GThom*'s version of the Lost Sheep (Q 15:4-7; *GThom* 107).

In view of the above tabulation, it does not seem likely that the kingdom formula was original to every parable even if it is securely attested in the case of the Mustard Seed and the Leaven. This does not mean that other (or all?) parables were not in some way about the kingdom at the stage of their earliest oral performance. But it does imply that this connection with the kingdom would have had to be part of the larger linguistic framework of oral performance. At any rate, when the parables are encountered in Q (as well as Mark 12–13 and Luke), most of this framework, if it ever existed, has been lost.

The Function of "Parables" in Q

Each of the ten parables of Q diplays signs of having been co-opted to serve the compositional ends of the document. The parables that belong to the formative layer of Q have been sub-

---

[49] It is common to argue that in the Fishnet (*GThom* 8), *prome* ("the man") replaced an original "kingdom". Thus Jeremias, *Parables of Jesus* 101 n. 56, 201; Stevan L. Davies, *The Gospel of Thomas and Christian Wisdom* (New York: 1983) 9. Against this, Ron Cameron ("Parable and Interpretation in the Gospel of Thomas," *Forum* 2/2 [1986] 29) has argued that the Fishnet is rather a wisdom parable "told about the discovery of one's destiny".

ordinated to the mainly didactic thrust of this stratum,[50] while those belonging to the second main redaction have been employed as allegorical illustrations of the failures of "this generation" or to embellish and dramatize the destablizing of the cosmos by the Day of the Son of Man (hereafter, "the Day").

1. Parables in the Secondary Layer

Four parables belong to this layer, Q 7:31-32; 12:42b-46; 14:16-24 and 19:12-26 and in each case, the parable has become part of a more extended argument.

The Children in the Agora

What is initially striking about the parable in Q 7:31-32 is that the introductory formula, τίνι (δὲ) ὁμοιώσω τὴν γενεὰν ταύτην, καὶ τίνι εἰσὶν ὅμοιοι; resembles the introductory formulae to the parables of the the Mustard (Q 13:18-19; Mk 4:30) and the Leaven (Q 13:20-21). But whereas those parables are about the kingdom, Q 7:31-32 offers a polemical commentary on "this generation". The parable itself is cleverly conceived, as Wendy J. Cotter has shown, depicting the children (παιδία) incongruously as *seated* in the ἀγορά like judges, and "summoning" (προσφωνοῦντα) their fellows.[51] Read in this way, the parable becomes a burlesque, mocking the self-importance of "this generation" by comparing it with children play-acting as judges in the agora.

What follows in Q shows that it was interested in a somewhat more specific application of the parable. John and Jesus, depicted as τέκνα Σοφίας, are set alongside the characters in the parable in an attempt to capitalize on the dynamics of the parable and to further Q's polemic against "this generation". This alignment is not entirely without its ambiguities, however. John, an ascetic, is presumably aligned with the first set of children and Jesus with the second set. It is not clear whether Jesus and John are meant to be

---

[50] On this distinction, see John S. Kloppenborg, *The Formation of Q: Trajectories in Ancient Wisdom Collections* (Studies in Antiquity and Christianity; Philadelphia: 1987); *idem*, "The Sayings Gospel Q: Literary and Stratigraphic Problems" in *ANRW* II.25.6 (forthcoming 1994).

[51] Wendy Cotter, "The Parable of the Children in the Market Place, Q (Luke) 7:31-35: An Examination of the Parable's Image and Significance," *NovT* 29 (1987) 289-304.

identified with those who call—in which case, there is an incongruity between the ascetic John and the first set of "piping" children and between the convivial Jesus and the dirge-players. Alternatively, John and Jesus may be identified, respectively, with those who refuse to dance and and those who refuse to mourn. However, the designation of John and Jesus as children of Sophia might lead us to expect an active role (i.e., summoning) for the two rather than a passive one. Moreover, the explanations that John might be demon-possessed and Jesus was a glutton and a drunk do not square in any obvious way with either the two summons or the two refusals.[52]

The imposition of an allegorical code suggests that Q was either unwilling or unable to leave the witticism stand on its own. Perhaps it is a little like feeling obliged to explain a joke; in any event, the appending of 7:33-35 illustrates the thoroughly literary and scribal character of Q. The parable has been preserved only by turning it to the main purposes of the secondary redactional layer: polemics and defence of the image of the founder(s). Q 7:33-35 shifts attention from the burlesque of the parable to an exegesis of the absurd way in which "this generation" has regarded John and Jesus, concluding with a characterization of John and Jesus as children of Sophia.[53]

The Great Supper

Allegorical application can also be seen in Q's use of the parable of the Great Supper (Q 14:16-24). The reconstruction of this parable is difficult, since Matthew especially has taken great liberties in recasting the parable as an allegory of salvation history and Luke as paradigm illustrating the preceding moralizing say-

---

[52] For a sketch of the positions on all sides of this debate, see Dieter Zeller, "Die Bildlogik des Gleichnisses Mt 11 16f / Lk 7 31f," *ZNW* 68 (1977) 252-257; Kloppenborg, *Formation of Q* 110-112.

[53] The woes in Q provide a partial analogy. The seven woes, in particular those regarding tithing and the washing of vessels, have the challenge / riposte character of oral culture. A much more learned perspective is achieved with the addition of Q 11:49-51 which, as Gerd Theissen rightly observes, presumes a knowledge that Zechariah was the last of prophets to be killed and assumes that 2 Chronicles is the last book of the collection of scriptures. See Gerd Theissen, *The Gospels in Context: Social and Political History in the Synoptic Tradition* (Minneapolis: 1991) 228. On the woes, see Leif E. Vaage, "The Woes in Q (and Matthew and Luke): Deciphering the Rhetoric of Criticism" in *SBLASP* 27 (1988) 582-607.

ings (Lk 14:7-14). Nevertheless, the agreements between Matthew and Luke indicate that an initial invitation was refused, that the householder reacted in anger (Q 14:21), and that a second invitation to others "in the roads" was successful.

By itself, the parable does not provide many clues as to how it would have been read in Q. The immediate context, however, suggests an allegorical reading. Two of the preceding sayings in Q are Q 13:28-29,[54] announcing a pilgrimage of those from east and west to participate in God's great supper, and Q 13:34-35, in which a divine figure, presumably Sophia, laments her rejection by Jerusalem and announces the desolation of that city. Given this context, it is difficult to avoid imposing an allegorical code upon the parable of the Great Supper and reading the first set of invitees in light of 13:34-35, and the second set in light of 13:28-29. This allegorizing of the parable becomes even clearer if Lk 14:24, λέγω γὰρ ὑμῖν ὅτι οὐδεὶς τῶν ἀνδρῶν ἐκείνων τῶν κεκλημένων γεύσεταί μου τοῦ δείπνου, can be ascribed to Q,[55] since this amounts to Jesus' own commentary, in which he identifies the parable's supper with "my supper", presumably that mentioned in 13:28-29.

A comparison with the version of the parable in *GThom* (64) is telling, for there is no evidence of allegorizing at all. At best, there is a slight moralizing tendency, witnessed in the final statement, "buyers and merchants will not enter the places of my Father." In Q, by contrast, the parable is preserved in the context of Q's campaign against "this generation" where it is used to dramatize the preceding polemical sayings, and to place Jesus and the Jesus movement, unsuccessful at summoning "this generation", on the side of Sophia and at table with the heroes of Israel, Abraham, Isaac and Jacob.

---

[54] Q 13:28-29: ⟦πολλοὶ⟧ ἀπὸ ἀνατολῶν καὶ δυσμῶν ἥξουσιν καὶ ἀνακλιθήσονται ⟦ ⟧ μετὰ Ἀβραὰμ καὶ Ἰσαὰκ καὶ Ἰακὼβ ἐν τῇ βασιλείᾳ τοῦ θεοῦ, ⟦ὑμ<εῖ>ς⟧ δὲ ⟦ ⟧ ἐκβ.λ⟦ηθήσ<εσθε>⟧...ἔξω...: ἐκεῖ ἔσται ὁ κλαυθμὸς καὶ ὁ βρυγμὸς τῶν ὀδόντων. Reconstruction: International Q Project, "The International Q Project Work Session 16 November 1990," *JBL* 110 (1991) 497.

[55] Thus Schulz, *Spruchquelle* 397-399; Wolfgang Schenk, *Synopse zur Redenquelle der Evangelien: Q-Synopse und Rekonstruktion in deutscher Übersetzung* (Düsseldorf: 1981) 108; Athanasius Polag, *Fragmenta Q: Textheft zur Logienquelle* (Neukirchen-Vluyn: 1979) 70 (in spite of the Lukanism ἀνήρ). In favour of this, it might be pointed out that Q elsewhere employs λέγω ὑμῖν statements to return from one level of discourse to Jesus' own commentary (Q 11:51b; 13:35b). See Kloppenborg, "The Sayings Gospel Q: Literary and Stratigraphic Problems."

The Faithful and Unfaithful Servants

While the first two parables are directed to polemical and apologetic ends, the parables of the Faithful and Unfaithful Servants (Q 12:42b-46) and the Entrusted Money (19:12-26), adopting the metaphor of household management, trade on apocalyptic fears in order to dramatize the importance of embracing the ethic of the Q folk.

The illative particle ἄρα in Q 12:42 shows that this parable was used by Q to illustrate Q 12:40. It is unclear whether the parable of the Faithful and Unfaithful Servants was an authentic parable that was secondarily allegorized[56] or whether it was a creation (in whole or in part) of the early Church.[57] The debate has turned on whether the phrase χρονίζει ὁ κύριός μου (12:45) can be anything other than an allusion to the delay of "the Day". But three other considerations favour the possibility of a secondary creation. First, the parable lacks an independent parallel. Second, it appears to be custom-tailored to the redactional verse 12:40,[58] elucidating the meaning of γίνεσθε ἕτοιμοι and adapting the phrase ὅτι ᾗ ὥρᾳ οὐ δοκεῖτε ὁ υἱὸς τοῦ ἀνθρώπου ἔρχεται in 12:46. Finally, the servant's musings in 12:45a as well as the statements in 12:43,

---

[56] Jeremias (*Parables of Jesus* 55-57) suggests that the original addressees were scribes. Marshall (*Luke* 534-535) thinks that the parable is authentic and was precisely Jesus' own teachings to his disciples regarding the parousia. Scott, *Hear Then the Parable* 210-212: "This parable makes the simple point that a servant who can be trusted only when his master is present is a worthless servant" (212). Alfons Weiser (*Die Knechtsgleichnisse der synoptischen Evangelien* [StANT 29; München: 1971] 204-214) also argues that the core is authentic.

[57] Erich Grässer, *Das Problem der Parusieverzögerung in den synoptischen Evangelien und in der Apostelgeschichte*, 3. Aufl. (BZNW 22; Berlin and New York: 1977) 84-95, especially 92: "Jedenfalls ist aber der Zug [to the delay] im jetzigen Gleichnis so fest mit dem Ganzen verbunden und der Bezug auf die Verzögerung der Parusie so deutlich, da man darin schwerlich einen unbetonten Nebenzug erblicken kann." Dieter Lührmann, *Die Redaktion der Logienquelle* (WMANT 33; Neukirchen-Vluyn: 1969) 70; Schulz, Spruchquelle 274. Gerhard Schneider, (*Parusiegleichnisse im Lukasevangelium* [SBS 74; Stuttgart: 1975] 28) considers the possibility that only the second part was a secondary creation.

[58] Note that a parallel to 12:40 is missing from *GThom* 21, 103. On Q 12:40, see Heinz Schürmann, "Observations on the Son of Man Title in the Speech Source: Its Occurrence in Closing and Introductory Expressions" in *The Shape of Q: Signal Essays on the Sayings Gospel*, ed. John S. Kloppenborg (Minneapolis: 1993) = "Beobachtungen zum Menschensohn-Titel in der Redenquelle" in *Gottes Reich, Jesu Geschick: Jesu ureigener Tod im Licht seiner Basileia-Verkündigung* (Freiburg and Basel: 1983) 169-170. Schürmann considers Q 12:40 to be a secondary expansion.

46 regarding the "coming" of the master do not follow from the opening of the parable. The situation outlined in Q 12:42b need not require that the master be absent at all. The appointment of a manager was normal on all large estates since owners normally preferred other activities to day-to-day supervision. Instead, 12:43, 45a and 46 are formulated with the departure-return scenario of 12:40 in view. In other words, the entire dynamics of the parable require that the master be absent and then return, something that the parable need not tell the reader, since it presupposes that s/he has seen Q 12:40. This of course means that the parable is probably a post-Easter creation. It is also worth noting that as in the parable of the Entrusted Money—also without an independent parallel—the reward mentioned involves status elevation (12:44; cf. 19:17, 19) and the punishment seems particularly brutal (12:46: διχοτομήσει!).

The parable forms part of an argument. Q takes for granted that "the Day" will come unheralded. For this reason, Q's advice is not to "watch"—that is Matthew's counsel (24:42 = MattR), presupposing the schema of Mark 13. Instead, Q advises to "be prepared." The nature of the preparation is not spelled out, either by 12:40 or by the parable, but the immediately preceding sayings would suggest that it entails embracing Q's disdain for wealth (12:33-34) and its search for the kingdom (12:31).

The allegorical identification of the ὁ κύριος of 12:46 with ὁ υἱὸς τοῦ ἀνθρώπου of 12:40 is inevitable given the close and deliberate structural similarities.[59] It does not follow, however, that Q means to allegorize all of the details of the parable, reading, for example, the servant (steward) as a "church leader" and the other servants as members of the "Q community". Nor does it follow that the parable recognizes a new situation characterized by the delay of "the Day". As Paul Hoffmann observes, the delay is not narrated objectively but is instead a (false) supposition of the manager.[60] The scenario is, in fact, quite normal: owners were

[59] This is the consensus of virtually all scholars. See most recently, Claus-Peter März, "Zur Vorgeschichte von Lk 12,35-48: Beobachtungen zur Komposition der Logientradition in der Redequelle" in *Christus bezeugen: Festschrift für Wolfgang Trilling zum 65. Geburtstag*, eds. Karl Kertelge, Traugott Holtz, and Claus-Peter März (EThSt 59; Leipzig: 1989) 175; Harry Fleddermann, "The Householder and the Servant Left in Charge" in *SBLASP* 25 (1986) 26.
[60] Paul Hoffmann (*Studien zur Theologie der Logienquelle*, 2. Aufl. [NTA NF 8; Münster: 1975] 47-48) observes that the phrase normally taken as an acknowledgement of the delay of the parousia is "in his heart" and that it "steht also im Gleichnis die Aussage des 'plötzlichen, überraschenden Kommens'

typically anxious that their managers might abuse their trust in their absence and, presumably, managers did so only when they thought that they would not be discovered.[61] Hence, while 12:42b-46 presupposes the departure-return scenario of 12:40, it is not a meditation upon a "new" situation caused by the delay of "the Day". Rather, it invokes a typical problem of agricultural management in order to dramatize just how unexpectedly "the Day" and its terrible consequences might arrive. The point is not to encourage responsible leadership within the church-household, but instead to conjure a vision of how "the Day", unforseen and unforseeable, will winnow and separate. The only means by which to avoid it is to embrace the ethos of Q.

The Entrusted Money

The parable of the Entrusted Money (Q 19:12-26) is perhaps the most difficult parable to reconstruct, since there is so little initial verbal agreement between Matthew and Luke. There is, however, agreement in the basic narrative structure (complicated by Luke's insertion of a story of a throne claimant).[62] In particular, both versions agree in indicating the distance (spatial or temporal) of the the master from the scene,[63] the third servant's characterization of the master as "harsh" (Matt: σκληρός; Luke: αὐστηρός), the castigation of the servant as "evil" and the assigning of his

---

gegenüber" (48). Hence, Hoffmann suggests that "die Verzögerung kennzeichnet die Haltung dessen, der sich auf die Botschaft von Q nicht einläßt, nicht aber notwendig einen internen Zweifel der Q-Gruppe" (*ibid*). This is part of a larger effort on Hoffmann's part to insert a third (transitional) term, "Parusieenttäuschung" (disappointment about the Parousia) between "Naherwartung" and "Parusieverzögerung". Fleddermann ("The Householder" 26) agrees that the parable is not simply about leaders but rejects Hoffmann's conclusion: "From now on...the prudent servant correctly sees the significance of the master's delay and acts on it—it is an opportunity to demonstrate his fidelity." This, however, construes the delay as objective.

[61] Authors on agricultural management suggest unannounced visits as a means for preventing such abuses. See Cato, *De agri cultura* 5.3-4 and the wideranging advice of Columella, *De re rustica* 1.7-8.

[62] See the summary of positions on vv. 12, 14-15a, 24a, 27 in Kloppenborg, *Q Parallels* 200.

[63] Matthew: ἀπεδήμησεν (25:14, 15); μετὰ δὲ πολὺν χρόνον ἔρχεται (25:19); Luke: ἐπορεύθη εἰς χώραν μακράν (19:12). In fact, Luke's introduction, in which an interlocutor supposes that the kingdom will appear παραχρῆμα also suggest that Luke presumes that the master will be absent for a long period, a supposition reinforced by the fact that two servants would require some time to make the profits described. In neither gospel, however, is a "delay" mentioned.

money to the ten-talent / mina servant. Matthew and Luke also concur by including the interpretative verse (Q 19:26) which provides a rationale for the master's seemingly harsh actions.

The appearance of independent parallels to Q 19:26 (but not to the remainder of the story[64] in Mk 4:25 and *GThom* 41 suggests that this verse was secondarily added to the story. It is worth noting that the Lukan version, like Q 14:24, introduces the interpretative saying with λέγω ὑμῖν ὅτι which, presumably, shifts the voice from the master to Jesus.[65]

The parable, whether in the Synoptics or Q, has normally been taken to be an object lesson in using time wisely and responsibly.[66] Schenk cites Wellhausen's comments on the Matthaean parable with approval: Christians "sind zum Dienst verpflichtet und nicht zur Entfaltung ihrer eigenen schönen Persönlichkeit,"[67] adding: "ein bloßes Bewahren und Verwalten ist angesichts dieses stetigen Gebers aller—der vorgegebenen, der möglichen wie der endgültigen—Gaben ein hoffnungsloses Unterfangen, das ihn betrügen und sich selbst Lügen strafen würde."[68]

What is normally missed in this story are its economic assumptions. Q is normally reconstructed following Luke's version (i.e., minas [100 drachmae] rather than talents [6000 drachmae]). The increases that are evidently expected and rewarded provide an indication of the kind of persons involved. Ten-fold or five-fold increases, while possible on a twentieth-century stock market, were conceivable in the first century only for persons who were prepared to make extremely high-risk maritime loans[69] or who

---

[64] The parable in *Gospel of the Nazarenes* 18 does not evidence an independent version of the parable, but like the rest of the *GNaz* materials is a secondary adaptation of canonical Matthew. See Philipp Vielhauer and Georg Strecker, "Jewish-Christian Gospels" in *New Testament Apocrypha. Volume One: Gospels and Related Writings*, rev. edn., ed. Wilhelm Schneemelcher (Louisville: 1991) 157-159.

[65] It is more difficult to account to Luke's insertion of λέγω ὑμῖν, which is so awkward after 19:25 and before 19:27, than it is to account for Matthew's deletion of the formula. The formula is included in the reconstructions by Schenk (*Synopse* 126); Polag (*Fragmenta* 82) and Schulz (*Spruchquelle* 292).

[66] Thus Lührmann, *Redaktion* 71; Schulz, *Spruchquelle* 294-295.

[67] Julius Wellhausen, *Das Evangelium Matthaei übersetzt und erklärt* (Berlin: 1904) 132.

[68] Schenk, *Synopse* 127-128.

[69] On this, see John H. D'Arms, *Commerce and Social Standing in Ancient Rome* (Cambridge, MA: 1981) 104-105; G. E. M. de Ste Croix, "Ancient Greek and Roman Maritime Loans" in *Debits, credits, finance and profits: Essays in Honor of W. T. Baxter*, eds. H. Edey and B. S. Yamey (London: 1974) 41-59; Paul Millett, "Maritime Loans and the Structure of Credit in Fourth Century Athens" in

could demand high interest because of their political position—for example, Brutus' loan to the city of Salamis which bore 48% interest[70]—or who could amass wealth though extortion or confiscation. As Scott rightly points out,[71] the strategy of the third servant was the more normal one to secure the investment against loss.[72] The interpretative verse (19:24), meant to rationalize the master's actions, is hardly a comforting assurance. Indeed, it serves to reinforce the master's self-description as someone who is "severe".

It is noteworthy that neither Matthew nor Luke regarded the concluding proverb as sufficient to turn the master into figure of Jesus or God. Matthew ties the parable, and hence its characters, into a web of significations found elsewhere in his gospel. By adding the command "enter into the joy of your Lord" Matthew connects this parable to the next one, in which the Son of Man invites those "blessed of his father" to come and inherit the kingdom prepared for them (25:34). The order to cast the servant into "outer darkness" (25:30) recalls two pericopae (8:12; 22:13) where those consigned to such a fate are unworthy in God's eyes and are so consigned as a matter of divine judgment. Matthew thus aligns the master with Jesus / God and further secures this interpretation by designating the man as τὸν ἀχρεῖον δοῦλον (25:30). For his part Luke has embedded the story of the entrusted money into a story about the rebel subjects of a king and thus creates a parallel between the punishment of the third servant and that of the rebellious subjects ("my enemies"). It should also be noted that the version of the story in the *Gospel of the Nazarenes* (18) solves the problem by displacing the punishment from the servant who hides the talent (who is only rebuked) to another servant, who had squandered the money on prostitutes.

Without the benefit of such expedients, Q is left with the proverbial saying in Q 19:26. Nothing in the context warrants the

---

Trade and Famine in Classical Antiquity, eds. Peter Garnsey and C. R. Whittaker (Proceedings of the Cambridge Philological Society, Supplement 8; Cambridge: 1983) 36-52.

[70] Cicero, *Letters to Atticus* 5.21.10-12; 6.1.5-7. See further, E. Badian, *Roman Imperialism in the Late Republic*, 2nd ed. (Oxford: 1968) 84-87. The legal limit on interest in the first century CE was 12%.

[71] Scott, *Hear Then the Parable* 228-229

[72] Petronius' *Satyricon* (53.3) has a treasurer announce to Trimalchio that 10 million sesterces were in a strong box "because they could not be invested." See also Demosthenes (27.9-11), where he distinguishes "active" from "inactive" capital, the latter including 8,000 drachmae in a strong-box (not an insignificant portion of his entire estate).

paraenetic message that interpreters like to find. When Zeller argues that the parable suggests that "anxious service according to the rules" is not sufficient and that 19:24 "might be a bitter fact in the economic realm; but in the realm of human freedom, it proves to be true: love will be reciprocated only if it takes risks,"[73] it should be pointed out that there is no indication at all that this is intended as a discourse on love or on the nature of Christian "duty". No one in the first century would dream that a ten- or fivefold increase on capital would come as a matter of course. If it occurred, it would be a matter of incredible good fortune. There is an air of unreality about the entire story.

The justification given for depriving the third servant of his money would hardly be consoling to most of the hearers of the parable, for it merely reiterates what most would know only too well: the rich get richer at the expense of the poor. Yet the parable cannot be meant as black irony, condemning the rapacity of the rich. The narrative structure of the parable, in which the master defines the outcomes, and his commendations of the first two servants as πιστοί (which has positive freighting in Q) and his elevation of their status forces the auditor / reader grudgingly to accept his judgments. Regardless of the sympathy the story might engender for the third servant, the exchange in 19:21-22 deprives the third servant (and the auditor) of the rhetorical high ground. The solution entertained in 19:23, even if the standard 12% interest would not increase the master's wealth by much, further undermines the servant's position. Thus, he has lost even before the actual punishment (19:24) and its rationalization (19:26).

A clue to Q's understanding of the story is found in its placement, after Q 17:23-24, 37, 26-30, 34-35 and before 22:28-30. While the discourse in Q 17:23-24, 37, 26-30, 34-35 has been called an apocalyptic discourse, it does not provide a timetable of "the Day" nor does it try to explain its delay—it does not even presume a delay. Instead, with a series of images it indicates the absolute impossibility of anticipating that day and sketches its truly ominous dimensions. It will appear in the midst, not of apocalyptic disasters (like Mark 13), but of the perfectly ordinary (Q 17:26-27, 28-30). There will be no signs (17:23). It will be as unheralded as the destruction of Sodom or the generation of Noah, and village bonds created by kinship and work will be torn

---

[73] Dieter Zeller, *Kommentar zur Logienquelle* (Stuttgarter kleiner Kommentar, Neues Testament 21; Stuttgart: 1984) 84.

apart (Q 17:34-35).[74] The function of such language is to call into question the security of everyday structures: all of this could be gone in the next instant. At the same time it explodes the false security of apocalyptic timetables: in fact, there will be no signs.

The parable of the Entrusted Money continues in this threatening tone, now depicting the actions of a rapacious landowner and the practically unattainable demands he makes of his retainers. The point of this parable is not the delay of "the Day" or what one ought to do in the meantime—indeed, there is no delay, only the absence of the master for some unspecified period of time. Nor is the point that the third servant was weak, or timid, or that he "hoarded" the money or was "over-cautious" or "unenterprising", or any of the other convenient moralizings found in the exegetical literature.[75] No paraenetic application refocuses attention on some other realm of discourse. If the "increase" were meant to be read as a metaphor for some virtue (love, service to others, etc.) or if the risks were intended in some transferred sense, those interpretative keys are now curiously absent in both the application and the context.

Instead, the reader / auditor is confronted with a particularly brutal and destablizing story of success and failure where the rules seem already to belong to foreign realm. As in 17:23-35, the ends are simply beyond calculation, and it is this fact that undermines the present. To view the world from inside the parable is terrifying; so also is Q's spectre of "the Day". Imaginative resolution is achieved only in the strongly pathetical appeal of the concluding verse of Q: ὑμεῖς οἱ ἀκολουθήσαντές μοι...καθήσεσθε ἐπὶ θρόνων τὰς δώδεκα φυλὰς κρίνοντες τοῦ Ἰσραήλ. Finally, the instability of servanthood and the fear of judgment is transcended in this promise of coregency. Adherence to Q's teachings of Jesus—serving God rather than mammon—is the only means by which to triumph over the frightening spectre of "the Day".

---

[74] On this point, see John S. Kloppenborg, "Symbolic Eschatology and the Apocalypticism of Q," *HThR* 80 (1987) 287-306, especially 301-302.

[75] The terms come from Dodd (*Parables of the Kingdom* 118-119) who thinks that the third servant represents a pious Jew who "seeks personal security in a meticulous observance of the Law" and thus, the parable commends risk-taking—the abandoning of the "scrupulous discipline of Pharisaism" and the embracing of the gospel. Scott (*Hear Then the Parable* 232-235) likewise suggests that the parable "marks out a fundamental difference between Jesus and the Pharisees". "The parable as a window onto the kingdom demands that the servant act neither as preserver nor as one afraid; but act boldly he must. If one is to act boldly, then the rules have been changed. They are no longer predictable" (234).

What is common to the four above mentioned parables is not allegorization—indeed, the Entrusted Money resists simple allegorization[76]—but the fact that each has become part of a larger rhetoric. Each parable occurs as the end to an argumentative sequence, providing a concluding visualization.[77] In the case of the Q 7:31-32 and 14:16-24, Q's argument is the indictment of "this generation": the illustration of its wrongheadedness and of the consequences of its refusals. The parables in Q 12:42b-46 and 19:12-26 serve a different argumentative end, the dramatization of "the Day" and its terrible consequences. In none of these instances is the parable intended as a "revelatory text" by itself. On the contrary, their autonomy (if 12:42b-46 was ever autonomous) has been subordinated to a larger rhetoric.

2. The Formative Stratum

Ancient theories of rhetorical composition imagined a relatively restricted role for parables. Recommending the use of enthymemes (rhetorical syllogisms) as demonstrative proofs, Aristotle allowed that in the absence of enthymemes parables might be used even though they were not ideally suited to that purpose. The more appropriate use was at the end of a speech, as an "epilogue", where parables serve as a "witness" (μάρτυς) to induce belief.[78] It was precisely the visual dimension of parables—

---

[76] Cf. Jeremias (*Parables of Jesus* 59-60), commenting on the implausibility of the synoptist's allegorical identification of the master with the Son of Man: "It is hardly conceivable that Jesus would have compared himself, either with a man 'who drew out where he had not paid in, and reaped where he had not sown' (Lk 19.21), that is, a rapacious man, heedlessly intent on his own profit: or with a brutal oriental despot, gloating over the sight of his enemies slaughtered before his eyes...."

[77] The Children in the Agora comes at the end of Q 7:1-10, 18-28, 31-35; the Faithful and Unfaithful Servants concludes Q 12:39-40, 42b-46; the Great Supper serves as a conclusion for 13:24-30, 34-35; 14:16-24; and the Entrusted Money and the Twelve Thrones are contrasting conclusions for 17:23-35.

[78] Aristotle, *Rhet.* 2.20.1394a.9: "If they [parables] stand first, they resemble induction, and induction is not suitable to rhetorical speeches except in very few cases; if they stand last they resemble evidence, and a witness is in every case likely to induce belief. Wherefore also it is necessary to quote a number of examples if they are put first, but one alone is sufficient if they are put last; for even a single trustworthy witness is of use." Cf. Quintilian (8.3.72-81): parables have a twofold function, as proofs and as ornamentation. "the invention of similes (similitudines) has also provided an admirable means of illuminating our decriptions. Some of these are designed for insertion among our arguments to help our proof (probationis gratia inter argumenta ponuntur), while others are

"putting the matter in plain sight"—that made them particularly well-suited to the kind of persuasion.[79]

It may be seen immediately that in addition to the foregoing parables, the parable of the builders (6:47-49) functions in this way, dramatizing the appeal of 6:46 to attend to the speaker's words: τί με καλεῖτε, κύριε κύριε, καὶ οὐ ποιεῖτε ἃ λέγω;[80] The parable is all the more appropriate, for it employs the image of housebuilding, a stock metaphor in didactic speeches.[81] The other parables from the formative stratum require slightly more discussion.

The Rich Farmer (Q 12:16-21)

The parable of the Rich Farmer (Q 12:16-21; cf. *GThom* 63) functions differently. It is, of course, not certain that either the parable or the preceding chreia (Q 12:13-14; cf. *GThom* 72) derived from Q, since a parallel is not attested in Matthew. However, the parallels in the *GThom* indicate that neither was a Lukan composition, and a variety of considerations make an origin in Q plausible.[82] If this was so, Q 12:16-21 may be seen as part of a complex and well-structured argument.

---

devised to make our pictures yet more vivid (ad exprimendam rerum imaginem)" (8.3.72). Cf. also *Ad Herennium* 4.45.59: "similitudo est oratio traducens ad rem quampriam aliquid ex re dispari. Ea sumitur aut ornandi causa aut probandi aut apertius dicendi aut ante oculos ponendi."

[79] See the discussion of vividness by Quintilian (above n. 78) and in *Ad Herennium* 4.47.60: "a similitude will be included for the sake of placing a matter in plain sight (of the audience)" (ante oculos ponendi negotii causa sumetur similitudo). See also Lucian, *Rhet. Praec.* 6, refering to *Cebes' Tablet*: Ἐθέλω δέ σοι πρῶτον ὥσπερ ὁ Κέβης ἐκεῖνος εἰκόνα γραψάμενος τῷ λόγῳ ἑκατέραν ἐπιδεῖξαι τὴν ὁδόν. See also Theon's account of ἔκφρασις, "description" in *Progymnasmata* 7.1-3: ἔκφρασίς ἐστι λόγος περιηγηματικὸς ἐναργῶς ὑπ' ὄψιν ἄγων τὸ δηλούμενον, "a description is an informative account which brings vividly into view what is being set forth". Theon later (7.52-55) states: ἀρεταὶ δὲ ἐκφράσεως αἵδε· σαφήνεια μὲν μάλιστα καὶ ἐνάργεια, τοῦ σχεδὸν ὁρᾶσθαι τὰ ἀπαγγελλόμενα, "desirable qualities of a description are these: above all, clarity and vividness, in order that what is being reported is virtually visible." (Text and translations: James R. Butts, *The "Progymnasmata" of Theon: A New Text with Translation and Commentary* [Ph.D. diss.; Claremont Graduate School: 1987]).

[80] Reconstruction: International Q Project, "The International Q Project Work Session 16 November 1990," *JBL* 110 (1991) 495.

[81] See Arland D. Jacobson, *Wisdom Christology in Q* (Diss.; Claremont Graduate School: 1978) 47, 110 n. 84.

[82] The main arguments are summarized by Kloppenborg, *Q Parallels* 128: (1) Lk 12:13-14 and 12:16-21 occur in a predominantly Q section of Luke; (2) there are a number of catchwords connecting it to the following sections of Q; (3) διὰ

On the one hand, the parable has been attached to the chria on inheritance and thereby serves to dramatize the folly of striving after wealth. The chreia depicts Jesus as refusing the role of a sage-king and an arbiter of disputes. It is not that Q regards Jesus as unqualified; rather, it is because the dispute—probably a controversy over the ancestral farm—is now seen as quite beside the point. The appending of the parable, which on its own may simply have dealt with the folly of greed,[83] preserves the focus on agricultural economics but creates an overpowering inertia favouring Jesus' statement of 12:14. The chreia moves quickly from the act of supplication to the opposition between the brother and Jesus. Similarly, the parable moves from the presumption of divine blessing (a plentiful harvest), to a willful and conspicuous display of wealth, described in first-person speech, to God's intrusion into the story—again, as direct speech—overpowering and negating the rich man's plans for conspicuous consumption. Both the chreia and the parable begin by raising one set of expectations and then subverting them, in the process indicating the great gulf that stands between the characters of the stories and Jesus / God. Thus while in the chreia Jesus offers no rationale for his refusal, the speech of God in the parable make that rationale patent. The point is cemented in the moralizing conclusion, οὕτως ὁ θησαυρίζων ἑαυτῷ καὶ μὴ εἰς θεὸν πλουτῶν ("thus [it is / goes with] one who piles up wealth for himself and does not get rich in

---

τοῦτο in Q 12:22a more logically follows on 12:13-14, 16-21 than it does on 12:11-12; (4) the criticism of riches is a theme that appears elsewhere in Q; and (5) Matthew may have omitted these sections because their forms did not fit within the Sermon on the Mount (i.e., where he moved the following materials), or because the rejection of a forensic function for Jesus interfered with Matthew's Christology. Nonetheless, there are clearly Lukan features in this section, e.g, 12:15 (see Jeremias, *Die Sprache* 215) and 12:16a (see above).

[83] Various readings for the parable have been proposed, e.g., Jülicher, *Gleichnisreden Jesu* 2.616: "Ursprünglich ist es m.E. dem Erfinder der Geschichte blos darauf angekommen, den Gegensatz zwischen den geplanten Genüssen und dem plötzlichen Tode drastisch zu beschreiben, so dass 16-20 eine Parallel zu Sir 11 18ff. 51 ψ 48 17f. 38 6ff. und ähnlich alttestamentlichen Stellen wäre, ein Hinweis auf die Vergänglichkeit des Reichtums, auf seine Hilflosigkeit gegenüber dem Tod." Scott (*Hear then the Parable* 138-140) suggests that the parable originally concerned the (in)appropriate use of wealth; Crossan (*In Parables* 85) [of the version in *GThom*]: "A very definite but utterly human example of failure to realize one's true situation." Richard A. Horsley, *Jesus and the Spiral of Violence: Popular Jewish Resistance in Roman Palestine* (San Francisco: 1987) 258: "It could originally have been a story directed to ordinary people illustrating the futility of building up a surplus that one holds onto for oneself."

God's sight", v. 21).[84] The focus is not merely upon the folly of greed, but the opposition between wealth and God.

On the other hand, the parable has been connected with Q 12:22-31, 33-34 in such a way that the argument begun in the parable is continued and developed. The "fit" between the parable and the following discourse is, in fact, remarkable. The mention of anxiety, eating, drinking[85] and clothing in Q 12:22b finds an almost perfect balance in the items mentioned in the rich man's soliloquy: rest, eating, drinking, and enjoying oneself. The address to the ψυχή, first by the Farmer who invites himself to enjoy his success (v. 15, bis) and then by God who deprives him of it, is balanced by Q 12:23, ἡ ψυχή πλεῖόν ἐστιν τῆς τροφῆς καὶ τὸ σῶμα τοῦ ἐνδύματος (not paralleled in POxy 655 1.1-17). Moreover, the agricultural activities that the birds do not undertake (Q 12:24)—sowing (σπείρουσιν), harvesting (θερίζουσιν) and storing in barns (ἀποθήκας)—correspond to those in which the farmer must necessarily engage. This link is all the more striking, since these activities are not mentioned in the parallel but independent POxy 655, which agrees with Q only in its second illustration of the lilies, which do not toil (κοπιᾷ) [or card, ξαίνει] or spin (νήθει). It would appear that both the mention of ψυχή and inclusion of the example of the birds had the parable in view, or vice versa.[86] The question in Q 12:25 (τίς δὲ ἐξ ὑμῶν μεριμνῶν δύναται ἐπὶ τὴν ἡλικίαν αὐτοῦ προσθεῖναι πῆχυν;) has the effect of shifting the nuance of μεριμνᾶν so that it now includes not only the anxiety of the poor regarding subsistence but also the

---

[84] That v. 16 is secondary is recognized by most: Jülicher, Die Gleichnisreden Jesu 2.614 ["dunkel und ziemlich überflüssig"]; Alfred F. Loisy, L'évangile selon Luc (Paris: 1924) 347; Fitzmyer, Luke 971 [who ascribes it to Luke]; Gerhard Schneider, Das Evangelium nach Lukas (ÖKTNT 3; Gütersloh and Würzburg: 1977-78) 283 [Lukan]; Jeremias, Parables of Jesus 106 [who unnecessarily understands the parable to imply an "eschatological warning" which v. 16 mitigates].

[85] ἢ τί πίητε is present only in Matthew, and not in all mss [it is absent in α λ 892 a b ff² l vg sy^c sa^mss; Cl]. It is sometimes argued that this is a Matthaean addition, following Q 12:29: Thus Gundry, Matthew 115; Ulrich Luz, Matthew 1–7 (Minneapolis: 1989) 401; Paul Hoffmann, "Jesu Verbot des Sorgen und seine Nachgeschichte in der synoptischen Überlieferung" in Jesu Rede von Gott und ihre Nachgeschichte im frühen Christentum: Festschrift für Willi Marxsen zum 70. Geburtstag, ed. Dietrich-Alex Koch (Gütersloh: 1989) 117.

[86] It is worth noting that GThom 63 uses the terms "sow", "reap", "plant", and "fill storehouses" but lacks "soul", "eating", "drinking" and "making merry".

"concern" of the farmer for a secure and long retirement.[87] The cares of the rich are every bit as ineffectual in prolonging life as the worries of the poor. When the figure of Solomon is invoked (also unparalleled in *POxy* 655), it is not as a sage-king who decides disputes, but was one whose finery was unsurpassed—that is, until one inspects the finery that God provides for the lilies.

Q 12:22-31, 33-34 establishes a rhetorical σύγκρισις which takes up the vocabulary and imagery of the parable, but casts it in another light. The farmer's concern to achieve an easy life through a surplus of food and his assurances to his soul are contrasted with the Q people's lack of concern over material sustenance and God's assurance of their supply. The farmer's productive agricultural land is contrasted with uncultivated land, producing lilies and grass (to be burned). His soul, captivated by the thought of pleasures but soon forfeit, is counterbalanced by the souls of 12:23-24 that are "greater" because of God's loving surveillance. When Q 12:30 notes that πάντα γὰρ ταῦτα τὰ ἔθνη ἐπιζητοῦσιν, the farmer, whose identity was hitherto unknown, it subtly placed on the side of the unbelieving nations. Thus, Q uses the opening chreia and the parable to demark lines of allegiance between the "easy" life of the landed gentry and life of the less privileged and to tarnish the image of wealth, first, by depicting Jesus' disdain for it, and then, by dramatizing its collapse. Once this is accomplished, a sustained set of comparisons establishes the superiority of a way of life that places the Q people's "justifiable anxieties about obtaining even basic necessities in the context and perspective of their overall longings and, now, God's overall care and renewing action."[88] This discourse concretizes what is said aphoristically in Q 6:20b (μακάριοι οἱ πτωχοί) in so far as it depicts both the unhappiness of the rich and the ways in which God sustains those in the kingdom.

---

[87] Paul Hoffmann ("Der Q-Text der Sprüche vom Sorgen Mt 6,25-33 / Lk 12,22-31: Ein Rekonstruktionsversuch" in *Studien zum Matthäusevangelium: Festschrift für Wilhelm Pesch*, ed. Ludger Schenke [SBS; Stuttgart: 1988] 139) points out that ἡλικία in Q 12:25 can refer to "stature" rather than "lifespan". The former meaning is clearly appropriate to the version in *POxy* 655 i 1-17: τίς ἂν προσθ<εί>η ἐπὶ τὴν εἰλικίαν ὑμῶν (which is embedded in the exhortations about clothing) and to Q 12:22-31 if it every circulated freely. In Q as it stands, however, Q 12:25 has been separated from the exhortations on clothing (12:26a καὶ περὶ ἐνδύματος τί μεριμνᾶτε begins a new topic) and seems to belong with 12:24 and 12:16-21 which concern provision of food (and hence the prolongation of life).

[88] Horsley, *Jesus and the Spiral of Violence* 257.

It is worth noting again that the editing of the discourse shows signs of learning and literary skill, not merely in the ways in which the chreia and the parable have been interlocked with the admonitions, but also in the invocation of general "philosophical" principles: οὕτως ὁ θησαυρίζων ἑαυτῷ καὶ μὴ εἰς θεὸν πλουτῶν (12:21), ἡ ψυχὴ πλεῖόν ἐστιν τῆς τροφῆς καὶ τὸ σῶμα τοῦ ἐνδύματος (12:23), τίς δὲ ἐξ ὑμῶν μεριμνῶν δύναται ἐπὶ τὴν ἡλικίαν αὐτοῦ προσθεῖναι πῆχυν; (12:25), and ὅπου γάρ ἐστιν ὁ θησαυρὸς ὑμῶν, ἐκεῖ ἔσται καὶ ἡ καρδία ὑμῶν (12:34). While the sayings which make up this discourse may have originally dealt rather concretely with the issues of subsistence,[89] in Q they have been woven into a scribal argument and betray the broader and more generalizing perspective of that social sector.[90]

The Mustard and the Leaven

Although a few critics thought that these two parables formed a pair from the beginnning,[91] the *GThom* (20, 96) now makes it

---

[89] Thus, Horsley, *Jesus and the Spiral of Violence* 257.

[90] I have argued elsewhere ("Literary Convention, Self-Evidence, and the Social History of the Q People" in *Early Christianity, Q and Jesus*, eds. John S. Kloppenborg with Leif E. Vaage [= *Semeia* 55; Atlanta: 1991] 77-102) that the first layer of Q was the product of the lower reaches of the town and village scribal sector, whose contact with and knowledge of the problems of poverty, debt, divorce and tenancy would be most immediate, and who would have had the intellectual and technical skills to compose a document such as Q. It would be unwise to exaggerate the distance between this type of scribe and the villagers whose debts, divorces, and taxation receipts they documented (*pace* Richard A. Horsley, "Questions about Redactional Strata and the Social Relations Reflected in Q" in *SBLASP* 28 [1989] 202).

[91] Thus Rudolf Schnackenburg, *God's Rule and Kingdom* (New York: 1963) 155. Jeremias (*Parables of Jesus* 92) notes that the Leaven is paired with the Mustard Seed in the Matthew and Luke, but with the Woman and the Jar (*GThom* 97) in the *GThom*, taking this to indicate that the Mustard and the Leaven may have been said on different occasions and variously combined. Nonetheless, he understands the two to refer to the same situation (defence of the mission) and thus to be happily paired in Matthew and Luke (*ibid.* 147-149). Jacques Dupont ("Le Couple parabolique du sénevé et du levain (Mt 13,31-33; Lc 13,18-21)" in *Jesus Christus in Historie und Theologie: Festschrift für Hans Conzelmann*, ed. Georg Strecker [Tübingen: 1975] 331-345) presents the best case for thinking that the parables were originally a couplet. He argues (1) that had the Markan tradition contained the Leaven, Mark would have omitted it since it did not, like the other parables in Mark 4, deal with seeds (just as Matthew omitted the Lost Drachma because it did not fit the pastoral context of Matthew 18); (2) the *GThom* is not evidence of the original independence of the two parables; "son témoignage serait plutôt de nature à illustrer la possibilité d'une

clear that the two did not always belong together.[92] The pairing of the parables, which perhaps first took place in the Sayings Gospel, represents an important interpretative manoeuvre. Rudolf Laufen has persuasively argued that one of the results of this pairing was an assimilation of the structure of the Mustard Seed to that of the Leaven.[93]

The Mustard Seed is attested in Mark and the *GThom* but in neither of these performances is an agent involved. Mark begins impersonally with ὡς κόκκῳ σινάπεως, ὃς ὅταν σπαρῇ ἐπὶ τῆς γῆς (Mk 4:31a), while the *GThom* has "it [the kingdom] is like a mustard seed" (*ectntōn aublbile nšltam, GThom* 20). Q, by contrast, introduces an agent: ὁμοία ἐστὶν κόκκῳ σινάπεως, ὃν λαβὼν ἄνθρωπος ἔβαλεν εἰς κῆπον αὐτοῦ (13:19a).[94] This parallels the introduction to Q's version of the Leaven: ὁμοία ἐστὶν ζύμῃ, ἣν λαβοῦσα γυνὴ ἐνέκρυψεν (13:21a).

Laufen has rightly observed that in the Mustard Seed the ἄνθρωπος has no proper function;[95] the sower immediately fades from sight and attention is turned to the seed. Indeed, the introduction of an agent creates the awkward image of the sower taking only one seed—an awkwardness that neither the Markan / *GThom* version of the Mustard nor the Q / *GThom* version of the Leaven shares.[96] This suggests that the impersonal presentation of Mark

---

dissociation secondaire de paraboles antérieurement associées" (338); (3) Mark's version is the result of Markan redaction, and thus not evidence of an earlier, independent form of the parable; (4) both parables represent "la même sagesse populaire"; and (5) in both cases the comparison is strange, producing a surprising or paradoxical effect (344-345).

Harry Fleddermann ("The Mustard Seed and the Leaven in Q, the Synoptics, and Thomas" *SBLASP* 28 [1989] 230) holds that the two formed an original pair and that Mark omitted the Leaven and the *GThom* was dependent primarily upon Mark for his version of the Mustard and chose to place the Leaven in a different cluster.

[92] Prior to the discovery of the *GThom* this point was already made by Dodd (*Parables of the Kingdom* 154-155). See, more recently, Laufen, *Doppelüberlieferungen* 178-179; Scott, *Hear Then the Parable* 323.

[93] This was earlier proposed by Wilhelm Michaelis, *Die Gleichnisse Jesu: Eine Einführung* 8. durchgehend neu bearb. Aufl. (Die urchristliche Botschaft 32; Hamburg: 1956) 56.

[94] Reconstruction: International Q Project, "The International Q Project Work Session 16 November 1990," *JBL* 110 (1991) 497. This reconstruction is in close agreement with those of Laufen (*Doppelüberlieferungen* 176) and Fleddermann ("The Mustard Seed and the Leaven" 224).

[95] Laufen, *Doppelüberlieferung* 178.

[96] Cf. Eduard Schweizer, *Das Evangelium nach Matthäus* (NTD 2; Göttingen: 1973; ³1981) 199: "...die Tatsache, daß Markus nur eines enthält und Q beim zweiten eine neue Einleitung setzt, spricht dafür, daß beide Gleichnisse zuerst getrennt überliefert und erst in der Gemeinde zusammengestellt worden sind. Das

and *GThom* is earlier and that Q 13:18-19 has been assimilated to the Leaven. The introduction of an agent and the assimilation of the present tenses (ἀναβαίνει καὶ γίνεται) to aorists (ἔβαλεν, ηὔξησεν, ἐγένετο) also transformed the Mustard from a similitude (*Gleichnis im strengen Sinn*) to a parable (*Parabel*).[97]

The interpretations of the "original" versions of the Mustard and the Leaven are controverted, but need not be explored here.[98] What is of interest for our purposes is the strategy employed by Q for dealing with these parables. Clues to the interpretation of the parables in Q are to be sought both in the way they have been structured, and in their placement in Q.

The structure of the Mustard has been assimilated to that of the Leaven, resulting in numerous parallel features: (1) both are introduced by a question about ἡ βασιλεία τοῦ θεοῦ; (2) the formula introducing the comparison is similar (ὁμοία ἐστὶν κόκκῳ σινάπεως / ζύμῃ); (3) both involve an agent who "takes" the mustard or leaven (ὃν λαβὼν ἄνθρωπος / ἣν λαβοῦσα γυνή); (4) both of the principal verbs are aorists and (5) both represent unusual choices, suggesting a furtive action (ἔβαλεν εἰς / ἐνέκρυψεν);[99] (6) both focus on the element of growth (ηὔξησεν)

---

erklärt auch die merkwürdige Formulierung, daß ein Mann ein(!) Senfkorn nimmt und in seinen Acker sät." Joel Marcus (*The Mystery of the Kingdom of God* [SBLDS 90; Atlanta: 1986] 207) points out that had Mark seen ἄνθρωπος in his sources he would doubtless have taken it over, since it would have created a better fit with his other two parables, the Sower and the Seed growing Secretly, both of which mention an agent.

Scott (*Hear Then the Parable* 383) includes the agent in his "originating structure" but does not refer to the arguments of Laufen or Schweizer, nor indeed does the agent have any significant function in Scott's reading of the parable.

[97] Laufen, *Doppelüberlieferung* 178. Similarly, Rudolf Pesch, *Das Markusevangelium* (HThK.NT 2/1-2; Freiburg i.B., Basel und Wien: 1976-80) 1:264 n. 20; Marcus, *Mystery* 207-208. Joachim Gnilka (*Das Evangelium nach Markus* [EKK.NT 2/1-2; Zürich and Neukirchen-Vluyn: 1978-79] 1:186-187) argues that Q has assimilated the Mustard to the Leaven, but allows for the possibility of two versions of the parable circulating, one a true parable with aorist verbs and one a similitude, with verbs in the present.

[98] See, most recently, John Dominic Crossan, *The Historical Jesus: The Life of a Mediterranean Jewish Peasant* (San Francisco: 1991) 276-279. Following Oakman (*Jesus and the Economic Questions* 127), Crossan argues that "the point...is not just that the mustard plant starts as a proverbially small seed and grows into a shrub of three or four feet, or even higher, it is that it tends to take over where it is not wanted, that it tends to get out of control, and that it tends to attract birds within cultivated areas where they are not particularly desired" (278-279).

[99] The more usual terms for planting would be Mark's σπείρω or φυτεύω and φυράω for kneading dough (cf. Gen 18:6). The use of βάλλω is attested, but

and increase (ἐζυμώθη ὅλον); and finally, (7) in both cases is the result extravagant. This creation of parallels accomplishes precisely what Aristotle recommends when he advised that if parables were used in the absence of other argument, several examples out to be quoted so as to make the induction clear (*Rhet.* 2.20.1394a.9).[100]

The deliberate creation of parallels between 13:18-19 and 13:20-21 has the effect of stressing (1) that the kingdom of God is the subject of the discourse, (2) that human action is involved in the initial "hidden" state, and (3) that the process of growth is, like mustard germination or leavening, rapid, dramatic, and incessant, producing results out of proportion to the initial state.

The significance of the placement of the parables in Q poses a more difficult problem. The Matthaean placement is clearly secondary, controlled by the structure of Mark 4. It must therefore be rejected as the original Q placement. It is much more likely that Luke's order reflects that of Q; there is no reason evident for Luke to have relocated the parables. But this raises the question of how precisely the parables related to their immediate context. Do they belong with the preceding sayings, or the following, or both?

In establishing general structures within Q, Polag grouped the parables in a rather amorphous cluster, "parabolae ac diversae sententiae", comprising Q 12:54-56, 58-59; 13:34-35; 13:18-19, 20-21, 24, 25-27, 28-29, 30; 14:16-24, 26-27, 34-35; 14:5; 15:4-10; 16:16-18; 16:13.[101] Apart from the unexplained transpositions of 13:34-35, 14:5 (!) and 16:13, this grouping ignores the close thematic relationship of 12:39-40, 42-46, 49, 51-53 with 12:54-59 and produces so unwieldy a unit that thematic or rhetorical

---

rarely with εἰς: 1 Clem 24.5: ἐξῆλθεν ὁ σπείρων καὶ ἔβαλεν εἰς τὴν γῆν ἕκαστον τῶν σπερμάτων.... More commonly the dative or ἐπὶ is used: Theocritus 25.25-26: "(labourers) casting seed in fallow, now three times ploughed, now four" (τριπόλοις σπόρον ἐν νειοῖσιν/ἔσθ᾽ ὅτε βάλλοντες καὶ τετραπόλοισιν ὁμοίως); Mk 4:26: ὡς ἄνθρωπος βάλῃ τὸν σπόρον ἐπὶ τῆς γῆς...; Diodorus Siculus 1.36.4: "farmers merely scatter the seed, then turn their herds and flocks (καὶ τὸ σπέρμα βάλλοντες ἐπάγειν τὰ βοσκήματα) into the field and after they have trampled it in, they return four or five months later for harvest."

[100] The importance of making the *tertium comparationis* clear is likewise emphasized in *Ad Herennium* 4.48.61 (non enim res tota totae rei necesse est similis sit, sed id ipsum quod conferetur similitudinem habeat oportet) and by Quintilian (8.3.73): debet enim, quod illustrandae alterius rei gratia assumitur, ipsum esse clarius eo quod illuminat.

[101] Polag, *Fragmenta* 66-74. In *Die Christologie der Logienquelle* (WMANT 45; Neukirchen-Vluyn: 1977) 5, Polag indicates that he regards the original position of 13:18-19, 23-24, 30; 14:5; 15:3-7 and 16:13 as uncertain.

structures are impossible to discern. Much to be preferred is the arrangement proposed by Wolfgang Schenk, who divided this material into two units, "Die erste Endzeitsrede" (12:39-59; 13:18-21), followed by "Die Zwei-Wege Rede" (13:24–17:6).[102] Schenk argued that as a conclusion for the eschatological sayings in Q 12:39-59, the two parables provide "Zeugnisse der Treue und Zuverlässigkeit des Schöpfungshandelns Gottes aus derselben Weisheit heraus, auf die man sich darum auch im Blick auf seine Gestaltung der zukünftigen Geschichte verlassen kann."[103] As such, they illustrate the "necessary connection" between small and hidden beginning of the kingdom in the past and its consummation at the coming of the Son of Man.

If the parables of the Mustard and Leaven formed the conclusion to 12:39-59, they were rather weak and ineffectual. There is no hint of the threats or ominous tones that permeate 12:39-59—housebreaking, severe punishment, fire, division, celestial signs, and imprisonment and, on the other hand, 13:18-19, 20-21 use language (the kingdom) and imagery (growth, spectacular results) that are foreign to the preceding section. Nor do the parable cohere with the "Two Ways" section that begins in 13:24. Schürmann senses the problem when he urges that 13:18-21 is a *Lukan* interpolation into 12:39-59 + 13:24-30.[104] Yet the two parables do not fit any better with Lk 13:1-9, 10-17, 22-30, which deals with grasping salvation and healing while it is near, and hence, it is difficult to assume that Luke interpolated them here.

Harry Fleddermann's understanding of the parables relies not upon the immediate literary context, but upon verbal connections with other portions of Q and upon the formal correspondences between the two parables. The mention of a mustard seed connects Q 13:18-19 with Q 17:6 (ὡς κόκκον σινάπεως) where mustard "symbolizes a small but powerful reality which can have

---

[102] Schenk, *Synopse* 94-101, 102-119. Similarly, T. W. Manson, *The Sayings of Jesus* (London: 1949; repr. 1971) 115.

[103] Schenk, *Synopse* 101.

[104] Heinz Schürmann, "Das Zeugnis der Redenquelle für die Basileia-Verkündigung Jesu" in *Logia: Les Paroles de Jésus—The Sayings of Jesus: Mémorial Joseph Coppens*, ed. J. Delobel (BETL 59; Leuven: 1982) 161: "Es müßte doch gefragt werden, ob nich der Abschnitt 12,39-59 sich bereits in Q in und hinter Lk 13,23-29 (30) mit der Thematik: «Wachsamkeit, Bereitschaft und Entschiedenheit in letzter Stunde», fortgesetzt hat....Wahrscheinlicher fügte aber nicht schon die Q-Redaktion die zwei zusammengefügten Parallelen [Parabele?] Lk 13,18f.20f. an dieser Stelle ein, sondern erst Lukas, der mit 13,22 redaktionell einen neuen Absatz beginnt und die doppelte Parabel als passenden Abschluß von 12,35-59, anfügt...."

extraordinary effects."[105] The verb κατεσκήνωσεν in 13:18 recalls κατασκηνώσεις in Q 9:58 used in reference to the homeless of the Son of Man. Similarly, the woman's act of "hiding" (ἐνέκρυψεν) the Leaven recalls ἔκρυψας of Q 10:21. For Fleddermann these correspondences suggest a reading. In spite of the fact that the kingdom is initially hidden and Jesus' followers homeless and poor, the kingdom is already at work, transforming all. The parables are, for Fleddermann, Q's explanation of the delay of the parousia. "The delay allows the tiny, hidden kingdom to grow and permeate the whole world."[106]

It is difficult to follow the subtlety of allusion that Fleddermann sees operative in Q. As Wendy Cotter puts it, "it is not certain that the use of an image in one saying defines its meaning wherever else it occurs."[107] Cotter focuses upon the secretive nature of the two actions, "casting into the garden" and "hiding the leaven", connecting these with the behaviour prescribed for Q's "missionaries" in Q 10. She interprets the "equipment instruction" (Q 10:4) to mean that Q's ἐργάται are to travel and conduct themselves in an unobtrusive manner and thereby avoid the hostile attention of officialdom but nonetheless secure stunning results. "These parables were probably joined in Q because they gave hope to a community obliged to adopt a strategy of secrecy for their missionary activities."[108]

This reading comes close to that of Laufen (whom Cotter cites). For Laufen, the parables are about the growth and manifestation of the kingdom, which is both result of missionary activities and the power of God. The notion of growth, made more prominent with the replacement of the more abstract ἀναβαίνει by ηὔξησεν,[109] is correlated with the spread of the church. The Q group saw in the two parables its own situation. While the present situation of confrontation with Israel was disheartening, the Q folk consoled themselves with the thought that growth of the kingdom,

---

[105] Fleddermann, "The Mustard Seed and the Leaven" 232.
[106] *Ibid.* 234.
[107] Wendy Cotter, "The Parables of the Mustard and Seed and the Leaven: Their Function in the Earliest Stratum of Q" in *Scriptures and Cultural Conversations: Essays for Heinz Guenther at 65*, eds. John S. Kloppenborg and Leif E. Vaage (= *Toronto Journal of Theology* 8/1 [1992] 45).
[108] Cotter, "The Mustard Seed and the Leaven" 47.
[109] Laufen, *Doppelüberlieferung* 190.

like that of mustard and leaven, could not ultimately be impeded.[110]

Read in this way, Q 13:18-19, 20-21 has little to do with the immediately preceding composition (12:39-59) and is not in any obvious way about the delay of "the Day" or of the devastating judgment that it brings. The parables do, however, cohere with the thrust of the material that precedes it, 12:2-12, 13-14, 16-21, 22-31, 33-34, which also concerns the kingdom of God (12:29) and involves human agency in its spread (12:3,[111] 31) and which, like the two parables, invokes natural processes (12:6, 24, 27-28) as analogies for the actions of the divine. Moreover, Q 12:2 states aphoristically what the two parables indicate metaphorically: that there is an ineluctable process at work that will bring to fruition what was initially small and hidden. This might suggest that prior to the interpolation of 12:39-59 (*ad voces* διορύσσω and κλέπτης),[112] the two parables served as a conclusion for Q 12:2-12, 13-14, 16-21, 22-31, 33-34, visualizing the process of the disclosure of the kingdom, and full of confidence in the ultimate outcome. Q 13:18-19, 20-21 would, then, function in much the same way as 6:47-49 to provide a concluding visualization and "witness" for the preceding argument.

The Lost Sheep and the Lost Drachma

The parables of the Lost Sheep and the Lost Drachma[113] present a special set of difficulties because the original literary context is not

---

[110] Laufen, *Doppelüberlieferung* 191: "Dabei ist die Q-Gemeinde sich wohl bewußt, daß dieses Ende nicht einfach die Verlängerung des missionarischen Bemühens ihrer Glaubensboten ist! Diese sammeln als Erntarbeiter (vgl. Mt 9,37f / Lk 10,2) das eschatologische Gottesvolk. Aber der Anbruch der endgültigen βασιλεία wird ein apokalyptisches Ereignis, d.h. ausschließlich die Tat Gottes sein."

[111] Reconstruction: International Q Project, "The International Q Project Work Session 17 November 1989," *JBL* 109 (1990) 501: Q 12:3 ὃ λέγω ὑμῖν ἐν τῇ σκοτίᾳ εἴπατε ἐν τῷ φωτί, καὶ ὃ εἰς τὸ οὖς ἀκούετε κηρύξατε ἐπὶ τῶν δωμάτων (based on the database of John S. Kloppenborg and responses by Jon Daniels).

[112] See Kloppenborg, *Formation of Q* 148-154.

[113] A number of reconstructions or treatments of Q simply ignore the question of whether 15:8-10 was in Q or not (e.g., Edwards, Harnack, Hoffmann, Schenk, Schulz, Streeter, Zeller). Those who do consider the issue are divided. While a small minority think that Luke composed the second parable on the pattern of the first (Hans Conzelmann, *The Theology of St. Luke* [New York: 1960] 111; John Drury, *The Parables in the Gospels: History and Allegory* [New York: 1985]

immediately clear, and because both Matthew and Luke have
edited the parable(s) in distinctive ways.

Matthew's placement is clearly secondary, for Matthew has attached several units of Q (15:4-7; 17:1-2; 17:3-4) to a Markan
context (Mt 18:1-5 / Mk 9:33-37; Mt 18:6-9 / Mk 9:42-50).
Matthew's parable is directed at church leaders, warning them to
care for "the little ones" and using the similitude of a shepherd's
interest in retrieving a lost sheep as the basis for the appeal.
Mt 18:14 is largely redactional, as evidenced by a cluster of
Matthaean vocabulary (θέλημα, ἔμπροσθεν, ὁ πατὴρ ὑμῶν ὁ ἐν
οὐρανοῖς, ἵνα + subj., ἓν τῶν μικρῶν τούτων).[114] But Dupont has
made a strong case for supposing that Matthew's πλανάω is also
redactional. In spite of the fact that Luke's ἀπόλλυμι fits the
structure of Luke 15,[115] Dupont observes that Matthew, who uses

155-156), the main disagreement is whether the parable came to Luke from Q or
from special materials. While a number of critics opt for the latter, the only real
argument is given by Fitzmyer (*Luke* 1073): it is "difficult to explain why
Matthew would have omitted the second [parable], thus disrupting the pair...."
This argument, in my view, has been successfully answered by Jacques Dupont
("Le Couple parabolique du sénevé et du levain" [see above n. 91] 337):
"Matthieu met la parabole de la Brebis perdue au service d'une exhortation
pastorale qui invite à prendre exemple sur la conduite du berger; il eût été
maladroit d'ajouter à cet exemple celui d'une femme cherchant sa drachme."
Similarly, Bernhard Weiss, *Die Quellen des Lukasevangeliums* (Stuttgart and
Berlin: 1907) 248; Josef Schmid, *Matthäus und Lukas: Eine Untersuchung des
Verhältnisses ihrer Evangelien* (BSt[F] 23/2-4; Freiburg: 1930) 305; Burton
Easton, *The Gospel according to St. Luke: A Critical and Exegetical Commentary*
(Edinburgh: 1926) 236; Schneider, *Lukas* 2.324-25; Jan Lambrecht, *Once More
Astonished: The Parables of Jesus* (New York: 1981) 38. Others have argued that
the striking parallels between the Lost Sheep and the Lost Drachma make it
likely that they belonged together from the beginning: Lambrecht, *Once More
Astonished* 28; Marshall *Luke* 602 (although Marshall is not sure that Matthew
and Luke were using the same source for the Lost Sheep); Helmut Koester,
Ancient Christian Gospels: Their history and development (Philadelphia and
London: 1990) 148. Walter Grundmann (*Das Evangelium nach Lukas*, 9. Aufl.
[ThHK.NT 3; Berlin: 1981] 306) even notes that like the Q Mustard / Leaven
pair, this pair also compares the actions of a man and a woman.

[114] See Wolfgang Schenk, *Die Sprache des Matthäus* (Göttingen: 1987) 236,
239, 284, 291-292, 308.

[115] The repetition of the verb ἀπόλλυμι throughout chap. 15 has led many
authors to suppose that it is redactional: e.g., Jülicher, *Gleichnisreden Jesu*
2.330; Marshall, *Luke* 601; Fitzmyer, *Luke* 1074. Others argue that Luke's formulation of the introduction (4a) required an active verb to replace Matthew's
(=Q's) passive: Adolf von Harnack, *The Sayings of Jesus: The Second Source of
St. Matthew and St. Luke* (New Testament Studies 2; London and New York:
1908) 92; Schulz, *Spruchquelle* 387. W. L. Peterson ("The Parable of the Lost
Sheep in the Gospel of Thomas and the Synoptics," *NovT* 23 [1981] 141) bases

ἀπόλλυμι in v. 14 to signify permanent loss, *cannot* keep ἀπόλλυμι as a description for the sheep straying.

> Au plan de l'image, il n'y a pas de différence entre une brebis «perdue» et une brebis «égarée», tandis que la différence est très importante au plan de l'application: un homme «égaré» peut encore être ramené, évitant ainsi l'irrémédiable «perdition». Mt fait donc une distinction entre «se perdre» et «s'égarer», distinction qui ne se justifie pas s'il s'agit d'une brebis, mais qui s'impose quand on parle d'un homme.[116]

It is obvious that the three parables in Luke 15 are part of a Lukan composition. Luke has prefaced the unit with a challenge to Jesus' table fellowship, to which the three parables provide the response. In each parable, the terms ἀπόλλυμι (4, 6, 8, 24, 32), εὑρίσκω (4, 5, 6, 8, 9, 24, 32) and (συγ)χαίρω / χαρά (5, 6, 7, 9, 10, 32) play key roles. The Lukan applications make it clear that he sees the three parables as paradigms of sinners repenting and being received back with celebration. But it is also clear that the narrative structure of the first two parables resist this application: neither the sheep nor the coin "repents". On the contrary, the focus is upon the actions of the shepherd and woman, not the items that were lost. For this reason it is probable that the use of μετάνοια / μετανοέω in vv. 7, 10 is Lukan and that Luke is responsible for shifting the attention from the actions of the shepherd to those of the "repentant sinner".[117] In spite of this, the similarity between Mt 18:13b and Lk 15:7b, both of which draw a comparison (χαίρει / χαρά...ἐπὶ...ἢ ἐπὶ [τοῖς] ἐνενήκοντα ἐννέα), indicates that in Q the parable concluded with some reference to celebration over the finding of the lost sheep. Lambrecht plausibly argues that vv. 5-6 (and 9) of Luke substantially represent Q.[118]

While it is not necessary to reconstruct the two parables in detail, several features are noteworthy. Like the Q parables of the Mustard and the Leaven, the Lost Sheep and the Lost Drachma have been assimilated in structure. (1) Both parables are framed as similitudes and introduced with questions expecting the answer, "everyone, of course" (cf. Mt 18:12 [οὐχί]; Lk 15:4 [οὐ], 8

---

his argument for the Matthaean wording on the observation that neither Matthew nor Luke seems to add πλανάω redactionally elsewhere.

[116] Jacques Dupont, "La Parabole de la brebis perdue (Mt 18,12-14; Lc 15,4-7)," *Gregorianum* 49 (1968) 275. Similarly, Lambrecht, *Once More Astonished* 38.

[117] Thus Dupont, "La parabole de la brebis perdue" 278; Schenk, *Synopse* 113.

[118] Lambrecht (*Once More Astonished* 40) thinks that "sinner" was in Q; but the likelihood that "repent" is Lukan casts serious doubt upon "sinner".

[οὐχί]). The two parables are framed as appeals to typical behaviour.[119] (2) In both similitudes, an agent is involved—and as in Q 13:18-21, first a man, then a woman. (3) A web of parallel features bind the two stories together: τίς ἄνθρωπος / τίς γυνὴ, ἔχων ἑκατὸν πρόβατα / δραχμὰς ἔχουσα δέκα, ἀπολέσας ἐξ αὐτῶν ἓν / ἐὰν ἀπολέσῃ δραχμὴν μίαν, πορεύεται ἐπὶ τὸ ἀπολωλὸς (Mt: ζητεῖ) / ζητεῖ ἐπιμελῶς, οὗ εὕρῃ, χαιρων / συγχάρητέ μοι, ὅτι εὗρον. (4) The narratives do not end merely with the finding of the item, but with a celebration. (5) In both instances it is not simply a matter of losing an item of significant value,[120] but of one of a larger group being lost. This is made clear by the comparison at the end of the Lost Sheep. And even though an explicit comparison is wanting in the Lost Drachma, the concluding celebration underscores the importance of the one, inspite of the numerical preponderance of the nine remaining drachmae. The point in mentioning the one hundred sheep and the ten drachmae in the first place is so that the comparative point can be scored.

The position of this parable-pair in Q presents some difficulties. Q 15:4-7, 8-10 does not appear to belong with the preceding material which, as I have argued elsewhere,[121] comes to an appro-

---

[119] Norman Perrin (*Rediscovering the Teaching of Jesus* [New York: 1967] 100) argues that the shepherd's abandoning of the sheep is a sign of unreasonable behaviour. It is arguable that the parable, circulating independently, was susceptible to this reading, inspite of the fact that, according to N. Levinson (*The Parables: Their Background and Local Setting* [Edinburgh: 1926] 152-153), E. F. F. Bishop ("The Parable of the Lost or Wandering Sheep: Matthew 18.10-14; Luke 15.3-7," *AThR* 44 [1962] 50) and Kenneth E. Bailey, *Poet and Peasant: A Literary-cultural Approach to the Parables in Luke* [Grand Rapids: 1976] 149-150), all of whom have lived in the mid-East, a flock—especially one so large—would normally be watched by several shepherds. However, in Q and Luke the parable was paired with the Lost Drachma, where there is no hint of irresponsibility or unconventional action. On the contrary, the actions are quite predictable. See J. Duncan M. Derrett, "Fresh Light on the Lost Sheep and the Lost Coin," *NTS* 26 (1979) 40-41.

[120] Scott (*Hear Then the Parable* 407) suggests that the lost item "has no intrinsic value". This appears to be a misunderstanding of the dynamics of subsistence economies. Scott seems to be influenced by *Song of Songs Rabbah* 1.1.9: "If a man losts a sela or an obol in his house, he lights lamp after lamp, wick after wick, till he finds it. Now does it stand to reason: if for these things which are only ephemeral and of this world a man will light so many lamps and lights till he finds where they are hidden, for the words of Torah which after the life both of this world and the next world, ought you not to seach as for hidden treasures?" But in this case the story has been created precisely to emphasize the insigificant of the item lost (an obol!).

[121] Kloppenborg, *Formation of Q* 232-234, 234-238.

priate conclusion with Q 14:34-35. Instead, the two parables, deliberately styled to emphasize the normalcy of seeking out lost items even when one has others, serves to set the stage for the following cluster of Q sayings: Q 16:16, 18; 17:1-2, 3-4, 6.[122]

One of the most cryptic sayings in Q, 16:16 appears minimally to be a reflection on the execution of John the Baptist, apparently viewing this event as a changing of the eras.[123] It is striking that the cause of John's execution, criticism of Herodian divorce and remarriage, is the subject of the next saying (16:18).[124] The peculiar formulation of this saying—claiming that the *male* can commit adultery against (i.e., damage the honour of) his wife—is an example of a "focal instance."[125] It reverses the logic of divorce, a mechanism designed to protect the honour of males, and insists that honour is (also) *gynecocentric*.[126] Q 16:18 is thus intentionally comparative, underscoring the honour of the lesser

---

[122] The placement of Q 16:13 is problematic. It position in Matthew (6:24) appears to be redactional, but Luke's placement, as the conclusion to sayings interpreting the Dishonoured Master (16:1-8a) is also suspect. Q 16:17 is excluded from consideration here since, as I have argued elsewhere, it belongs to a tertiary glossing of Q: *"Nomos* and *Ethos* in Q" in *Gospel Origins and Christian Beginnings: In Honor of James M. Robinson*, eds. James E. Goehring, Jack T. Sanders, and Charles W. Hedrick (Sonoma: 1990) 35-48.

[123] On the problem of the placement of this saying, see Weiss, *Predigt Jesu* 192. The Lukan placement is so difficult, and the Matthaean placement so convenient, that it is difficult to argue that Luke's placement is secondary. See, most recently, Daniel Kosch, *Die eschatologische Tora des Menschensohnes: Untersuchungen zur Rezeption der Stellung Jesu zur Tora in Q* (NTOA 12; Freiburg and Göttingen: 1989) 430. Kosch is probably correct in arguing that 16:16 was not intended to suggest an abrogation of the law, even if the editor responsible for 16:17 saw this danger in the saying. "Vielmehr wird man (gerade auch im Blick auf den zweiten Teil des Logions) verstehen müssen: Bis Johannes waren Gesetz und Propheten Ausdruck der Forderung Gottes, die erhoben, aber immer auch missachtet wurde. Seitdem bricht sich die Basileia Gottes Bahn, aber auch sie stösst auf Widerspruch und Ablehnung"(439).

[124] Q 16:18: πᾶς ὁ ἀπολύων τὴν γυναῖκα αὐτοῦ [[]] μοιχεύ[ει]], καὶ ὁ [[]] ἀπολελυμένην [[]] γαμ[ῶν]] μοιχ.... Reconstruction: International Q Project, "The International Q Project Work Session 17 November 1989," *JBL* 109 (1990) 501.

[125] See Robert C. Tannehill, "The 'Focal Instance' as a Form of New Testament Speech: A Study of Matthew 5:39b-42," *JR* 50 (1970) 372-385. Also Robert W. Funk, "Unravelling the Jesus Tradition: Criteria and Criticism," *Forum* 5/2 (1989) 31-62.

[126] This point is worked out in greater detail in John S. Kloppenborg, "Alms, Debt and Divorce: Jesus' Ethics in their Mediterranean Context," *Toronto Journal of Theology* 6 (1990) 182-200, especially 193-196. See now Crossan, *The Historical Jesus* 301-302.

(female) partner in marriage over against that of the dominant partner.

The issue of status and rank are fully exposed in the following saying, Q 17:1b-2,[127] which so elevates *one* (ἕνα) of the "little ones" that it pronounces a death-sentence on those who would offend them. This is obviously another example of a "focal instance", this time trading on an inversion of the roles of strong and weak, statussed and unstatussed. The next saying in sequence, Q 17:3b-4,[128] provides another perspective on local conflict, suggesting that those wronged take steps to resolve tension (instead of retaliating), and even imagining a scenario of virtually unlimited forebearance and forgiveness (cf. Q 6:29, 30). When the cluster concludes with 17:6,[129] the same dynamics of small / insignificant versus powerful and the inversion of roles are present again. The personal formulation, εἰ ἔχετε πίστιν, is framed with the addressees of 16:18; 17:1b-2, 3b-4 in view: if they will embrace this social experiment in reconciliation,[130] like mustard (or leaven!) it will grow and vindicate itself. The same optimism that characterized Q 12:2-3; 13:18-19, 20-21 recurs here.[131]

The entire section from Q 15:4 to 17:6 deals with reconciliation and peacemaking in a social situation where the categories of

---

[127] Q 17:1b-2: <...> ἀνάγκη ἐλθεῖν τὰ σκάνδαλα, πλὴν οὐαὶ δι' οὗ ἔρχεται. 2 λυσιτελεῖ αὐτῷ [εἰ] μύλος ὀνικὸς περίκειται περὶ τὸν τράχηλον αὐτοῦ καὶ ἔρριπται ε[ἰς] τὴ[ν] θάλασσ[αν] ἢ ἵνα σκανδαλίσῃ τῶν μικρῶν τούτων ἕνα. Reconstruction: International Q Project, "The International Q Project Work Session 16 November 1990," *JBL* 110 (1991) 498.

[128] Q 17:3b-4: ἐὰν ἁμαρτήσῃ ὁ ἀδελφός σου ἐπιτίμησον αὐτῷ, καὶ ἐὰν [σου ἀκούσῃ, ἄφες αὐτῷ]. 4 καὶ ἐὰν ἑπτάκις τῆς ἡμέρας ἁμαρτήσῃ εἰς σὲ καὶ ἑπτάκις [] ἀφήσεις αὐτῷ. Reconstruction: *ibid.*

[129] Q 17:6: εἰ ἔχετε πίστιν ὡς κόκκον σινάπεως, ἐλέγετε ἂν τῇ συκαμίνῳ ταύτῃ· ἐκριζώθητι καὶ φυτεύθητι ἐν τῇ θαλάσσῃ· καὶ ὑπήκουσεν ἂν ὑμῖν. Reconstruction: *ibid.*

[130] It is worth noting that Thomas' formulation of the saying (*GThom* 48) is explicit about reconciliation: "If two make peace with each other in a single house, they will say to the mountain, 'Move from here!' and it will move." *GThom* 106, "When you make the two into one, you will become children of humankind, and when you say, 'Mountain, move from here!' it will move." The latter saying betrays more influence on Thomas' theology of becoming a single one.

[131] Ferdinand Hahn ("Jesu Wort vom bergversetzenden Glauben," *ZNW* 73 [1985] 149-169), although he see nothing more than an isolated saying in Q (151), rightly suggests that the focus of the saying is that "a little faith is enough." "Wo in der Bibel vom Samenkorn die Rede ist, geht es immer auch im das Fruchttragen. Das Samenkorn enthält in sich alles, was zum Fruchtbringen nötig ist. Der Glaube, zu dem Jesus ruft, ist ein lebendiger und wirksamer Glaube" (166).

honour and status threaten stability by valuing the large, the numerous, the male, the elder, the "just" and the powerful over their
opposites. As an introduction to this unit, the two similitudes
appeal to what is self-evident in village life. Of course, no shepherd will let one sheep go astray, even if there are still 99 left; of
course, no woman will ignore the loss of one drachma, even if she
still has nine left. Why then in community relationships should
there be differential valuations according to the standards of
gender or standing or honour and why should those standards be
permitted to destroy and dishonour the one or the weak? Like the
ethics proposed by Q 6:27-35, this section of Q imagines the reduction of local conflict by a re-evaluation of the values
(protection of honour) operative in Palestinian (and indeed
Mediterranean) village culture.

The Kingdom, Jesus and the Rhetoric of Q

The parables in the formative stratum of Q, like those in the secondary stratum, have been made part of a larger argumentative
strategy. In the case of Q 6:47-49 and 13:18-19, 20-21 they fall at
the end of a sequence, providing a concluding dramatization. In
Q 12:16-21 and 15:4-7, 8-10 the parables introduce ideas upon
which the following discourse elaborates. The differences between
the two principal strata of Q with regard to their use of parables is
not a difference in technique. Although only the secondary
stratum (Q^2) employs allegory, even this is not used consistently.
Rather it is a difference of subject matter. While the secondary
stratum parables are yoked to Q's polemic against "this
generation" and its invocation of "the Day" in order to subvert
confidence in the "status quo", the parables of formative stratum
(Q^1) function to illustrate and dramatize the hortatory and paraenetic materials of Q. They appear, typically, either at the beginning or at the end of an argument.

We began by observing the paradox that none of the parables in
Q functioned "parabolically"[132] and that only two are parables

---

[132] James G. Williams ("Parable and Chreia. From Q to Narrative Gospel,"
Semeia 43 [1988] 89-90) notes that only the Mustard Seed, the Great Supper, and
Serpents and Doves [Mt 10:16b, which he ascribes to Q] function
"paradoxically". Nevertheless, he notes that most of the Q sayings are rather
common and he later (94) concedes that "extravagance" is not the best term with
which to describe the parables in Q. He prefers to speak of intensification and
heightening, but as we have seen above, this is better described in the language
of ancient rhetoric: parables were used because they were vivid. Williams' view

"of the kingdom". These two features are related. It is often
observed of the parables in the *GThom* that they are less allegorized than their synoptic counterparts;[133] this is certainly true of
the parable of the Great Supper, whose parabolic function is
GThom is less obscured. On the other hand, the *GThom* has eight
kingdom-parables, far more than Q. Unlike Q, however, the
framers of the *GThom* made little or no attempt to realise an argumentative function in their use of parables. Parables and other
sayings are simply serialized (apart from a few catchword collections). The incipit, which designates the sayings as "secret",
whose true significance is available only to those who "seek"
their meaning, was perhaps a key element in the framing of
GThom's parables that *prevented* their being furnished with interpretative glosses or allegorizing transformations. In the *GThom*,
the parables, like the other sayings, remain mysteries for wise to
ponder and to be transformed in the very act of pondering.[134]

The intention is quite otherwise in the Sayings Gospel. Q is, from
the beginning, a work of scribal imagination that transforms
individual sayings and stories into an argument, that is, into a
rhetorical composition. The decision to make individual sayings
of Jesus part of a larger literary composition meant that parables
had to be treated not in the way in which they might have functioned in the give and take of oral culture, but in accordance with
the norms of literary composition: as a concluding "witness" or
illustration or as an initial story which the subsequent argument
develops. Free-standing parables like those offered by the *GThom*
were no longer an option. Correspondingly, the connection
between the kingdom and parabolic narrative was effectively
severed, except in the single instance (13:18-19, 20-21) where the
kingdom and its ethic was the topic under discussion in the discourse. Whether or not the remainder of the parables were originally about the kingdom one cannot know. In Q, they are not. It is
perhaps noteworthy that Q 7:31-32 appears to imitate the
interrogative introduction to the kingdom parables (e.g., Q 13:18,

---

that Q was a parable-chreia collection is possible only because he overlooks the
literary context into which the parables have been set and continues to treat them
as individual, separable (i.e., oral) units.

[133] See Helmut Koester, "Three Thomas Parables" in *The New Testament and
Gnosis: Essays in Honour of Robert McLaughlan Wilson*, eds. A. H. B. Logan
and A. J. M. Wedderburn (Edinburgh: 1983) 195-203.

[134] On the notion of "sapiential research", see Kloppenborg, *Formation of Q*
304-306.

20; Mk 4:30), but substitutes "this generation" and uses the parable in a thoroughly polemical way.

The outcome of this investigation is that while Q may stand only a decade or so from Jesus the parabler, it is the *GThom*, framed perhaps several decades later,[135] that provides better (i.e., less edited) access to the parables. In the Sayings Gospel, as in Mark, we already witness literary experimentation at work. Both Q and Mark know and value the tradition that Jesus told lively stories. But as a writer Mark was unable to preserve the parables as they functioned in oral back-and-forth. Yet his treatment of parables as speech that divided friends from foes, insiders from outsiders, at least reflected the challenging, subversive and provocative dimension of Jesus' parables even if Mark also turned them into allegories. Enigmatic speech that provoked decision easily modulated into enigmatic speech in need of decoding.

In the Sayings Gospel, especially in Q[1], we see the first attempts at Christian rhetoric (at least in the Jesus tradition). Here parables function much as they do in other rhetorical speeches, as "witnesses". The locus of challenge and provocation is not the parable as such, but the entire speech to which they were attached and which they either introduce or conclude. Jesus the parabler became scribalized, grounding an alternative ethic in enthymemes, rhetorical inductions and concluding visualizations. By the secondary redactional strata, the parable had become familiar enough to function in general argumentation—the polemic against this generation. The connection with the kingdom was further weakened, and the way was prepared for Matthew's thoroughgoing allegorizing hermeneutic where parables are turned into meditations on church polity and salvation history. But it would be a mistake simply to regard Q's use of parables as the first stage in loss of parabolic meaning. The Saying Gospel's successful incorporation of the parable into a literary format was a key step in the scribalizing of the Jesus tradition. And it provided an important antecedent for Matthew's and Luke's much more ambitious use of parables a few decades later.

---

[135]The dating of *GThom* is, of course, much discussed, but probably beyond determination. The *termini* provided by the dating of the Oxyrhynchus fragments is not any more helpful that the dating of the first fragments of Matthew ($\mathfrak{P}^{64}$) to the dating of the composition of Matthew.

CHAPTER THIRTEEN

ON THE GOSPEL OF THOMAS AND Q

Bradley H. McLean

After the discovery of a Coptic *Gospel of Thomas* (*GThom*) in 1945, and its subsequent identification three years later, it became apparent that this Nag Hammadi codex preserved the same Gospel as that which was partially preserved in three Oxyrhynchus papyri discovered about fifty years earlier.[1] This unexpected discovery coincided with a growing scholarly appreciation for another gospel, that of the Sayings Source Q. In fact, the publication of the Greek fragments of *GThom* (1897 / 1903 / 1904) closely coincided with Adolf von Harnack's publication of his Q reconstruction in 1907 which precipitated scholarly awareness of Q as a distinct document.[2] The subsequent attempts to reconstruct the Q text by Schenk (1981), Polag (1979), and most recently by the ongoing International Q Project parallel the efforts to reconstruct the text of *GThom*.[3] As a result of these achievements,

---

[1] *POxy* 1=*GThom* 28-33, 77a; *POxy* 654=*GThom* 1-7; *POxy* 655= *GThom* 24, 36-39; see B. P. Grenfell and A. S. Hunt, *Logia Iesou. Sayings of Our Lord* (London: 1897); idem, *New Sayings of Jesus and Fragment of a Lost Gospel from Oxyrhynchus* (London: 1903); idem, *The Oxyrhynchus Papyri, Part IV* (London: 1904) 28. For a critical edition of Coptic, Greek with ET, see B. Layton (ed.), "The Gospel According to Thomas" in *Nag Hammadi Codex II,2-7 Together with XIII,2*, Brit. Lib. Or. 4926(1) and P.Oxy. 1, 654, 655* (NHS 20-21; Leiden: 1989) 38-109.

[2] A. von Harnack, *Sprüche und Reden Jesu* (Leipzig: 1907); also: G. H. Müller, *Zur Synopse: Untersuchung über die Arbeitsweise des Luke und Matt. und ihre Quellen* (FRLANT 11; Göttingen: 1908). As John Kloppenborg has pointed out: "Prior to Harnack's reconstruction of Q, various discussions of the synoptic problem had used the notion of 'Q' virtually as an algebraic variable for solving the relationship among the extant Synoptics....With Harnack's reconstruction, the mathematical, almost whimsical, use of the idea of Q vanished and Q as a document of early Christianity appeared" (Review of Helmut Koester's *Ancient Christian Gospels* [unpublished; delivered to SBL, Nov. 1991, p. 2]).

[3] W. Schenk, *Synopse zur Redenquelle der Evangelien: Q Synopse und Rekonstruktion in deutscher Übersetzung mit kurzen Erläuterungen* (Düsseldorf: 1981); A. Polag, *Fragmenta Q: Textheft zur Logienquelle* (Neukirchen-Vluyn: 1979); James M. Robinson, "The International Q Project: Work Session 17

GThom and Q have never been as concretely available for study as they are today. Accordingly, scholars have endeavored to determine their relation to the synoptic gospels, to each other, and to apply them to the larger problem of Christian origins. This essay will discuss the advances being made in these areas.

1. The Relationship of the Gospel of Thomas to the Synoptic Gospels

Given the striking similarity between many of the sayings of *GThom* and the synoptic gospels, sharp controversy has arisen over the relationship between these textual traditions: is *GThom* dependent upon or independent of the synoptic Gospels? The ranks of scholars on both sides of this question are very impressive.[4] Yet this history towards polarization amongst scholars must not discourage one from posing the question again since it is no

---

November 1989," *JBL* 109 (1990) 499-501; *idem,* "The International Q Project: Work Session 16 November 1990," *JBL* 110 (1991) 494-498; *idem,* "The International Q Project: Work Sessions 12-14 July, 22 November 1991," *JBL* 111 (1992) 500-508.

[4] Advocates of dependency: R. Kasser, *L'Évangile selon Thomas: Présentation et commentaire théologique* (Neuchatel: 1961); B. Dehandschutter, "Évangile selon Thomas: témoin d'une tradition prélucanienne?" in *Évangile de Luc,* ed. Frans Neirynck (BETL 32; Gembloux: 1973) 287-297; *idem,* "L'Évangile de Thomas comme collection des paroles de Jésus" in *Logia: les paroles de Jesus: Mémorial Joseph Coppens,* ed. J. Delobel (Leuven: 1982) 507-515; J.-M. Sevrin, "L'Évangile selon Thomas: Paroles de Jésus et révélation gnostique," *RTL* 8 (1977) 265-292; C. Tuckett, *Nag Hammadi and the Gospel Tradition: Synoptic Tradition in the Nag Hammadi Library* (Edinburgh: 1986); H. E. W. Turner, "The Gospel of Thomas: its history, tranmission and sources" in *Thomas and the Evangelists,* eds. Turner and Montefiore (London: 1962) 11-39; W. G. Kümmel, *Introduction to the New Testament,* trans. H. C. Kee, ([14]1965/rev. Eng. edn. 1973/1975) 75-76. Others have argued against dependency from the synoptic tradition: John Dominic Crossan, *In Fragments: Aphorisms of Jesus* (San Francisco: 1983) x; *idem,* "The Seed Parables of Jesus," *JBL* 92 (1973) 244-266; Helmut Koester, *Ancient Christian Gospels* (Philadelphia: 1990) 84-86; G. Quispel, "The Gospel of Thomas and the New Testament," *VigChr* 11 (1957) 189-207; *idem,* "L'Évangile selon Thomas et les Clémentines," *VigChr* 12 (1958) 181-196; *idem,* "Jewish-Christian Gospel Tradition," *ATR Suppl* 3 (1974) 112-116; *idem,* "L'Évangile selon Thomas et le Diatessaron," *VigChr* 13 (1959) 87-117; R. McL. Wilson, *Studies in the Gospel of Thomas* (London: 1960) 144-148; O. Cullmann, *The Gospel of Thomas and the Problem of the Age of the Tradition*; J. H. Sieber, "Redactional Analysis of the Synoptic Gospels with Regard to the Question of the Sources of the Gospel According to Thomas" (Ph.D. diss.; Yale University: 1962).

exaggeration to say that meaningful comparison of Q with *GThom* is inconceivable without first settling this prior problem.

The question of the relationship of *GThom* to the synoptic gospels was led astray from the beginning by two erroneous misconceptions: the first involved the confinement of *GThom* to second century Gnosticism; the second comprised the notion that the text of *GThom* is a fixed, that is stable, text. It is hardly necessary to mention that the Coptic *GThom* was discovered in the library of a Gnostic sect in Nag Hammadi. Perhaps it was this simple fact that led to the assumption that *GThom* reflects the atmosphere of Gnosticism of the second and third centuries. As Davies observes: "Arguments for an early or mid-[second]-century date are based entirely (to the best of my knowledge) on the idea that since Thomas is gnostic it must necessarily be a second-century text."[5] If *GThom* is dated almost a century later than the synoptic gospels, it is but a small step to conclude that the text of *GThom* must be dependent on the synoptics, given the linear model of textual transmission which has so dominated scholarship. Differences between *GThom* and the synoptic gospels have been explained in terms of *GThom*'s assumed Gnostic proclivity. Some scholars have even attempted to identify the particular school to which the author of *GThom* belonged, whether it be the Naassene school,[6] the Valentian school,[7] or some other ascetic Gnostic school.[8]

In order to sustain the theory that *GThom* is indeed dependent upon the synoptic gospels, it was necessary to account for *GThom*'s lack of connective narrative. Ernst Haenchen attempted to account for the absence of narrative arguing that it had been eliminated because it was not pertinent to the Gnostic message contained in the word of revelation. According to this view, *GThom* is a derivative of the synoptic gospels formed by stripping off narrative in accordance with Gnostic theology and exegetical practice.[9] Similarly, the lack of the allegorization of parables

---

[5] S. L. Davies, *The Gospel of Thomas and Christian Wisdom* (New York: 1983) 33.

[6] R. M. Grant, "Notes on the Gospel of Thomas," *VigChr* 13 (1959) 170-180; R. M. Grant and D. N. Freedman, *The Secret Sayings of Jesus* (New York: 1960) 100-101.

[7] B. Gärtner, *The Theology of the Gospel according to Thomas* (New York: 1961) 272.

[8] E. Haenchen, *Die Botschaft des Thomas-Evangeliums* (Berlin: 1961) 10.

[9] Haenchen, *Botschaft* 11.

which is notably absent in *GThom*,[10] was attributed, not to the author's ignorance of the synoptic tradition but, to the deliberate reworking in accordance with Gnostic theology.[11]

Two obstacles stand in the face of the above theory. First, James M. Robinson has demonstrated that other Nag Hammadi tractates indicate that Gnosticism tended to reinterpret problematic traditions rather than eliminate them.[12] Concrete proof of this is found in the retention and reinterpretation of the passion narratives in the Second Treatise of the Great Seth (*NHC* VII, 2) and the Apocalypse of Peter (*NHC* VII, 3).

Secondly, in answer to the assertion that *GThom* has stripped the synoptic parables of their allegorical component, Helmut Koester has demonstrated that *GThom* does not presuppose a written narrative precursor. In the early Christian period, parables were transmitted in two fundamentally different ways, orally and scribally. Orality and scribality exhibit different characteristics. When transmitted orally, parables are not allegorized, interpreted or redacted, though they naturally give rise to what Dominic Crossan refers to as *performancial* variations. The oral repetition of a parable is a repetition *ad sensum* and *ad structuram*, but is not a verbatim reproduction. In contrast to orality, it is through scribal transmission that so-called *hermeneutical* variations occur which supply an interpretation (e.g., allegorization) in addition to a "performance".[13] It follows that if *GThom* were dependent on the synoptic gospels it would manifest either deliberate dependence on, or conscious avoidance of, synoptic hermeneutical variants, in addition to performancial variants. Since this is not the case,

---

[10] Cf. *GThom* 9 / Mk 4:13-20; *GThom* 57 / Mt 13:36-43; *GThom* 64 / Mt 22:11-14.

[11] R. M. Grant, "Notes"; W. R. Schoedel, "Parables in the Gospel of Thomas: Oral Tradition or Gnostic Exegesis?" *CTM* 43 (1972) 548-560; J. B. Sheppard, "A Study of the Parables Common to the Synoptic Gospels and the Coptic Gospel of Thomas" (Ph.D. diss.; Claremont Graduate School: 1966); A. Lindemann, "Zur Gleichnisinterpretation im Thomas-Evangelium," *ZNW* 71 (1980) 214-243.

[12] James M. Robinson, "LOGOI SOPHON: On the Gattung of Q" in *Trajectories through Early Christianity*, eds. Robinson and Koester (Philadelphia: 1971) 102, n. 69.

[13] Koester, "Three Thomas Parables" in *The New Testament and Gnosis: Essays in Honour of Robert McL. Wilson*, eds. A. H. B. Logan and A. J. M. Wedderburn (Edinburgh: 1983) 195-203, especially 195; Crossan describes five types of performancial variants: contraction, expansion, or transposition of stichs, the conversion from positive to negative (or vice versa), and the substitution of synonyms (*In Fragments* 38-41).

Koester concludes that *GThom* did not evolve from an editing of synoptic parables but from independent *oral* transmission. The absence of allegorical features in *GThom* suggests that its originator is "a collector rather than a (Gnostic) interpreter"[14] Finally, the random order of sayings in *GThom* in comparison with their synoptic parallels indicates that *GThom* is not simply a synoptic gospel stripped of its narrative.

Robinson contends that Haenchen has construed the developmental process backwards: it is not a matter of *narrative* gospels being stripped down to *sayings* gospels but the reverse. To cite a parallel example, it was the Sayings Gospel Q which was absorbed and ultimately replaced by narrative *Gattung* of the emerging synoptic gospels. The same may be said of the parables collection in Mark 4.[15] *GThom* survived as a sayings gospel, whereas Q did not, because it remained independent of the synoptic tradition and thereby was preserved from absorption.

We have yet to address the principal argument, *viz.* that *GThom* is a Gnostic document and therefore belongs to the second century. In actual fact, the supposed Gnostic character of *GThom* is in no way decisive in the determination of dependency. First, the traditional definition of Gnosticism as a second-century heresy resulting from the fusion of second-century Christianity with Greek philosophy is no longer viable. There are at the very least affinities with Gnostic thought found in much earlier writings. Far from being confined to second-century Christianity, scholars now recognize the diffuse and complex character of Gnosticism, exhibiting diverse expressions in Graeco-Roman, Jewish and Christian forms. There is now strong evidence of Jewish Gnosticism which pre-dates Christianity.[16] Ithamar Gruenwald, for example, thinks that the majority of Gnostic systems came into existence out of apocalyptic and sapiential traditions of Judaism.[17] This is not the place to discuss whether the pre-second century systems should be called pre-gnostic, proto-gnostic, Gnosis, or Gnosticism.[18] Rather, as Helmut Koester remarks, what is more

---

[14] Koester, "Parables" 195.

[15] Koester, "Parables" 198.

[16] Rudolph, *Gnosis: The Nature and History of an Ancient Religion* (Edinburgh: 1983) 275-294.

[17] I. Gruenwald, "Knowledge and Vision," *Israel Oriental Studies* 3 (1973) 63-107.

[18] For a discussion of the problem posed by terminology see: Robinson, "On Bridging the Gulf from Q to the Gospel of Thomas (or Vice Versa)," in *Nag*

important [than opinions about the origins of Gnosticism] is the recognition of the indebtedness of Christianity as a whole to a theological development that bears many marks of what is customarily designated as "gnostic".[19] The fact that forms of Gnosticism existed in the first century cannot be contradicted by arguing that the *full* Gnostic system was *not* present, for as Robinson points out, if one subjected first-century Christianity to the same analysis there would be as little orthodox Christianity in primitive Christianity as Gnosticism in the first century:

> Hence, the strategy implicit in limiting gnosticism to the second century and thereafter, namely the resultant allocation of first-century Christianity to orthodoxy, cannot be carried through, lest on the same logic the absence of second-century othrodoxy in the first century lead to the allocation of first-century Christianity to—heresy![20]

Secondly, the identification of "Gnosticism" in *GThom* is a moot point. Koester argues that, given the lack of allegorical features in the *GThom* parables, it is impossible on internal grounds either to clearly demonstrate that a Gnostic interpretation is intended or, to infer what these parables might have suggested to a Gnostic author.[21] Robert Grant comes close to admitting as much: "The sayings actually preserved in the Greek version [of *GThom*] do not sound very Gnostic, and it is tempting to suppose that in the early third century the Gospel of Thomas had not yet undergone the process of Gnosticizing".[22] Indeed, many of the readings found in *GThom* occur in other sources, many of which did not have Gnostic tendencies (Diatessaron, Clement of Alexandria, the "Western" text of the Gospels, Macarius, etc.).[23] Schrage agrees with Koester in so far as he finds no evidence in the Coptic *GThom* for the view that it represents an advanced stage of Gnosticism, nor are accretions from the synoptic gospels, such

Hammadi, Gnosticism, and Early Christianity, eds. C. W. Hedrick and R. Hodgson Jr. (Peabody, MA: 1986) 127-175, especially 128-135.

[19] Koester, "GNOMAI DIAPHOROI: The Origin and Nature of Diversification in the History of Early Christianity" in *Trajectories* (see note 12 above) 114-157, especially 116.

[20] Robinson, "Bridging the Gulf " 134.

[21] Koester, "Parables" 201.

[22] Grant-Freedman, *Secret Sayings* 71.

[23] G. C. Quispel, *Makarius: das Thomasevangelium, und das Lied von der Perle* (Leiden: 1967) 7-8.

as they exist, introduced in order to compromise "orthodoxy".[24] Similarly, Steven L. Davies argues that *GThom* is in no meaningful sense "gnostic".[25]

The argument for dependency must be founded principally on textual grounds—not preconceived notions about Gnosticism. There are several Thomas texts which exhibit a degree of synoptic dependence.[26] These instances of dependence must be addressed in any theory which deals with the relationship between *GThom* and the synoptic gospels.

Wolfgang Schrage was the first to provide a detailed exposition of the relationship of *GThom* to the synoptic gospels based upon a detailed comparison of Coptic *GThom* (*GThom*^{co}) with the Sahidic translation of the NT (NT^{sa}).[27] He concludes that the wording of *GThom*^{co} can best be explained by supposing that *GThom*^{co} received its sayings from the NT^{sa}. The argument is essentially one of analogy for it presumes that the Greek version of *GThom* (*GThom*^{gr}) has the same relationship to the Greek NT as *GThom*^{co} has to NT^{sa}.[28]

Schrage's argument also depends on the presupposition that NT^{sa} pre-dates *GThom*^{co}. However, given the existence of second-century papyri fragments of *GThom*^{gr}, his theory is unlikely since NT^{sa} is customarily dated in the third century.[29] Contrary to Schrage, textual agreements between NT^{sa} and *GThom*^{co} suggest the dependency of NT^{sa} on *GThom*^{co}, though there are also

---

[24] W. Schrage, "Evangelienzitate in Oxyrhynchus-Logien und im koptischen Thomas-Evangelium" in *Apophoreta: Festschrift für Ernst Haenchen*, ed. W. Eltester (Berlin: 1964) 251-268, especially 267-268.

[25] Davies, *Thomas and Wisdom* 32-33.

[26] *GThom* 32 (cf. Mt 5:14b); *GThom* 39 (cf. Mt 23:13); *GThom* 45b (cf. Lk 6:45); *GThom* 104a (cf. Lk 5:33); *GThom* 104b (cf. Lk 5:33-35). J. Horman argues that *GThom* 12 (cf. Mt 16:13-20) depends on the Synoptics since it seems to contradict, point by point, Matthew's detailed version (Mt 16:13-20): J. Horman, "The Source of the Version of the Parable of the Sower in the Gospel of Thomas," *NovT* 21 (1979) 326-343, especially 327-328 n. 8. There are also instances were the synoptic order of sayings has influenced *GThom* (*GThom* 32, 33b [cf. Mt 5:14b-15]; *GThom* 65, 66 [cf. Mk 12:31-35]; *GThom* 92a, 93-94 [cf. Mt 7:6-7]).

[27] W. Schrage, *Das Verhältnis des Thomas-Evangelium zur synoptischen Tradition und zu den koptischen Evangelienübersetzungen. Zugleich ein Beitrag zur gnostischen Synoptikerdeutung* (BZNW 29; Berlin: 1964).

[28] Robinson, "LOGOI SOPHON" 102 n. 69.

[29] B. Metzger, *The Text of the New Testament: Its Transmission, Corruption, and Restoration* (New York: 1964) 79-81.

grammatical differences between the two which must be reckoned with.[30]

More important is the fact that synoptic influence on *GThom*, to the extent that it can be demonstrated, may not be due to the Greek version of *GThom*, but to scribal harmonization at the level of the Coptic translation. Three points are sufficient to illustrate this point. First, Schrage's examination of the Greek fragments provides evidence against his own thesis: the text of *GThom*[co] bears a closer resemblance to the NT than does *GThom*[gr] (e.g., Saying 33 in *GThom*[co] and *POxy* 1). This does not imply that the Coptic translator of GThom was working with a written NT at his side. He may simply have had a memory of individual sayings. The Coptic translators are noted for their imprecision and proclivity for harmonizing with the synoptic gospels. In his comparison of the Greek and Coptic texts, Attridge catalogues differences between *GThom*[gr] and *GThom*[co] resulting from loose translation (Sayings 6, 10, 11, 16, 17, 22-25), accidental omission (2, 3, 8, 12, 13), deliberate deletion or expansion (5, 7, 9), and deliberate editorial alteration (1, 14, 19).[31] Koester remarks:

> It is quite likely that the Coptic text of the Gospel of Thomas does not directly reflect the original text of this Gospel; differences between the Coptic version and the Greek fragments from Oxyrhynchus show that the text was not stable; similar observations can be made for the transmission of other Gospels during the 2d century.[32]

The fact that the three extant Greek fragments belong to three different manuscripts suggests that *GThom*[gr] was frequently copied, as well as perhaps *GThom*[co]. In any case, it is clear that the *GThom*[co] was not a straight translation of the *GThom*[gr] but an adapted translation into which some synoptic influences were intruded.[33] The synoptic harmonizations at the level of the Coptic translation of *GThom* are of no assistance in answering the question of the relationship of *GThom*[gr] to the NT. Robinson notes,

---

[30] K. Rudolph, "Gnosis, ein Forschungsbericht," *ThR* 34 (1969) 121-175, 181-231, 358-361, especially 361; cf. Peter Nagel, "Grammatische Untersuchungen zu Nag Hammadi Codex II" in *Die Araber in der alten Welt*, ed. F. Altheim (Berlin: 1968-69) 5.2, 393-469; especially 447 n. 24, 453-454, 462.

[31] Harold Attridge, "The Greek Fragments [of the Gospel of Thomas]" in *Nag Hammadi Codex*, ed. B. Layton, 98-109, especially 100-101; also: J. Horman, "Sower" 335 n. 30, 336-338.

[32] Koester, "Apocryphal and Canonical Gospels," *HThR* 73 (1980) 105-130, especially 116.

[33] J. Fitzmyer, *Essays on the Semitic Background of the New Testament* (Missoula, Mo.: 1974) 416; ref. in Crossan, *In Fragments* 32-33.

"the latest trait in a sayings collection is far from being an assured indication of the date when the basic collection was made", or, for that matter, the relationship between collections.[34] Schrage's thesis in effect confuses the original text of *GThom* with its surviving manuscript in that it asserts textual dependency based upon scribal harmonization in the latest extant document. Robinson remarks:

> The late date of [the translation of, interpolations into, the final redaction of, the scribe of?] the Gospel of Thomas cannot be validly used as an argument for leaving this text out of the study of the Synoptic tradition, any more than it would be legitimate to eliminate the Synoptic Gospels themselves, dating from the last third of that century, about whom they contain traditions going back to his lifetime.[35]

John Sieber has accused Schrage of misunderstanding the nature of the editorial process. Redactional features in *GThom* do not necessarily connote synoptic dependence: "In order to call a reading a redactional trace, one must be able to attribute that reading to a particular evangelist's theological intent".[36] Similarly, Wilson maintains that any theory of dependency must demonstrate that the differences between *GThom* and the NT serve a particular purpose.[37] Such explanations have not been forthcoming.

Besides the many problems which attend any attempt to argue the synoptic dependence of *GThom* at the level of the Coptic translation, there is strong evidence in favour of the independence of *GThom*. Form-critical characteristics such as allegorization of parables, the pairing of sayings sharing a similar form or content, and the use of septuagintal language are all recognized as secondary accretions to primitive tradition. According to this criterion, the form of sayings in *GThom* are generally more primitive than their counterparts in the synoptic gospels. For ex-

---

[34] Robinson, "Bridging the Gulf" 160.

[35] Robinson, "Bridging the Gulf" 164. Ménard concludes: "La méthode de cet auteur est toutefois fausse de vouloir prouver que le texte de Thomas coïncide avec celui des différentes versions coptes et qu'il leur est par conséquent postérieur. C'est peut-être le dernier rédacteur de l'Évangile qui a harmonisé son texte avec celui des version" (J.-E. Ménard, *L'Évangile selon Thomas* [NHS 5; Leiden: 1975] 23).

[36] J. H. Sieber, *Redactional Analysis* 17. For an overview of Schrage's work on *GThom* 55ab (cf. Mt 10:37 / Lk 14:26), *GThom* 55b (cf. Mk 8:34b / Mt 10:38 / Lk 14:27), *GThom* 65 (Mt 21:33-46 / Mk 12:1-12 / Lk 20:9-19) and Sieber's refutations, see F. T. Fallon and R. Cameron, "The Gospel of Thomas: A Forschungsbericht and Analysis," *ANRW* 2.25/5, pp. 4195-4251, especially 4221-4223.

[37] R. McL. Wilson, *Studies in the Gospel of Thomas* (London: 1960) 148.

ample, the primitive character of *POxy* 1.6 (=*GThom* 31; cf. Mt 6:1-6) as demonstrated by Wendling and Bultmann remains uncontested.[38]

Similarly, the parables in *GThom* rarely have the allegorical features which abound in the synoptic versions (see above). For example, in his careful analysis of the Parable of the Sower in the synoptic gospels and *GThom*, John Horman concludes not only that the version in *GThom* is independent, but that it "does indeed permit us to recover an earlier version of this parable".[39] The conclusion is unavoidable that secondary features are absent in *GThom* because they were absent in its source.

Hugh Montefiore has analyzed the *GThom* parables according to a series of so-called "laws of transformation" based upon the same categories which Jeremias employed of the synoptic tradition. He concludes that on those occasions when the *GThom* sayings *do* exhibit secondary features, they are usually unique to the *GThom*.[40] Thus, even though *GThom* exhibits some secondary characteristics, this process of development is independent. Based on the above criteria, Montefiore concludes that *GThom* is a distinct and sometimes superior source to the synoptic gospels.[41] Similarly, Gilles Quispel concludes that the sayings of *GThom* derive from a different and independent tradition.[42]

The analytical paradigm presupposed by past assertions of *GThom*'s synoptic dependency is typical of much Thomas scholarship in so far as it treats the text of *GThom* as a stable entity. For example, H. K. McArthur argues that once a few sayings have been shown to be dependent on the synoptic gospels, the whole text of *GThom* should be presumed to be dependent until proven

---

[38] Emil Wendling, *Die Entstehung des Marcus-Evangeliums* (Oxford: 1908) 53-56; R. Bultmann, *The History of the Synoptic Tradition*, (Oxford: 1963) 31-32. Koester describes many such examples of more primitive sayings (e.g., *GThom* 68 / Lk 6:22; *GThom* 95 / Lk 6:34; *GThom* 47ab / Mt 6:24 / Lk 16:13; *GThom* 89 / Lk 11:39-40; *GThom* 39 / Lk 11:52;*GThom* 44 / Lk 12:10; *GThom* 63 / Lk 12:16-21; *GThom* 10 / Lk12:49-50; *GThom* 16 / Lk 12:51-53; *GThom* 91 / Lk 12:56): *Ancient Christian Gospels* 89-94.

[39] Horman, "Sower" 343.

[40] Categories include: embellishment, change of audience, hortatory use of parables by the church, influence of the church's changing situation, allegorization, collection and conflation of parables, and setting (H. Montefiore, "A Comparision of the Parables of the Gospel According to Thomas and the Synoptic Gospels" in *Thomas and the Evangelists* [see note 4 above] 40-78).

[41] Montefiore, "Comparision" 78.

[42] G. Quispel, "The Gospel of Thomas and the NT," *VigChr* 11 (1957) 189-207.

otherwise.[43] However, if the text of *GThom* were fixed and dependent upon the synoptic gospels, one would expect a consistent and extensive pattern of dependence, and the reproduction of redactional changes unique to the various synoptic gospels. This is not indeed what one actually finds.

A more sophisticated approach is now emerging which recognizes the fluid dimension of *GThom*'s textual history. While the synoptic tradition tended to fix sayings by embedding them in narrative contexts such as pronouncement stories,[44] the *logia* of *GThom* lack this imaginative realism. Given the lack of narrative, and the fact that the sayings in *GThom* are not organized according to some overarching master plan,[45] it was very easy for new sayings to be added, and old sayings to be reorganized. In the words of Robinson:

> Not only does the Gospel of Thomas share a fluidity of text with other non- or not-yet-canonical literature, but also a fluidity of text particularly characteristic of sayings collections, where there is no train of thought or causal nexus to stabilize the text from saying to saying. A saying can be added or subtracted, a sequence can be altered, quite imperceptibly.[46]

This explains why there is even variability in the respective order of the sayings between the Greek and Coptic versions of *GThom*.[47] Kenneth Neller argues that the Thomas tradition was not fixed even in its written form.[48] Given the fragmentary nature of the

---

[43] H. K. McArthur, "The Gospel According to Thomas" in *New Testament Sidelights: Essays in Honor of Alexander C. Purdy*, ed. McArthur (Hartford: 1960) 43-77.

[44] Bultmann, *Synoptic Tradition* 61-64.

[45] Despite attempts to deduce a rationale for the compositional arrangement of *GThom*, no theory has received general recognition. Attempts are surveyed in: R. McL. Wilson, *Studies in the Gospel of Thomas* (London: 1960) 8-9; Fallon & Cameron, "Gospel of Thomas" (see note 36 above) 4208-4209. Besides the incidental organizing by catchwords (e.g., *GThom* 2, 3), verbal associations, or form (e.g., *GThom* 63, 64, 65), sayings seem to be randomly compiled, each saying having a meaning unto itself. Koester concludes that apart from the introduction (Sayings 1-2), central section (Sayings 49-61) and conclusion (Sayings 113-114), there are no thematic arrangements ("Introduction [to the Gospel of Thomas]" in *Nag Hammadi Codex*, ed. B. Layton, 38-45, especially 41).

[46] Robinson, "Bridging the Gulf" 160-161.

[47] In *POxy* 1, lines 23-30 contain one saying that is found in two separate contexts in *GThom*co (Sayings 30, 77b). Therefore, there are at least two different versions of *GThom*.

[48] K. V. Neller, "Diversity in the Gospel of Thomas," *Second Century* 7 (1989-90) 1-18; cf. R. McL. Wilson, *VigChr* 20 (1966) 121.

extant Greek text, the degree to which sayings were added, rearranged, and redacted is inscrutable. The final text of *GThom*co is probably a cumulative product which expanded over time by the interpolation of new sayings. While some synoptic features where introduced at the level of the Coptic translation, one cannot rule out the possibility that some synoptically-influenced sayings were also interpolated at the latest stage of the collection.

> If in fact the text of the *Gospel of Thomas* (or Q) was never stable, but continued its own life throughout the whole period from the earliest sources embedded in it down to the copying of the *Gospel of Thomas* in Codex II (or of Q in Matthew or Luke), one must reconceptualize the procedures for dating: rather than the whole text of the *Gospel of Thomas* (or Q) being read synchronically, so that all the sayings contribute to establishing the one date of authorship and all the sayings are interpreted in terms of the one dating, one must learn to read diachronically, placing the individual sayings and indeed specific traits in them along the trajectory of the life of the text.[49]

Similarly, Ronald Cameron distinguishes between the basic composition of *GThom* containing the least developed sayings, with later segments which are secondary accretions in the process of transmission of the already-composed document.

> Even though *GTh* does not exhibit the literary sophistication of Q, a controlled use of the thematic criterion of conceptual coherence can serve as a literary tool to peel back stratigraphic levels. Utopian language and conceptuality characterize the final redaction of *GTh*. Therefore, esoteric sayings that depict salvation as liberation through insight into one's origin, identity, and destiny (e.g., *GTh* 13, 49-51, 83-84, 114) can be assigned to the latest compositional layer of the text, which marks the shift in discourse from a locative to a utopian world view.[50]

Given the problems inherent in scribal tradition, and the fact that there are at least sixty-eight parallels between *GThom* and the NT, a few unrelated cases of dependence do not present a strong case for an over-all compositional theory involving direct dependence upon synoptic texts. The compositional history of *GThom* suggests that instances of dependency are attributable either to scribal harmonization at level of Coptic translation, or to the late incorporation of synoptically-influenced sayings into *GThom*. This alone can account for four features of the text: first, form-critical evidence that the majority of the sayings are more primi-

---

[49] Robinson, "Bridging the Gulf" 162.

[50] R. Cameron, "Theses Toward a Stratigraphy of the *Gospel According to Thomas*" (Unpublished lecture delivered 24 Oct. 1991) 1-7, especially 5; cf. *idem, The Other Gospels* 17.

tive than their synoptic parallels; secondly, the lack of a consistent or extensive pattern of synoptic dependency, or theological rationale for changes. Thirdly, it accounts for isolated instances of synoptic dependence. Such instances are capricious, isolated, and unrelated. This explains the absence of any consistent or extensive pattern of dependency. Finally, since forty-one percent of *GThom* has no NT parallels, it is clear that *GThom* had access to canonically independent sources. Given the fluidity of the text, each case for dependency must be assessed on its own merits using form-critical criteria.

To sum up: the blanket theory that *GThom* is dependent on the synoptic tradition was founded upon a naïve understanding of Gnosticism and *GThom*'s textual history. As such, it is no longer useful as a point of departure. Adherents of the dependency theory exhibit the same genealogically-oriented mind set which has so characterized the historical-critical method. The genealogical model, which attempts to compress all traditions onto a single linear trajectory conceals the preunderstanding that a pure, pristine oral tradition was first written down (Q / Mark), then redacted (e.g, *Matthew / Luke*), and subsequently corrupted (e.g., *GThom*). This approach fails to recognize that the period of earliest Christian origins was far more diverse than previously suspected, and that a multiplicity of oral sayings and lists of sayings circulated amongst various Jesus groups alongside the emergent pre-canonical texts.

2. The Gospel of Thomas and Q Stratigraphy

Of *GThom*'s one hundred and fourteen sayings, sixty-eight (= 59%) have parallels in the New Testament. Forty of these sixty-eight NT parallels are Q texts. This remarkable overlap between *GThom* and Q has spurred attempts to apply *GThom* to the problem of Q's compositional history and the question of the nature of their shared sources.

Dieter Lührmann and John Kloppenborg have demonstrated that, far from being a random collection of sayings, the Sayings Source Q exhibits a definite structure as a product of distinct moments of compositional activity.[51] Delineation of strata is accomplished by a compositional approach which analyzes Q texts

---

[51] D. Lührmann, *Der Redaktion der Logienquelle* (WMANT 33; Neukirchen-Vluyn: 1969); John S. Kloppenborg, *The Formation of Q: Trajectories in Ancient Wisdom Collections* (Philadelphia: 1987); *idem*, "Tradition and Redaction in the Synoptic Sayings Source," *CBQ* 46 (1984) 34-62.

according to two criteria: continuity (of theme, implied audience, and forms of speech); and discontinuity, or redactional breaks, between and within defined blocks of text. Through the application of these criteria, Kloppenborg has delineated three compositional strata in Q, a sapiential layer (=Q^1) which constitutes the most primitive stratum of Q, a secondary redactional stage which incorporates apocalyptic and other themes (=Q^2), and finally a third stage in which the temptation story (Q 4:1-13; 11:42c; 16:17) is appended (=Q^3).

This compositional approach begins with the final form of Q, as best as it can be deduced, and then works backwards to distinguish its constituitive layers. Thus, the delineation of strata does not begin with individual sayings but with Q's unifying structures which subsume compositional clusters of sayings and single sayings into a cohesive literary composition.[52] Such an compositional approach disengages the analysis from *a priori* sociological judgments about nature of primitive Christianity, whether it be characterized as being sapiential, prophetic or apocalyptic. Instead, the criteria are internal and literary.

Kloppenborg has isolated five complexes of sayings which constitute the redactional, i.e. second, stratum of Q based on continuity of theme, implied audience, and forms (see *Figure 3* below).[53] From this redactional stratum, he distinguishes a more primitive layer (Q^1) which consists of six well-rounded clusters of sapiential instructions (see *Figure 2* below).[54] Though parallels to

---

[52] Kloppenborg remarks: "The detection of the presence of redaction in a sayings collection such as Q cannot proceed simply by cataloguing and sorting the individual Q sayings into two or three "piles" either on the basis of common form, or shared motifs, or the extent of external attestation. Rather than beginning with the individual saying, it must start with the larger composed units, i.e., with the form in which the sayings are now framed. This, of course, implies, that the issue of the original order of Q is a necessarily preliminary" ("The Formation of Q Revisited: A Response to R. Horsley" in *SBLASP* [1989] 204-225, especially 205).

[53] Continuity of theme: judgement themes such as imminence of parousia, Israel's obstinate rejection of John, Jesus and Q prophets. Implied audience: impenitents and opponents of Q preaching. Forms: chriae criticizing the response of Israel, i.e. "this generation", to the preaching of the kingdom (Kloppenborg, *Formation* 102-165). In the case of Lk 11:27-28, while Lührmann and *Formation* do not regard it as a Q text, Kloppenborg argues for its inclusion in *Q Parallels* [Somona, Calif.: 1988] 96).

[54] Kloppenborg, *Formation* 171-245. Each begins with programmatic aphorisms prefacing a series of second person plural imperatives, usually with motive clauses. Properly understood, the classification 'sapiental' offers no difficulty. Kloppenborg has situated the Q^1 sayings within the definable range of non-

GThom exist in both Q^1 and Q^2, most of the correspondences are found in Q^1.

	Q^1	Q^2	Q^3	Total
No. Q Sayings	28	12	0	40
% of Q Sayings	24%	11%	0	35%

Figure 1. Q Overlap with *GThom*'s 114 Sayings

It might be supposed that Q and *GThom* shared a documentary source, but the evidence does not bear this out. For example, Leif Vaage has demonstrated that the Q Sermon did not exist independently prior to its composition in Q^1.[55] The lack of a documentary precursor can be proven elsewhere in Q, for, as Kloppenborg observes, "in several Q^1 / *GThom* overlaps (Q 12:16-21 / *GThom* 63; Q 15:4-7 / *GThom* 107; Q 16:13 / *GThom* 47a) the *GThom* lacks elements present in Q but which, had Thomas know Q, would surely have taken over."[56] A documentary hypothesis for the relationship between Q and *GThom* must be ruled out.

Jewish sayings collections, Near Eastern instruction, the hellenistic gnomologium, and the chriae-collection (*Formation* 263-316). Though Q^1 materially differs from classic sapiental texts such as Prov 1-9 and Sirach, it *is* sapiential when compared with structure of contemporary conventional wisdom purveyed in the instructional genre of Egyptian and Near East sapiental instructions. Kloppenborg uses this classification in a more formal and literary sense: "it [the Sayings Source Q] is *framed* in the form of wisdom teachings, and the structuring of the material conforms rather impressively to the conventions in organizing wisdom materials" ("Formation of Q Revisited" 210; *Formation* 263-316).

[55] In Leif Vaage's thorough examination of this question, he demonstrates that the Sermon was never known apart from Q^1. (For example, he points out that sayings in the Q Sermon exhibit no shared sequence of sayings with *GThom*; "Composite Texts and Oral Myths: The Case of the 'Sermon' (6:20b-49)," *SBLSP* ([1989] 424-439).

[56] Kloppenborg, "Review" 5; cf. Koester, *Ancient Christian Gospels* 96-97.

Cluster	Text	Subject	*GThom* Parallels	No.
1	Q 6:20b-49 + 16:13 + 13:26-27	Inaugural Sermon	Q 6:20b/*GTh* 54 Q 6:21a/*GTh* 69b Q 6:22/*GTh* 68 Q 6:23/*GTh* 69a Q 6:34/*GTh* 95 Q 6:39/*GTh* 34 Q 6:41-42/*GTh* 26 Q 6:43/*GTh* 43 Q 6:44b-45/*GTh* 45	9
2	Q 9:57-62 + 10:2-16, 21-24	Discipleship and Mission	Q 9:58/*GTh* 86 Q 10:2/*GTh* 73 Q 10:8-9/*GTh* 14b Q 10:23-24/*GTh* 17	4
3	Q 11:2-4, 9-13	Prayer	Q 11:9-10/*GTh* 92, 94	1
4	Q 12:2-12	Anxiety	Q 12:2/*GTh* 5, 6 Q 12:3/*GTh* 33a Q 12:10/*GTh* 44	3
5	Q 12:22-34	Necessities and wealth	Q 12:22-30/*GTh* 36 Q 12:33/*GTh* 76b	2
6	Q 13:24-30, 34-35 + 14:16-24, 26-27 + 17:33 + 14:34-35	Discipleship	Q 14:16-24/*GTh* 64 Q 14:26-27/ *GTh* 55, 101	2
Other Q[1] texts			Q 12:13-14/*GTh* 73 Q 12:16-21/*GTh* 63 Q 13:18-19/*GTh* 20 Q 13:20-21/*GTh* 96 Q 15:4-6/*GTh* 107 Q 16:13/*GTh* 47 Q 17:6/*GTh* 48	7
Total				28

Figure 2. Parallels Between Q[1] and *GThom*

The shared tradition between Q and *GThom* was of two kinds, oral sayings and lists of sayings. These two forms of transmission exhibit different characteristics. Werner Kelber has demonstrated the compositional, transitory, and ever-changing disposition of orality.[57] Orally transmitted sayings tend to proliferate ceaselessly in a multiplicity of versions. Orality always involves composition. According to Robinson, both Q and *GThom* share the same relationship to the oral tradition of Jesus sayings, "directly feeding upon and growing out of the oral tradition of Jesus' sayings and smaller collections".[58]

Alongside *orally* transmitted sayings were sayings transmitted in the form of lists. Scholars have only begun to explore the importance of lists in Christian origins. According to Jonathan Z. Smith, "The list is, perhaps, the most archaic and pervasive of genres".[59] In John Dominic Crossan's discussion of sayings lists, miracle lists, and prophecy lists, he states that the activity of listing is "an inaugural genre for the first move from orality to literacy".[60] Similarly, John Kloppenborg observes that, even though first-century Palestine was not in transition between oral and literate cultures, the Jesus people, who did not inherit a ready-made corpus of literature, *were* undergoing such a transition. As such "the listing of sayings (and stories) may have been at the beginning of Christian literary activity".[61] Such lists would have permitted experimentation with various kinds of sortings of material since, and once formed, they could be reorganized according to new categories by recopying.[62] There is evidence that sayings lists continued to have a shadowy existence through the

---

[57] As Werner Kelber writes: "In speaking, transmission involves an act of composition, or at least recreation. All too often when we think of transmission of traditions, we think of it primarily as the passing on of fixed forms. In other words, we think of it in literary terms. In orality, tradition is almost always composition in transmission. From this perspective, too, oral transmission enacts a multiplicity of discrete instances of speech rather than a continuous process of solidification of speech into written forms" (*The Oral and the Written Gospel* [Philadelphia: 1983] 30, cf. 4, 29-31).

[58] Robinson, "Bridging the Gulf" 167.

[59] Jonathan Z. Smith, *Imagining Religion: From Babylon to Jonestown.* (Chicago: 1982) 44.

[60] John Dominic Crossan, "Lists in Early Christianity: A Response to Early Christianity, Q and Jesus," *Early Christianity, Q and Jesus*, eds. J. S. Kloppenborg, with L. E. Vaage (Semeia 55; Atlanta: 1991) 235-243, especially 237.

[61] Kloppenborg, "Review" 7.

[62] Kloppenborg, "Review" 7-8; cf. J. Goody, *The Interface between the Written and the Oral: Studies in Literacy, Family, Culture, and the State* (Cambridge: 1987) 202-203; cf. *idem*, *The Domestication of the Savage Mind: Themes in the Social Sciences.* (Cambridge: 1977) 108.

second century despite their partial eclipse by the canonical gospels.[63]

The dual nature of the sources shared by Q and *GThom* has implications for Q studies. When Matthew and Luke differ on the wording of Q, scholars are often tempted to solve the conflict by reference to *GThom* when a parallel exists. Unfortunately, the mixed nature of sayings traditions shared by Q and *GThom* makes this an uncertain exercise. Shared sayings which are drawn from one of the early circulating lists are of course more dependable, even though they are still subject to editing and redaction. Shared sayings based on oral traditions are of much less value since they are by nature unstable and compositional. However, this theoretical separation between written and oral sources has little usefulness for Q text reconstruction since it is not yet possible, practically speaking, to discriminate between the mode of transmission for any given saying. However, to the extent that *GThom* preserves a more primitive form of a saying preserved in Q, *GThom* is useful in determining the prehistory of Q sayings. Compare, for example, the saying about the coming of the thief in Q 12:39 and *GThom* 21b / 101 where the former concerns the unexpected coming of the Son of Man, while the latter preserves the more natural interpretation about watchfulness as a safeguard against thieves.

Of the 40 *GThom* sayings paralleled in Q, 28 belong to Q[1], its most primitive stratum. The overlaps are especially numerous between Q[1]'s "Sermon" with nine parallels (see *Figure 2*). In several of the "Sermon" parallels, *GThom* frequently preserves a more original form of the saying than Q.[64]

The redacted form of Q (i.e., Q[2]) has subordinated this sapiential collection to apocalyptic traditions unparalleled in *GThom*. *GThom* lacks Q[2]'s polemic against "this generation", its apocalyptic expectation, and Son of Man sayings.[65] Moreover, there is

---

[63] Koester, *Überlieferung bei den apostolischen Vätern* (TU 65; Berlin: 1957); Robinson, "LOGOI SOPHON" 99-101.

[64] E.g., *GThom* 68 / Q 6:22; *GThom* 95 / Q 6:34; *GThom* 47ab / Q 16:13 (Koester, *Ancient Christian Gospels* 89-90).

[65] Cf. Q 14:16-23 with *GThom* 64; cf. J. D. Crossan, *Four Other Gospels* (Minneapolis: 1985) 39-52. "Son of Man" occurs only once in *GThom*, and here in the non-technical sense, 'human being' (*GThom* 86). In fact *GThom* is anti-apocalyptic. It actually opposes this interpretation of Jesus (cf. *GThom* 113). *GThom* sees the coming of the kingdom primarily as something which takes places inside the believer as he gains a new understanding of himself (*GThom* 3).

no mention of John's preaching (Q 3:2-4, 7-9, 16-17), Jesus' baptism or temptation (Q 3:21-22[66]; Q 4:1-13).[67] Thus, *GThom* attests to a stage in the *logoi Gattung* shared by Q and *GThom* which had not yet been redacted under the influence of apocalyptic expectation. It can be concluded from this that *GThom* is not dependent on redacted Q. According to Koester, "the *Gospel of Thomas* is either dependent upon the earliest version of Q or, more likely, shares with the author of Q one or several early collections of Jesus' sayings."[68]

It is clear that Q^1's sapiential material incorporates the highest number of *GThom* parallels. Equally clear is the fact that the apocalyptic sayings which are proper to Q^2 are not paralleled in *GThom*. But this does not complete the picture. There are twelve Q^2 sayings which do have parallels in *GThom*.

It is striking that eight of these Q^2 sayings are not randomly dispersed in Q but collected in a single block (Q 11:27–12:26) with some sayings from Q^1 (Q 11:27–12:26). Q^1 sayings (in clusters 4 and 5) are bracketed by four Q^2 sayings (complexes 3 and 4) on each side (see *Figure 4* below).

These Q^2 sayings display more redaction than their *GThom* counterparts. A second block of Q^2 material appears in Q 7:24b-25, 28 (cluster 2), where again they are more redacted. Unlike Q 7:24b-25, *GThom* 78 lacks a reference to John. Moreover, *GThom* 46 lacks the polemic application found in Q 7:28.

How are the textual parallels between Q^2 and *GThom* to be explained? If Kloppenborg's stratigraphic analysis were abandoned, Q^1 could be redefined as the sum of Q's sapiential material plus all other Q texts which find a parallel in *GThom*. This, in effect, would be to use *GThom*, albeit in a mechanical way, to distinguish between Q^1 and Q^2.[69]

---

[66] Though Q 3:21-22 is not universally ascribed to Q, many scholars argue for its inclusion on the basis of (1) Matthew-Luke agreements against Mark; (2) the statements in Q 4:3, 9 presuppose some narrative in which Jesus' divine sonship is manifested (Kloppenborg, *Formation* 16).

[67] Though John is mentioned once (*GThom* 46 = Q 7:28).

[68] Koester, *Ancient Christian Gospels* 95.

[69] This seems to be Koester's position: "Analogous to the *GTh*, however, is the earlier sayings tradition which preceded the final redaction of Q, in which the title Son of Man was introduced" (*Introduction to the New Testament* 2.152-153). Similarly, Ron Cameron remarks "*GTh* is comparable to an early version of Q in which the apocalyptic Son of Man is missing" ("The Gospel of Thomas and Christian Origins," in *The Future of Early Christianity*, ed. B. A. Pearson [Minneapolis: 1991] 381-393, especially 389).

In my opinion, it would be perilous to use *GThom* to determine Q stratigraphy. First, I have argued above that the textual tradition of *GThom* was fluid with some additional sayings being interpolated over time. Therefore, the textual history of *GThom* is too indeterminate to be used to determine Q^1.

Complex	Text	*GThom* Parallels	No.
1	Q 3:7-9, 16-17		0
2	Q 7:1-10, 18-28, (16:16), 31-35	Q 7:24-25/ *GTh* 78 Q 7:28/*GTh* 40	2
3	Q 11:14-32, 39-52	Q 11:27-28/*GTh* 79 Q 11:33/*GTh* 33b Q 11:39-40/*GTh* 89 Q 11:52/*GTh* 39	4
4	Q 12:39-40, 42-46, 49, 51-53, 54-56, 57-59	Q 12:39/*GTh* 21b, 103 Q 12:49/*GTh* 10 Q 12:51-53/*GTh* 16 Q 12:56/*GTh* 91	4
5	Q 17:23-24, 26-30, 34-35, 37	Q 17:34/*GTh* 61a	1
Other		Q 19:26/*GTh* 41	1
Total			12

Figure 3. Parallels Between Q^2 and *GThom*

Secondly, Kloppenborg's compositional approach respects the role of context in determining the compositional identity of a given saying. He distinguishes between the "possible meaning(s) and function(s) of the sayings considered as free-floating units, and the compositional effect of their juxtaposition with other sayings, and the effect that one saying exerts on another".[70] Therefore, before such Q sayings can be assigned to Q^1 it would be necessary to demonstrate their plausible literary function in the sapiential stratum. The mere fact that a given Q text is paralleled in *GThom* is insufficient for the determination of Q stratigraphy: the context supplied by Q's overarching literary structures is vital in the determination of stratigraphy.

---

[70] Kloppenborg, "Formation of Q Revisited" 205.

Thirdly, since the shared tradition between Q and *GThom* was of two kinds, oral sayings and lists of sayings, it should be assumed until proven otherwise that the respective compilers of Q and *GThom* did not have access to an identical collection of sayings simultaneously. One would expect that the discrete sayings collections available to Q and *GThom* would have been varied in content and been made available at different times. It follows that the bare fact of commonly held sayings between Q and *GThom* is not instructive of the *timing* of the incorporation of these sayings into Q. Indeed, this understanding of textual transmission suggests a different explanation for Q^2 / *GThom* parallels.

Q^1	Q^2
	Complex 3
	Q 11:27-28/*GTh* 79
	Q 11:33/*GTh* 33b
	Q 11:39-40/*GTh* 89
	Q 11:52/*GTh* 39
Cluster 4	
Q 12:2/*GTh* 5, 6	
Q 12:3/*GTh* 33a	
Q 12:10/*GTh* 44	
Q 12:13-14/*GTh* 73[71]	
Q 12:16-21/*GTh* 63	
Cluster 5	
Q 12:22-31/*GTh* 36	
Q 12:33/*GTh* 76b	
Q 12:35/*GTh* 21c	
	Complex 4
	Q 12:39/*GTh* 21b, 103
	Q 12:49/*GTh* 10
	Q 12:51-53/*GTh* 16
	Q 12:56/*GTh* 91

Figure 4.

---

[71] Though Q 12:13-14, 16-21, are without a parallel in Matthew, many scholars assign this section to Q because it is closely related to the following section, Q 12:22-46, by style and wording (Kloppenborg, *Formation* 215; *idem, Q Parallels* 128).

Kloppenborg thinks "that the Q^2 / *GThom* overlaps represent early materials incorporated into Q at a later stage".[72] This theory is corroborated by the fact that the Q^2 parallels evince more redactional activity than *GThom* and that they are inserted as clearly defined blocks which frame Q^1 material (cf. *Figure 4*). Given the fact that *GThom* had exclusive access to 46 sayings, not to mention the characteristic fluctuating nature of early oral and written sayings collections, it is likely that *GThom* also had access to sayings which were not available to the Q^1 compiler, but were subsequently available to the Q^2 redactor. Alternatively, Koester suggests that Q^2 verses such as Q 7:24b-25, 28 may have originally belonged to the Q^1 stratum and referred to Jesus instead of John, and were subsequently reworked by the Q^2 redactor.[73]

3. The Gospel of Thomas, Q, and Christian Origins

The obvious implication of W. G. Kümmel's assertion that *GThom* was dependent upon the synoptics was to dissociate *GThom* from Q. As Kümmel himself remarks: "The document [*GThom*] is as such certainly no late form of the same literary *Gattung* as Q, but rather a late stage, different in kind, of the development of the tradition of Jesus' sayings."[74] It follows that if *GThom* is indeed independent of, and generally more primitive than the synoptic gospels, then the obverse of Kümmel's statement is true. Q no longer stands as an isolated example of the sayings tradition.

I have argued above that *GThom* does not represent a reductionist or derivative genre in which the sayings of the synoptic gospels have been stripped of their biographical framework, christological titles, redaction, and then rearranged. Kloppenborg has established that "meaning in text is *genre-bound*...the act of understanding the genre of a text is always constitutive to the act of understanding [the text itself]."[75] It follows that the differences between *GThom* and Q, on the one hand, and the synoptic gospels are attributable to the dissimilarity between the distinct genres which they represent. The *Gattung* of *GThom* is specified in its incipit as *logoi*. It is now widely recognized that Q^1 *also* preserves

---

[72] Kloppenborg, "Review" 7.
[73] Koester, *Ancient Christian Gospels* 139, 151.
[74] W. G. Kümmel, *Introduction* 58.
[75] Kloppenborg, *Formation* 2.

this *logoi Gattung*, termed *logoi sophōn* by Robinson.[76] *GThom* is a pure instance of the *logoi Gattung* in that it did not suffer synoptic redaction as Q did.[77] Once Q's *Gattung* is appreciated, it is no longer possible to treat Q as a paraenetic supplement to the synoptic gospels. Q, like *GThom*, is a gospel of a different kind.[78] Given the primitiveness of this *Gattung*, Q and *GThom* have much to contribute towards the reappraisal of the origins of Christianity.

Having identified both the *Gattung* of Q and *GThom* as *logoi sophōn*, other texts come to the fore that embody this same *Gattung*. For example, 1 Cor 1–4 reports of Christians who claimed that secret wisdom was revealed to them by Jesus.[79] In his attack on this wisdom theology, Paul employs a saying which also appears in *GThom* 17 (1 Cor 2:9). Similarly, Mark's *parables* approach what *GThom* calls *secret sayings*. They are really allegorical riddles intended to obscure of the mystery of the Kingdom to outsiders (e.g., 4:10-12, 21-22, 33-34; 7:17), but to be revealed to the inner circle of Jesus' followers.[80]

In the course of time, the *logoi Gattung* suffered two significant modifications. First, the *Gattung* bifurcated: while *GThom* remained true to its *Gattung*, the Q[2] redactor subjugated the Q[1] sapiential sayings to apocalyptic themes.[81] This forking of the trajectory of the *logoi Gattung* continued and widened further when Matthew and Luke superimposed Mark's narrative kerygma upon Q.[82] According to Robinson, the *logoi Gattung* was absorbed by the narrative *Gattung* of the synoptic tradition because it was unacceptable to orthodox Christianity without a

---

[76] Robinson, "LOGOI SOPHON" 74-85; Koester, "GNOMAI DIAPHOROI" 135-136. Robinson has demonstrated that the incipit *logoi* is more primitive than the subscription *gospel* ("LOGOI SOPHON" 78-80).

[77] Crossan, *Four Other Gospels* 26-27; Koester, "One Jesus" 186; Koester, "Dialog und Spruchüberlieferung in den gnostischen Texten von Nag Hammadi," *EvTh* 39 (1979) 532-556; *idem*, "Überlieferung und Geschichte der frühchristlichen Evangelienliteratur," *ANRW* 2.25.2 (Berlin: 1984) 1512-1524; Fallon & Cameron, "Gospel of Thomas" (see note 36 above) 4205. Robinson traces the history of this *Gattung* in early Christianity ("LOGOI SOPHON" 71-103).

[78] Robinson, "Bridging the Gulf " 164.

[79] Davies, *Thomas and Wisdom* 145.

[80] Robinson, "LOGOI SOPHON" 91-94; Boring, *Sayings of the Risen Jesus* 80-81 (cf. 1 Cor 2:6-7; Lk 12:2-3).

[81] Koester, "One Jesus" 186-87; *idem*, "GNOMAI DIAPHOROI" 138.

[82] J. M. Robinson, "Jesus-From Easter to Valentius (or to the Apostles' Creed)," *JBL* 101 (1982) 5-37, especially 22, 36.

radical alteration of its form and theological intention.[83] Unlike Q, *GThom* continued to be controlled by the original principle of the *logoi Gattung*, *viz.* that the word of wisdom has authority because "the teacher is present in the word which he has spoken".[84]

Both *GThom* and Q[1] presuppose that Jesus' importance lay in his words alone. Jesus is portrayed as a teacher of wisdom or a spokesperson of heavenly wisdom. His death and resurrection have no theological import. *GThom*'s incipit which refers to the living Jesus does not seem to imply a resurrected Jesus but rather, as Koester points out, Jesus is simply referred to "without any concern for the problem of his death, and without any recognition of the fact that his life has become past history".[85] An awareness of the primitive and widespread nature of the wisdom sayings *Gattung* requires a re-evaluation of the taxonomies of Christian origins.

Taken together, as Koester observes, *GThom* and Q "challenge the assumption that the early church was unanimous in making Jesus' death and resurrection the fulcrum of Christian faith".[86] The extant archaeological evidence supports this view. Graydon Snyder observes: "From 180 to 400 artistic analogies of self-giving, suffering, sacrifice, or incarnation are totally missing. The suffering Christ on a cross first appeared in the fifth century, and then not very convincingly."[87] Snyder interprets these exemplars of early Christian iconography as representative of *popular* Christian religion as opposed to *official* Christian religion. Taken together they provoke the scholar to reconsider the character of first- and second-century Christianity. One should not discount the possibility that Paul's Gospel of the Cross which commanded such centrality in the post-Constantinian Church, partly on account of the sheer bulk of his letters, may have been a minority voice in the first century.

---

[83] Robinson, "LOGOI SOPHON" 112-113; Robinson, "The Problem of History in Mark, Reconsidered," *USQR* 20 (1965) 135.

[84] Koester, "GNOMAI DIAPHOROI" 138; Robinson, "Bridging the Gulf" 168.

[85] Koester, "One Jesus" 167-168; contra B. E. Gärtner, *The Theology of the Gospel According to Thomas* (New York: 1960/ET 1961) 112-113.

[86] Koester, *Ancient Christian Gospels* 86.

[87] *Ante Pacem: Archaeological Evidence of Church Life Before Constantine* (Mercer, GA: 1985) 165. Cf. "There is no place in the third century [or earlier] for a crucified Christ, or a symbol of divine death. Only when Christ was all powerful, as in the iconography of the Emperor, could that strength be used for redemption and salvation as well as deliverance" (*idem, Ante Pacem* 29).

Taken together, *GThom* and Q testify to the presence of a primitive form of the Jesus tradition which was originally independent of, parallel to, and in tension with, the emerging synoptic and Pauline traditions.[88] They demonstrate the fact that Jesus, and the ever-evolving Jesus sayings, were interpreted with remarkable freedom and diversity. The challenge of future scholarship will be to construct a descriptive model of Christian origins which is able to encompass this multiplicity of responses to Jesus.

---

[88] Koester considers *GThom* to be the oldest form of Christianity in Edessa, antedating both Marcionite and "orthodox" Christianity in that area. Koester, "GNOMOI DIAPHOROI" 129, 133, cf. 130-131: *GThom* "represents the eastern branch of the gattung *logoi*, the western branch being represented by the synoptic *logoi* of Q, which was used in western Syria by Matthew and later by Luke" ("GNOMAI DIAPHOROI" 136).

CHAPTER FOURTEEN

ITINERANT PROPHETESSES:
A FEMINIST ANALYSIS OF THE SAYINGS SOURCE Q

Luise Schottroff

The following observations[1] are based on minimal Q, that is those overlapping sayings of the Gospels of Matthew and Luke not found in Mark.[2]

The Androcentric Opposition to Patriarchy
in the Sayings Source and Its Limits

By patriarchy I mean a social organization based on the husband's domination over his wife in a patriarchal "house", which includes further dominative relationships, for example over children and slaves. The state in turn is based on an analogous domination by the ruling class over the masses. Society's hierarchical structures of domination are likewise repeated in its conception of God.[3] Throughout the sayings source Q, an androcentric language corresponding to this patriarchal ideology is spoken. Women are never acknowledged as independently operative outside of the home—the Queen of the South (Q 11:31[4]) being the exception that proves the rule. They are the *objects* of men's transactions in marriage (Q 16:18, 17:27) and in divorce (Q 16:18). Women are only acknowledged as operative within the domestic realm in their chores (by milling in Q 17:35; by baking in Q 13:20f.). The conflict in the patriarchal

---

[1] This essay arose in connection with the Q Seminar of the Society of Biblical Literature. Translated by Jonathan Reed, Associate Director, Institute for Antiquity and Christianity in Claremont, and also published in the Institute's *Occasional Papers* 21 (1991).

[2] For a detailed discussion of the possibilities and limits of reconstructing Q, see Luise Schottroff, "Das Gleichnis vom grossen Gastmahl in der Logienquelle," *EvTh* 47 (1987) 192-211.

[3] On the concept of patriarchy, see Elisabeth Schüssler Fiorenza, *In Memory of Her: A Feminist Theological Reconstruction of Christian Origins* (New York: 1983) and Luise Schottroff, *Lydias ungeduldige Schwestern. Feministische Sozialgeschichte des frühen Christentums* (Gütersloh, 1994) 40-68.

[4] As is the case with other essays in this volume, the Lukan versification is used for Q according to the current scholarly convention, without prejudicing either the order or reading in favor of Luke.

household brought about by Jesus' message is acknowledged only in the conflict regarding a son's duties towards his father (Q 9:59-60). Matthew's androcentric version of Q 12:51-53 therefore likely preserves Q. Luke's more egalitarian version *also* presupposes a patriarchal household, in which the young bride moves in with the groom's parents. Matthew's "person" (ἄνθρωπος) is the young man in the patriarchal household of his father. Female companions of Jesus or encounters with women on the road—described in the other synoptic sources—are sought for in vain in the sayings source. Except for the household, the world of the sayings source is—seemingly—strictly a society of males. Yet the relegation of women to the household should not be understood as their confinement to the "private" realm. The household was at that time also in some sense "public". Their confinement was based on the patriarchal ideology, according to which women were defined by matrimony.

The sayings source criticizes the reality of patriarchal domination in a radical way, but exclusively from the perspective of men, who oppose any domination as contrary to the divine will. I would like to illustrate an example of this androcentric opposition to patriarchy in some detail. An eschatological logion of the sayings source reads as follows:[5]

> As were the days of Noah, so will be the coming of the Son of man. For just as (*in those days before the flood*) they were eating and drinking, marrying and giving in marriage,[6] up to the day when Noah went into the ark and *(they did not notice until)* the flood came and destroyed them all (Q 17:26-27).

The periphrastic imperfect tense[7] in Matthew's version as well as the imperfect tenses in Luke's version emphasize the usual pursuit of daily life and the habitual behavior of Noah's generation. They continue on as always. But their behavior is seen as culpable and obstinate in God's eyes, which leads to their eschatological destruction, to eternal death. Numerous exegetes have claimed that this logion finds Noah's generation innocent: "Their activities are in no way evil in and of themselves" (D. Zeller[8]); "the regularity of daily life is sur-

---

[5] The Lukan and Matthean overlap is sufficient for an understanding of the saying. The text cited represents the Matthean version, with those portions of the Matthean text without a Lukan parallel in parentheses.

[6] Matthew's version ("marrying and giving in marriage") has in mind the groom and the bride's father; Luke's version ("they married, they were being married") the groom and the bride. In both cases, women are the objects of men's transactions.

[7] "They were eating..."

[8] Dieter Zeller, *Kommentar zur Logienquelle* (Stuttgart: 1984) 91.

prisingly and unexpectedly confronted by God's judgement"
(W. Schenk[9]). But this logion does not portray a confrontation between confident certainty on the part of those engaged in "instinctive
busyness" (S. Schulz[10]) and God's judgement. Rather, it portrays a
confrontation between those who heard God's voice but *chose not to
listen*. The form of this logion (some kind of monitory saying), the
Jewish traditions pondering the guilt of Noah's generation[11] and its
context in the sayings source (see Q 13:34 in the Matthean order:
"...and you refused!") demonstrate that the issue lies not in the inap-
prehensive attitude of Noah's generation, but in the culpable persistence of living on as before. The offence of Noah's generation is essentially described as the persistence of an intact patriarchal household: "...eating and drinking, marrying and being married ("were being married" in Luke)" constitute unassailable pillars of daily life.
The patriarchal household is described from an androcentric perspective: in Luke as arranged by the *paterfamilias*, the master of the
household, and in Matthew as arranged by the father and the son.
Women are the objects of men's transactions and their work is invisible. Women produce the "eating and drinking", but they are not
mentioned. This rigid arrangement ought to have been shattered by
Jesus' message, had it been heard. His message should have induced
disputes and conflicts, as other Q logia show (Q 12:51-53; 14:25-27;
17:33; 9:58-60). The persistent, stubborn endurance of the patriarchal
household is held in defiance by the community through their
imminent expectation of judgement—but this defiance lacks a conscious interest in the emancipation of women. Indeed the patriarchal
house is not demurred as an oppressive place, rather its privileged
men are chided for their disinclination to hear Jesus' words.

The sayings source's androcentric opposition to patriarchy gets at
the root of men's patriarchal behavior; nevertheless, it disregards the
situation of women: they are implicated in the text, without having
been operative for themselves, for they too are subjected to the
judgement on Noah's generation. Elsewhere in the sayings source, a
similar androcentric opposition to patriarchy critiques the worldly
political domination of Rome,[12] the hierarchical structures of military

---

[9] Wolfgang Schenk, *Synopse zur Redenquelle der Evangelien* (Düsseldorf: 1981)
122.

[10] Siegfried Schulz, *Q. Die Spruchquelle der Evangelisten* (Zürich: 1972) 285.

[11] Collected in H. Strack and P. Billerbeck, *Kommentar zum Neuen Testament aus
Talmud und Midrasch* I (München: 1922) 961-964.

[12] Q 4:5.

authority,[13] the luxury of Herod's palaces,[14] and the reliance upon kinship with Abraham.[15] Nevertheless, this opposition to patriarchy falls short of a critique of the patriarchal structures imposed on both God and the lives of the women followers of Jesus: believers are *sons* of God (Q 6:35); Jesus is the *Son* of God (Q 4:3); believers are compared to a *man* building a house upon a rock (Q 6:48). The sayings source's androcentric descriptions as well as its limited opposition to patriarchy are taken into consideration in the following attempt to say something about the history of the women in the Jesus movement recorded in Q.

A Woman's Labor and Its Theological Implications

The sayings source juxtaposes the parable of the leaven (Q 13:20-21), a parable about a woman, with the parable of the mustard seed. The sowing of mustard seeds, a man's chore (only in Q[16]), is juxtaposed with the baking of bread, a woman's chore. Similarly, the description of the woman's chore of grinding at the millstone is juxtaposed with a man's chore in Q 17:34-5.[17] Again in Q 12:27 ("toil nor spin"), a woman's household chore is coupled with a man's chore as an equitable pair. An acknowledgement of women's labor is unusual in patriarchal societies. Normally, a woman's labor is not even considered "labor" in the sense that a man's is—as a rule it is not even mentioned. Even the sayings source—with a certain inconsistency—reflects the patriarchal concealment (as in Q 17:27 "eating and drinking") and even the expropriation of women's labor: in Q 11:11-

---

[13] Q 7:8. The faith of the Capernaum Centurion does not consist in his understanding of Jesus' authority over demons as analogous to his authority over his soldiers. Rather it consists in his realization that his own realm of authority is limited to killing, while Jesus' realm of authority extends to healing. The military command and the healing words of Jesus are essentially incomparable. On the history of interpretation see Uwe Wegner, *Der Hauptmann von Kapernaum (Mt 7,28a; 8,5-10.13 par Lk 7,1-10)* (WUNT 2/14; Tübingen: 1985), who in his own exegesis stresses the difference in the magnitude of authority between the Centurion and Jesus, but who neglects any qualitative difference between military authority and the authority to heal.

[14] Q 7:25.

[15] Q 3:8.

[16] The "person" (ἄνθρωπος) who in Q 13:19 sows the mustard seed is (unlike in Mk 4:31) a man, as the following saying about the woman and the leaven makes clear.

[17] The similarities between Mt 24:40 and Lk 17:34 are insufficient accurately to ascertain the activities of the two men. Because of Q's interest in the theme of labor, one could argue that Mt = Q.

12 the mealtime role of the *paterfamilias* is equated with God's role (which God surpasses)—he gives the son bread (or an egg) and a fish. The distribution of bread, of the food, by the *paterfamilias* is a clear symbolic expropriation of the woman's household chores. Women grind at the millstone, bake the bread, prepare the fish, yet the *paterfamilias* hands the food to the son, he is the actual donor. The sayings source embraces both a conspicuously equitable perception of women's household chores, as well as an unconscious patriarchal concealment and expropriation of women's labor. It should also be noted that the sayings source does not acknowledge women's labor outside of the household (in trade, in textile production, in the fields, in prostitution), since according to patriarchal ideology, women exist only *in* the household.

The parable of the leaven, the saying about the women who grind at the millstone and the admonition not to worry all place women's labor alongside men's labor with theological implications. The *parable of the leaven* most obviously shatters the laws of patriarchal perceptions of women's labor, since it equates a woman's labor with God's activities. The parable tells of a particular situation during the baking of leaven bread: the woman takes the leaven (mixes it with flour) and covers the dough,[18] so that it can rise. She can then patiently await the permeation of the dough by the leaven. The baking of bread by women was common to all societies of antiquity, as it still is in the so-called "third world;" it is the daily labor which sustains all people. For people in a famine stricken land, as the sayings source presupposes ("give us today bread" Q 11:3), a glimpse at a full vat of dough,[19] which would only have been possible in well-off

---

[18] Most exegetes have viewed the woman's "hiding" of the leaven as an inaccurate description how dough is prepared. Walter Bauer's *TDNT* III.958 adds "to mix in" as a translation in addition to "conceal." Other authors solve this alleged problem by assuming that the parable is speaking of the concealment of the kingdom. Even the geographically and technologically oriented exegetes fail to appeal to the covering of dough in order to let it rise: Cf. Gustav Dalman, *Arbeit und Sitte in Palästina* IV (Gütersloh: 1935) 46; Samuel Krauss, *Talmudische Archäologie* I (Leipzig: 1910) 99f; Hugo Blümner, *Technologie und Terminologie der Gewerbe und Künste bei Griechen und Römern* I (Leipzig: 1912) 61. The distance of men who work in the humanities and sciences from the procedure of baking bread is apparent here. The procedure is accurately described in cookbooks, such as Helene Caspari and Elisabeth Kleemann, *Das Landkochbuch,* 2nd ed. (Berlin: 1918). Joachim Jeremias, *Die Gleichnisse Jesu*, 7th ed. (Göttingen: 1965) 147, and Adolf Jülicher, *Die Gleichnisreden Jesu* II (Tübingen: 1910) 578, correctly describe the procedure, presumably from their own observation.

[19] The above-mentioned cookbook presupposes 30 kg of flour for the baking of bread in a large rural household. Leaven bread was baked for storage, so that the

households, would have been a sign of the promised kingdom of God. Jesus' parables tend to equate items of everyday life with the kingdom of God.[20] This particular parable directs attention to the hands of a woman, who *takes* the leaven and *covers* the dough and then waits with clasped hands. Her hands are compared to God's hands; in them the hungry see a sign from God. God too intervened[21] and now awaits with tranquil certainty the transformation of all creation into the kingdom of God. The parable speaks of that moment of comprehensive hope, in which the Jesus movement is recognized as the mustard seed which will become a tree. The time to cover the dough is now. God and God's children look to the future with the patient hope of a woman baking bread.

In Q 17:35 the strenuous labor of two women grinding at a millstone is portrayed as a typical situation of daily life,[22] which is interrupted by God's judgement as they are separated: one woman is taken, the other is left...one will thus live, the other will die an eternal death. Judgement will separate those who did God's will, who listened to God, from those who did not listen. This saying harries its audience: "Is it me or is it my neighbor?" "Am I alert, did I listen to the voice of God?" There are a series of logia which portray the confrontation of God's judgement and the activities of daily life. They each emphasize a different aspect: an *obstinate perpetuity* in Q 17:27 (see above), and the *separation of two*, who had been only inches apart, in this logion.[23] It is difficult to decide what Q's parallel to the women who were grinding at the mill was: Was it two men who were

---

amount of flour mentioned in the parable (3 measures = 39.4 liters) need not be seen as a "divine reality" (so J. Jeremias, *Die Gleichnisse Jesu* 146 n. 16).

[20] See Luise Schottroff in Christine Schaumberger and Luise Schottroff, *Schuld und Macht. Studien zu einer feministischen Befreiungstheologie* (1988: München) 137-140.

[21] The concern of theologians of the "first" world not to speak of a human co-laboring in the kingdom of God ("synergism") has led to the bifurcation of God's activity and human activity in following Jesus. God's intervention in this text is tied to the work and person of Jesus as well as that of his followers. The feminist interpretation of Elizabeth Waller ("The Parable of the Leaven: A Sectarian Teaching and the Inclusion of Women," *USQR* 35 [1979-80] 99-109) de-emphasizes the theme of women's labor and the significance of leaven and bread for people, and places the theme of the conception of God in the foreground: "A woman is the locus of sacred activity." Sharon H. Ringe appropriately emphasizes the connection between the significance of women's labor and of bread in a famine stricken land ("Matthäus 13:33: Das Brot geht auf" in *Feministisch gelesen* I, ed. Eva Renate Schmidt, Mieke Korenhof and Renate Jost [Stuttgart: 1988] 159).

[22] See especially G. Dalman, *Arbeit und Sitte in Palästina* III (1933) 219f.

[23] Mk 13:15 par and Mk 13:16 par deal with the admonition to be ready immediately. Mk 13:17 par deals with the perils of those who are pregnant and nursing.

still in bed while the women were working (Luke), or was it two men who were working in the fields (Matthew)? In any case, the aim of this logion is to harry its audience—in this case men—with the thought of imminent judgement. In Q 17:35 women are addressed in their daily toil: Judgement is near, it will fall upon you too, if you do not listen. Here women are accorded their own decision and their own behavior in following Jesus (as opposed to the previous logion).

In the admonition to avoid enslavement by earthly anxieties (Q 12:22-32), the labor of men and women is likened to imprisonment. The anxiety over food and clothing, as well as the strenuous labor of men and women, ensnares people and renders them incapable of seeking the kingdom of God (Q 12:31). In this instance people are admonished, in spite of their poverty, to avoid being crushed by their poverty.[24] Here too, women are addressed in the midst of their daily toil—they are credited with the ability to liberate themselves from the enslavement of anxieties.

Despite the androcentrism of the sayings source, despite its inconsistency in the perception of women's labor, in these texts the lives of women are acknowledged, and they are given the same opportunities as men to follow Jesus—in the parable of the leaven their labor is even compared to God's labor for the creation. The inconsistency with regard to the liberation of women is not unique to the sayings source; it is also encountered in Paul and in the other synoptic traditions. Nevertheless, with due caution, I would like to point out a particularly striking difference: Q's androcentrism is particularly pronounced,[25] rendering its equitable perception of women's labor unique[26] in the early Christian traditions or in the social reality of its time.

---

[24] Luise Schottroff and Wolfgang Stegemann, *Jesus and the Hope of the Poor* (New York: 1986) 42ff.

[25] When, for example, marriage is portrayed as the exclusive activity of men (see above note 6).

[26] On contempt for women's labor, see Luise Schottroff, "DienerInnen der Heiligen. Der Diakonat der Frauen im Neuen Testament," in G. K. Schäfer and Th. Strohm, *Diakonie—Biblische Grundlagen und Orientierungen* (Heidelberg: 1990). I see the reasons for the beginnings of justice for women—in spite of Elisabeth Schüssler Fiorenza's critique (*In Memory of Her* 140ff.)—as the experience of equity in a famine stricken society and in the hope of God's rule, and not as a conscious espousal of the liberation of women in the Jesus tradition.

Family Conflicts of Women

The followers of Jesus spread a message that created conflict in the
patriarchal household, the evidence of which crops up in a variety of
logia: in the enmity between the members of a household who continued to live together (Q 12:51-53), and in the abandonment of family and the imitation of Jesus' homeless lifestyle (Q 9:58; the mission
speech according to Q;[27] perhaps also Q 14:26). It should already be
clear from the analysis of Q 17:27 that the notion of itinerant
prophets, who were economically dependant on a sedentary and pa-
triarchally structured community, is inapplicable.[28] In such a model
itinerant charismatics are discarded as moral freaks, while the early
Christian community is adopted as the model for a patriarchal Church
and society.[29] The sayings source and other early Christian sources
paint a different picture: the message of Jesus effectively questions—
in the resultant conflicts, and structurally (even though
androcentrically)—the patriarchal order. Men who plod along as if
nothing had happened (Q 17:27) are deaf to the voice of God. And
Jesus demands: "Let the dead bury the dead" (Q 9:60). This undermines one of the foundational pillars of the inter-generational con-
tract, based on the Decalogue's commandment to honor one's parents.[30] There were then, except for the itinerant followers of Jesus, no
"normal" family structures, nor was there a "love-patriarchy" as an
organizational principle in the community.[31] This raises the question
of the impact upon women of an actual and fundamental breakdown
of the patriarchal household. According to Q 12:53, it meant that the
young women of the household (daughters and daughters-in-law) re-
belled against their mothers (so Matthew); in the Lukan version, it
also meant the rebellion of the old against the young. According to
Q 16:18, the gospel often led to divorce,[32] after which the woman

---

[27] See Luise Schottroff in L. Schottroff and W. Stegemann, *Jesus and the Hope of
the Poor* 45ff.

[28] So Gerd Theissen, *Studien zur Soziologie des Urchristentums* (Tübingen: 1979),
especially in his 1973 essay on "Wanderradikalismus."

[29] For a criticism of Theissen's model, see Luise Schottroff in L. Schottroff and
W. Stegemann, *Jesus von Nazareth* 66f.; Elisabeth Schüssler Fiorenza, *In Memory of
Her* 145f.

[30] See especially Martin Hengel, *Nachfolge und Charisma* (Berlin: 1968) 9ff.

[31] 1 Timothy and Titus are particularly interested in re-establishing the patriarchal
arrangements instead of the existing non-patriarchal community structures.

[32] See Luise Schottroff, "Ehe—Familie—Gemeinde," *Reader der Sommeruni-
versität Kassel 1989* (Universität Kassel: 1990). Based on the logia on divorce in the
Synoptic tradition, it is inappropriate to speak of Jesus forbidding divorce. Divorce is

was not permitted to remarry, but was to remain single. It is thus clear that women too could be counted among the itinerant messengers of Jesus, who lived according to Jesus' homeless lifestyle.[33] With this, however, the women's assigned roles in the patriarchal structure were made obsolete. Texts like the so-called "household codes", which force women into specific roles of the patriarchal structure, are absent from the sayings source and the entire synoptic tradition. Even though the sayings source's androcentric language conceals the presence of women among the messengers of Jesus (especially in the mission speech Q 10:2-12), they are nevertheless to be counted among those who considered their labor to be for the kingdom of God, and not for the patriarchal household: there were women laborers for God's harvest (Q 10:2). Whether sedentary or itinerant, they lived as messengers of God in a new community. Traces of this community are present in the portrayal of solidarity among the male and female disciples, who together lived as sheep among wolves (Q 10:3).

The Gospel of the Poor and Divine Sophia

At the suggestion of the so-called "history-of-religions" school (R. Reitzenstein, W. Bousset[34]), Rudolf Bultmann[35] tried to reconstruct a Sophia myth, whose traces he detected not only in the Jewish wisdom literature, but also in the sayings source. Over the past sixty years his method of reconstructing a myth based on common motifs

---

presupposed, and the logia's interest is to hinder remarriage. 1 Cor 7 can be read as a commentary on the gospels' logia on divorce.

[33] At this point I agree with Elisabeth Schüssler Fiorenza (*In Memory of Her* 145f) as well as with her critique of Theissen's scheme. Monika Fander (*Die Stellung der Frau im Markusevangelium* [Altenberge: 1989]) adopts Theissen's theories without addressing the arguments of E. Schüssler Fiorenza, and imagines that the wives of the radically itinerant men stayed at home (329f.). She also notes that it is difficult to prove the existence of radically itinerant women. But Mk 15:40f. is unequivocal. Even aside from the sayings source, it is clear that women are to be counted among the itinerant prophets. See especially Mary R. D'Angelo, "Women Partners in the New Testament" in *Journal of Feminist Studies in Religion* 6 (1990) 65-86.

[34] See R. Bultmann, "Der religionsgeschichtliche Hintergrund des Prologs zum Johannesevangelium" (1923) in *Exegetica. Aufsätze zur Erforschung des Neuen Testaments* (Tübingen: 1967) 10-35, especially 26f.

[35] R. Bultmann, "Der religionsgeschichtliche Hintergrund des Prologs zum Johannesevangelium," and *Die Geschichte der synoptischen Tradition*, 4th ed. (Göttingen: 1958) 120.

has been called into question by various scholars:[36] with this method myths can be reconstructed that did not exist. In the process, the sources in which traces of the alleged myth are posited are not examined in their own right. Rudolf Bultmann's suggestion was pursued, among others, by James Robinson.[37] He noticed in the sayings source both texts in which Jesus is a messenger of Sophia (such as Q 7:35) and texts that understand Jesus to be Sophia (Q 10:22; Mt 11:28-30). According to Robinson, sapiential traditions and sapiential motifs tend to develop in a Christological direction, without necessarily emanating from a "wisdom myth." This hypothesis was accepted by other exegetes who built on the work of R. Bultmann, as for example S. Schulz.[38]

This thesis has gained widespread acceptance among those engaged in the feminist theological quest for an egalitarian spirituality. Elisabeth Schüssler Fiorenza[39] sees in Jesus as divine Sophia and in the later Jesus-Sophia-Christology of the New Testament (especially in the pre-Pauline hymns) a concept of God, a praxis and a Christology, which liberate women both spiritually and practically. Those texts of the Jewish wisdom literature oppressive to women are, according to Elisabeth Schüssler Fiorenza, in tension with their own portrayal of Sophia, and they are imperilled by it.[40] Unlike Rosemary Ruether,[41] she does not think of Sophia, the mediator of revelation, as a feminine supplement to God, a male notion of femininity in heaven. Elisabeth Schüssler Fiorenza believes that the struggle

---

[36] Carsten Colpe, *Die religionsgeschichtliche Schule. Darstellung und Kritik ihres Bildes vom gnostischen Erlösermythos* (Göttingen: 1961); Luise Schottroff, *Der Glaubende und die feindliche Welt. Studien zum gnostischen Dualismus und seiner Bedeutung für Paulus und das Johannesevangelium* (Neukirchen: 1970). See also Willy Schottroff's review of W. Fauth's *Aphrodite Parakyptusa* in *ZDPV* 83 (1967) 206-208.

[37] James Robinson, "ΛΟΓΟΙ ΣΟΦΩΝ. Zur Gattung der Spruchquelle Q" in *Zeit und Geschichte. Dankesgabe an R. Bultmann,* ed. Erich Dinkler (Tübingen: 1964) 77-96; "Jesus as Sophos and Sophia: Wisdom Tradition and the Gospels" in *Aspects of Wisdom in Judaism and Early Christianity,* ed. Robert L. Wilken (Notre Dame: 1975) 1-16.

[38] S. Schulz, *Q. Die Spruchquelle der Evangelisten* 213-228, who nevertheless recognizes the non-sapiential thought of Mt 11:25 par; see below note 50.

[39] Elisabeth Schüssler Fiorenza, *In Memory of Her* 208-218. See also her "Wisdom Mythology and the Christological Hymns of the New Testament" in *Aspects of Wisdom in Judaism and Early Christianity,* ed. Robert L. Wilken (Notre Dame: 1975) 17-41.

[40] Elisabeth Schüssler Fiorenza, *In Memory of Her* 133-134.

[41] Rosemary R. Ruether, *Sexism God Talk* (Boston: 1983), especially 61: "...that simply ratify on the divine level the patriarchal split of the masculine and the feminine."

against a "divine dimorphism"[42] in the Jewish wisdom literature made possible the notion of divine Sophia. In addition to James Robinson's work, Felix Christ's 1970 book *Jesus Sophia*[43] is also foundational for Elisabeth Schüssler Fiorenza. She adopts from Felix Christ the notion that divine Sophia was already connected with the gospel of the poor in the Jewish wisdom literature. She speaks of a "divine Sophia of the poor." Though I applaud her presentation of the synoptic traditions as a gospel of the poor, I can not agree that it understood *divine Sophia* as partial towards the poor.

F. Christ did not succeed in finding texts in the wisdom literature that demonstrated the sapiential character of the sayings source's gospel of the poor.[44] The idea that wisdom turned to fools and infants in order to make them wise, or the idea that wisdom did not reveal herself to the powerful and renowned,[45] is not what Mt 11:25 has in mind: "thou hast *hidden* these things from the wise and understanding and revealed them to infants." The infants or the uneducated are not transformed into sages by wisdom, but rather they become, as it were, children of God. This is a resumption of the prophetic tradition (like Isa 29:14-20, for example), which was also decisive for Paul in 1 Cor 1:27-28. God chooses the lowly and brings to naught the wisdom of the wise; the community translated the election of the lowly into practical behavior. Without trying to play wisdom and prophecy off each other, it is noteworthy that in the writings that we call sapiential (Wisdom of Solomon, Sirach, Proverbs, and others), the gospel of the poor plays no role. Rather, the concern is for the wise and pious man, and for how the *paterfamilias* might attain a prosperous patriarchal household. The wisdom literature provides instructions for grooming a sage endowed with all the proper traits of a pa-

---

[42] *In Memory of Her* 134.

[43] Felix Christ, *Jesus Sophia. Die Sophia-Christologie bei den Synoptikern* (Zürich: 1970). See Elisabeth Fiorenza Schüssler, *In Memory of Her* 132 n. 76 and the connection between speculations of Sophia and the gospel of the poor.

[44] Note, for example, his lists of sapiential motifs (158-163) with the alleged sapiential examples of "associating with tax collectors and sinners".

[45] Wisdom of Solomon 10:21 (and elsewhere): "Wisdom opened the mouth of the dumb and made the tongues of infants speak clearly"—that is to say the dumb and the infants are made wise by wisdom. See Sirach 3:19 or Baruch 3 for the idea that there were powerful and renowned who did not receive a revelation from wisdom; see also Marcion's version of Mt 11:25 (in Adolf von Harnack, *Marcion* [1924] [Darmstadt: 1960] 205 f: "I thank you and I praise you..., because that which was hidden from the wise and the prudent, you revealed to infants.") For a discussion of parallels to Mt 11:25, see G. Bertram in *TDNT* IV.921-922, and F. Christ, *Jesus Sophia* 83ff.

triarchal *paterfamilias*, or even a king (Wisdom of Solomon). A reading of the wisdom literature critical of patriarchy is still pending.

It is striking that some of the constituent motifs of wisdom as the
mediator of revelation crop up in the sayings source—and elsewhere
in the New Testament. Wisdom is involved as the sender of prophetic
messengers in Q 11:49. However, I do not assume that sapiential
motifs are present in Mt 11:28-30 (nor in Q 10:22[46]). Mt 11:28-30
criticizes forms of domination[47] and can hardly be considered sapiential. Yet where sapiential motifs do occur, it is necessary to consider the associations of these motifs in a methodologically sound
manner: the meaning of the adopted motif must be understood *in its
new context*. The sayings source subjugates the relatively few sapiential fragments under the rubric of its gospel of the poor. Those
texts mentioning the rejection of Jesus' messengers are spiritually
heir to the prophetic tradition, not the sapiential tradition. The messengers of Jesus were killed by those who rejected them. Sophia
withdrew to heaven after she was rejected.[48]

All in all, I consider the sapiential motifs of the sayings source, and
indeed of the entire synoptic tradition, to be marginal and essentially
irrelevant in the Jesus traditions: their meaning is derived from other
traditions (prophecy and apocalyptic) and from other experiences.

Another exegetical tradition appropriately states that Q 10:21 and
other such passages contain no sapiential motifs, but then inappropriately interprets the text in an anti-Jewish manner: Jesus sarcas-

---

[46] On the apocalyptic background of Q 10:22, see Paul Hoffmann, *Studien zur
Theologie der Logienquelle* (Münster: 1972) 122-138.

[47] See Luise Schottroff, "Das geschundene Volk und die Arbeit in der Ernte
Gottes" in *Mitarbeiter der Schöpfung*, eds. L. and W. Schottroff (München: 1983)
161f. Sirach 6:18-31; 51:26 (which F. Christ [*Jesus Sophia* 108 n. 9] suggests as
parallel to Mt 11:28-30) speaks of the yoke of wisdom in the struggle for learning.
The yoke of those "who labor and are heavy laden" is imposed by unjust domination,
which Jesus the gentle king will replace with an easy yoke.

[48] 1 Enoch 42. Further material on this motif is cited in F. Christ, *Jesus Sophia*
162 n. 40. On the prophetic tradition of texts like Q 11:49-51, see Jer 5:3; 6:10; 7:13;
on the unwillingness in Q 13:34, see O. H. Steck, *Israel und das gewaltsame
Geschick der Propheten* (Neukirchen: 1967). He believes that Prov 1:20ff. and
Baruch 3:9ff., texts that report the rejection of Wisdom, have been influenced by the
Deuteronomistic tradition of the rejection of the prophets (233 and n. 7; compare
with F. Christ, *Jesus Sophia* 139 n. 40, and 144 "Weisheitstradition"). Decisive for
any explication of a motif's meaning (in this case the rejection of God or Sophia) is
its application within its context. The rejection of Wisdom does not mean that Wisdom is killed. But in the prophetic tradition the historical experiences of Israel killing
its own prophets were central (Neh 9:26). Q 11:49-51 and 13:34-35 point to both
Jesus and his messengers: they too were prophets who had been killed.

tically refutes the Jewish claim to be wise by offering revelation to infants.[49]

In their 1986 book titled *Sophia*,[50] Susan Cady, Marian Ronan and Hal Taussig base their interpretation of the synoptic tradition[51] on Felix Christ as well. As a whole they are more cautious in their appropriation of the Sophia traditions for a feminist spirituality. They see in the sapiential traditions a starting point, from which a feminist spirituality could be developed (p. 14). Yet their work—despite F. Christ and especially despite Elisabeth Schüssler Fiorenza's influence—neglects the gospel of the poor in the synoptic tradition; they therefore operated with a limited perspective on the Jesus traditions. The gospel of the poor must remain central for any feminist spirituality, as they themselves tentatively suggest (p. 91: "experience of marginality").

The infants, to whom God is revealed (Q 10:21-22), include both women and men, though one expects more women to be νήπιοι— "infants", in this case "the uneducated." The text states that God is revealed to those who, according to the wise, have no access to wisdom (and no claim to revelation). Q 10:21 indicates why Jesus' good news to the poor is also good news to women. I believe that herein, and not so much in the presence of Sophia in the synoptic traditions, lies the starting point for a feminist spirituality. God's election of infants, the poor and children opens the eyes of the androcentric Jesus movement to the fate of women and admonishes women to act with the self confidence of a daughter of God. By overcoming the androcentrism of the synoptic tradition, our eyes can be opened to a justice that excludes no one, that leaves no victims invisible and that works towards the liberation of women. My criticism of a feminist Sophia theology or Sophia Christology is rooted in historical and theological reasons. The historical reason is my assessment of the sapiential tradition, which is *not* as a whole oriented towards the goal of a comprehensive justice. The theological reason is the significance of the interrelationship of the gospel of the poor and justice for women and women's liberation.

---

[49] Walter Grundmann, *Das Evangelium nach Lukas* (Berlin: 1961) on Lk 10:21f. S. Schulz, *Q. Die Spruchquelle der Evangelisten* 219; R. Schnackenburg, *Matthäusevangelium* I (Würzburg: 1985) on Mt 11:25.

[50] Susan Cady, Marian Ronan and Hal Taussig, *Sophia: The Future of Feminist Spirituality* (New York: 1986).

[51] *Ibid*. 47f.

Conclusion

Despite the androcentric perspective of the sayings source Q, it nevertheless radically criticizes the persistent state of affairs of the patriarchal household (Q 17:27). A woman's labor in the house is considered equivalent to a man's labor (Q 13:20-21; Q 12:26-27; Q 17:35)
and is even compared to God's labor (Q 13:20-21). In the sayings
source women are addressed as capable of making their own decisions and are deemed responsible for their own behavior (Q 17:35;
Q 12:22-31). Despite the androcentrism of the sayings source, one
can conclude from those passages dealing with women's family conflicts that itinerant prophetesses did exist. In the sayings source, as in
the rest of the synoptic tradition, a Jesus movement is presupposed in
which women were independently operative—whether sedentary or
itinerant. Fundamental to the history of women in the Jesus movement was the gospel of the poor, which is also central in the sayings
source (Q 10:21). While a critical reading of the texts of the sayings
source points to the existence of itinerant prophetesses who followed
Jesus, it is apparent that the sayings source's androcentric perspective
also obscured the extent of the liberation of women. The sayings
source—as the entire synoptic tradition—points to a Jesus movement
that questioned the hierarchies of the patriarchal household, thereby
questioning the entire structure of the patriarchal household.
Therefore, the fact that women too left their houses to become
itinerant prophetesses is of utmost significance for those who still
live—usually in conflict—at home. Both women and men who live
as itinerant messengers, as well as those who live in villages, in the
same way live a gospel of the poor that destroys and subverts the
patriarchal structures.

CHAPTER FIFTEEN

DIVIDED FAMILIES AND CHRISTIAN ORIGINS

Arland D. Jacobson

"The hostility of Christianity to the family dates back 2,000 years", writes Ferdinand Mount in his popularisation of modern research on the family entitled *The Subversive Family* (p. 6). "Hostility" may be a bit sensational, but it is not hard to document *de facto* opposition to the family from the very beginning. Gerd Theissen called attention to the a-familial ethos of the Jesus movement.[1] Some of the sayings of Jesus which are most offensive to modern ears are his anti-family sayings. For example, "If any one comes to me and does not hate his own father and mother...and brothers and sisters...he cannot be my disciple" (Lk 14:26). These sayings are found in all the gospels except the Fourth, including Mark, Thomas and Q. Whether they are deliberately anti-family or only anti-family in their effect, they will herein be called "anti-family" sayings. This paper, then, will focus on these sayings in Q, and on a series of questions related to these sayings, questions which will lead us to consider their social context and some aspects of the larger question of Christian origins.

The Texts

Q 9:59-60a

The most obviously anti-family sayings in Q are Q 9:59-60a and 14:26. In the first, Jesus says to a prospective disciple, "Follow me." The disciple says, "Master, let me first go and bury my father." And Jesus replies, "Let the dead bury their dead." This saying is shocking both because of the sacredness of the duty of burying one's father which is here contravened, and because of the presumed precipitous nature of the call.

---

[1] *Sociology of Early Palestinian Christianity* (Philadelphia: 1978) 11-12.

Burial apparently took place as quickly as possible (cf. Acts 5:6, 7-10; 8:2). "Leaving a corpse unburied through the night, for any reason, was considered to be sinfully disrespectful."[2] One would therefore presume that the death had just happened. Among the various tasks a son was expected to perform was that of obligatory grief and mourning and the rending of garments.[3] But the call of Jesus would require the son to trample on all of these family pieties, including the most solemn one of all, the duty of burying one's father. Since the burial would take place quickly, it is hardly a matter of a significant delay, though the period of mourning would have extended the delay much longer. Jesus' call is, in any context but especially that of first-century Palestine, utterly insensitive. It is an insult to the most inviolate of all bonds, those of the family.

Many interpretations of this saying have been proposed. We cannot review them all here.[4] Recently, Byron McCane has proposed that secondary burial of the dead lies behind this saying.[5] It was, he claims, common practice in first-century Palestine to "bury" a person (that is, place the body in a niche in the wall of a burial cave) for a period of about one year during which the flesh would decompose; then the bones would be reburied in an ossuary or other repository where the bones of other members of the family had also been placed. This, it is claimed, is what is meant when the Bible speaks of someone as being "gathered to his people" (Gen 25:8 and elsewhere).[6] Secondary burial was not, apparently, limited to elites but was employed generally.[7] McCane thinks that "let the dead bury their dead" really means: let the dead whose bones are in an ossuary rebury the bones of the dead father. In the

---

[2] S. Safrai, "Home and Family" in *The Jewish People in the First Century* II, eds. S. Safrai and M. Stern (Compendia Rerum Iudaicarum ad Novum Testamentum I.2; Philadelphia: 1976) 774.

[3] *Ibid.*

[4] See H. G. Klemm, "Das Wort von der Selbstbestattung der Toten," *NTS* 16 (1969-70) 60-75; J. Fitzmyer, *The Gospel According to Luke X-XXIV* (AncB 28a; Garden City, NY: 1985) 835-836; U. Luz, *Das Evangelium nach Matthäus,* vol. 2 (EKK I/2; Zurich and Neukirchen-Vluyn: 1990) 25-27; J. D. Kingsbury, "On Following Jesus," *NTS* 34 (1988) 45-59; and Jacobson, *The First Gospel. An Introduction to Q* (Sonoma, CA: 1992) 135-136.

[5] "'Let the Dead Bury Their Own Dead'," *HThR* 83 (1990) 31-43.

[6] See E. Meyers, "Secondary Burials in Palestine," *BA* 33 (1970) 15-17. There are differences of opinion as to the prevalence and antiquity of secondary burial; see R. Hachlili, "Burials, Ancient Jewish" in *Anchor Bible Dictionary* 1.789-794.

[7] E. Meyers, "Secondary Burials" 18; Hachlili, "Burials" 793.

Jewish texts cited by McCane with reference to secondary burial, however, the word bury refers to the initial burial, not to the reburial; "gather" is used for reburial. Nevertheless, McCane's interpretation could be correct, but, as he emphasizes, on this interpretation the saying would still be offensive to Jewish familial piety. Indeed, since secondary burial is an expression of kinship with the dead, the demand to sever that kinship would be all the more offensive.

Q 14:26

The second clearly anti-family saying is Q 14:26 which in Luke reads, "If any one comes to me and does not hate his own father and mother and wife and children and brothers and sisters, yes, and even his own life, he cannot be my disciple." The parallel in Mt 10:37 reads, "he who loves father or mother more than me is not worthy of me, and he who loves son or daughter more than me is not worthy of me." It is generally assumed that Luke's version more closely approximates Q because it is more radical.[8] It is easy to see why Matthew might have made the saying a bit less radical, but hard to see why Luke would have made it more offensive than it was. However, Luke's saying has also been subjected to redaction. Schüssler Fiorenza is probably correct that Q did not refer to "wife and children".[9] Matthew lacks these words, and most significantly, Luke has inserted them in 18:29 as well (cf. Mk 10:29). In other words, Luke assumed that only male followers left home and family; Q assumed both men and women did so.

Q 14:26 no doubt means that one must be prepared to abandon one's family for the sake of following Jesus. Especially shocking is the first to be mentioned, the father. To be sure, one was to honour both father and mother but Jewish families, like most other Mediterranean families, were strongly patriarchal. Filial obedience was expected. The penalty for the "stubborn and rebellious son" was death by stoning (Deut 21:18-21), though it is not likely this penalty was ever imposed. Q 14:26 is not just radical; it would have been profoundly offensive. However, it need not mean that hatred of one's family is as such a prerequisite for discipleship. "Hate"

---

[8] For the probable Q wording of the saying, see Jacobson, *The First Gospel* 221-222 n. 92.

[9] *In Memory of Her* (New York: 1983) 145-146; cf. J. D. Crossan, *In Fragments: The Aphorisms of Jesus* (San Francisco: 1983) 132.

here probably does not mean "dislike intensely" but "sever one's relationship with" the family.[10]

Both Q 9:59-60a and 14:26 represent radical calls to follow Jesus, calls that entail a *de facto* attack on the family. But they do not call for behaviour essentially different from that of Jesus himself. So far as we know—and Q offers no evidence at all one way or the other—Jesus was unmarried, and the synoptic gospels give the clear impression that he was not on very good terms with his family (e.g., Mk 3:19b-21, 31-35; 6:4). Whether this is historically credible or not one may debate, but it does seem odd that the gospels would call attention to this if there were not some truth to it. However that may be, Q does present a Jesus who is homeless (Q 9:58). Moreover, the two Q anti-family sayings are consistent with the lifestyle demanded of missioners in Q 10, especially Q 10:4, where provisions for travelling are prohibited. So offensive as the sayings are, they are hardly aberrant within the gospel tradition.

Q 12:51-53

Like the two previous sayings, Q 12:51-53 is an anti-family saying, but it is different from them in other respects. The previous sayings deal with priorities, and state unequivocally that obligations to one's family cannot be allowed to conflict with the demands of following Jesus, that, indeed, one must sever one's connection to one's family. Q 12:51-52, on the other hand, has to do with discord within the family, discord generated by Jesus. Nothing is said here explicitly of discipleship. The saying seems to indicate that family dissension will involve not only "itinerant charismatics", as Theissen calls them, but all who belong to the Jesus movement. The saying reads, in its Lukan version (cf. Mt 10:34-35): "Do you think that I have come to give peace on earth? No, I tell you, but rather division; for henceforth in one house there will be five divided, three against two and two against three; they will be divided, father against son and son against father, mother against daughter and daughter against her mother, mother-in-law against

---

[10] "Love" and "hate" can mean something like "recognize one's obligation to someone" or to refuse to do so (= hate); see, e.g., Deut 21:15-18; cf. Gen 29:31, 33. This is true in Q 16:13 as well. One would not, as a slave, love or hate one's master so much as inwardly recognize one's obligation to him or her, or refuse to do so; cf. Josephus, *Antiq* 6.255, 324; 7.254. See also R. H. Stein, "Luke 14:26 and the Question of Authenticity," *Forum* 5/2 (1989) 188.

her daughter-in-law and daughter-in-law against her mother-in-law."

Though Luke's version may be secondary at a number of points, his version is at least more clear than Mt 10:34-35 about the nature of the discord. Lk 12:52 has no parallel in Matthew, but since it is independently attested in *GThom* 16, it may well have been in Q as well. But even without 12:52, we are presented with a household of five persons (small children not included, if there are any): mother, father, married son and his wife (the daughter-in-law) and a younger, unmarried daughter. This is a slightly "extended" family. The conflict is between the generations: parents against children–father against son, son against father, and so on. This is clearly true for Matthew's version as well. This may, indeed, reflect a situation in which it was the young who were most attracted to the Jesus movement, and this led to dissension. Both Matthean and Lukan versions of the saying seem to be loosely based on Micah (7:6), where we also have a five-member family. Luke's version, however, differs from Matthew's in that it presumes that the conflict goes both ways. That is, we do not have just rebellious behaviour on the part of the young; we also have the active opposition of the old: not only son against father but father against son, and so on. In this respect, the Q saying differs significantly from Mic 7:6 where we have the young dishonouring and rebelling against the old; in Q, there is bitter generational conflict but it is not blamed on the young. As in Q 14:26, here too it is presumed that both men and women are involved.

The original wording of this saying is uncertain because of the differences between Matthew and Luke.[11] Schulz has pointed out that Matthew's version is modelled after Mt 5:17; and that Luke's is modelled after Lk 13:2-3 and Lk 13:4-5. As noted earlier, Lk 12:52, though without parallel in Matthew, may have been in Q since it is attested also in *GThom* 16 (cf. Ps-Clem *Recog* II.28-29.12),[12] in my judgement independently (though *GThom* 16.4 is secondary). However, the opening part of Lk 12:52 ("from henceforth") is Lukan (cf. 1:48; 5:10; 22:69). Mt 10:36 has been introduced by Matthew from Mic 7:6. For our purposes, however, it is not necessary to reconstruct the Q version of these sayings because the content is essentially the same. Koester notes that

---

[11] See the attempts at reconstruction by P. Sellew, "Reconstruction of Q 12:33-59," *SBLSP* (1987) especially 622, 647-653 and S. J. Patterson, "Fire and Dissension," *Forum* 5/2 (1989) 121-139.

[12] See also S. Patterson, "Fire and Dissension" 123.

GThom 16 lacks a parallel to Q 12:53 beyond the initial father against son and son against father; he regards this part of Q as a "pedantic, and certainly secondary, enlargement of the family relationships".[13] Even if it is secondary, it was clearly in Q, and it may not have been "pedantic", since it shows that the whole family is divided, women as well as men. Matthew's version of Q 12:53 is more radical than Luke's in that Luke merely predicts family dissension in the future whereas Matthew has Jesus as the direct cause of it. However, Q 12:51 has already made clear that Jesus is, in fact, the agent of dissension.

It is certainly telling that this saying moves from the cosmic ("peace on earth") directly to the household. The division envisioned is not sectarian *per se*, nor does it entail cities or villages, much less nations. The *household* is the primary focus of attention, as though it were the only place the Q document could imagine conflict occurring. Perhaps it was. After all, the mission in Q was directed precisely to houses (Q 10:2-16), homes in fact to which the word of peace had been addressed (Q 10:5).

Q 12:51-53 is often characterized as an apocalyptic saying, perhaps because Luke's version takes the form of a prediction (but not of the distant or even near future, but "from henceforth"), or because of the similar saying in Mk 13:12 where the context is apocalyptic, or because the end-time is occasionally said to be characterized by dissension in apocalyptic texts such as 1 En 56:7; 99:5; 100:1-2; 4 Ezra 5:9; 6:24; Jub 23:26, 29; cf. Is 3:1-5; 2 Bar 70:3, 6; Mal 4:6.[14] But there is no real justification for regarding the saying as apocalyptic; instead the saying provides a rationale for the dissension among families that the Q group is experiencing–it was intended by Jesus. It does not refer to the persecution experienced by the Q community.[15] It would appear that there were some in the Q group who saw Jesus' mission and their own as one of bringing peace. There is ample material in Q which points precisely in that direction. At its earliest stage, in fact,

---

[13] *Ancient Christian Gospels: Their History and Development* (London and Philadelphia: 1990) 94; Patterson, "Fire and Dissension" 129; M. Sato, *Q und Prophetie* (WUNT 2/29; Tübingen: 1988) 295.

[14] For the apocalyptic interpretation, see e.g. P. Hoffmann, *Studien zur Theologie der Logienquelle* (NTA 8; Münster: 1972) 72-73; S. Schulz, *Q: Die Spruchquelle der Evangelisten* (Zürich: 1972) 260; W. Schenk, *Synopse zur Redenquelle der Evangelien* (Düsseldorf: 1981) 97; J. Kloppenborg, *The Formation of Q* (Studies in Antiquity and Christianity; Philadelphia: 1987) 151-152.

[15] *Pace* Hoffmann, *Studien* 72-73; Schenk, *Synopse* 97; Kloppenborg *Formation* 152.

the Q group may have been a "peace movement"; perhaps the Sermon on the Mount / Plain was its "Bible". But they began to experience cognitive dissonance when their experience of families being torn apart contradicted the peace lifestyle which they had come to adopt. That is why the saying begins, "Do you think that I have come to bring peace on earth?" Q 12:51-53 thus would seem to represent a critical shift in the self-understanding of the Q group. Unfortunately, however, it is not possible here to pursue this thesis further.

Q 16:13

The Lukan version of this saying reads, "No servant can serve two masters; for either he will hate the one and love the other, or he will be devoted to the one and despise the other. You cannot serve God and Mammon." The wording of this saying is identical in Mt 6:24 and Lk 16:13 except for a single Greek word; Luke had "no household servant" rather than simply "no one", as in Matthew.

There is a parallel, probably literarily independent, in *GThom* 47.2, but it lacks the concluding, "You cannot serve God and Mammon." Bultmann had suspected that this concluding application of a proverbial saying was a later addition,[16] and the reading in Thomas suggests he was right.[17] If this is true it suggests that "You cannot serve God and Mammon", being peculiar to Q, may reflect a particular concern of the Q group.

Further, Thomas attests the word "servant", which agrees with Luke against Matthew, and suggests that Luke may have the correct Q reading.[18]

It seems clear that here we have two sayings, either of which could stand alone, but, in their present position, the second interprets the first. The first saying represents conventional wisdom; the second interprets it by identifying who the two "masters" are: God and Mammon. The personification of mammon and its collocation with God indicate that the issue here is ultimately obedience or idolatry.

---

[16] R. Bultmann, *History of the Synoptic Tradition* (rev. ed.; New York: 1963) 87.

[17] See also Koester, *Ancient Christian Gospels* 90.

[18] Cf. *ibid*. However, see H. Koester, *Synoptische Überlieferungen bei den apostolischen Vätern* (TU 65; Berlin: 1957) 74-75, where Koester judged 2 Clem 6:1, which also has the word *oiketes*, to be based on Luke.

Anthony Blasi has claimed that God and Mammon in this saying refer to the choice between "the religious work of the 'Q' stratum" and "the security of the household-centred economic system of the day".[19] This could be the case. The interpretation of the word "mammon" does not itself settle the issue. It can mean "property", or more specifically "money" or "wealth", without any necessary negative connotations.[20]

For the interpretation of the saying, it would be helpful to know its context in Q. Unfortunately, Matthew and Luke have it in different locations. The most intricate argument concerning the context of Q 16:13 (= Mt 6:24) is that offered by R. A. Piper.[21] Piper argues that Q 16:13 was part of a small, pre-Lukan cluster now in Lk 16:9-13 which is structurally similar to other sayings clusters he has identified. Matthew, probably under the influence of Sir 31 (Hebrew), created a kind of echo collection (Mt 6:19-24) out of Q material which Luke had elsewhere. Thus Piper seems to presume that Luke's order for this material is that of Q. However, I am not able to accept his analysis, for a variety of reasons.[22] It seems more likely to me that (a) Matthew has best preserved the Q linkage of

---

[19] *Early Christianity as a Social Movement* (Toronto Studies in Religion 5; New York: 1988) 133.

[20] The word does not occur in the Hebrew Bible, but it is found occasionally in the Mishnah, Qumran documents, and later Jewish writings. See *m.*Abot 2:12; *m.*Sanh. 1:1; *m.*Ber 9:5; 1QS 6:2; CD 14:20; 1Q27.1.2.5; Sir 31:8 (Hebrew). In these instances, as in others, mammon has no negative connotations, with H. P. Rüger, "Mamonas," *ZNW* 64 (1973) 129, and Max Wilcox, "Mammon" in *Anchor Bible Dictionary* 4.490; *pace* Hauck, "*Mamōnas*" in *TDNT* 4. 389. See also Jastrow in *A Dictionary of the Targumim* 794; Fitzmyer, *Luke* 1109.

[21] *Wisdom in the Q Tradition* (MSSNTS 61; Cambridge: 1989) 86-99.

[22] The reasons are: (a) Lk 16:9 does not belong to this cluster but rather to the parable in Lk 16:1-9; v. 9 is based on Lk 16:4 (so also Fitzmyer, *Luke* 1105), and it functions exactly like the other "I say to you" sayings which are appended to Lukan parables (Lk 11:8; 12:35-44; 14:15-24; 15:3-7; 15:8-10; 18:18; 18:9-14; 19:11-27; cf. B. B. Scott, *Hear Then the Parable* [Minneapolis: 1989] 257 n. 11), even though admittedly the Greek of this "I say to you" introduction differs from the others. (b) If Lk 16:9-13 was an early collection, what is its relation to Q? According to Piper, Lk 16:13 is "clearly a saying added here from Q" (93). But if Luke did not compose this collection, who added it? It could not have been Q because Lk 16:10-12 is not Q material. (c) If Q 16:13 is understood in relation to Lk 16:9-12, its radicality is lost; in that context, it must, as Piper correctly notes, have to do with the right use of mammon, but the saying means that mammon is an idol to be avoided, not just used properly. It should be noted that their respective contexts indicate that Matthew understood "mammon" as nothing more than ordinary possessions, like the ordinary things treated in Mt 6:25-34, whereas Luke (mis)understood "mammon" as riches.

the God and mammon saying with the pericope on anxiety (both Matthew and Luke have the saying in close proximity to this pericope), but that (b) Luke has best preserved the Q location of the anxiety pericope. In short, Q 16:13 probably stood just before Q 12:22-31. If so, the more ordinary meaning of "property" or "money" or, as we might say, "a living", was probably intended in Q.

Q 16:13 does not deal merely with the *love* of money or the right use of it. It declares that money or possessions or property is a "master" which demands one's allegiance and attention, and therefore it is incompatible with God, who is also a master. It is anachronistic to read into the saying modern dreams of amassing great wealth and the possibilities of doing so, which were far more remote to a first century Galilean Jew than to a 20th century Westerner. The saying is more radical than that. It means that "making a living" is, or least may be, incompatible with following God—which would make the saying consistent both with other passages in Q such as Q 10:4 and the passage which follows it, Q 12:22-31. And since the "economy" of first-century Palestinians was essentially an economy of the household,[23] the saying would seem to imply a call to either serve God or be caught up into the network of the household and its economy, whether based on agriculture, crafts, fishing or whatever. The effect of the saying, in short, is to assert that the religious calling must be pursued, and the claims and responsibilities of family life must be rejected.[24]

Q 16:18

The Lukan version of this saying reads, "Everyone who divorces his wife and marries another commits adultery, and he who (or: whoever) marries a woman divorced from her husband commits adultery."

The Matthean parallel to this saying reads, "But I say to you that everyone who divorces his wife, except on the grounds of fornication, causes her to commit adultery; and if he marries a divorced woman, he commits adultery."

---

[23] See B. Malina, "Wealth and Poverty in the New Testament and Its World," *Interp.* 41 (1987) 354-367.

[24] Cf. Schulz, *Q* 460: "so gibt es auch hier Paktieren mit dem Kapital, mit Besitz, Vermögen oder Geld", though I do not agree that the basis for this is the apocalyptic expectation of the imminent End. See also P. Hartin, *James and the Q Sayings of Jesus* (JSOT Supplement Series 47; Sheffield: 1991) 184.

The prevailing view is that Matthew's version, with its exceptive clause, is secondary. This can be argued not only on the basis that the exceptive clause represents a later concession but also on the basis of structural symmetry, which the exceptive clause ruins.[25] Sometimes *kai gamon heteran* ("and marries another") in Lk 26:28a is regarded as secondary (inserted by Luke from Mk 10:11),[26] but since remarriage is the basis of the charge of adultery in Lk 16:18b, it probably was also in 16:18a. Thus Luke's text may be taken as probably the closest to Q.[27]

Enormous amounts of ink have been spilt on this and other divorce sayings of Jesus, so one is reticent to enter the debate, much less propose an interpretation which varies from the prevailing one. Nevertheless, I wish to propose for consideration a variant interpretation.

Assuming that Luke's reading is close to that of Q, I would emphasize first that the saying seems to concern primarily *remarriage*, not divorce. Moreover, remarriage is not, strictly speaking, prohibited; rather, it is stigmatized, socially a quite different process, though it is not possible to explore that here.

It should be noted that there is no adultery until there is remarriage; divorce itself does not constitute adultery, though it is often said that it does. But why does remarriage constitute adultery? Because, it is presumed, marriage is indissoluble.[28] So even if, in the legal sense, a divorce has occurred, the marriage has not ceased, and intercourse between a man thus "divorced" and another woman is adultery.

Q 16:18b reads, "And one marrying a woman divorced from her husband commits adultery." In this case, it is presumed that the man has never married before, but marries a divorced woman; that too constitutes adultery, for the same reason as above. Q 16:18 thus covers two of three possible scenarios: divorced man marries single woman, and single man marries divorced woman. The third scenario–divorced man marries divorced woman–is obviously excluded by the same reasoning.

---

[25] On this, see Ulrich Luz, *Matthew 1-7* (Minneapolis: 1989) 300.

[26] See, e.g., Schenk, *Synopse* 116; Schulz, *Q* 117.

[27] See Bultmann, *History of the Synoptic Tradition* 132; R. Laufen, *Die Doppelüberlieferungen der Logienquelle und des Markusevangeliums* (BBB 54; Bonn: 1980) 344-347. Cf. R. Wall, "Divorce" in *Anchor Bible Dictionary* 2.218.

[28] It is possible that this explains the connection between Q 16:17 and 16:18–one deals with the indissolubility of the Law, the other with the indissolubility of marriage.

Q 16:18 does *not* say that divorce is prohibited. However, it may be noted that "and marries another", which was discussed earlier, can be interpreted differently. Ulrich Luz interprets it as specifying when the divorce is final and the man liable to judgement.[29] But this is highly improbable; it would mean that divorce itself is adultery, but that it does not become divorce until the divorce is "finalised" by remarriage. In any case, how divorce itself can constitute adultery remains unexplained. The presumption must be that divorce would occur solely for the purpose of remarriage, and so remarriage is merely assumed.[30] This may be the case in Mt 5:32a which is the only one of the parallel sayings (cf. Lk 16:18a; Mk 10:11; Mt 19:9a) to omit "and marries another". It is not the case in Lk 16:18, which best represents the Q version. Thus it would seem that, in fact, divorce is not prohibited in Lk 16:18. That is true as well of Mk 10:11-12 (despite the context, where divorce is indeed rejected) and of Mt 19:9.[31] Mt 5:32a is ambiguous in this respect.

Q 16:18 assumes that there are divorced people for whom the question now is: what about remarriage? It is remarriage that is stigmatized. Who might these divorced people be? Probably the persons to whom Jesus directed such sayings as Q 14:26, which instructed them to sunder family ties and follow him. Having left their families and joined the Jesus movement, they might now wish to marry a "believer". Q in 16:18 stigmatizes any who would do that.

The view that divorce is permissible and that it is remarriage that is prohibited could be construed as an exceedingly cruel set of rules. Luz notes that "This prohibition [of remarriage] could be devastating for the divorced woman."[32] It would mean that she would have to return to her family, if they were still alive, or be bereft of any other source of support, not to mention possible denial of the right to bear children. However, if the prohibition is understood in the context proposed, it has the effect of prohibiting the creation of new families within the Jesus movement, but also of

---

[29] *Matthew 1-7* 303.

[30] See J. P. Louw and E. A. Nida, eds., *Greek English Lexicon* 88.276 (p. 772).

[31] Mk 10:11-12 must be interpreted apart from its context because it did not belong with Mk 10:2-9; see Bultmann, *History of the Synoptic Tradition* 26-27; A. Hultgren, *Jesus and his Adversaries* 143 n. 88; J. A. Fitzmyer, "The Matthean Divorce Texts and Some New Palestinian Evidence,"*TS* 37 (1976) 203-205.

[32] *Matthew 1-7* 302.

effectively eliminating divorce where both spouses are members of the movement.[33]

This focus on remarriage as adultery is hardly eccentric within the context of the early church. Paul, like Q 16:18, assumes that marriage is indissoluble. Thus, a woman is bound to her husband as long as he lives (Rom 7:2; 1 Cor 7:39). "Accordingly she will be called an adulteress if she lives with another man while her husband is still alive" (Rom 7:3). Here, divorce is presumed, and remarriage constitutes adultery.

Paul's discussion of celibacy, marriage and divorce in 1 Cor 7 takes the same line, though here it is quite clear that Paul prefers that people not marry at all (1 Cor 7:1, 8, 25-26, 29-38), but he regards celibacy as a gift which not all have received. This may well have been the position of the Q group as well–that people who have left their spouses should remain single. In 1 Cor 7:10-11, Paul sets forth this view: "To the married I give this command, not I but the Lord, that the wife should not separate from her husband–but if she does, let her remain single or else be reconciled to her husband–and that the husband should not divorce his wife." Needless to say, the interpretation of this verse is controverted, but it quite clearly says that divorce, while strongly discouraged, is permissible–but that remarriage is not permissible. This view is repeated later (1 Cor 7:15), in the case of an unbelieving partner who wishes to separate. Not every marriage, apparently, was regarded as indissoluble ("in such a case the brother or sister is not bound"). This may be the presumption for the Jesus movement as well: separation and divorce were possible, indeed required, of those whose spouses or families refused to become members of the Jesus movement. This would explain how Jesus' saying could be understood by some as a simple prohibition of divorce; that is, divorce *was* prohibited within the believing community.

The same position is found in Her. *Mand.* 4.1.6. Here, the question is raised (*Mand.* 4.1.4-6) whether a male believer should divorce his believing wife if she commits adultery. The answer is yes,

---

[33] Kloppenborg ("Alms, Debt and Divorce: Jesus' Ethics in their Mediterranean Context," *Toronto Journal of Theology* 6 [1990] 193-196) interprets Mk 10:11-12 / Q 16:18 as at once "social protest" against the frequency of divorce among the elite and as a critique of "androcentric honour" for the sake of the honour of the woman. I am not persuaded of either view: it is not clear that divorce was more common among elites than among peasants (cf. T. F. Carney, *The Shape of the Past* 89-90), and the linkage of remarriage with fornication in CD 4:20-21 suggests that Jesus' association of remarriage with adultery was neither innovative nor intended to protect the honour of women.

if he knows about it. But if he divorces her, "let her husband remain by himself" because "if he put his wife away and marry another he also commits adultery himself." Athenagoras, in his "Plea Regarding Christians" (33), says that many Christians are married, but many "have grown to old age unmarried, in the hope of being closer to God". And he continues,

> "We hold that a man should either remain as he is born or else marry only once. For a second marriage is a veiled adultery. The Scripture says, 'Whoever puts away his wife and marries another, commits adultery.' Thus a man is forbidden both to put her away whose virginity he has ended, and to marry again."[34]

The position set forth in Q 16:18 may have an earlier antecedent in CD 4:20-21, though the passage is much disputed. It says that the corrupt priests are trapped "in lust by taking two wives during their lifetime, whereas the principle of creation is 'male and female He created them'."[35] The saying seems to document the association of remarriage with lust or fornication (Hebrew *zenut*). However, it is unclear whether the saying refers to divorce followed by remarriage, or to polygamy.

But why is remarriage such an issue? In all likelihood, it is because marriages were being broken up by the Jesus movement, and the question arose as to whether a woman, for example, who had left her husband because he refused to join the movement could now remarry. In short, we may suppose that within the Q group there were divorces or at least separations. This would hardly be surprising given injunctions such as Q 14:26!

In any case, it seems quite clear that far from being pro-marriage and thus in tension with Jesus' anti-family sayings,[36] Q 16:18 fits them hand in glove. It is a *de facto* anti-family saying, because it effectively prohibits the formation of new families after the dissolution of old ones. One may speculate that the intention is to facilitate communal life within a new community.

---

[34] Cited from C. Richardson, ed., *Early Christian Fathers* (LCC 1) 337; cf. also Justin, *1 Apol* 15.

[35] Cited from the translation in P. R. Davies, *The Damascus Covenant* (JSOT Supplement Series, 25; Sheffield: 1983) 242-245. See J. R. Mueller, "The Temple Scroll and the Gospel Divorce Texts," *Revue de Qumran* 10 (1980) especially 253-254, and cf. Fitzmyer, "The Matthean Divorce Texts" 216-221. 11Q Temple Scroll 57.17-19 attests the idea that marriage is indissoluble while the partners are alive.

[36] See, e.g., J. Eckert, "Wessen und Funktion der Radikalismen in der Botschaft Jesu," *MThZ* 24 (1973) 314-315.

Q 17:26-27

Recently, Luise Schottroff has claimed to have found in Q 17:26-
27 evidence of an "androcentric critique of patriarchy".[37] The
Lukan version reads, "And as it was in the days of Noah, so also
will it be in the days of the Son of man; they were eating, drinking,
marrying and being married, until the day Noah entered into the
ark, and the flood came and destroyed all of them."

Schottroff argues that the problem with the people in Noah's day
according to this text was not that they carried out the ordinary
activities of life heedless of the danger until it was too late, but that
they did not hear God's voice and chose deliberately to ignore it.[38]

The description of the Flood generation in Q 17:26-27 differs
dramatically from that of Genesis 6, where we are told that "every
inclination of the thoughts of their hearts was only evil
continually" (Gen 6:5) and that "the earth was cor-
rupt...and...filled with violence" (6:11). Instead of this, Q 17:26-
27 portrays people simply carrying out their ordinary lives. But
precisely this makes them culpable. In fact, this culpable insou-
ciance is a regular theme in Q. For example, Q 11:31—"The queen
of the south will arise at the judgement with the people of this
generation and condemn them; for she came from the ends of the
earth to hear the wisdom of Solomon, and behold, something
greater than Solomon is here." Schottroff is correct: continuing to
carry on with the ordinary activities of life as if nothing has
changed is precisely what one must not do. Whether this constitutes
a critique of the patriarchal household is another question. It seems
clear that the Q group was a potential menace to the patriarchal
household. But there is only scant evidence that the patriarchal
household was rejected because it was patriarchal; rather, it appears
that the patriarchal household was simply eclipsed by more urgent
matters. There are, to be sure, a few hints of an anti-patriarchal
spirit (evidence noted above that the Q group consisted of both
women and men), but no explicit critique in language such as
Mk 3:31-35 or Mt 23:9. If we knew how the Q group organized
itself, whether along the lines of a fictive or ritual family which was
non-patriarchal, we would have a good basis for deciding the
attitude of the Q group to the patriarchal household. But aside
from the apparent fact that God functioned as the fictive father for

[37] "Wanderprophetinnen," *EvTh* 51 (1991). The English translation of this
essay appears in the present volume.
[38] "Wanderprophetinnen" 333-334.

the group, little else can be discerned from the texts; and God as fictive father *could* be anti-patriarchal but need not be, since patriarchal Jewish texts can speak of God as "father" too.

Summary and Conclusions

The texts discussed above are often treated as "hard sayings" of Jesus for which an explanation is sought. But they are not so frequently used as a window into the origins of Christianity. That cults and sects are often *de facto* subversive of families is, of course, well known.[39] That the Q group was a sect has not been demonstrated; however, the anti-family sayings in Q may themselves be evidence of the sectarian character of the Q group.

The picture that emerges from these sayings is one of people who have severed ties to families and, presumably, come together as a group, or as groups. There is some evidence in Q that households were the focus of activity (Q 10:5-7; 12:51-53; and further possible hints in Q 7:6; 12:3; 12:42; 13:25-26; 13:29; 14:23). There are hints too that meals may have been important times of gathering (Q 7:34; 10:7; 12:42; 13:29; 14:21-24), but no indication that these were ritual meals. Evidence of fictive family formation is not strong, but not entirely absent. The members of the group regarded each other as "brothers" (Q 6:41-42; 17:3), and among them had already arisen some problems of living together such as spiritual direction (Q 6:41-42) and the limits of forgiveness (Q 17:3-4). They may have thought of themselves as "children" (Q 3:7; 7:35; 13:34); in fact, Blasi thinks that the Q group recruited young people in particular, and that this led to controversy and opposition.[40] Religious symbolism in Q is consistent with fictive family formation: God is a "father" who provides for his family (Q 11:2-3; 11:13; 12:22-31), sets an example for them (Q 6:36) and, probably at a later stage, was regarded as bearer of special revelation (Q 10:21-22). Members are

---

[39] Sensational accounts abound; but see, e.g., Bromley, Busching and Shupe, "The Unification Church and the American Family: Strain, Conflict, and Control" in *New Religious Movements: A Perspective for Understanding Society*, ed. Eileen Barker (Studies in Religion and Society 3; New York: 1982) 302-323; also Gene G. James (ed.), *The Family and the Unification Church* (New York, 1983). On the Unification Church as a fictive family see, e.g., A. Parsons, "Messianic Personalism: A Role Analysis of the Unification Church," *JSSR* (1986) 141-161.

[40] Blasi, *Early Christianity as Social Movement* 118-119, 124, 130, 140-142. But at least "babes" in Q 10:21 will not sustain his interpretation (p. 124).

"sons" of this "father" (Q 6:35). If, as probable, Lk 11:27-28 is to be assigned to Q,[41] then we have further evidence that ties to families had been eclipsed by membership in the Jesus group.

Q and the Origins of Christianity

The Q document is not, I have argued elsewhere, "Christian".[42] It has no "christology" in the strict sense of a view of Jesus as the messiah, or in the sense of Jesus as a redeemer. Jesus' death, while not explicitly mentioned in Q, was almost certainly understood in the context of the deuteronomistic tradition expressed most clearly in Q 11:49-51 and 13:34-35. Personified Sophia occurs in Q (7:35; 11:49), but Jesus is not identified with her, and there is little connection between Q and the elaborated cosmic sophiology of later Christian tradition. Theologically, Q gives the impression of being underdeveloped. Moreover, there are no named disciples to legitimate traditions, no sacraments, no indication of the formation of a "church" in the sense that we know it from other New Testament and later documents.

Yet if Q seems pre-Christian, just as clearly it came from a group which was in severe tension with other Jews or Jewish groups, whoever they might have been. They have a sense of identification with the prophets who preceded them and who, it is claimed, endured violent opposition (Q 6:23; 11:49-51; 13:34-35).

The anti-family sayings in Q may help us to understand the situation of this group behind Q. These sayings have not received the attention they deserve.[43] And they deserve more attention than is

---

[41] See Jacobson, *The First Gospel* 155-156.

[42] *The First Gospel* 32, 212, 251, 255-256.

[43] A few such studies may be mentioned: R. A. Harrisville, "Jesus and the Family,"*Interp.* 23 (1969) 425-438; Jacques Dupont, "Jesus, His Family and His Disciples," *JSNT* 15 (1982) 3-19; I. Ellis, "Jesus and the Subversive Family," *SJTh* 38 (1985) 173-188; B. Lang, "Charisma and the Disruption of the Family in Early Christianity" in *Die Vielfalt der Kultur*, eds. K.-H. Kohl, H. Muzinski and I. Strecker (Mainzer Ethnologica 4; Berlin: 1990) 278-287. I did not have access to A. George, "La venue de Jésus, cause de division entre les hommes Lc 12,49-53," *Assemblées du Seigneur* 51 (1972) 62-71. Focusing on Markan texts are H. Furst, "Verlust der Familie–Gewinn einer neuen Familie" in *Studia Historico-Ecclesiastica*, ed. I. Vázquez (Rome: 1977) 17-47; and David May, "Leaving and Receiving: A Social Scientific Exegesis of Mark 10:29-31," *Perspectives in Religious Studies* 17 (1990) 141-151, 154. Other works place the anti-family sayings within various contexts, e.g.: M. Hengel, *The Charismatic Leader and His Followers* (New York: 1981); O. Betz, "Jesu heiliger Krieg," *NT* 2 (1958) 116-137 (especially 129-130); J. Eckert, "Wesen und Funktion der Radikalismen in

possible in this brief essay. In particular, we need to go beyond the gospel texts and, indeed, texts in general to consider such issues as the shape of the family and the household in first-century CE Galilee,[44] distinctions between elite and non-elite family systems,[45] domestic architecture,[46] fictive or ritual family formation,[47] religious symbolism in fictive families, and the like.

We need to disabuse ourselves of the notion that the synagogue was the locus of religious life in first-century CE Galilee. Archaeological investigations have located many synagogues in Palestine, but nearly all are 3rd century CE or later.[48] Only a few structures

---

der Botschaft Jesu," *MThZ* 24 (1973) 301-325; E. Schüssler Fiorenza, *In Memory of Her*, especially 140-151; G. Lohfink, "Der ekklesiale Sitz im Leben der Aufforderung Jesu zum Gewaltverzicht," *ThQ* 162 (1982) 236-253; A. J. Blasi, *Early Christianity as a Social Movement* [cf. L. M. White, "Sociological Analysis of Early Christian Groups," *SocAn* 47 (1986) 250-257]; L. Schottroff, "Wanderprophetinnen"; Robert Nisbet, *The Social Philosophers* (New York: 1973), especially 174-181.

[44] See *inter alia*, P. Laslett (ed.), *Household and Family in Past Time* (Cambridge: 1972); Jack Goody, *The Development of the Family and Marriage in Europe* (Cambridge: 1983); M. Mitterauer and R. Sieder, *The European Family* (Chicago and Oxford: 1982); S. A. Queen, R. W. Habenstein, and J. S. Quadagno, *The Family in Various Cultures* (5th ed.; New York: 1985); J. Davis, *People of the Mediterranean* (London: 1977); P. Lampe, "Zur gesellschaftlichen und kirchlichen Funktion der 'Familie' in neutestamentlicher Zeitrechnung Streiflichter," *Ref.* 31 (1982) 533-542; M. Goodman, *State and Society in Roman Galilee* (Totowa, NJ: 1983); D. A. Fiensy, *The Social History of Palestine in the Herodian Period* (Studies in the Bible and Early Christianity 20; Lewiston, NY: 1991); B. Malina, *The New Testament World* (Atlanta: 1981); idem, "Dealing with Biblical (Mediterranean) Characters," *BTB* 19 (1989) 127-141; idem, "Mother and Son," *BTB* 20 (1990) 54-64; K. C. Hanson, "The Herodians and Mediterranean Kinship," *BTB* 19 (1989) 75-84, 142-151; *BTB* 20 (1990) 10-21; D. A. Knight, "Family" in *Mercer Dictionary of the Bible* 294-296; C. J. H. Wright, "Family" in *Anchor Bible Dictionary* 2.761-769.

[45] See the brief but helpful comments of T. F. Carney, *The Shape of the Past* (Lawrence, KS: 1975) 89-93, and G. Sjoberg, *The Preindustrial City. Past and Present* (New York and London: 1960) ch. 6.

[46] See, e.g., L. E. Stager, "The Archaeology of the Family in Ancient Israel," *BASOR* 260 (1985) 1-35; H. K. Beebe, "Domestic Architecture and the New Testament," *BA* 38 (1975) 89-104; J. S. Holladay, Jr., "House, Israelite" in *Anchor Bible Dictionary* 3.308-318; and D. A. Fiensy, *The Social History of Palestine in the Herodian Period* (see note 44 above).

[47] For this distinction, see J. Pitt-Rivers, "Pseudokinship" in *International Encyclopaedia of the Social Sciences* 8.408-413.

[48] See M. J. S. Chiat, *Handbook of Synagogue Architecture* (Brown Judaic Studies 29; Chico, CA: 1982); L. Levine (ed.), *Ancient Synagogue Revealed* (Jerusalem: 1981); J. Gutmann (ed.), *Ancient Synagogues: The State of Research* (Brown Judaic Studies 22; Chico, CA: 1981); J. Gutmann (ed.), *The Synagogue: Studies in Origins, Archaeology and Architecture* (Library of Biblical Studies;

have been identified as Second Temple synagogues (Masada, Herodium, Capernaum, Gamala, Magdala), and some or all of these are dubious.[49] Even if some or all of the identifications are correct, what they show us is that the synagogue in first-century CE Palestine was at an embryonic stage of development. It was not yet architecturally distinct, and probably people met as often in houses or meeting halls; liturgies, lectionaries, and synagogue organization were only beginning to emerge, if they had emerged at all. Accordingly, there was no organizational network, certainly no Jewish "denomination", nor even probably party control of synagogues, including that of the Pharisees.[50] Judaism outside of the Temple and its organization was decentralized and locally variable, as even later synagogues indicate.[51] So a scenario of the Q group being opposed by some dominant group in the synagogue is probably pure fancy.

The locus of Jewish religious life outside of the Temple was not the synagogue but primarily the household. That was also the battleground, and the echoes of these battles can be heard in Q as well as in Mark. Of course, we know that much of what a Jew would do religiously would be done in the home, from circumcision to instruction to marriage and death rituals, not to mention food and purity laws, and so on. We also know that family solidarity was a powerful reality throughout the Mediterranean, at least among those above subsistence levels, and we know that religion was em-

New York: 1975); M. Dothan, "Research on Ancient Synagogues in the Land of Israel" in *Recent Archaeology in the Land of Israel*, eds. H. Shanks and B. Mazar (Washington D.C. and Jerusalem: 1981) 89-96; S. B. Hoenig, "The Ancient City-Square: The Forerunner of the Synagogue" in *ANRW* 19.1.2, 448-476; L. Levine (ed.), *The Synagogue in Late Antiquity* (Philadelphia: 1987).

[49] See especially J. Gutmann, "Synagogue Origins: Theories and Facts" in *Ancient Synagogues*, ed. J. Gutmann; L. M. White, "The Delos Synagogue Revisited," *HThR* 80 (1987) 133-160; L. Grabbe, "Synagogues in Pre-70 Palestine: A Re-assessment," *JThS* 39 (1988) 401-410; P. V. M. Flesher, "Palestinian Synagogues before 70 CE: A Review of the Evidence" in *Approaches to Ancient Judaism* VI, eds. J. Neusner and E. S. Frerichs (Brown Judaic Studies; Atlanta: 1989) 67-81; H. C. Kee, "The Transformation of the Synagogue after 70 CE: Its Import for Early Christianity," *NTS* 36 (1990) 1-24; E. M. Meyers, "Synagogue" in *Anchor Bible Dictionary* 6.251-260.

[50] See, e.g., S. J. D. Cohen, *From the Maccabees to the Mishnah* (Library of Early Christianity; Philadelphia: 1987) especially 111-115; and L. Grabbe, "Synagogues in Pre-70 Palestine" 48.

[51] See, e.g., E. M. Meyers, "The Current State of Galilean Synagogue Studies" in *The Synagogue in Late Antiquity*, ed. Levine, 127-137; and A. T. Kraabel, "Unity and Diversity among Diaspora Synagogues" in the same volume 51-60.

bedded in the family or household. Pursuit of an alternative or deviant religious vision, therefore, would almost inevitably entail conflict with the family and departure or eviction from it.

Capernaum, Jesus' presumed hometown, has been studied by archaeologists.[52] They found a city of some size–perhaps 12,000 to 15,000 people. The plan of the city was Roman: a *cardo maximus* or *via principalis* with intersecting streets or *decumani*, forming a grid. The blocks contain what are perhaps somewhat inaccurately called *insulae*. The *insulae* of Rome and other Roman cities were extensive apartment complexes, sometimes four or five stories high. Corbo speaks of "clan" buildings "arranged around internal courts, which numbered at times as many as three".[53] The courtyard house was the dominant form of domestic architecture in Roman Palestine. Its thick stone walls supported a roof of branches, mud, etc., often constructed well enough to allow another room in the second storey. The courtyard house was flexible, accommodating families as they expanded or contracted. For the same reason, it would have been ideal for communal living, with individual rooms for sleeping and for cooking and so on. There is, in fact, evidence of nuclear families living in clusters as production units based, e.g., on crafts, all living in interconnected units.

This is the specific social context that I would suggest for the Q group(s). Whether in Capernaum or elsewhere, such houses would have lent themselves readily to fictive family formation. Indeed, it would be possible for some members of the group to be itinerant, but I would suggest that most were not. Rather, they belonged to family-like groups which could together sustain a modest living. The groups included women as well as men, but some individuals, perhaps most, were either single or separated without remarrying.

Such religious fictive families would hardly have been unique. According to Neusner, the locus for the religious life of Pharisees was also the home,[54] and some or many probably belonged to

---

[52] See, e.g., E. M. Meyers and James F. Strange, *Archaeology, the Rabbis and Early Christianity* (Nashville: 1981) 59-60; and V. Corbo, "Capernaum" in *Anchor Bible Dictionary* 866-869.

[53] Corbo, "Capernaum" 867. Cf. Meyers and Strange, *Archeology, the Rabbis and Early Christianity* 58: "The town was laid out in regular blocks of one-storey houses. Each block was about 40 by 40 meters... Each block...would contain three or four houses with common walls. Each house...would contain rooms around a central courtyard."

[54] See J. Neusner, *From Politics to Piety* (Englewood Cliffs, NJ: 1973) especially 82-90; *idem*, "'Pharisaic-Rabbinic' Judaism: A Clarification," *HR* 12 (1973) 250-270; cf. A. J. Saldarini, *Pharisees, Scribes and Sadducees in Pales-*

fictive families called *haburoth*.[55] The Essenes described by Josephus and Philo seem to have been similar in that they formed
communal groups, perhaps also resembling families, though celi-
bate.[56] It is well known, of course, that the early Christian church
was a house-church movement.[57] It could hardly have been different early on. Indeed the continuity between Q and early Christianity is probably not to be found in its theology so much as in its
ecclesiology. The persistence of group formation, that is, may have
been a more powerful factor in early Christianity than the persistence of theological conceptions, and that, in turn, may indicate
that we need to pay at least as much attention to the specific social
context of the early church as to its theology.

---

tinian Society: A Sociological Approach (Wilmington, DE: 1988) especially 50-
75.

[55] See J. Neusner, *Fellowship in Judaism* (London: 1963).

[56] The evidence is conveniently gathered in G. Vermes and M. D. Goodman,
The Essenes According to the Classical Sources (Sheffield: 1989).

[57] See, e.g., F. Filson, "The Significance of the Early House Churches," *JBL*
58 (1939) 105-112; E. A. Judge, *The Social Pattern of the Christian Groups in
the First Century* (London: 1960); *idem*, "The Early Christians as a Scholastic
Community," *JRH* 1 (1960) 4-15 and 2 (1961) 125-137; R. Banks, *Paul's Idea of
Community: The Early House Churches in Their Historical Setting* (London and
Grands Rapids, MI: 1980); H.-J. Klauck, *Hausgemeinde und Hauskirche im frühen
Christentum* (SBS 103; Stuttgart: 1981); A. Malherbe, "House Churches and their
Problems" in *Social Aspects of Early Christianity* (2nd ed.; Philadelphia: 1983);
L. M. White, *Building God's House in the Roman World* (Baltimore: 1990);
H. O. Maier, *The Social Setting of the Ministry as Reflected in the Writings of
Hermas, Clement and Ignatius* (Waterloo, Ont: 1991).

INDEX TO MODERN AUTHORS

INDEX TO ANCIENT SOURCES

11:49-51 140, 170, 173, 175-176,
192, 214, 291, 358, 376
11:49f. 191, 271
11:49 38, 124, 132, 141, 192, 243,
358, 376
11:51 125, 192, 292
11:52 227, 340-341

12–17 183, 185
12:1 72
12:2ff. 174, 176
12:2-34 189
12:2-12 186, 311, 336
12:2-10 174
12:2-9 151
12:2-7 117, 170, 260
12:2f. 316
12:2 143, 148-149, 174, 177, 182,
184, 311, 336, 341
12:3 148, 311, 336, 341, 375
12:4-7 118, 123, 151
12:6f. 143, 151
12:6 154, 311
12:8f. 117, 126, 132, 137, 154, 170,
181, 190, 261
12:8 161, 184
12:9 128
12:10 117, 236-238, 261, 336,
341
12:11f. 117-118, 127, 132, 260,
302
12:12 236, 238
12:13f. 301-302, 311, 336, 341
12:14 302
12:16-21 301-302, 304, 311, 317,
335-336, 341
12:16-20 287, 289
12:16 303
12:21 303, 305
12:22-34 336
12:22-32 353
12:22-31 16, 117-118, 151-153, 174,
183, 185-186, 222-224, 260,

265, 303-304, 311, 341, 360, 369,
375
12:22-30 336
12:22 284, 302-303
12:23 303-305
12:24 143, 152-153, 303-304, 311
12:25 303-305
12:26f. 152, 360
12:27f. 143, 152-153, 311
12:27 118, 125, 350
12:29 303, 311
12:30 118, 265, 304
12:31 119, 152-153, 220,224, 263,
265, 268, 294, 311, 353
12:33-59 284
12:33f. 117-118, 186, 260, 294,
303-304, 311
12:33 155, 336, 341
12:34 143, 155-156, 305
12:35 341
12:39-59 187, 309-311
12:39-46 127, 192
12:39f. 117, 137, 143, 146, 156,
170, 183, 185, 261, 300, 308, 340
12:39 146-147, 153, 338, 340
12:40 178, 181, 184, 186, 242, 293-
295
12:42-46 117, 137, 144, 148, 150,
156, 170, 181, 184, 261, 287, 290,
293, 295, 300, 308, 340
12:42 293-294, 375
12:43 293-294
12:44 294
12:45 293-294
12:46 293-294
12:49-53 127
12:49 117, 261, 308, 340
12:51-59 117, 261
12:51-53 17, 308, 340, 348-349,
354, 364, 366-367, 375
12:51f. 364
12:51 366
12:52f. 125, 132

.20.1393b.4-8   286

ato, De agricultura

..3f.   295

icero, Letters to Atticus

.21.10-12   297
.1.5-7   297

icero, Pro Flaccus

6   133

olumella, De re rustica

.7f.   295

seudo-Crates, ep.

1   220
8   221

emetrius, On Style

9   286

emosthenes

7.9-11   297

io Cassius, Roman History

2.36   130
).6.6   135

io Chrysostom, Orationes

:15f.   223-224
2   204
.4   215

odorus Siculus

36.4   308

Diogenes Laertius

6.22f.   209
6.27f.   226
6.28   225
6.39   227
6.42   225
6.45   226
6.49   213
6.78f.   227
6.87   212
6.89   215
6.92   210
6.102   209, 222
6.104   216
7.148f.   203

pseudo-Diogenes, _ep._

7   216
16   203
42   203

Epictetus, _Dissertations_

1.1.3   118
1.24.6   211
1.29.46f.   211
2.16.47   211
3.22.23f.   211
3.22.26   211
3.22.38   211
3.22.56   211
3.22.59   211
3.22.69   211
3.22.97   211
3.23.34   211
3.23.53f.   217
3.24.112f.   211
4.8.30f.   211

Livy

1.1-2,6   131

SUPPLEMENTS TO NOVUM TESTAMENTUM

ISSN 0167-9732

Recent volumes in the series:

60. MILLER, E.L. *Salvation-History in the Prologue of John.* The Significance of John 1: 3-4. 1989. ISBN 90 04 08692 7

61. THIELMAN, F. *From Plight to Solution.* A Jewish Framework for Understanding Paul's View of the Law in Galatians and Romans. 1989. ISBN 90 04 09176 9

64. STERLING, G.E. *Historiography and Self-Definition.* Josephos, Luke-Acts and Apologetic Historiography. 1992. ISBN 90 04 09501 2

65. BOTHA, J.E. *Jesus and the Samaritan Woman.* A Speech Act Reading of John 4:1-42. 1991. ISBN 90 04 09505 5

66. KUCK, D.W. *Judgment and Community Conflict.* Paul's Use of Apologetic Judgment Language in 1 Corinthians 3:5-4:5. 1992. ISBN 90 04 09510 1

67. SCHNEIDER, G. *Jesusüberlieferung und Christologie.* Neutestamentliche Aufsätze 1970-1990. 1992. ISBN 90 04 09555 1

68. SEIFRID, M.A. *Justification by Faith.* The Origin and Development of a Central Pauline Theme. 1992. ISBN 90 04 09521 7

69. NEWMAN, C.C. *Paul's Glory-Christology.* Tradition and Rhetoric. 1992. ISBN 90 04 09463 6

70. IRELAND, D.J. *Stewardship and the Kingdom of God.* An Historical, Exegetical, and Contextual Study of the Parable of the Unjust Steward in Luke 16: 1-13. 1992. ISBN 90 04 09600 0

71. ELLIOTT, J.K. *The Language and Style of the Gospel of Mark.* An Edition of C.H. Turner's "Notes on Marcan Usage" together with other comparable studies. 1993. ISBN 90 04 09767 8

72. CHILTON, B. *A Feast of Meanings.* Eucharistic Theologies from Jesus through Johannine Circles. 1994. ISBN 90 04 09949 2

73. GUTHRIE, G.H. *The Structure of Hebrews.* A Text-Linguistic Analysis. 1994. ISBN 90 04 09866 6

74. BORMANN, L., K. DEL TREDICI & A. STANDHARTINGER (eds.) *Religious Propaganda and Missionary Competition in the New Testament World.* Essays Honoring Dieter Georgi. 1994. ISBN 90 04 10049 0

75. PIPER, R.A. (ed.) *The Gospel Behind the Gospels.* Current Studies on Q. 1995. ISBN 90 04 09737 6

76. PEDERSEN, S. (ed.) *New Directions in Biblical Theology.* Papers of the Aarhus Conference, 16-19 September 1992. 1994. ISBN 90 04 10120 9